WORLD FACTBOOK

PHILIP'S

WORLD FACTBOOK

NEW 2008–2009 EDITION

KABUL

Area 47,000 sq km
[18,147 sq mi]
Population 2,186,000
Capital (population)
Thimphu (35,000)
Government
Constitutional monarchy
Ethnic groups
Bhutanese 50%,
Nepalese 35%
Languages Dzongkha

Text *Keith Lye*
Editor *Lester Hawksby*
Executive art editor *Mike Brown*
Designers *Chris Bell, Caroline Ohara*
Production *Sally Banner*

First published in Great Britain in 1995
by Philip's, a division of
Octopus Publishing Group Limited,
2–4 Heron Quays, London E14 4JP

An Hachette Livre UK Company

Fifth Edition 2008
Copyright © 2008 Philip's

Cartography by Philip's

ISBN 978–0–540–09237–6

A CIP catalogue record for this book is
available from the British Library.

Printed in Hong Kong

FRONT COVER : *Street in Hong Kong, CORBIS;
Mozambique, Philip's; Flag of Lebanon, Philip's;
Climate of Kabul, Philip's; Polar bears on an iceberg
near Greenland, CORBIS.*
BACK COVER : *Flags of South Africa, Switzerland,
Suriname, Tuvalu, Sri Lanka and Iraq, Philip's; Maps of
Costa Rica and Ivory Coast, Philip's.*

Other titles from Philip's

Philip's publish a range of titles of
geographical interest in the same
format as this book, including:

Philip's Guide to Wetlands
Philip's Guide to Mountains
Philip's Guide to Oceans
Philip's Guide to Weather
Philip's Guide to Minerals, Rocks and Fossils
Philip's Guide to Gems
Philip's Guide to Fossils
Philip's Guide to Global Hazards
Philip's Guide to the State of the World

For details of Philip's products
website **www.philips-maps.co.uk**
email **philips@philips-maps.co.uk**

Introduction

Philip's World Factbook contains articles and maps for all the countries of the world, arranged in alphabetical order. A simple locator map shows the position of the country within its region, and the national flag is illustrated with an explanation of its origin. The smallest countries or islands, such as the islands of the Atlantic Ocean, are grouped together within their region. A few very small countries are found alongside their larger neighbours; for example, Andorra and Gibraltar are included in the entry for Spain.

In addition to the main article, each country features a separate piece about the capital city; a statistics box detailing area, population, capital city, government, ethnic groups, languages, religions, currency and website; and a climate graph.

The country maps are physically coloured and are usually a column width in size, but a country's shape and area have sometimes merited a larger map. Where neighbouring countries are in dispute, the maps show the de facto boundary between nations; that is, the boundary that exists in the real world rather than the boundary that a particular country may wish to be shown on a map.

Each map contains a number of symbols indicating the major towns and cities, principal roads and railways, with the main border crossings. Major international airports and the highest point in most countries are also shown. A scale bar indicates the distances between places, and the lines of latitude and longitude show the country's position on the globe.

The spellings of the placenames on the maps match the forms that are used in everyday English; for example, Rome (not Roma), Munich (not München), Moscow (not Moskva). Only the more common accented characters of the Western European languages have been used.

KEY		
	✈ Major airport	⟋ Railway
■● City or town	△ Highest point in country	⤨ Road
★ Capital city	↷ International boundary	〰 River

Contents

WORLD STATISTICS

Country / Territory	Area (1,000 sq km)	Area (1,000 sq mi)	Population (1,000s)	Capital City	Annual income US $
Afghanistan	652	252	31,057	Kabul	800
Albania	28.7	11.1	3,582	Tirana	5,600
Algeria	2,382	920	32,930	Algiers	7,700
American Samoa (US)	0.2	0.08	58	Pago Pago	5,800
Andorra	0.47	0.18	71	Andorra La Vella	38,800
Angola	1,247	481	12,127	Luanda	4,300
Anguilla (UK)	0.1	0.04	13	The Valley	8,800
Antigua & Barbuda	0.44	0.17	69	St John's	10,900
Argentina	2,780	1,074	39,922	Buenos Aires	15,000
Armenia	29.8	11.5	2,976	Yerevan	5,400
Aruba (Netherlands)	0.19	0.07	72	Oranjestad	21,800
Australia	7,741	2,989	20,264	Canberra	32,900
Austria	83.9	32.4	8,193	Vienna	35,500
Azerbaijan	86.6	33.4	7,962	Baku	7,300
Azores (Portugal)	2.2	0.86	243	Ponta Delgada	N/A
Bahamas	13.9	5.4	304	Nassau	21,300
Bahrain	0.69	0.27	699	Manama	25,300
Bangladesh	144	55.6	147,365	Dhaka	2,200
Barbados	0.43	0.17	280	Bridgetown	18,200
Belarus	208	80.2	10,293	Minsk	7,800
Belgium	30.5	11.8	10,379	Brussels	31,800
Belize	23	8.9	288	Belmopan	8,400
Benin	113	43.5	7,863	Porto-Novo	1,100
Bermuda (UK)	0.05	0.02	66	Hamilton	69,900
Bhutan	47	18.1	2,280	Thimphu	1,400
Bolivia	1,099	424	8,989	La Paz/Sucre	3,000
Bosnia-Herzegovina	51.2	19.8	4,499	Sarajevo	5,500
Botswana	582	225	1,640	Gaborone	11,400
Brazil	8,514	3,287	188,078	Brasília	8,600
Brunei	5.8	2.2	379	Bandar Seri Begawan	25,600
Bulgaria	111	42.8	7,385	Sofia	10,400
Burkina Faso	274	106	13,903	Ouagadougou	1,300
Burma (Myanmar)	677	261	47,383	Naypyitaw	1,800
Burundi	27.8	10.7	8,090	Bujumbura	700
Cambodia	181	69.9	13,881	Phnom Penh	2,600
Cameroon	475	184	17,341	Yaoundé	2,400

Listed above are the principal countries and territories of the world. If a territory is not completely independent, then the country it is associated with is named where space permits. The area figures give the total area of land, inland water and ice. The annual income is the Gross Domestic Product per capita in US dollars. [Gross Domestic Product per capita has been measured using the purchasing power parity method. This enables comparisons to be made between countries through their purchasing power (in US dollars), showing real price levels of goods and services rather than using currency exchange rates.] The figures are the latest available, usually 2006 estimates. *OPT: Occupied Palestinian Territory; N/A: Not available.

Country/Territory	Area (1,000 sq km)	Area (1,000 sq mi)	Population (1,000s)	Capital City	Annual income US $
Canada	9,971	3,850	33,099	Ottawa	35,200
Canary Is. (Spain)	7.4	2.9	1,673	Santa Cruz & Las Palmas	N/A
Cape Verde	4	1.6	421	Praia	6,000
Cayman Is. (UK)	0.26	0.1	45	George Town	43,800
Central African Rep.	623	241	4,303	Bangui	1,100
Chad	1,284	496	9,944	Ndjamena	1,500
Chile	757	292	16,134	Santiago	12,700
China	9,597	3,705	1,313,974	Beijing	7,600
Colombia	1,139	440	43,593	Bogotá	8,400
Comoros	2.2	0.84	691	Moroni	600
Congo	342	132	3,702	Brazzaville	1,300
Congo (Dem. Rep.)	2,345	905	62,661	Kinshasa	700
Cook Is. (NZ)	0.29	0.11	21	Avarua	9,100
Costa Rica	51.1	19.7	4,075	San José	12,000
Croatia	56.5	21.8	4,495	Zagreb	13,200
Cuba	111	42.8	11,383	Havana	3,900
Cyprus	9.3	3.6	784	Nicosia	22,700
Czech Republic	78.9	30.5	10,235	Prague	21,600
Denmark	43.1	16.6	5,451	Copenhagen	37,000
Djibouti	23.2	9	487	Djibouti	1,000
Dominica	0.75	0.29	69	Roseau	3,800
Dominican Republic	48.5	18.7	9,184	Santo Domingo	8,000
East Timor	14.9	5.7	1,063	Dili	800
Ecuador	284	109	13,548	Quito	4,500
Egypt	1,001	387	78,887	Cairo	4,200
El Salvador	21	8.1	6,822	San Salvador	4,900
Equatorial Guinea	28.1	10.8	540	Malabo	5,200
Eritrea	118	45.4	4,787	Asmara	1,000
Estonia	45.1	17.4	1,324	Tallinn	19,600
Ethiopia	1,104	426	74,778	Addis Ababa	1,000
Faeroe Is. (Denmark)	1.4	0.55	47	Tórshavn	31,000
Fiji	18.3	7.1	906	Suva	6,100
Finland	338	131	5,231	Helsinki	32,800
France	552	213	60,876	Paris	30,100
French Guiana	90	34.7	200	Cayenne	8,300
French Polynesia	4	1.5	275	Papeete	17,500
Gabon	268	103	1,425	Libreville	7,200

WORLD STATISTICS

Country/Territory	Area (1,000 sq km)	Area (1,000 sq mi)	Population (1,000s)	Capital City	Annual income US $
Gambia, The	11.3	4.4	1,642	Banjul	2,000
Georgia	69.7	26.9	4,661	Tbilisi	3,800
Germany	357	138	82,422	Berlin	31,400
Ghana	239	92.1	22,410	Accra	2,600
Gibraltar (UK)	0.006	0.002	28	Gibraltar Town	27,900
Greece	132	50.9	10,688	Athens	23,500
Greenland	2,166	836	56	Nuuk (Godthåb)	20,000
Grenada	0.34	0.13	90	St George's	3,900
Guadeloupe (France)	1.7	0.66	453	Basse-Terre	7,900
Guam (US)	0.55	0.21	171	Agana	15,000
Guatemala	109	42	12,294	Guatemala City	4,900
Guinea	246	94.9	9,690	Conakry	2,000
Guinea-Bissau	36.1	13.9	1,442	Bissau	900
Guyana	215	83	767	Georgetown	4,700
Haiti	27.8	10.7	8,309	Port-au-Prince	1,800
Honduras	112	43.3	7,326	Tegucigalpa	3,000
Hungary	93	35.9	9,981	Budapest	17,300
Iceland	103	39.8	299	Reykjavik	38,100
India	3,287	1,269	1,095,352	New Delhi	3,700
Indonesia	1,905	735	245,453	Jakarta	3,800
Iran	1,648	636	68,688	Tehran	8,900
Iraq	438	169	26,783	Baghdad	2,900
Ireland	70.3	27.1	4,062	Dublin	43,600
Israel	20.6	8	6,352	Jerusalem	26,200
Italy	301	116	58,134	Rome	29,700
Ivory Coast	322	125	17,655	Yamoussoukro	1,600
Jamaica	11	4.2	2,758	Kingston	4,600
Japan	378	146	127,464	Tokyo	33,100
Jordan	89.3	34.5	5,907	Amman	4,900
Kazakhstan	2,725	1,052	15,233	Astana	9,100
Kenya	580	224	34,708	Nairobi	1,200
Kiribati	0.73	0.28	105	Bairiki	2,700
Korea, North	121	46.5	23,113	Pyongyang	1,800
Korea, South	99.3	38.3	48,847	Seoul	24,200
Kuwait	17.8	6.9	2,418	Kuwait City	21,600
Kyrgyzstan	200	77.2	5,214	Bishkek	2,000
Laos	237	91.4	6,368	Vientiane	2,100

Country/Territory	Area (1,000 sq km)	Area (1,000 sq mi)	Population (1,000s)	Capital City	Annual income US $
Latvia	64.6	24.9	2,275	Riga	15,400
Lebanon	10.4	4	3,874	Beirut	5,500
Lesotho	30.4	11.7	2,022	Maseru	2,600
Liberia	111	43	3,042	Monrovia	1,000
Libya	1,760	679	5,901	Tripoli	12,700
Liechtenstein	0.16	0.06	34	Vaduz	25,000
Lithuania	65.2	25.2	3,586	Vilnius	15,100
Luxembourg	2.6	1	474	Luxembourg	68,800
Macedonia	25.7	9.9	2,051	Skopje	8,200
Madagascar	587	227	18,595	Antananarivo	900
Madeira (Portugal)	0.79	0.31	253	Funchal	N/A
Malawi	118	45.7	13,014	Lilongwe	600
Malaysia	330	127	24,386	Kuala Lumpur	12,700
Maldives	0.3	0.12	359	Malé	3,900
Mali	1,240	479	11,717	Bamako	1,200
Malta	0.32	0.12	400	Valletta	20,300
Marshall Is.	0.18	0.07	60	Majuro	2,900
Martinique (France)	1.1	0.43	436	Fort-de-France	14,400
Mauritania	1,026	396	3,177	Nouakchott	2,600
Mauritius	2	0.79	1,241	Port Louis	13,500
Mayotte (France)	0.37	0.14	201	Mamoundzou	4,900
Mexico	1,958	756	107,450	Mexico City	10,600
Micronesia	0.7	0.27	108	Palikir	2,300
Moldova	33.9	13.1	4,467	Chisinau	2,000
Monaco	0.001	0.0004	33	Monaco	30,000
Mongolia	1,567	605	2,832	Ulan Bator	2,000
Montenegro	14	5.4	631	Podgorica	3,800
Montserrat (UK)	0.1	0.04	9	St John's	3,400
Morocco	447	172	33,241	Rabat	4,400
Mozambique	802	309	19,687	Maputo	1,500
Namibia	824	318	2,044	Windhoek	7,400
Nauru	0.02	0.008	13	Yaren	5,000
Nepal	147	56.8	28,287	Katmandu	1,500
Netherlands	41.5	16	16,491	Amsterdam/The Hague	31,700
Netherlands Antilles	0.8	0.31	222	Willemstad	16,000
New Caledonia (Fr.)	18.6	7.2	219	Nouméa	15,000
New Zealand	271	104	4,076	Wellington	26,000
Nicaragua	130	50.2	5,570	Managua	3,000
Niger	1,267	489	12,525	Niamey	1,000
Nigeria	924	357	131,860	Abuja	1,400

WORLD STATISTICS

Country/Territory	Area (1,000 sq km)	Area (1,000 sq mi)	Population (1,000s)	Capital City	Annual income US $
Northern Marianas	0.46	0.18	82	Saipan	12,500
Norway	324	125	4,611	Oslo	47,800
Oman	310	119	3,102	Muscat	14,100
Pakistan	796	307	165,804	Islamabad	2,600
Palau	0.46	0.18	21	Koror	7,600
Panama	75.5	29.2	3,191	Panamá	7,900
Papua New Guinea	463	179	5,671	Port Moresby	2,700
Paraguay	407	157	6,506	Asunción	4,700
Peru	1,285	496	28,303	Lima	6,400
Philippines	300	116	89,469	Manila	5,000
Poland	323	125	38,537	Warsaw	14,100
Portugal	88.8	34.3	10,606	Lisbon	19,800
Puerto Rico (US)	8.9	3.4	3,927	San Juan	19,300
Qatar	11.5	4.4	885	Doha	29,400
Réunion (France)	2.5	0.97	788	St-Denis	6,200
Romania	238	92	22,304	Bucharest	8,800
Russia	17,075	6,593	142,894	Moscow	12,100
Rwanda	26.3	10.2	8,648	Kigali	1,600
St Kitts & Nevis	0.26	0.1	39	Basseterre	8,200
St Lucia	0.54	0.21	168	Castries	4,800
St V. & Grenadines	0.39	0.15	118	Kingstown	3,600
Samoa	2.8	1.1	177	Apia	2,100
San Marino	0.06	0.02	29	San Marino	34,100
São Tomé & Príncipe	0.96	0.37	193	São Tomé	1,200
Saudi Arabia	2,150	830	27,020	Riyadh	13,800
Senegal	197	76	11,987	Dakar	1,800
Serbia	88	34.1	9,396	Belgrade	4,400
Seychelles	0.46	0.18	82	Victoria	7,800
Sierra Leone	71.7	27.7	6,005	Freetown	900
Singapore	0.68	0.26	4,492	Singapore City	30,900
Slovak Republic	49	18.9	5,439	Bratislava	17,700
Slovenia	20.3	7.8	2,010	Ljubljana	23,400
Solomon Is.	28.9	11.2	552	Honiara	600
Somalia	638	246	8,863	Mogadishu	600
South Africa	1,221	471	44,188	Cape Town/ Pretoria/Bloemfontein	13,000
Spain	498	192	40,398	Madrid	27,000
Sri Lanka	65.6	25.3	20,222	Colombo	4,600

Country/Territory	Area (1,000 sq km)	Area (1,000 sq mi)	Population (1,000s)	Capital City	Annual income US $
Sudan	2,506	967	41,236	Khartoum	2,300
Suriname	163	63	439	Paramaribo	7,100
Swaziland	17.4	6.7	1,136	Mbabane	5,500
Sweden	450	174	9,017	Stockholm	31,600
Switzerland	41.3	15.9	7,524	Bern	33,600
Syria	185	71.5	18,881	Damascus	4,000
Taiwan	36	13.9	23,036	Taipei	29,000
Tajikistan	143	55.3	7,321	Dushanbe	1,300
Tanzania	945	365	37,445	Dodoma	800
Thailand	513	198	64,632	Bangkok	9,100
Togo	56.8	21.9	5,549	Lomé	1,700
Tonga	0.65	0.25	115	Nukúalofa	2,200
Trinidad & Tobago	5.1	2	1,066	Port of Spain	19,700
Tunisia	164	63.2	10,175	Tunis	8,600
Turkey	775	299	70,414	Ankara	8,900
Turkmenistan	488	188	5,043	Ashkhabad	8,900
Turks & Caicos	0.43	0.17	21	Cockburn Town	11,500
Tuvalu	0.03	0.01	12	Fongafale	1,600
Uganda	241	93.1	28,196	Kampala	1,800
Ukraine	604	233	46,711	Kiev	7,600
United Arab Emirates	83.6	32.3	2,603	Abu Dhabi	49,700
United Kingdom	242	93.4	60,609	London	31,400
USA	9,629	3,718	298,444	Washington, DC	43,500
Uruguay	175	67.6	3,432	Montevideo	10,700
Uzbekistan	447	173	27,307	Tashkent	2,000
Vanuatu	12.2	4.7	209	Port Vila	2,900
Venezuela	912	352	25,730	Caracas	6,900
Vietnam	332	128	84,403	Hanoi	3,100
Virgin Is. (UK)	0.15	0.06	23	Road Town	38,500
Virgin Is. (US)	0.35	0.13	109	Charlotte Amalie	14,500
Wallis & Futuna	0.2	0.08	16	Mata-Utu	3,800
Western Sahara	266	103	273	El Aaiún	N/A
Yemen	528	204	21,456	San'a	900
Zambia	753	291	11,502	Lusaka	1,000
Zimbabwe	391	151	12,237	Harare	2,000

THE WORLD: POLITICAL

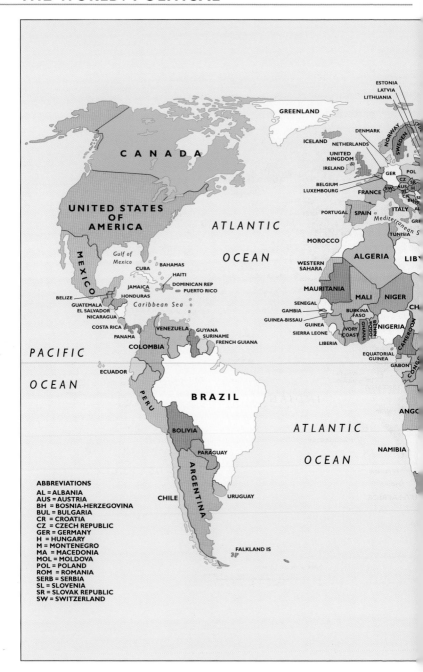

GREENLAND

ESTONIA
LATVIA
LITHUANIA

DENMARK

ICELAND   NETHERLANDS

NORWAY

SWEDEN

CANADA

UNITED
KINGDOM

IRELAND

POL

GER
CZ
SR
AUS
H

BELGIUM
LUXEMBOURG

FRANCE

SW
SL
CR
BH

UNITED STATES
OF
AMERICA

ATLANTIC

PORTUGAL   SPAIN

ITALY

GRE

AL

Mediterranean S

OCEAN

MOROCCO

TUNISIA

Gulf of
Mexico

M
E
X
I
C
O

BAHAMAS

CUBA

HAITI

JAMAICA

DOMINICAN REP
PUERTO RICO

WESTERN
SAHARA

ALGERIA

LIB

MAURITANIA

MALI

NIGER

BELIZE

GUATEMALA
EL SALVADOR
NICARAGUA

HONDURAS

Caribbean Sea

SENEGAL

CH

GAMBIA

GUINEA-BISSAU

BURKINA
FASO

COSTA RICA

PANAMA

VENEZUELA

GUYANA
SURINAME
FRENCH GUIANA

GUINEA

SIERRA LEONE

IVORY
COAST

BENIN
TOGO
GHANA

NIGERIA

COLOMBIA

LIBERIA

CAMEROON

PACIFIC

EQUATORIAL
GUINEA

ECUADOR

GABON

CONG

OCEAN

BRAZIL

PERU

ATLANTIC

ANGO

BOLIVIA

OCEAN

NAMIBIA

PARAGUAY

A
R
G
E
N
T
I
N
A

ABBREVIATIONS
AL = ALBANIA
AUS = AUSTRIA
BH = BOSNIA-HERZEGOVINA
BUL = BULGARIA
CR = CROATIA
CZ = CZECH REPUBLIC
GER = GERMANY
H = HUNGARY
M = MONTENEGRO
MA = MACEDONIA
MOL = MOLDOVA
POL = POLAND
ROM = ROMANIA
SERB = SERBIA
SL = SLOVENIA
SR = SLOVAK REPUBLIC
SW = SWITZERLAND

CHILE

URUGUAY

FALKLAND IS

BELARUS

R U S S I A

KAZAKHSTAN MONGOLIA

RAINE
L

GEORGIA UZBEKISTAN KYRGYZSTAN
ARMENIA AZER- TURKMENISTAN
TURKEY BAIJAN TAJIKISTAN
RUS SYRIA AFGHAN-
BANON ISTAN PAKISTAN
ISRAEL IRAQ IRAN
JORDAN KUWAIT
GYPT SAUDI NEPAL BHUTAN
ARABIA QATAR BANGLA-
UNITED DESH
ARAB INDIA BURMA
EMIRATES
UDAN YEMEN OMAN

NORTH
KOREA JAPAN

SOUTH
KOREA

C H I N A

TAIWAN

PACIFIC

OCEAN

Red Sea
Persian Gulf

ERITREA THAILAND CAMBODIA

VIETNAM
LAOS

PHILIPPINES

TRAL
CAN ETHIOPIA DJIBOUTI

SRI
LANKA

SOMALIA

UGANDA BRUNEI
NGO P.) KENYA MALAYSIA
RWANDA SINGAPORE
BURUNDI
TANZANIA I N D O N E S I A

PAPUA
NEW
GUINEA

INDIAN OCEAN

EAST
TIMOR

MBIA MALAWI
MOZAMBIQUE
BABWE
A MADAGASCAR

AUSTRALIA

SWAZILAND
LESOTHO
UTH AFRICA

NEW
ZEALAND

Scale along the Equator
0   1000   2000   3000   4000 km
0   1000   2000 miles

15

AFGHANISTAN

Introduced in January 2002, this flag replaces that of the Mujaheddin ('holy warriors'), who defeated Afghanistan's socialist government but lost power at the end of 2001. The flag is the 19th different design used by the country since 1901.

The Islamic Republic of Afghanistan is a landlocked country bordered by Turkmenistan, Uzbekistan, Tajikistan, China, Pakistan and Iran. The main regions are the northern plains, highlands in the centre of the country, and lowlands in the south-west.

The central highlands, comprising most of the Hindu Kush and its foothills, with peaks rising to more than 6,400 m [21,000 ft], cover nearly three-quarters of the land. Many Afghans live in the deep valleys of the highlands. The River Kabul flows east to the Khyber Pass on the border with Pakistan.

Much of the south-west is desert, while the northern plains contain most of the country's small amount of agricultural land. Grasslands cover much of the north, while the vegetation in the dry south is sparse.

Trees are rare in both regions, but forests of such coniferous trees as pine and fir grow on the higher mountain slopes, with cedars lower down. Alder, ash, juniper, oak and walnut grow in the mountain valleys.

Area 652,090 sq km [251,772 sq mi]
Population 31,057,000
Capital (population) Kabul (3,288,000)
Government Transitional regime
Ethnic groups Pashtun (Pathan) 44%, Tajik 25%, Hazara 10%, Uzbek 8%, others 8%
Languages Pashtu, Dari/Persian (both official), Uzbek
Religions Islam (Sunni Muslim 84%, Shiite Muslim 15%), others
Currency Afghani = 100 puls
Website www.afghan-web.com

CLIMATE

The height of the land and the country's remote position have a great effect on the climate. In winter, northerly winds bring cold, snowy weather in the mountains, but summers are hot and dry. The rainfall decreases to the south, where temperatures are higher throughout the year.

HISTORY

In ancient times, the area was invaded by Aryans, Persians, Greeks and Macedonians, and warrior armies from central Asia. Arab armies introduced Islam in the late 7th century. It has always occupied a strategic position, because the Khyber Pass was both the gateway to India and the back door to Russia.

Its modern history began in 1747, when the first unified Afghan state was established. A civil war was fought between 1819 and 1835, and in 1839 British troops invaded Afghanistan in an attempt to reduce Russian influence. Over the next 80 years, Britain fought three Anglo-Afghan wars to maintain control over the region. The British withdrew after the last, in 1919, and Afghanistan became independent.

POLITICS

In 1964, Afghanistan adopted a democratic constitution, but the country's ruler King Zahir and the legislature failed to agree on reforms. Muhammad Daoud Khan, the king's cousin, seized power in 1973 and abolished the monarchy. He ruled as president until 1978, when he was killed during a left-wing coup. The new regime's socialist policies conflicted with Islam and provoked a rebellion.

In 1987, Soviet troops invaded Afghanistan to support the left-wing regime. The Soviet occupation led to a protracted civil war. Various Muslim groups united behind the banner of the Mujaheddin to wage a guerrilla campaign, financed by the United States and aided by Pakistan. Soviet forces withdrew in 1989.

By 1992, the Mujaheddin had overthrown the government. The fundamentalist Muslim Taliban became the dominant group and, by 2000, their regime controlled 90% of the land.

In October 2001, the Taliban regime refused to hand over Osama bin Laden, the man suspected of masterminding the attacks on New York City and Washington D.C. on 11 September 2001, to US authorities. An American-led coalition and US air strikes backed local Northern Alliance troops to depose the Taliban and attack al-Qaeda. In November the Taliban regime collapsed, though conflict continued, and a coalition government led by Hamid Karzai was set up.

A draft constitution was approved in January 2004. The first democratic elections for president were held in October 2004 and won by Hamid Karzai, but the government's power outside Kabul and surrounding regions is limited. Much of the country is ruled by local warlords, who have encouraged the drug trade. Taliban insurgents remained in the south. In 2005 NATO took command of the US-led peacekeeping force, and in 2006 fighting intensified between the Taliban and NATO troops. In 2007 the insurgency spread beyond the southern region into the rest of the country.

ECONOMY

Afghanistan is one of the world's poorest countries. About 60% of the people are farmers or semi-nomadic herders. The largest economic activity, c. 30% of GDP, is the illegal farming of opium poppies to manufacture over 90% of the world's heroin. Rich mineral and natural gas resources remain underexploited.

KABUL

Capital of Afghanistan situated on the River Kabul in the eastern part of the country. It is strategically located in a high mountain valley in the Hindu Kush. The city was taken by Genghis Khan in the 13th century. Later it became part of the Mogul Empire, from 1526 to 1738. It has been the capital since 1776 and was occupied by the British during the Afghan Wars in the 19th century. Following the Soviet invasion in 1979, Kabul was the scene of bitter fighting. Unrest continued into the mid-1990s as rival Muslim groups fought for control. Industries include textiles, leather goods, and furniture.

ALBANIA

Albania's official name, Shqiperia, means 'Land of the Eagle', and the black double eagle was the emblem of the 15th-century hero Skanderbeg. A star placed above the eagle in 1946 was removed in 1992 when a non-Communist government was formed.

The Republic of Albania lies in the Balkan Peninsula. It faces the Adriatic Sea in the west and is bordered by Serbia, Montenegro, Macedonia and Greece. About 70% of the land is mountainous, with the highest point, Korab, reaching 2,764 m [9,068 ft] on the Macedonian border. Most Albanians live in the west on the coastal lowlands – the main farming region. Albania lies in an earthquake zone and severe earthquakes occur occasionally.

Area 28,748 sq km [11,100 sq mi]
Population 3,582,000
Capital (population) Tirana (300,000)
Government Multiparty republic
Ethnic groups Albanian 95%, Greek 3%, Macedonian, Vlachs, Gypsy
Languages Albanian (official)
Religions A majority of Albania's people claim no religious belief. Among the believers, 70% follow Islam and 30% follow Christianity (Orthodox 20%, Roman Catholic 10%).
Currency Lek = 100 qindars
Website www.parlament.al

CLIMATE

The coastal areas of Albania have a typical Mediterranean climate, with fairly dry, sunny summers and cool, moist winters. The mountainous regions have a severe climate, with heavy winter snow.

HISTORY

Albania was originally part of a region called Illyria. In 167 BC, it became part of the Roman Empire. When the Roman Empire broke up in AD 395, much of Albania became part of the Byzantine Empire. The country was subsequently conquered by Goths, Bulgarians, Slavs and Normans, although southern Albania remained part of the Byzantine Empire until 1204.

Much of Albania became part of the Serbian Empire in the 14th century and in the 15th century, a leader named Skanderbeg, now regarded as a national hero, successfully led the Albanians against the invading Ottoman Turks. After his death in 1468 the Turks took over the country. Albania was part of the Ottoman Empire until 1912, when it declared its independence.

Italy invaded Albania in 1939, but German forces took over the country in 1943. At the end of World War II, an Albanian People's Republic was formed under the Communist leaders who had led the partisans against the Germans. Pursuing a modernization programme on rigid Stalinist lines, the regime of Enver Hoxha at various times associated politically and economically with Yugoslavia (to 1948), the Soviet Union (1948–61) and China (1961–77), before following a fiercely independent policy. After Hoxha died in 1985, his successor, Ramiz Alia, continued the dictator's austere policies, but by the end of the decade, even Albania was affected by the sweeping changes in Eastern Europe.

POLITICS

In 1990, the more progressive wing of the Communist Party, led by Ramiz Alia, tee took over, but it collapsed within six months. Elections in 1992 finally brought to an end the last Communist regime in Europe when the non-Communist Democratic Party won power.

In 1997, amid a financial crisis caused by the collapse of fraudulent pyramid selling schemes, fresh elections took place. The socialist-led government that took power was re-elected in 2001. The stability of the region was threatened when Albanian-speaking Kosovars and Macedonians, many favouring the creation of a Greater Albania, fought with government forces in north-western Macedonia.

ECONOMY

Albania is Europe's poorest country. Agriculture employs 62% of the population. Major crops include fruits, maize, olives, potatoes, sugar beet, vegetables and wheat. Livestock farming and the fishing industry are also important.

Private ownership has been encouraged since 1991, but change has been slow. Albania has some minerals, and chromite, copper and nickel are exported. There is also some oil, brown coal and hydroelectricity.

won the struggle for power. The new government instituted a wide programme of reform, including the legalization of religion, the encouragement of foreign investment, the introduction of a free market for peasants' produce and the establishment of pluralist democracy. The Communists comfortably retained their majority in 1991 elections, but the government was brought down two months later by a general strike. An interim coalition 'national salvation' commit-

TIRANA (TIRANË)

Capital of Albania situated on the banks of the River Ishm in central Albania. Tirana was founded in the early 17th century by the Ottoman Turks and became the capital in 1920. In 1946 the communists came to power and the industrial sector of the city was developed. Industries include metal goods, agricultural machinery and textiles. Places of interest include Skanderbeg Square with the main historical buildings. Also the 18th century Haxhi Ethem Bey Mosque; Art Gallery (Albanian); National Museum of History.

ALGERIA

The star and crescent and the colour green on Algeria's flag are traditional symbols of the Islamic religion. The liberation movement which fought for independence from French rule from 1954 used this flag. It became the national flag when Algeria became independent in 1962.

The People's Democratic Republic of Algeria is Africa's second largest country after Sudan. Most Algerians live in the north, on the fertile coastal plains and hill country. South of this region lie high plateaux and ranges of the Atlas Mountains. Four-fifths of Algeria is in the Sahara, the world's largest desert.

Area 2,381,741 sq km [919,590 sq mi]
Population 32,930,000
Capital (population) Algiers (Alger, 3,260,000)
Government Socialist republic
Ethnic groups Arab-Berber 99%
Languages Arabic and Berber (both official), French
Religions Sunni Muslim 99%
Currency Algerian dinar = 100 centimes
Website www.algeria-un.org

CLIMATE

The coast has a Mediterranean climate, with warm and dry summers and mild and moist winters. The northern highlands have warmer summers and colder winters. The arid Sahara is hot by day and cool by night. Annual rainfall is less than 200 mm [8 in].

HISTORY

In early times, the region was ruled by the Carthaginians before it came under the control of the Roman empire. A major Roman province, it was captured by the Vandals in the 5th century. Arabs invaded the area in the 600s AD, converting the local Berbers to Islam and introducing Arabic. Intermarriage has made it difficult to distinguish Arabs from Berbers, though Berber dialects are still spoken and a 1998 law making Arabic the only official language met with much opposition.

POLITICS

Algeria experienced French colonial rule and colonization by settlers, finally achieving independence in 1962 following years of bitter warfare between nationalist guerrillas and French armed forces. After independence, the socialist FLN (National Liberation Party) formed a one-party government. Opposition parties were permitted in 1989.

ALGIERS

Capital and largest city of Algeria, north Africa's chief port on the Mediterranean. Founded by the Phoenicians, it has been ruled by Romans, Berber Arabs, Turks and Muslim Barbary pirates. In 1830 the French made Algiers the capital of the colony of Algeria. In World War II it was the headquarters of the Allies and seat of the French provisional government. During the 1950s and 1960s it was a focus for the violent struggle for independence. The old city is based round a 16th-century Turkish citadel. The 11th-century Sidi Abderrahman Mosque is a major destination for pilgrims.

In 1991, a Muslim party, the FIS (Islamic Salvation Front) won an election. The FLN cancelled the results and declared a state of emergency. Terrorist activities mounted and, between 1991 and 1999, about 100,000 people were killed. A proposal to ban political parties based on religion was approved in a 1996 referendum. In 1999 Abdelaziz Boutflika, a candidate favoured by the army, was elected president. The scale of the violence was reduced. In 2005, the government agreed to accept the demands of the Berber community, including official recognition of the Berber language. In

September an amnesty for Islamist guerrillas was approved in a referendum and terrorism reduced, but soon returned.

ECONOMY

Algeria is a developing country, whose main income is from its two main natural resources, oil and natural gas. Its natural gas reserves are among the world's largest. Oil and gas account for around two-thirds of the country's total revenues and more than 90% of the exports. Algeria's crude oil refining capacity is the biggest in Africa. Agriculture employs about 16% of the population.

ANGOLA

The flag is based on the flag of the MPLA (the Popular Movement for the Liberation of Angola) during the independence struggle. The emblem includes a star symbolizing socialism, one half of a gearwheel to represent industry, and a machete symbolizing agriculture.

The Republic of Angola is a large country, more than twice the size of France, on the south-western coast of Africa. The majority of the country is part of the plateau that forms most of southern Africa, with a narrow coastal plain in the west.

Angola has many rivers. In the northeast, several rivers flow northwards to become tributaries of the River Congo, while in the south, some rivers, including the Cubango (Okavango) and the Cuando, flow south-eastwards into inland drainage basins in the interior of Africa.

Area 1,246,700 sq km [481,351 sq mi]
Population 12,127,000
Capital Luanda (2,839,000)
Government Multiparty republic
Ethnic groups Ovimbundu 37%, Kimbundu 25%, Bakongo 13%, others 25%
Languages Portuguese (official), many others
Religions Traditional beliefs 47%, Roman Catholic 38%, Protestant 15%
Currency Kwanza = 100 lwei
Website www.angola.org

CLIMATE

Angola has a tropical climate, with temperatures of over 20°C [68°F] all year round, although upland areas are somewhat cooler. Coastal regions are dry, increasingly so to the south of Luanda, but the rainfall increases to the north and east. The rainy season lasts from November to April. Tropical forests flourish in the north, but the vegetation along the coast is sparse. The south of the country is semi-desert.

HISTORY

Bantu-speaking peoples from the north settled in Angola around 2,000 years ago. In the late 15th century, Portuguese navigators, seeking a route to Asia around Africa, explored the coast and, in the early 16th century, the Portuguese set up trading stations.

Angola became important as a source of slaves for Brazil, Portugal's huge colony in South America. After the decline of the slave trade, Portuguese settlers began to develop the land. The Portuguese population increased gently in the early 20th century.

In the 1950s, local nationalists began to demand independence. In 1956, the MPLA (Popular Movement for the Liberation of Angola) was founded with support from the Mbundu and mestizos (people of African and European descent). The MPLA led a revolt in Luanda in 1961, but it was put down by Portuguese troops.

Other opposition groups developed. In the north, the Kongo set up the FNLA (Front for the Liberation of Angola), while, in 1966, southern peoples, including many Ovimbundu, formed UNITA (National Union for the Total Independence of Angola).

POLITICS

The Portuguese agreed to grant Angola independence in 1975, after which rival the conflict. Angola then started the lengthy process of rebuilding its devastated infrastructure. Millions of refugees have begun to be resettled, but landmine clearance work proceeds slowly and is a major obstacle to redevelopment.

ECONOMY

Angola is a developing country, where 70% of the people are poor farmers, although agriculture contributes only about 9% of the gross domestic product. The main food crops include cassava, maize, sweet potatoes and beans, while bananas, coffee, palm products, seed cotton and sugar cane are grown for export. Cattle are the leading livestock, but sheep and goats are raised in drier areas.

Despite the poverty of most of its people and its low per capita GNP, Angola has much economic potential. It has oil reserves near Luanda and in the enclave of Cabinda, which is separated from Angola by a strip of land belonging to the Democratic Republic of Congo. Oil and mineral fuels are the leading exports.

Other resources include diamonds (the second most important export), copper and manganese. Angola also has a growing industrial sector. Manufactures include cement, chemicals, processed food and textiles.

nationalist forces began a struggle for power. A long-running civil war developed between the government forces, the FNLA in the north, and UNITA in the south. The government received Soviet and Cuban military aid, and as the war developed both the FNLA and UNITA turned to the West for support. UNITA was also aided by South Africa. FNLA guerrilla activity ended in 1984, but UNITA took control of large areas. Economic progress was hampered not only by the vast spending on defence and security, but also by the MPLA government's austere Marxist policies.

In 1991, a peace accord was agreed and multiparty elections were held, in which the MPLA, which had renounced Marxism-Leninism, won a majority. Jose Eduardo Dos Santos, president since 1979, retained power. UNITA's leaders rejected the election result and civil war resumed in 1994. In 1997 the government invited UNITA leader Jonas Savimbi to join a coalition but he refused.

Savimbi was killed in action in February 2002, raising hopes of peace and the army and rebels signed a cease-fire to end

LUANDA

Capital, chief port, and largest city of Angola, on the Atlantic coast. Luanda was first settled by the Portuguese in 1575. Its economy thrived on the shipment of more than 3 million slaves to Brazil until the abolition of slavery in the 19th century. Today, it exports crops from the province of Luanda.

ANTARCTICA

Antarctica is the fifth-largest continent (larger than Europe or Australasia), covering almost 10% of the world's total land area. Surrounding the South Pole, it is bordered by the Antarctic Ocean and the southern sections of the Atlantic, Pacific, and Indian Oceans. Almost entirely within the Antarctic Circle, it is of great strategic and scientific interest.

No people live there permanently, though scientists frequently stay for short periods to conduct research and exploration. Seven nations lay claim to sectors of it. Covered by an ice-sheet with an average thickness of c. 1,800 m (5,900 ft), it contains c. 90% of the world's ice and more than 70% of its fresh water and plays a crucial role in the circulation of the atmosphere and ocean, and hence in determining the planetary climate.

Area 14 million sq km [280,000 sq km ice-free, 13.72 million sq km ice-covered]
5,405,430 sq mi [108,108 sq mi ice-free, 5,297,322 sq mi ice-covered]
Government The Antarctic Treaty
Websites www.antarctica.ac.uk; www.aad.gov.au

LAND
Resembling an open fan, with the Antarctic Peninsula as a handle, the continent is a snowy desert covering approximately 14.2 million sq km [5.5 million sq mi]. The land is a high plateau with an average elevation of 1,800 m [6,000 ft] and rising to 4,897 m [16,066 ft] in the Vinson Massif. Mountain ranges occur near the coasts.

The interior, or South Polar Plateau, lies beneath c. 2,000 m [6,500 ft] of snow, accumulated over tens of thousands of years. Mineral deposits exist in the mountains, but their recovery is not practicable. Coal may be plentiful, but the value of known deposits of copper, nickel, gold, and iron will not repay the expense, both financial and environmental, of their extraction and export.

SEAS AND GLACIERS
Antarctic rivers are frozen, inching towards the sea, and instead of lakes there are large bodies of ice along the coasts. The great Beardmore Glacier creeps down from the South Polar Plateau, and eventually becomes part of the Ross Ice Shelf. The southernmost part of the Atlantic is the portion of the Antarctic Ocean known as the Weddell Sea.

CLIMATE AND VEGETATION
The coldest, windiest, highest (on average), and driest continent. During summer, more solar radiation reaches the surface at the South Pole than is received at the Equator in an equivalent period.

Mostly uninhabitable, Antarctica remains cold all year, with only a few coastal areas being free from snow or ice in summer (December to February). On most of the continent the temperature remains below freezing, and in August it has been recorded at nearly –90°C [–130°F]. Precipitation is generally 18–38cm [7–15in] of snow a year, but it melts at a slower rate, allowing a build-up over the centuries.

Mosses manage to survive on rocks along the outer rim of the continent. Certain algae grow on the snow, and others appear in pools of fresh water when they form during thaws.

HISTORY
Antarctic islands were sighted first in the 18th century, and in 1820 Nathaniel Palmer reached the Antarctic Peninsula. Between 1838 and 1840, US explorer Charles Wilkes discovered enough of the coast to prove that a continent existed, and the English explorer James Clark Ross made coastal maps. Towards the end of the 19th century, exploration of

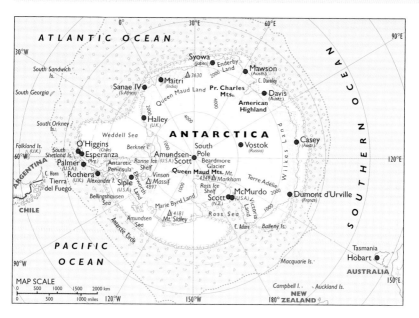

the interior developed into a race for the South Pole. Roald Amundsen reached the Pole on 14 December 1911, a month before Captain Robert Scott. The aeroplane brought a new era of exploration, and Richard E. Byrd became the best-known of the airborne polar explorers.

ANTARCTIC TREATY

The Antarctic Treaty in 1961 set aside the area for peaceful uses only, guaranteeing freedom of scientific investigation, banning waste disposal and nuclear testing, and suspending the issue of territorial rights. By 1990 the original 12 signatories had grown to 25, with a further 15 nations granted observer status in subsequent deliberations. However, the Treaty itself was threatened by wrangles between different countries, government agencies and international pressure groups.

Finally in July 1991, the belated agreement of the UK and the USA assured unanimity on a new accord to ban all mineral exploration for a further 50 years. This can only be rescinded if all the present signatories, plus a majority of any future adherents, agree. While the treaty has always lacked a formal mechanism for enforcement, it is firmly underwritten by public concern generated by the efforts of environmental pressure groups such as Greenpeace, which has been foremost in the campaign to have Antarctica declared as a 'World Park'.

The continent appears to be under threat from global warming. Some scientists believe this was the cause of the break-up of ice shelves along the Antarctic peninsula. Rising temperatures have also disturbed the breeding patterns of the Adelie penguins.

ANTARCTIC CIRCLE

Southernmost of the Earth's parallels, 66.5° south of the Equator. At this latitude the sun neither sets on the day of summer solstice (22 December) nor rises on the day of winter solstice (21 June).

ARGENTINA

The 'celeste' (sky blue) and white stripes were the symbols of independence around the city of Buenos Aires, where an independent government was set up in 1810. It became the national flag in 1816. The gold Sun of May, another symbol of independence, was added two years later.

The Argentine Republic is the largest of South America's Spanish-speaking countries. Its western boundary lies in the Andes, with basins, ridges and peaks of more than 6,000 m [19,685 ft] in the north. South of latitude 27°S, the ridges merge into a single high cordillera. Aconcagua, at 6,962 m [22,849 ft], is the tallest mountain in the western hemisphere.

In the south, the Andes are lower, with glaciers and volcanoes. Eastern Argentina is a series of alluvial plains, from the Andean foothills to the sea. The Gran Chaco in the north slopes down to the Paraná River, from the high desert of the Andean foothills to lowland swamp forest. Between the Paraná and Uruguay rivers is Mesopotamia, a fertile region. Further south are the damp and fertile pampa grasslands. Thereafter, the pampa gives way to the dry, windswept plateaux of Patagonia towards Tierra del Fuego.

Area 2,780,400 sq km [1,073,512 sq mi]
Population 39,922,000
Capital (population) Buenos Aires (13,349,000)
Government Federal republic
Ethnic groups European 97%, Mestizo, Amerindian
Languages Spanish (official)
Religions Roman Catholic 92%, Protestant 2%, Jewish 2%, others
Currency Peso = 10,000 australs
Website www.sectur.gov.ar

CLIMATE

The climate varies from subtropical in the north to temperate in the south. Rainfall is abundant in the north-east, but is lower to the west and south. Patagonia is a dry region, crossed by rivers that rise in the Andes.

HISTORY

Spanish explorers first reached the coast in 1516, landing on the shores of the Rio de la Plata. They were soon followed by others in search of gold and silver. Early prosperity based on stock raising and farming, combined with stable government, was boosted from 1870 by a massive influx of European immigrants, particularly Italians and Spaniards, for whom Argentina was a viable alternative to the United States. They settled lands recently cleared of Native Americans, often organized by huge land companies.

Development of a good railway network to the ports, plus steamship services to Europe, and, from 1877, refrigerated vessels, helped to create the strong meat, wool and wheat economy that carried Argentina into the 20th century. Before the Great Depression in the 1930s, Argentina was one of the world's more prosperous nations.

POLITICS

The collapse in the economy during the Great Depression led to a military coup in 1930. This was the start of a long period of military intervention in the politics of the country.

From 1976, the 'dirty war' saw the torture, wrongful imprisonment and murder ('disappearance') of up to

Islands, the first since 1982. Argentines were allowed to visit the Falkland Islands and erect a memorial to their war dead, and Argentina agreed to allow flights from the Falkland Islands to Chile.

In 2001, violent protests broke out when the peso was devalued and the government introduced severe austerity measures aimed at restoring the failing economy. 2003 and 2004 saw a slow return to economic growth. In 2007, during a dispute with the UK over oil rights, Argentina renewed its claims to the Falkland Islands.

ECONOMY

An 'upper-middle-income' developing country and one of the richest in South America in terms of natural resources, especially its fertile farmland. The economic base is mainly agricultural. Chief products are beef, maize and wheat. Sheep are raised in drier parts of the country, while other crops include citrus fruits, cotton, flax, grapes, potatoes, sorghum, sugar cane, sunflower seeds and tea.

Oilfields in Patagonia and the Piedmont make Argentina almost self-sufficient in oil and natural gas, which are a valuable export.

15,000 people by the military with 2 million people fleeing the country. In 1982, the government, blamed for the poor state of the economy, launched an invasion of the Falkland Islands (Islas Malvinas), which they had claimed since 1820. Britain regained the islands by sending an expeditionary force. After losing the conflict Argentina's President Galtieri resigned. Constitutional govern-ment was restored in 1983, though the army remained influential.

In 1999, Argentina and Britain signed an agreement concerning the Falkland

BUENOS AIRES

Capital of Argentina, on the estuary of the Río de la Plata, 240 km (150 mi) from the Atlantic Ocean. Originally founded by Spain in 1536, it was refounded in 1580 after being destroyed by the indigenous population. It became a separate federal district and capital of Argentina in 1880. Buenos Aires later developed as a commercial centre for beef, grain and dairy products.
It is the seat of the National University (1821). Industries include meat processing, flour milling, textiles, metal works, car assembly.

ARMENIA

Armenia's flag was first used between 1918 and 1922, when the country was an independent republic. It was readopted on 24 August 1990. The red represents the blood shed in the past, the blue the land of Armenia, and the orange the courage of the people.

The Republic of Armenia is a landlocked country in south-western Asia. Mostly consisting of a rugged plateau, criss-crossed by long faults. Movements along the faults cause earth tremors and occasionally major earthquakes. Armenia's highest point is Mount Aragats, at 4,090 m [13,149 ft] above sea level. The lowest land is in the north-west, where the capital Yerevan is situated. The largest lake is Ozero (Lake) Sevan in the east of the country.

The vegetation in Armenia ranges from semi-desert to grassy steppe, forest, mountain pastures and treeless tundra at the highest levels. Oak forests are found in the south-east, with beech being the most common tree in the forests of the north-east. Originally it was a much larger kingdom centred on Mount Ararat incorporating present-day north-east Turkey and parts of north-west Iran.

Area 29,800 sq km [11,506 sq mi]
Population 2,976,000
Capital (population) Yerevan (1,066,000)
Government Multiparty republic
Ethnic groups Armenian 93%, Russian 2%, Azeri 1%, others (mostly Kurds) 4%
Languages Armenian (official)
Religions Armenian Apostolic 94%
Currency Dram = 100 couma
Website www.armeniaforeignministry.com

CLIMATE

The height of the land, which averages 1,500 m [4,920 ft] gives rise to severe winters and cool summers. The highest peaks are snow-capped, but the total yearly rainfall is low, between and 200 and 800 mm [8 and 31 in].

HISTORY

Armenia was an advanced ancient kingdom, considered to be one of the original sites of iron and bronze smelting. A nation was established in the 6th century BC and Alexander the Great expelled the Persians in 330 BC. In 69 BC Armenia was incorporated into the Roman Empire. In AD 303, Armenia became the first country to adopt Christianity as its state religion. From 886 to 1046 Armenia was an independent kingdom. From the 11th to 15th centuries the Mongols were the greatest power in the region. By the 16th century Armenia was controlled by the Ottoman Empire. Despite religious discrimination, the Armenians generally prospered under Turkish rule. Eastern Armenia was the battleground between the rival Ottoman and Persian empires. In 1828 Russia acquired Persian Armenia and (with many promises of religious tolerance) many Armenians moved to the Russian-controlled area. In Turkish Armenia, British promises of protection encouraged nationalist movements. The Turkish response was uncompromising, killing about 200,000 in 1896 alone. In the Russian sector, a process of Russification was enforced.

During World War I, Armenia was the battleground for the Turkish and Russian armies. Armenians were accused of aiding the Russians and Turkish atrocities republic. In 1922, it became, with Azerbaijan and Georgia, part of the Transcaucasian Republic within the Soviet Union. But the three territories became separate Soviet Socialist Republics in 1936. Earthquakes in 1984 and 1988 killed more than 80,000 people and destroyed many cities.

After the break-up of the Soviet Union in 1991, Armenia became an independent republic and joined the Commonwealth of Independent States (CIS).

POLITICS

Armenia has long disputed the status of Nagorno-Karabakh, an Armenian-majority enclave in Azerbaijan. In 1992 Armenia occupied the territory between its border and Nagorno-Karabakh. A 1994 cease-fire left Armenia in control of about 20% of Azerbaijan's land area. Azerbaijan and its ally Turkey blockaded the borders, making Armenia dependent on Iran and Georgia for access to the outside world.

In 1998 Robert Kocharian, former leader of Nagorno-Karabakh, became president. Elections are frequently held, most recently in 2007, but are marked by alleged fraud by the ruling party.

intensified. More than 600,000 Armenians were killed by Turkish troops and 1.75 million were deported to Syria and Palestine. The Armenian Autonomous Republic was set up in the area held by Russia in 1918, but the western part of historic Armenia remained in Turkey, and the north-west was held by Iran. In 1920, Armenia became a Communist

YEREVAN

Capital of Armenia, on the River Razdan, southern Caucasus. One of the world's oldest cities, it was capital of Armenia from as early as the 7th century (though under Persian control). A crucial crossroads for caravan routes between India and Transcaucasia, it is the site of a 16th-century Turkish fortress. It is a traditional wine-making centre. Industries include chemicals, plastics, cables, tyres, metals, vodka.

ECONOMY

The World Bank classifies Armenia as a 'lower-middle-income' economy. Conflict with Azerbaijan in the early 1990s and the earthquakes have damaged the economy, but since 1992 the government has encouraged free enterprise.

Poverty, corruption and political assassinations contributed to Armenia losing 20% of its population in the 1990s. The country is highly industrialized with production dominated by mining and chemicals. Copper is the chief metal, but gold, lead and zinc are also mined. Agriculture is the second-largest sector, with cotton, tobacco, fruit and rice the main products.

ATLANTIC ISLANDS

AZORES

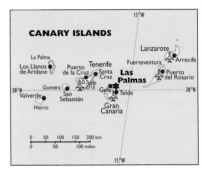

The Azores consist of nine large and several small islands, forming three groups, lying about 1290 km [800 mi] west of Lisbon in Portugal. Rising from the Mid-Atlantic Ridge in the North Atlantic Ocean, they are of relatively recent volcanic origin and mostly mountainous. Pico Alto, at 2351 m [7713 ft], is Portugal's highest mountain.

The Azores may have been known to Phoenician and Norse explorers, but were uninhabited when found by Portuguese sailors in the 15th century. Portugal laid claim to the islands and settled them, installing a Portuguese governor. They became a supply point for ships heading to the Americas in the 16th and 17th centuries and for whaling ships in the 19th. The Azores served as military bases in both World Wars and were particularly important in the second, when the allies leased a base which was used by anti-submarine forces against German U-boats. The US still leases an air base at Lages on Terceira island.

From 1938 until 1978, the islands were governed as three districts of Portugal. In 1976 they became an autonomous region with their own government. The capital and chief port is Ponta Delgada on São Miguel.

Farming and fishing are the main occupations, and the islands export a variety of fruits, vegetables and fish. Tourism has become the Azores' major source of income.

Area 2,247 sq km [868 sq mi]
Population 243,000
Capital (population) Ponta Delgada (21,000)
Government Autonomous region of Portugal
Ethnic groups Azorean
Languages Portuguese (official)
Religion Roman Catholic
Currency Euro = 100 cents
Website www.drtacores.pt

BERMUDA

Bermuda comprises some 150 small islands, the coral caps of ancient volcanoes rising from the floor of the North Atlantic Ocean 940 km [580 mi] east of North Carolina. When discovered in 1503 by the Spaniard Juan Mermúdez, the islands were uninhabited. They were claimed for Britain by Sir George Somers in the early 17th century. English colonists and slaves brought from Virginia settled and founded tobacco plantations, but found more success in shipbuilding and trade. The islands became a crown colony in 1684.

During the American War of Independence the islands became the western Atlantic headquarters of the British navy, and in the American Civil War they experienced a brief boom in 'blockade running' trade with the Confederacy. In World War II a US military base was built to protect Atlantic shipping, and US presence continued until 1995.

In 1968 the Bermudas were granted internal self-government, while the British crown retained control over security and international relations. Independence from Britain was rejected in a 1995 referendum.

Very low taxes and light regulation have made the Bermudas rich as a tax haven for overseas companies. Financial services are the largest industry, and the islands have a thriving stock exchange. GDP per capita is one of the highest in the world. The remainder of the Bermu-

das' income derives from tourism. There is little agriculture, principally bananas and citrus fruits, and most foods and other needs are imported.

Area 53 sq km [21 sq mi]

Population 66,000

Capital (population) Hamilton (1,000)

Government Parliamentary British overseas territory with internal self-government

Ethnic groups Black 55%, White 34%, others

Languages English (official), Portuguese

Religion Anglican 23%, Roman Catholic 15%, African Methodist Episcopal 11%, others

Currency Bermudian dollar = 100 cents

Website www.bermudatourism.com

ATLANTIC ISLANDS

CANARY ISLANDS

The Canary Islands are a group of seven large islands and many small ones, situated off southern Morocco. Formed by volcanic activity, they are steeply mountainous and have fertile soils. Teide, on Tenerife, is Spain's highest mountain and the third largest volcano in the world. The Canaries' climate is sub-tropical, dry at sea level, and wetter in the mountains.

The Canary Islands were probably known to the Phoenicians and Ancient Greeks, but were forgotten in the Middle Ages. They were rediscovered in the 14th century and claimed by Portugal. From 1400 Spanish expeditions began to conquer the native population, who had only stone age technology. Portugal accepted Spanish rule of the islands in 1479 and the Spanish established an economy based on sugar cane and wine production. After the discovery of the Americas, the Canary Islands became an important stopping point for Spanish ships.

The Canary Islands were divided into two separate provinces of Spain in 1927. In 1982 they together became an autonomous region which elects its own regional government.

Tourism forms the largest part of the economy, and its growth has also fuelled a large construction sector. Farming remains important, and exports include fruit, vegetables and tobacco.

Area 7,447 sq km [2,875 sq mi]
Population 1,672,689
Capital
Santa Cruz (Tenerife),
Las Palmas (Gran Canaria)
Government Constitutional monarchy
Ethnic groups Spanish
Languages Spanish (official)
Religion Roman Catholic
Currency Euro = 100 cents
Website www.icanarias.com

CAPE VERDE

The Republic of Cape Verde consists of ten large and five small islands, divided into the Barlavento (windward) and Sotavento (leeward) groups. They are volcanic and mainly mountainous, with steep cliffs and rocky headlands. The highest point is on the island of Fogo, an active volcano standing at 2,829 m [9,281 ft]). The climate is tropical, being hot for most of the year and mainly dry at sea level. The higher ground is cooler.

Portuguese since the 15th century, Verde included Portuguese Guinea (now Guinea-Bissau) until the mainland territory was separated in 1879. It was used chiefly as a provisioning station and assembly point for slaves in the trade from West Africa.

Cape Verde became fully independent in 1975 as a one-party state. Union with Guinea-Bissau was attempted but abandoned in 1980 after a coup in the mainland nation. In 1991 the country's first multiparty elections were held. A newly legalized opposition party, the Movement for Democracy (MPD), took control. The former ruling African Independence Party (PAICV) regained power in 2001.

Bananas, beans, coffee, fruit, groundnuts, maize and sugar cane are grown on the wetter, higher ground, when they are not ruined by endemic droughts. Cape Verde's principal exports are fish and bananas. Economic problems include high unemployment, but rising tourism has led to economic growth.

Area 4,033 sq km [1,557 sq mi]
Population 415,000
Capital (population) Praia (95,000)
Government Multiparty republic
Ethnic groups Creole (mulatto) 71%, African 28%
Languages Portuguese and Crioulo
Religion Roman Catholic and Protestant
Currency Cape Verdean escudo = 100 centavos
Website www.caboverde.com

FALKLAND ISLANDS

MADEIRA

The Falkland Islands (Islas Malvinas) lie 480 km [300 mi] to the west of Argentina and consist of two main islands, and more than 200 small ones.

Discovered in 1592 by the English navigator John Davis, the Falklands were first occupied nearly 200 years later by the French (East) and the British (West). The French interest, bought by Spain in 1770, was assumed by Argentina in 1806. The British, who had withdrawn in 1774, returned in 1832. They dispossessed the Argentinian settlers and founded a settlement of their own, which became a colony in 1892.

Argentina continues to claim possession of the Falkland Islands. In 1982 Argentinian forces launched an invasion which quickly overran the islands, but a large British expeditionary force returned possession to the United Kingdom within a few months. In 1999, a formal agreement between Britain and Argentina permitted Argentinians to visit the islands and improved air connections.

Sheep farming is the main employer and agricultural activity, and wool is the most significant export. Since the war, the fishing industry and in tourism have become the largest parts of the economy and have caused rapid economic growth. The sale of fishing licenses to other nations' fleets is a particularly strong source of income. Since the 1970s substantial oil reserves have been discovered, but have yet to be exploited.

Area 12,173 sq km [4,700 sq mi]
Population 3,000
Capital (population) Stanley (2,000)
Government Overseas British territory
Ethnic groups British
Languages English (official)
Religions Anglican
Currency Falkland pound = 100 pence
Website www.falklandislands.com

Madeira is the largest of the group of volcanic islands lying 550 km [350 mi] west of the Moroccan coast. Porto Santo, the uninhabited Islas Selvagens (not shown on the map) and the Desertas complete the group. The island of Madeira, at 745 sq km [288 sq mi], makes up more than 90% of the total land area.

With a warm climate and fertile soils, the Madeira Islands are known for their rich exotic plant life. The abundance of species is all the more surprising because rainfall is confined to the winter months.

Known to the Genoese in the 14th century, Madeira was discovered again by the Portuguese in the 1419. The present name, meaning 'wood', was given by the Portuguese when they first saw the forested islands. Portuguese settlers cleared most of the forests to establish a plantation farming industry. Spain held the islands between 1580 and 1640, while Britain occupied the islands twice in the early 19th century. Since 1976 the islands have formed an autonomous region of Portugal.

Major crops include bananas, maize, mangoes, oranges and sugar cane. Grapes are grown to make Madeira wine, and wine, sugar and bananas are the major exports. Other income derives from fishing and a large tourism sector. Financial services are a growth area as international companies are drawn by tax incentives.

Area 794 sq km [307 sq mi]
Population 253,000
Capital (population) Funchal (5,618)
Government Autonomous region of Portugal
Ethnic groups Portuguese
Languages Portuguese (official)
Religions Roman Catholic
Currency Euro = 100 cents
Website www.madeiratourism.org

ATLANTIC ISLANDS

ST HELENA

Saint Helena is a remote island in the South Atlantic, 1,920 km [1,190 mi] from the coast of west Africa. It is volcanic, though far from the main line of the Mid-Atlantic ridge, and consists of a high tableland dissected by valleys and bounded by steep cliffs. Relatively little of its 122 sq km [47 sq mi] is flat enough for habitation. Standing in the trade winds, it has a cool tropical maritime climate, dry at sea level but moist enough for limited farming on the heights.

Discovered by the Portuguese in 1502, it was captured by the Dutch in 1633 and passed to the British East India Company in 1659. It became a British crown colony in 1834 and is chiefly known as the place of Napoleon I's final exile. Nearby Ascension Island, one of St Helena's territories, served as an allied airbase in the Second World War and was extensively used by the UK in the Falklands War. St Helena itself is inaccessible to aircraft and can be visited only by ship.

St Helena is now a UK dependent territory and administrative centre for the islands of Ascension and Tristan da Cunha. It services ships, exports fish and handicrafts, and has some small scale farming. Ascension's military bases and communications relays provide some employment. However, jobs on St Helena are scarce and many are unemployed. The island is too remote to attract much tourism, and largely depends on financial assistance from the British government.

Area 122 sq km [47 sq mi]
Population 7,000
Capital (population) Jamestown
Government British overseas territory
Ethnic groups British
Languages English (official)
Religion Anglican
Currency Pound sterling = 100 pence
Website www.sainthelena.gov.sh

ST PIERRE & MIQUELON

A group of eight small islands in the Gulf of St Lawrence, south-west of Newfoundland. Miquelon is the largest. Rugged and barren, the islands have a cold, damp climate and harsh winters.

The group was claimed for France in 1535, but visited only seasonally by fishermen. In the 17th century, permanent French settlement began. In the 18th century, France's wars with Britain led to attacks on the islands, and British troops took control several times. After the defeat of Napoleon in 1815 the islands were permanently returned to France.

The Prohibition era in the US (1920–1933) led to an economic boom for St Pierre and Miquelon as a base for alcohol smugglers. When prohibition ended in 1933, the economy collapsed. During the Second World War the islands were controlled by occupied France's Vichy government, and Canada considered but rejected plans for an invasion. In 1941 the islands were suddenly captured by Free French forces. They are now a French overseas collectivity.

There is little farming. Fishing is the most important activity, but from the 1970s disputes with Canada arose over territorial waters and fishing rights. In 1992 they were resolved, with the islands receiving less than a quarter of the sea area France had claimed. The collapse of the Grand Banks cod fisheries furthered the fishing industry's decline.

Area 242 sq km [93 sq mi]
Population 6,100
Capital (population) St Pierre (5,500)
Government
Self-governing territorial collectivity of France
Ethnic groups Basques and Bretons
Languages French (official)
Religions Roman Catholic
Currency Euro = 100 cents
Website www2.st-pierre-et-miquelon.info

SÃO TOMÉ & PRÍNCIPE

São Tomé and Principe are two mountainous, volcanic and heavily forested islands in the Gulf of Guinea, 300 km [200 mi] off the west coast of Africa. São Tome is the larger and more developed of the two and has the pair's highest point, Pico di São Tomé, at 2,024 m [6,640 ft]. The native vegetation is mainly tropical rainforest, though much has been cleared for agriculture.

São Tomé and Principe were discovered by the Portuguese in 1471, nd became a Portuguese colony in 1522. Large sugar plantations were established, using African slave labour, and the islands became a major supplier of sugar to Europe. The plantations declined in the 17th century after far more efficient ones had been established in South America and the Caribbean, and the islands became a transit point for ships involved in the slave trade. In the early 19th century, new plantations were established growing coffee and cocoa. These became the mainstay of the economy, though the use of forced labour caused frequent unrest.

The islands became an independent nation in 1975 when Portugal abandoned its empire. They formed a one-party state, which adopted hardline socialist policies and aligned itself with the Soviet Union. Attempts to centralize the economy caused it to deteriorate, and poor management and droughts led to a decline in cocoa production. This wiped out export earnings, and the country became dependent on foreign aid.

In the late 1980s reliance on the Soviet Union was lessened, and the cocoa industry began to be revived. Palm oil and pepper were added to the island's exports and tourism began to be encouraged. Pressure from aid donors, principally France, improved the political situation. In 1990 Marxism was officially abandoned, and free elections were held in 1991 and won by the opposition party.

Since then, multiparty democracy has been maintained, despite being threatened by occasional coups d'etat.

Cocoa, coffee, bananas, and coconuts are grown on plantations, and their export is the republic's major source of income. Instability in cocoa prices causes major fluctuations in income. The government has begun to develop oil deposits in the Gulf of Guinea, which it is hoped will broaden the economy and control foreign debt.

Area 964 sq km [372 sq mi]
Population 19e,000
Capital (population) São Tomé (6,000)
Government Republic
Ethnic groups
Mestico, Angolares, Forros, Servicais, Tongas, Europeans (primarily Portuguese)
Languages Portuguese (official)
Religions Roman Catholic
Currency Dobra = 100 céntimos
Website www.saotome.st

TRISTAN DA CUNHA

Tristan da Cunha is one of a group of four islands in the south Atlantic Ocean, between South Africa and South America. The group was discovered in 1506 by the Portuguese and annexed by Britain in 1816. In 1961, Tristan, the only inhabitable island, suffered a volcanic eruption and was temporarily evacuated. Tristan da Cunha is administered from St Helena.

Area 98 sq km [38 sq mi]
Population 275
Capital (population) Edinburgh (275)
Government British overseas territory
Ethnic groups British
Languages English (official)
Religions Anglican
Currency Pound sterling = 100 pence
Website www.tristandc.com

AUSTRALIA

The national flag (above left) was adopted in 1901. It includes the British Union Flag, revealing Australia's historic links with Britain. In 1995, the Australian government put the flag used by the country's Aboriginal people (above right) on the same footing as the national flag.

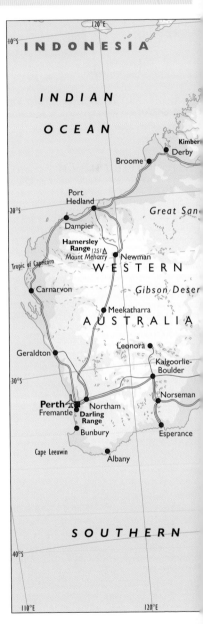

Australia is the world's sixth-largest country. The huge Western Plateau makes up 66% of its land area, and is mainly flat and dry. Off the coast of north-east Queensland lies the Great Barrier Reef. The Great Dividing Range extends down the entire east coast and into Victoria. The mountains of Tasmania are a southerly extension of the range. The highlands separate the east coastal plains from the Central Lowlands and include Australia's highest peak, Mount Kosciuszko, in New South Wales. The capital, Canberra, lies in the foothills. The south-east lowlands are drained by the Murray and Darling, Australia's two longest rivers. Lake Eyre is the continent's largest lake. It lies on the edge of the Simpson Desert and is a dry salt flat for most of the year. Alice Springs lies in the heart of the continent, close to Ayers Rock (Uluru).

Much of the Western Plateau is desert, although areas of grass and low shrubs are found on its margins. The grasslands of the Central Lowlands are used to raise live-stock. The north has areas of savanna and rainforest. In dry areas, acacias are common. Eucalyptus grows in wetter regions.

CLIMATE

Only 10% of Australia has an average annual rainfall greater than 1,000 mm [39 in]. These areas include some of the tropical north (where Darwin is situated), and the north-east coast, and the south-east. The coasts are usually warm and many parts of the south and south-west, including Perth, enjoy a Mediterranean climate of dry summers and moist winters. The interior is dry and many rivers are only seasonal.

AUSTRALIA

HISTORY

Native Australians (Aborigines) entered the continent from south-east Asia more than 50,000 years ago. They settled throughout the country and remained isolated from the rest of the world until the first European explorers, the Dutch, arrived in the 17th century. The Dutch

Area 7,741,229 sq km [2,988,885 sq mi]
Population 20,264,000
Capital (population) Canberra (309,000)
Government Federal constitutional monarchy
Ethnic groups Caucasian 92%. Asian 7%. Aboriginal 1%
Languages English (official)
Religions Roman Catholic 26%, Anglican 26%, other Christian 24%, non-Christian 24%
Currency Australian dollar = 100 cents
Website www.australia.gov.au

AYERS ROCK (ULURU)

Outcrop of rock, 448 km [280 mi] south west of Alice Springs, Northern Territory, Australia. Named after the South Australian politician Sir Henry Ayers (1821–97), it remained undiscovered by Europeans until 1872. It stands 348 m [1,142 ft] high, and is the second largest single rock in the world – the distance around its base is c. 10 km [6 mi]. The rock, caves of which are decorated with ancient paintings, is of great religious significance to Native Australians.

Commonwealth of Australia. In 1911 the Northern Territory joined the federation. A range of progressive social welfare policies were adopted, such as old-age pensions in 1909. The federal capital was established in 1927 at Canberra, Australian Capital Territory. Australia fought as a member of the Allies in both world wars. The Battle of the Coral Sea in 1942 prevented a full-scale attack on the continent.

POLITICS

After 1945 Australia steadily realigned itself with its Asian neighbours. Robert Menzies, Australia's longest-serving prime minister, oversaw many economic and social reforms and dispatched Australian troops to the Vietnam War. In 1977 Prime Minister Gough Whitlam was removed from office by the British governor general. He was succeeded by Malcolm Fraser. In 1983 elections, the Labour Party defeated Fraser's Liberal

did not settle. In 1770 British explorer Captain James Cook reached Botany Bay and claimed the east coast for Great Britain. In 1788 Britain built its first settlement, for convicts, on the site of present-day Sydney. The first free settlers arrived three years later.

In the 19th century, the economy developed rapidly, based on mining and sheep-rearing. At this time the continent was divided into colonies, which later were to become states. In 1901 the states of Queensland, Victoria, Tasmania, New South Wales, South Australia and Western Australia, federated to create the

Party, and Bob Hawke became prime minister. His shrewd handling of industrial disputes and economic recession helped him win a record four terms in office. In 1991 Hawke was forced to

CANBERRA

Capital of Australia on the River Molonglo, Australian Capital Territory, south-eastern Australia. Settled in the early 1820s, it was chosen in 1908 as the new site for Australia's capital (succeeding Melbourne). The transfer of all governmental agencies was not completed until after World War II. Canberra has the Australian National University (1946), Royal Australian Mint (1965), Royal Military College and Stromlo Observatory. The new Parliament House was opened in 1988. Other important buildings include the National Library, National Museum, and National Gallery. Tidbinbilla Nature Reserve is located just outside the city.

resign as leader and was succeeded by Paul Keating. Backed by a series of opinion polls, Keating proposed that Australia should become a republic by 2001.

Keating won the 1993 general election and persevered with his free market reforms. In 1996 elections, Keating was defeated by a coalition led by John Howard. In 1998 Howard narrowly secured a second term in office. In a referendum of 1999 Australia voted against becoming a republic. In 2000 Sydney hosted the 28th Summer Olympic Games, nicknamed the 'Friendly Games'.

The historic maltreatment of Native Australians remains a contentious political issue. In 1993 the government passed the Native Title Act which restored to Native Australians land rights over some traditional hunting and sacred areas, and

further land rights improvements followed However, native peoples still suffer extensive poverty and low life expectancy.

Howard secured a fourth term in 2004 elections and vowed to stay leader of the Liberal Party for as long as the members want him. His government has acted slowly on global warming, despite rising temperatures already causing devastating bush fires and severe drought.

ECONOMY

Australia is a prosperous country. Originally an agrarian economy, although crops grow on only 6% of the land. The country remains a major producer and exporter of farm products, particularly cattle, wheat and wool. Grapes grown for winemaking are also important. Australia is rich in natural resources and is a major producer of minerals, such as bauxite, coal, copper, diamonds, gold, iron ore, manganese, nickel, silver, tin, tungsten and zinc. Some oil and natural gas is also produced.

The majority of Australia's imports are manufactured products. They include machinery and other capital goods required by factories. The country has a highly developed manufacturing sector; the major products include consumer goods, notably foodstuffs and household articles. Tourism is a vital industry.

GREAT BARRIER REEF

World's largest coral reef, in the Coral Sea off the north east coast of Queensland. It was first explored by James Cook in 1770. It forms a natural breakwater and is up to 800 m [2,600 ft] wide. The reef is separated from the mainland by a shallow lagoon, 11–24 km [7–15 mi] wide. It is a world heritage site. The reef is 2,000 km [1,250 mi] in length, with an area of approximately 207,000 sq km [80,000 sq mi].

AUSTRIA

According to legend, the colours on Austria's flag originate from a battle in the Third Crusade in 1191 when an Austrian duke's tunic was stained with blood, remaining white under his belt. Actually based on 13th-century heraldry, the design only became the official flag in 1918.

The Republic of Austria is a landlocked country in the heart of Europe. About three-quarters of the land is mountainous. Northern Austria contains the valley of the River Danube, and the Vienna Basin. This is Austria's main farming region.

Southern Austria contains ranges of the Alps, which rise to their highest point of 3,797 m [12,457 ft] at Grossglockner.

Area 83,859 sq km [32,378 sq mi]
Population 8,193,000
Capital (population) Vienna (2,190,000)
Government Federal republic
Ethnic groups Austrian 90%, Croatian, Slovene, others
Languages German (official)
Religions Roman Catholic 78%, Protestant 5%, Islam and others 17%
Currency Euro = 100 cents
Website www.austria.info

CLIMATE

The climate is influenced both by westerly and easterly winds. The moist westerly winds bring rain and snow. They also moderate the temperatures. Dry easterly winds bring very cold weather during the winter, and hot weather during the summer.

HISTORY

Following the collapse of the Roman Empire, of which Austria south of the Danube formed a part, the area was invaded and settled by waves of Asian, Germanic and Slav peoples. In the late 8th century, Austria came under the rule of Charlemagne, but in the 10th century, the area was overrun by Magyars.

In 955, the German king Otto I brought Austria under his rule, and in 962 it became part of what later became known as the Holy Roman Empire. German emperors ruled the area until 1806, when the Holy Roman Empire broke up.

The Habsburg ruler of the Holy Roman Empire became Emperor Francis I of Austria. In 1867, Austria and Hungary set up the powerful dual monarchy of Austria-Hungary.

Austria-Hungary was allied to Germany in World War I, but the defeated empire collapsed in 1918. Austria's present boundaries derive from the Versailles Treaty, signed in France in June 1919. In 1933, the Christian Socialist Chancellor Engelbert Dollfuss ended parliamentary democracy and ruled as a dictator. He was assassinated in 1934 due to his opposition to the Austrian Nazi Party's aim of uniting Austria and Germany.

The *Anschluss* (union with Germany) was achieved by the German invasion in March 1938. Austria became a province of the Third Reich called Ostmark until the defeat of the Axis powers in 1945.

POLITICS

After World War II, Austria was occupied by the Allies, Britain, France and the United States and it paid reparations for a 10-year period. After agreeing to be permanently neutral, Austria became an independent federal republic in 1955.

In 1994, two-thirds of the people voted in favour of joining the European Union and the country became a member in 1995. Austria became a centre of controversy in 1999, when the extreme right-wing Freedom Party, led by Jörg Haider, who had described Nazi Germany's employment policies as 'sound', came second in national elections. A coalition government was formed, divided equally between the Freedom Party and the conservative People's Party. Elections in 2002 halved the Freedom Party's share of the vote, but the coalition continued. In 2006 elections it was replaced by a coalition between the People's Party and the Social Democrat party.

ECONOMY

Austria is a prosperous country with plenty of hydroelectric power, some oil and gas, and reserves of lignite (brown coal). The country's leading economic activity is manufacturing metals and metal products, including iron and steel, vehicles, machinery, machine tools and ships. Craft industries, making such things as fine glassware, jewellery and porcelain are also important. Dairy and livestock farming are the leading agricultural activities. Major crops include barley, potatoes, rye, sugar beet and wheat.

VIENNA (WIEN)

Capital of Austria, on the River Danube. Vienna became important under the Romans, but after their withdrawal in the 5th century it fell to a succession of invaders from eastern Europe. The first Habsburg ruler was installed in 1276. It was the seat of the Holy Roman Empire from 1558 to 1806. Occupied by the French during the Napoleonic Wars, it was later chosen as the site of the Congress of Vienna. As the capital of the Austro-Hungarian Empire, it was the cultural and social centre of 19th-century Europe under Emperor Franz Joseph. After World War II, it was occupied (1945–55) by joint Soviet-Western forces. Historical buildings include the 12th-century St Stephen's Cathedral, the Schönbrunn, and the Hofburg.

AZERBAIJAN

Azerbaijan's flag was adopted in 1991. Light blue is a traditional Turkic colour. At the centre of the red stripe is a white crescent and star, traditional symbols of Islam. The points of the star represent the eight groups of people in Azerbaijan.

The Republic of Azerbaijan lies in eastern Transcaucasia, bordering the Caspian Sea to the east. The Caucasus Mountains are in the north and include Azerbaijan's highest peak, Mount Bazar-Dyuzi, at 4,466 m [14,652 ft]. Another highland region including the Little Caucasus Mountains and part of the rugged Armenian plateau, lies in the south-west.

Between these regions lies a broad plain drained by the River Kura. Its eastern part, south of the capital Baku, lies below sea level. Azerbaijan also includes the Nakhichevan Autonomous Republic on the Iran frontier, an area cut off from the rest of Azerbaijan by Armenian territory.

Forests grow on the mountains, while the lowlands comprise grassy steppe or semi-desert.

Area 86,600 sq km [33,436 sq mi]
Population 7,962,000
Capital (population) Baku (1,830,000)
Government Federal multiparty republic
Ethnic groups Azeri 90%, Dagestani 3%, Russian, Armenian, others
Languages Azerbaijani (official),Russian, Armenian
Religions Islam 93%, Russian Orthodox 2%, Armenian Orthodox
Currency Azerbaijani manat = 100 gopik
Website www.president.az

migrated to the area from the east by the 9th century.

Azerbaijan was ruled by the Mongols between the 13th and 15th centuries and then by the Persian Safavid dynasty. By the early 19th century it was under Russian control.

CLIMATE

Azerbaijan has hot summers and cool winters. The plains have low rainfall ranging from c. 130 to 380 mm [5 to 15 in] a year. The uplands have much higher rainfall as does the subtropical south east coast.

HISTORY

In ancient times, the area now called Azerbaijan was invaded many times. Arab armies introduced Islam in 642, but most modern Azerbaijanis are descendants of Persians and Turkic peoples who

CAUCASUS

Mountain region in south-east Europe, Russia, Georgia, Armenia and Azerbaijan, extending south-east from the mouth of the River Kuban on the Black Sea to the Apscheron Peninsula in the Caspian Sea. It stretches for 1,210 km [750 mi].The system includes two major regions: north Caucasia (steppes) and Transcaucasia. It forms a natural barrier between Asia and Europe. There are deposits of oil, iron and manganese, and cotton, fruit and cereal crops are grown. The highest peak is Mount Elbrus 5,637 m [18,493 ft].

After the Russian Revolution of 1917, attempts were made to form a Transcaucasian Federation made up of Armenia, Azerbaijan and Georgia. When this failed, Azerbaijanis set up an independent state. But Russian forces occupied the area in 1920. In 1922, the Communists set up a Transcaucasian Republic consisting of Armenia, Azerbaijan and Georgia, and placed it under Russian control. In 1936, the areas became separate Soviet Socialist Republics within the Soviet Union.

POLITICS

Following the break-up of the Soviet Union in 1991, Azerbaijan became independent. In 1992, Abulfaz Elchibey became president in Azerbaijan's first contested election. In 1993 Elchibey fled and Heydar Aliev, former head of the Communist Party and the KGB in Azerbaijan, assumed the presidency. He was elected later that year and Azerbaijan joined the Commonwealth of Independent States (CIS).

In 1992 conflict with Armenia arose over Nagorno-Karabakh, an enclave in Azerbaijan where the majority of the people are Christian Armenians. A cease-fire in 1994 left Armenia in control of about 20% of Azerbaijan's land area, but negotiations remain inconclusive and neither side has been able to safely re-settle.

In 1998 Aliev was re-elected. In 2003 his son Ilham became president, and was re-elected in 2005 despite charges of fraud. In 2006-7 Russia threatened to reduce subsidies on Azerbaijan's gas supplies, doubling the price. Azerbaijan responded by stopping oil supplies to Russia and opening new pipelines to Turkey to allow direct access to European markets.

ECONOMY

In the mid-1990s, the World Bank classified Azerbaijan as a 'lower-middle-income' economy. Yet, by the late 1990s, the oil reserves in the Baku area on the Caspian Sea, and in the sea itself, held great promise. Oil extraction and manufacturing, including oil refining and the production of chemicals, machinery and textiles, are now the most valuable sources of revenue.

Large areas of land are irrigated and crops include cotton, fruit, grains, tea, tobacco and vegetables. Fishing is still important although the Caspian Sea is becoming increasingly polluted. Private enterprise is now encouraged.

BAKU

Capital of Azerbaijan, a port on the west coast of the Caspian Sea. A trade and craft centre in the Middle Ages, Baku prospered under the Shirvan shahs in the 15th century. Commercial oil production began in the 1870s. At the beginning of the 20th century, Baku lay at the centre of the world's largest oilfield. Industries include oil processing and equipment, shipbuilding, electrical machinery, chemicals.

BAHRAIN

Red and white are traditional colours of the Gulf States. The white historically identified friendly Arab states. The five steps in the serration denote the five Pillars of Islam.

The Kingdom of Bahrain, a former Emirate and now a constitutional hereditary monarchy, is an archipelago consisting of more than 30 islands in the Persian Gulf. The largest of the islands, also called Bahrain, makes up seven-eighths of the country. Causeways link the island of Bahrain to the second largest island of Al Muharraq to the northeast and also to the Arabian peninsula.

Sandy, desert plains make up most of this small, low-lying island country. In the northern coastal areas of Bahrain, freshwater springs provide water for drinking and also for irrigation.

Area 694 sq km [268 sq mi]
Population 699,000
Capital (population) Manama (140,000)
Government Constitutional hereditary monarchy
Ethnic groups Bahraini 62%, others
Languages Arabic, English, Farsi, Urdu
Religions Muslim (Shi'a and Sunni) 81%, Christian 9%, other
Currency Bahraini dinar = 1000 fils
Website www.bahrain.gov.bh

CLIMATE

Bahrain has a hot and humid climate. Winters are mild, with temperatures ranging from about 10°C [50°F] to 27°C [80°F]. Summers are hot and humid, with temperatures often soaring to more than 38°C [100°F]. The average annual rainfall is low. The rain occurs mainly in winter, and rainfall is almost non-existent in summer months. Northern Bahrain is furthest from mainland Arabia and is the wettest area, with about 80 mm [3 in] of rain a year.

HISTORY

Bahrain was part of a trading civilization called Dilmun, which prospered between about 2000 and 1800 BC. This civilization was linked to the Sumerian, Babylonian and Assyrian civilizations to the north, and with the Indus Valley civilization in what is now Pakistan. Bahrain later came under Islamic Arab influence from the 7th century.

Portugal seized the archipelago from its Arab rulers in 1521, but the Persians conquered the islands in 1603, holding them against attacks by the Portuguese and Omanis. However, in 1782, the Al Khalifah Arabs from Saudi Arabia took over the islands and have controlled them ever since.

In the early 19th century, Britain helped Bahrain to prevent annexation by Saudi Arabian invaders. As a result, Bahrain agreed to let Britain take control of its foreign affairs. Bahrain effectively became a British protectorate, though it was not called one. In the 1920s and 1930s, the Bahrainis established welfare systems, which were later funded by revenue from oil, which was discovered in 1932.

Political reforms began in the 1950s and, in 1970, the Emir turned over some of his power to a Council of State, which became a Cabinet. Britain withdrew from the Persian Gulf region in 1971 and Bahrain became fully independent.

POLITICS

Bahrain adopted a new constitution in 1973. This created a National Assembly with 30 elected members. However, relations between the National Assembly and the ruling Al Khalifa family were difficult and the National Assembly was dissolved in 1975. The country was then ruled by the Emir and his cabinet, headed by the prime minister, the Emir's appointee.

In February 2002, a new constitution changed the country from an Emirate into a constitutional hereditary monarchy and the ruler Sheikh Hamad bin Isa Al-Khalifa became king. Elections for a new directly elected House of Deputies took place later that year, with women allowed to vote for the first time. The 40-member House of Deputies together with a second chamber, a Shura Council, consisting of experts appointed by the king, made up the National Assembly, Bahrain's first parliament since 1975.

Political problems in recent years have included tensions between ruling Sunni Muslims and the Shiite majority. During the Iran-Iraq War Bahrain supported Iraq against Iran, but in the Gulf War it joined the coalition against its former ally.

Since 1991, the US Navy has used Bahrain as its permanent headquarters in the Persian Gulf. This has provoked terrorist incidents. Although the people have more freedom than others in the region, opposition groups continue to press for further progress, including greater powers for the elected House of Deputies. After large public rallies and demonstrations, the opposition Shiite Al-Wefaq party won over 40% of parliamentary seats in 2005 elections.

ECONOMY

The people of Bahrain enjoy one of the highest standards of living in the Persian Gulf region. The average life expectancy at birth (2005 estimate) is 74 years and free medical services are available. The adult literacy rate is 89%.

Bahrain's prosperity is based on oil, although the country lacks major reserves. Petroleum and petroleum products accounted for 68% of the exports in 2002. Its aluminium smelting plant is the Persian Gulf's largest non-oil industrial complex and aluminium, in all forms, accounted for 15% of the exports in 2002. Textiles and clothing accounted for another 8%.

Bahrain is a major banking and financial centre, and it is home to numerous multinational companies that operate in the Persian Gulf region. It is a popular tourist destination.

MANAMA (AL-MANAMAH)

Capital of Bahrain, on the north coast of Bahrain Island, in the Persian Gulf. It was made a free port in 1958, and a deepwater harbour was built in 1962. It is the country's principal port and commercial centre. Industries include oil refining, banking, boatbuilding.

BANGLADESH

Bangladesh adopted this flag in 1971, following the country's break from Pakistan. The green is said to represent the fertility of the land. The red disc is the sun of independence. It commemorates the blood shed during the struggle for freedom.

The People's Republic of Bangladesh is one of the world's most densely populated countries. Apart from the hilly regions in the far north-east and south-east, most of the land is flat and covered by fertile alluvium spread over the land by the Ganges, Brahmaputra and Meghna rivers. These rivers overflow when they are swollen by the annual monsoon rains. Floods also occur along the coast, 575 km [357 mi] long, when tropical cyclones (the name for hurricanes in this region) drive seawater inland. These periodic storms cause great human suffering. The most devastating tropical cyclone ever recorded occurred in Bangladesh in 1970, when an estimated 1 million people were killed. Most of Bangladesh is cultivated, but forests cover about 16% of the land. They include bamboo forests in the north-east and mangrove forests in the swampy Sundarbans region in the south-west, which is a sanctuary for the Royal Bengal tiger.

Area 143,998 sq km [55,598 sq mi]
Population 147,365,000
Capital (population) Dhaka (12,560,000)
Government Multiparty republic
Ethnic groups Bengali 98%, tribal groups
Languages Bangali (official), English
Religions Islam 83%, Hinduism 16%
Currency Taka =100 paisas
Website www.bangladeshonline.com

CLIMATE

Bangladesh has a tropical monsoon climate. Dry northerly winds blow during the winter months, but, in summer, moist winds from the south bring monsoon rains. In 1998, around two-thirds of the entire country was submerged, causing extensive damage. In December 2004, Bangladesh emerged relatively unscathed by the tsunami in the Indian Ocean.

HISTORY

For 300 years after the mid-8th century AD, Buddhist rulers governed eastern Bengal, the area that now makes up Bangladesh. In the 13th century, Muslims from the north extended their rule into Bengal and, in 1576, the area became part of the Muslim Mughal Empire which was ruled by the emperor Akbar. This empire, which also included India, Pakistan and Afghanistan, began to break up in the early 18th century. Europeans, who had first made contact with the area in the 16th century, began to gain influence.

The East India Company, chartered by the English government in 1600 to develop trade in Asia, became the leading trade power in Bengal by the mid-18th century. In 1757, following the defeat of the nawab of Bengal in the Battle of Plessey, the East India Company effectively ruled Bengal. Discontent with the company led to the Sepoy Rebellion in 1857. In 1858, the British government took over the East India Company and its territory became known as British India.

MAP SCALE
0   50   100 km
0   50 miles

By 1990 protests toppled Ershad from power and, after the first free parliamentary elections since independence, a coalition government was formed in 1991. Many problems arose in the 1990s, including increasing Muslim fundamentalism and severe cyclone damage. In 1996, Sheikh Hasina Wajed of the Awami League became prime minister, but, in 1999, she was defeated by Khaleda Zia of the Nationalist Party. Elections scheduled for January 2007 were postponed after accusations of unfairness led to rioting. An army-backed administration took control, claiming it intended to clean up politics before holding elections in 2008.

ECONOMY

Bangladesh is one of the world's poorest countries. Agriculture employs more than half of the workforce. Rice is the chief crop and Bangladesh is the world's fourth largest producer. Other important crops include jute, sugar cane, tobacco and wheat.

Clothing manufacture is the largest industry and dominant export. Shipbreaking is also important. The country has some gas reserves, which may allow future exonomic expansion.

POLITICS

In 1947 British India was partitioned between mainly Hindu India and Muslim Pakistan. Pakistan consisted of two parts, West and East Pakistan, separated by about 1,600 km [1,000 mi] of Indian territory. Differences developed between West and East Pakistan as people in the east felt themselves victims of ethnic and economic discrimination by the Urdu and Punjabi-speaking peoples of the west.

In 1971 resentment turned to war when Bengali irregulars, aided by Indian troops, established the independent nation of 'Free Bengal' with Sheikh Mujibur Rahman as head of state. The Sheikh's assassination in 1975, one of four military coups in the first 11 years of independence, led finally to a takeover by General Zia Rahman. He created an Islamic state before his assassination in 1981. General Ershad took over in a coup in 1982 and resigned as army chief in 1986 to become a civilian president.

DHAKA (DACCA)

Capital of Bangladesh, a port on the Ganges delta, eastern Bangladesh. Its influence grew as the 17th century Mogul capital of Bengal. In 1765 it came under British control. At independence (1947) it was made capital of the province of East Pakistan. Severely damaged during the war of independence from Pakistan, it became capital of Bangladesh (1971). Sights include the Dakeshwari Temple, Bara Katra Palace (1644) and mosques. It is in the centre of the world's largest jute-producing area. Industries include engineering, textiles, printing, glass, chemicals.

BELARUS

In September 1991, Belarus adopted a red and white flag, replacing the flag used in the Soviet era. In June 1995, following a referendum in which Belarussians voted to improve relations with Russia, it was replaced with a design similar to the old flag, but without the hammer and sickle.

The Republic of Belarus is a land-locked country in Eastern Europe, formerly part of the Soviet Union. The land is low-lying and mostly flat. In the south, much of the land is marshy. This area contains Europe's largest marsh and peat bog, the Pripet Marshes.

A hilly region extends from north-east to south-west and includes the highest point in Belarus, situated near the capital Minsk. This hill reaches a height of 342 m [1,122 ft] above sea level. Over 1,000 lakes, mostly small, dot the landscape. Forests cover large areas. Belarus and Poland jointly control a remnant of virgin forest, which contains a herd of rare wisent (European bison). This is the Belovezha Forest, which is known as the Bialowieza Forest in Poland.

Area 207,600 sq km [80,154 sq mi]
Population 10,293,000
Capital (population) Minsk (1,709,000)
Government Multiparty republic
Ethnic groups Belarusian 81%, Russian 11%, Polish, Ukrainian, others
Languages Belarusian, Russian (both official)
Religions Eastern Orthodox 80%, others 20%
Currency Belarusian rouble = 100 kopecks
Website www.mfa.gov.by/eng

CLIMATE

The climate of Belarus is affected by both the moderating influence of the Baltic Sea and continental conditions to the east. The winters are cold and the summers warm.

HISTORY

Slavic people settled in what is now Belarus about 1,500 years ago. In the 9th century, the area became part of the first East Slavic state, Kievan Rus, which became a major European power in the 10th and 11th centuries. Mongol invaders captured the eastern part of Kievan Rus in the 13th century, while Germanic tribes threatened from the west. Belarus allied itself with Lithuania, which also became a powerful state. In 1386, the Lithuanian Grand Duke married the queen of Poland and Lithuanian-Polish kings ruled both countries until 1569, when Lithuania with Belarus merged with Poland. In the 18th century, Russia took most of eastern Poland, including Belarus. Yet the people of Belarus continued to maintain their individuality.

Following the Russian Revolution of 1917, a Communist government replaced tsarist rule in Russia, and, in March 1918, Belarus became an independent, non-Communist republic. Later that year, Russian Communists invaded Belarus, renaming it Byelorussia, a name derived from the Russian *Belaya Rus*, or White Russia. They established a Communist government there in 1919, and in 1922, the country became a founder republic of the Soviet Union. In 1939, Russia occupied what is now western Belarus, which had been part of Poland since 1919. Nazi troops occupied the area between 1941 and 1944, during which one in four citizens died. Byelorussia became a founding member of the United Nations in 1945.

alleged fraud, saying that the vote was neither free nor fair. In 2005 Belarus was described as Europe's last remaining outpost of tyranny by the US.

In 2006, Russian attempts to end gas subsidies escalated into a major dispute. Belarus briefly blocked Russian oil pipelines to the EU, and in 2007 Lukashenko rejected earlier plans for union with Russia.

ECONOMY

The World Bank classifies Belarus as an 'upper-middle-income' economy. Like other former republics of the Soviet Union, it faces many problems in turning from Communism to a free-market economy.

Under Communist rule many manufacturing industries were set up, producing chemicals, trucks and tractors, machine tools and textiles. Farming is important and major products include barley, eggs, flax, meat, potatoes and other vegetables, rye and sugar beet. Leading exports include machinery and transport equipment, chemicals and food products.

POLITICS

In 1990, the Byelorussian parliament declared that its laws took precedence over those of the Soviet Union. On 25 August 1991, many observers were very surprised that this most conservative and Communist-dominated of parliaments declared its independence, playing a supporting role in its deconstruction and the creation of the Commonwealth of Independent States (CIS). In September 1991, the republic changed its name back to its Belarusian form, Belarus.

The Communists retained control in Belarus after independence. A new constitution introduced in 1994 led to presidential elections that brought Alexander Lukashenko to power. Economic reform began, though the country remained pro-Russian. Lukashenko favoured a union with Russia and, in 1999, signed a treaty committing the countries to a confederal state. However, Russia insisted that a referendum would have to take place before any. In 2001 Lukashenko was re-elected amid accusations of electoral fraud. A referendum in 2004 claimed overwhelming support for the removal of the two-term limit on his rule, while Western observers

MINSK

Capital of Belarus, on the River Svisloch. Founded c. 1060, it was under Lithuanian and Polish rule before becoming part of Russia in 1793. During World War II the city was almost completely destroyed and only a few historical buildings were left standing. The city was rebuilt as the showplace city of a modern republic. In 1974 Minsk was awarded the Soviet title of 'Hero City' for its sufferings in World War II and speedy reconstruction. In 1991, Minsk became the administrative centre of the newly formed CIS. Industries include textiles, machinery, motor vehicles, electronic goods.

BELGIUM

Belgium's national flag was adopted in 1830, when the country won its independence from the Netherlands. The colours came from the arms of the province of Brabant, in central Belgium, which rebelled against Austrian rule in 1787.

The Kingdom of Belgium is a densely populated country in western Europe. Behind the 63 km [39 mi] long coastline on the North Sea, lie its coastal plains. Some low-lying areas, called polders, are protected from the sea by dykes (sea walls).

Central Belgium consists of low plateaux and the only highland region is the Ardennes in the south-east. The Ardennes, reaching a height of 694 m [2,277 ft], consists largely of moorland, peat bogs and woodland. The country's chief rivers are the Schelde, which flows through Tournai, Gent (or Ghent) and Antwerp in the west, and the Sambre and the Meuse, which flow between the central plateau and the Ardennes.

Area 30,528 sq km [11,787 sq mi]
Population 10,379,000
Capital (population) Brussels (964,000)
Government Federal constitutional monarchy
Ethnic groups Belgian 89% (Fleming 58%, Walloon 31%), others
Languages Dutch, French, German (all official)
Religions Roman Catholic 75%, others 25%
Currency Euro = 100 cents
Website www.belgium.be

CLIMATE

The moderating effects of the sea give much of Belgium a temperate climate, with mild winters and cool summers. Moist winds from the Atlantic Ocean bring significant amounts of rainfall throughout the year, especially in the Ardennes. During January and February, much snow falls in the Ardennes, where temperatures are more extreme. Brussels has mild winters and warm summers.

HISTORY

Due to its strategic position, Belgium has often been called the 'cockpit of Europe'.

In the Middle Ages, the area was split into small states, but, with the Netherlands and Luxembourg, it was united and made prosperous by the dukes of Burgundy in the 14th and 15th centuries. Later, at various times, Belgium, came under Austrian, Spanish and French rule.

From 1815, following the Napoleonic Wars, Belgium and the Netherlands were united as the 'Low Countries' but, in 1830, a National Congress proclaimed independence from the Dutch. In 1831, Prince Leopold of Saxe-Coburg became Belgium's king.

The division between Belgium and the Netherlands rested on history rather than geography. Belgium was a mainly Roman Catholic country while the Netherlands was mainly Protestant. Both were neutral in foreign policy, but both were occupied by the Nazis from 1940 until September 1944.

After World War II, Belgium achieved rapid economic progress, first through collaboration with the Netherlands and Luxembourg by forming a customs union called Benelux, and later as a founder member of what is now the European Union. In 1960 Belgium ber of Deputies has had 150 members, and the Senate 71. The regional assembly of Flanders had 118 deputies, while the assemblies of Brussels and Wallonia had 75 each.

ECONOMY

Belgium is a major trading nation, with a highly developed economy. Almost 75% of its trade is with other EU nations.

With few natural resources it must import a large percentage of the raw materials required for industry. Its main products include chemicals, processed food and steel. The steelworks lie near ports because they are reliant on imported petroleum for power. In 2002, parliament voted to phase out the use of nuclear energy by 2025.

Agriculture employs less than 2% of the people, but Belgian farmers produce most of the food needed by the people. The chief crops are barley and wheat, but the most valuable activities are dairy farming and livestock rearing.

granted independence to the Belgian Congo (now the Democratic Republic of the Congo) and, in 1962, its supervision of Ruanda-Urundi (now Rwanda and Burundi) was ended.

POLITICS

Belgium has always been an uneasy marriage of two peoples: the majority Flemings, who speak a language closely related to Dutch, and the Walloons, who speak French. The dividing line between the two communities runs east–west, just south of Brussels, although the capital is officially bilingual.

Since the inception of the country, the Flemings have caught up and overtaken the Walloons in cultural influence as well as in numbers. In 1971, the constitution was revised and three economic regions were established: Flanders (Vlaanderen), Wallonia (Wallonie) and Brussels. However, tensions remained.

In 1993, Belgium adopted a federal system of government, with each of the three regions being granted its own regional assembly. Further changes in 2001 gave the regions greater tax-raising powers, plus responsibility for agriculture and the promotion of trade. Elections under this system were held in 1995 and 1999. Since 1995, the Cham-

BRUSSELS (BRUXELLES)

Capital of Belgium and of Brabant province, central Belgium. During the Middle Ages, it achieved prosperity through the wool trade and became capital of the Spanish Netherlands. In 1830 it became capital of newly independent Belgium. Places of interest include a 13th-century cathedral, the town hall, splendid art nouveau buildings, and academies of fine arts. The main commercial, financial, cultural, and administrative centre of Belgium, it is also the headquarters of the European Union (EU) and of the North Atlantic Treaty Organization (NATO). Industries include textiles, chemicals, electronic equipment, electrical goods, brewing.

BELIZE

Above the shield is a mahogany tree, beside it stand two woodcutters denoting the two main ethnic groups of Belize. A ring of 50 laurel leaves marks the year 1950, the start of the liberation struggle. The country's motto is also shown - Sub umbra floreo (I flourish in the shade).

Belize is a small country in Central America, lying on the Caribbean Sea. It is a monarchy whose ceremonial head of state is Britain's monarch. A governor-general represents the monarch. An elected government, headed by a prime minister, actually rules the country day-to-day.

Behind the swampy coastal plain in the south, the land rises to the low Maya Mountains, which reach 1,120 m [3,675 ft] at Victoria Peak. Northern Belize is mostly low lying and swampy. The main river, the River Belize, flows across the centre of the country. Rainforest covers large areas. A barrier reef stretches 297 km (185 mi) along the coast, the longest of its kind in the Western Hemisphere.

Area 22,966 sq km [8,867 sq miles]
Population 288,000
Capital (population) Belmopan (12,000)
Government Constitutional monarchy
Ethnic groups Mestizo 49%, Creole 25% ,Mayan Indian 11%, Garifuna 6%, others 9%
Languages English (official), Spanish, Creole
Religions Roman Catholic 50%, Protestant 27%, others
Currency Belizean dollar = 100 cents
Website www.belize.gov.bz

CLIMATE

Belize has a humid tropical climate with high temperatures all year round. The average annual rainfall ranges from 1,300 mm [52 in] in the north to over 3,800 mm [150 in] in the south. Hurricanes sometimes occur. One in 2001 killed 22 people and left 12,000 homeless.

HISTORY

Between 300 BC and AD 1000 Belize was part of the Maya Empire, which was in decline long before Spanish explorers reached the coast in the 16th century. Spain claimed the area but did not set-

MAYA

The outstanding culture of central American civilization, occupying south Mexico and north Central America. The civilization divides into three periods. The pre-classic era was from 1000 BC to AD 300. The classic era, when it was at its height, was from the 3rd to the 9th centuries. The Maya built great temple cities with buildings surmounting stepped pyramids. They were skilful potters and weavers and productive farmers. They worshipped gods and ancestors and blood sacrifice was an important element of religion. The post-classic era extended from AD 100 to 1500 when the Maya civilization declined.

Much was destroyed after the Spanish conquest in the 16th century. The modern Maya, numbering about 4 million, live in the same area and speak a variety of languages related to those of their ancestors.

relations in the early 1990s led Guatemala to recognize Belize's independence and in 1992, Britain agreed to withdraw its troops from the country. Mayan land rights remain a contentious political issue.

High levels of unemployment are a major problem as is a growing involvement in the South American drug trade which has brought with it increasing levels of violent crime.

ECONOMY

The World Bank classifies Belize as a 'lower-middle-income' developing country. Tourism has become the mainstay of the economy and in recent years cruise ships have called there, bringing additional income.

Agriculture is still important, and cane sugar is the chief commercial crop and export. Other crops include bananas, beans, citrus fruits, maize and rice. Forestry is of longstanding importance, the timber trade even features on the flag. Fishing is now the second biggest earner.

BELMOPAN

Capital of Belize, on the River Belize. It replaced Belize City, 80 km [50 mi] upstream, as capital in 1971, the latter having been largely destroyed by a hurricane in 1961. The building of Belmopan began in 1966 and was completed in 1971. As an inland city temperatures are high in the daytime but much cooler at night. Belmopan is the centre of government. In its centre are the National Assembly Building and the majority of central government offices. The residents of Belmopan are mostly government employees and their families. As the city is relatively new the inhabitants originate from all other areas of the country, with only a small indigenous population.

tle. In 1638 the first European settlement was founded by shipwrecked soldiers. Over the next 150 years Britain gradually took control of Belize and established sugar plantations using imported African slave labour.

In 1862 Belize became the colony of British Honduras. Renamed Belize in 1973, it gained full independence in 1981. Guatemala, which had claimed the area since the early 19th century, opposed Belize's independence. This led to British troops remaining deployed in Belize to prevent a possible invasion.

POLITICS

In 1983, Guatemala reduced its claim to the southern half of Belize. Improved

BENIN

The colours on this flag, used by Africa's oldest independent nation, Ethiopia, symbolize African unity. Benin adopted this flag after independence in 1960. A flag with a red (Communist) star replaced it between 1975 and 1990, after which Benin dropped its Communist policies.

The Republic of Benin, formerly called Dahomey, is one of Africa's smallest countries. It extends north-south for about 620 km [390 mi]. The coastline on the Bight of Benin, which is about 100 km [62 mi] long, is lined by lagoons. It lacks natural harbours and the harbour at Cotonou, the main port and commercial centre, is artificial.

Behind the coastal lagoons is a flat plain. Beyond this plain is a marshy depression, but the land rises to a low plateau in central Benin. The highest land is in the north-west.

Savanna covers most of northern Benin. The north is home to many typical savanna animals, such as buffaloes, elephants and lions. The north has two national parks, the Penjari and the 'W', which Benin shares with Burkina Faso and Niger.

Area 112,622 sq km [43,483 sq mi]
Population 7,863,000
Capital (population) Porto-Novo (233,000)
Government Multiparty republic
Ethnic groups Fon, Adja, Bariba, Yoruba, Fulani
Languages French (official), Fon, Adja, Yoruba
Religions Traditional beliefs 50%, Christianity 30%, Islam 20%
Currency CFA franc = 100 centimes
Website www.gouv.bj/en/

CLIMATE

Benin has a hot, wet climate. The average annual temperature on the coast is 25°C [77°F], while the average annual rainfall is 1,330 mm [52 in]. The forested inland plains are wetter than the coast, but the rainfall decreases to the north, which has rainy summer season and a very dry winter.

HISTORY

The ancient kingdom of Dahomey, a prominent West African kingdom which developed in the 15th century, had its capital at Abomey in what is now south-western Benin. In the 17th century, the kings of Dahomey became involved in supplying slaves to European slave traders, including the Portuguese, who shipped many Dahomeans to the Americas. The shoreline of present-day Benin became part of what was called the Slave Coast. Many slaves were shipped to Brazil. Traces of the culture and religion of the slaves still survive in parts of the Americas. For example, the voodoo cult in Haiti originated in Dahomey.

After slavery was ended in the 19th century, France began to gain influence in the area. Around 1851 France signed a treaty with the kingdom of Dahomey. In the 1890s the area, which also included some other small African states, became a French colony. From 1904, they ruled Dahomey as part of a huge region called French West Africa, which also included what are now Burkina Faso, Guinea, Ivory Coast, Mauritania, Mali, Niger and Senegal. Dahomey became an overseas territory of France in 1946 and a self-governing nation in the French Community in 1958. Full independence was achieved in 1960.

MAP SCALE
0   50   100 km
0   50 miles

in 1977, it became a one-party state. This regime, headed by President Kérékou, held power until 1989, when, following the lead of several East European countries in abandoning Communism, Kérékou announced that his country would also abandon Marxism-Leninism and, instead, follow liberal economic policies.

In 1990, a new democratic constitution with a presidential system was introduced. Presidential elections were held in 1991 and Nicéphore Soglo, a former World Bank executive and prime minister, defeated Kérékou. However, in 1996, Kérékou defeated Soglo and returned to power. Kérékou, who was re-elected in 2001, worked to restore Benin's fragile economy. Many observers have praised Benin's transition from a Marxist-Leninist state into one of Africa's most stable democracies.

ECONOMY

Benin is a poor developing country. About half of the population depends on agriculture, but farming is largely at subsistence level. The main food crops include beans, cassava, millet, rice, sorghum and yams. The chief cash crops are cotton, palm oil and palm kernels. Forestry is also important.

Benin produces some oil, but manufacturing remains on a small scale. It depends heavily upon Nigeria for trade.

POLITICS

Dahomey suffered from instability and unrest in the early years of independence. The first president, Hubert Maga, was removed in 1963 in a military coup led by General Christophe Soglo. A presidential council was set up in 1970 and Hubert Maga became one of three rotating presidents. But this regime was overthrown in 1973 by a coup led by Lt-Col Matthieu Kérékou. In 1975, Kérékou announced that the country would be renamed Benin after the powerful state known for its magnificent sculptures in south-western Nigeria. Benin became a Marxist-Leninist People's Republic and,

PORTO-NOVO

Capital of Benin, a port on the Gulf of Guinea near the border with Nigeria. Settled by 16th-century Portuguese traders, it later became a shipping point for slaves to America.
It was made the country's capital at independence in 1960, but Cotonou is assuming increasing importance. Today it is a market for the surrounding agricultural region.

BHUTAN

The dragon dates to the 17th century. The jewels in the dragon's claws represent Bhutan's wealth. The white symbolizes purity. The gold represents the secular power of the *Druk Gyalpo* (Dragon King), and the orange, the spiritual power of Buddhism.

The Kingdom of Bhutan is a small, landlocked country in the eastern Himalayas, between India and the Tibetan plateau of China.

Southern Bhutan, along the border with India, is the lowest land region, ranging between about 50 and 900 m [160 to 3,000 ft] above sea level. North of the plains is a mountainous region between about 1,500 and 4,250 m [4,900 to 13,950 ft]. The northernmost region lies in the Great Himalayan range, reaching more than 7,500 m [24,600 ft]. Most people live in the fertile valleys of rivers which flow generally from north to south.

Area 47,000 sq km [18,147 sq mi]
Population 2,280,000
Capital (population) Thimphu (35,000)
Government Constitutional monarchy
Ethnic groups Bhutanese 50%, Nepalese 35%
Languages Dzongkha (official)
Religions Buddhism 75%, Hinduism 25%
Currency Ngultrum = 100 cetrum
Website www.bhutan.gov.bt

CLIMATE

The altitude determines the climate. The southern plains have a subtropical, rainy climate, with an average annual rainfall of around 5,000 mm [197 in]. Dense vegetation covers much of the region, with savanna in the far south. Central Bhutan has a moderate climate, though winters are cold.

HISTORY

Tibetan invaders settled in the area around 1,200 years ago. In the early 17th century, Bhutan became a separate state when a Tibetan lama (Buddhist monk), who was both a spiritual and temporal ruler, took power. The country was divid- ed into districts ruled by governors and fort commanders. The 19th century was plagued by civil wars in which rival governors battled for power. In 1907, Bhutan became a monarchy when Ugyen Wangchuk, the powerful governor of Tongsa district, made himself Maharajah (now King) and set up the country's first effective central government. The monarch was hereditary and the Maharajah's successors have ruled the country ever since.

Britain took control of Bhutan's foreign affairs in 1910, but it did not interfere in internal affairs. This treaty was renewed with newly independent India in 1949. India also returned some parts of Bhutan which had been annexed by Britain and agreed to help Bhutan develop its economy. Later, India also began to assist with Bhutan's defence.

POLITICS

Bhutan's remote but strategic position cut it off from the outside world for centuries and it only began to open up to outsiders in the 1970s. The roots of reform go back to 1952 when Jigme Dorji Wangchuk succeeded to the throne and established a national assembly to advise him. Slavery was abolished in antagonized the minority Nepalis, and violence in 1990 caused many to flee. In 2005 the king declared that the country would become a democracy in 2008. In 2006 he abdicated in favour of his son, Prince Namgyal, and 2007 saw mock elections to prepare the population.

ECONOMY

Bhutan is a poor country. The rugged terrain makes the building of roads and other infrastructure difficult. Agriculture, mainly subsistence farming, cattle rearing and forestry, accounts for 93% of the workforce. Barley, rice and wheat are the chief food crops. Other products include citrus fruits, dairy products and maize. Industry is small scale, some coal is mined in the south.

The country's economy is closely linked to that of India with nearly 90% of Bhutan's total exports going to India. Bhutan has considerable hydroelectric power potential and electricity is exported to India. However, economic development is hampered by Bhutan's desire to maintain its traditional culture. The controls placed by the government on outside groups have inevitably restricted foreign investment.

1958. In 1959 Bhutan admitted several thousand refugees after China annexed Tibet. A cabinet was set up in 1968.

In 1972, King Jigme Dorji Wangchuk died and was succeeded by his son, Jigme Singye Wangchuk. The new king continued Bhutan's policy of slow modernization. The first foreign tourists were admitted in 1974, although tourism was restricted to people on prepackaged or guided tours. Independent travel was discouraged as Bhutan sought to preserve its majority Buddhist culture. A television service was not introduced until 1999.

The king gave up some of the monarch's absolute powers in 1998, giving up his role as head of the government. Instead, he ruled in conjunction with the government, a National Assembly and a royal advisory council. In 2005, the government published a new draft constitution, which would make Bhutan a democracy with a parliament consisting of two elected houses. The parliament would have the right to impeach the king by a two-thirds vote.

Ethnic conflict has marred Bhutan's recent history. In 1986, a new law came into force making citizenship dependent on length of residence in Bhutan. Many ethnic Nepalis living in the south were made illegal immigrants. Other measures emphasizing Buddhist culture further

THIMPHU

Bhutan's capital is located in the west of the country. The city is modern in age only (established in 1952) as all new buildings are built following traditional designs. Among its sights are the Memorial Chorten (dedicated to the king's late father Jigme Dorji Wangchuck) and the Tashicho Dzong a 350-year-old structure built by Shabdrung Ngawang Namgyal and refurbished in 1961 to house government departments and ministries.

BOLIVIA

This flag, which has been Bolivia's national and merchant flag since 1888, dates back to 1825 when Bolivia became independent. The red stands for Bolivia's animals and the courage of the army, the yellow for its mineral resources, and the green for its agricultural wealth.

The Republic of Bolivia is a landlocked country in South America. It can be divided into two regions. The west is dominated by two parallel ranges of the Andes Mountains. The western cordillera forms Bolivia's border with Chile. The eastern range runs through the heart of Bolivia. Between the two, lies the Altiplano. The Altiplano is the most densely populated region of Bolivia and the site of its famous ruins, it includes the seat of government, La Paz, close to Lake Titicaca. Sucre, the legal capital, lies in the Andean foothills.

The east is a relatively unexplored region of lush, tropical rainforest, inhabited mainly by Native South Americans. In the south-east lies the Gran Chaco.

The windswept Altiplano is a grassland region. The semi-arid Gran Chaco is a largely unpopulated vast lowland plain, drained by the River Madeira, a tributary of the Amazon. The region is famous for its quebracho trees which are a major source of tannin.

Area 1,098,581 sq km [424,162 sq mi]
Population 8,989,000
Capital (population) La Paz (seat of government, 1,533,000); Sucre (legal capital/seat of judiciary, 177,000)
Government Multiparty republic
Ethnic groups Mestizo 30%, Quechua 30%, Aymara 25%, White 15%
Languages Spanish, Aymara, Quechua (all official)
Religions Roman Catholic 95%
Currency Boliviano = 100 centavos
Website www.bolivia.com

HISTORY

American Indians have lived in Bolivia for at least 10,000 years. The main groups today are the Aymara and Quechua people.

When Spanish soldiers arrived in the early 16th century, Bolivia was part of the

CLIMATE

Bolivia's climate varies greatly according to the to altitude with the highest Andean peaks permanently covered in snow. In contrast, the eastern plains have a humid tropical climate. The principal rainy season takes place between December and February.

TITICACA

Lake in the Andes on the Peru-Bolivia border, draining s through the River Desaguader into Lake Poopó. At an altitude of 3,810 m [12,500 ft], it is the world's highest navigable body of water. The constant supply of water has enabled the region to grow crops since ancient times. The lake is home to giant edible frogs, and is famed for its totora reeds, from which the Uru make their floating island homes and fishing rafts. It covers an area of 8,290 sq km [3,200 sq mi] with a maximum depth of 280 m [920 ft].

ther instability. Elections were held in 1980, but the military again intervened until 1982.

Presidential elections were held in 1989, 1993 and 1997, when General Hugo Bánzer Suárez, who had ruled as a dictator in the 1970s, became president. In 2005 Evo Morales, a left-wing Aymaran Indian and peasant leader, was elected president. In 2006 he nationalized the oil and gas industries and began controversial reforms of land ownership.

ECONOMY

Bolivia is one of the poorest countries in South America. It has several natural resources, including tin, silver and natural gas, but the chief activity is agriculture, which employs 47% of the people. Potatoes, wheat and a grain called quinoa are important crops on the Altiplano, while bananas, cocoa, coffee and maize are grown at the lower, warmer levels.

Inca empire. Following the defeat of the Incas, Spain ruled from 1532 to 1825, when Antonio José de Sucre, one of revolutionary leader Simón Bolívar's generals, defeated the Spaniards.

Since independence, Bolivia has lost much territory to its neighbours. In 1932, Bolivia fought with Paraguay for control of the Gran Chaco region. Bolivia lost and most of this area passed to Paraguay in 1938.

Manufacturing is small-scale and the main exports are mineral ores and fossil fuels. Coca, which is used to make cocaine, is exported illegally. In 2002–3, the production of coca plummeted, causing social unrest. In 2004, the people voted in favour of a government plan to export natural gas via a port in Peru.

POLITICS

Following the Chaco War, Bolivia entered a long period of instability. It had ten presidents, six of whom were members of the military, between 1936 and 1952, when the Revolutionary Movement replaced the military. The new government launched a series of reforms, which included the break-up of large estates and the granting of land to Amerindian farmers. Another military uprising occurred in 1964, heralding fur-

LA PAZ

Administrative capital and largest city of Bolivia, in the west of the country. Founded by the Spanish in 1548 on the site of an Inca village, it was one of the centres of revolt in the War of Independence (1809–24). Located at 3,600 m [12,000 ft] in the Andes, it is the world's highest capital city. Industries include chemicals, tanning, flour-milling, electrical equipment, textiles, brewing and distilling.

Bosnia-Herzegovina adopted a new flag in 1998, because the previous flag was thought to be synonymous with the wartime Muslim regime. The blue background and white stars represent the country's links with the EU, and the triangle stands for the three ethnic groups in the country.

Bosnia-Herzegovina is one of the five republics to emerge from the former Federal People's Republic of Yugoslavia. Much of the country is mountainous or hilly, with an arid limestone plateau in the south-west. The River Sava, which forms most of the northern border with Croatia, is a tributary of the River Danube. Because of the country's odd shape, the coastline is limited to a short stretch of 20 km [13 mi] on the Adriatic coast.

Area 51,197 sq km [19,767 sq mi]
Population 4,499,000
Capital (population) Sarajevo (529,000)
Government Federal republic
Ethnic groups Bosnian 48%, Serb 37%, Croat 14%
Languages Bosnian, Serbian, Croatian
Religions Islam 40%, Serbian Orthodox 31%, Roman Catholic 15%, others 14%
Currency Convertible marka = 100 convertible pfenniga
Website www.fbihvlada.gov.ba/engleski/

CLIMATE

The coast benefits from a Mediterranean climate. Summers are dry and sunny, while winters are moist and mild. Inland, the weather is more severe, with hot, dry summers and bitterly cold, snowy winters. The weather reaches its greatest extremes in the north.

HISTORY

Slavs settled in the area that is now Bosnia-Herzegovina around 1,400 years ago. In the late 15th century, the area was taken by the Ottoman Turks. In 1878, the dual monarchy of Austria-Hungary gained temporary control over Bosnia-Herzegovina and it formally took over the area in 1908. The assassination of Archduke Franz Ferdinand of Austria-Hungary in Sarajevo, in June 1914, was the catalyst for the start of World War I. In 1918, Bosnia-Herzegovina became part

of the Kingdom of the Serbs, Croats and Slovenes, renamed Yugoslavia in 1929. Germany occupied Yugoslavia during World War II, and Bosnia-Herzegovina came under a puppet regime in Croatia. A Communist government took over in Yugoslavia in 1945, and a new constitution in 1946 made the country a federal state, with Bosnia-Herzegovina as one of its six constituent republics.

Under Communism, Bosnia-Herzegovina was a potentially explosive area due to its mix of Bosnian Muslims, Orthodox Christian Serbs and Roman Catholic Croats, as well as Albanian, gypsy and Ukrainian minorities. The ethnic and religious differences started to exert themselves after the death of Yugoslavia's president Josip Broz Tito in 1980, among increasing indications that Communist economic policies were failing to work.

POLITICS

Free elections were held in 1990 and non-Communists won a majority, with a Muslim, Alija Izetbegovic, as president. In 1991, Croatia and Slovenia declared themselves independent republics and

In 1995, the warring parties agreed to a solution to the conflict, the Dayton Peace Accord. The country was split into two self-governing provinces, one Bosnian Serb and the other Muslim-Croat, under a central, unified, multi-ethnic government. A NATO force helped stabilize the country. European forces took over in 2004, and began to leave in 2007 as stability returned.

ECONOMY

The economy of Bosnia-Herzegovina, was shattered by the war in the early 1990s. Manufactures include electrical equipment, machinery and transport equipment, and textiles. Farm products include fruits, maize, tobacco, vegetables and wheat, but the country has to import food.

seceded from Yugoslavia. Bosnia-Herzegovina held a referendum on independence in 1992. Most Bosnian Serbs boycotted the vote, but the Muslims and Croats voted in favour and Bosnia-Herzegovina proclaimed its independence. War then broke out.

At first, the Muslim-dominated government allied itself uneasily with the Croat minority, but it was at once under attack by local Serbs supported by their co-nationals from beyond Bosnia-Herzegovina's borders. In their 'ethnic cleansing' campaign, heavily equipped Serb militias drove poorly-armed Muslims from towns they had long inhabited. By early 1993, the Muslims controlled less than a third of the former federal republic. Even the capital, Sarajevo, became disputed territory suffering constant shelling.

The Muslim-Croat alliance rapidly disintegrated and refugees approached the million mark. Tougher economic sanctions on Serbia in April 1993 had little effect on the war in Bosnia. A small UN force attempted to deliver relief supplies to civilians and maintain 'safe' Muslim areas to no avail.

SARAJEVO

Capital of Bosnia-Herzegovina, on the River Miljacka. It fell to the Turks in 1429, and flourished as a commercial centre in the Ottoman Empire. Passing to the Austro-Hungarian Empire in 1878, the city was a centre of Serb and Bosnian resistance to Austrian rule. In June 1914 a Serb nationalist assassinated Austrian Archduke Franz Ferdinand in the city, an act that precipitated World War I. In 1991 Sarajevo became the focal point of the civil war between Bosnian-Serb troops and Bosnian government forces. The city lay under prolonged siege, often without water, electricity, or basic medical supplies. After the 1995 Dayton Peace Accord, it in effect became a Bosnian city , though with a reduced population as many Serbs fled.

BOTSWANA

The black-and-white zebra stripe in the centre of Botswana's flag symbolizes racial harmony. The blue represents rainwater, because water supply is the most vital need in this dry country. This flag was adopted in 1966, when Botswana became independent from Britain.

The Republic of Botswana is a land-locked country which lies in the heart of southern Africa. The majority of the land is flat or gently rolling, with an average height of about 1,000 m [3,280 ft]. More hilly country lies in the east. The Kalahari, a semi-desert area covers much of Botswana.

Most of the south has no permanent streams, but large depressions occur in the north. In one, the Okavango River, which flows from Angola, forms a large delta, an area of swampland. Another depression contains the Makgadikgadi Salt Pans. During floods, the Botletle River drains from the Okavango Swamps into the Makgadikgadi Salt Pans.

Area 581,730 sq km [224,606 sq mi]
Population 1,640,000
Capital (population) Gaborone (186,000)
Government Multiparty republic
Ethnic groups Tswana (or Setswana) 79%, Kalanga 11%, Basarwa 3%, others
Languages English (official), Setswana
Religions Traditional beliefs 85%, Christianity 15%
Currency Pula = 100 thebe
Website www.gov.bw

HISTORY

The earliest inhabitants of the region were the San, who are also called Bush-men. They had a nomadic way of life, hunting wild animals and collecting plant foods.

The Tswana, cattle-herding Bantu speakers, settled in eastern Botswana over 1,000 years ago. Their arrival drove the San into the Kalahari, and Tswana now form the majority of the population. San are now a tiny minority, most of

CLIMATE

Temperatures are high during the summer which runs from October to April, but the winter months are much cooler. Night-time temperatures in winter sometimes drop below freezing. The average rainfall ranges from over 400 mm [16 in] in the east to less than 200 mm [8 in] in the south-west.

Gaborone, the capital of Botswana, lies in the wetter eastern part of the country, where the majority of the population lives. The rainy season occurs during summer, between the months of November and March. Frosts sometimes occur in parts of the east when the temperature drops below freezing.

KALAHARI

A desert region in southern Africa covering parts of Botswana, Namibia and South Africa between the Orange and Zambezi rivers. Thorn scrub and forest grow in some parts of the desert and it is possible to graze animals in the rainy season. The Kalahari is inhabited by the San as well as by Africans and Europeans primarily engaged in rearing cattle. It has an area of approximately 260,000 sq km [100,000 sq mi]).

the virus, and the average life expectancy fell from 60 to 40 years. Botswana does, however, have one of Africa's most progressive programmes in place to deal with the disease.

ECONOMY
In 1966, Botswana was one of Africa's poorest countries, depending on meat and live cattle for its exports. But the discovery of minerals, including coal, cobalt, copper and nickel, has helped to diversify the economy. The mining of diamonds at Orapa, started in 1971 and was the chief factor in the transformation of the economy. By 1997, Botswana had become the world's leading producer, overtaking Australia and the Democratic Republic of the Congo. Diamonds accounted for about 74% of Botswana's exports, followed by copper-nickel matte, textiles and meat products. Another major source of income comes from tourists, the majority of whom come from South Africa, which continues to have a great influence on Botswana.

The development of mining and tourism has reduced the relative importance of farming, though agriculture still employs about a fifth of the population. The most important type of farming is livestock raising, particularly cattle, which are mostly reared in the wetter east. Crops include beans, maize, millet, sorghum and vegetables.

whom live in permanent settlements and work on cattle ranches. San land rights remain a contentious issue.

POLITICS
Britain ruled the area as the Bechuanaland Protectorate between 1885 and 1966. When the country became independent, it adopted the name of Botswana. Since then, unlike many African countries, Botswana has been a stable multiparty democracy.

The economy has undergone a steady process of diversification under successive presidents. Botswana's first president, Sir Seretse Khama, who died in 1980, and his successor, Sir Ketumile Masire, who served from 1980 until 1998, when he retired in favour of Festus Mogae. Despite a severe drought, the economy expanded and the government introduced major social programmes. Tourism also grew as huge national parks and reserves were established. However, by the early 2000s, Botswana was suffering a very high rate of HIV infection. Around one in five of the population had

GABORONE
Capital of Botswana, close to the border with South Africa. First settled in the 1890s, it served as the administrative headquarters of the former Bechuanaland Protectorate. In 1966 it became the capital of an independent Botswana.

BRAZIL

The green on the flag symbolizes Brazil's rainforests and the yellow diamond its mineral wealth. The blue sphere bears the motto 'Order and Progress'. The 27 stars, arranged in the pattern of the night sky over Rio de Janeiro, represent the states and the federal district.

The Federative Republic of Brazil is the world's fifth largest country. Structurally, it has two main regions. In the north is the vast Amazon basin, once an inland sea and now drained by a river system that carries one-fifth of the world's running water. The largest area of river plain is in the upper part of the basin, along the frontiers with Bolivia and Peru. Downstream, the flood plain is relatively narrow.

The Brazilian Highlands make up the country's second main region and consist largely of hard crystalline rock dissected into rolling uplands. They include the heartland (Mato Grosso) and the whole western flank of the country from the bulge to the border with Uruguay. The undulating plateau of the northern highlands carries poor soils.

The typical vegetation is thorny scrub which, in the south, merges into wooded savanna. Conditions are better in the south, where rainfall is more reliable. More than 60% of the population lives in the four southern and south-eastern states, the most developed part of Brazil, though these account for only 17% of Brazil's total area.

CLIMATE

Manaus has high temperatures all through the year. The rainfall is heavy, though the period from June to September is drier than the rest of the year. The capital, Brasília, and the city Rio de Janeiro also have tropical climates, with much more marked dry seasons than Manaus. The far south has a temperate climate. The north-eastern interior is the driest region, with an average annual rainfall of only 250 mm [10 in] in places. The rainfall is also unreliable and severe droughts are common in this region.

The Amazon basin contains the world's largest rainforests, which the

BRAZIL

Brazilians call the selvas. The forests contain an enormous variety of plant and animal species, but many species are threatened by loggers and those who wish to exploit the forests. The destruction of the forest is also ruining the lives of the last surviving groups of Amazonian Indians.

Forests grow on the north-eastern coasts, but the dry interior has large areas of thorny scrub. The south-east contains fertile farmland and large ranches.

HISTORY

The Portuguese explorer Pedro Alvarez Cabral claimed Brazil for Portugal in 1500. While Spain was occupied in the western parts of South America, the first Portuguese colonists settled in the north-east in the 1530s. They were followed by other settlers, missionaries, explorers and prospectors who gradually penetrated the country during the 17th and 18th centuries. They found many groups of Amerindians, some of whom lived semi-nomadic lives, hunting, fishing and gathering fruits, while others lived in farming villages, growing cassava and other crops.

Area 8,514,215 sq km [3,287,338 sq mi]
Population 188,078,000
Capital (population) Brasília (3,341,000)
Government Federal republic
Ethnic groups White 55%, Mulatto 38%, Black 6%, others 1%
Languages Portuguese (official)
Religions Roman Catholic 80%
Currency Real = 100 centavos
Website www.turismo.gov.br

The Portuguese enslaved many Amerindians who were used for plantation work, while others were driven into the interior. The Portuguese also introduced about 4 million African slaves, notably in the sugar-cane-growing areas in the north-east. For many decades following the early settlements, Brazil was mainly a sugar-producing colony, with most plantations centred on the rich coastal plains of the north-east. These areas later produced cotton, cocoa, rice and other crops. In the south, colonists penetrated the interior in search of slaves and minerals, especially gold and diamonds. The city of Ouro Preto in Minas Gerais was built and Rio de Janeiro grew as a port for the area.

Initially little more than a group of rival provinces, Brazil began to unite in 1807 when the Portuguese royal court transferred from Lisbon to Rio de Janeiro. The eldest son of King Joao VI of Portugal was chosen as the 'Perpetual Defender' of Brazil by a national congress. In 1822, he proclaimed the independence of the country and was chosen as the constitutional emperor with the title of Pedro I. He became increasingly unpopular and was forced to abdicate in 1831. He was succeeded by his five-year-old son, Pedro II, who officially took office in 1841. Pedro's liberal policies included the gradual abolition of slavery.

During the 19th century, São Paulo state became the centre of a huge coffee-growing industry. While the fortunes made in mining helped to develop Rio de Janeiro, profits from coffee were invested in the city of São Paulo. Immigrants from Italy and Germany settled in the south, introducing farming in the fertile valleys, in co-existence with the cattle ranchers and gauchos of the plains. The second half of the 19th century saw the development of the wild rubber industry in the Amazon basin, where the city of Manaus, with its world-famous opera house, served as a centre and market. Although Manaus lies 1,600 km [1,000 mi] from the mouth of the Amazon, rubber from the hinterland could be shipped out directly to world markets in ocean-going steamers. Brazil enjoyed a virtual monopoly of the rubber trade until the early 20th century, when Malaya began to compete, later with massive success.

A federal system was adopted for the United States of Brazil in the 1881 constitution and Brazil became a republic in 1889. Until 1930, the country experienced very strong economic expansion and prospered, but social unrest in 1930 resulted in a major revolt. From then on the country was under the control of President Getulio Vargas, who established a strong corporate state similar to that of fascist Italy, although Brazil entered World War II on the side of the Allies. Democracy, often corrupt, prevailed from 1956, 1964 and 1985. In between there were five military presidents of illiberal regimes.

POLITICS

A new constitution came into force in October 1988 – the eighth since Brazil became independent from Portugal in 1822. The constitution transferred powers from the president to the congress and paved the way for a return to democracy. In 1989, Fernando Collor de Mello was elected to cut inflation and combat corruption. But he made little progress and in 1992, with inflation soaring, his vice-president, Itamar Franco, took over as president. He served until 1994 when the Social Democrat Fernando Henrique Cardoso, a former finance minister, was elected president.

In 2002 elections Luiz Inácio Lula da Silva of the left-wing Workers' Party became president. Known as 'Lula', he promised social reforms but has proved to be a pragmatist following moderate economic policies. In 2005 his government was hit by corruption charges, but in 2006 he was re-elected in a landslide victory.

ECONOMY

Brazil's total volume of production is one of the largest in the world, but many people, including poor farmers and residents of the *favelas* (city slums), do not share in the country's fast economic growth. Widespread poverty, together with high inflation and unemployment, cause political problems.

Industry is the most valuable activity, employing about 20% of the workforce. Brazil is among the world's top producers of bauxite, chrome, diamonds, gold, iron ore, manganese and tin. Its manufactures include aircraft, cars, chemicals, processed food, raw sugar, iron and steel, paper and textiles.

Agriculture employs 28% of workers.Coffee is a major export. Other leading products include bananas, citrus fruits, cocoa, maize, rice, soya beans and sugar cane. Brazil is the top producer of eggs, meat and milk in South America.

Forestry is a major industry, though the exploitation of the rainforests, with 1.5% to 4% of Brazil's forest being destroyed every year, is a disaster for the entire world.

BRASÍLIA

Capital city, located in west central Brazil. Although the city was originally planned in 1891, building did not start until 1956. The city was laid out in the shape of an aircraft, and Oscar Niemeyer designed the modernist public buildings. It was inaugurated as the capital in 1960, in order to develop Brazil's interior.

BULGARIA

This flag, first adopted in 1878, uses the colours associated with the Slav people. The national emblem, incorporating a lion – a symbol of Bulgaria since the 14th century – was first added to the flag in 1947. It is now added only for official government occasions.

The Republic of Bulgaria is a country in the Balkan Peninsula, facing the Black Sea in the east. There are two main lowland regions. The Danubian lowlands in the north consists of a plateau that descends to the Danube, which forms much of the boundary with Romania. The other lowland region is the warmer valley of the River Maritsa, where cotton, fruits, grains, rice, tobacco and vines are grown.

Separating the two lowland areas are the Balkan Mountains (Stara Planina), rising to heights of over 2,000 m [6,500 ft]. North of the capital Sofia (Sofiya), the Balkan Mountains contain rich mineral veins of iron and non-ferrous metals.

In south-facing valleys overlooking the Maritsa Plain, plums, tobacco and vines are grown. A feature of this area is Kazanluk, from which attar of roses is exported worldwide to the cosmetics industry. South and west of the Maritsa Valley are the Rhodope (or Rhodopi) Mountains, which contain lead, zinc and copper ores.

Area 110,912 sq km [42,823 sq mi]
Population 7,385,000
Capital (population) Sofia (1,045,000)
Government Multiparty republic
Ethnic groups Bulgarian 84%, Turkish 9%, Gypsy 5%, Macedonian, Armenian, others
Languages Bulgarian (official), Turkish
Religions Bulgarian Orthodox 83%, Islam 12%, Roman Catholic 2%, others
Currency Lev = 100 stotinki
Website www.government.bg/English

HISTORY

Most of the Bulgarian people are descendants of Slavs and nomadic Bulgar tribes who arrived from the east in the 6th and 7th centuries. A powerful Bulgar kingdom was set up in 681, but the country became part of the Byzantine Empire in the 11th century.

Ottoman Turks ruled Bulgaria from 1396 and ethnic Turks still form a sizable minority in the country. In 1879, Bulgaria became a monarchy, and in

CLIMATE

The average temperature in Sofia is 15°–21°C (60–70°F) in the summer and between –1° and 5°C (30°–40°F) in the winter. Other regions experience even more extreme ranges of temperature but winters are rarely severe. Rainfall is moderate all through the year.

BALKAN MOUNTAINS

Major mountain range of the Balkan Peninsula, extending from eastern Serbia through central Bulgaria to the Black Sea. The range is a continuation of the Carpathian Mountains. It is rich in minerals and forms a climatic barrier for the interior. The highest pass is Shipka Pass, c. 1,270 m [4,166 ft], and the highest peak is Botev, 2,375 m [7,793 ft].

elections in 2005. Bulgaria joined the EU in January 2007, but six months on was criticized for making little progress against corruption.

ECONOMY

According to the World Bank, Bulgaria in the 1990s was classed as a 'lower-middle-income' developing country, though in the early 21st century growth has been rapid Bulgaria has some deposits of minerals, including brown coal, manganese and iron ore. Manufacturing is the leading economic activity and source of exports, though problems arose in the early 1990s due to outdated equipment. The main products are chemicals, processed foods, metal products, machinery and textiles. Bulgaria trades mainly with countries in Eastern Europe.

Wheat and maize are the chief crops of Bulgaria. Fruit, oilseeds, tobacco and vegetables are also important. Livestock farming, particularly the rearing of dairy and beef cattle, sheep and pigs, is an important source of revenue.

1908 became fully independent. Bulgaria was an ally of Germany in World War I (1914–18) and again in World War II (1939–45). In 1944, Soviet troops invaded Bulgaria. After the war, the monarchy was abolished and the country became a Communist ally of the Soviet Union.

POLITICS

After World War II, and especially under President Zhikov from 1954, Bulgaria became dependent on the Soviet Union. In 1990 the Communist Party held on to power under increasing pressure by ousting Zhikov, renouncing its leading role in the nation's affairs and changing its name to the Socialist Party. It won the first free elections since the war, albeit unconvincingly and against confused opposition. With improved organization, the Union of Democratic Forces defeated the old guard in the following year and began the transition to a free-market economy. Subsequent governments faced numerous problems including inflation, food shortages, rising unemployment, strikes, a large foreign debt, a declining manufacturing industry, increased prices for raw materials and a potential drop in the expanding tourist industry. In 2001 former king Siméon Saxe-Coburg-Gotha, who had left Bulgaria in 1948 when the monarchy was abolished, became prime minister. He left office when his party lost

SOFIA (SOFIJA)

Capital of Bulgaria and Sofia province, in west central Bulgaria, at the foot of the Vitosha Mountains. Known for its hot mineral springs, Sofia was founded by the Romans in the 2nd century AD. From 1018 to 1185, it was ruled by the Byzantine Empire (as Triaditsa). Sofia passed to the second Bulgarian Empire (1186–1382), and then to the Ottoman Empire (1382–1878). In 1877, Sofia was captured by Russia and chosen as the capital of Bulgaria by the Congress of Berlin. Industries include steel, machinery, textiles, rubber, chemicals, metallurgy, leather goods, food processing.

BURKINA FASO

This flag was adopted in 1984, when Upper Volta was renamed Burkino Faso. The red, green and yellow colours used on this flag symbolize the desire for African unity. This is because they are used on the flag of Ethiopia, Africa's oldest independent country.

The Democratic People's Republic of Burkina Faso is a landlocked country in West Africa. It is a little larger than the United Kingdom, but has only one-sixth of the population of the UK.

Burkina Faso consists of a plateau, between about 300 m and 700 m [650–2,300 ft] above sea level. The plateau is cut by several rivers. Most of the rivers flow south into Ghana or east into the River Niger. During droughts some of the rivers stop flowing, becoming marshes.

The northern part of the country is covered by savanna, consisting of grassland with stunted trees and shrubs. It is part of a region called the Sahel, where the land merges into the Sahara Desert. Overgrazing of the land and deforestation are common problems in the Sahel, causing desertification in many areas of the country. Climate change threatens to worsen the problem.

Woodlands border the rivers and parts of the south-east region are swampy. The south-east contains the 'W' National Park, which Burkina Faso shares with Benin and Niger, and the Arly Park. A third wildlife area is the Po Park situated south of Ouagadougou.

Area 274,000 sq km [105,791 sq mi]
Population 13,903,000
Capital (population) Ouagadougou (637,000)
Government Multiparty republic
Ethnic groups Mossi 40%, Gurunsi, Senufo, Lobi, Bobo, Mande, Fulani
Languages French (official), Mossi, Fulani
Religions Islam 50%, traditional beliefs 40%, Christianity 10%
Currency CFA franc = 100 centimes
Website www.burkinaembassy-usa.org

CLIMATE

Burkina Faso has three main seasons. From October to February, it is relatively cool and dry. From March to April, it is hot and dry, while it is hot and humid between May and September.

HISTORY

The people of Burkina Faso are divided into two main groups. The Voltaic group includes the Mossi, who form the largest single group, and the Bobo. The other main group is the Mande family. Burkina Faso also contains some Fulani herders and Hausa traders, who are related to the people of northern Nigeria. In early times, the ethnic groups in Burkina Faso were divided into kingdoms and chiefdoms. The leading kingdom, which was ruled by an absolute

---

FULANI

A west African people numbering 6 million. Their language belongs to the Niger-Congo group. Originally a pastoral people, they helped to spread Islam throughout West Africa from the 16th century, establishing an empire that lasted until British colonialism in the 19th century.

1987, Sankara was assassinated and Captain Blaise Campaore seized power. Campaore became president in unopposed elections in 1991. Elections in 1992 were the first multiparty ballots since 1978, but Campaore remained in power then and in subsequent polls, most recently in 2005. Burkina Faso struggles with one of the world's highest rates of HIV infection.

ECONOMY

Burkina Faso is one of the world's 20 poorest countries and has become extremely dependent on foreign aid. Approximately 90% of the people earn their living by farming or by raising livestock. Grazing land covers around 37% of the land and farmland covers around 10%.

Most of Burkina Faso is dry with thin soils. The country's main food crops are beans, maize, millet, rice and sorghum. Cotton, groundnuts and shea nuts, whose seeds produce a fat used to make cooking oil and soap, are grown for sale abroad. Livestock is also important.

The country has few resources and manufacturing is on a small scale. There are deposits of manganese, zinc, lead and nickel in the north of the country, but exploitation awaits improvements to the transport system. Many young men work abroad in Ghana and Ivory Coast. The money they send to their families is important to the country's economy.

monarch called the Moro Naba, was that of the Mossi. It has existed since the 13th century. The semi-autonomous states fiercely resisted domination by the larger Mali and Songhai Empires.

The French conquered the Mossi capital of Ouagadougou in 1897 and they made the area a protectorate. In 1919, the area became a French colony called Upper Volta. In 1947, Upper Volta gained semi-autonomy within the French Union, and in 1958 became an autonomous republic within the French Community.

POLITICS

Upper Volta achieved independence in 1960 and adopted a strong presidential form of government. Persistent drought and austerity measures led to a military coup in 1966. Civilian rule partially returned in 1970 but the military, led by Sangoule Lamizana, regained power in 1974. Lamizana became president after elections in 1978, but was overthrown in 1980. Parliament and the constitution were suspended and a series of military regimes ensued. In 1983 Thomas Sankara gained power in a bloody coup.

In 1984, as a symbolic break from the country's colonial past, Sankara changed Upper Volta's name to Burkina Faso 'land of the incorruptible'. In

OUAGADOUGOU

Capital city lying in the centre of Burkina Faso. Founded in the late 11th century as capital of the Mossi empire, it remained the centre of Mossi power until captured by the French in 1896. Industries include handicrafts, textiles, food processing, groundnuts, vegetable oil.

BURMA (MYANMAR)

The colours on Burma's flag were adopted in 1948 when the country became independent from Britain. The socialist symbol, added in 1974, includes a ring of 14 stars representing the country's 14 states. The gearwheel represents industry and the rice plant symbolizes agriculture.

The Union of Burma is now officially known as the Union of Myanmar; its name was changed in 1989. Mountains border the country in the east and west, with the highest mountains in the north. Burma's highest mountain is Hkakabo Razi, which is 5,881 m [19,294 ft] high. Between these ranges is central Burma, which contains the fertile valleys of the Irrawaddy and Sittang rivers. The Irrawaddy delta on the Bay of Bengal is one of the world's leading rice-growing areas. Burma also includes the long Tenasserim coast in the south-east.

Area 676,578 sq km [261,227 sq mi]
Population 47,383,000
Capital (population) Rangoon (4,082,000), Naypyitaw (seat of government)
Government Military regime
Ethnic groups Burman 68%, Shan 9%, Karen 7%, Rakhine 4%, Chinese, Indian, Mon
Languages Burmese, minority ethnic languages
Religions Buddhism 89%, Christianity, Islam
Currency Kyat = 100 pyas
Website www.burmaproject.org

CLIMATE

Burma has a tropical monsoon climate. There are three seasons. The rainy season runs from late May to mid-October. A cool, dry season follows, between late October and the middle part of February. The hot season lasts from late February to mid-May, though temperatures remain high during the humid rainy season.

HISTORY

Conflict between the Burmans and Mons dominated Burma's early history. In 1044 the Burman King Anawratha unified the Irrawaddy delta region. In 1287 Kublai Khan conquered the Burman capital, Pagan. Burma was divided: the Shan controlled north Burma, while the resurgent Mons held the south. In the 16th century, the Burmans subjugated the Shan. In 1758 Alaungapaya reunified Burma, defeating the Mons kingdom and establishing the Konbaung dynasty.

Wars with British India marked much of the 19th century. The first war, in 1824, resulted in the British gaining the coastal regions of Tenasserim and Arakan. The second war in 1852 saw the British gain control of the Irrawaddy delta. British India annexed Burma in the third war of 1885 and the British set up a capital at Rangoon (or Yangon) on the Rangoon River. Rangoon became the country's largest city and chief port.

In 1937 Burma gained limited self-government. Helped by the Burmese Independent Army led by Aung San, Japan conquered the country in 1942. The installation of a puppet regime led Aung San to form a resistance movement. In 1947 Aung San was murdered. Burma achieved independence in 1948.

POLITICS

The socialist AFPFL government, led by U Nu, faced secessionist revolts by communists and Karen tribesmen. In 1958 U Nu invited General Ne Win to re-

League for Democracy (NLD) led by Aung San Suu Kyi won elections in 1990, but SLORC annulled the result and placed her under house arrest. In 1997 SLORC became the State Peace and Development Council (SPDC). In 1998, NLD calls for the reconvening of Parliament led to mass detention of political opponents by the SPDC. Aung San Suu Kyi, effectively leader of the opposition, was released in 2002 but arrested again from 2003. Her continued imprisonment, along with thousands of other political prisoners, attracted widespread international criticism.

In 2006 the government abruptly moved the capital to Naypyidaw. September 2007 saw mass protests, the largest since the 1980s, which were brutally suppressed.

ECONOMY

Agriculture is the main activity, employing 66% of the workforce. The chief crop is rice. Groundnuts, maize, plantains, pulses, seed cotton, sesame seeds and sugar cane are also produced. Forestry is important and teak is a major product. Fish and shellfish are another industry. The varied natural resources are mostly underdeveloped, although the country is famous for its precious stones, especially rubies. Burma is almost self-sufficient in oil and natural gas.

NAYPYIDAW

Capital of Burma, in the Pyinmana area 400km (250mi) north of Rangoon. Construction on the formerly uninhabited site began in 2005. It is specifically designed for easy military access to allow demonstrations to be rapidly suppressed. The city is closed to the Burmese public and most international visitors. Secrecy is high and little information is available.

establish order. Civilian rule returned in 1960, but in 1962 Ne Win mounted a successful coup. His military dictatorship faced mass insurgency. In 1974 Ne Win became president. Mass demonstrations forced Ne Win to resign in 1988, but the military retained power under the guise of the State Law and Order Restoration Council (SLORC), led by General Saw Muang. In 1989 the country's name changed to Myanmar. The National

BURUNDI

This flag was adopted in 1967 when Burundi became a republic. It contains three red stars rimmed in green, symbolizing the nation's motto of 'Unité, Travail, Progrès'. The green represents hope for the future, the red the struggle for independence, and the white the desire for peace.

The Republic of Burundi is a small country in east central Africa. A section of the Great Rift Valley, lies in the west. It contains part of Lake Tanganyika, whose shoreline is 772 m [2,533 ft] above sea level. East of the Rift Valley is a mountain zone, rising to 2,670 metres [8,760 ft]. The land descends to the east in a series of steppe-like plateaux. Burundi forms part of the Nile-Congo watershed and contains the headwaters of the River Kagera, the most remote source of the Nile.

Grassland covers much of Burundi, because much of the original forest has been cleared by farming and overgrazing. New forests are now being planted to halt the loss of soil fertility caused by erosion.

Area 27,834 sq km [10,747 sq mi]
Population 8,090,000
Capital (population) Bujumbura (235,000)
Government Republic
Ethnic groups Hutu 85%, Tutsi 14%, Twa (Pygmy)
Languages French, Kirundi (both official)
Religions Roman Catholic 62%, traditional beliefs 23%, Islam 10%, Protestant 5%
Currency Burundi franc = 100 centimes
Website www.burundi-embassy-berlin.com

CLIMATE

Bujumbura has an average annual temperature of 23°C [73°F]. June to August and December-January are dry, but the rest of the year rainy. The mountains and the central plateaux are distinctly cooler and wetter than the Rift Valley floor, but the rainfall decreases to the east.

HISTORY

The first known inhabitants of the area were the Twa, a pygmy group of hunting and gathering people, who now make up just 1% of the population. Around 1,000 years ago, a Bantu-speaking, iron-using farming people from the west, the Hutu, began to settle, pushing the Twa into remote areas. A third group, the cattle-owning Tutsi from the north-east, arrived around 600 years ago. They gradually took control of the area and, although in the minority, formed the ruling class. The Tutsi created a feudal state, making the Hutu serfs. The explorers Richard Burton and John Hanning Speke visited the area in 1858 in their quest to find the source of the Nile.

A powerful Tutsi kingdom under Mwami (king) Rugamba, that developed in the late 18th century, had broken up by the 1880s. Germany conquered what are now Burundi and Rwanda, in the late 1890s. The area, called Ruanda-Urundi, became part of German East Africa. After Germany's defeat in World War I, Belgium took control.

In 1961, the people of Urundi voted to become a monarchy under Mwami Mwambutsa IV, who had ruled since 1915, while the people of Ruanda voted to become a republic.

POLITICS

The two territories finally became fully independent as Burundi and Rwanda on

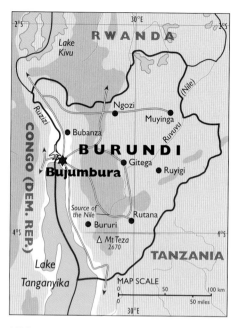

In 1992 a new constitution gave the country a multiparty system. In 1993 Melchior Ndadaye, a Hutu, beat Buyoya in presidential elections but supporters of Bagaza assassinated Ndadaye. In 1994 the new president, Cyprien Ntaryamira, a Hutu, was killed in a plane crash together with the Rwandan president, causing more ethnic violence. In 1996 Buyoya staged another coup and suspended the constitution. In 1999, peace talks began which led, in 2001, to the setting up of a transitional, power-sharing government. However, some Hutu rebel groups refused to sign the cease-fire. In 2003, Domitien Ndayizeye succeeded Buyoya as president, under the power-sharing agreement. In 2004, the disarming of rebels and soldiers began. In 2005 the people voted in favour of the new power-sharing constitution. In 2006 the last rebel group signed a cease-fire, but peace remains fragile.

1 July 1962. Since then, Burundi has suffered severe conflict caused by ethnic rivalry between the Hutu majority and the Tutsi. Around 300,000 people have been killed, and a great many more displaced or made refugees. In 1965 Mwambutsa refused to appoint a Hutu prime minister, although the Hutu were in the majority. An attempted coup was brutally put down. In 1966, Mwambutsa was deposed by his son who became Mwami Ntare V, but Tutsi prime minister Michel Micombero deposed Ntare and declared Burundi to be a republic with himself as president.

Between 1966 and 1972 most Hutu and some Tutsi were removed from high office. This culminated in a rebellion, when between 100,000 and 200,000 mostly Hutu were killed. In 1976 Jean-Baptiste Bagaza, a Tutsi, deposed Micombero. In 1981 Burundi became a one-party state, but Bagaza was deposed in 1987 by a coup led by Pierre Buyoya. Another uprising in 1988 led to the slaughter of thousands of Hutus.

ECONOMY

Burundi is one of the world's poorest countries. 94% of the people depend on farming, mainly at subsistence level. The main food crops are bananas, beans, cassava, maize and sweet potatoes. Cattle, goats and sheep are raised, and fishing is important.

The economy depends on coffee and tea, which account for 90% of foreign exchange earnings, and cotton.

BUJUMBURA

Capital and chief port of Burundi, east central Africa, at the north-east end of Lake Tanganyika. Founded in 1899 as part of German East Africa, it was the capital of Ruanda-Urundi after World War I and remained capital of Burundi upon independence in 1962.

CAMBODIA

Red is the traditional colour of Cambodia. The blue symbolizes the water resources that are so important to the people, three-quarters of whom depend on farming for a living. The silhouette is the historic temple at Angkor Wat.

The Kingdom of Cambodia is a country in South-east Asia. Low mountains border the country, except in the south-east. Most of Cambodia consists of plains drained by the River Mekong, which enters Cambodia from Laos in the north and exits through Vietnam in the south-east. The north-west contains Tonlé Sap (or Great Lake). In the dry season this lake drains into the River Mekong, but in the wet season the level of the Mekong rises and water flows in the opposite direction, from the river into Tonlé Sap. The lake then becomes the largest freshwater lake in Asia.

Area 181,035 sq km [69,898 sq mi]
Population 13,881,000
Capital (population) Phnom Penh (1,174,000)
Government Constitutional monarchy
Ethnic groups Khmer 90%, Vietnamese 5%, Chinese 1%, others
Languages Khmer (official), French, English
Religions Buddhism 95%, others 5%
Currency Riel = 100 sen
Website www.cambodia.gov.kh

CLIMATE

Cambodia has a tropical monsoon climate, with high temperatures all through the year. The dry season, when winds blow from the north or north-east, runs from November to April. During the rainy season, from May to October, moist winds blow from the south or south-east. The high humidity and heat often make conditions unpleasant. The rainfall is heaviest near the coast, and rather lower inland.

HISTORY

From 802 to 1431, the Hindu-Buddhist Khmer people ruled a great empire. Its zenith came in the reign of Suryavarman II (1113–50), who built the great funerary temple of Angkor Wat. Together with Angkor Thom, the Angkor site contains the world's largest group of religious buildings. The wealth of the kingdom rested on fish from the lake and rice from the flooded lowlands, for which an extensive system of irrigation channels and strong reservoirs was developed. Thai forces captured Angkor in 1431 and forests covered the site. Following its rediscovery in 1860, it has been gradually restored and is now a major tourist attraction.

France ruled the country from 1863 as part of Indo-China until it achieved independence in 1954. In a short period of stability during the late 1950s and 1960s, the country developed its small-scale agricultural resources and rubber plantations. It remained predominantly rural, but achieved self-sufficiency in food, with some exports.

POLITICS

In 1969, during the Vietnam War, US planes bombed North Vietnamese targets in Cambodia. In 1970, King Norodom Sihanouk was overthrown and Cambodia became a republic. Under assault from South Vietnamese troops, the Communist Vietnamese withdrew deep into

However, the Khmer Rouge continued hostilities and were banned in 1994. In 1997, Hu Sen, the second prime minister, engineered a coup against Ranariddh, exiling him and taking his place as Prime Minister. In 1998 Ranariddh returned, alleging electoral fraud when elections resulted in victory for Hu Sen. A coalition government was formed in December 1998, with Hu Sen as prime minister. In 2001, the government set up a court to try leaders of the Khmer Rouge. In 2004, Sihanouk abdicated due to ill health and was succeeded by his son Prince Norodom Sihamoni.

ECONOMY
Cambodia is a poor country whose economy has been wrecked by war and relies heavily on aid. Recovery has been slow. Farming is the main activity and rice, rubber and maize important. Tourism is increasing, and the Angkor temples are a major attraction. In 2005 oil and gas were discovered in Cambodia's territorial waters, promising future economic improvement.

Cambodia. US raids ended in 1973, but fighting continued as Cambodia's Communists in the Khmer Rouge fought against the government. The Khmer Rouge, led by Pol Pot, were victorious in 1975. They began a reign of terror, murdering government officials and educated people. Up to 2 million people are estimated to have been killed. After the overthrow of Pol Pot by Vietnamese forces in 1979, civil war raged between the Vietnamese-backed government led by Heng Samrin and the US-backed Democratic Kampuchea faction. This was a coalition of Prince Sihanouk, the Khmer Liberation Front, and the Khmer Rouge who, from 1982, claimed to have abandoned Communist ideology.

Devastated by war and denied almost any aid, Cambodia continued to decline. It was only the withdrawal of Vietnamese troops in 1989, sparking fear of a Khmer Rouge revival, that forced a settlement. In October 1991, a UN-brokered peace plan for elections in 1993 was accepted by all parties. A new constitution was adopted in September 1993, restoring democracy and the monarchy. Sihanouk again became king, with his son Prince Norodom Ranariddh as prime minister.

PHNOM PENH (PHNUM PÉNH)
Capital of Cambodia, in the south of the country, a port at the confluence of the rivers Mekong and Tonlé Sap. Founded in the 14th century, the city was the capital of the Khmers after 1434. In 1865, it became the capital of Cambodia. Occupied by the Japanese during World War II, it was extensively damaged during the Cambodian civil war. After the Khmer Rouge took power in 1975, the city shrank drastically as its inhabitants were forcibly removed to work in the countryside. Industries include milling, brewing, distilling.

CAMEROON

Cameroon uses the colours that appear on the flag of Ethiopia, Africa's oldest independent nation. These colours symbolize African unity. The flag is based on the tricolour adopted in 1957. The design with the yellow liberty star dates from 1975.

The Republic of Cameroon in West Africa got its name from the Portuguese word *camarões*, or prawns. This name was used by Portuguese explorers who fished for prawns along the coast.

Behind the narrow coastal plains on the Gulf of Guinea, the land rises to a series of plateaux. In the north, the land slopes down towards the Lake Chad (Tchad) basin. The mountain region in the south-west of the country includes Mount Cameroon, a volcano which is still occasionally active. The vegetation varies greatly from north to south. The deserts in the north merge into dry and moist savanna in central Cameroon, with dense tropical rainforests in the humid south.

Area 475,442 sq km [183,568 sq mi]
Population 17,341,000
Capital (population) Yaoundé (649,000)
Government Multiparty republic
Ethnic groups Cameroon Highlanders 31%, Bantu 27%, Kirdi 11%, Fulani 10%, others
Languages French and English (both official), many others
Religions Christianity 40%, traditional beliefs 40%, Islam 20%
Currency CFA franc = 100 centimes
Website www.camnet.cm

CLIMATE

The rainfall is heavy, especially in the highlands. The rainiest months near the coast are from June to September. The rainfall decreases to the north and the far north has a hot, dry climate. Temperatures are high on the coast, whereas the inland plateaux are cooler.

HISTORY

Among the early inhabitants of Cameroon were groups of Bantu-speaking people. There are now more than 160 ethnic groups, each with their own language. In the late 15th century Portuguese explorers, who were seeking a sea route to Asia around Africa, reached the Cameroon coast. From the 17th century, southern Cameroon was a centre of the slave trade, but slavery was ended in the early 19th century. The area became a German protectorate in 1884, but was captured by Allied troops during World

YAOUNDÉ

Capital of Cameroon, West Africa. Located in beautiful hills on the edge of dense jungle, German traders founded it in 1888. During World War I, it was occupied by Belgian troops, and later acted as capital (1921–60) of French Cameroon. Since independence, it has grown rapidly as a financial and administrative centre with strong Western influences. It is the site of the University of Cameroon (1962). The city also serves as a market for the surrounding region, notably in coffee, cacao and sugar.

population, Cameroon joined the Commonwealth. In 2002, the International Court of Justice gave Cameroon sovereignty over the disputed oil-rich Bakassi peninsula. Nigeria failed to reach the deadline for the handover of the area in 2004, but finally withdrew and handed over Bakassi in 2006.

Presidential elections in 2004 saw Paul Biya win a new seven-year term with more than 70% of the vote. The result was accepted by Commonwealth observers, but opposition parties alleged widespread fraud.

ECONOMY
Like most countries in tropical Africa, Cameroon's economy is based on agriculture, which employs 73% of the people. Chief food crops include cassava, maize, millet, sweet potatoes and yams.

Cameroon is fortunate in having some oil, the country's chief export, and bauxite. Although Cameroon has few manufacturing and processing industries, its mineral exports and its self-sufficiency in food production make it one of the wealthier countries in tropical Africa. Another important industry is forestry, ranking second among the exports after oil. Other exports are cocoa, coffee, aluminium and cotton.

War I. The country was then divided into two parts, one ruled by Britain and the other by France.

POLITICS
In 1960, French Cameroon became the independent Cameroon Republic. In 1961, after a vote in British Cameroon, part of the territory joined the Cameroon Republic to become the Federal Republic of Cameroon. The other part joined Nigeria. In 1972, Cameroon became a unitary state called the United Republic of Cameroon. It adopted the name Republic of Cameroon in 1984, but the country had two official languages. Opposition parties were legalized in 1992, and Paul Biya was elected president in 1993 and 1997. In 1995, partly to placate the English-speaking part of the

DOUALA
Chief port of Cameroon, on the Bight of Biafra, West Africa. As Kamerunstadt, it was capital of the German Kamerun Protectorate (1885–1901), became Douala (1907), and was capital of French Cameroon (1940–46). Industries include ship repairing, textiles and palm oil. It has a population of 1,239,100.

CANADA

Canada's flag, with its simple 11-pointed maple leaf emblem, was adopted in 1965 after many attempts to find an acceptable design. The former flag, used from 1892, was the British Red Ensign. The British ensign was unpopular with Canada's French community.

A vast confederation of ten provinces and three territories, Canada is the world's second largest country after Russia, with an even longer coastline – about 250,000 km [155,000 mi]. It is sparsely populated because it contains vast areas of virtually unoccupied mountains, cold forests, tundra and polar desert in the north and west. About 80% of the population of Canada lives within about 300 km [186 mi] of the southern border.

Forests of cedars, hemlocks and other trees grow on the western mountains, with firs and spruces at the higher levels. The mountain forests provide habitats for bears, deer and mountain lions, while such animals as the sure-footed Rocky Mountain goats and bighorn sheep roam above the tree line (the upper limit of tree growth).

The interior plains were once grassy prairies. While the drier areas are still used for grazing cattle, the wetter areas are used largely for growing wheat and other cereals. North of the prairies are boreal forests which, in turn, merge into the treeless tundra and Arctic wastelands in the far north. The lowlands in south-eastern Canada contain forests of deciduous trees, such as beech, hickory, oak and walnut.

CLIMATE

Canada has a cold climate. In winter, temperatures fall below freezing point throughout most of the country. But the south-western coast has a relatively mild climate. Along the Arctic Circle, the temperatures are, on average, below freezing for seven months a year. By contrast, hot winds from the Gulf of Mexico warm

Area 9,970,610 sq km [3,849,653 sq mi]
Population 33,099,000
Capital (population) Ottawa (1,120,000)
Government
Federal multiparty constitutional monarchy
Ethnic groups
British origin 28%, French origin 23%, other European 15%, Amerindian/Inuit 2%, others
Languages English and French (both official)
Religions Roman Catholic 46%, Protestant 36%, Judaism, Islam, Hinduism
Currency Canadian dollar = 100 cents
Website http://canada.gc.ca

southern Ontario and the St Lawrence River lowlands in summer. As a result, southern Ontario has a frost-free season of nearly six months.

The coasts of British Columbia are wet, with an average annual rainfall of more than 2,500 mm [98 in] in places. The prairies however are arid or semi-arid, with an average annual rainfall of 250 mm to 500 mm [10–20 in]. The rainfall in south-eastern Canada ranges from around 800 mm [31 in] in southern Ontario to about 1,500 mm [59 in] on the coasts of Newfoundland and Nova Scotia. Heavy snow falls across eastern Canada in winter.

HISTORY

Canada's first people, ancestors of the Native Americans, arrived from Asia around 40,000 years ago. The Inuit arrived later, also from Asia.

Norse voyagers and fishermen were probably the first Europeans to visit Canada. John Cabot's rediscovery of North America in 1497 led to a race to annex lands and wealth, with France and Britain the main contenders. Canada came under British rule after wars with France in the eighteenth century.

The creation of the British Commonwealth in 1931 made Canada a sovereign nation under the crown. Canada is now a constitutional monarchy. Under the Constitution Act of 1982, Queen Elizabeth II is head of state and a symbol of the close ties between Canada and Britain. She is represented by an appointed governor-general, but the country is ruled by a prime minister and an elected, two-chamber parliament.

POLITICS

Canada combines the cabinet system with a federal form of government, in which each province has its own government. The federal government can reject any law passed by a provincial legislature, though this seldom happens in practice. The territories are self-governing, but the federal government plays a large part in their administration.

Canada and the United States of America have the largest bilateral trade flow in the world. This economic co-operation was further enhanced in 1993 when Canada, the United States and Mexico set up NAFTA – the North American Free Trade Agreement.

A constant problem facing those who want to maintain the unity of Canada is the persistence of French culture in Québec, which has fuelled a separatist movement seeking to turn the province into an independent French-speaking republic. More than two-thirds of the population of Québec are French speakers. In 1994, the people of Québec voted the separatist Parti Québécois into provincial office. The incoming prime minister announced that independence for Québec would be the subject of a referendum in 1995. In that referendum, 49.4% voted 'Yes' (for separation) while 50.5% voted 'No'.

Provincial elections in 1998 resulted in another victory for the Parti Québécois, but while the separatist party won 75 out of the 125 seats in the provincial assembly, it won only 43% of the popular vote compared with 44% for the anti-secessionist Liberal Party and 12% for the floating Action Démocratique de Québec. Also significant was a ruling by Canada's highest court that, under Canadian law, Québec does not have the right to secede unilaterally. The court ruled that, should the people in the province vote by 'a clear majority' to a 'clear question' in favour of independence, the federal government and the other provinces would then have to negotiate Québec's secession. In 2006 the national parliament symbolically recognized Québec as 'a nation within a united Canada' in an attempt at reconciliation. Support for secession fell in elections held in 2007.

OTTAWA

Capital of Canada, in south-east Ontario, on the Ottawa River and the Rideau Canal. Founded in 1826 as Bytown, it acquired its present name in 1854. Queen Victoria chose it as capital of the United Provinces in 1858, and in 1867 it became the national capital of the Dominion of Canada. Industries include glass-making, printing, publishing, sawmilling, pulp-making, timepieces.

Other problems involve the rights of the aboriginal Native Americans and the Inuit, who together numbered about 470,000 in 1991. In 1999, a new Inuit territory was created. Called Nunavut, it is made up of 64% of the former Northwest Territories, and covers 2,201,400 sq km [649,965 sq mi]. Nunavut, whose capital is Iqaluit (formerly Frobisher Bay), will depend on aid. Mineral extraction and ecotourism will be developed in the region to attempt to lessen this dependence.

ECONOMY

Canada is a highly developed and prosperous country. Although farmland covers only 8% of the country, Canadian farms are highly productive, Canada is one of the world's leading producers of barley, wheat, meat and milk. Forestry and fishing are other important industries. The country is rich in natural resources, especially oil and natural gas. Canada exports minerals, including copper, gold, iron ore, uranium and zinc. Manufacturing is important, main-ly in the cities where 79% of the population lives. Canada processes farm and mineral products. Its industries produce cars, chemicals, electronic goods, machinery, paper, timber and timber products.

Tourism is an important source of income, with both winter and summer popular tourist seasons.

ANGUILLA

Most northerly of the Leeward Islands, Anguilla is named after the Spanish for eel. Long and thin, it is a low coral atoll covered with poor soil and scrub. It measures 96 sq km [37 sq mi].

Discovered by French explorers in the 1550s, Anguilla was settled by English colonists in 1650. They farmed food and tobacco, but were barely able to subsist. Attempts to establish plantations failed due to the poor soils.

In 1967 Britain granted the St Kitts-Nevis-Anguilla group its own constitution and limited self-government as a move towards a separate state. Anguilla, rejecting this arrangement, seceded from the group and declared independence. In 1980 it rejoined Britain as a self-governing overseas dependency.

The island's economy is based on fishing and tourism. Offshore banking is also important due to low taxation.

Area 96 sq km [37 sq mi]
Population 13,000
Capital The Valley
Government Overseas territory of the UK
Ethnic groups Black 90%, Mixed 5%, White 3%
Languages English
Religions Anglican 29%, Methodist 24%, Protestant 30%, Roman Catholic 6%
Currency East Caribbean dollar = 100 cents
Website www.anguilla-vacation.com

ANTIGUA & BARBUDA

Part of the Lesser Antilles in the Leeward Islands. Antigua is mountainous, rising to 405 m [1,328 ft] at is highest, but unlike other mountainous Leeward Islands has no rivers or forests. Barbuda, by contrast, is a wooded, low coral atoll. Barbuda is principally a wildlife preserve and tourist attraction, with a population of only 1,400.

The islands were discovered by Columbus in 1493, and early settlements by the Spanish and French wiped out the native population. Britain later took control of the islands, and established a colony in 1667. Antigua and Barbuda gained internal self-government in 1967, and independence in 1981. The islands' economy depends on tourism.

Area 442 sq km [171 sq mi]
Population 69,000
Capital St John's
Government Constitutional monarchy
Ethnic groups Black, British, others
Languages English, Local dialects
Religions Christian
Currency
East Caribbean dollar = 100 cents
Website www.antigua-barbuda.org

CARIBBEAN ISLANDS

ARUBA

Dutch island in the Caribbean, off the coast of north-west Venezuela. It was part of the Netherlands Antilles until 1986. Independence was revoked in 1990, at Aruba's request, and it is now an autonomous part of the Netherlands. Oil refining, phosphates and tourism are the key sources of revenue.

Area 193 sq km [75 sq mi]
Population 72,000
Capital Oranjestad
Government Parliamentary democracy
Ethnic groups Mixed White/Amerindian 80%
Languages Dutch (official), Papiamento, English
Religions Roman Catholic 82%, Protestant 8%
Currency Aruban guilder/florin = 100 cents
Website www.aruba.com

BAHAMAS

The Bahamas consists of a coral and limestone archipelago of more than 700 low-lying islands, centred on the Grand Bahama Bank off eastern Florida and Cuba. Only around 30 are inhabited. Most of the islands are low, flat, and riverless, with rocky terrain poorly suited to agriculture, and bordered by mangrove swamps. The climate is subtropical, with average temperatures of 21–32°C [70–90°F].

The island of San Salvador in the Bahamas was the site of Christopher Columbus' first landfall in the New World. Within a few decades of the arrival of the Spanish, the native people were wiped out by enslavement and disease, and the islands became uninhabited. English settlers arrived in 1647, and the Bahamas became a British crown colony in 1717.

In 1973 the Bahamas gained independence from Britain under a democratic constitution, though the British monarch remains the ceremonial head of state. Since independence it has developed close ties with the USA.

Tourism is the most important source of revenue, though it has proved vulnerable to fluctuatons in the US economy. Zero income taxes have drawn a large financial services and offshore banking sector, though it shrank after new laws in 2000 aimed to control money laundering. Small export earnings are provided by fruit, salt and rum.

Area 13,878 sq km [5,358 sq mi]
Population 304,000
Capital Nassau
Government Constitutional parliamentary democracy
Ethnic groups Black 85%, White 12%, others
Languages English (official), Creole
Religions Christian
Currency Bahamian dollar = 100 cents
Website www.bahamas.gov.bs

BARBADOS

An island state in the Windward Islands of the West Indies, Barbados is the easternmost Caribbean country and the first to be hit by the region's seasonal hurricanes. It is formed of limestone capped with coral. Mt Hillaby, the highest point at 340 m [1,115 ft], is fringed by marine terraces marking stages in the island's emergence from the sea. Soils are fertile and deep, and the island has a warm climate with a long wet season.

British settlers arrived in 1627 and soon set up an economy based on sugar plantations. Early plantations were worked by indentured servants from Ireland and Scotland, but slaves from Africa soon became the main source of labour. Slavery was abolished in the British Empire in 1834, but most former slaves continued to work on plantations and the island was effectively ruled by plantation owners until political reform movements began in the 1930s and 1940s. Barbados became independent from Britain in 1966, though the Queen is still the ceremonial head of state.

From the 1990s, tourism and manufacturing outgrew sugar to become the mainstays of the economy. Tourism has in turn fuelled growth in the construction sector. Agriculture is limited, though sugarcane production still takes up the majority of cropped land and is a significant employer. Much sugar is converted to rum for export.

Area 430 sq km [166 sq mi]
Population 280,000
Capital Bridgetown
Government Parliamentary democracy
Ethnic groups Black 90%, Asian, White
Languages English
Religions Protestant 67%, Roman Catholic 4%
Currency Barbadian dollar = 100 cents
Website www.barbados.org

CAYMAN ISLANDS

British dependency in the West Indies, comprising Grand Cayman, Little Cayman, and Cayman Brac, 325 km (200 mi) north-west of Jamaica, in the Caribbean Sea. The islands were discovered by Columbus in 1503, and ceded to Britain in the 17th century. The islanders voted against independence in 1962. Tourism, international finance and turtle and shark fishing are sources of revenue.

Area 264 sq km [102 sq mi]
Population 45,000
Capital George Town
Government Overseas territory of the UK
Ethnic groups Mixed 40%, White 20%, Black 20%
Languages English
Religions Protestant, Roman Catholic
Currency Caymanian dollar = 100 cents
Website www.gov.ky

DOMINICA

An independent island nation in the east Caribbean Sea, it is the largest of the Windward Islands. The present population are mainly the descendants of African slaves. Dominica is mountainous and heavily forested, and the climate is tropical. It achieved complete independence in 1978. Dominica is one of the poorest Caribbean countries. Agriculture dominates the economy.

Area 751 sq km [290 sq mi]
Population 69,000
Capital Roseau
Government Parliamentary democracy
Ethnic groups Black, Mixed, European
Languages English (official), French patois
Religions Roman Catholic 77%, Protestant 15%
Currency East Caribbean dollar = 100 cents
Website www.avirtualdominica.com

CARIBBEAN ISLANDS

GRENADA

Independent island nation in the south east Caribbean Sea, consisting of Grenada and the small islands of the Southern Grenadines, 160 km [100 mi] north of Venezuela. Grenada itself is volcanic in origin, with a ridge of mountains running north–south. The climate is tropical, supporting lush vegetation.

Grenada first became known to Europeans when discovered by Columbus in 1498. Unlike many Caribbean islands, the native Caribs survived the arrival of the Spanish. Grenada was not permanently settled by Europeans until the 1650s, when French colonists defeated the Caribs and seized the island.

The French settlers established a plantation economy, using African slave labour to produce sugar. The colony was ceded to the UK in the 1760s. Under British control, production shifted from sugar to spices and cacao.

Grenada became a self-governing colony in 1967 and achieved independence in 1974. In 1979 the unpopular government was toppled by a Marxist coup. Maurice Bishop, the new president, established links with Cuba but was killed in 1983 by more hardline Marxists. The US military intervened and established a pro-US government.

The agrarian economy is based on cash crops, with spices the dominant export, though 2004 hurricanes caused heavy damage. In the 1990s, tourism and offshore finance industries arose.

Area 344 sq km [133 sq mi]
Population 90,000
Capital St George's
Government Constitutional monarchy
Ethnic groups Black 82%, others
Languages English (official), French patois
Religions Roman Catholic 53%, Protestant 47%
Currency East Caribbean dollar = 100 cents
Website www.gov.gd

GUADELOUPE

French overseas department, consisting of seven islands in the Leeward Islands. Basse-Terre, which makes up over 90% of the area, is volcanic and mountainous. Its highest peak, La Soufrière, is the highest point in the Lesser Antilles. The smaller Grande-Terre is a flat island of limestone separated from Basse-Terre by a narrow sea channel called Rivière-Salée, Salt River.

Discovered in 1493 by Columbus, Guadeloupe was settled by the French in 1635. Under French rule many of the indigenous Carib were killed and a prosperous plantation economy was established. Briefly held by Britain and Sweden, Guadeloupe reverted to French rule in 1816. In 1946 it became an Overseas Department of France. Saint-Martin and Saint-Barthélemy were formerly part of the Guadeloupe administration, but acquired their own governments as French overseas territories after a referendum in 2003.

Guadeloupe's weak economy is heavily dependent on French subsidies and government-created jobs. The island's other main source of income is tourism, mostly from France and from passing cruise ships. Unemployment is high. Agriculture is a significant sector, principally for sugar cane and bananas grown for export. The industry is diversifying to produce other fruits and flowers.

Area 1,705 sq km [658 sq mi]
Population 453,000
Capital Basse-Terre
Government Overseas department of France
Ethnic groups
Black or mulatto 90%, White 5%
Languages English (official), Spanish, Creole
Religions
Roman Catholic 95%, Hindu and pagan African 4%
Currency Euro = 100 cents
Website www.guadeloupe.pref.gouv.fr

MARTINIQUE

Island in the Windward group of the Lesser Antilles, consisting of three groups of forested volcanic hills joined by lowlands. The highest peak is Mt Pelée, at 1,397 m [4,583 ft], which is still intermittently active. When it last erupted, in 1902, it completely destroyed the original capital St Pierre leaving only a handful of survivors. Today it is closely monitored to warn of future activity.

Martinique was inhabited by Carib Indians until they were displaced by French settlers after 1635. The French established a plantation economy, which rapidly became prosperous. The island was briefly taken over by the British several times, but became a permanent French possession after the Napoleonic Wars. Napoleon's first wife, Josephine, was the daughter of wealthy Martinique plantation owners.

Demands for independence grew through the 20th century. In 1982 Martinique became an Overseas Department of France with its own government.

In the 20th century, tourism overtook sugar cane to become the largest sector of the economy. Sugar production remains important, though most is now used for the production of rum and exported in that form. Some oil products are exported, refined from imported Venezuelan crude. The economy is bolstered by subsidies from France.

Area 1,102 sq km [425 sq mi]
Population 436,000
Capital Fort-de-France
Government Overseas department of France
Ethnic groups
African and African-white-Indian mixture 90%
Languages French, Creole patois
Religions
Roman Catholic 85%, Protestant 10%
Currency Euro = 100 cents
Website www.martinique.org

MONTSERRAT

Montserrat is one of the Leeward Islands in the Lesser Antilles. It is dominated by an active volcano in the Soufrière Hills.

The island was inhabited by Carib and Arawak peoples when discovered by Christopher Columbus in 1493. The first European colonization was by the British in 1632, at first with predominantly Irish settlers. A plantation economy was set up, using African slave labour to produce sugar and a South American cotton plant called sea island cotton. The island was briefly captured by the French during the American War of Independence, but soon returned to British control.

Slavery was abolished in 1834. Unlike most islands with plantation economies, many of Montserrat's plantations broke up into smallholdings in the course of the 19th century. Falling sugar prices led to the conversion of failing sugar estates to lime-growing. Montserrat formed part of the Leeward Island colony from 1871 until 1956, when it became a separate, dependent territory of the UK.

In 1997 the Soufrière Hills volcano erupted. It devastated half the island and buried Plymouth, the capital. Few were killed, but most of the population had to evacuate. Many remain abroad.

The island's economy was mainly based on tourism, offshore finance and sea island cotton. British and EU aid is assisting reconstruction.

Area 102 sq km [40 sq mi]
Population 9,000
Capital St John's
Government Overseas territory of the UK
Ethnic groups Black, White
Languages English
Religions Christian
Currency East Caribbean dollar = 100 cents
Website www.gov.ms

CARIBBEAN ISLANDS

NETHERLANDS ANTILLES

The Netherlands Antilles consists of two very different island groups - Curaçao and Bonaire of the coast of Venezuela, and Saba, Saint Eustatius, and the southern half of Saint Maarten at the northern end of the Leeward Islands some 800 km [500 mi] away. The other half of Saint Maarten is shared with France as St Martin. Curaçao, the largest island, has nearly 45% of the land area and over 80% of the population.

Both sets of islands were discovered by Columbus in 1493 and settled by the Spanish in the early 16th century. In 1633–40 they were captured by the Dutch. The Dutch West India Company used the islands, particularly Curaçao, as centres for the slave trade. Slavery was not abolished until 1863.

The territory was granted internal self-government in 1954. Aruba split off in 1986 to become a separate Dutch territory. In 2005 the leaders of the remaining islands reached an agreement with the Dutch government to break up the federation, making Curaçao and St Maarten separate Dutch territories in 2008. The remaining islands will receive a status equivalent to Dutch cities.

Most revenue comes from the refining of Venezuelan oil and its conversion to petrochemicals for export. Tourism is also important, as is offshore finance.

Area 800 sq km [309 sq mi]
Population 222,000
Capital Willemstadt (Curacao)
Government Autonomous country within the Kingdom of the Netherlands
Ethnic groups Mixed Black 85%, others
Languages Papiamento 65%, English 16%, Dutch 7% (official)
Religions Roman Catholic 72%, others
Currency Netherlands Antillean guilder = 100 cents
Website www.gov.an

PUERTO RICO

Easternmost of the major Greater Antilles, Puerto Rico has a mountainous interior and a narrow coastal plain. The south coast is relatively dry, but the north is well-watered and fertile.

Puerto Rico was inhabited by the Taino people when discovered by Christopher Columbus in 1493. Spanish colonists arrived in the early 1500s, and the Taino were soon wiped out by disease and forced labour. The Spanish imported African slaves to set up a plantation economy. In the 17th and 18th centuries the island developed slowly, as Spanish attention was focused on their empire in mainland South America.

In 1898, during the Spanish-American war, Puerto Rico was invaded by the United States. After the war the island was among the territories Spain was forced to cede to the US, and fell under US military rule. From 1917 Puerto Rico was permitted to elect its own government and Puerto Ricans were given US citizenship. In the 1940s and 1950s, poverty drove a large number of Puerto Ricans to emigrate to the US. The island

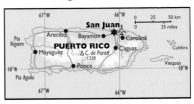

Area 8,875 sq km [3,427 sq mi]
Population 3,927,000
Capital San Juan
Government
US Territory with commonwealth status
Ethnic groups
White Spanish 80%, Black 8%, Mixed 10%
Languages English, Spanish
Religions Roman Catholic, other Christian
Currency United States dollar = 100 cents

has not decided whether to seek independence or full US statehood.

Puerto Rico is the most industrialized island in the Caribbean, with large chemical, pharmaceutical and manufacturing sectors. Cash crops such as sugar, coffee and bananas are exported. Tourism is a major source of income.

ST KITTS & NEVIS

Self-governing state in the Leeward Islands, West Indies. It comprises the islands St Kitts and Nevis, both mountainous volcanic islands rising to about 1,000 m [3,300 ft] at their highest.

When discovered by Columbus in 1493 the islands were populated by the Kalinago people. The first English colony in the Caribbean was established on St Kitts in 1623, and the first French colony in 1625. The Kalinago were wiped out after a failed attempt to drive the settlers out. Anglo-French disputes over possession lasted until 1783. The islands gained self-government in 1967 and became independent in 1983.

Sugar was formerly the mainstay of the economy. The sugar industry was nationalized in 1975. In 2005 it was closed down, having become unprofitable. The islands' income now derives from tourism and offshore banking; strict secrecy laws and poor regulation have made them a haven for money laundering, though since 2003 there have been attempts to control this.

Area 261 sq km [101 sq mi]
Population 39,000
Capital Basseterre (St Kitts)
Government Constitutional monarchy
Ethnic groups Black
Languages English
Religions Anglican, Roman Catholic
Currency
East Caribbean dollar = 100 cents
Website www.stkittsnevis.net

ST LUCIA

Island in the Windward group, West Indies. It is mountainous and forested, composed of extinct volcanoes which are represented on its flag. The twin Piton mountains are a famous landmark.

When discovered by Europeans in the early 16th century, the islands were inhabited by a Carib people. The English attempted to settle in 1639 but were wiped out by the natives. French and English settlers arrived in the 1650s and 1660s. They fought over the island during Britain's wars with France, and it was repeatedly exchanged in treaty negotiations throughout the 18th century. St Lucia changed hands 14 times between France and Britain before finally being ceded to Britain in 1814. It remained a British colony until achieving full independence in 1979.

Historically, the mainstay of the island's economy was sugar plantations. In the 20th century banana production took over, and sugar exports ceased in the 1960s. Bananas remain the major export. Difficult conditions in the banana market have led to unemployment problems, though the remainder of St Lucia's economy is diverse by Caribbean standards and there is a significant light manufacturing sector. Tourism is the largest source of foreign earnings, especially from visiting cruise ships. Offshore banking and financial services provide additional income.

Area 539 sq km [208 sq mi]
Population 168,000
Capital Castries
Government Parliamentary democracy
Ethnic groups Black 90%
Languages English (official), French patois
Religions Roman Catholic 68%, Protestant
Currency
East Caribbean dollar = 100 cents
Website www.stlucia.gov.lc

CARIBBEAN ISLANDS

ST VINCENT & GRENADINES

Island state of the Windward Islands, between St Lucia and Grenada. It comprises St Vincent and five islands of the Grenadine group, including Mustique. St Vincent is mountainous and volcanic, with lush vegetation. Soufrière, its highest peak at 1,178 m [3,866 ft], is an active volcano which last erupted in 1979. Like the actively volcanic Soufrière Hills on Martinique and La Soufrière on Guadeloupe's Basse-Terre, the name derives from the French for a source of sulphur.

When discovered by the Spanish in the 1500s, St Vincent was inhabited by indigenous Carib people. The Caribs aggressively resisted European colonization, and in the 17th century were reinforced by escaped African slaves from neighbouring islands. French settlers finally gained a foothold in 1719 and the island was disputed by France and Britain through the 18th century. Conflict with the indigenous Carib continued until 1796, when the British finally ended Carib resistance.

St Vincent and the Grenadines gained self-government in 1969 and finally became independent from Britain in 1979, the last of the Windwards to do so.

The weak local economy relies upon tourism. Agriculture is principally for bananas, the major export. Tightening of laws against money laundering has reduced the financial sector. Unemployment remains high despite emigration.

Area 388 sq km [150 sq mi]
Population 118,000
Capital Kingstown
Government Parliamentary democracy
Ethnic groups Black 66%, Mixed 19%
Languages English, French patois
Religions Anglican 47%, Methodist 28%, Roman Catholic 13%
Currency East Caribbean dollar = 100 cents
Website www.svgtourism.com

TURKS & CAICOS

Turks and Caicos are two island groups in the West Indies. They include more than 40 islands, eight of which are inhabited. Inhabited by a Carib people when discovered in 1512 by Ponce de León, the islands were not immediately settled but raided by the Spanish for slave labour. The Turks islands were first occupied by Europeans in the late 17th century, when British colonists from Bermuda arrived to set up a salt industry. The Caicos were not colonized until the 18th century. French forces twice occupied the Turks islands during wars with Britain.

Once the islands were permanently under British control, Britain's Bermuda and Bahama colonial administrations disputed which took authority over them and could levy taxes. The war of 1812 between Britain and the US destroyed the lucrative salt trade, which exported to US markets, and ended the dispute. In 1873 administration passed from the Bahamas to Jamaica.

In 1962, when Jamaica became independent, the Turks and Caicos separated to become a Crown Colony of Britain. Independence from Britain was considered and rejected in the 1980s.

The islands' main sources of income are tourism and offshore banking. Unemployment is widespread. There is little agriculture. Conch are farmed, and fresh conch and conch shells are exports.

Area 430 sq km [166 sq mi]
Population 21,000
Capital Cockburn Town (Grand Turk Island)
Government Overseas territory of the UK
Ethnic groups Black 90%
Languages English (official)
Religions Baptist 40%, Methodist 16%, Anglican 18%, Church of God 12%
Currency US dollar = 100 cents
Website www.turksandcaicosislands.gov.tc

BRITISH VIRGIN ISLANDS

US VIRGIN ISLANDS

British colony in the West Indies. It is a group of 36 islands and cays, which form the most northerly part of the Antilles group between the Caribbean Sea and the Atlantic Ocean. Tortola is the main island, with about three quarters of the population.

The islands were first inhabited by an Arawak people, but had been taken over by Caribs by the time Columbus reached them in 1493. They were claimed by the Spanish, but never settled. In the mid 17th century they were colonized by the Dutch. The British conquered and annexed the islands in the later 17th century and introduced plantation farming for sugar cane, importing African slaves. The islands prospered until the 19th century, when the abolition of slavery combined with increased competition in the sugar trade caused the plantations to decline.

The islands formed part of Britain's Leeward Islands colony until 1956. They became a separate colony in 1960 and were granted their own autonomous government in 1967.

Since the 1960s the islands have diversified away from plantation agriculture, which is no longer a significant employer. Tourism has grown to become the major source of income, and from the 1980s a financial sector has grown up based on the islands' status as a tax haven with tight commercial confidentiality laws.

Area 151 sq km [58 sq mi]
Population 23,000
Capital Road Town (Tortola)
Government Overseas territory of the UK
Ethnic groups Black 84%
Languages English (official)
Religions
Protestant 86%, Roman Catholic 10%
Currency US dollar = 100 cents
Website www.bvitourism.com

Group of 68 islands in the Lesser Antilles. Chief islands are St Croix and St Thomas. Most are hilly, formed of volcanic rocks, but others including St Croix are flatter coral formations. Soils are poor and rainfall low.

The islands were inhabited by a number of native peoples when discovered by Columbus in 1493. They were settled by Spain in 1553. Other settlers included the French and British, but from the later 17th century the Danish took over or purchased the islands. In 1754 they formally became Danish colonies. Sugar plantations were established using African slave labour, but declined after the abolition of slavery in 1848.

In 1917 the US, fearing that the Virgin Islands might become a base for German submarines to attack shipping passing through the Panama Canal, purchased the islands from the Danes for US$25 million (about $400 million in today's terms). US Virgin Islanders became US citizens in 1927. The Virgin Islands send non-voting delegates to both US Houses. The US has offered the islands the choice of independence or statehood, but each referendum has failed due to low voter turnout.

Tourism is by far the biggest earner. There is also a petrochemicals sector based on refining imported Venezuelan crude for the US market. St Croix has one of the world's largest oil refineries.

Area 347 sq km [134 sq mi]
Population 109,000
Capital Charlotte Amalie (St Thomas)
Government Unincorporated territory of the US
Ethnic groups Black 76%, White 13%
Languages English 75%, Spanish or Spanish Creole 17%, French or French Creole 7%
Religions Baptist 42%, Roman Catholic 34%
Currency US dollar = 100 cents
Website www.usvi.net

CENTRAL AFRICAN REPUBLIC

The red, yellow and green colours on this flag were originally used by Ethiopia, Africa's oldest independent nation. They symbolize African unity. The blue, white and red recall the flag of France, the country's colonial ruler. This flag was adopted in 1958.

The Central African Republic is a remote landlocked country in central Africa. It lies on a plateau, mostly 600–800 m (2,000–2,600 ft) above sea level, forming a watershed between the headwaters of two river systems. In the south, the rivers flow into the navigable River Ubangi (a tributary of the Congo). The Ubangi and the Bomu form much of its southern border. In the north, most rivers are headwaters of the River Chari, which flows north into Lake Chad.

Wooded savanna covers much of the country, with open grasslands in the north and rainforests in the south-west. The country has many forest and savanna animals, such as buffalo, leopards, lions and elephants, as well as many bird species. About 6% of the land is protected in national parks and reserves, but tourism is on a small scale because of the republic's remoteness.

Area 622,984 sq km [240,534 sq mi]
Population 4,303,000
Capital (population) Bangui (553,000)
Government Multiparty republic
Ethnic groups Baya 33%, Banda 27%, Mandjia 13%, Sara 10%, Mboum 7% Mbaka 4%, others
Languages French (official), Sangho
Religions Traditional beliefs 35%, Protestant 25%, Roman Catholic 25%, Islam 15%
Currency CFA franc = 100 centimes
Website www.banguinet.net

reduced by slavery, and the country is still thinly populated. France first occupied the area in 1887, and in 1894 established the colony of Ubangi-Shari at Bangui. In 1906 the colony was united with Chad, and in 1910 was subsumed into French Equatorial Africa (which included Chad, Congo and Gabon). Forced-labour rebellions occurred in

CLIMATE

The climate is warm throughout the year, with an average annual rainfall in Bangui totalling 1,574 mm [62 in]. The north is drier, with an average annual rainfall total of about 800 mm [31 in].

HISTORY

Little is known of the country's early history. Between the 16th and 19th centuries, the population was greatly

UBANGI (OUBANGI)

The River Ubangi is a major tributary of the River Congo in central Africa, beginning at the junction of the Mbomou and Uele rivers. The Ubangi defines the boundary between the Central African Republic and the Democratic Republic of the Congo (DRC), passing through Bangui, after which it forms the boundary between the DRC and the Republic of Congo before emptying into the River Congo. It is an important artery for river boats between Bangui and Brazzaville.

1928, 1935 and 1946. During World War II Ubangi-Shari supported the Free French. Post-1945 the colony received representation in the French parliament. In 1958 the colony voted to become a self-governing republic within the French community, and became the Central African Republic.

POLITICS

In 1960 Central African Republic declared independence. The next six years, under President David Dacko, saw a deterioration in the economy and increasing government corruption and inefficiency. The country became a one-party state in 1962. In 1966 Colonel Jean Bédel Bokassa assumed power in a blood-less coup, abrogated the constitution and dissolved the National Assembly.

In 1976 Bokassa transformed the republic into an empire, and proclaimed himself Emperor Bokassa I. The country was renamed the Central African Empire. His rule became increasingly brutal, and in 1979 he was deposed in a French-backed coup led by Dacko. Dacko, faced with continuing unrest, was replaced by André Kolingba in 1981. The army quickly banned all political parties.

The country adopted a new, multipar-ty constitution in 1991. Elections were held in 1993. An army rebellion in 1996 was finally put down in 1997 with the assistance of French troops. In 2001

President Ange-Félix Patassé, who had served as president since 1993, stopped a coup attempt with Libyan help. A 2003 coup brought General François Bozize to power and Patassé went into exile in Togo. In 2006 the country descended into civil war between Bozize's forces and a guerilla movement associated with the Patassé government. The country has also struggled to cope with refugees from Sudan.

ECONOMY

The World Bank classifies the Central African Republic as a 'low-income' developing country. Approximately 10% of the land is cultivated and over 80% of the workforce are engaged in subsistence agriculture. The main food crops are bananas, maize, manioc, millet and yams. Coffee, cotton, timber and tobacco are the main cash crops.

Diamonds, the only major mineral resource, are the most valuable export. Manufacturing is on a very small scale. Products include beer, cotton fabrics, footwear, leather, soap and sawn timber. The country's development has been greatly impeded by its remote position, poor transport and an untrained work-force. The country is heavily dependent on aid, especially from France.

BANGUI

Capital of the Central African Republic, on the River Ubangi, near the border with the Democratic Republic of Congo. Founded in 1889 by the French, it is the nation's chief port for international trade. Places of interest include the triumphal arch dedicated to Jean-Bédel Bokassa, the Boganda Museum and the central market. Industries include textiles, shoes, food processing, beer and soap.

CHAD

Chad's flag was adopted in 1959 as the country prepared for independence in 1960. The blue represents the sky, the streams in southern Chad and hope. The yellow symbolizes the sun and the Sahara in the north. The red represents national sacrifice.

Chad is Africa's fifth largest country. It is more than twice as big as the former colonial power, France. Southern Chad is crossed by rivers that flow into Lake Chad, on the western border with Nigeria. The capital, Ndjamena, lies on the banks of the River Chari. Beyond a large depression northeast of Lake Chad are the Tibesti Mountains, which rise steeply from the sands of the Sahara Desert. The mountains contain Chad's highest peak, Emi Koussi, at 3,415 m [11,204 ft]. The far south contains forests, while central Chad is a region of savanna, merging into the dry grasslands of the Sahel. Plants are rare in the northern desert. Droughts are common in north central Chad. Long droughts, overgrazing, and felling for firewood have exposed the Sahel's soil and wind erosion is increasing desertification.

Area 1,284,000 sq km [495,752 sq mi]
Population 9,944,000
Capital (population) Ndjamena (530,000)
Government Multiparty republic
Ethnic groups 200 distinct groups: mostly Muslim in the north and centre; mostly Christian or animist in the south
Languages French and Arabic (both official), many others
Religions Islam 51%, Christianity 35%, animist 7%
Currency CFA franc = 100 centimes
Website www.chadembassy.org

CLIMATE

Central Chad has a hot tropical climate. There is a marked dry season from November to April. The south is wetter, with an average annual rainfall of about 1000 mm [39 in]. Conversely, the hot northern desert has an average annual rainfall of less than 130 mm [5 in].

HISTORY

Chad straddles two, often conflicting worlds: the north, populated by nomadic or semi-nomadic Muslim peoples such as Arabs and Tuaregs, and the dominant south where a sedentary population practise Christianity or animist traditional religions. Lake Chad was an important watering point for the trans-Saharan caravans. Around AD 700 North African nomads founded the Kanem Empire. In the 14th century, the kingdom of Bornu expanded to incorporate Kanem. In the late 19th century the region was taken over by a Sudanese kingdom.

The first major European explorations were by the French in 1890. The French

LAKE CHAD (TCHAD)

Lake in north-central Africa, mainly in the Republic of Chad and partly in Nigeria, Cameroon and Niger. The chief tributary is the River Chari. The lake has no outlet. Depending on the season, the area of the surface varies from 10,000 to 26,000 sq km [3,850–10,000 sq mi] with a maximum depth: of 7.6 m (25 ft).

pied northern Chad. In 1982 two leaders of Frolinat, Hissène Habré and Goukouni Oueddi, formed rival regimes. Libya's bombing of Chad in 1983 led to the deployment of 3,000 French troops. The Libyans retreated, retaining only the uranium-rich Aozou Strip. A cease-fire took effect in 1987. In 1990, Habré was removed in a coup led by Idriss Déby. In 1994, the Aozou Strip was returned to Chad. In 1996, a new democratic constitution was adopted and multiparty elections confirmed Déby as president. He was re-elected in 2001. In 2002 a peace treaty, signed by the government and the Movement for Democracy and Justice, ended three years of civil war. From 2004 Chad's forces clashed with pro-Sudanese militia as conflict in Sudan's Darfur province spilled over the border. Clashes worsened in 2006-7.

ECONOMY
Chad is one of the world's poorest countries. Agriculture dominates the economy, more than 80% of the workforce are engaged in farming, mainly at subsistence level. Groundnuts, millet, rice and sorghum are major crops in the wetter south. The most valuable crop is cotton.

defeated the Sudanese in 1900, and in 1908 Chad became the largest province of French Equatorial Africa. In 1920 it became a separate colony.

POLITICS
In 1958 Chad gained autonomous status within the French Community, and in 1960 achieved full independence. Divisions between north and south rapidly surfaced. In 1965, President François Tombalbaye declared a one-party state. The north's Muslims, led by the Chad National Liberation Front (Frolinat), rebelled. By 1973 the government, helped by the French, quashed the revolt. In 1980 Libya occu-

NDJAMENA
Capital of Chad, a port on the River Chari. Founded by the French in 1900, it was known as Fort Lamy until 1973. Ndjamena grew rapidly after independence in 1960. An important market for the surrounding region, which produces livestock, dates, and cereals. The main industry is meat processing.

CHILE

Chile's flag was adopted in 1817. It was designed in that year by an American serving in the Chilean army who was inspired by the US Stars and Stripes. The white represents the snow-capped Andes, the blue the sky, and the red the blood of the nation's patriots.

The Republic of Chile stretches 4,260 km [2,650 mi] from north to south, while the maximum east-west distance is only 430 km [270 mi]. The Andes mountains form Chile's eastern borders with Argentina and Bolivia. Ojos del Salado, at 6,863 m [22,516 f], is the second-highest peak in South America. Easter Island lies 3,500 km [2,200 mi] off Chile's west coast.

Area 756,626 sq km [292,133 sq mi]
Population 16,134,000
Capital (population) Santiago (5,623,000)
Government Multiparty republic
Ethnic groups Mestizo 95%, Amerindian 3%
Languages Spanish (official)
Religions Roman Catholic 89%, Protestant 11%
Currency Chilean peso = 100 centavos
Website www.chileangovernment.cl

Western Chile contains three main land regions. In the north is the sparsely populated Atacama Desert, stretching 1,600 km [1,000 mi] south from the Peruvian border. The Central Valley, which contains the capital, Santiago, Valparaíso and Concepción, is by far the most densely populated region. In the south, the land has been heavily glaciated, the coastal uplands have been worn into islands, while the inland valleys are arms of the sea.

In the far south, the Strait of Magellan separates the Chilean mainland from Tierra del Fuego. Punta Arenas is the world's southernmost city.

CLIMATE

Chile has three principal climate zones. The Atacama Desert in the north is arid, but temperatures are moderated by the cold Peru Current. Central Chile has a Mediterranean climate with hot, dry summers and mild, moist winters. The south has a cool and stormy climate. Chile is one of the countries most affected by the El Niño, which periodically disrupts the Peru Current and causes extreme weather conditions.

HISTORY

Amerindian people reached the southern tip of South America at least 8,000 years ago. In 1520, the Portuguese navigator Ferdinand Magellan became the first European to sight Chile. The country became a Spanish colony in the 1540s. Under Spain the economy in the north was based on mining. Huge ranches, or *haciendas*, were set up in central Chile. Chile became independent in 1818. Valparaiso developed as a port exporting produce from central Chile to California and Australia. During a war with Peru and Bolivia from 1879–83, Chile acquired mineral-rich territories. In the 20th century, revenue from nitrate exports fuelled industrial growth.

POLITICS

After World War II Chile faced economic problems, partly caused by falls in world copper prices. A Christian Democrat was elected president in 1964, but was replaced by Salvador Allende Gossens in 1970. Allende's administration, the

Augusto Pinochet Ugarte took power as a dictator, banning all political activity in a repressive regime.

A new constitution took effect from 1981, allowing for an eventual return to democracy. Patrico Aylwin became president after 1989 elections, but Pinochet secured continued office as commander-in-chief of the armed forces. Chile became a successful democracy, holding regular presidential elections usually won by a broad centre-left coalition. In 1999 General Pinochet, who was visiting Britain for medical treatment, was faced with extradition to Spain to answer charges that he had presided over acts of torture when he was Chile's dictator. In 2000 he was allowed to return to Chile where, in 2001, he was found to be too ill to stand trial. New charges were brought against him in 2004, and he was placed under house arrest. He died in 2006.

ECONOMY

The World Bank classifies Chile as a 'lower-middle-income' developing country. Mining is important, and minerals dominate Chile's exports. The most valuable activity is manufacturing. Products include processed foods, metals, iron and steel, wood products, and textiles.

Agriculture employs 18% of the workforce. The chief crop is wheat. Beans, fruits, maize and livestock products are also important. Chile's fishing industry is one of the world's largest.

SANTIAGO

Capital of Chile, in central Chile on the River Mapocho, 90 km [55 mi] from the Atlantic coast. Founded in 1541, it was destroyed by an earthquake in 1647. Most of Santiago's architecture dates from after 1850. It is the nation's administrative, commercial, and cultural centre, accounting for nearly a third of the population.

world's first democratically elected Marxist government, was overthrown in a CIA-backed coup in 1973. General

CHINA

China's flag was adopted in 1949, when the country became a Communist People's Republic. Red is the traditional colour of both China and Communism. The large star represents the Communist Party programme. The smaller stars symbolize the four main social classes.

The People's Republic of China is the world's third largest country. Most people live on the eastern coastal plains, in the highlands or the fertile valleys of the rivers Huang He and Yangtze. The Yangtze, at 6,380 km [3,960 mi], is Asia's longest river.

Western China includes the bleak Tibetan plateau, bounded by the Himalayas. Everest, the world's highest peak, lies on the border with Nepal. Other ranges include the Tian Shan and Kunlun Shan. China contains part of the Gobi Desert on the Mongolian border.

Large areas in the west are covered by sparse grasses or desert. The most luxuriant forests, including the bamboo forest habitat of the rare giant panda, are in the south-east.

CLIMATE

The capital, Beijing in north-east China, has cold winters and warm summers with moderate rainfall. Shanghai, in the east-central region, has milder winters and more rain. The south-east region has a wet, subtropical climate. In the west, the climate is colder and more severe.

Area 9,596,961 sq km [3,705,387 sq mi]
Population 1,313,974,000
Capital (population) Beijing (7,362,000)
Government Single-party Communist republic
Ethnic groups Han Chinese 92%, many others
Languages Mandarin Chinese (official)
Religions Atheist (official)
Currency Renminbi yuan= 10 jiao = 100 fen
Website www.china.org.cn/english

HISTORY

The first documented dynasty was the Shang (1523–1030 BC), when bronze casting was perfected. The Zhou dynasty (1030–221 BC) was the age of Chinese classical literature, in particular Confucious and Lao Tzu. China was unified by Qin Shihuangdi, whose tomb near Xian contains the famous terracotta army. The Qin dynasty (221–206 BC) also built the majority of the Great Wall. The Han dynasty (202 BC–AD 220) developed the Empire, a bureaucracy based on Confucianism, and also introduced Buddhism. China then split into three kingdoms (Wei, Shu, and Wu) and the influence of Buddhism and Taoism grew. The T'ang dynasty from 618–907 was a golden era of artistic achievement, especially in poetry and fine art. Genghis Khan conquered most of China in the 1210s and established the Mongol empire. Kublai Khan founded the Yüan dynasty

BEIJING (PEKING)

Capital of the People's Republic of China, between the Pei and Hun rivers, north-east China. A settlement since 1000 BC, Beijing served as China's capital from 1421 to 1911. After the establishment of the Chinese Republic (1911–12), Beijing remained the political centre of China. The seat of government was transferred to Nanking in 1928. Beijing ('northern capital') became known as Pei-p'ing ('northern peace'). Occupied by the Japanese in 1937, it was restored to China in 1945 and came under Communist control in 1949. Its name was restored as capital of the People's Republic. The city comprises two walled sections: the Inner (Tatar) City, including the Forbidden City (imperial palace complex), and the Outer (Chinese) city. Beijing is the political, cultural, educational, financial, and transport centre of China. Heavy industry expanded after the end of the Civil War, and products now include textiles, iron and steel.

The Communist Party of China initially allied with the Kuomintang. In 1926, the Kuomintang, led by Chiang Kai-shek, emerged victorious and turned on their Communist allies. In 1930 a rival communist government was established, but was uprooted by Kuomintang troops and began the Long March (1934). Japan took over Manchuria as Manchukuo in 1932 and Chiang was forced to ally with the Communists. Japan launched a full-scale invasion in 1937, and conquered

HONG KONG

(XIANGGANG SPECIAL ADMINISTRATIVE REGION)

Former British Crown Colony off the coast of south-east China; the capital is Victoria on Hong Kong Island. Hong Kong comprises: Hong Kong Island, ceded to Britain by China in 1842; the mainland peninsula of Kowloon, acquired in 1860; the New Territories on the mainland, leased for 99 years in 1898; and some 230 islets in the South China Sea. The climate is subtropical, with hot, dry summers. In 1984, the UK and China signed a Joint Declaration in which it was agreed that China would resume sovereignty over Hong Kong in 1997. It also provided that Hong Kong would become a special administrative region, with its existing social and economic structure unchanged for 50 years. It would remain a free port. The last British governor, Chris Patten (1992–97), introduced a legislative council. The handover to China completed on 1 July 1997, and Chief Executive Tung Chee-hwa was sworn in and a provisional legislative council appointed. Hong Kong is a vital international financial centre with a strong manufacturing base.

(1271–1368), an era of dialogue with Europe. The Ming dynasty (1368–1644) re-established Chinese rule and is famed for its fine porcelain. The Manchu Qing dynasty (1644–1912) began by vastly extending the empire, but the 19th century was marked by foreign interventions, such as the Opium War (1839–42), when Britain occupied Hong Kong. Popular disaffection culminated in the Boxer Rebellion (1900). The last Emperor (Henry Pu Yi) was overthrown in a revolution led by Sun Yat-sen and a republic established (1912).

China rapidly fragmented between a Beijing government supported by warlords, and Sun Yat-sen's nationalist Kuomintang government in Guangzhou.

much of north and east China. From 1941 Chinese forces, with Allied support, began to regain territory. At the end of World War II civil war resumed. The nationalists were supported by the USA, and the Communists by Russia. The Communists, with greater popular support, triumphed and the Kuomintang fled to Taiwan.

POLITICS

Mao Zedong established the People's Republic of China in 1949 and seized Tibet in 1950. Mao began to collectivize agriculture and nationalize industry. In 1958, the Great Leap Forward failed to boost industrial production. The Cultural Revolution (1966–76) promoted indoctrination, purged intellectuals and

Jiang Zemin succeeded Deng as paramount leader and in 2002 was succeeded by Hu Jintao. The government remains authoritarian, exercising repression and heavy censorship.

ECONOMY

China's economy has grown extraordinarily rapidly in recent years, over 10% a year, and has become one of the world's largest. The rise of private enterprise has led to massive investments in manufacturing, making China a major exporter of every class of goods. Economic inequality is increasing, and a middle class has arisen and is growing rapidly. The countryside has seen few of the economic benefits and remains very poor, leading to mass migration to cities and attendant social problems. Industrial growth has also led to severe environmental damage.

MACAU (MACAO)

Former Portuguese overseas province in south-east China, 64 km [40 mi] west of Hong Kong, on the River Pearl estuary; it consists of the 6 sq km [2 sq mi] Macau Peninsula and the islands of Taipa and Colôane. Santa Nome de Deus de Macao connects via a narrow isthmus to the Chinese province of Guangzhou. Vasco da Gama discovered Macau in 1497, and the Portuguese colonized the island in 1557. In 1849, Portugal declared it a free port. In 1887, the Chinese government recognized Portugal's right of 'perpetual occupation'. Competition from Hong Kong and the silting of Macau's harbour led to the port's decline at the end of the 19th century. In 1974, Macau became a Chinese province under Portuguese administration. It returned to China in 1999. Gambling and tourism are dominant in the economy.

destroyed cultural heritage. By 1971 China had nuclear weapons and a seat on the UN security council. Following Mao's death in 1976, a power struggle developed. Deng Xiaoping took power and began a process of modernization, forging closer links with the West. In 1989 a pro-democracy demonstration was crushed in Tiananmen Square. In 1997

COLOMBIA

The yellow on Colombia's flag depicts the land, which is separated from the tyranny of Spain by the blue, symbolizing the Atlantic Ocean. The red symbolizes the blood of the people who fought to make the country independent. The flag has been used since 1806.

Area 1,138,914 sq km [439,735 sq mi]
Population 43,593,000
Capital (population) Bogotá (7,594,000)
Government Multiparty republic
Ethnic groups Mestizo 58%, White 20%, Mulatto 14%, Black 4%
Languages Spanish (official)
Religions Roman Catholic 90%
Currency Colombian peso = 100 centavos
Website www.gobiernoenlinea.gov.co/ingles

Colombia is the only South American country to have coastlines on both the Pacific Ocean and the Caribbean Sea. Cartagena is the main Caribbean port. Colombia is dominated by three ranges of the Andean Mountains. On the edge of the western Cordillera lies the city of Cali. The Central Cordillera is a chain of volcanoes that divide the valleys of the rivers Magdalena and Cauca. It includes the city of Medellín. The eastern Cordillera contains the capital, Bogotá, at 2,800 m [9,200 ft]. East of the Andes lie plains drained by headwaters of the Amazon and Orinoco rivers.

Vegetation varies from dense rainforest in the south east to tundra in the snow-capped Andes. Coffee plantations line the western slopes of the eastern Cordillera. The ancient forests of the Caribbean lowlands have mostly been cleared. Savanna (*llanos*) covers the north eastern plains.

CLIMATE

Altitude greatly affects the climate. The Pacific lowlands have a tropical, rainy climate, but Bogotá has mild annual temperatures. The lowlands of the Caribbean and the Magdalena valley both have dry seasons.

HISTORY

Before the arrival of the Spanish, the eastern cordillera was inhabited by the Chibcha culture. In 1525 the Spanish established the first European settlement at Santa Marta. By 1538 conquistador Gonzalo Jiménez de Quesada conquered the Chibcha and established the city of Bogotá. Colombia became part of the New Kingdom of Granada, whose territory also included Ecuador, Panama, and Venezuela.

In 1819 Simón Bolívar defeated the Spanish at Boyacá and established Greater Colombia. Bolívar became president. In 1830 Ecuador and Venezuela

---

MEDELLÍN

City in north-west central Colombia; capital of Antioquia department and the second-largest city in Colombia. Founded in the early 17th century by Spanish refugees, it became the centre of Colombia's illegal cocaine trade. The surrounding region has gold and silver mines. Industries include food processing, coffee, chemicals, steel. It has a population of over 2,000,000.

tive Party (PSC) leader Andrés Pastrana Arango won the 1998 presidential elections and, in an effort to end the 30-year guerrilla war, negotiated with the Revolutionary Armed Forces of Colombia (FARC) and the National Liberation Army (ELN). Pastrana granted FARC a safe haven in southeast Colombia.

In 1999, the worst earthquake in Colombia's history killed more than 1,000 people and left thousands homeless. In 2002 Pastrana declared war on FARC, sending the army into FARC's 'safe haven'. Alvaro Uribe defeated Pastrana in 2002 presidential elections. Uribe promised even tougher action against terrorism.

ECONOMY
Colombia is a lower-middle income developing country. It is the world's second-largest coffee producer. Other crops include bananas, cocoa and maize. Colombia also exports coal, oil, emeralds, and gold. In 1997 a collapse in the world coffee and banana markets led to a budget deficit. In 1998 Colombia devalued the peso. This triggered a 20-day general strike, the longest in Colombia's history.

gained independence. In 1885, the Republic of Colombia was formed. Differences between republican and federalist factions led to civil war from 1899–1902, killing nearly 100,000 people. In 1903 Panama gained independence with US help. A second civil war, in 1949–57, was even more bloody and is known as La Violencia.

POLITICS
In 1957 Liberal and Conservative parties formed a National Front Coalition, which held power until 1974. In the 1970s the illegal trade in cocaine grew steadily, creating wealthy drug barons. In the 1980s, armed cartels destabilized Colombia with frequent assassinations of political and media figures.

A new constitution in 1991 aimed to protect human rights. Social Conserva-

BOGOTÁ
Capital of Colombia, in the centre of the country on a fertile plateau. Bogotá was founded in 1538 by the Spanish on the site of a Chibcha Indian settlement. In 1819 it became the capital of Greater Colombia, part of which later formed Colombia. Today, it is a centre for culture, education and finance. Industries include tobacco, sugar, flour, textiles, engineering, chemicals.

CONGO

Congo's red flag, with the national emblem of a crossed hoe and mattock (a kind of pick-axe), was dropped in 1990, when the country officially abandoned the Communist policies it had followed since 1970. This new flag was adopted in its place.

The Republic of Congo lies on the River Congo in west central Africa. The Equator runs through the centre of the country. Congo has a narrow coastal plain on which stands its main port, Pointe Noire, which itself lies on the Gulf of Guinea. Behind the plain are forested highlands through which the River Niari has carved a fertile valley. To the east lies Malebo Pool, formerly Stanley Pool, a large lake where the River Congo widens.

Central Congo consists of luxuriant savanna. Tree species include the valuable okoumé and mahogany. The north contains large swamps in the tributary valleys of the Congo and Oubangi rivers.

Area 342,000 sq km [132,046 sq mi]
Population 3,702,000
Capital (population) Brazzaville (1,153,000)
Government Military regime
Ethnic groups Kongo 48%, Sangha 20%, Teke 17%, M'bochi 12%
Languages French (official), many others
Religions
Christianity 50%, animist 48%, Islam 2%
Currency CFA franc = 100 centimes
Website www.congo-site.com

CLIMATE

Most of the country has a humid, equatorial climate, with rain throughout the year. Brazzaville has a dry season between June and September. The narrow treeless coastal plain is drier and cooler than the rest of the country because the cold Benguela current flows northwards along the coast.

HISTORY

The Loango and Bakongo kingdoms dominated the Congo when the first Europeans arrived in 1482. Between the 15th and 18th centuries, part of Congo belonged to the huge Kongo kingdom, whose centre lay to the south. Portuguese explorers reached the coast of Congo in the 15th century and the area soon became a trading region, the main commodities being slaves and ivory. The slave trade continued until the 19th century.

European exploration of the interior did not occur until the late 19th century. In 1880 Pierre Savorgnan de Brazza

---

RIVER CONGO

The River Congo (formerly the River Zaïre) in central and west Africa; the second-longest in the continent. It rises in southern Democratic Republic of Congo and flows in a massive curve to the Atlantic Ocean for 4,670 km [2,900 mi]. Its rate of flow and size of drainage basin make it Africa's largest untapped source of hydroelectric power. The chief ocean port is Matadi, and the major river ports are Kinshasa and Kisangani. The main headstream is the Lualaba, and the Kasai and Oubangi are among its many large tributaries.

1997 Sassou-Nguesso, assisted by his personal militia and by troops from Angola, launched an uprising which overthrew the government. Lissouba fled the country, taking refuge in Burkina Faso, but forces loyal to him fought back and started a civil war. Cease-fires were agreed in 1999. Sassou-Nguesso took the presidency after rigged elections in 2002. A peace accord was signed in 2003, but militia remnants have yet to fully disarm.

ECONOMY

The World Bank classifies Congo as a 'lower-middle-income' developing country. Agriculture is the most important activity, employing about 60% of the workforce, but many only farm at a subsistence level. Chief food crops include cassava, maize, plantains, rice and yams, while cash crops include cocoa, coffee and sugar.

Congo is one of Africa's major producers of oil, and oil remains the major export, but production is declining. Timber is also exported. Manufacturing is relatively unimportant, hampered by poor transport links. Inland, rivers form the main lines of communication, and Brazzaville is linked to the port of Pointe-Noire by the Congo-Ocean Railway.

explored the area and it became a French protectorate. It became known as Middle Congo, a country within French Equatorial Africa, which also included Chad, Gabon, and Ubangi-Shari (now the Central African Republic). In 1910 Brazzaville became the capital of French Equatorial Africa. In 1960 the Republic of Congo gained independence.

POLITICS

In 1964 Congo adopted Marxism-Leninism as the state ideology. The military, led by Marien Ngouabi, seized power in 1968. Ngouabi created the Congolese Workers Party (PCT) and was assassinated in 1977. The PCT retained power under Colonel Denis Sassou-Nguesso. In 1990 it renounced Marxism and Sassou-Nguesso was deposed. The Pan-African Union for Social Democracy (UPADS), led by Pascal Lissouba, won multiparty elections in 1992. In

BRAZZAVILLE

Capital and largest city of the Congo, West Africa, on the River Congo, below Stanley Pool. Founded in 1880, it was capital of French Equatorial Africa (1910–58) and a base for Free French forces in World War II. It has a university (1972) and a cathedral. It is a major port, connected by rail to the main Atlantic seaport of Pointe-Noire.

CONGO, DEMOCRATIC REPUBLIC OF

The Democratic Republic of the Congo adopted a new flag in 1997 after Laurent Kabila rose to power. The blue represents the UN's role in securing independence for the country, and the six small stars represent the original provinces of the independent state.

Democratic Republic of Congo is Africa's third-largest country. It is dominated by the River Congo. North-central Congo consists of a high plateau. In the east, the plateau rises to 5,109 m [16,762 ft] in the Ruwenzori mountains. Lakes Albert and Edward form much of Congo's border with Uganda. Lake Kivu lies along its border with Rwanda. Lake Tanganyika forms the border with Tanzania. All the lakes lie in an arm of the Great Rift Valley. Dense equatorial rainforests grow in the north, with savanna and swamps in the south.

Area 2,344,858 sq km [905,350 sq mi]
Population 62,661,000
Capital (population) Kinshasa (5,717,000)
Government Single-party republic
Ethnic groups Over 200; the largest are Mongo, Luba, Kongo, Mangbetu-Azande
Languages French (official), tribal languages
Religions Roman Catholic 50%, Protestant 20%, Islam 10%, others
Currency Congolese franc = 100 centimes
Website www.monuc.org

CLIMATE

Much of Congo has an equatorial climate with high temperatures and heavy rainfall throughout the year. The south has a more subtropical climate.

HISTORY

From the 14th century, large Bantu kingdoms emerged. In 1482, a Portuguese navigator became the first European to reach the mouth of the River Congo. In the 19th century, ivory and slave traders formed powerful states. Henry Morton Stanley's explorations from 1874–77 established the route of the Congo. In 1878, King Leopold II of Belgium employed Stanley to found colonies along the Congo.

In 1885 Leopold established the Congo Free State under his personal rule. Lucrative rubber plantations were established, and even by colonial standards the exploitation and repression of the African population was exceptional. In 1908, after international criticism, the Belgian government took control from the King as the colony of Belgian Congo.

POLITICS

In 1960, the Republic of the Congo gained independence and Patrice Lumumba became prime minister. Joseph Mobutu, commander of the Congolese National Army, seized power later that year. Lumumba was later murdered. In 1964 the country plunged into civil war and Belgian troops intervened. In 1965 Mobutu proclaimed himself president and began a campaign of 'Africanization'. The country and river became Zaïre in 1971 and Mobutu adopted the name Mobutu Sese Seko. Zaïre became a one-party state. Mobutu finally accepted opposition parties in 1990, though elections were repeatedly deferred. In 1995, millions of Hutus fled from Rwanda into east Zaïre to escape Tutsi reprisals. In 1996 rebels led by Laurent Kabila overthrew Mobuto. Zaïre became the Democratic Republic of Congo. In 1998 Congo descended into civil war between government forces and the Tutsi-dominated Congolese Rally for Democracy (RCD). The Lusaka agreement (1999) brought a cease-fire and 5,500 UN peace-keeping troops, but fighting continued. By 2001 the civil war had claimed more than 2.5 million lives. In 2001, Kabila was assassinated. Under a 2003 peace agreement his son Joseph Kabila was installed as interim president of a transitional government, but fighting continued. In 2006 Joseph Kabila won DRC's first contested elections in 40 years. In 2007 fighting worsened between the army and militia loyal to opposition leader Jean-Pierre Bemba, who was driven into exile.

ECONOMY

Congo is a low-income developing country. It is the world's leading producer of cobalt and the second-largest producer of diamonds. Agriculture employs 71% of the workforce, mainly at subsistence level. Palm oil is the most vital cash crop.

KINSHASA

Capital of Democratic Republic of Congo, a port on the River Congo. Founded in 1881, it replaced Boma as the capital of the Belgian Congo in 1923. An important music centre.

COSTA RICA

Costa Rica's flag is based on the blue-white-blue pattern used by the Central American Federation (1823–39). This Federation consisted of Costa Rica, El Salvador, Guatemala, Honduras and Nicaragua. The red stripe, which was adopted in 1848, reflects the colours of France.

The Republic of Costa Rica in Central America is bordered by Nicaragua to the north and Panama to the south. It has coastlines on both the Pacific Ocean and on the Caribbean Sea. Central Costa Rica consists of mountain ranges and plateaux with many volcanoes. The Meseta Central, where the capital San José is situated, and the Valle del General in the south-east have rich, volcanic soils and are the most thickly populated parts of Costa Rica.

The highlands descend to the Caribbean lowlands and the Pacific Coast region, with its low mountain ranges. San José stands at about 1,170 m [3,840 ft] above sea level.

Evergreen forests cover around 50% of Costa Rica. Oaks grow in the highlands, palm trees along the Caribbean coast and mangrove swamps are common on the Pacific coast.

Area 51,100 sq km [19,730 sq mi]
Population 4,075,000
Capital (population) San José (1,145,000)
Government Multiparty republic
Ethnic groups White (including Mestizo) 94%, Black 3%, Amerindian 1%, Chinese 1%, others
Languages Spanish (official), English
Religions Roman Catholic 76%, Evangelical 14%
Currency Costa Rican colón = 100 céntimos
Website www.visitcostarica.com

HISTORY

Christopher Columbus reached the Caribbean coast in 1502 and named the land Costa Rica, Spanish for 'rich coast'. Rumours of treasure attracted many Spaniards to settle in the country from 1561. Spain ruled the country until 1821, when Spain's Central American colonies broke away to join the Mexican empire in 1822.

In 1823, the Central American states broke with Mexico and set up the Central American Federation, the members being Costa Rica, Guatemala, Honduras, Nicaragua and El Salvador. Later, this large union broke up and Costa Rica

CLIMATE

The Meseta Central benefits from a pleasant climate and an average annual temperature of 20°C [68°F], compared with more than 27°C [81°F] on the coast. The coolest months are December and January. The north-east trade winds bring heavy rain to the Caribbean coast. There is only half as much rainfall in the the highlands and on the Pacific coastlands as occurs on the Caribbean coast.

SAN JOSÉ

Capital and largest city of Costa Rica, in central Costa Rica, capital of San José province. Founded around 1736, it succeeded Cartago as capital in 1823, and soon became the centre of a prosperous coffee trade. Products include coffee, sugar cane, cacao, vegetables, fruit, tobacco.

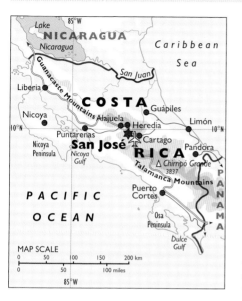

oping country. It is one of the most prosperous countries in Central America. There are high educational standards, and a high average life expectancy of 78 years.

Agriculture employs 24% of the workforce. Major crops include coffee, pineapples, bananas and sugar. Other crops include beans, citrus fruits, cocoa, potatoes, rice and maize. Cattle ranching is important.

The country's resources include its forests, but it lacks minerals apart from some bauxite and manganese. Manufacturing is increasing with electronics to the fore. It also has hydroelectric power.

Tourism is a fast-growing industry with eco-tourism gaining in importance. The United States is Costa Rica's chief trading partner.

became fully independent in 1838. From the late 19th century, Costa Rica experienced a number of revolutions, with both periods of dictatorship and democracy. In 1917–19 General Tinoco formed a dictatorship. In 1948, following a revolt, the armed forces were abolished.

POLITICS

Jose Figueres Ferrer served as president from 1953 to 1958 and again from 1970 to 1974. In 1987 President Oscar Arias Sanchez was awarded the Nobel Peace Prize for his efforts to end the civil wars in Central America.

In 2002 Abel Pancho won the presidential elections. Costa Rica's image was tarnished in 2004 when two former presidents were imprisoned on charges of corruption, but the country remains an example of political stability in the region and continues to maintain this without having to resort to armed forces. In 2006 Oscar Arias was re-elected president.

ECONOMY

Costa Rica is classified by the World Bank as a 'lower-middle-income' devel-

COSTA RICAN BUTTERFLIES

In Costa Rica the butterfly is omnipresent, whether on the plains or at a volcanic summit. Of the 20,000 butterfly species that exist worldwide about 1,000 or 5% can be found in Costa Rica. The butterfly is a day-flying insect of the order Lepidoptera. The adult has two pairs of scale-covered wings that are often brightly coloured. The female lays eggs on a selected food source and the caterpillar larvae emerge within days or hours. The larvae have chewing mouthparts and often do great damage to crops until they reach the 'resting phase' of the life cycle, the pupa (chrysalis). Within the pupa, the adult (imago) is formed with wings, wing muscles, antennae, a slender body and sucking mouth parts. The adults mate soon after emerging from the chrysalis, and the four-stage life cycle begins again.

CROATIA

Croatia adopted a red, white and blue flag in 1848. Under Communist rule, a red star appeared at the centre. In 1990, the red star was replaced by the present coat of arms, which symbolizes the various parts of the country.

The Republic of Croatia was part of Yugoslavia until becoming independent in 1991. The region bordering the Adriatic Sea is called Dalmatia. It includes the coastal ranges, which contain large areas of bare limestone, reaching 1,913 m [6,276 ft] at Mount Troglav. Other highlands lie in the north-east. Most of the rest of the country consists of the fertile Pannonian Plains, which are drained by Croatia's two main rivers, the Drava and the Sava.

Area 56,538 sq km [21,829 sq mi]
Population 4,495,000
Capital (population) Zagreb (1,067,000)
Government Multiparty republic
Ethnic groups Croat 90%, Serb 5%, others
Languages Croatian 96%
Religions Roman Catholic 88%, Orthodox 4%, Islam 1%, others
Currency Kuna = 100 lipas
Website www.vlada.hr/default.asp?ru=2

CLIMATE

The coastal area has a climate akin to the Mediterranean Sea's, with hot, dry summers and mild, moist winters. Inland, the climate does become more continental . The winters are cold, while temperatures often soar to 38°C [100°F] in the summer months.

HISTORY

Slav peoples settled in the area around 1,400 years ago. In 803, Croatia became part of the Holy Roman Empire. In 1102, the king of Hungary also became king of Croatia, creating a union that lasted 800 years. In 1526, much of Croatia and Hungary came under the Ottoman Turks. At about the same time, the Austrian Habsburgs gained control of the rest of Croatia. In 1699 the Habsburgs drove out the Turks and Croatia again came under Hungarian rule. In 1809

Croatia became part of the Illyrian provinces of Napoleon I of France, but the Habsburgs took over in 1815.

In 1867 Croatia became part of the dual monarchy of Austria-Hungary, and in 1868 Croatia signed an agreement with Hungary guaranteeing Croatia some of its historic rights. During World War I, Austria-Hungary fought on the side of the defeated Axis powers, and in 1918 the empire was broken up. Croatia declared its independence and joined with neighbouring states to form the Kingdom of the Serbs, Croats and Slovenes. Serbian domination provoked Croatian opposition. In 1929 the king changed the country's name to Yugoslavia and began to rule as a dictator. He was assassinated in 1934 by a Bulgarian employed by a Croatian terrorist group, provoking more hostility between Croats and Serbs.

Germany occupied Croatia in World War II. After the war, Communists took power in Yugoslavia, with Josip Broz Tito as its leader. After Tito's death in 1980, economic and ethnic rivalries threatened stability. In the early 1990s, Yugoslavia split into five nations. Croatia declared itself independent in 1991.

nals and co-operate with the war crimes tribunal in The Hague. In 2005 Croatia began negotiations to join the EU in 2010.

ECONOMY

The wars of the early 1990s disrupted Croatia's economy. Tourism on the Dalmatian coast had formerly been a major industry, has gradually recovered, and is once again thriving. The manufacturing industries are the chief exports. Manufactures include cement, chemicals, refined oil and oil products, ships, steel and wood products. Agriculture is important, and major farm products include fruits, livestock, maize, soya beans, sugar beet and wheat.

POLITICS

After Serbia supplied arms to Serbs living in Croatia, war broke out between the two republics causing great damage, large-scale movements of refugees and disruption of the economy.

In 1992 the United Nations sent a peace-keeping force to Croatia, effectively ending the war with Serbia. However, in 1992, war broke out in Bosnia-Herzegovina and Bosnian Croats occupied parts of the country. In 1994 Croatia helped to end the Croat-Muslim conflict in Bosnia-Herzegovina, and in 1995, after retaking some areas occupied by Serbs, it contributed to the drawing up of the Dayton Peace Accord which ended the civil war.

Croatia's arch-nationalist president, Franco Tudjman, died in December 1999. In January 2000, Tudjman's Croatian Democratic Union was defeated in a general election by a westward-leaning alliance of Social Democrats and Social Liberals. Stipe Mesic, the last head of state of the former Yugoslavia before it disintegrated in 1991, became president. In 2000 the government announced that it would prosecute suspected war crimi-

ZAGREB

Capital of Croatia, on the River Sava. Founded in the 11th century, it became capital of the Hungarian province of Croatia and Slavonia during the 14th century. The city was an important centre of the 19th-century Croatian nationalist movement. In 1918 it was the meeting place of the Croatian Diet (parliament), which severed all ties with Austria-Hungary. In World War II, Zagreb was the capital of the Axis-controlled, puppet Croatian state. It was wrested from Axis control in 1945, and became capital of the Croatian Republic of Yugoslavia. Following the break-up of Yugoslavia in 1992, Zagreb remained capital of the newly independent state of Croatia. The city has many places of historical interest, including a Gothic cathedral and a Baroque archiepiscopal palace. Zagreb has a university (founded 1669) and an Academy of Arts and Sciences (1861).

CUBA

Cuba's flag, the 'Lone Star' banner, was designed in 1849. It was not adopted as the national flag until 1901, after Spain had withdrawn from the country. The red triangle represents the Cuban people's bloody struggle for independence.

The Republic of Cuba is the largest island country in the Caribbean Sea. It consists of one large island, Cuba, the Isle of Youth (Isla de la Juventud) and about 1,600 small islets.

Mountains and hills cover about a quarter of Cuba. The highest mountain range, the Sierra Maestra in the southeast, reaches 1,972 m [6,470 ft] above sea level at the Pico Real del Turquino. The rest of the land consists of gently rolling country or coastal plains, crossed by fertile valleys that have been carved by several short, mostly shallow and narrow rivers.

Farmland covers about half of Cuba and 66% of this is given over to sugar cane. Pine forests still grow, especially in the south east. Mangrove swamps line some coastal areas.

Area 110,861 sq km [42,803 sq mi]
Population 11,383,000
Capital (population) Havana (2,192,000)
Government Socialist republic
Ethnic groups
Mulatto 51%, White 37%, Black 11%
Languages Spanish (official)
Religions Christianity
Currency Cuban peso = 100 centavos
Website www.cubagob.gov.cu/ingles/

CLIMATE
Cuba lies in the tropics, but sea breezes moderate the temperature, warming the land in winter and cooling it in summer.

HISTORY
In 1492 Christopher Columbus discovered the island. Spaniards began to settle there from 1511. Spanish rule ended in 1898, when the United States defeated Spain in the Spanish-American War. The United States ruled Cuba from 1898 until 1902, when the people elected Tomás Estrada Palma as president of the independent Republic of

Cuba, though American influence remained strong. In 1933, an army sergeant named Fulgencio Batista seized power and ruled as dictator. Under a new constitution, he was elected president in 1940, serving until 1944. He again seized power in 1952 but, on 1 January 1959, he fled Cuba following the overthrow of his US-backed regime by revolutionaries. Their leader Fidel Castro, a young lawyer, became president.

POLITICS
Castro nationalized many US-owned industries, and many Cubans who were opposed to Castro fled to the US. In 1961 the US broke off diplomatic ties, imposed a trade embargo and backed Cuban exiles in an invasion attempt at the Bay of Pigs which failed disastrously. Castro turned to the Soviet Union for assistance. In 1962 the US learned that the Soviet Union had established nuclear missile bases in Cuba, and ordered their removal. Many feared that a world war might break out, but eventually the Soviets backed down and withdrew.

Cuba's relations with the Soviet Union remained strong until 1991, when the Soviet Union was broken up. The loss of Soviet aid greatly damaged Cuba's economy and the new situation undermined Castro's considerable social achievements, though the government remained popular. In 1998, hopes of a thaw in relations with the United States were raised when the US government announced that it was lifting the ban on flights to Cuba. The Pope, making his first visit to Cuba, criticized the 'unjust and ethically unacceptable' US blockade. In 2000, the United States lifted its food embargo on Cuba. The last Russian base in Cuba closed in 2002. In 2004, following a United States crackdown on currency and travel, Cuba declared that US dollars would no longer be accepted on the island. In 2006, after a serious health crisis, Fidel Castro transferred power to his brother Raul.

ECONOMY
The World Bank classifies Cuba as a 'lower-middle-income' country. Sugar cane remains Cuba's outstandingly important cash crop, accounting for more than 60% of the country's exports. It is grown on more than half of the island's cultivated land and Cuba is one of the world's top ten producers of the product. Before 1959, the sugar cane was grown on large estates, many of them owned by US companies. Following the Revolution, they were nationalized and the Soviet Union and Eastern European countries replaced the United States as the main market. The other main crop is tobacco, which is grown in the north-west. Cattle raising, milk production and rice cultivation have also been encouraged to help diversify the economy, and the Castro regime has devoted considerable efforts to improving the quality of rural life, making standards of living more homogeneous throughout the island.

Minerals and concentrates rank second to sugar among Cuba's exports, followed by fish products, tobacco and tobacco products, including the famous cigars, and citrus fruits. In the 1990s, Cuba sought to increase its trade with Latin America and China. Tourism is a major source of income, but the industry was badly hit following the terrorist attacks on the United States in 2001.

HAVANA (LA HABANA)
Capital of Cuba, on the north west coast. It is the largest city and port in the West Indies. Havana was founded by the Spanish explorer Diego Velázquez in 1515, and moved to its present site in 1519. It became Cuba's capital at the end of the 16th century. Industries include oil refining, textiles, sugar and cigars.

CYPRUS

This flag became the official flag when the country became independent from Britain in 1960. It shows an outline map of the island, with two olive branches. Since Cyprus was divided, the separate communities have flown the Greek and Turkish flags.

The Republic of Cyprus is an island nation which lies in the north-eastern Mediterranean Sea. Geographers regard it as part of Asia, but it resembles southern Europe in many ways. Cyprus has scenic mountain ranges, including the Kyrenia Range in the north and the Troodos Mountains in the south, which rise to 1,951 m [6,401 ft] at Mount Olympus.

The island also contains fertile lowlands used extensively for agriculture, including the broad Mesaoria Plain. Pine forests grow on the mountain slopes.

Area 9,251 sq km [3,572 sq mi]
Population 784,000
Capital (population) Nicosia (200,000)
Government Multiparty republic
Ethnic groups Greek Cypriot 77%, Turkish Cypriot 18%, others
Languages
Greek and Turkish (both official), English
Religions Greek Orthodox 78%, Islam 8%
Currency Cypriot pound = 100 cents
Website www.cyprus.gov.cy

CLIMATE

Cyprus experiences hot, dry summers and mild, wet winters. Summers are hotter than those further west in the Mediterranean as Cyprus lies close to the hot mainland of southwestern Asia.

HISTORY

The history of Cyprus dates back to 7000 BC. Greeks settled on Cyprus around 3,200 years ago. By 1050 BC Cyprus was fully established as a Greek island, having embraced the language and culture of Greece. In 333 BC it became part of the empire of Alexander the Great and in 58 BC part of the Roman Empire. From AD 330, the island was under the Byzantine empire.

Cyprus was conquered in 1191 by Richard the Lionheart and the island was sold to the Knights Templar. Catholicism became the official religion. The island was under Venetian control from 1489 and fortifications were added to the towns of Nicosia and Famagusta. In the 1570s it was captured by the Turks, who made the island part of the Ottoman Empire and introduced Islam.

FAMAGUSTA

A fortified port on the east coast of Northern Cyprus. Famagusta was founded by the King Ptolemy II in the 3rd century BC. Christian refugees fleeing the Holy Lands in 1291 transformed it into a rich city . In 1571 it fell to the Ottoman Empire. The old walled town is now only partially inhabited. Under the British from 1878-1960 it developed as a tourist resort. In 1974 it came under siege by Greek Cypriots. 11,000 Turkish Cypriots defended the city until the arrival of Turkish troops. Nearby, stands the ancient city of Salamis, a spectacular archaeological site.

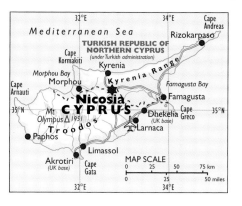

Turkish rule continued until 1878 when Cyprus, although still part of the Ottoman Empire, was leased to Britain. When the Ottomans entered World War I in 1914 on the side of Germany, the island was annexed by Britain. It was proclaimed a Crown Colony in 1925.

In the 1950s, Greek Cypriots, who made up four-fifths of the population, led by Greek Orthodox Archbishop Makarios, began a campaign for enosis (union) with Greece. A guerrilla force called EOKA attacked the British, who exiled Makarios but eventually were forced to negotiate the island's independence.

POLITICS

Cyprus became an independent country in 1960, with Makarios as president. Britain retained two military bases. The constitution of Cyprus provided for power-sharing between the Greek and Turkish Cypriots. But this arrangement proved unworkable and fighting broke out. In 1964 the UN sent in a peace-keeping force.

In 1974, Cypriot forces led by Greek officers overthrew Makarios. This led Turkey to invade northern Cyprus, a territory occupying about 40% of the island. Many Greek Cypriots fled from the north, which, in 1983, was proclaimed an independent state called the Turkish Republic of Northern Cyprus. However, the only country to recognize

its status was Turkey. The UN regards Cyprus as a single nation under the Greek-Cypriot government in the south. It is estimated that more than 30,000 Turkish troops are deployed in northern Cyprus. Despite UN-brokered peace negotiations, there are still frequent border clashes.

In 2002, the European Union invited Cyprus to become a member. In April 2004, the people voted on a UN plan to reunify the island. Turkish Cypriots voted in favour of the plan, but Greek Cypriots voted against. As a result, only the south was admitted to membership of the EU on 1 May 2004. The dispute over Cyprus threatens Turkey's application for EU membership.

ECONOMY

Cyprus got its name from the Greek word *kypros*, meaning copper, but little copper remains. The chief minerals are asbestos and chromium. The most valuable activity in Cyprus is tourism.

Industry employs 37% of the workforce and manufactures include cement, clothes, footwear, tiles and wine. In the early 1990s, the United Nations reclassified Cyprus as a developed rather than developing country, though the economy of the Turkish-Cypriot north lags behind that of the more prosperous Greek-Cypriot south.

NICOSIA (LEVKOSÍA)

Capital of Cyprus, in the centre of the island. Known to the ancients as Ledra, the city was later held by Byzantines, French crusaders and Venetians. The Ottoman Turks occupied the city from 1571 to 1878, when it passed to Britain. It is now divided into Greek and Turkish sectors. Industries: cigarettes, textiles, footwear.

CZECH REPUBLIC

After independence, on 1 January 1993, the Czech Republic adopted the former flag of Czechoslovakia. It features the red and white of Bohemia in the west, together with the blue of Moravia and Slovakia. Red, white and blue are the colours of Pan-Slavic liberation.

The Czech Republic is the western three-fifths of the former country of Czechoslovakia. It contains two regions: Bohemia in the west and Moravia in the east. Mountains border much of the country in the west. The Bohemian basin in the north-centre is a fertile lowland region, with Prague, the capital city, as its main centre. Highlands cover much of the centre of the country, with lowlands in the south-east. Some rivers, such as the Elbe (Labe) and Oder (Odra) flow north into Germany and Poland. In the south, rivers flow into the Danube Basin.

Area 78,866 sq km [30,450 sq mi]
Population 10,235,000
Capital (population) Prague (1,164,000)
Government Multiparty republic
Ethnic groups Czech 81%, Moravian 13%, Slovak 3%, Polish, German, Silesian, Gypsy, Hungarian, Ukrainian
Languages Czech (official)
Religions Atheist 40%, Roman Catholic 39%, Protestant 4%, Orthodox 3%, others
Currency Czech koruna = 100 haler
Website www.czech.cz

CLIMATE

The climate of the Czech Republic is influenced by its landlocked position in east-central Europe. The country experiences a humid continental climate, with warm summers and cold winters. The average rainfall is moderate, with 500 mm to 750 mm [20 in to 30 in] annually in lowland areas.

HISTORY

The ancestors of the Czech people began to settle in what is now the Czech Republic around 1,500 years ago. Bohemia, in the west, became important in the 10th century as a kingdom within the Holy Roman Empire. By the 14th century, Prague was one of Europe's major cultural cities. Religious wars in the first half of the 15th century led many Czech people to become Protestants. From 1526, the Roman Catholic Habsburgs from Austria began to rule the area, but, in 1618, a Czech Protestant rebellion started the Thirty Years' War. From 1620, most Czechs were made to convert to Catholicism and adopt German as their language.

Czech nationalism grew throughout the 19th century. During World War I, Czech nationalists advocated the creation of an independent nation. At the end of the war, when Austria-Hungary collapsed, the new republic of Czechoslovakia was founded. The 1920s and 1930s were generally a period of stability and economic progress, but problems arose concerning the country's minority groups. Many Slovaks wanted a greater degree of self-government, while Germans living in Sudetenland, in western Czechoslovakia, were unhappy under Czech rule.

In 1938 Sudetenland was turned over to Germany, and in March 1939 Germany occupied the rest of the country. In 1945, following the Nazi defeat, a coalition government including Czech Communists was formed to rule the country. In 1948 Communist leaders seized control and made the country an ally of the Soviet Union in the Cold War. In 1968 the Communist government introduced reforms, which were known as the 'Prague Spring'. However, Russian and other East European troops invaded and suppressed the reform group.

POLITICS

When democratic reforms were introduced in the Soviet Union in the 1980s, the Czechs also demanded change. In 1989 the Federal Assembly elected Václav Havel, a noted playwright and dissident, as the country's president. Free elections were held in 1990 and the smooth transition from Communism to democracy became known as the 'Velvet Revolution'. The road to a free-market economy was not easy, with resulting inflation, falling production, strikes and unemployment, though tourism has partly made up for some of the economic decline. Political problems also arose when Slovaks began to demand independence. Finally, on 1 January 1993, the more statist Slovakia broke away from the free-market Czech Republic. However, the split was generally amicable and border adjustments were negligible. The Czechs and Slovaks maintained a customs union and other economic ties. Meanwhile the Czech government continued to develop links with Western Europe when it became a member of NATO in 1992. On 1 May 2004 the Czech Republic became a member of the European Union.

ECONOMY

Under Communist rule the Czech Republic became one of the most industrialized parts of Eastern Europe. The country has deposits of coal, uranium, iron ore, magnesite, tin and zinc. Manufactures include such products as chemicals, iron and steel and machinery, but the country also has light industries making such things as glassware and textiles for export. Manufacturing employs about 40% of the Czech Republic's entire workforce.

Farming is important. The main crops include barley, fruit, hops for beer-making, maize, potatoes, sugar beet, vegetables and wheat. Cattle and other livestock are raised. The country was admitted into the Organization for Economic Co-operation and Development (OECD) in 1995.

PRAGUE (PRAHA)

Capital of the Czech Republic, on the River Vltava. Founded in the 9th century, it grew rapidly after Wenceslaus I established a German settlement in 1232. In the 14th century it was the capital of Bohemia. It was the capital of the Czechoslovak Republic (1918–93). Occupied in World War II by the Germans it was liberated by Soviet troops in 1945. Prague was the centre of Czech resistance to the Soviet invasion of 1968. Sights include Hradcany Castle and Charles Bridge. An important commercial centre, industries include engineering, iron and steel.

DENMARK

Denmark's flag is called the Dannebrog, or 'the spirit of Denmark'. It may be the oldest national flag in continuous use. It represents a vision thought to have been seen by the Danish King Waldemar II before the Battle of Lyndanisse, which took place in Estonia in 1219.

The Kingdom of Denmark is the smallest country in Scandinavia. It consists of a peninsula called Jutland (Jylland), which is joined to Germany, and more than 400 islands, 89 of which are inhabited. The land is flat and mostly scattered with rocks dropped there by huge ice sheets during the last Ice Age. The highest point in Denmark is on Jutland and is only 173 m [568 ft].

Area 43,094 sq km [16,639 sq mi]
Population 5,451,000
Capital (population) Copenhagen (1,091,000)
Government Parliamentary monarchy
Ethnic groups Scandinavian, Inuit, Faeroese, German
Languages Danish (official), English, Faerose
Religions Evangelical Lutheran 95%
Currency Danish krone = 100 øre
Website http://denmark.dk

CLIMATE

Denmark has a cool but pleasant climate. During cold spells in the winter, The Sound between Sjælland and Sweden may freeze over. Summers are warm. Rainfall occurs throughout the year.

HISTORY

Danish Vikings terrorized much of Western Europe for about 300 years after AD 800. Danish kings ruled England in the 11th century. Control of the entrances to the Baltic Sea contributed to the power of Denmark in the Middle Ages, when the kingdom dominated its neighbours and expanded its territories to include Norway, Iceland, Greenland and the Faroe Islands. The link with Norway was broken in 1814, and with Iceland in 1944. But Greenland and the Faroes retained connections with Denmark. The granite island of Bornholm, off the southern tip of Sweden, also remains a Danish possession. This island was occupied by Germany in World War II, but it was liberated by the Soviet Union and returned to Denmark in 1946. Denmark was also occupied by Germany in 1940, but it was liberated in 1945. The Danes then set about rebuilding their industries and restoring their economy.

POLITICS

Denmark is a generally comfortable mixture of striking political opposites. The Lutheran tradition and the cradle of Hans Christian Andersen's fairy tales coexist with open attitudes to pornography and one of the highest illegitimacy rates in the West.

The country is one of the 'greenest' of the developed nations, with a pioneering Ministry of Pollution. In 1991, it became the first government anywhere to fine industries for emissions of carbon dioxide, the primary 'greenhouse' gas.

It joined the North Atlantic Treaty Organization (NATO) in 1949, and in 1973 it joined the European Community (now the European Union). However, it remains one of the European Union's least enthusiastic members and was one of the four countries that did not adopt the euro, the single EU currency, on

ECONOMY

Denmark has few mineral resources, though there is now some oil and natural gas from the North Sea. It is one of Europe's wealthiest industrial nations. Farming employs only 4% of workers, but it is highly scientific and productive. Dairy farming and pig and poultry breeding are the chief areas.

From a firm agricultural base, Denmark has developed a wide range of industries. Some, including brewing, meat canning, fish processing, pottery, textiles and furniture making, use Danish products, but others, such as shipbuilding, oil refining, engineering and metal-working, depend on imported raw materials. Copenhagen is the chief industrial centre and draws more than a million tourists each year. At the other end of the scale is Legoland, the famous miniature town of plastic bricks, built at Billand, north-west of Vejle in eastern Jutland. It was here that Lego was created before it became the world's best-selling construction toy and a prominent Danish export.

1 January 2002. In 1972, in order to join the EC, Denmark had become the first Scandinavian country to break away from the other major economic grouping in Europe, the European Free Trade Association (EFTA), but it continued to co-operate with its five Scandinavian partners through the consultative Nordic Council which was set up in 1953.

The Danes enjoy some of the world's highest living standards. The cost of welfare provisions has been high, although the election of a Liberal-Conservative coalition in 2001 led to cutbacks. Under Prime Minister Anders Fogh Rasmussen, who won a second term in 2005, the government tightened immigration controls. This led to criticism from the UN High Commissioner for Refugees.

Denmark granted home rule to the Faeroe Islands in 1948, although in 1998, the government of the Faeroes announced plans for independence. In 1979, home rule was also granted to Greenland, which demonstrated its new-found independence by withdrawing from the European Community in 1985. Denmark is a constitutional monarchy, with a hereditary monarch, and its constitution was amended in 1953 to allow female succession to the throne.

COPENHAGEN (KØBENHAVN)

Capital and chief port of Denmark on east Sjaelland and north Amager Island, in the Øresund. A trading and fishing centre by the early 12th century, it became Denmark's capital in 1443. It has a 17th-century stock exchange, the Amalienborg palace (home of the royal family) and the Christianborgs Palace. Other sights include the Tivoli Amusement Park and the Little Mermaid sculpture. The commercial and cultural centre of the nation, it has shipbuilding, chemical and brewing industries.

DENMARK

FAEROE ISLANDS

The Faeroe (or Faroe) Islands are an autonomous region of Denmark. Situated in the North Atlantic Ocean between Iceland and the Shetland Islands, the region consists of 18 islands, 17 of which are inhabited. The main islands are Streymoy, on which the capital Tórshavn stands, Vágar, Suduroy and Sandoy. The islands have rugged coasts with abundant bird life. Most people live on the small coastal lowlands.

Area 1,399 sq km [545.3 sq mi]
Population 47,000
Capital (population) Tórshavn (18,000)
Government Self-governing overseas administrative division of Denmark
Ethnic groups Scandinavian
Languages Faroese, Danish
Religions Evangelical Lutheran
Currency Danish krone = 100 ore
Website www.tourist.fo

CLIMATE
Winters are mild under the influence of the North Atlantic Drift, the extension of the warm Gulf Stream. Summers are cool and the weather is often overcast. Fogs are common and winds are often strong.

HISTORY
Irish monks settled on the islands in the 6th century AD, though most of the islanders today are descendants of Vikings. The Faeroe Islands were part of the Kingdom of Norway from the 11th century until 1380. The islands came under Danish control when Norway joined the Kingdom of Denmark. British troops occupied the islands during World War II (1939–45), but they reverted to Danish control after the war.

POLITICS
The Danes granted the islands self-government in 1948, making them a self-governing overseas administrative division of Denmark, with Denmark responsible for defence and foreign relations. The islands have their own parliament, consisting of 32 members elected on a proportional basis from the seven constituencies. The parliament elects the leader of the majority group as prime minister. Two members are elected to the Danish parliament.

In 2001, a planned referendum on independence was cancelled when the Danish government stated that it would cut off all financial aid to the islands within four years of independence.

ECONOMY
The people enjoy a high standard of living. Fishing is the main activity and the country has benefited, since the 1990s, from increased production, together with high export prices. Faeroese fishermen have traditionally hunted pilot whales, but animal rights activists have called for the abandonment of the cull.

The government hopes to diversify the economy and explore the prospects of offshore oil and gas fields. The islands benefit from a Danish subsidy which accounts for 15% of the GDP.

TÓRSHAVN
Capital city in the centre of the Faeroe Islands. In 800, Norwegian settlers replaced an Irish settlement on the islands. Tórshavn became the central meeting place. Christianity was introduced in about 1000. The isles came under Norwegian rule in 1035 and under Danish rule in 1816.

Tórshavn became the seat of government in 1856. The Faeroese seafishing trade started in Tórshavn. Since 1974 the town has joined with Kaldbak, Hoyvík, Argir and Kollafjørur.

GREENLAND

Situated in the north-west Atlantic Ocean and lying mostly within the Arctic Circle, Greenland is regarded by geographers as the world's largest island. It is almost three times larger than the second largest island, New Guinea.

An ice sheet, the world's second largest after Antarctica, covers more than 85% of its area with an average depth of 1,500 m [5,000 ft]. Settlement is confined to the rocky south west coast.

Area 2,166,086 sq km [836,330 sq mi]
Population 56,000
Capital (population) Nuuk (14,000)
Government Self-governing overseas administrative division of Denmark
Ethnic groups Greenlander 88% (Inuit and Greenland-born whites), Danish and others 12%
Languages Greenlandic (East Inuit), Danish, English
Religions Evangelical Lutheran
Currency Danish krone = 100 ore
Website http://dk.nanoq.gl

CLIMATE

The south west coast, where the capital Nuuk (Godthåb) is situated, is warmed by Atlantic currents. Even so, it has more than seven months in which average temperatures are below freezing.

HISTORY

European discovery of Greenland is credited to Erik the Red, who settled in 982, founding a colony that lasted more than 500 years. Greenland became a Danish possession in 1380 and an integral part of the Danish kingdom in 1953.

POLITICS

Greenland was taken into the European Community (EC) in 1973, despite a majority of Greenlanders voting against this. In 1979, after another referendum, home rule was introduced, with full internal self-government in 1981. In 1985 Greenland withdrew from the EC, halving the Community's land area.

ECONOMY

Greenland still relies heavily on Danish aid and Denmark is its main trading partner. The chief rural occupations are sheep-rearing and fishing, with shrimps, prawns and molluscs being exported. The only major manufacturing industry is fish canning, which has drawn many Inuit to the towns. Few Inuit now follow the traditional life of nomadic hunting.

Most Greenlanders live precariously between the primitive and the modern. Yet a nationalist mood prevails, buoyed by rich fish stocks, lead and zinc from Uummannaq in the north-west, untapped uranium in the south and, possibly, oil in the east. In addition, an adventure-oriented tourist industry is expanding. In 1997, the nationalist resurgence was evident when Greenland made Inuit name forms official.

NUUK
(Danish, GODTHÅB)

Capital and largest town of Greenland. The mouth of a group of fjords on the south-west coast. Founded in 1721, it is the oldest Danish settlement in Greenland. Places of interest include the Greenlandic National Museum and Archives, the Katuaq Cultural Centre (with Greenland's only cinema) and Niels Lynges' House.

DJIBOUTI

Based on the banner of the African People's League for Independence. Blue is the colour of the Issas people and also the sky and the sea. Green is the colour of the Afars people and symbolizes fertile earth. The white triangle signifies peace and equality, the red star is a symbol of unity.

The Republic of Djibouti is a small country on the north-east coast of Africa, the capital is also Djibouti. Djibouti occupies a strategic position around the Gulf of Tadjoura, where the Red Sea meets the Gulf of Aden. Behind the coastal plain lie the Mabla Mountains, rising to Moussa Ali at 2,063 m [6,769 ft]. Djibouti contains the lowest point on the African continent, Lake Assal, at 155 m [509 ft] below sea level.

Nearly 90% of the land is semi-desert, and shortage of pasture and water make farming difficult.

Area 23,200 sq km [8,958 sq mi]
Population 487,000
Capital (population) Djibouti (317,000)
Government Multiparty republic
Ethnic groups Somali 60%, Afar 35%
Languages Arabic and French (both official)
Religions Islam 94%, Christianity 6%
Currency Djiboutian franc = 100 centimes
Website www.presidence.dj

CLIMATE

Djibouti has one of the world's hottest and driest climates with summer temperatures regularly exceeding 42°C [100°F]. Average annual rainfall is only 130 mm [5 in]. In the wooded Mabla Mountains average annual rainfall is much higher, and can reach 500 mm [20 in].

HISTORY

Islam arrived in the 9th century. The subsequent conversion of the Afars led to conflict with Christian Ethiopians who lived in the interior. By the 19th century, Somalian Issas moved north and occupied much of the Afars' grazing land.

France gained influence in 1862, with its interest centred around Djibouti, the French commercial rival to the port of Aden. French Somaliland was established in 1888.

A referendum in 1967 saw 60% of the electorate vote to retain links with France, though most Issas favoured independence. The country was renamed French Territory of the Afars and Issas.

POLITICS

In 1977 the Republic of Djibouti gained full independence, and Hassan Gouled Aptidon of the Popular Rally for Progress (RPP) was elected president. He declared a one-party state in 1981.

RED SEA

Narrow arm of the Indian Ocean between north-east Africa and the Arabian Peninsula, connected to the Mediterranean by the Gulf of Suez and the Suez Canal. With the building of vessels too large for the canal and the construction of pipelines, the Red Sea's importance as a trade route has diminished. Its widest point is 320 km [200 mi]. It covers an area of 438,000 sq km [169,000 sq mi].

boycotted 1993 elections, and Aptidon was re-elected for a fourth six-year term. FRUD rebels continued an armed campaign for political representation. In 1996, government and FRUD forces signed a peace agreement, recognizing FRUD as a political party.

In 1999, Ismael Omar Gelleh succeeded Aptidon as president in the country's first multiparty presidential elections. He pursues a policy of closer links with France, which still has a strong military presence in Djibouti, and with the US. The only US military base in sub-Saharan Africa is stationed here. In 2005 elections Gelleh was the only candidate.

ECONOMY

Djibouti is a poor nation, heavily reliant on food imports and revenue from the capital city. A free-trade zone, it has no major resources and manufacturing is on a very small scale. The only important activity is livestock raising, and 50% of the population are pastoral nomads.

Its location at the mouth of the Red Sea is of great economic importance as it serves as a vital trans-shipment point.

Protests against the Issas-dominated regime forced the adoption of a multiparty constitution in 1992. The Front for the Restoration of Unity and Democracy (FRUD), supported primarily by Afars,

GULF OF ADEN

A body of water that makes up the western arm of the Arabian Sea, meeting the Red Sea at the Bab el Mandeb strait. The gulf runs in a west–east direction, between Yemen and Somalia, meeting Djibouti at the western end. It is about 900 km [560 mi] long, and 500 km [310 mi] wide at the eastern end, between Ra's Asir of Somalia and the city of al-Mukalla in Yemen. The Gulf of Aden is an important route for commercial shipping.

DJIBOUTI (JIBUTI)

Capital of Djibouti, on the western shore of an isthmus in the Gulf of Tadjoura, north-east Africa. Founded in 1888, it became capital in 1892, and a free port in 1949. Ethiopian emperor Menelik II built a railway from Addis Ababa, and Djibouti became the chief port for handling Ethiopian trade. While Eritrea was federated with Ethiopia (1952–93), it lost this status to the Red Sea port of Assab. Now home to two-thirds of the country's population.

DOMINICAN REPUBLIC

Blue represents liberty, red stands for blood shed during the struggle for liberation and the white cross is a symbol of sacrifice. The coat of arms features a Bible open at the Gospel of St John, symbolizing the Trinitarian movement that led the movement for independence.

The Dominican Republic is the second largest of the Caribbean nations in both area and population, it shares the island of Hispaniola with Haiti, the Dominican Republic occupying the eastern two-thirds.

Of the steep-sided mountains that dominate the island, the country includes the northern Cordillera Septentrional, the huge Cordillera Central, which rises to Pico Duarte, at 3,175 m [10,414 ft] the highest peak in the Caribbean, and the southern Sierra de Bahoruco. Between them and to the east lie fertile valleys and lowlands, including the Vega Real and the coastal plains where the main sugar plantations are found.

Area 48,511 sq km [18,730 sq mi]
Population 9,184,000
Capital (population) Santo Domingo (2,563,000)
Government Multiparty republic
Ethnic groups
Mulatto 73%, White 16%, Black 11%
Languages Spanish (official)
Religions Roman Catholic 95%
Currency Dominican peso = 100 centavos
Website www.dominicanrepublic.com

CLIMATE

Typical of the Caribbean region, the climate is humid and hot throughout the year close to sea level, while cooler conditions prevail in the mountains. Rainfall is heavy, especially in the north-east.

HISTORY

Hispaniola was inhabited by Amerindians when it was discovered by Columbus in 1492. The city of Santo Domingo, now the capital and chief port, was founded by Columbus' brother Bartholomew four years later and is the oldest in the Americas. The native population died out within a few decades of the arrival of the Spanish. Hispaniola was initially the centrepiece of the Spanish empire, but was later to become less significant.

In 1795 it became French, then Spanish again in 1809. In 1821, when it was called Santo Domingo, the country won its independence. Haiti held the territory from 1822 until 1844. When the country's sovereignty was restored, it became the Dominican Republic.

Growing American influence culminated in US occupation between 1916 and 1924. This was followed by a period of corrupt dictatorship. From 1930 until his assassination in 1961, the country was ruled by Rafael Trujillo, one of Latin America's most notorious dictators, who imprisoned or killed many of his opponents. A power struggle developed between the military, the upper class, those who wanted the country to become a democracy and others who favoured making it a Communist regime.

POLITICS

In 1962 Juan Bosch became president, but was ousted in 1963. Bosch supporters tried to seize power in 1965, but were met with strong military opposition. This led to US military intervention in 1965. In 1966, a new constitution was adopted

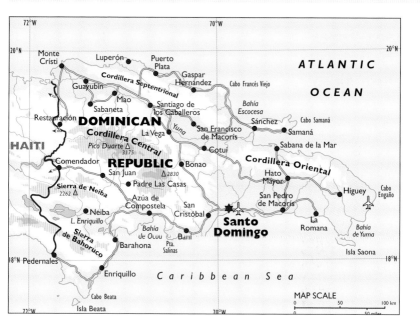

and Joaquín Balaguer was elected president (1966–78, 1986–96). Elections have been known to be violent and the United States has kept a watchful eye.

Leonel Fernandez was elected president for a second time in 2004. He had campaigned on a ticket that promised to tackle inflation, and once in office he introduced austerity measures which included cuts to state spending.

ECONOMY

The World Bank describes the Dominican Republic as a 'lower-middle-income' developing country. Since the 1990s, industrial growth that exploited the country's huge hydroelectric potential, mining and tourism has augmented the traditional agricultural economy, though the country is far from being politically stable. Agriculture is a major activity. Leading crops include avocados, bananas, beans, mangoes, oranges, plantains, rice, sugar cane and tobacco.

Gold and nickel are mined. Sugar refining is a major industry, with the bulk of the production exported to the United States. Leading exports are ferronickel, sugar, coffee, cocoa and gold. The main trading partner is the United States.

SANTO DOMINGO
(formerly CIUDAD TRUJILLO, 1936–61)

Capital and chief port of the Dominican Republic, on the south coast of the island, on the River Ozama. Founded in 1496, the city is the oldest continuous European settlement in the Americas. It was the seat of the Spanish viceroys in the early 1500s, and base for the Spaniards' conquering expeditions until it was devastated by an earthquake in 1562. It houses more than a third of the country's population, many of whom work in the sugar industry.

127

EAST TIMOR

Yellow represents the vestiges of East Timor's colonial past. Black stands for the darkness to be overcome, while red recalls the struggle for liberation. The five-pointed star is the guiding light of peace.

The Democratic Republic of Timor-Leste is a small island nation in south-east Asia. It became part of Indonesia in 1975, but it became independent in 2002, ending almost 500 years of foreign domination.

The Timor Sea separates East Timor from Australia, which lies about 500 km [310 mi] away. East Timor occupies the north-eastern part of the island of Timor. It also includes some small islands and the enclave of Oscùsso-Ambeno on the north-western coast of West Timor, the Indonesian part of the island. The land is largely mountainous, rising to about 2,960 metres [9,711 ft].

Area 14,874 sq km [5,743 sq mi]
Population 1,063,000
Capital (population) Dili (52,000)
Government Multiparty republic
Ethnic groups
Austronesian (Malayo-Polynesian), Papuan
Languages Tetum, Portuguese (both official),
Indonesian, English
Religions Roman Catholic 90%, Muslim 4%,
Protestant 3%
Currency US dollar = 100 cents
Website www.gov.east-timor.org

CLIMATE

East Timor has a monsoon climate, with high temperatures throughout the year. The average temperature is more than 24°C [75°F], although the mountainous zone is cooler. The monsoon extends from November to May. The average annual rainfall is less than 1,500 mm [59 in]. The mountainous zone is wetter, with a shorter dry period of four months.

HISTORY

Europeans first visited the island of Timor in the 16th century and, following skirmishing between the Dutch and the Portuguese, East Timor came under Portuguese rule by treaties in 1859 and 1893. Japan occupied Timor between 1942 and 1945 during World War II, but the Portuguese returned after Japan was defeated. Following a coup in Portugal in 1974, the new government announced that its colonies should prepare for independence. The Portuguese withdrew from East Timor in August 1975 and Fretilin (the Revolutionary Front for an Independent East Timor) declared the territory independent, but in December 1975, Indonesia seized the territory.

The territory became the 27th province of Indonesia named Timor Timur. Indonesian rule proved oppressive and guerrilla resistance grew. In 1999, Indonesia agreed to let the people of East Timor vote on independence or local autonomy in a UN-supervised referendum. The people voted by almost 99% for independence. East Timor declared itself independent. However, pro-Indonesian militias, who were widely believed to have the backing of the Indonesian government, caused massive destruction until an international peacekeeping force restored order. An estimated 1,400 people were killed and 250,000 were displaced.

POLITICS

East Timor gained full independence on 20 May 2002 and became the 191st member of the United Nations in September. The UN set up a Mission of Support to help the Timorese authorities. Xanana Gusmao became the country's first president, a ceremonial head of state, in a 2002 election. Gusmao was the former leader of the separatist guerrilla fighters and had been jailed by the Indonesians between 1992 and 1999.

Following independence, the new government replaced the UN-supervised transitional government. In 2005 the United Nations withdrew the last of its troops. Some Australian troops remained to train a Timorese army. East Timor has an elected National Parliament, which elects the country's head of state.

A major problem arising in independent East Timor was the bringing to trial of individuals responsible for atrocities committed during the country's violent transition. An Indonesian court tried people for human rights abuses in East Timor in 1999, while a joint Indonesian and East Timorese Truth and Friendship Commission was established to heal the wounds of the past. Some organizations have criticized the Truth and Friendship Commission, arguing that it is an attempt to bury the past rather than providing justice. However, the governments of East Timor and Indonesia have argued that it is important for the two countries to build a strong relationship with each other. In 2006 violence broke out after 600 soldiers were sacked, but it was brought under control with Australian assistance.

ECONOMY

Agriculture is the main activity. Arable farms cover about 5% of the land and coffee is widely grown. Crops include bananas, cassava, maize, rice, soya beans and sweet potatoes. Coffee, sandalwood and marble are exported.

Following independence, the new country, with its shattered economy and infrastructure, was heavily dependent on foreign aid. However, offshore oil and gas deposits hold out hope for future development. Production of natural gas began in 2004. The oil and gas deposits are located under the Timor Sea and, following independence, East Timor denounced the maritime boundary given to Australia by Indonesia because it gave Australia control over what was probably the richest oil field region. In 2005 Australia agreed on a division of the expected revenues on the oil and gas deposits, while East Timor agreed to postpone discussions on the disputed maritime boundary.

DILI

Capital of East Timor, on the north coast of Timor. Originally settled in 1520 by the Portuguese, who made it the capital of Portuguese Timor in 1596. Occupied by the Japanese during World War II. Occupied by Indonesian forces from 1975, but finally independent in 2002. The city retains links with its Portuguese past but has rebuilt itself after the massive destruction of 1999.

ECUADOR

Ecuador's flag was created by a patriot, Francisco de Miranda, in 1806. The armies of Simón Bolívar, the South American general, won victories over Spain, and flew this flag. At the centre is Ecuador's coat of arms, showing a condor over Mount Chimborazo.

The Republic of Ecuador straddles the Equator on the west coast of South America. Three ranges of the high Andes Mountains form the backbone of the country. Between the towering, snow-capped peaks of the mountains, some of which are volcanoes, lie a series of high plateaux, or basins. Nearly half of Ecuador's population lives on these plateaux.

West of the Andes lie the flat coastal lowlands, which border the Pacific Ocean and average 100 km [60 mi] in width. The eastern alluvial lowlands, often called the Oriente, are drained by headwaters of the River Amazon.

Area 283,561 sq km [109,483 sq mi]
Population 13,548,000
Capital (population) Quito (1,514,000)
Government Multiparty republic
Ethnic groups Mestizo 65%, Amerindian 25%, White 7%, Black 3%
Languages Spanish (official), Quechua
Religions Roman Catholic 95%
Currency US dollar = 100 cents
Website www.vivecuador.com

CLIMATE

The climate in Ecuador is greatly influenced by altitude. The coastal lowlands are hot, despite cooling by the cold offshore Peru Current. The Andes have spring temperatures throughout the year, while the eastern lowlands are hot and humid. The rainfall is heaviest in the east and the northern coastal lowlands. The El Niño effect in Pacific ocean currents intermittently causes rainstorms, flooding and other severe weather.

HISTORY

The Inca people of Peru conquered much of what is now Ecuador in the late 15th century. They introduced their language, Quechua, which is widely spoken today. In 1532 a colony was founded by the Spaniards in the territory, which was then called Quito. The country became independent in 1822, following the defeat of a Spanish force by an army led by General Antonio Jose de Sucre in a battle near Quito. Ecuador became part of Gran Colombia, a confederation which also included Colombia and Venezuela. Ecuador became a separate nation in 1830.

In 1832 Ecuador annexed the volcanic Galapagos Islands, which lie 970 km [610 mi] west of Ecuador, of which they form a province. The archipelago, which contains six main islands and more than 50 smaller ones, later became world-famous through the writings of Charles Darwin, who visited the islands in 1835. His descriptions of the unique endemic flora and fauna gave him crucial evidence for his theory of evolution through natural selection.

POLITICS

The failure of successive governments to tackle the country's social and economic problems caused great instability in Ecuador throughout the 20th century. A 1941 war with Peru led to loss of territory, and border disputes flared up again in 1995. A peace treaty was signed in 1998.

Military regimes ruled the country between 1963 and 1966 and again from 1976 to 1979. However, under a new constitution introduced by the second of these military juntas and approved by a national referendum, civilian government was restored. Civilian governments have ruled Ecuador since multiparty elections in 1979. But the volatile character of politics here was evident throughout the 1980s and 1990s. For example, a state of emergency, albeit of short duration, was declared in 1986 and, in 1995, the vice-president was forced to leave the country after accusations that he had bribed opposition deputies.

In 1996, the president was deposed on the grounds of mental incompetence and, in 1998, accusations of fraud marred the victory of President Jamil Mahaud of the centre-right Popular Democracy Party. The early years of the 21st century were marked by political instability as successive presidents faced opposition from the military and public demonstrations. In 2000, economic problems made Ecuador adopt the US dollar as its sole unit of currency. In 2006 elections Rafael Correa became president, promising anti-corruption reforms.

ECONOMY

The World Bank classifies Ecuador as a 'lower-middle-income' developing country. Agriculture employs 10% of the population. Bananas, cocoa and coffee are all important export crops. Other products in the hot coastal lowlands include citrus fruits, rice and sugar cane, while beans, maize and wheat are important in the highlands. Cattle are raised for dairy products and meat, while fishing is important in the coastal waters. Forestry is a major activity. Ecuador produces balsa wood and such hardwoods as mahogany. Mining is important and oil and oil products now play a major part in the economy. Ecuador started to export oil in the early 1970s and is a member of the Organization of Petroleum Exporting Countries. Manufactures include cement, Panama hats, paper products, processed food and textiles. Major exports are food and live animals, and mineral fuels. Ecuador's main trading partners are the United States and Colombia.

QUITO

Capital of Ecuador, at 2,850 m [9,260 ft], Quito lies almost on the Equator. The site was first settled by Quito Native Americans, and was captured by the Incas in 1487. It was taken by Spain in 1534, and liberated in 1822 by Antonio José de Sucre. A cultural and political centre, it is the site of the Central University of Ecuador (1787). Products include textiles and handicrafts.

131

EGYPT

A flag consisting of three bands of red, white and black, the colours of the Pan-Arab movement, was adopted in 1958. The present design has a gold eagle in the centre. This symbolizes Saladin, the warrior who led the Arabs in the 12th century.

The Arab Republic of Egypt is Africa's second largest country by population, after Nigeria. Most of Egypt is desert. Almost all the people live either in the Nile Valley and its fertile delta or along the Suez Canal, the artificial waterway between the Mediterranean and Red seas. This canal shortens the sea journey between the United Kingdom and India by 9,700 km [6,027 mi]. Recent attempts have been made to irrigate parts of the Western Desert.

Apart from the Nile Valley, Egypt has three other main regions. The Western and Eastern deserts are part of the Sahara. The Sinai Peninsula (Es Sina), to the east of the Suez Canal, is very mountainous and contains Egypt's highest peak, Gebel Katherina (2,637 m [8,650 ft]); few people live in this area.

Area 1,001,449 sq km [386,659 sq mi]
Population 78,887,000
Capital (population) Cairo (11,146,000)
Government Republic
Ethnic groups Egyptians/Bedouins/Berbers 99%
Languages Arabic (official), French, English
Religions Islam (mainly Sunni Muslim) 94%, Christian (mainly Coptic Christian) and others 6%
Currency Egyptian pound = 100 piastres
Website www.egypt.gov.eg/english/default.asp

CLIMATE

Egypt has a desert climate and is one of the world's sunniest countries. The country's low rainfall occurs in winter, if at all. Winters are mild. In summer conditions are hot, and become unpleasant when hot and dusty winds blow from the deserts into the Nile Valley.

HISTORY

Ancient Egypt, which was founded about 5,000 years ago, was one of the great early civilizations. Throughout the country, pyramids, temples and richly decorated tombs are memorials to its great achievements. After Ancient Egypt declined, the country came under successive foreign rulers. Arabs occupied Egypt in AD 639–42. They introduced the Arabic language and Islam. Their influence was so great that many Egyptians now regard themselves as Arabs.

Egypt came under British rule in 1882, but it gained partial independence in 1922, becoming a monarchy.

POLITICS

In 1952, following a military revolution led by General Muhammad Naguib, the monarchy was abolished and Egypt became a republic. Naguib became president, but he was overthrown in 1954 by Colonel Gamal Abdel Nasser. President Nasser sought to develop Egypt's economy, and he announced a major project to build a new dam at Aswan to provide electricity and water for irrigation. When Britain and the United States failed to provide finance for building the dam, Nasser seized the Suez Canal Company in July 1956. In retaliation, Israel, backed by British and French troops, invaded the Sinai Peninsula and the Suez Canal region. However, under international ing as independents, made gains in parliament. In 2007 Mubarak altered the constitution to strengthen his control, increase police powers and further outlaw the Muslim Brotherhood.

ECONOMY

Egypt is Africa's second most industrialized country after South Africa, but remains a developing country. The people are poor, farming employs 34% of the workers. Most *fellahin* (peasants) grow food crops such as beans, maize, rice, sugar cane and wheat, but cotton is the chief cash crop. Egypt depends increasingly on the Nile. Its waters are seasonal, and control and storage have become essential in the last 100 years. The Aswan High Dam is the greatest Nile dam, and the water behind it

pressure, they were forced to withdraw. Construction of the Aswan High Dam began in 1960 and it was fully operational by 1968.

In 1967, Egypt lost territory to Israel in the Six-Day War and Nasser tendered his resignation, but the people refused to accept it. After his death in 1970, Nasser was succeeded vice-president Anwar el-Sadat. In 1973 Egypt launched a surprise attack in the Sinai Peninsula, but its troops were forced back to the Suez Canal. In 1977 Sadat began peace negotiations with Israel. Finally, in 1979, Egypt and Israel signed a peace treaty and Egypt regained the Sinai Peninsula. Extremists opposed contacts with Israel, and in 1981 Sadat was assassinated. He was succeeded by Hosni Mubarak.

In the 1990s attacks on foreign visitors severely damaged tourism, despite efforts to curb the activities of Islamic extremists. In 1997 terrorists killed 58 foreign tourists near Luxor. Unrest continued in the 21st century. In 2005 Mubarak claimed victory in the first contested presidential elections, but members of the banned Muslim Brotherhood, stand-

in Lake Nasser makes desert reclamation possible. The electricity produced is important for industrial development.

CAIRO (AL-QAHIRAH)

Capital of Egypt and port on the River Nile. The largest city in Africa, Cairo was founded in 969 by the Fatimid dynasty and subsequently fortified by Saladin. Medieval Cairo became capital of the Mamluk empire, but declined under Turkish rule. During the 20th century it grew dramatically in population and area. Nearby are world-famous archaeological sites, the sphinx and the Pyramids of Giza. Old Cairo is a world heritage site containing over 400 mosques and other fine examples of Islamic art and architecture. Its five universities include the world's oldest, housed in the mosque of Al Azhar (972) and the centre of Shiite Koranic study.

EL SALVADOR

This flag was adopted in 1912, replacing the earlier 'Stars and Stripes'. The blue and white stripes are featured on the flags of several Central American countries which gained their independence from Spain at the same time in 1821.

El Salvador is the smallest and most densely populated country in Central America. It has a narrow coastal plain along the Pacific Ocean. The majority of the interior is mountainous with many extinct volcanic peaks, overlooking a heavily populated central plateau. Earthquakes are common; in 1854, an earthquake destroyed the capital, San Salvador. In October 1986, another earthquake killed 400 people and caused widespread damage.

The highlands were once heavily wooded, but have suffered widespread deforestation. The central plateau and valleys have areas of grass and deciduous woodland, while tropical savanna or forest cover the coastal regions.

Area 21,041 sq km [8,124 sq mi]
Population 6,822,000
Capital (population) San Salvador (1,472,000)
Government Republic
Ethnic groups Mestizo 90%, White 9%, Amerindian 1%
Languages Spanish (official)
Religions Roman Catholic 83%
Currency US dollar = 100 cents
Website www.elsalvadorturismo.gob.sv

El Salvador declared independence in 1841 but was continually subject to foreign interference, especially from Guatemala and Nicaragua. An economy based on coffee plantations developed.

POLITICS

Following a collapse in coffee prices, Maximiliano Hernández Martínez seized power in a palace coup in 1931. In 1944 a general strike overthrew his brutal dictatorship. After a period of progressive government, a military junta headed by Julio Adalberto Rivera from 1962 to 1967 and Fidel Sánchez Hernández from

CLIMATE

The coast has a hot tropical climate. Inland, the climate is moderated by altitude. The centre region has similar day temperatures but cooler nights. Rainfall is frequent between May and October.

HISTORY

In 1524–6 Spanish explorer Pedro de Alvarado conquered Native American tribes such as the Pipil, and the region became part of the Spanish Viceroyalty of Guatemala. Independence was achieved in 1821, and in 1823 El Salvador joined the Central American Federation. The federation dissolved in 1839.

COFFEE

Plant and the popular caffeine beverage produced from its seeds (coffee beans). The plants of the genus Coffea are evergreen with white fragrant flowers. Originally native to Ethiopia, they are now cultivated in the tropics, especially Brazil, Colombia and the Ivory Coast. Family Rubiaceae.

Commission led to the removal of senior army officers for human rights abuses and the decommissioning of FMLN arms. Armando Calderón Sol became president in 1994 elections; Francisco Flores succeeded him in 1999.

In 2001, earthquakes killed about 1,200 people and left a million homeless. Tony Saca won 2004 elections to become the fourth successive ARENA president. His government has privatized many state-owned services.

1967 to 1972 seized power. Honduras' discriminatory immigration laws exacerbated tension on the border between the two countries. The 'Soccer War' of 1969 broke out following an ill-tempered World Cup qualifying match. Within four days, El Salvador captured much of Honduras. Troops withdrew after a cease-fire.

In the 1970s, the repressive National Republican Alliance (ARENA) regime compounded El Salvador's problems of overpopulation, unequal distribution of wealth, and social unrest. Civil war broke out in 1979 between US-backed government forces and the Farabundo Marti National Liberation Front (FMLN). The 12-year war killed 75,000 and made millions homeless. A cease-fire held from 1992, and the FMLN became a recognized political party. In 1993 a UN Truth

ECONOMY

El Salvador is a lower-middle-income developing country. Farmland and pasture account for approximately 60% of land use. El Salvador is the world's 10th largest producer of coffee, and reliance on the crop caused economic structural imbalance. Sugar and cotton grow on the coastal lowlands. Fishing is important, but manufacturing is on a small scale. The civil war devastated the economy. Between 1993 and 1995, El Salvador received more than US$100 million of credit from the International Monetary Fund. In 2001 the failing local currency, the colón, was abandoned in favour of the US dollar. Money sent home by Salvadorans working abroad makes a major contribution to the economy.

SAN SALVADOR

Capital and largest city of El Salvador in central El Salvador. Founded in 1524 near the volcano of San Salvador, which rises to 1,885 m [6,184 ft] and last erupted in 1917. The city has frequently been damaged by earthquakes. The main industry is the processing of the coffee which is grown on the rich volcanic soils of the area. Other manufactures include beer, textiles and tobacco.

LAGUNA EL JOCOTAL

Freshwater lagoon 12 km (7.5 mi) south of San Miguel, lying in a volcanic crater, the lagoon varies in size from 5 sq km (2 sq mi) to 15 sq km (6 sq mi) between dry and rainy seasons. The tree duck and over 130 other species of aquatic bird use the lagoon, which is an internationally recognized conservation area.

EQUATORIAL GUINEA

Green equals agriculture, white is peace and red is for the blood shed in the fight for independence. Blue is for the Atlantic Ocean. The tree on the coat of arms is the tree under which the 1843 treaty with Spain was signed. The six stars represent the mainland and the five islands.

The Republic of Equatorial Guinea is located in west-central Africa and is one of the smallest countries on the African continent. It consists of a mainland territory between Cameroon and Gabon, called Río Muni (Mbini), and five islands in the Bight of Biafra (Bonny), the largest of which is Bioko (Fernando Póo).

Bioko is a volcanic island with fertile soils and a steep rocky coast. Malabo's harbour is part of a submerged volcano. Bioko is mountainous, rising to a height of 3,008 m [9,869 ft] at the Pico de Basilé. It has varied vegetation with trees such as teak, mahogany, oak, walnut and rosewood, and grasslands at higher levels.

Mainland Río Muni, 90% of the country, consists mainly of hills and plateaux behind the coastal plains. Its main river, the Lolo, rises in Gabon. Dense forest covers most of Río Muni and provides a habitat for animals such as lions, gazelles and elephants.

Area 28,051 sq km [10,830 sq mi]
Population 540,000
Capital (population) Malabo (30,000)
Government Multiparty republic (transitional)
Ethnic groups Bubi (on Bioko), Fang (in Rio Muni)
Languages Spanish and French (both official)
Religions Christianity
Currency CFA franc = 100 centimes
Website www.ceiba-guinea-ecuatorial.org

HISTORY

In 1472 Portuguese navigator Fernão do Pó sighted the largest island of Bioko. In 1778, Portugal ceded the islands and commercial mainland rights to Spain in exchange for some Brazilian territories. Yellow fever hit Spanish settlers on Bioko, and they withdrew in 1781. In 1827, Spain leased bases on Bioko to Britain, and the British settled some freed slaves. Descendants of these former slaves (*Fernandinos*) remain on the island. Spain returned in the mid-19th century and developed plantations on Bioko.

In 1956, the islands became the Overseas Provinces in the Gulf of Guinea. In 1959, the territory was divided into two

CLIMATE

Situated on the equator, Equatorial Guinea has a tropical climate. High temperatures and high humidity are the norm with an average annual temperature of 25°C [77°F]. Bioko has heavy rainfall and there is a dry season from December to February. Río Muni has a similar climate to Bioko, though rainfall diminishes inland.

COCOA

Drink obtained from the seeds of the tropical American evergreen tree *Theobroma cacao*. The seeds are crushed and some fatty substances are removed to produce cocoa powder. Cocoa is the basic ingredient of chocolate. The Ivory Coast is the world's largest producer. Family Sterculiaceae.

EQUATORIAL GUINEA

provinces, Fernando Póo and Río Muni, and named Spanish Guinea. The two territories reunified in 1963 and were renamed the Autonomous Territories of Equatorial Guinea. In 1968 the combined territory gained independence as the Republic of Equatorial Guinea.

POLITICS

In 1969, social unrest broke out as a result of ethnic conflict and economic problems. President Francisco Macías Nguema responded by annulling the constitution and setting up a military dictatorship. Up to 100,000 refugees fled to neighbouring countries and more than 40,000 people were killed during Nguema's dictatorship, which endured from 1968 to 1979.

In 1979, Lieutenant-Colonel Teodoro Obiang Nguema Mbasogo deposed Nguema in a military coup. A 1991 referendum voted to set up a multiparty democracy, consisting of the ruling Equatorial Guinea Democratic Party (PDGE) and ten opposition parties. The main parties and most of the electorate boycotted elections in 1993, and the PDGE formed a government. 1996 and 2004 elections were again boycotted by most opposition parties and President Obiang claimed to have won by a massive majority. Human rights organizations accuse his regime of routine arrests and torture of opponents and the president is seen to control all the political parties.

In 2004 a coup attempt by foreign mercenaries was foiled and the leaders were arrested.

ECONOMY

Equatorial Guinea is a poor country. Agriculture employs around 60% of the people, though many farmers live at subsistence level, contributing little to the economy. The main food crops are bananas, cassava and sweet potatoes. The chief cash crop is cocoa, grown on Bioko, though this has been hit by a worldwide dip in cocoa prices.

Oil has been produced off Bioko since 1966. By 2002 it accounted for more than 80% of exports. It has caused rapid expansion of the economy and massive increase in revenue, but greatly widened the gap between rich and poor. One UN human rights report stated that 65% of the people still live in 'extreme poverty'.

The government has promised that agriculture will benefit from the large amounts of revenue gained from oil, but this has yet to materialize. Other natural resources that have yet to be developed include titanium, iron, manganese and uranium. The country has forfeited much aid from the World Bank and the IMF due to corruption and mismanagement.

MALABO

Seaport capital of Equatorial Guinea, on Bioko island, in the Gulf of Guinea in west central Africa. Founded in 1827 as a British base to suppress the slave trade, it was known as Santa Isabel until 1973. Malabo stands on the edge of a volcanic crater that acts as a natural harbour. Industries include fish processing, hardwoods, cocoa, coffee.

137

ERITREA

Based on the flag of the EPLF, the red triangle symbolizes blood shed in the fight for freedom, the blue triangle represents the Red Sea, the green triangle stands for agriculture. From 1952–9 Eritrea's flag bore a green wreath and olive branch in the centre of a field of United Nations' blue.

The State of Eritrea occupies a strategic geopolitical position on the Red Sea in north-eastern Africa. The coastal plain extends inland between 16 and 64 km [10–40 mi]. Inland are mountains. In the south-west, the mountains descend to the Danakil Desert. This desert contains Eritrea's lowest point at 75 m [246 ft] below sea level.

Area 117,600 sq km [45,405 sq miles]
Population 4,787,000
Capital (population) Asmara (358,000)
Government Transitional government
Ethnic groups Tigrinya 50%, Tigre and Kunama 40%, Afar 4%, Saho 3% and others
Languages Afar, Arabic, Tigre and Kunama, Tigrinya
Religions Islam, Coptic Christian, Roman Catholic
Currency Nakfa = 100 cents
Website www.shabait.com

CLIMATE

The temperature ranges from 16°C [61°F] in the highlands to 27°C [81°F] on the coastal plain. Rainfall on the coastal plain is between 150 and 250 mm [6–10 in] with up to 610 mm [24 in] in the highlands. The rainy season is from June to September.

HISTORY

The first settlers were from Africa, followed by others from the Arabian peninsula. Between AD 50 and 600, Eritrea was part of the Ethiopian kingdom of Axum. The people of Axum were converted to Christianity in the 4th century, but Muslims gained control of the area in the 7th century, introducing Islam to the coastal areas. Christianity survived inland.

In the 16th century, the Ottoman Empire took over the coastal area. Italy made Eritrea a colony in 1890. In 1935, Italy also conquered Ethiopia. During World War II, a British force drove the Italians out off north-eastern Africa.

After the war, a British military administration ruled Eritrea.

In 1950, the UN made Eritrea a self-governing part of Ethiopia. Ethiopian rule proved unpopular and, in 1958, Eritrean nationalists formed the Eritrean Liberation Front (ELF). War broke out in 1961 between the ELF and the Ethiopians. In 1962, Ethiopia declared Eritrea to be a province, sparking off a war of independence.

The Eritrean People's Liberation Front (EPLF) was formed in 1970, replacing the ELF as the main anti-Ethiopian organization. In 1974, Ethiopian Emperor Haile Selassie was overthrown and a military government took power. EPLF victories gradually weakened Ethiopia's government. and the regime collapsed in 1991. The EPLF then formed a provisional government.

POLITICS

Eritrea declared independence in 1993, with Isaias Afewerki as president. The ruling People's Front for Democracy and Justice is the only party permitted, and the government has been criticized for repressing opposition and closing the private press in 2001. Eritrea's relations with Ethiopia deteriorated in 1998 over a border dispute around the town of Badme. Ethiopia bombed Asmara airport, Eritrea attacked Mekele in northern Ethiopia, and war broke out. In 2000 UN intervened to support a peace plan. In 2001 the two countries agreed to allow a UN mediator to demarcate the border, and in 2003 the mediator ruled that Badme lies in Eritrea. Tension continued and, in late 2005, Eritrea ordered UN peace-keeping troops to leave the country. In 2006 both countries boycotted border demarcation meetings. In 2007 Eritrea declared support for the Islamists opposing the Ethiopian-backed transitional government in Somalia.

ECONOMY

One of Africa's poorest countries; half the population lives below the poverty line and life expectancy is 52 years. Since 1993, the economy has been set back by droughts, border conflict and high population increase. The main activity is farming, mostly at subsistence level. Agriculture employs 80% of the workforce.

ASMARA (ASMERA)

Capital of Eritrea, north-east Africa. Occupied by Italy in 1889 then their colonial capital and main base for the invasion of Ethiopia (1935–6). In the 1950s, the US built Africa's biggest military communications centre here. Absorbed by Ethiopia in 1952, it was the main garrison in the fight against independence-seeking Eritrean rebels. In 1993 it became the capital of independent Eritrea.

ESTONIA

Estonia's flag was used between 1918 and 1940, when the country was an independent republic. It was readopted in June 1988. The blue is said to symbolize the sky, the black Estonia's black soil, and the white the snow that blankets the land in winter.

The Republic of Estonia is the smallest of the three states on the east coast of the Baltic Sea, formerly part of the Soviet Union, which became independent in the early 1990s. Estonia consists of a generally flat plain which was covered by ice sheets during the Ice Age. The land is strewn with moraine rocks deposited by the ice.

The country is dotted with more than 1,500 small lakes. Water, including the large Lake Peipus (Ozero Chudskoye) and the River Narva, makes up much of Estonia's eastern border with Russia. Estonia has more than 800 islands, which together comprise about a tenth of the country. The largest island is Saaremaa (Sarema).

Farmland and pasture account for more than 33% of land use.

Area 45,100 sq km [17,413 sq mi]
Population 1,324,000
Capital (population) Tallinn (418,000)
Government Multiparty republic
Ethnic groups Estonian 65%, Russian 28%, Ukranian 2%, Belarusian 2%, Finnish 1%
Languages Estonian (official), Russian
Religions Lutheran, Russian and Estonian Orthodox, Methodist, Baptist, Roman Catholic
Currency Estonian kroon = 100 senti
Website www.riik.ee/en

CLIMATE

Despite its position to the north, Estonia has a fairly mild climate due to its proximity to the sea. Sea winds tend to warm the land during winter and cool it in summer. Rainfall averages from 480 to 580 mm (19–23 in).

HISTORY

The ancestors of the Estonians, who are related to the Finns, settled in the area several thousand years ago. Divided into several separate states, they were vulnerable to Viking attacks, but in the early 13th century, German crusaders, known as the Teutonic Knights, introduced Christianity. Germany took control of the southern part of Estonia and Denmark took control of the north. The Danes sold the north to the Germans in 1324 and Estonia became part of the Holy Roman Empire.

In 1561, Sweden took over northern Estonia and Poland ruled the south. Sweden controlled the entire country from 1625 until 1721 but, following the victory of Peter the Great over Sweden in the Great Northern War (1700–21), the area became part of the Russian Empire. On 24 February 1918, Estonia declared its independence. A democratic government was established in 1919, but a fascist coup in 1934 ended democratic rule.

POLITICS

In 1939 Germany and the Soviet Union agreed to take over large areas of eastern Europe, and it was agreed that the Soviet Union would take over Estonia. The Soviet Union forcibly annexed the country in 1940. Germany invaded Estonia in 1941, but the Soviet Union regained control in 1944 and created the Estonian were placed on Russians applying for Estonian citizenship.

ECONOMY

Despite the fact that it had the highest standard of living among the 15 former Soviet republics, Estonia found the change to a free-market economy difficult. After initial problems the economy entered rapid growth, particularly in IT and finance. This has brought high inflation, which has postponed Estonia's intended adoption of the Euro.

The timber industry is important, alongside metal-working, ship-building, clothing, textiles, chemicals and food processing. Food processing is based primarily on efficient dairy farming and pig breeding, but oats, barley and potatoes are suited to the cool climate and the average soils.

Like the other two Baltic states, Estonia is not rich in natural resources, though its oil shale is an important mineral deposit; enough gas is extracted to supply St Petersburg, Russia's second largest city. The leading exports are mineral fuels and chemical products, followed by food, textiles and cloth, and wood and paper products. Finland and Russia are the leading trading partners.

Soviet Socialist Republic. Many Estonians opposed Soviet rule and were deported to Siberia. About 100,000 Estonians settled in the West.

Resistance to Soviet rule was fuelled in the 1980s when the Soviet leader Mikhail Gorbachev began to introduce reforms and many Estonians called for independence. In 1990, the Estonian parliament declared Soviet rule invalid and called for a gradual transition to full independence. The Soviet Union regarded this as illegal, but finally the Soviet State Council recognized the Estonian parliament's proclamation of independence in September 1991. The Soviet Union itself was dissolved in December 1991.

Since independence, Estonia has sought to increase links with Europe. It was admitted to the Council of Europe in 1993; has been a member of the World Trade Organization since 1999, and a member of NATO and the European Union since 2004.

Other problems facing Estonia include crime, rural under-development and the status of its non-Estonian citizens, including Russians who make up about 30% of the population. In the country's first free elections in 1992, only Estonians were permitted to vote and all Russians were excluded. Tension on this issue continued through the 1990s. Dual citizenship was outlawed, while restrictions

TALLINN

Capital and largest city of Estonia, on the Gulf of Finland, opposite Helsinki. Founded in 1219 by the Danes, it became a member of the Hanseatic League in 1285. It passed to Sweden in 1561, and was ceded to Russia in 1721. Developed in the 19th century for Russia's Baltic Fleet, it remains a major port and industrial centre. It was badly damaged in World War II. Tourism is increasing. Industries include machinery, cables, paper.

ETHIOPIA

The tricolour flag of Ethiopia first appeared in 1897. The central pentangle was introduced in 1996, and represents the common will of the country's 68 ethnic groups, and the present sequence was adopted in 1914.

Ethiopia is dominated by the Ethiopian Plateau, a block of volcanic mountains. Its average height is 1,800 m to 2,450 m [6,000 ft to 8,000 ft], rising in the north to 4620 m [15,157 ft], at Ras Dashen. The Great Rift Valley bisects the plateau. The Eastern Highlands include the Somali Plateau and the desert of the Ogaden Plateau. The Western Highlands include the capital, Addis Ababa, the Blue Nile (Abbay), and its source Lake Tana. Lake Tana is Ethiopia's largest lake. The Danakil Desert forms Ethiopia's contested border with Eritrea.

Grass, farmland, and trees cover most of the highlands. Semi-desert and tropical savanna cover parts of the lowlands. Dense rainforest grows in the south-west.

Area 1,104,300 sq km [426,370 sq mi]
Population 74,778,000
Capital (population) Addis Ababa (2,424,000)
Government Federation of nine provinces
Ethnic groups Oromo 40%, Amhara and Tigre 32%, Sidamo 9%, Shankella 6%, Somali 6% , others
Languages Amharic (official), many others
Religions Islam 47%, Ethiopian Orthodox 40%, traditional beliefs 12%
Currency Birr = 100 cents
Website www.mfa.gov.et

CLIMATE

Ethiopia's climate is greatly affected by altitude. Addis Ababa, at 2,450 m [8,000 ft], has an average annual temperature of 20°C [68°F]. Rainfall is generally more than 1,000 mm [39 in], with a rainy season from April to September. The north-east and south-west lowlands are extremely hot and arid, with less than 500 mm [20 in] rainfall and frequent droughts.

HISTORY

According to legend Menelik I, son of King Solomon and the Queen of Sheba, founded Ethiopia in about 1000 BC. In AD 321, the northern kingdom of Axum introduced Coptic Christianity. Judaism flourished in the 6th century. The expansion of Islam isolated Axum, which broke up in the 16th century.

In 1855 Kasa re-established unity and proclaimed himself Negus (Emperor) Theodore, thereby founding the modern state. European intervention marked the late 19th century, and Menelik II became

ADDIS ABABA (AMHARIC, 'NEW FLOWER')

Capital and largest city in Ethiopia, located on a plateau at 2,440 m [8,000 ft] in the highlands of Shewa province. Addis Ababa was made capital of Ethiopia in 1889. It is the headquarters of the African Union (AU). It is the main centre for the country's vital coffee trade. Industries include food, tanning, textiles, wood products.

tion. Much international aid was sent, but appropriated for Mengistu's armed forces. 10,000 Ethiopian Jews were airlifted to Israel.

In 1991, the Tigrean-based Ethiopian People's Revolutionary Democratic Front (EPRDF) and the Eritrean People's Liberation Front (EPLF) deposed Mengistu. In 1995 the Federal Democratic Republic of Ethiopia was created, with Meles Zenawi as prime minister. A border war with Eritrea occurred in 1998-2000. Elections in 2005 led to protests and a crackdown on the opposition and press. Ethiopia intervened against Somalia's Islamist government in 2006, and in 2007 continued supporting the transitional administration with Ethiopian troops.

emperor with Italian support. He expanded the empire, made Addis Ababa his capital in 1889, and defeated an Italian invasion in 1895. In 1930 Menelik II's grandnephew, Ras Tafari Makonnen, was crowned Emperor Haile Selassie I. Italian troops invaded Ethiopia (Abyssinia) in 1935 and incorporated the country into Italian East Africa in 1936. During World War II, British and South African forces recaptured Ethiopia. Haile Selassie was restored as emperor in 1941.

POLITICS

In 1952 Eritrea federated with Ethiopia. The 1960s witnessed violent demands for Eritrean secession and economic equality. In 1962 Ethiopia annexed Eritrea. When Haile Selassie was killed in 1974, the Provisional Military Administrative Council (PMAC) abolished the monarchy. Military rule was repressive, and civil war broke out. The new PMAC leader, Mengistu Mariam, recaptured territory in Eritrea and the Ogaden with Soviet military assistance.

In 1984-5 widespread famine caused by Mengistu's policies drew global atten-

ECONOMY

Having been afflicted by drought and civil war in the 1970s and 1980s, Ethiopia is now one of the world's poorest countries. Agriculture is the main activity. In 2004, a UN report stated that Ethiopia remained on the brink of disaster, with spiralling population growth, slow economic growth and environmental degradation. Coffee is the leading cash crop and export, followed by hides, skins and pulses.

AFRICAN UNION (AU)

Intergovernmental organization. Previously known as the Organization of African Unity (OAU). Founded in 1963 and renamed in 2001, it aims to safeguard the interests and independence of all African states, encourage the continent's development, and settle disputes among member states. Its headquarters are in Addis Ababa, Ethiopia. In 2003, the AU elected its first president, Alpha Oumar Konaré.

FIJI

A modified version of the colonial flag, Fiji's flag includes that of the UK and the country's coat of arms. The blue represents the Pacific Ocean. Each quarter of the St George cross features products or symbols of Fiji: sugar cane, coconut palm, bananas, dove of peace and lion with cocoa pod.

The Republic of the Fiji Islands consists of more than 800 Melanesian islands situated in the South Pacific Ocean. The larger ones are mountainous and volcanic, and they are surrounded by coral reefs. There are also fertile coastal plains and river valleys. The rest of the islands are low, sandy coral atolls. Easily the biggest islands are Viti Levu (meaning 'Big Island'), with the capital Suva on its south coast, and Vanua Levu ('Big Land'), which is just over half the size of the larger island.

Tropical forests cover more than half of the area of the islands.

Area 18,274 sq km [7,056 sq mi]
Population 906,000
Capital (population) Suva (70,000)
Government Republic
Ethnic groups
Fijian 51% (predominantly Melanesian with a Polynesian admixture), Indian 44%, others
Languages English (official), Fijian, Hindustani
Religions Christian 52% (Methodist 37%, Roman Catholic 9%), Hindu 38%, Muslim 8%, others
Currency Fiji dollar = 100 cents
Website www.fiji.gov.fj

CLIMATE

Fiji has a tropical oceanic climate, with south-east trade winds blowing throughout the year, Average temperatures vary between 16°C [60°F] and 32°C [90°F]. The average annual rainfall in Suva is 3,000 mm [118 in]. Heavy rains occur, especially between November and April. Much of the rain comes in short, heavy showers often after a sunny morning. But rains may last all day during the rainy season.

HISTORY

Melanesians, possibly from Indonesia, settled on the islands thousands of years ago, while a small group of Polynesians also reached the islands about 1,900 years ago. In 1643. the Dutch navigator

Abel Janszoon Tasman became the first European to reach the islands. The British Captain James Cook arrived on Vatoa, one of the southern islands in 1774. Christian missionaries began to arrive in the 1830s.

Following conflict between various Fijian tribes in the mid-19th century, a local Christian chief named Cacobau, took control of western Fiji after having helped to restore peace there. Another Christian, Ma'afu, controlled the east. In 1871, European settlers named Cacobau king of Fiji. In 1874 Fiji, at the request of Cacobau and other chiefs, became a British crown colony. In the late 19th century, European traders, missionaries and escaped convicts from Australia also settled in Fiji. Additionally, between 1879 and 1916 the British brought more than 60,000 indentured labourers from India to work on the sugar plantations.

POLITICS

Fiji finally became independent on 10 October 1970, with Ratu Sir Kamisese Mara as prime minister. Fiji's colonial past caused problems of ethnic tension.

Until the late 1980s, the Indian workers and their descendants outnumbered the native Fijians. Mixing between the two groups was minimal and the ethnic Indians were second-class citizens in terms of electoral representation, economic opportunity and land ownership. However, they played an important role in the economy. In 1987 two military coups led by Lt-Colonel Sitiveni Rabuka, overthrew the elected (and first) Indian majority government, although it had been led by an ethnic Fijian, Timoci Bavadra. The leaders suspended the constitution and set up a Fijian-dominated republic outside the Commonwealth.

The country returned to civilian rule in 1990. In 1992 elections were held under a new constitution guaranteeing Melanesian supremacy and Rabuka became prime minister. However, thousands of ethnic Indians had already emigrated before these elections, taking their valuable skills with them and causing severe economic problems. Fiji was readmitted to the Commonwealth in 1997 after introducing a non-discriminatory constitution. Peaceful elections in 1999 led to victory for the Fiji Labour Party, whose leader, an ethnic Indian, Mahendra Chaudhry, became prime minister, defeating Rabuka.

In May 2000, ethnic Fijians, led by businessman George Speight, seized parliament and held the prime minister, his cabinet and several MPs hostage. They were eventually disarmed and arrested, but Chaudhry was dismissed as prime minister. The army appointed an ethnic Fijian, Laisenia Qarase of the nationalist Fiji United Party, as the new prime minister. His party won 2001 elections and the ethnic Indian Fijian Labour Party became the official opposition. Following the 2000 coup the Commonwealth again expelled Fiji, but it was readmitted in 2002. In 2004 George Speight was sentenced to death, but the president commuted the sentence to life imprisonment. In 2004 Fiji sent soldiers to Iraq for peace-keeping. In 2006 a military coup put Commodore Frank Bainimarama in power. US aid and Fiji's Commonwealth membership were again suspended.

ECONOMY

Fiji is one of the more developed of the Pacific island states, but remains poor. Agriculture, which employs 70% of the population, remains the mainstay of its economy. Sugar cane, copra and ginger are the main cash crops, and fish and timber are also exported. Other crops include bananas, cassava, coconuts, sweet potatoes and rice.

Fiji mines and exports gold, silver and limestone. Sugar processing is the major industrial activity. Other manufactures include beer, cement and cigarettes. Tourism is another important activity, with 300,000 to 400,000 visitors arriving annually. However, ethnic and political tensions and frequent coups have slowed the development of the tourist industry.

The leading markets for Fiji's exports are Australia, the United Kingdom, the United States and Japan. Imports come from Australia, New Zealand, the United States and Japan. Fiji is heavily dependent on foreign aid, which is subject to suspension during political instability, causing serious economic disruption.

SUVA

Seaport on the south-east coast of Viti Levu Island. Fiji's capital, it is the manufacturing and trade centre of the islands, with an excellent harbour. Exports include fruit, copra and gold.

FINLAND

The flag of Finland was adopted in 1918, after the country had become an independent republic in 1917, following a century of Russian rule. The blue represents Finland's many lakes. The white symbolizes the blanket of snow which masks the land in winter.

The Republic of Finland (Suomi) has four geographical regions. In the south and west, on the Gulfs of Bothnia and Finland, is a low, narrow coastal strip, where most Finns live. The capital and largest city, Helsinki, is here. The Åland Islands lie in the entrance to the Gulf of Bothnia. Most of the interior is a beautiful wooded plateau, with more than 60,000 lakes. The Saimaa area is Europe's largest inland water system. A third of Finland lies within the Arctic Circle; this 'land of the midnight sun' is called Lappi (Lapland).

Forests (birch, pine, and spruce) cover 60% of Finland. The vegetation becomes more and more sparse to the north, until it merges into Arctic tundra.

Area 338,145 sq km [130,558 sq mi]
Population 5,231,000
Capital (population) Helsinki (937,000)
Government Multiparty republic
Ethnic groups Finnish 93%, Swedish 6%
Languages Finnish and Swedish (both official)
Religions Evangelical Lutheran 89%
Currency Euro = 100 cents
Website www.government.fi

CLIMATE

Finland has short, warm summers; Helsinki's July average is 17°C [63°F]. In Lapland, the temperatures are lower, and in June the sun never sets. Winters are long and cold; Helsinki's January average is 26°C [21°F]. The North Atlantic Drift keeps the Arctic coasts free of ice.

HISTORY

In the 8th century, Finnish-speaking settlers forced the Lapps to the north. Between 1150 and 1809, Finland was under Swedish rule. The close links between the countries continue today.

Swedish remains an official language in Finland and one of the legacies of this period is a Swedish-speaking minority of 6% of the total population. In some localities on the south and west coasts, Swedish speakers are in the majority and Åland, an island closer to the Swedish coast than to Finland, is a self-governing province. Many towns use both Finnish and Swedish names. For example, Helsinki is Helsingfors, and Turku is Åbo in Swedish. Finnish bears little relation to the Swedish or any other Scandinavian language. It is closest to Magyar, the language of Hungary.

Lutheranism arrived in the 16th century. Wars between Sweden and Russia devastated Finland. Following the Northern War (1700–21), Russia gained much Finnish land. In the Napoleonic Wars, Russia conquered Finland and in 1809, it became an independent grand duchy of the Russian Empire, though the Russian tsar was its grand duke. Nationalist feelings developed during the 19th century, but in 1899 Russia sought to enforce its culture on the Finns. In 1903, the Russian governor suspended the constitution and became dictator. After much resistance, self-government was restored in 1906. Finland proclaimed its

Finland became a full member of EFTA in 1986, in a decade in which its economy was growing rapidly.

POLITICS

In 1992 Finland, which after the fall of the Soviet Union no longer needed to remain neutral, applied for membership of the European Union (EU). In 1994 the Finnish people voted in favour of membership of the EU, and the country joined on 1 January 1995. On 1 January 2002 the euro became Finland's sole unit of currency. Finland has also discussed the possibility of joining NATO. However, polls since the events of 11 September 2001 suggest that the majority of Finns favour non-alliance. In 2000 elections Tarja Halonen became Finland's first female president, and she was re-elected in 2006.

ECONOMY

Although the fall of the Soviet Union caused a major recession, Finland recovered rapidly and has a prosperous economy. Engineering, high technology electronics, and paper and wood products are the major sectors and the largest exports. Within these, shipbuilding and mobile telephones are particularly important. Forests are Finland's most valuable natural resource, and most other raw materials are imported. Farming employs less than 5% of the workforce.

independence in 1917 after the Russian Revolution and the collapse of the Russian Empire. In 1919, it adopted a republican constitution. During World War II the Soviet Union declared war on Finland and took the southern part of Karelia, where 12% of the Finnish people lived. Finland allied itself to Germany and Finnish troops regained southern Karelia. At the end of the war, Russia regained southern Karelia and other parts of Finland, which also had to pay massive reparations to the Soviet Union.

After World War II, Finland pursued a policy of neutrality to placate the Soviets, but also strengthened its links with other north European countries and became an associate member of the European Free Trade Association (EFTA) in 1961.

HELSINKI

Capital of Finland, in the south of the country, on the Gulf of Finland. Founded in 1550 by Gustavus I (Vasa), it became the capital in 1812. It has two universities (1849, 1908), a cathedral (1852), museums and art galleries. The commercial and administrative centre of the country, it is Finland's largest port. Industries include shipbuilding, engineering, food processing, ceramics, textiles.

FRANCE

The colours of this flag originated during the French Revolution of 1789. The red and blue are said to represent Paris, while the white represented the monarchy. The present design was adopted in 1794, and is meant to symbolize republican principles.

The Republic of France is the largest country in Western Europe. The scenery is extremely varied. The Vosges Mountains overlook the Rhine Valley in the north-east, the Jura Mountains and the Alps form the borders with Switzerland and Italy in the south-east, while the Pyrenees straddle France's border with Spain. The only large highland area entirely within France is the Massif Central between the Rhône-Saône Valley and the basin of Aquitaine. This dramatic area, covering one-sixth of the country, has peaks rising to more than 1,800 m [5,900 ft]. Volcanic activity dating back 10 to 30 million years ago appears in the form of steep-sided volcanic plugs. Brittany (Bretagne) and Normandy (Normandie) form a scenic hill region. Fertile lowlands cover most of northern France, including the densely populated Paris Basin. Another major lowland area, the Aquitanian Basin, is in the south-west, while the Rhône-Saône Valley and extensive Mediterranean lowlands are in the south-east.

Area 551,500 sq km [212,934 sq mi]
Population 60,876,000
Capital (population) Paris (9,630,000)
Government Multiparty republic
Ethnic groups Celtic, Latin, Arab, Teutonic, Slavic
Languages French (official)
Religions Roman Catholic 85%, Islam 8%, others
Currency Euro = 100 cents
Website www.elysee.fr

CLIMATE

The climate varies from west to east and from north to south. The west comes under the moderating influence of the Atlantic Ocean, giving generally mild weather. To the east, summers are warmer and winters colder. The climate also becomes warmer as one travels from north to south. The Mediterranean Sea coast experiences hot, dry summers and mild, moist winters. The Alps, Jura and Pyrenees mountains have snowy winters. Winter sports centres are found in all three areas. Large glaciers occupy high valleys in the Alps.

HISTORY

The Romans conquered France, then known as Gaul, in the 50s BC. Roman rule began to decline in the 5th century AD. In 486, the Frankish realm, as France was by then called, became independent under a Christian king, Clovis. In 800 Charlemagne, who had been king of the Franks since 768, became emperor of the

Romans. Through conquest, his empire extended from central Italy to Denmark, and from eastern Germany to the Atlantic Ocean. However, in 843, the empire was divided into three parts and the area of France contracted.

After the Norman invasion of England in 1066, large areas of France came under English rule. By 1453, after the Hundred Years' War, France drove most of the English out. In this war, the French kings lost much power to French nobles, but Louis XI, who reigned from 1461 to 1483, laid the foundations for absolute rule by French kings.

France later became a powerful monarchy, but the French Revolution (1789–99) ended absolute rule by

French kings. In 1799 Napoleon Bonaparte took power and fought a series of brilliant military campaigns before his final defeat in 1815. The monarchy was restored until 1848, when the Second Republic was founded. In 1852, Napoleon's nephew became Napoleon III, but the Third Republic was established in 1875. France was the scene of much fighting during World War I (1914–18) and World War II (1939–45), causing great loss of life and much damage to the economy.

Post-war aid from the United States started a revival in its economy, but Communist-led strikes often crippled production. France also faced growing support for independence movements in its overseas empire. After a bitter war, France withdrew from French Indo-China in 1954 and then faced a long and costly struggle in Algeria, finally ending

PARIS

The capital of France is situated on the River Seine. When the Romans took Paris in 52 BC, it was a small village on the Ile de la Cité on the Seine. Under their rule it became an important administrative centre.

During the 14th century Paris rebelled against the Crown and declared itself an independent commune. It suffered further civil disorder during the Hundred Years' War. In the 16th century, it underwent fresh expansion, its architecture strongly influenced by the Italian Renaiassance. In the reign of Louis XIII, Cardinal Richelieu established Paris as the cultural and political centre of Europe. The French Revolution began in Paris when the Bastille was stormed by crowds in 1789. Under Emperor Napoleon I the city began to assume its present-day form. The work of modernization was continued under Napoleon III, when Baron Haussmann was commissioned to plan the boulevards, bridges and parks. Although occupied during the Franco-Prussian War (1870–71) and again in World War II, Paris was not badly damaged. The city proper consists of the Paris department, Ville de Paris. Its many famous buildings and landmarks include the Eiffel Tower, Arc de Triomphe, the Louvre, Notre Dame and the Pompidou Centre. Paris is an important European cultural, commercial and communications centre and is noted for its fashion industry and for the manufacture of luxury articles.

with Algeria's independence in 1962. The problems in Algeria caused considerable unrest in France in the 1950s and, in 1958, De Gaulle was recalled to power as prime minister. His government prepared a new constitution, establishing the Fifth Republic. It gave the president greater executive powers and reduced the power of parliament. The Electoral College elected De Gaulle as president for a seven-year term.

De Gaulle gave independence to many of its overseas territories and made France a major player in an alliance of western European nations. In 1957, France became a founder member of the European Economic Community (EEC). De Gaulle opposed British membership in 1963, considering that Britain's links with the United States would give it too much influence in Europe's economy, but his popularity waned in the late 1960s when huge student demonstrations and workers' strikes paralyzed the country and he resigned as president in 1969. His successor, Georges Pompidou, changed course in foreign affairs by re-establishing closer contacts with the United States and supporting the entry of Britain into the EEC.

POLITICS

Rapid urban growth has resulted in overcrowding and the growth of poorly built districts to house immigrants, especially those from North Africa. The 4 million underprivileged workers from Africa's Maghreb region became a major political issue in the 1990s, leading to political successes in some areas for the extreme right. Other problems faced by France include unemployment, pollution and the growing proportion of elderly people.

A socialist government under Lionel Jospin was elected in 1997. He increased the minimum wage, shortened the working week, and adopted the euro. However, in 2002 centre-right parties won a resounding victory and Jean-Pierre Raffarin replaced Jospin as Prime Minister. In 2003 the government angered the US and some of its EU allies by opposing the invasion of Iraq, arguing that the UN weapons inspectors should be given more time to search for weapons of mass destruction. Some US congressmen called for a boycott of French goods, and the number of US tourists to France fell.

A 'no' vote in the referendum on the European constitution in May 2005 led to the resignation of Raffarin and further decline in the relationship between President Jacques Chirac and UK Prime Minister Tony Blair over the UK rebate and EU subsidies for French farmers.

Unemployment is a major problem, particularly among the young. 2006 attempts to liberalize the labour market led to widespread rioting. In 2007 elections the right-wing candidate Nicolas Sarkozy became president, promising pro-market reforms and tax cuts to boost economic growth.

ECONOMY

France is one of the world's most developed countries. Its post-war economic growth was built on a high level of state control and national ownership of major industries. Since the 1980s the country has mostly made the transition to a free market system, but adjustments have been difficult. The government retains major stakes in sectors such as energy, defence, transport and telecommunications. In addition to services and design, France has managed to maintain a large manufacturing sector. Major manufactures include aircraft, cars, chemicals, electronic products, machinery, metal products, processed food, steel and textiles. Some natural resources are exploited, including bauxite, coal, iron ore, natural gas, and potash.

Agriculture employs only about 2% of the people, but France is the largest producer of farm products in Western Europe, producing most of its own food and extensive exports. Wheat, livestock and dairy, and wine production are all of major importance. Fishing and forestry are significant industries. Tourism is a major source of income, and France is a popular year-round destination both for its cities and its countryside.

MONACO

The tiny Principality of Monaco consists of a narrow strip of coastline and a rocky peninsula on the French Riviera. Like the rest of the Riviera, it has mild, moist winters and dry, sunny summers. Average temperatures range from 10°C [50°F] in January to 24°C [75°F] in July. The average annual rainfall is about 800 mm [31 in].

Area 1 sq km [0.4 sq mi]
Population 33,000
Capital (population) Monaco (30,000)
Government Constitutional monarchy
Religions Roman Catholic 62%, Protestant 30%
Currency Euro = 100 cents
Website www.visitmonaco.com

The Genoese from northern Italy gained control of Monaco in the 12th century and, from 1297, it has been ruled for most of the time by the Genoese Grimaldi family. Monaco attracted little attention until the late 19th century when it developed into a major tourist resort. World attention was focused on Monaco in 1956 when Prince Rainier III of Monaco married the actress Grace Kelly. Their son, Prince Albert, became ruler upon Rainier's death in 2005. The country's wealth comes mainly from banking, finance, gambling and tourism. There are three casinos, a marine museum, a zoo and botanical gardens. It also stages the Monte Carlo Rally and the Monaco Grand Prix. Manufactures include chemicals, electronic goods and plastics. In 2001, France threatened to break its ties with Monaco unless it revised its legal system and prevented money laundering.

FRENCH GUIANA

French Guiana flies the French flag. The colours originated during the French Revolution of 1789. The red and blue are said to represent Paris, while the white represented the monarchy. The present design was adopted in 1794, and is meant to symbolize republican principles.

French Guiana is a French overseas department and the smallest country in mainland South America. The coastal plain is swampy in places, but dry areas are cultivated, particularly near the capital, Cayenne. The River Maroni forms the border with Suriname, and the River Oyapock its eastern border with Brazil. Inland lies a plateau, with the low Tumuchumac Mountains in the south. Most of the rivers run north towards the Atlantic Ocean.

Rainforest covers approximately 90% of the land and contains valuable hardwood species. Mangrove swamps line parts of the coast; other areas are covered by tropical savanna.

Area 90,000 sq km [34,749 sq mi]
Population 200,000
Capital (population) Cayenne (51,000)
Government Overseas department of France
Ethnic groups Black or Mulatto 66%, East Indian/Chinese and Amerindian 12%, White 12%, others 10%
Languages French (official)
Religions Roman Catholic
Currency Euro = 100 cents
Website www.guyane.pref.gouv.fr

French merchants founded Cayenne in 1637. The area became a French colony in the late 17th century, with a plantation economy dependent on African slaves. It

CLIMATE

French Guiana has a hot equatorial climate with high temperatures throughout the year. Rainfall is heavy, especially between December and June, but it is dry between August and October. North-east trade winds blow across the country all year round.

HISTORY

The first people to live in what is now French Guiana were Amerindians. Today only a few of them survive in the interior. The first Europeans to explore the coast arrived in 1500 and they were followed by adventurers seeking El Dorado. The French were the first settlers in 1604 and

CENTRE SPATIAL GUYANAIS (CSG)

In 1964 the French Government chose Kourou as a satellite-launching base. An agreement in 1975 led to the newly formed European Space Agency (ESA) sharing the facility in return for financial aid. The ESA now funds two-thirds of the CSG's annual budget. The CSG also counts among its clients industries from Brazil, Canada, India, Japan and the United States. Kourou's geographical position makes it ideal for satellite launching. It is possible to launch both eastwards and northwards over the sea, without encountering populated areas meaning that the risks to human life are negligible.

were introduced to work the land. From the time of the French Revolution, France used the colony as a penal settlement, and between 1852 and 1945 the country was notorious for the harsh treatment of prisoners. Captain Alfred Dreyfus was imprisoned on the famed Île du Diable, Devil's Island.

POLITICS

In 1946, French Guiana became an overseas department of France, and in 1974 it also became an administrative region. An independence movement developed in the 1980s, but most of the people want to retain links with France and continue to obtain financial aid to develop their territory.

ECONOMY

Although it has rich forest and mineral resources, such as bauxite (aluminium ore), French Guiana is a developing country with high unemployment. It depends greatly on France for money to run its services and the government is the country's biggest employer. Since 1975, Kourou has been the European Space Agency's rocket-launching site and has earned money for France by sending communications satellites into space.

The main industries are fishing, forestry, gold mining and agriculture. Crops include bananas, cassava, rice and sugar cane. French Guiana exports shrimps, timber and rosewood essence.

remained French except for a brief period in the early 19th century. Slavery was abolished in 1848, and Asian labourers

DEVIL'S ISLAND (ÎLE DU DIABLE)

The smallest island of the three Iles du Salut off the coast of French Guiana. A notorious French penal colony from 1852 to 1945 and most famous for the prison and the harsh treatment of its inmates whether they be political prisoners or murderers. Few prisoners made it off the island due to the high levels of disease and escape was almost impossible. The publicity surrounding the case of Captain Alfred Dreyfus in 1894 brought the horrors of this prison to the fore.

CAYENNE

Capital and chief port of French Guiana, on the Atlantic coast. Founded in 1643 and named after an Indian Chief. Places of interest include the cathedral, the ruined 17th century Fort Cépérou,Hôtel de Ville and museums of local history.

GABON

Gabon's flag was adopted in 1960 when the country became independent from France. The central yellow stripe symbolizes the Equator which runs through Gabon. The green stands for the country's forests. The blue symbolizes the sea.

The Gabonese Republic lies on the Equator in west-central Africa. In area, it is a little larger than the United Kingdom, with a coastline 800 km [500 mi] long. Behind the narrow, partly lagoon-lined coastal plain, the land rises to hills, plateaux and mountains divided by deep valleys carved by the River Ogooué and its tributaries.

Dense rainforest covers about 75% of Gabon, with tropical savanna in the east and south. The forests teem with wildlife, and Gabon has several national parks and wildlife reserves.

Area 267,668 sq km [103,347 sq mi]
Population 1,425,000
Capital (population) Libreville (362,000)
Government Multiparty republic
Ethnic groups Bantu tribes: Fang, Bandjabi, Bapounou, Eshira, Myene, Nzebi, Obamba and Okande
Languages French (official), Fang, Myene, Nzebi, Bapounou/Eschira, Bandjabi
Religions Christianity 75%, animist, Islam
Currency CFA franc = 100 centimes
Website www.senat.ga

CLIMATE
Most of Gabon has an equatorial climate. There are high temperatures and humidity throughout the year. The rainfall is heavy and the skies are often cloudy.

HISTORY
Explorers from Portugal reached the Gabon coast in the 1470s, and the area later became a source of slaves.

In 1839 France established the first European settlement. In 1849 freed slaves founded Libreville. Gabon became a French colony in the 1880s and achieved full independence in 1960.

Léon Mba was Gabon's first president from 1960 to 1967. In 1964, an attempted coup was put down when French troops intervened and crushed the revolt. Following the death of Léon Mba in 1967, Bernard-Albert Bongo became president. He later renamed himself El Hadj Omar Bongo, and made Gabon a one-party state in 1968.

POLITICS
Free elections took place in 1990. The Gabonese Democratic Party (PDG) won a majority in the National Assembly.

RIVER OGOOUÉ (OGOWE)
The main river of Gabon, its basin drains nearly the entire country. Some of its tributaries can be found in Cameroon the Republic of Congo, and Equatorial Guinea. The Ogooué is about 900 km [560 mi] in length, rising in the north-west of the Bateke Plateau. It empties into the Gulf of Guinea, south of Port Gentil. The delta is approximately 100 km [62 mi] long and 100 km wide. The total water basin is 223,856 sq km [86,431sq mi], and is largely made up of forest.

President Bongo, of the PDG, won the presidential elections in 1993, although accusations of fraud and corruption led to riots in Libreville. The international community condemned Bongo for his harsh suppression of popular demonstrations. He was re-elected in 1998. In 2003, constitutional changes enabled Bongo to stand as president as many times as he wished. In November 2005 he was again elected president. Despite the opposition's protests of unfairness, the elections were deemed acceptable by international observers. Opposition parties remain weak.

ECONOMY

Gabon's abundant natural resources include its forests, oil and gas deposits near Port Gentil, and manganese and uranium. These mineral deposits make Gabon one of Africa's wealthiest countries. However, oil production has begun to decline.

Agriculture still employs about 75% of the workforce, most farmers producing little more than they need to support their families. Crops include bananas, cassava, maize and sugar cane. Cocoa and coffee are grown for export. Other exports include oil, manganese, timber and wood products and uranium.

BANTU

Group of African languages generally considered as forming part of the Benue-Congo branch of the Niger-Congo family. Swahili, Xhosa, and Zulu are among the most widely spoken of the several hundred Bantu languages spoken from the Congo Basin to South Africa, and almost all are tone languages, that is to say languages that use pitch to signal a difference in meaning between words. There are more than 70 million speakers of Bantu.

LIBREVILLE

Capital and largest city of Gabon, at the mouth of the River Gabon, on the Gulf of Guinea. Founded by the French in 1843, and named Libreville (French for Freetown) in 1849, it was initially a refuge for escaped slaves. The city expanded with the development of the country's minerals and is now also an administrative centre. Places of interest include the Musée des Arts et Traditions, the French cultural centre, the presidential palace, St Marie's Cathedral, the Eglise St Michel with its carved wooden columns, Nkembo, the Arboretum de Sibang and two cultural villages. Other industries include timber (hardwoods), palm oil and rubber.

GAMBIA, THE

The colours represent features of the Gambian landscape. Green symbolizes the land and agricultural produce. Blue stands for the River Gambia, a vital trade route. Red represents the hot African sun. The two white bands stand for peace and unity.

The Republic of the Gambia is the smallest country in mainland Africa. It consists of a narrow strip of land bordering the River Gambia. The Gambia is almost entirely enclosed by Senegal, except along the short Atlantic coastline. The land is flat near the sea.

Mangrove swamps line the river banks. Much tropical savanna has been cleared for farming. The Gambia is rich in wildlife and has six national parks and reserves as well as several forest parks.

Area 11,295 sq km [4,361 sq mi]
Population 1,642,000
Capital (population) Banjul (42,000)
Government Military regime
Ethnic groups Mandinka 42%, Fula 18%, Wolof 16%, Jola 10%, Serahuli 9%, others
Languages English (official), Mandinka, Wolof, Fula
Religions Islam 90%, Christianity 9%, traditional beliefs 1%
Currency Dalasi = 100 butut
Website www.gambia.gm

CLIMATE

The Gambia has hot and humid summers, but between November and May temperatures drop to around 16°C [61°F]. In the summer, moist winds heading south-west bring rain, which is heaviest on the coast.

HISTORY

Portuguese mariners reached Gambia's coast in 1455, when the area was part of the Mali empire. In the 16th century, Portuguese and English slave traders operated in the area. English traders bought rights to trade on the River Gambia in 1588, and in 1664 the English established a settlement on an island in the river estuary. In 1765, the British founded a colony called Senegambia, which included parts of present-day Gambia and Senegal.

In 1783, Britain handed this colony over to France. During the 1860s and 1870s, Britain and France discussed the

MANGROVE

Common name for any one of 120 species of tropical trees or shrubs found in marine swampy areas. Also known as coastal woodland, tidal forest and mangrove forest.Its stilt-like aerial roots, which arise from the branches and hang down into the water, produce a thick undergrowth, useful in the reclaiming of land along tropical coasts. The composition varies greatly from region to region. Even within the same delta the composition of the mangrove can vary substantially according to the conditions of salinity, tidal system and substrate (soil foundation). Some species also have roots that rise up out of the water. It grows to a height of 20 m [70 ft].

exchange of the Gambia for some other French territory. No agreement was reached and Britain made the Gambia a British colony in 1888. It remained under British rule until it achieved full independence in 1965 with Dawda Jawara as prime minister. In 1970 the Gambia became a republic.

POLITICS

Relations between the French-speaking Senegalese and the English-speaking Gambians are a major political issue. In 1981 a coup attempt in the Gambia was put down with Senegalese help In 1982 the Gambia and Senegal set up a defence alliance called the Confederation of Senegambia. It was dissolved in 1989.

In 1992, Jawara was re-elected as president for a fifth term. In July 1994, he was overthrown in a military coup and fled into exile. The coup was led by Yahya Jammeh who was elected president in 1996. His regime faced charges of political repression. In 2001, Jammeh lifted the ban on opposition parties and was re-elected, though he is still criticized for impinging on press freedom. In 2006 he claimed election victory yet again.

ECONOMY

Agriculture is the main activity, employing more than 80% of the workforce. The main food crops include cassava, millet and sorghum. Peanuts are the chief export, and fluctuations in peanut prices seriously affect the economy. The money sent home by Gambians living abroad is a vital source of income. Tourism is a growing industry. In 2004 the government claimed large oil discoveries, but these have yet to be exploited.

RIVER GAMBIA

The dominant feature of the Gambia, rising in the Fouta Djallon highlands in the Republic of Guinea and flowing to the Atlantic Ocean. The river valley runs along the entire length and breadth of the country. It provides precious sanctuary for many birds and fish through the creeks that adjoin it, these areas are very important to bird watchers and lovers of nature as a whole. The river is also the habitat for much of the country's wildlife such as hippopotamus and crocodiles.

BANJUL

Capital of the Gambia, the city lies on St Mary's Island, where the River Gambia enters the Atlantic Ocean. It was founded as a trading post by the British in 1816 and originally named Bathurst after Henry Bathurst, the secretary of the British Colonial Office. Banjul is Gambia's chief port and commercial centre. The main industry is groundnut processing, though tourism is growing rapidly.

157

GEORGIA

The Republic of Georgia adopted a new flag in 2004. The flag had been in use some 500 years before as that of the medieval Georgian kingdom. It was subsequently used as the official symbol of the political party –United National Movement.

Georgia is located on the borders of Europe and Asia, facing the Black Sea. The land is rugged, with the Caucasus Mountains forming its northern border. The highest mountain in this range, Mount Elbrus (5,642 m [18,506 ft]), lies over the border in Russia.

Lower ranges run through southern Georgia, through which pass the borders with Turkey and Armenia. The Black Sea coastal plains are in the west. In the east a low plateau extends into Azerbaijan. The main river in the east is the River Kura, on which the capital Tbilisi stands.

Area 69,700 sq km [26,911 sq mi]
Population 4,661,000
Capital (population) Tbilisi (1,406,000)
Government Multiparty republic
Ethnic groups Georgian 70%, Armenian 8%, Russian 6%, Azeri 6%, Ossetiam 3%, Greek 2%, Abkhaz 2%, others
Languages Georgian (official), Russian
Religions Georgian Orthodox 65%, Islam 11%, Russian Orthodox 10%, Amenian Apostolic 8%
Currency Lari = 100 tetri
Website www.parliament.ge

CLIMATE

The Black Sea plains have hot summers and mild winters, when the temperature seldom drops below freezing. Rainfall is heavy, but inland Tbilisi has moderate rainfall, with the heaviest rains in the spring and early summer.

HISTORY

The first Georgian state was set up nearly 2,000 years ago and, by the 3rd century BC, most of what is now Georgia was united as a single kingdom. For much of its history, Georgia was ruled by various conquerors. For example, between about 60 BC and the 11th century, the area was ruled successively by Romans, Persians, Byzantines, Arabs and Seljuk Turks. Christianity was introduced in AD 330 and most Georgians are now members of the Georgian Orthodox Church. Georgia freed itself from foreign rule in the 11th and 12th centuries, but Mongol armies invaded in the 13th century. From the 16th to the 18th centuries, Iran and the Turkish Ottoman Empire struggled for control of the area.

In the late 18th century, Georgia sought the protection of Russia and, by the early 19th century was part of the Russian Empire. After the Russian Revolution of 1917, Georgia declared itself independent and was recognized by the League of Nations. However, Russian troops invaded in 1921, making Georgia part of the Soviet regime. From 1922, Georgia, Armenia and Azerbaijan were linked, forming the Transcaucasian Republic. But, in 1936, the territories became separate republics within the Soviet Union. Renowned for their longevity, the people of Georgia are famous for producing Josef Stalin, who was born in Gori, 65 km [40 mi] northwest of the capital Tbilisi. Stalin ruled the Soviet Union from 1929 until his death in 1953.

and Abkhazia signed a peace accord and agreed to the safe return of refugees. In 2002, Russian and Georgian troops attacked Chechen rebels in Pankisi Gorge in north-eastern Georgia. US officials believed that Taliban fighters from Afghanistan and other Islamic terrorists had also moved into this region. In 2004 Mikhail Saakashvili was elected president, but his authority was challenged by separatists in the three minority regions. In 2006 Saakashvili criticised Russian support for the separatists as relations with Russia worsened.

POLITICS

A maverick among the Soviet republics, Georgia was the first to declare its independence after the Baltic states (April 1991) and deferred joining the Commonwealth of Independent States (CIS) until 1993.

In 1991 Zviad Gamsakhurdia, a non-Communist who had been democratically elected president of Georgia in 1990, was besieged in Tblisi's KGB headquarters by rebel forces. They represented widespread opposition to his government's policies, ranging from the economy to the imprisonment of his opponents. In January 1992, following the break-up of the Soviet Union, Gamsakhurdia fled the country and a military council took power.

Georgia contains three regions of minority peoples. In South Ossetia, in north-central Georgia, civil war broke out in the early 1990s when nationalists demanded the right to set up their own governments. Abkhazia, in the northwest, proclaimed its sovereignty in 1994 with fierce fighting continuing until the late 1990s. Adjaria or Adzharia, in the south-west, gained autonomy recognized in Georgia's constitution in 2000.

In March 1992 Eduard Shevardnadze, former Soviet Foreign Minister, was named head of state. He was elected, unopposed, later that year. Shevardnadze was re-elected in 1995 and 2000, but Georgia faced mounting problems which threatened its stability. In 2001, Georgia

ECONOMY

Georgia is a developing country. Agriculture is important. Major products include barley, citrus fruits, grapes for wine-making, maize, tea, tobacco and vegetables. Food processing, and silk- and perfume-making are other important activities. Sheep and cattle are reared.

Barium ore, coal, copper and manganese are mined, and tourism is a major industry on the Black Sea coast. Georgia's mountains have huge potential for hydroelectric power, but most electricity is imported from Russia or Ukraine.

TBILISI (TIFLIS)

Largest city and capital of Georgia, on the upper River Kura. It was founded in the 5th century AD, and ruled successively by the Iranians, Byzantines, Arabs, Mongols, and Turks, before coming under Russian rule in 1801. Tbilisi's importance lies in its location on the trade route between the Black Sea and Caspian Sea. It is now the administrative and economic focus of modern Transcaucasia. Industries include chemicals, petroleum products, locomotives, electrical equipment.

GERMANY

This flag, adopted by the Federal Republic of Germany (West Germany) in 1949, became the flag of the reunified Germany in 1990. The red, black and gold colours date back to the Holy Roman Empire. They are associated with the struggle for a united Germany from the 1830s.

The Federal Republic of Germany lies in the heart of Europe. It is the fifth-largest country in Europe. Germany divides into three geographical regions: the north German plain, central highlands, and the south Central Alps.

The rivers Elbe, Weser, and Oder drain the fertile northern plain, which includes the industrial centres of Hamburg, Bremen, Hanover and Kiel. In the east, lies the capital, Berlin, and the former East German cities of Leipzig, Dresden and Magdeburg. North-west Germany (especially the Rhine, Ruhr and Saar valleys) is Germany's industrial heartland. It includes the cities of Cologne, Essen, Dortmund, Düsseldorf and Duisburg.

The central highlands include the Harz Mountains and the cities of Munich, Frankfurt, Stuttgart, Nuremberg and Augsburg.

Southern Germany rises to the Bavarian Alps on the border with Switzerland and Germany's highest peak, Zugspitze, (2,963 m [9,721 ft]). The Black Forest, overlooking the Rhine valley, is a major tourist attraction. The region is drained by the River Danube.

Area 357,022 sq km [137, 846 sq mi]
Population 82,422,000
Capital (population) Berlin (3,387,000)
Government Federal multiparty republic
Ethnic groups German 92%, Turkish 3%, Serbo-Croatian, Italian, Greek, Polish, Spanish
Languages German (official)
Religions Protestant (mainly Lutheran) 34%, Roman Catholic 34%, Islam 4%, others
Currency Euro = 100 cents
Website www.deutschland.de

CLIMATE

Germany has a temperate climate. The north-west is warmed by the North Sea. The Baltic lowlands in the north-east are cooler. In the south, the climate becomes more continental.

HISTORY

Around 3,000 years ago, various tribes from northern Europe began to settle in what is now Germany, occupying the valleys of the Rhine and the Danube. The Romans called this region Germania after the Germani, the name of one of the tribes. In the 5th century, the Germanic tribes attacked the Roman Empire and plundered Rome. The western part of the Roman Empire split up into several kingdoms, the largest of which was the Kingdom of the Franks.

In 486, Clovis, a Frankish king, extended his rule to include both Gaul (now France) and western Germany, introducing Christianity and other Roman practices. The Frankish ruler, Charlemagne, came to power in 768 and established his capital at Aachen. From 962, much of the German Empire became part of what was later known as the Holy Roman Empire under King Otto II of Germany. In 1517, a German monk, Martin Luther, began to criticize many of the practices and teachings of the Roman Catholic Church. A Protestant movement called the Reformation soon attracted much support. By the early 17th century, the people of Germany were deeply divided by political and religious rivalries. The Thirty Years' War, which began in 1618 and lasted for 30 years, ravaged much of the country with Germany losing territory to France and Sweden, and itself being split into hundreds of states and free cities. It took almost 200 years for Germany to recover

In the 17th century, the Hohenzollern family began to assume importance in eastern Germany, gradually extending their power and building a professional civil service and army.

Prussia stayed out of the Napoleonic wars until 1806, but following defeats by Napoleon, lost its territories west of the Elbe. Prussia did help to defeat Napoleon's armies at the battles of Leipzig (1813) and Waterloo (1815) and following the Napoleonic wars, gained the Rhineland, Westphalia and much of Saxony.

In the early 1860s, the Prussian king, Wilhelm I, appointed Otto von Bismarck as prime minister. Bismarck set about strengthening Prussian power through three short wars. One conflict led to the acquisition of Schleswig-Holstein from Denmark, another led to the annexation of territory from Austria. The third was the Franco-Prussian War (1870–1), following which victorious Germany was granted Alsace and part of Lorraine. In 1871, Wilhelm I was crowned the first Kaiser of the new German Empire and Bismarck became the chancellor and head of government. Bismarck sought to consolidate German power and avoid conflict with Austria-Hungary and Russia, but was forced to resign in 1890 when Wilhelm II wanted to establish his own authority and extend Germany's influence. Wilhelm's ambitions led Britain and France to establish the Entente Cordiale in 1904, with Britain and Russia signing a similar agreement in 1907. This left Europe divided, with Germany, Austria-Hungary and Italy forming the Triple Alliance.

After Germany and its allies were defeated in World War I, Germany became a republic and lost territories. Overseas, it lost its colonies. Germany's humiliation under the terms of the Versailles Treaty caused much resentment, made worse by the economic collapse of 1922–3. Support grew for the Nazi Party and its leader Adolf Hitler, who became chancellor in 1933. Hitler's order to invade Poland in 1939 triggered off World War II. His armies were finally defeated in 1945 and the country left in ruins. Germany was obliged to transfer the area east of the Oder and Neisse rivers to Poland and the Soviet Union. German-speaking inhabitants were expelled and the remainder of Germany was occupied by the four victorious Allied powers. In 1948, West Germany, consisting of the American, British and French zones, was proclaimed the Federal Republic of Germany with its provisional capital at Bonn, while the Soviet zone became the German Democratic Republic with its capital in East Berlin.

POLITICS

The post-war partition of Germany, together with its geographical position, made it a central focus of the Cold War. West Germany became a showpiece of the West through its phenomenal recovery and sustained growth, the so-called 'economic miracle'. It played a major part, together with France, in the revival of Western Europe through the development of the European Community and eventually the European Union. Although East Germany achieved the highest standard of living in the Soviet bloc, it fell short of Western Europe. East Germany dissolved itself in 1990, at the start of the fall of Communism, and was reunited with the rest of Germany in October of that year.

Following reunification, the new country adopted the name the Federal Republic of Germany. Massive investment was needed to rebuild the East's failing infrastructure and industrial base, leading to an increased tax burden on the West. In addition, the new nation found itself funnelling aid into Eastern Europe. Germany led the EU in recognizing the independence of Slovenia, Croatia and the former Soviet republics. The transition to a free market economy in the East caused rapid de-industrialization, leading to large scale unemployment and its attendant social problems.

The creation of a unified state was far more complicated, expensive and lengthy an undertaking than envisaged when the Berlin Wall came down. In 1998 the centre-right government of Helmut Kohl, who had presided over reunification, was defeated by the left-of-centre Social Democratic Party (SPD) led by Gerhard Schröder. Schröder led an SPD-Green Party coalition which set about tackling Germany's high unemployment and sluggish economy. Following the attacks on the United States on 11 September 2001 Schröder declared Germany's support for the campaign against terrorism, although Germany opposed the invasion of Iraq in 2003. In 2005, Schröder was narrowly defeated in elections. A broad left-right coalition was set up and Angela Merkel, a conservative Christian Democrat, became Germany's first female Chancellor.

ECONOMY

Despite the problems associated with reunification, Germany still has one of the world's largest and most successful economies and is one of the largest exporters of manufactured goods. The foundation of the 'economic miracle' that led to Germany's astonishing post-war recovery was manufacturing. Germany's industrial strength was based on its coal reserves, though oil-burning and nuclear generating plants have become increasingly important since the 1970s. Lower Saxony has oilfields, while southern Germany has some hydroelectricity. In the early 2000s the government resolved to phase out nuclear power by 2020, but this plan was questioned in 2007 after oil supplies from Russia were disrupted. Mineral resources include potash and rock salt, and smaller quantities of copper, lead, tin, uranium and zinc.

The leading industrial region is the Ruhr, which produces iron and steel, chemicals and textiles. Germany is a major producer of cars, while other manufactures include electronic equipment, fertilizers, processed food, plastics, scientific instruments, ships, tools and wood and pulp products.

Agriculture employs less than 3% of the workforce, and Germany imports about a third of its food. Barley, fruits, grapes, oats, potatoes, rye, sugar beet, vegetables and wheat are grown. Beef and dairy cattle are raised, together with pigs, poultry and sheep.

BERLIN

Capital and largest city of Germany, on the River Spree, north-east Germany. Berlin was founded in the 13th century. It became the residence of the Hohenzollerns and the capital of Brandenburg, and later of Prussia. It rose to prominence as a manufacturing town and became the capital of the newly formed state of Germany in 1871. Virtually destroyed at the end of World War II, Berlin was divided into four sectors; British, French, US and Soviet. On the formation of East Germany, the Soviet sector became East Berlin, the rest West Berlin. In 1961 East Germany erected the Berlin Wall, which divided the city until 1989. On the reunification of Germany in 1990, East Berlin and West Berlin amalgamated. Sights include the Brandenberg Gate, the Kaiser Wilhelm Memorial Church and the Victory Column in the Tiergarten. Parts of the Berlin Wall remain as a monument.

GHANA

Ghana's flag has red, green and yellow bands like the flag of Ethiopia, Africa's oldest independent nation. These colours symbolize African unity. The black star is a symbol of African freedom. Ghana's flag was adopted when the country became independent in 1957.

The Republic of Ghana faces the Gulf of Guinea in West Africa. This hot country, just north of the Equator, was formerly called the Gold Coast. Behind the thickly populated southern coastal plains, which are lined with lagoons, lies a plateau region in the south-west.

Northern Ghana is drained by the Black and White Volta Rivers, which flow into Lake Volta. This lake, which has formed behind the Akosombo Dam, is one of the largest artificially created lakes in the world.

Rainforests grow in the south-west. To the north, the forests merge into savanna (tropical grassland with some woodland). More open grasslands dominate in the country's far north.

Area 238,533 sq km [92,098 sq mi]
Population 22,410,000
Capital (population) Accra (1,970,000)
Government Republic
Ethnic groups Akan 44%, Moshi-Dagomba 16%, Ewe 13%, Ga 8%, Gurma 3%, Yoruba 1%
Languages English (official), Akan, Moshi-Dagomba, Ewe, Ga
Religions Christianity 63%, traditional beliefs 21%, Islam 16%
Currency Cedi = 100 pesewas
Website www.ghana.gov.gh

CLIMATE

Ghana has a tropical climate. A cool offshore current reduces temperatures on the coast, and the north is hotter. The heaviest rains occur in the south-west. There are marked dry seasons in northern and eastern Ghana.

HISTORY

Ghana was a great African empire which flourished to the north-west of present-day Ghana between the AD 300s and 1000s. Portuguese explorers reached the area in 1471 and named it the Gold Coast. The area became a centre of the slave trade in the 17th century. The slave trade was ended in the 1860s and the British gradually took control of the area. The country became independent in 1957, and was renamed Ghana after the ancient state. Modern Ghana was the first country in the Commonwealth to be ruled by black Africans.

LAKE VOLTA

The largest artificial lake in Africa. Created in 1964 by the closure of the Akosombo Dam 100 km [60 mi] upstream from the mouth of the Volta. The reservoir covers 850,000 sq km [330,000 sq mi] and stretches 320 km [190 mi] from north to south and 400 km [250 mi] east to west. Built to provide hydroelectricity, the dam has rarely achieved full capacity as it takes 3 or 4 years of consecutive flood to fill the lake to its full capacity. The construction of the dam led to a substantial reduction in the fisheries of the Volta Delta.

MAP SCALE
0   50   100   150 km
0   50   100 miles

in 2000. The economy expanded in the 1990s, largely because the government followed World Bank policies. When Rawlings retired John Agyekum Kufuor, the leader of the opposition New Patriotic Party, defeated Rawlings' vice-president and was elected president. He was re-elected in 2004.

ECONOMY

The World Bank classifies Ghana as a 'low-income' developing country. Most people are poor farmers. Food crops include cassava, groundnuts, maize, millet, plantains, rice and yams. Cocoa is the most valuable export crop, and timber and gold are also exported. Other valuable crops include tobacco, coffee, coconuts and palm kernels.

Many small factories produce goods, such as beverages, cement and clothing, for local consumption. The aluminium smelter at Tema, a port near Accra, is the country's largest factory. There are plans to construct around 600 km [378 mi] of pipeline which will form part of the West African Gas Pipeline Project. The aim is to lessen the dependence of electricity production on hydroelectric stations. In 2007 the government announced offshore oil discoveries.

POLITICS

After independence, attempts were made to develop the economy by creating large state-owned manufacturing industries. Debt and corruption together with falls in the price of the chief export, cocoa, caused economic problems. This led to instability and frequent coups. In 1981, power was invested in a Provisional National Defence Council, led by Flight-Lieutenant Jerry Rawlings.

The government steadied the economy and introduced several new policies, including the relaxation of government controls. In 1992, a new constitution was introduced which allowed for multiparty elections. Rawlings was re-elected later that year, and served until his retirement

ACCRA

Capital and largest city of Ghana, on the Gulf of Guinea. Occupied by the Ga people since the 15th century, it became the capital of Britain's Gold Coast colony in 1875. Today it is a major port and economic centre and is increasingly popular with tourists. Industries include engineering, timber, textiles, chemicals. The principal export is cacao.

GREECE

Blue and white became Greece's national colours during the war of independence (1821–9). The nine horizontal stripes on the flag, which was finally adopted in 1970, represent the nine syllables of the battle cry 'Eleutheria i thanatos' ('Freedom or Death').

The Hellenic Republic, the official name of Greece, is a rugged country lying at the southern end of the Balkan Peninsula. Olympus (Ólimbos), at 2,917 m [9,570 ft], is the highest peak. Nearly a fifth of the land area is made up of around 2,000 islands, mainly in the Aegean Sea, east of the main peninsula, but also in the Ionian Sea to the west. Only 154 are inhabited. The island of Crete is structurally related to the main Alpine fold mountain system to which the mainland Pindos Range belongs.

Area 131,957 sq km [50,949 sq mi]
Population 10,688,000
Capital (population) Athens (3,238,000)
Government Multiparty republic
Ethnic groups Greek 98%
Languages Greek (official)
Religions Greek Orthodox 98%
Currency Euro = 100 cents
Website www.culture.gr

CLIMATE

Low-lying areas in Greece have mild, moist winters and hot, dry summers. The east coast has more than 2,700 hours of sunshine a year and only about half of the rainfall of the west. The mountains have a more severe climate, and snow lies on the higher slopes in winter.

HISTORY

Around 2,500 years ago, Greece became the birthplace of Western civilization. Crete was the centre of the Minoan civilization, an early Greek culture, between about 3000 and 1400 BC. Following the end of the related Mycaenean period on the mainland in about 1200 BC, a 'dark age' lasted until about 800 BC. In about 750 BC, the Greeks began to colonize the Mediterranean, creating wealth through trade. The city-state of Athens reached its peak in the 461-431 BC, but in 338 BC Macedonia became the dominant power. In 334–331 BC, Alexander the Great conquered south-western Asia. Greece became a Roman province in 146 BC and, in AD 365, part of the Byzantine Empire. In 1453, the Turks defeated the Byzantine Empire. But between 1821 and 1829, the Greeks defeated the Turks. The country became an independent monarchy in 1830.

GREEK ART AND ARCHITECTURE

Ancient Greek art divides into four periods: Geometric (late 11th–late 8th century BC), Archaic (late 8th century–480 BC), Classical (480–323 BC), and Hellenistic (323–27 BC). Little survives from the Geometric period. During the Archaic period stone sculpture appeared, vase painting proliferated and the human figure became a common subject. In the Classical period public art was used to display city-states' wealth. The Hellenistic period is noted for increasingly dramatic works.

GREECE

little progress has been made. Territorial and boundary disputes in the Aegean Sea are the most problematic issues.

ECONOMY

Manufacturing is important. Products include processed food, cement, chemicals, metal products, textiles and tobacco. Lignite, bauxite and chromite are mined.

Farmland and grazing land cover about 75% of the land. Major crops include barley, grapes for wine-making, dried fruits, olives, potatoes, sugar beet and wheat. Poultry, sheep, goats, pigs and cattle are raised. The vital tourist industry is based on the warm climate, beautiful scenery, and the historic sites dating back to the days of classical Greece.

After World War II (1939–45), when Germany had occupied Greece, a civil war broke out between Communist and nationalist forces. This war ended in 1949. and a military dictatorship took power in 1967. The monarchy was abolished in 1973 and democratic government restored in 1974.

POLITICS

Greece joined the European Community in 1981. Despite efforts to develop the economy, Greece remained one of the poorer countries in the European Union for some time. Only in the 2000s has growth improved, though the government has struggled to control expenditure and national debt. The cost of hosting the 2004 Olympic Games has caused particular problems. Greece adopted the euro as the sole unit of currency on 1 January 2002.

Relations with Turkey have long been difficult. In 1999, the two countries helped each other when both were hit by major earthquakes. In 2000 Greece and Turkey signed agreements aimed at improving relations between them, but

ATHENS (ATHÍNAI)

Capital and largest city of Greece, situated on the Saronic Gulf. The ancient city was built around the Acropolis, a fortified citadel, and was the greatest artistic and cultural centre in ancient Greece, gaining importance after the Persian Wars (500–449 BC). Athens prospered under Cimon and Pericles during the 5th century BC and provided a climate in which the great classical works of philosophy and drama were created. The most noted artistic treasures are the Parthenon (438 BC), the Erechtheum (406 BC), and the Theatre of Dionysus (500 BC, the oldest of the Greek theatres). Modern Athens and its port of Piraeus form a major Mediterranean transport and economic centre. Overcrowding and severe air pollution are damaging the ancient sites and the tourist industry.

167

GUATEMALA

Guatemala's flag was adopted in 1871, but its origins go back to the days of the Central American Federation (1823–39), which was set up after the break from Spain in 1821. The Federation included Costa Rica, El Salvador, Guatemala, Honduras and Nicaragua.

The Central American republic of Guatemala contains a densely populated, fertile mountain region. The capital, Guatemala City, is situated here. The highlands run east–west and contain many volcanoes. Guatemala is subject to frequent earthquakes and volcanic eruptions. Tajumulco, an inactive volcano, is the highest peak in Central America at 4,211 m [13,816 ft].

South of the highlands lie the Pacific coastal lowlands. North of the highlands is the thinly populated Caribbean plain and the vast Petén tropical forest. Guatemala's largest lake, Izabal, drains into the Caribbean Sea.

Hardwoods such as mahogany, rubber, palm, and chicozapote (from which chicle, used in chewing gum, is obtained), grow in the tropical forests in the north, with mangrove swamps on the coast. Oak and willow grow in the highlands, with fir and pine at higher levels. Much of the Pacific plains is farmland.

Area 108,889 sq km [42,042 sq mi]
Population 12,294,000
Capital (population) Guatemala City (3,242,000)
Government Republic
Ethnic groups Ladino (mixed Hispanic and Amerindian) 55%, Amerindian 43%, others 2%
Languages
Spanish (official), Amerindian languages
Religions Christianity, indigenous Mayan beliefs
Currency US dollar; Quetzal = 100 centavos
Website
www.visitguatemala.com/site/home/index_3.html

HISTORY

Between AD 300 and 900, the Quiché branch of the Maya ruled much of Guatemala, but inexplicably abandoned their cities on the northern plains. The Quiché ruins at Tikal are the tallest temple pyramids in the Americas.

In 1523–4, the Spanish conquistador Pedro de Alvarado defeated the native tribes. In 1821, Guatemala became independent. From 1823–39, it formed part of the Central American Federation. Var-

CLIMATE

Guatemala lies in the tropics. The low-lands are hot and wet, with the central mountain region being cooler and drier. Guatemala City, at about 1,500 m [5,000 ft] above sea level, has a pleasant, warm climate, with a marked dry season between November and April.

GUATEMALA CITY (CIUDAD GUATEMALA)

The capital of Guatemala lies on a plateau in the Sierra Madre. It is the largest city in Central America. Founded in 1776, the city was the capital of the Central American Federation from 1823–39. It was badly damaged by earthquakes in 1917–18 and 1976. Industries include mining, furniture, textiles, handicrafts.

MAP SCALE
0 50 100 km
0 50 miles

sion was set up to bring the killers to justice. Progress has been very slow, and no trials had occurred by 2007. Alfonso Portillo became president in 1999 elections, despite admitting to killing two men. Oscar Berger was elected president in 2004.

ECONOMY

The World Bank classifies Guatemala as a 'lower-middle-income' developing country. Inequalities are severe. Agriculture employs nearly half of the workforce and coffee, sugar, bananas and beef are the leading exports. Other important crops include cardamom and cotton. Maize is the chief food crop, but is insufficient to feed the population, and Guatemala is dependent upon food imports.

Tourism and manufacturing are growing in importance. Manufactures include processed farm products, textiles, wood products, and handicrafts. Money sent home by Guatemalans working in the US is the primary source of foreign income.

ious dictatorial regimes interfered in the politics of other Central American states, arousing resentment and leading to the creation of the Central American Court of Justice. In 1941, the state took over the German-owned coffee plantations. After World War II, Guatemala nationalized the remainder of its plantations.

POLITICS

In 1960, the mainly Quiché Guatemalan Revolutionary National Unity Movement (URNG) began a guerrilla war that claimed more than 200,000 lives. During the 1960s and 1970s, terrorism and political assassinations beset Guatemala. In 1976 an earthquake devastated Guatemala City and killed 22,000 people.

In 1985, Guatemala elected its first civilian president for 15 years. Alvaro Arzú Irigoyen became president in 1996 elections, and a peace agreement with the URNG ended 35 years of civil war. The vast majority of the civil war's atrocities were carried out by security forces, rather than the guerrillas, and a Truth Commis-

THE PETEN

The largest province of Guatemala, situated in the northern third of the country. it is a vast lowland region which, until recently, had only a small population and has thereby retained much of its original forest. This small population is due partly to the hot, moist climate and harsh dry season, and partly to the presence of anti-government guerrilla armies during the civil war. The Peten's forests, along with areas of Belize and southern Mexico, make up the largest unbroken stretch of tropical forest north of the Brazilian Amazon.

GUINEA

Guinea's flag was adopted when the country became independent from France in 1958. It uses the colours of the flag of Ethiopia, Africa's oldest nation, which symbolize African unity. The red represents work, the yellow justice and the green solidarity.

The Republic of Guinea, which faces the Atlantic Ocean in West Africa, can be divided into four regions: an alluvial coastal plain, which includes the capital, Conakry; the highland region of the Fouta Djallon, the source of one of Africa's longest rivers, the Niger; the north-east savanna; and the south-east Guinea Highlands, which rise to 1,752 m [5,748 ft] at Mount Nimba.

Mangrove swamps grow along parts of the coast. Inland, the Fouta Djallon is largely open grassland. North eastern Guinea is tropical savanna, with acacia and shea scattered across the grassland. Rainforests of ebony, mahogany, and teak grow in the Guinea Highlands.

Area 245,857 sq km [94,925 sq mi]
Population 9,690,000
Capital (population) Conakry (1,465,000)
Government Multiparty republic
Ethnic groups Peuhl 40%, Malinke 30%, Soussou 20%, others 10%
Languages French (official)
Religions
Islam 85%, Christianity 8%, traditional beliefs 7%
Currency Guinean franc = 100 cauris
Website www.guinee.gov.gn

CLIMATE

Guinea has a tropical climate. Conakry on the coast has heavy rains during its relatively cool season between May and November. Hot, dry harmattan winds blow south-westwards from the Sahara in the dry season. The Fouta Djalon is cooler than the coast. The driest region is in the north-east. This region and the south-eastern highlands have greater temperature variations than on the coast.

HISTORY

The north-east Guinea plains formed part of the medieval Empire of Ghana. The Malinke formed the Mali Empire, which dominated the region in the 12th century. The Songhai Empire supplanted the Malinke in the 15th century.

Portuguese explorers arrived in the mid-15th century and the slave trade began soon afterwards. From the 17th century, other European slave traders became active in Guinea. In the early 18th century, the Fulani embarked on a *jihad* (holy war) and gained control of the Fouta Djallon. Following a series of wars, France won control in the mid-19th cen-

> ### SONGHAI
> West African empire, founded around AD 700. In 1468, Sonni Ali captured the market city of Timbuktu, and the Songhai Empire acquired control of most of the trade in western Africa. Askia Muhammad I succeeded Sonni, and further increased the stranglehold on trade routes. The Empire began to disintegrate because of factional in-fighting. The Songhai peoples still control much of the trans-Saharan trade.

2000 rebel incursions from these countries killed more than 1,000 people, caused massive population displacement, and threatened to destablilize Guinea. Conté was re-elected in 2003, although the poll was boycotted by the opposition. Despite his age and poor health Conté survived an assassination attempt in 2005. 2006 and 2007 saw mass riots protesting against his corrupt, repressive government and economic mismanagement.

ECONOMY

The World Bank classifies Guinea as a 'low-income' developing country. It is the world's second-largest producer of bauxite which accounts for 90% of its exports. Guinea has 25% of the world's known reserves.

Other natural resources include diamonds, gold, iron ore and uranium. Due to the mining industry, the rail and road infrastructure is improving. Agriculture (mainly at subsistence level) employs 78% of the workforce. Major crops include bananas, cassava, coffee, palm kernels, pineapples, rice and sweet potatoes. Cattle and other livestock are raised in highland areas.

tury and, in 1891, it made Guinea a French colony. France exploited Guinea's bauxite deposits, and mining unions developed.

In 1958, Guinea voted to become an independent republic and France severed all aid. Its first president, Sékou Touré (1958–84), adopted a Marxist programme of reform and embraced Pan-Africanism. Opposition parties were banned, and dissent brutally suppressed. In 1970, Portuguese Guinea (now Guinea-Bissau) invaded Guinea. Conakry later acted as the headquarters for independence movements in Guinea-Bissau. A military coup followed Touré's death in 1984, and Colonel Lansana Conté established the Military Committee for National Recovery (CMRN). Conté improved relations with the West and introduced free-enterprise policies.

POLITICS

Civil unrest forced the introduction of a multiparty system in 1992. Elections in 1993 confirmed Conté as president, amid claims of voting fraud. In February 1996, Conté foiled an attempted military coup. He was re-elected in 1998.

By 2000, Guinea was home to about 500,000 refugees from the wars in neighbouring Sierra Leone and Liberia. In

CONAKRY

Capital city of Guinea. Conakry is located on Tombo Island, in the Atlantic Ocean and is connected to the mainland via a causeway. Founded in 1884, then occupied by French forces in 1887, it is Guinea's largest city. It is a major port and the administrative and commercial centre of Guinea. Its economy revolves largely round the port, from which it exports alumina and bananas. Manufactures include food products, automobiles, and beverages. The city is noted for its botanical gardens.

The red symbolizes the blood shed in the liberation struggle. Yellow stands for the hot African sun. Green represents the fertile land and hope for the future. The black star represents the African continent and pays homage to the flag of Ghana, the first African colony to gain independence.

The Republic of Guinea-Bissau is a small country in West Africa. The land is mostly low-lying, with a broad, swampy, coastal plain. There are many flat offshore islands, including the Bijagós Archipelago.

Mangrove forests line the coasts, and dense rainforest covers much of the coastal plain.

Area 36,125 sq km [13,948 sq mi]
Population 1,442,000
Capital (population) Bissau (200,000)
Government Interim government
Ethnic groups Balanta 30%, Fula 20%, Manjaca 14%, Mandinga 13%, Papel 7%
Languages Portuguese (official),Crioulo
Religions Traditional beliefs 50%, Islam 45%, Christianity 5%
Currency CFA franc = 100 centimes
Website www.republica-da-guine-bissau.org

CLIMATE

The country has a tropical climate, with its dry season from December to May and its rainy season from June to November.

HISTORY

It was first visited by Portuguese navigators in 1446. From the 17th to the early 19th century, Portugal used the coast as a slave-trading base. Portugal appointed a governor to administer Guinea-Bissau and the Cape Verde Islands in 1836, but in 1879 the territories separated and Guinea-Bissau became a colony, then called Portuguese Guinea. Development was slow, partly because the territory did not attract settlers on the same scale as Portugal's much healthier African colonies of Angola and Mozambique.

In 1956, African nationalists in Portuguese Guinea and Cape Verde founded the African Party for the Independence of Guinea and Cape Verde (PAIGC). Because Portugal seemed determined to

hang on to its overseas territories, the PAIGC began a guerrilla war in 1963. By 1968, it held two-thirds of the country. In 1972, a rebel National Assembly, elected by the people in the PAIGC-controlled areas, voted to make the country independent as Guinea-Bissau.

POLITICS

In 1974, it formally achieved independence (followed by Cape Verde in 1975). The independent nation faced many problems arising from its under-developed economy and its lack of trained personnel. Guinea-Bissau's leaders favoured

BISSAU

Capital of Guinea-Bissau, near the mouth of the River Geba, western Africa. Established by the Portuguese as a slave-trading centre in 1687, Bissau became a free port in 1869. It replaced Bonama as capital in 1941. The port has recently been improved. Industries include oil processing.

on national policies and socialist reforms.

In 1991, the PAIGC voted to introduce a multiparty system. The PAIGC won the 1994 elections, and Vieira was elected president. In 1998 an army rebellion sparked a civil war. The army rebels took power in 1999, but elections were held in 1999–2000. Kumba Ialá became president in 2000 but was overthrown in a coup in 2003. Civilian government was restored in 2004. Elections in 2005 made Vieira president once again.

union with Cape Verde. This objective was abandoned in 1980, when an army coup, led by Major João Vieira, overthrew the government. The Revolutionary Council which took over opposed unification with Cape Verde; it concentrated

ECONOMY

Guinea-Bissau is a poor country. Agriculture employs more than 70% of the workforce, but most farming is at subsistence level. Major crops include beans, coconuts, groundnuts, maize and rice. Fishing is also important.

BIJAGOS ARCHIPELAGO

Formed by the prehistoric delta of the Rio Grande de Buba and the Rio Geba, the Bijagos Archipelago consists of 88 islands and islets spread over 10,000 sq km [4,000 sq mi]. The rainy season brings fresh water into the coastal zone, while coastal currents from north and south meet, making the delta region vulnerable yet biologically rich. Between the islands, extensive mud flats are drained by a network of canals and creeks as the tide recedes. The characteristic vegetation of the islands are the palm groves which have replaced the once extensive forest. The tidal areas remain relatively untouched, forming a unique mosaic of mangroves and tidal flats. Hippos have adapted to life in sea water and can be seen plodding along the beaches, while otters hunt for shellfish or wallow in the creeks together with manatees for which the archipelago forms one of the most important strongholds in the region. Two species of dolphin live here. Reptiles include two species of crocodile and four species of marine turtle, including the green turtle for which the Bijagos Archipelago is the most important breeding site in West Africa. Some 7,000 female green turtles nest here each year, and satellite tracking of turtles equipped with transmitters has shown that, after laying, they move north along the coast towards the waters of the Gulf d'Arguin in Mauritania. The archipelago is inhabited almost exclusively by the Bijagos ethnic group, 25,000 of whom live year round on 20 islands, with 20 others used at particular times of the year. The Bijagos assiduously maintain the palms from which they extract oil and palm wine; they also harvest shellfish from the mud flats and catch fish.

GUYANA

Guyana's flag was adopted in 1966 when the country became independent from Britain. The colours symbolize the people's energy in building a new nation (red), their perseverance (black), minerals (yellow), rivers (white) and agriculture and forests (green).

The Co-operative Republic of Guyana borders the Atlantic Ocean. It is the only English-speaking country in mainland South America and. The coastal plain, where the majority live, is between 3 and 48 km [2–30 mi] wide. Much of it is below sea level, with dykes to prevent flooding. Inland is hilly and forested, and this terrain makes up Guyana's largest region. The land rises to 2,810 m [9,219 ft] in the Pakaraima Mountains, part of the Guiana Highlands on Guyana's western border. Other highlands are in the south and southwest. Guyana has impressive waterfalls, such as the King George VI Falls (488 m [1,601 ft]), the Great Falls (256 m [840 ft]) and Kaieteur Falls (226 m [741 ft]).

The coastal plain is largely farmed, but wet savanna covers some areas. Inland, rainforests, rich in plant and animal species, cover about 85% of the country. Savanna occurs in the south-west.

Area 214,969 sq km [83,000 sq mi]
Population 767,000
Capital (population) Georgetown (213,000)
Government Multiparty republic
Ethnic groups East Indian 50%, Black 36%, Amerindian 7%, others
Languages English (official), Creole, Hindi, Urdu
Religions Christianity 50%, Hinduism 35%, Islam 10%, others
Currency Guyanese dollar = 100 cents
Website www.guyana-tourism.com

CLIMATE

Guyana has a hot, humid equatorial climate. Rainfall ranges from 2,280 mm [90 in] on the coast to 3,560 mm [140 in] in the rainforest region. The rainfall decreases to the west and south.

HISTORY

The first inhabitants of Guyana were Arawak, Carib and Warrau Amerindians. The Dutch founded a settlement in what is now Guyana in 1581 and, in 1620, the Dutch West India Company began to set up armed bases and to import African slaves to work on the sugar plantations. However, between 1780 and 1813, the territory changed hands between the Dutch, French and British. Britain occupied Guyana in 1814 during the Napoleonic Wars, and, in 1831, Britain founded the colony of British Guiana. After slavery was abolished in 1834, many former slaves set up their own farms with East Indian and Chinese labourers introduced to replace them. Gold was discovered in 1879. In 1889,

GEORGETOWN

Capital and largest city of Guyana, at the mouth of the River Demerara. Founded in 1781 by the British, it was the capital of the united colonies of Essequibo and Demerara and was known as Stabroek during the brief Dutch occupation from 1784. It was renamed Georgetown in 1812. Industries, shipbuilding, brewing.

prime minister. Riots, strikes and racial conflict broke out in the early 1960s. Elections in 1964 were won by the PNC and its ally, the United Force and Burnham became prime minister

POLITICS

British Guiana became independent as Guyana on 26 May 1966 with Burnham as prime minister. In 1970, Guyana became a republic but remained a member of the Commonwealth. In 1980 Burnham became president and served in that post until his death in 1985. He was succeeded by the prime minister Desmond Hoyte, but, in 1992, the PPP won the elections and Cheddi Jagan was elected president. On his death in 1997, he was succeeded by his wife Janet, who herself retired on health grounds in 1999. Her successor Bharrat Jagdeo, a former finance minister, was re-elected in 2001 when the PPP won both the presidential and parliamentary elections. Venezuela continues to claim Guyanese territory west of the Essequibo river, while Suriname is in dispute with Guyana over the headwaters of the Corentyne River, which forms part of the border between the two countries. Guyana also has a long-standing dispute with Suriname over their sea boundary, which runs through a potentially important offshore oilfield.

Venezuela claimed part of the territory, but its claims were over-ruled by an international arbitration tribunal. In 1953, the left-wing Guyanese Progressive People's Party (PPP) led by East Indian Cheddi Jagan won the elections. Britain then sent in troops and set up an interim administration. The constitution was restored in 1957, when the PPP split into a mostly Indian party, led by Jagan, and another group, led by a black lawyer, Forbes Burnham. Burnham's party, the more moderate People's National Congress (PNC), consisted mainly of the descendants of Africans. In 1961, British Guiana became self-governing, with Jagan as

ECONOMY

Guyana is a poor developing country. Its resources include gold, bauxite (aluminium ore) and other minerals, its forests and fertile soils. Agriculture and mining are the chief activities. The leading crops are sugar cane and rice, but citrus fruits, cocoa, coffee and plantains are also important. Farmers also produce beef, pork, poultry and dairy products. Fishing and forestry are other activities.

HAITI

Blue represents Haitians of African and French descent. Red represents blood shed in the struggle for independence. The coat of arms features a liberty cap on a royal palm tree and two cannons flanked by flags with a scroll reading l'Union Fait la Force (Strength in Unity).

The Republic of Haiti occupies the western third of Hispaniola, the Caribbean's second largest island. It is best known for political instability and for voodoo, which is practised by around 80% of the people, often together with Christianity. The land is mainly rugged, with mountain chains forming peninsulas in the north and south. The highest peak, at 2,680 m [8,793 ft] is in Massif de la Selle in the south-east. Between the two peninsulas is the Golfe de la Gonâve, which contains the large Isle de la Gonâve. Haiti's long coastline, which extends about 1,770 km [1,100 miles], is deeply indented.

Area 27,750 sq km [10,714 sq mi]
Population 8,309,000
Capital (population) Port-au-Prince (2,090,000)
Government Multiparty republic
Ethnic groups Black 95%, Mulatto/White 5%
Languages French and Creole (both official)
Religions Roman Catholic 80%, Voodoo
Currency Gourde = 100 centimes
Website www.haititourisme.org

CLIMATE

Haiti has a hot and humid tropical climate. Annual rainfall in the northern highlands is about 2,000 mm [79 in], more than twice that of the southern coast. The country is subject to violent tropical storms, which frequently cause widespread damage.

HISTORY

In 1496 Spain established a settlement at Santo Domingo, now capital of the neighbouring Dominican Republic. This was the first European settlement in the Western Hemisphere. The local Arawak Amerindians were annihilated by Spanish settlers in barely 25 years. Spain ceded the western part of Hispan-iola to France in 1697, and this area became Haiti. With an economy based on sugar cultivation and forestry, Haiti soon became prosperous.

In 1801 former slave Toussaint L'Ouverture led a revolt and proclaimed himself governor-general. A French force failed to conquer the interior of Haiti and the country became independent in 1804. Another former slave, Jean-Jacques Dessalines, declared himself emperor. In 1915, following conflict between black and mulatto Haitians, the United States invaded the country to protect its interests. The troops withdrew in 1934, although the United States maintained control over the economy until 1947.

POLITICS

In 1956 François Duvalier ('Papa Doc') seized power in a military coup. He was elected president in 1957. Duvalier established a brutal dictatorship. He died in 1971 and his son Jean Claude Duvalier ('Baby Doc') became president. Like his father, Baby Doc used a murderous militia, the Tontons Macoutes, to conduct a reign of terror and maintain rule. In 1986, popular unrest forced Baby Doc to flee and a military regime took over.

The country's first multiparty elections were held in December 1990; the winner was radical Roman Catholic priest, Fr Jean-Bertrand Aristide, who promised sweeping reforms. He was re-elected in 1994, but stood down in 1995 and was succeeded by René Préval. Violence and poverty prevailed and, in 1999, Préval dissolved parliament and declared that he would rule by decree. In the elections of 2000 Aristide again became president amid accusations of electoral irregularities, surviving an attempted coup in 2001. In 2004 rebels seized several towns and cities in an anti-government uprising, and Aristide fled the country. Boniface Alexandre was sworn in as interim president and an interim government led by prime minister Gerald Latortue, a former foreign secretary and UN official, took control. A UN peace-keeping force was sent to restore order. Floods in May 2004 caused major loss of life in Haiti and the Dominican Republic while, later that year, Hurricane Jeanne killed nearly 3,000 people in the north-west. The interim government failed to solve the country's problems and was accused of a poor human rights record. By 2006, UN forces had managed to suppress gangs and political violence enough for elections to be held. René Préval became president.

ECONOMY

Haiti is the poorest country in the Western Hemisphere and 80% of the people live below the poverty line. Agriculture is the occupation of two-thirds of the people, but coffee is the only significant cash crop. Money-laundering, corruption and drug-trafficking are rife.

PORT-AU-PRINCE

Capital of Haiti, a port on the southeast shore of the Gulf of Gonâve, on the west coast of Hispaniola. Founded by the French in 1749, Port-au-Prince became the capital of Haiti in 1770. Industries include tobacco, textiles, cement, coffee, sugar.

HONDURAS

Honduras adopted its present flag officially in 1866. It is based on the flag of the Central American Federation, set up in 1823, consisting of Costa Rica, El Salvador, Guatemala, Honduras and Nicaragua. Honduras left the Federation in 1838.

The Republic of Honduras is the second largest country in Central America. It has two coastlines. The north Caribbean coast extends for about 600 km [375 mi]. Deep offshore waters led the Spanish to name the country Honduras, Spanish for 'depths'. On the Pacific there is a narrow coast to the Gulf of Fonseca. Along the north coast are vast banana plantations. To the east lies the Mosquito Coast. The Cordillera highlands make up 80% of Honduras, including the capital, Tegucigalpa.

Pine forests cover 75% of Honduras. The northern coastal plains contain rainforest and tropical savanna. The Mosquito Coast contains mangrove swamps and dense forests. Mahogany and rosewood forest grow on lower mountain slopes.

Area 112,088 sq km [43,277 sq mi]
Population 7,326,000
Capital (population) Tegucigalpa (1,061,000)
Government Republic
Ethnic groups Mestizo 90%, Amerindian 7%, Black (including Black Carib) 2%, White 1%
Languages Spanish (official), Amerindian dialects
Religions Roman Catholic 97%
Currency Honduran lempira = 100 centavos
Website www.letsgohonduras.com

CLIMATE

The climate is tropical, though the uplands, where the capital Tegucigalpa is situated, are cooler than the coastal plains. The heaviest rainfall occurs from November to May. The coast is often battered by hurricanes. In October 1998, Honduras and Nicaragua were hit by Hurricane Mitch, which caused floods and mudslides.

HISTORY

From AD 400 to 900, the Maya civilization flourished. The Spanish discovered their magnificent ruins at Copán in western Honduras in 1576, but these became covered in dense forest and were rediscovered only in 1839. Columbus sighted the coast in 1502. Pedro de Alvarado founded the first Spanish settlements in 1524. The Spanish gradually subdued the native population and established gold and silver mines.

In 1821 Honduras gained independence, and formed part of the Mexican Empire. From 1823 to 1838, Honduras

MOSQUITO COAST (MOSQUITIA)

Coastal region bordering the Caribbean Sea, 65 km (40 mi) wide, now divided between Nicaragua and Honduras. A British protectorate from 1740, it returned to its original inhabitants (the Miskito) in 1860. In 1894, it became part of Nicaragua. International arbitration awarded the northern part to Honduras in 1960. The region, which consists mainly of tropical forest, swamp and lagoons, is only thinly populated.

Nicaragua, after which the Contra bases were closed down.

In 1992 Honduras signed a treaty with El Salvador, settling the disputed border. Liberal Party leader Carlos Flores became president in 1997 elections. In 1998, Hurricane Mitch killed more than 5,500 people and left 14 million people homeless. Human rights organizations estimated that 'death squads', often backed by the police, killed more than 1,000 street children in 2000. National Party leader Ricardo Maduro was elected president in 2001 but was unable to stem rising violent crime. In 2005 Manuel Zelaya became president.

was a member of the Central American Federation. Throughout the rest of the 19th century, Honduras was subject to continuous political interference, especially from Guatemala. Britain controlled the Mosquito Coast.

In the 1890s, American companies developed plantations in Honduras to grow bananas. These soon became the country's chief source of income. The companies exerted great political influence and the country became known as a 'banana republic', a term later applied to several other Latin American nations.

After World War II, demands grew for greater national autonomy and workers' rights. A military coup overthrew the Liberal government in 1963. In 1969, Honduras fought the short 'Soccer War' with El Salvador. The war was sparked off by the treatment of fans during a World Cup soccer series, though the real reason was that Honduras had forced Salvadoreans in Honduras to give up land.

POLITICS
Civilian government returned in 1982. During the 1980s, Honduras allowed US-backed Contra rebels from Nicaragua to operate in Honduras against Nicaragua's left-wing Sandinista government. Honduras was heavily dependent on US aid. Popular demonstrations against the Contras led to the declaration of a state of emergency in 1988. A ceasefire was then signed in

ECONOMY
Honduras is the least industrialized country in Central America, and the poorest developing nation in the Americas. Unemployment is very high, leading to high crime and drug trafficking.

Agriculture dominates the economy, forming 78% of exports and employing 38% of the workforce. Bananas and coffee are the leading exports, and maize the principal food crop. Cattle are raised in the mountain valleys and on the southern Pacific plains.

Fishing and forestry are also important. There are substantial timber resources but very few minerals, other than silver, lead and zinc. Lack of an adequate transport infrastructure hampers development.

TEGUCIGALPA

Capital and largest city of Honduras, located in the mountainous central Cordilleras. Founded in the 16th century by the Spanish as a silver and gold mining town, it became the national capital in 1880. Industries include sugar, textiles, chemicals, cigarettes.

HUNGARY

Hungary's flag was adopted in 1919. A state emblem was added in 1949 and removed in 1957. The colours of red, white and green had been used in the Hungarian arms since the 15th century. The tricolour design became popular during the 1848 rebellion against Habsburg rule.

The Republic of Hungary is a land-locked country in central Europe. The land is mostly low lying and drained by the Danube (Duna) and its tributary, the Tisza. Most of the land east of the Danube belongs to a region called the Great Plain, or Nagyalföld, which covers about half of Hungary.

West of the Danube is a hilly region, with some low mountains, called Trans-danubia. This region contains the country's largest lake, Lake Balaton. In the north-west is a small, fertile and mostly flat region which is called the Little Plain or Kisalföld.

Much of Hungary's original vegetation has been cleared. Large forests remain in the scenic northeastern highlands

Area 93,032 sq km [35,920 sq mi]
Population 9,981,000
Capital (population) Budapest (1,670,000)
Government Multiparty republic
Ethnic groups Magyar 90%, Gypsy, German, Serb, Romanian, Slovak
Languages Hungarian (official)
Religions Roman Catholic 68%, Calvinist 20%, Lutheran 5%, others
Currency Forint = 100 fillér
Website www.magyarorszag.hu/angol

CLIMATE

Hungary lies far from the moderating influence of the sea. As a result, summers are warmer and sunnier, and the winters colder than in Western Europe.

HISTORY

Magyars first arrived in the area from the east in the 9th century. In the 11th century, Hungary's first king, Stephen I, made Roman Catholicism the official religion. Hungary became a powerful kingdom, but in 1526 it was defeated by Turkish forces, who later occupied much of Hungary. In the late 17th century, the Austrian Habsburgs conquered Hungary. In 1867, Aus-tria granted Hungary equal status in a 'dual monarchy', called Austria-Hungary. In 1914, a Bosnian student killed Archduke Franz Ferdinand, the heir to the Austria-Hungary throne. This led to World War I, when Austria-Hungary fought alongside Germany. Defeat in 1918 led to nearly 70% of its territory being apportioned by the Treaty of Versailles to Czechoslovakia, Yugoslavia and Romania. Some 2.6 million Hungarians live in these countries today.

The government hoped to regain these territories by siding with Hitler's Germany in World War II, but the Germans occupied the country in 1944 and later that year the Red Army invaded. Elections were held in 1945 and, in 1946, the country was declared a republic. Although the smallholders had won a clear majority of the votes in the 1945 elections, the Communists gradually took control even after failing to win a majority of the votes cast in new elections in 1947.

POLITICS

Hungary became a Communist state in 1949, with a constitution based on that

Free Democrats. In 1998 elections Victor Orbán, leader of the Fidesz-Hungarian Civic Party, became prime minister. In 2002, the Socialists and the Free Democrat coalition, led by Peter Medgyessy, won a majority in parliament. Hungary became a member of NATO and the EU in 2004. In 2006 Socialist PM Ferenc Gyurcsany's admissions of government lies about the state of the economy led to massive protests, but he refused to resign.

of the Soviet Union. The first leader of the Communist government was Mathias Rákosi, who was replaced in 1953 by Imre Nagy. Nagy sought to relax Communist policies and was forced from office in 1955. He was replaced by Rákosi in 1956 and this led to a major uprising in which many Hungarians were killed or imprisoned. Nagy and his co-workers were executed for treason in 1958. Janos Kádár came to power in the wake of the suppression, but his was a relatively progressive leadership, including an element of political reform and a measure of economic liberalism. However, in the late 1970s, the economic situation worsened and new political parties started to appear.

Kádár resigned in 1989 and the central Committee of the Socialist Workers' Party (the Communist Party) agreed to sweeping reforms, including the introduction of a pluralist system and a democratic parliament, which had formally been little more than a rubber-stamp assembly. The trial of Imre Nagy and his co-workers was declared unlawful and their bodies were reburied with honour in June 1989.

In 1990, Hungarians voted into office a centre-right coalition headed by the Democratic Forum. In 1994 the Hungarian Socialist Party, made up of ex-Communists, won a majority and governed in coalition with the Alliance of

ECONOMY

Under communism the economy was transformed from agrarian to industrial under state ownership. From the late 1980s the government worked to increase private ownership, a change of policy which caused problems including inflation and high unemployment.

Manufacturing is the most valuable activity. Major products include aluminium made from local bauxite, chemicals, electrical and electronic goods, processed food, iron and steel, and vehicles. Agriculture remains important. Major crops include grapes, maize, potatoes, sugar beet and wheat.

BUDAPEST

Capital of Hungary, on the River Danube. It was created in 1873 by uniting the towns of Buda (capital of Hungary since the 14th century) and Pest, on the opposite bank. It became one of the two capitals of the Austro-Hungarian Empire. In 1918, it was declared capital of independent Hungary. Budapest was the scene of a popular uprising against the Soviet Union in 1956. The old town contains a remarkable collection of buildings, including Buda Castle, the parliament building, the National Museum and Roman remains.

ICELAND

Iceland's flag dates from 1915. It became the official flag in 1944, when Iceland became fully independent. The flag, which uses Iceland's traditional colours, blue and white, is the same as Norway's flag, except that the blue and red colours are reversed.

The Republic of Iceland, in the North Atlantic Ocean, though deemed part of Europe, is closer to Greenland than to Scotland. Iceland sits astride the Mid-Atlantic Ridge, the geological boundary between Europe and North America. The island is slowly getting wider as the ocean is stretched apart by the forces of plate tectonics.

Iceland has around 200 volcanoes, and eruptions are frequent. An eruption under the Vatnajökull ice cap in 1996 created a subglacial lake which subsequently burst, causing severe flooding. Geysers and hot springs are other volcanic features. During the thousand years that Iceland has been settled, between 150 and 200 volcanic eruptions have occurred. Ice caps and glaciers cover about one-eighth of the land. The only regions suitable for habitation are the coastal lowlands.

Vegetation is sparse or non-existent on 75% of the land. Treeless grassland and bogs cover some areas. Deep fjords fringe the coast.

Area 103,000 sq km [39,768 sq mi]
Population 299,000
Capital (population) Reykjavik (110,000)
Government Multiparty republic
Ethnic groups Icelandic 97%, Danish 1%
Languages Icelandic (official)
Religions Evangelical Lutheran 87%, other Protestant 4%, Roman Catholic 2%, others
Currency Icelandic króna = 100 aurar
Website www.icetourist.is

CLIMATE

Although it lies far to the north, Iceland's climate is moderated by the warm waters of the Gulf Stream. The port of Reykjavik is ice free all the year round.

HISTORY

Iceland was colonized by Vikings from Norway in AD 874 and the population grew as more settlers arrived from Norway and from the Viking colonies in the British Isles. In 930, the settlers founded the oldest, and what is thought to be the world's first, parliament (the Althing). One early settler was Erik the Red, a Viking who sailed to Greenland in about 982 and founded another colony there in about 985.

Iceland was an independent country until 1262 when, following a series of civil wars, the Althing recognized the rule of the king of Norway. When Norway united with Denmark in 1380, Iceland came under the rule of Danish kingdoms. Life on Iceland was never easy. The Black Death, which swept the island in 1402, claimed two-thirds of the population, while in the late 18th century volcanic eruptions destroyed crops, farmland and livestock, causing a famine. Then, during the Napoleonic Wars in the early 19th century, food supplies from Europe failed to reach the island and many people starved.

When Norway was separated from Denmark in 1814, Iceland remained under Danish rule. In the late 19th century, the invention of motorized craft, which changed the fishing industry, led

2002, but in 2003 undertook its first whale hunt for 15 years, claiming that it was to study the impact of whales on fish stocks. In 2006 Iceland resumed commercial whaling despite condemnation from environmental groups.

Iceland has no armed forces of its own. However, it joined NATO in 1949 and, under a NATO agreement, the United States maintains a base on the island. This became unpopular after the Cold War ended, and in 2006 the US agreed to withdraw.

to mounting demands for self-government. In 1918, Iceland was acknowledged as a sovereign state, but remained united with Denmark through a common monarch. During World War II, when Germany occupied Denmark, British and American troops landed in Iceland to protect it from invasion by the Germans. Finally, following a referendum in which 97% of the people voted to cut all ties with Denmark, Iceland became a fully independent republic on 17 June 1944.

POLITICS

Fishing, on which Iceland's economy is based, is a major political issue. In 1975 Iceland extended its territorial waters to 200 nautical miles, causing skirmishes between Icelandic and British vessels. The issue was resolved in 1977 when Britain agreed not to fish in the disputed waters. In the late 1980s Iceland reduced the allowable catches in its waters because overfishing was causing the depletion of fishing stocks, especially of cod. The reduced catch led to a slowdown in the economy and eventually to a recession, though the economy recovered in the mid-1990s when the conservation measures appeared to have been successful. Iceland left the International Whaling Commission in 1992, accusing it of having anti-whaling policies. It rejoined in

ECONOMY

Fishing and fish processing are major industries which dominate Iceland's overseas trade, though overfishing threatens economic problems. Agriculture is minimal, and much food is imported. Barely 1% of the land is used to grow crops, mainly root vegetables and fodder. 23% of the land is used for grazing sheep and cattle, making Iceland self-sufficient in meat and dairy products.

Manufacturing is important. Products include aluminium, cement, clothing, electrical equipment, fertilizers and processed foods. Geothermal power is an important energy source, and hydroelectric power is being developed to aid the aluminium industry. Tourism is also a significant sector.

REYKJAVÍK

Capital of Iceland, a port on the south-west coast. Founded in 870, it was the island's first permanent settlement. It expanded during the 18th century, and became the capital in 1918. During World War II, it served as a British and US air base. Tourism is now important. Industries include food processing, fishing, textiles, metallurgy, printing and publishing, and shipbuilding.

INDIA

The Indian flag was adopted shortly after the country gained independence from Britain in 1947. The saffron (orange) represents renunciation, the white represents truth and the green symbolizes mankind's relationship with nature. The central wheel represents dynamism and change.

The Republic of India, the world's seventh largest country, extends from the Himalayas, through the Tropic of Cancer, to the Indian Ocean at Cape Comorin. India is the world's second most populous nation after China, and the largest democracy. The north contains the mountains and foothills of the Himalayan range. Rivers such as the Brahmaputra and Ganges (Ganga) rise in the Himalayas and flow across the fertile northern plains. Southern India consists of a large plateau called the Deccan plateau which is bordered by two mountain ranges known as the Western Ghats and the Eastern Ghats.

The Karakoram Range, in the far north, has snow-covered peaks year round. The eastern Ganges delta has mangrove swamps. Between the gulfs of Kutch and Cambay are the deciduous forest habitats of the last of India's wild lions. Areas in the north-east and in the Western Ghats have heavy rainfall.

CLIMATE

India has three seasons. The weather during the cool season, from October to February, is mild in the northern plains, but southern India remains hot, though temperatures are a little lower than during the rest of the year. Temperatures on the northern plains sometimes soar to 49°C [120°F] during the hot season from March to the end of June. The monsoon season starts in the middle of June and continues into September. At this time,

INDIA

Area 3,287,263 sq km [1,269,212 sq mi]
Population 1,095,352,000
Capital (population) New Delhi (295,000)
Government Multiparty federal republic
Ethnic groups Indo-Aryan (Caucasoid) 72%, Dravidian (Aboriginal) 25%, others (mainly Mongoloid) 3%
Languages Hindi, English,Telugu, Bengali, Marathi, Tamil, Urdu, Gujurati, Malayalam, Kannada, Oriya, Punjabi, Assamese, Kasmiri, Sindhi and Sanskrit (all official)
Religions Hinduism 82%, Islam 12%, Christianity 2%, Sikhism 2%, Buddhism and others
Currency Indian rupee = 100 paisa
Website www.incredibleindia.org

moist south-easterly winds from the Indian Ocean bring heavy rains to India. Darjeeling in the north-east has an average annual rainfall of 3,040 mm [120 in], but parts of the Thar Desert in the northwest have only 50 mm [2 in] of rain a year. The monsoon rains are essential for India's farmers. If they arrive late, crops may be ruined. If the rainfall is considerably higher than average, floods may cause great destruction.

HISTORY

India's early settlers were scattered across the subcontinent in the Stone Age. The first of its many civilizations began to flourish in the Indus Valley in what is now Pakistan and western India around 4,500 years ago, and in the Ganges Valley from about 1500 BC, when Aryan people arrived in India from central Asia. The earlier, darker-skinned people, the Dravidians, moved southwards, ahead of the Aryans, and their descendants are now the main inhabitants of southern India.

India was the birthplace of several major religions including Hinduism, Buddhism and Sikhism. Islam was introduced from about AD 1000. The Muslim Mughal empire was founded in 1526. From the 17th century Britain began to gain influence through the East India Company, and from 1858 to 1947, India was ruled as part of the British empire.

An independence movement began in India after the Sepoy Rebellion (1857–9) and, in 1885, the Indian National Congress was founded. In 1906, Indian Muslims, concerned that Hindus formed the majority of the members of the Indian National Congress, founded the Muslim League. In 1920, Mohandas K. Gandhi, a former lawyer, became leader of the Indian National Congress, which soon became a mass movement. Gandhi's policy of non-violent disobedience proved highly effective, and in response Britain began to introduce political reforms. In the 1930s, the Muslim League called for the establishment of a Muslim state, called Pakistan.

In 1947, it was agreed that British India be partitioned into the mainly Hindu India and the Muslim Pakistan. Both countries became independent in August 1947, but the events were marred by mass slaughter as Hindus and Sikhs fled from Pakistan and Muslims flocked to Pakistan from India. In the boundary disputes, violence and mass migrations that followed, between 500,000 and 1 million people died or were killed.

POLITICS

Gandhi was assassinated in 1948 by a Hindu extremist who hated him for his tolerant attitude towards Muslims. The country adopted a new constitution in 1948 making the country a democratic republic within the Commonwealth, and elections were held in 1951 and 1952. India's first prime minister was Jawaharlal Nehru. The government sought to develop the economy and raise living standards at home, while, on the international stage, Nehru won great respect for his policy of non-alignment and neutrality. The disputed status of Kashmir posed a difficult security problem.

In 1966 Nehru's daughter, Indira Gandhi, took office. Her Congress Party lost support because of food shortages, unemployment and other problems. In 1971 India helped the people of East Pakistan achieve independence from

West Pakistan to become Bangladesh. India tested its first atomic bomb in 1974, but pledged to use nuclear power for peaceful purposes only. In 1977 Mrs Gandhi lost her seat in parliament and her Congress Party was defeated by the Janata Party, a coalition led by Morarji R. Desai. Disputes in the Janata Party led to Desai's resignation in 1979 and, in 1980, Congress-I (the I standing for Indira) won the elections. Mrs Gandhi again became prime minister, but her government faced many problems. Many Sikhs wanted more influence over the Punjab, and Sikh radicals began to commit acts of violence to draw attention to their cause. In 1984 armed Sikhs occupied the sacred Golden Temple in Amritsar. In response, Indian troops attacked the temple, causing deaths and much damage. In October 1984 two of Mrs Gandhi's Sikh guards assassinated her. Her son Rajiv was chosen to succeed her as prime minister but, in 1989, Congress lost its majority in parliament. Rajiv Gandhi resigned as prime minister, and during elections in 1991 he was assassinated by Tamil extremists.

India is a vast country with an enormous diversity of cultures. It has more than a dozen major languages, and many minor languages. Hindi, the national language, and the Dravidian languages of the south (Kannada, Tamil, Telugu and Malayam) are Indo-European. Sino-Tibetan languages are spoken in the north and east.

Hinduism is all-pervasive and Buddhism is slowly reviving in the country of its origin. Jainism is strong in the merchant towns around Mount Abu in the Aravallis hills north of Ahmadabad. Islam has contributed many mosques and monuments, the Taj Mahal being the best known, and India retains a large Muslim minority. The Punjab's militant Sikhs now seek separation. However, India's most intractable problem remains the divided region of Kashmir, the subject of a long conflict between India and Pakistan. In 2004 and 2005 both countries sought ways of easing the tension, including the opening up of cross-border transport services. In 2006 bombings in Mumbai were blamed on Pakistan, causing setbacks, but the peace process was resumed.

ECONOMY

According to the World Bank, India is a 'low-income' developing country. While it ranked 11th in total gross national product in 2004, its per capita GNP of US$440 placed it among the world's poorer countries. Despite initiatives, socialist policies failed to raise living standards. In the 1990s, the government introduced private enterprise policies which have stimulated growth. Manufacturing has expanded, adding electronics and high technology to the country's industries. India also produces iron and steel, machinery, refined petroleum, textiles and transport equipment. In the 2000s a booming IT and services sector has brought massive economic growth, but severe inequality remains a major problem and about two thirds of the people remain impoverished farmers. Major crops include rice, wheat, millet, sorghum, peas and beans.

NEW DELHI

Capital of India, in the north of the country, on the River Yamuna in Delhi Union Territory. Planned by the British architects Edwin Lutyens and Herbert Baker, it was constructed in 1912–29 to replace Calcutta (now Kolkata) as the capital of British India. Whereas Old Delhi is primarily a commercial centre, New Delhi has an administrative function. Places of interest include the Coronation Durbar Site, the Crafts Museum and Humayun's Tomb. Industries include textile production, chemicals, machine tools, plastics, electrical appliances and traditional crafts.

CHRISTMAS ISLAND

Area 135 sq km [52 sq mi]
Population 1,500
Capital The Settlement
Government Territory of Australia
Ethnic groups
Chinese 70%, European 20%, Malay 10%
Languages English (official), Chinese, Malay
Religions Buddhist 36%, Muslim 25%, Christian 18%, others
Currency Australian dollar = 100 cents
Website www.christmas.net.au

Island in the east Indian Ocean 320 km [200 mi] south of Java. Once under British domination, it was annexed to Australia in 1958. Phosphate deposits were once exploited but are now exhausted. Australian Government attempts to revitalize the economy with a casino and proposed spaceport have stalled. Two-thirds of the island is national park, and tourists visit for bird-watching.

COCOS ISLANDS

Area 14 sq km [5.4 sq mi]
Population 600
Capital (population) West Island
Government Territory of Australia
Ethnic groups Europeans, Cocos Malays
Languages Malay (Cocos dialect), English
Religions Sunni Muslim 80%, others
Currency Australian dollar = 100 cents
Website
www.dotars.gov.au/terr/cocos/index.aspx

The Territory of the Cocos (Keeling) Islands is made up of 27 coral islands. Discovered in 1609 by Captain William Keeling, they were uninhabited until the 19th century. The islands were annexed by the UK in 1857 and transferred to the Australian Government in 1955. Only two of the islands are inhabited and the population of the two is split along ethnic lines, with ethnic Europeans on West Island and ethnic Malays on Home Island.

Coconuts are the sole cash crop and there is a small tourist industry.

COMOROS

Area 2,170 sq km [838 sq mi]
Population 691,000
Capital (population) Moroni (30,000)
Government Independent republic
Ethnic groups Antalote, Cafre, Makoa, Oimatsaha, Sakalava
Languages
Arabic and French (both official), Shikomoro
Religions Sunni Muslim 98%, Roman Catholic 2%
Currency Comoran franc = 100 centimes
Website www.arab.net/comoros

The Union des Isles Comoros consists of three large volcanic islands and several smaller ones at the northern end of the Mozambique Channel. The three major islands are Grande Comore (site of the capital), Anjouan and Mohéli. They are mountainous, with a tropical climate and fertile soil.

France took over one of the islands, Mayotte, in 1843. In 1886, the other islands came under French protection. The Comoros became independent in 1974, but the people of Mayotte opted to remain French. In the late 1990s, separatists on Anjouan and Mohéli islands sought to secede, but in 2004 each of the large islands was granted autonomy with its own president and legislature. The Comoros is a poor country. It exports cloves, perfume oils, coconuts, copra and vanilla.

MALDIVES

The Republic of the Maldives, Asia's smallest independent country, comprises some 1,200 low-lying coral islands grouped into 26 atolls; 202 of the islands are inhabited. They are scattered along a broad north–south line in the Indian Ocean about 640 km [400 mi] south west of Sri Lanka.

Area 298 sq km [112 sq mi]
Population 359,000
Capital (population) Malé (74,000)
Government Republic
Ethnic groups South Indians, Sinhalese, Arabs
Languages Maldivian Dhivehi (dialect of Sinhala, script derived from Arabic), English
Religion Sunni Muslim
Currency Rufiyaa = 100 laari
Website www.maldivesinfo.gov.mv

189

The islands are prone to flooding. They have a tropical climate and the monsoon season lasts from April to October.

HISTORY AND POLITICS
Sri Lanka settled the islands in about 500 BC. From the 14th century, the ad-Din dynasty ruled the Maldives. In 1518, the Portuguese claimed them. From 1665 to 1886, the Maldives were a dependency of Ceylon (Sri Lanka).

They became a British protectorate in 1887. In 1965 they achieved independence as a sultanate and then became a republic when the sultan was deposed in 1968. Maumoon Abdul Gayoom has served as president since 1978. In 1982, the Maldives joined the Commonwealth. In 1988, Indian troops helped suppress an attempted coup.

A tsunami struck the islands in December 2004 killing 82 people.

Political parties are banned, though political activity is permitted, at least nominally. The president is chosen in a yes-no referendum. The voters are presented with just one candidate, chosen on their behalf by parliament. President Gayoom came under increasing pressure from human rights groups to ease up on his autocratic style of governance. There was anti-government violence on the streets. In 2005 he promised a multiparty democracy, but later postponed it indefinitely.

ECONOMY
The chief crops are bananas, coconuts, copra, mangoes, sweet potatoes and spices, but much food is imported. Fishing is important and the leading export is the bonito (Maldives tuna). Since 1972 growth in tourism has boosted foreign reserves, but the Maldives remains one of the world's poorest countries.

MAYOTTE

Area 373 sq km [144 sq mi]
Population 201,000
Capital (population) Mamoudzou (4,000)
Government Territorial collectivity of France
Ethnic groups Comorian (mixture of Bantu, Arab, and Malagasy) 92%
Languages
Mahorian (a Swahili dialect), French (official)
Religions Muslim 97%, Christian (mostly Roman Catholic)
Currency Euro = 100 cents
Website
http://ctt.mayotte.free.fr/anglais/Eaccueil.htm

A French-administered archipelago in the Indian Ocean to the east of the Comoros. The two major islands are Grande Terre and Petite Terre (Pamanzi). Grande Terre includes the new capital, Mamoudzou. Pamanzi is the site of the old capital, Dzaoudzi.

Mayotte has a tropical climate. It is generally hot and humid. The rainy season is from November to May, during the north-eastern monsoon. The dry season, from May to November, is cooler.

HISTORY AND POLITICS
Mayotte was a French colony from 1843 to 1914 when it was attached to the Comoro group and collectively achieved administrative autonomy as a French Overseas Territory. In 1974 the rest of the Comoros became independent, while Mayotte voted to remain a French

dependency. In 1976 it became an overseas collectivity of France.

ECONOMY
The economy is primarily agricultural, and the chief products and exports are fruits, spices and coconut.

RÉUNION

Area 2,510 sq km [969 sq mi]
Population 788,000
Capital (population) St-Denis (122,000)
Government Overseas department of France
Ethnic groups French, African, Malagasy, Chinese, Pakistani, Indian
Languages French (official), Creole
Religions Roman Catholic 86%, Hindu, Muslim, Buddhist
Currency Euro = 100 cents
Website
www.la-reunion-tourisme.com/gb_entree.htm

The Department of Réunion is a volcanic island in the Mascarene group lying about 700 km [440 mi] east of Madagascar in the Indian Ocean. It has a mountainous, wooded centre, surrounded by a fertile coastal plain. The climate is tropical, but the temperature moderates with elevation. It is cool and dry from May to November and hot and rainy from November to April.

HISTORY AND POLITICS
Discovered in 1513 by the Portuguese, Réunion was claimed by France in 1638. It became a French department in 1946. The island became part of an administrative region in 1973. There is increasing pressure on France for independence.

ECONOMY
Sugar cane dominates the economy, though vanilla, perfume oils and tea also produce revenue. Tourism is the big hope for the future, but unemployment is high and the island relies on French aid.

SEYCHELLES

Area 455 sq km [176 sq mi]
Population 82,000
Capital (population) Victoria (24,000)
Government Republic
Ethnic groups French, African, Indian, Chinese, and Arab
Languages Creole 92%, English 5% (both official)
Religions Roman Catholic 82%, Anglican 6%, others
Currency Seychelles rupee = 100 cents
Website www.virtualseychelles.sc

The Republic of Seychelles includes a group of four large and 36 small granitic islands, plus a wide scattering of coralline islands, 14 of them inhabited, lying to the south and west. The islands experience a tropical oceanic climate.

Formerly part of the British Indian Ocean Territory (BIOT), Farquhar, Des Roches and Aldabra (famous for its unique wildlife) were returned to the Seychelles in 1976. The BIOT now consists only of the Chagos Archipelago, with Diego Garcia, the largest island, supporting a US Navy base.

HISTORY AND POLITICS
French from 1756 and British from 1814, the islands gained their independence in 1976. A year later, a coup resulted in the setting up of a one-party socialist state under President France-Albert René. In 1992 he declared a return to multiparty democracy, but claimed victory in each subsequent election until he stepped down in 2004. Former vice-president James Michel won 2006 elections, though the opposition claimed that the system is not yet fair.

ECONOMY
The Seychelles produces copra, cinnamon and tea, although rice is imported. Fishing and luxury tourism are the two main industries.

INDONESIA

This flag was adopted in 1945, when Indonesia proclaimed itself independent from the Netherlands. The colours, which date back to the Middle Ages, were adopted in the 1920s by political groups in their struggle against Dutch rule.

The Republic of Indonesia, in Southeast Asia, consists of about 13,600 islands, less than 6,000 of which are inhabited. The island of Java covers only 7% of the country's area but it contains more than half of Indonesia's population. Three-quarters of the country is made up of five main areas: the islands of Sumatra, Java and Sulawesi (Celebes), together with Kalimantan (southern Borneo and Papua (western New Guinea). The islands are mountainous and many have extensive coastal lowlands. Indonesia contains more than 200 volcanoes. The highest peak is Puncak Jaya, in West Papua, which reaches 5,029 m [16,503 ft] above sea level.

Area 1,904,569 sq km [735,354 sq mi]
Population 245,453,000
Capital (population) Jakarta (13,194,000)
Government Multiparty republic
Ethnic groups Javanese 45%, Sundanese 14|%, Madurese 7%, coastal Malays 7%, approximately 300 others
Languages Bahasa Indonesian (official), many others
Religions Islam 88%, Roman Catholic 3%, Hinduism 2%, Buddhism 1%
Currency Indonesian rupiah = 100 sen
Website www.indonesiamission-ny.org

CLIMATE
Indonesia has a hot and humid monsoon climate. Only Java and the Sunda Islands have a relatively dry season. From December to March, moist prevailing winds blow from mainland Asia. Between mid-June and October, dry prevailing winds blow from Australia.

HISTORY
From the 8th century, the empire of Sri Vijaya, which was centred on Palembang, held sway until it was replaced in the 14th century by the kingdom of Madjapahit, whose centre was east-central Java. Indonesia is the world's most populous Muslim nation, though Islam was introduced as recently as the 15th century. The area came under the domination of the Dutch East India Company in the 17th century. The Dutch government took over the islands in 1799. Japan occupied the islands in World War II and Indonesia declared its independence in 1945. The Dutch finally recognized Indonesia's independence in 1949.

POLITICS
Indonesia's first president, the anti-Western Achmed Sukarno, plunged his coun-

KRAKATOA
Small, volcanic island (813 m [2,667 ft]) in western Indonesia, in the Sunda Strait between Java and Sumatra. In 1883, one of the world's largest recorded volcanic eruptions destroyed most of the island. The resulting tidal waves caused 50,000 deaths and great destruction.

try into chaos. In 1962, Indonesia invaded Dutch New Guinea (now West Papua), and between 1963 and 1966 Sukarno sought to destabilize the Federation of Malaysia through incursions into northern Borneo. In 1965-7 Sukarno suppressed an allegedly Communist uprising, killing 80,000. In 1967 General Suharto took over in a coup. Suharto's military regime, with US help, achieved significant economic growth though corruption was rife. In 1975 Indonesian troops invaded East Timor, opposed by the local people. Suharto was forced to stand down in 1998 and his deputy, Bacharuddin Jusuf Habibie, succeeded him. In June 1999 Habibie's ruling Golkar Party was defeated in elections and, in October, the parliament elected Abdurrahman Wahid as president. However, Wahid, charged with corruption and general incompetence, was dismissed in 2001. He was succeeded by his vice-president Megawati Sukarnoputri, the daughter of President Sukarno.

East Timor seceded in 2002, while secessionist groups in Aceh province, northern Sumatra, and the Free Papua Movement in West Papua also demanded independence. Muslim-Christian clashes broke out in the Moluccas at the end of 1999, while indigenous Dyaks in Kalimantan clashed with immigrants from Madura. In December 2004, more than 120,000 people in Indonesia were killed by a tsunami. Worst hit was Aceh, though the tragedy was followed by peace talks in 2005. The separatist conflict ended and Aceh gained some autonomy. In 2006 Aceh held its first independent elections.

ECONOMY

The World Bank describes Indonesia as a 'lower-middle-income' developing country. Agriculture employs more than 40% of the workforce and rice is the main food crop. Bananas, cassava, coconuts, groundnuts, maize, spices and sweet potatoes are also grown. Major cash crops include coffee, palm oil, rubber, sugar cane, tea and tobacco. Fishing and forestry are also important.

There are important mineral reserves. Bauxite, coal, iron ore, nickel and tin are mined. There is some oil and natural gas, but production is declining.

JAKARTA

Capital of Indonesia, on the northwest coast of Java. It was founded in 1619 as Batavia by the Dutch as a fort and trading post, and it became the headquarters of the Dutch East India Company. It became the capital after Indonesia gained its independence in 1949. Industries include ironworking, printing and timber.

IRAN

Iran's flag was adopted in 1980 by the country's Islamic government. The white stripe contains the national emblem, which is the word for Allah (God) in formal Arabic script. The words Allah Akbar (God is Great) is repeated 11 times on both the green and red stripes.

The Islamic Republic of Iran contains a barren central plateau which covers about half the country. It includes the Great Salt Desert (Dasht-e-Kavir) and the Great Sand Desert (Dasht-e-Lut). The Elburz Mountains (Alborz), which border the plateau to the north, contain Iran's highest peak, Damavand (5,604 m [18,386 ft]). North of the Elburz Mountains are the fertile, densely populated lowlands around the Caspian Sea, with a mild climate and abundant rainfall. Bordering the plateau to the west are the Zagros Mountains which separate the central plateau from the Khuzistan Plain, a region of sugar plantations and oil fields, which extends to the Iraqi border.

Area 1,648,195 sq km [636,368 sq mi]
Population 68,688,000
Capital (population) Tehran (7,352,000)
Government Islamic Republic
Ethnic groups Persian 51%, Azeri 24%, Gilaki and Mazandarani 8%, Kurd 7%, Arab 3%, Lur 2%, Baluchi 2%, Turkmen 2%
Languages Persian, Turkic 26%, Kurdish
Religions Islam (Shi'ite Muslim 89%)
Currency Iranian rial = 100 dinars
Website www.netiran.com

CLIMATE

Much of Iran has a severe, dry climate, with hot summers and cold winters. Rain falls only about 30 days a year in Tehran and the annual temperature range is of more than 25°C [45°F]. The lowlands are generally milder.

HISTORY

Ancient Persia was a powerful empire. It flourished from 550 BC, when its king, Cyrus the Great, conquered the Medes, to 331 BC, when the empire was conquered by Alexander the Great. Arab armies introduced Islam in AD 641 and made Iran a great centre of learning.

Britain and Russia competed for influence in the area in the 19th century, and in the early 20th century the British began to develop the country's oil resources. In 1925, the Pahlavi family took power. Reza Khan became Shah (king) and worked to modernize the country. Persia was renamed Iran in 1935. The Pahlavi Dynasty ended in 1979 when the government was overthrown and the Shah fled. Ayatollah Ruhollah Khomeini tok control and established an Islamic republic.

POLITICS

Iran and Iraq fought over disputed borders from 1980–8. Iran suffered heavy casualties, and the war's cost and damage to oil production caused severe problems for the economy. Khomeini died in 1989 but his views and anti-Western attitudes continued to dominate. In 1997 and 2001 the liberal Mohammad Khatami was elected president, but conservative clerics and unelected branches of government blocked his reform plans. From 2003 onwards the United States accused Iran of developing nuclear weapons, a charge Iran denied. In 2005 elections

Khatami was replaced by the highly conservative Mahmoud Ahmedinejad. In 2006 Iran began enriching uranium, and the UN began to impose sanctions.

ECONOMY

Iran's prosperity is based on its oil, which accounts for 95% of the country's exports. Oil revenues have been used to develop a manufacturing sector, but agriculture still accounts for 25% of the gross domestic product, even though farms cover only a tenth of the land. The main crops are wheat and barley. Livestock farming and fishing are also important.

TEHRAN

Capital of Iran, 105 km [65 mi] south of the Caspian Sea. Strategically placed on the edge of the plains, in the foothills of the country's highest mountains. In 1788, it replaced Isfahan as the capital of Persia. In the early 20th century, the old fortifications were demolished and a planned city established by the Shah. Now Iran's industrial, commercial, administrative and cultural centre.

IRAQ

Iraq's flag was adopted in 1963, when the country was planning to federate with Egypt and Syria. It uses the four Pan-Arab colours. The three green stars symbolize the three countries. Iraq retained these stars even though the union failed to come into being.

The Republic of Iraq is a south-west Asian country at the head of the Persian Gulf. Deserts cover western and south-western Iraq, including part of the Hamad (or Syrian) Desert. Part of the Zagros Mountains, where farming can be practised without irrigation, occupies the north-east. Western Iraq contains lower valleys of the rivers Euphrates (Nahr al Furat) and Tigris (Nahr Dijlah). The region is arid, but has fertile alluvial soils. The Euphrates and Tigris join south of al Qurnah to form the Shatt al Arab. The Shatt al Arab's delta is an area of irrigated farmland and marshes. This waterway is shared with Iran, and the boundary has often been disputed.

Area 438,317 sq km [169,234 sq mi]
Population 26,783,000
Capital (population) Baghdad (5,910,000)
Government Republic
Ethnic groups Arab 77%, Kurdish 19%, Assyrian and others
Languages Arabic (official), Kurdish (official in Kurdish areas), Assyrian, Armenian
Religions Islam 97%, Christianity and others
Currency New Iraqi dinar
Website www.un.int/iraq/homepage.htm

CLIMATE

The climate of Iraq varies from temperate in the north to subtropical in the south and east. Baghdad, in central Iraq, has cool winters, with occasional frosts, and hot summers. Rainfall is generally low.

HISTORY

Mesopotamia was the home of several great civilizations, including Sumer, Babylon and Assyria. It later became part of the Persian Empire. Islam was introduced in AD 637 and Baghdad became the brilliant capital of the powerful Arab Empire. However, Mesopotamia declined after the Mongols invaded it in

1258. From 1534, Mesopotamia became part of the Turkish Ottoman Empire. Britain invaded the area in 1916. In 1921, Britain renamed the country Iraq and set up an Arab monarchy. Iraq finally became independent in 1932.

By the 1950s, oil dominated Iraq's economy. In 1952, Iraq agreed to take 50% of the profits of the foreign oil companies. This revenue enabled the government to pay for welfare services and development projects, but many Iraqis felt that they should benefit more from the country's oil.

Since 1958, when army officers killed the king and made Iraq a republic, the country has undergone turbulent times. In the 1960s, the Kurds, who live in northern Iraq, Iran, Turkey, Syria and Armenia, asked for self-rule. The government rejected their demands and war broke out. A peace treaty was signed in 1975, but conflict continued.

POLITICS

In 1979, Saddam Hussein became Iraq's president. Under his leadership, Iraq invaded Iran in 1980, starting an eight-year war which devastated both countries.

Iraqi government, Coalition troops and civilians by opposing insurgent forces escalated in 2004 and continue to the present.

Multiparty elections took place in 2005 but were boycotted by Sunni Arabs, 20% of the population. Reconstruction of the nation's damaged infrastructure was halted by widespread corruption. In 2006 a US Congress report urged withdrawal of American forces, but President Bush instead increased them. In December 2006 an Iraqi court executed Saddam Hussein for 'crimes against humanity' against opposition groups during his rule. In 2007 the US accused Iran of backing insurgents.

ECONOMY

Civil war and war damage in 1991 and 2003, UN sanctions', and economic mismanagement have all contributed to economic chaos. Oil remains Iraq's main resource, but the industry is severely disrupted. Farmland covers around a fifth of the land, and Iraq has to import much of its food.

Iraq used chemical weapons both against Iran and against Iraqi Kurds.

In 1990 Iraqi troops occupied Kuwait, but an international force drove them out in 1991. From 1991, Iraqi troops attacked Shi'ite Marsh Arabs and Kurds. In 1996, the government aided the forces of the Kurdish Democratic Party in an offensive against the Patriotic Union of Kurdistan, a rival Kurdish faction. In 1998, Iraq's failure to allow full access to UNSCOM, the UN body charged with disposing of Iraq's biological and chemical weapons, led to Western bombardment of military sites. Periodic bombing and severe economic sanctions continued, but the UN allowed Iraq to export a limited amount of oil in exchange for food and some medicines.

In late 2002 Iraq finally allowed the return of UN inspectors, who found no material evidence of chemical weapons. In 2003 a US-led coalition invaded the country and toppled Saddam's regime. Saddam Hussein was captured, but no biological or chemical weapons were found. Attacks on the Coalition-backed

BAGHDAD

Capital of Iraq, on the River Tigris. Established in 762 as capital of the Abbasid caliphate, it became a centre of Islamic civilization and focus of caravan routes between Asia and Europe. It was almost destroyed by the Mongols in 1258. In 1921 Baghdad became the capital of newly independent Iraq. Notable sites include the 13th-century Abbasid Palace. In 1991 and 2003 Baghdad was badly damaged by bombing in the two Gulf Wars. Industries once included building materials, textiles, tanning and bookbinding.

IRELAND

Ireland's flag was adopted in 1922 after the country had become independent from Britain, though nationalists had used it as early as 1848. Green represents Ireland's Roman Catholics, orange the Protestants, and the white a desire for peace between the two.

The Republic of Ireland consists of a large lowland region surrounded by a broken rim of low mountains. The lowlands include peat bogs. The uplands include the Mountains of Kerry with Carrauntoohill, Ireland's highest peak (1,041 m [3,415 ft]). The River Shannon is the longest in Ireland, flowing through three large loughs: Allen, Ree and Derg. Forests cover approximately 5% of Ireland. Much of the land is under pasture and a very small percentage is set aside for crops.

Area 70,273 sq km [27,132 sq mi]
Population 4,062,000
Capital (population) Dublin (985,000)
Government Multiparty republic
Ethnic groups Irish 94%
Languages Irish (Gaelic) and English (both official)
Religions Roman Catholic 92%, Protestant 3%
Currency Euro = 100 cents
Website www.irlgov.ie

CLIMATE

Ireland has a mild, damp climate influenced by the Gulf Stream current which warms the west coast, with Dublin in the east somewhat cooler. Frequent rainfall occurs throughout the year.

HISTORY

Celts settled in Ireland from about 400 BC. They were followed by the Vikings, Normans and the English. Vikings raided Ireland from the 790s, establishing settlements in the 9th century, but Norse domination was ended in 1014 when they were defeated by Ireland's king, Brian Boru. The Normans arrived in 1169 and, gradually, Ireland came under English influence.

In 1801, the Act of Union created the United Kingdom of Great Britain and Ireland. But Irish discontent intensified in the 1840s when a potato blight caused a famine in which a million people died and nearly a million emigrated. Britain was blamed for not having done enough to help. In 1905, Arthur Griffith founded Sinn Féin ('We Ourselves'), a movement

DUBLIN (BAILE ÁTHA CLIATH)

Capital of the Republic of Ireland, at the mouth of the River Liffey on Dublin Bay. In 1014, Brian Boru recaptured it from the Danish. In 1170, it was taken by the English and became the seat of colonial government. Dublin suffered much bloodshed in nationalist attempts to free Ireland from English rule. Strikes beginning in 1913 finally resulted in the Easter Rising (1916). Dublin was the centre of the late 19th-century Irish literary renaissance. It is now the commercial and cultural centre of the Republic. Notable sites include Christ Church Cathedral (1053), St Patrick's Cathedral (1190), Trinity College (1591) and the Abbey Theatre (1904).

accepted the Act, but fighting broke out in southern Ireland. In 1921, a treaty was agreed allowing southern Ireland to become a self-governing dominion, called the Irish Free State, within the British Commonwealth. With one Irish group accepting the treaty and another group wanting complete independence, civil war occurred between 1922 and 1923.

POLITICS

Ireland became a republic in 1949 and has subsequently played an independent role in Europe, joining the EEC in 1973 and adopting the euro in 2002. The government of Ireland worked with British governments in attempts to solve the problems of Northern Ireland. In 1998, it supported the creation of a Northern Ireland Assembly, the setting-up of north–south political structures and the amendment of the 1937 constitution removing from it the republic's claim to Northern Ireland. A referendum showed strong support for the proposals and amendments to the constitution. The 1998 Good Friday Agreement in Northern Ireland aimed to end the long-standing conflict: it met with much support but stalled when the Irish Republican Army (IRA) refused to disarm. In July 2005 the IRA issued a statement of full disarmament. The Northern Ireland Assembly resumed in 2007.

advocating self-government for Ireland. Another secret organization, the Irish Republican Brotherhood, was also active in the early 20th century and its support-ers became known as republicans. In 1916, republicans launched what was called the Easter Rebellion in Dublin, but the uprising was crushed. The republi-cans took over the Sinn Féin movement in 1918. They won a majority of Ireland's seats in the British parliament, but instead of going to London, they set up the Dáil Éireann (House of Representa-tives) in Dublin and declared Ireland an independent republic in January 1919.

In 1920, the British parliament passed the Government of Ireland Act, parti-tioning Ireland. The six Ulster counties

ECONOMY

Manufacturing is now the leading activi-ty, with high-tech industries producing chemicals and pharmaceuticals, electron-ic equipment, machinery, paper and tex-tiles. Aided by EU grants, farming is now prosperous; products include livestock, potatoes and barley. Racehorses are a sig-nificant part of the rural economy. Tourism is also important.

ISRAEL

Israel's flag was adopted when the Jewish state declared itself independent in 1948. The blue and white stripes are based on the tallit, a Hebrew prayer shawl. The ancient, six-pointed Star of David is in the centre. The flag was designed in America in 1891.

The State of Israel is a small country on the eastern Mediterranean. Inland lie the Judaeo-Galilean highlands, from northern Israel to the northern tip of the Negev Desert in the south. To the east lie part of the Great Rift Valley, River Jordan, Sea of Galilee and Dead Sea, 418 m [1,371 ft] below sea level, the world's lowest point on land.

Area 20,600 sq km [7,954 sq mi]
Population 6,352,000
Capital (population) Jerusalem (685,000)
Government Multiparty republic
Ethnic groups Jewish 80%, Arab and others 20%
Languages Hebrew and Arabic (both official)
Religions Judaism 80%, Islam (mostly Sunni) 14%, Christianity 2%, Druze and others 2%
Currency New Israeli shekel = 100 agorat
Website www.mfa.gov.il/MFA
Statistics exclude the Palestinian Territories

CLIMATE

Israel has hot, dry summers. Winters are mild and moist on the coast. Annual rainfall decreases west to east and north to south with only 70 mm [2.5 in] in the Dead Sea region.

HISTORY

Israel is part of a region historically called Palestine. Most modern Israelis are descendants of immigrants who began to settle from the 1880s. Britain ruled Palestine from 1917. Large numbers of Jews escaping Nazi persecution arrived in the 1930s, provoking an Arab uprising against British rule. In 1947 the UN agreed to partition Palestine into an Arab and a Jewish state. Fighting broke out after Arabs rejected the plan. The State of Israel came into being in May 1948, but fighting continued into 1949. The Six Day War in 1967 led to the acquisition by Israel of the West Bank, East Jerusalem, the Gaza Strip, Egypt's Sinai Peninsula and the Syrian Golan Heights. Israel invaded Lebanon in 1982 to destroy the

stronghold of the PLO (Palestine Liberation Organization), but left in 1985.

POLITICS

Israel returned the Sinai Peninsula to Egypt in 1979. Conflict continued between Israel and the PLO. In 1993 the PLO and Israel agreed to establish Palestinian rule in the Gaza Strip and in Jericho on the West Bank. In 1995 this was extended to over 30% of the West Bank. Israeli PM Yitzhak Rabin, who sought a 'land for peace' settlement, was assassinated in 1995. Right-wing hardliner Binyamin Netanyahu became PM in 1996.

JERUSALEM

Repeatedly occupied and destroyed through history, it is a sacred site for Christians, Jews and Muslims. In 1948, it was divided between Jordan (east) and Israel (west). In 1967, the Israeli army captured the Old City of East Jerusalem. In 1980 the united city became the capital of Israel, but the UN refuses to recognize it.

ments in the occupied areas and attacks on Israel by the Lebanese militant Islamic group, Hezbollah. In 2001 former general Ariel Sharon was elected prime minister, adopting a hardline policy against the Palestinians. After negotiations failed, Israel unilaterally withdrew from Gaza in 2005, forcibly evicting its own settlers. In 2006 a stroke left Ariel Sharon in a permanent coma, and he was succeeded by his deputy Ehud Olmert. Israel responded to Hezbollah kidnappings of Israeli soldiers with a massive invasion of Lebanon, but withdrew after a few months.

ECONOMY

Israel has a high standard of living, while Palestinian areas remain poor. Israel's strong economy is based on the export of high technology manufacturing, military equipment and agricultural produce.

PALESTINIAN TERRITORIES

The West Bank and Gaza together form the Palestinian Territories. Arab districts in the 1947 partition plan, they were taken by Egypt and Jordan respecively after the first Arab-Israeli War (1948). After their capture by Israel in the Six-Day War (1967), Israeli settlers moved in.

Israel withdrew from Gaza and part of the West Bank in 2005 but still controls most access, and Israeli border controls effectively form an economic blockade. In 2006 elections the Islamist group Hamas, which refuses to acknowledge Israel or renounce violence, won a majority in the Territories' legislative council. In response, the EU and US cut off aid. In 2007, fighting between Hamas and the President's Fatah party split Palestine. The Gaza Strip fell entirely under Hamas control, while the West Bank remained in the hands of Fatah.

In 1999 the left-wing Ehud Barak won elections, promising to resume the peace process. Problems included Jewish settle-

ITALY

The Italian flag is based on the military standard carried by the French Republican National Guard when Napoleon invaded Italy in 1796, causing great changes in Italy's map. It was finally adopted as the national flag after Italy was unified in 1861.

The Republic of Italy is bordered to the north by the Alps which overlook the northern plains, Italy's most fertile and densely populated region, drained by the River Po. The Apennines (Appennini), which form the backbone of southern Italy, reach their highest peaks (3,000 m [9,800 ft]), in the Gran Sasso Range overlooking the Adriatic coast, near Pescara. Limestone is the most common rock. Between the mountains are long, narrow basins, some with lakes.

Southern Italy contains a string of volcanoes, stretching from Vesuvius, near Naples (Nápoli), through the Lipari Islands, to Mount Etna on Sicily. Traces of volcanic activity are found throughout Italy. Ancient lava flows cover large areas and produce fertile soils. Italy is still subject to earthquakes and volcanic eruptions. Sicily is the largest island in the Mediterranean. Sardinia is more isolated from the mainland and its rugged, windswept terrain and lack of resources have set it apart.

Area 301,318 sq km [116,339 sq mi]
Population 58,134,000
Capital (population) Rome (2,469,000)
Government Multiparty republic
Ethnic groups Italian 94%, German, French, Albanian, Slovene, Greek
Languages Italian (official),German, French, Slovene
Religions Roman Catholic
Currency Euro = 100 cents
Website www.enit.it

HISTORY

Magnificent ruins throughout Italy testify to the glories of the ancient Roman Empire, which was founded in 753 BC. It reached its peak in the AD 100s and finally collapsed in the 400s, although the Eastern Roman Empire survived another 1,000 years as the Byzantine Empire.

By the Middle Ages, Italy was split into many small states. In the Renaissance, they made a huge contribution to the revival of Classical art and learning after which the era is named. Cities such as Florence and Venice testify to the artistic achievements of this period.

The struggle for unification, the Risorgimento, began early in the 19th century. Little progress was made until an alliance between France and Piedmont drove Austria from Lombardy in 1859. Tuscany, Parma and Modena joined Piedmont-Lombardy in 1860, and the Papal States, Sicily, Naples – including most of the southern peninsula – and Romagna were brought into the alliance. King Victor Emmanuel II was proclaimed ruler of a united Italy the following year. Venetia was acquired from Austria in 1866 and Rome was finally

CLIMATE

The north has cold, snowy winters, but warm and sunny summer months. Rainfall is plentiful, with brief but powerful thunderstorms in summer. Southern Italy has mild, moist winters and warm, dry summers.

annexed in 1871. Since then, Italy has been a unified state, though the pope and his successors disputed the takeover of the Papal States. This dispute was resolved in 1929, when Vatican City was established as a fully independent state.

After unification the population grew rapidly, in what was then a poor country attempting to develop its resources, forcing millions of Italians to emigrate during the first quarter of the 20th century. Large numbers settled in the United States, South America and Australia. Later, emigrants headed for northern Europe. Today Italy's population growth rate is one of the slowest in the EU.

In 1915 Italy entered World War I alongside the Allied powers, Britain, France and Russia. After the war, Italy was given nearly 23,000 sq km [9,000 sq mi] of territory that had belonged to Austria-Hungary. Benito Mussolini became Fascist prime minister of Italy in 1922 and ruled as a dictator from 1925. In 1936 Italian forces invaded Ethiopia, and military personnel were sent to support the rebellion of General Franco in Spain. Italy agreed to fight alongside Germany in the event of war, though did not enter World War II until June 1940. During the war Italy lost its colonial empire to the Allies and, in late 1943, declared war on Germany. Mussolini was captured and shot by partisans in 1945 when he tried to escape to Switzerland.

Italy became a republic in 1946 following a referendum. Allied troops left in 1947. Italy was a founder member of NATO in 1949 and of the EEC, now the European Union, in 1957. After the establishment of the EEC, Italy's economy began to expand. Much of the economic development took place in the industrialized north. Central Italy is less developed and represents a transition zone between the developed north and the poor agrarian south known as the Mezzogiorno.

POLITICS

In 1992 the old political establishment was driven from office, with several prominent leaders accused of links to organized crime and some imprisoned. In 1996 the left-wing Olive Tree alliance led by Romano Prodi took office, but Prodi was forced to resign in 1998 following his rejection of demands made by his Communist allies. He was replaced by Massimo D'Alemo, the first former Communist to become prime minister. His attempts to create a two-party system in Italy failed in 1999.

By the late 1990s, Italy had the world's sixth largest economy. On 1 January 2002, the euro became its currency. In 2001, Italy moved towards the political right when centre-right parties won a substantial majority in parliament. Media tycoon Silvio Berlusconi, who had briefly served as prime minister in 1994 and who had spent several years fighting tax evasion charges, became prime minister. Accusations of corruption continued throughout his premiership and he was narrowly defeated by Prodi in 2006.

ECONOMY

Fifty years ago, Italy was a mainly agricultural society. Today it is a major industrial power. It imports most raw materials used in industry. Manufactures include cars, chemicals, processed food, machinery and textiles. Major crops include grapes for wine-making and olives, citrus fruits, sugar beet and vegetables. Cattle, pigs, poultry and sheep are raised.

ROME (ROMA)

Capital of Italy, on the River Tiber, west central Italy. Founded in the 8th century BC. The Roman Republic was founded around 500 BC. By the 3rd century BC, Rome ruled most of Italy and began to expand overseas. In the 1st century AD, the city was transformed as successive emperors built temples, palaces, public baths, arches and columns. It remained the capital of the Roman Empire until AD 330. In the 5th century, Rome was sacked during the Barbarian invasions, and its population fell rapidly. In the Middle Ages, Rome became the seat of the papacy. In 1527, it was sacked by the army of Charles V. The city flourished once more in the 16th and 17th centuries. Italian troops occupied it in 1870, and in 1871 it became the capital of a unified Italy. The 1922 Fascist march on Rome brought Mussolini to power; he did much to turn Rome into a modern capital city.

SAN MARINO

The Republic of San Marino, the world's smallest republic, lies 20 km [12 mi] south-west of the Adriatic port of Rimini and is wholly surrounded by Italy. It consists largely of the limestone mass of Monte Titano (725 m [2,382 ft]) around which cluster wooded mountains, pastures, fortresses and medieval villages. San Marino has pleasant, mild summers and cool winters.

Area 61 sq km [24 sq mi]
Population 29,000
Capital San Marino
Government Republic
Ethnic groups Sanmarinese, Italian
Languages Italian (official)
Religions Roman Catholic
Currency Euro = 100 cents
Website www.visitsanmarino.com

The republic was named after St Marinus, the stonemason saint who is said to have first established a community here in 301 AD. It has a friendship and co-operation treaty with Italy dating back to 1862 and uses Italian currency, but issues its own stamps, which are an important source of revenue. The state is governed by an elected council and has its own legal system. San Marino has no armed forces and its police are from the Italian constabulary. Most of the people live in the medieval city of San Marino, which receives more than 3 million tourists a year.

Chief occupations are tourism, limestone quarrying, ceramics, textiles and wine-making. The customs union with Italy makes San Marino an easy conduit for the illegal export of currency and certain kinds of tax evasion for Italians.

VATICAN CITY

The State of the Vatican City, the world's smallest independent nation, is an enclave on the west bank of the River Tiber in Rome. It forms an independent base for the Holy See, the governing body of the Roman Catholic Church. The state includes St Peter's Square, St Peter's Basilica and the Vatican Palace.

Area 0.44 sq km [0.17 sq mi]
Population 821
Capital (population) Vatican City (821)
Government Ecclesiastical
Ethnic groups Italian, Swiss, others
Languages Italian, Latin, French, others
Religions Roman Catholic
Currency Euro = 100 cents
Website www.vatican.va

The treasures of the Vatican, including Michelangelo's frescoes in the Sistine Chapel, attract tourists from the world. The Vatican Library contains a priceless collection of Christian and pre-Christian manuscripts. Popes have lived in the Vatican almost continuously since the 5th century. Sustained by investment income and voluntary contributions, Vatican City is all that remains of the Papal States which, until 1870, occupied most of central Italy. In 1929 Mussolini recognized the Vatican's independence in return for papal recognition of the kingdom of Italy.

The population, including the country's armed force of 100 Swiss Guards, consists entirely of unmarried males. The Commission appointed by the Pope to administer the affairs of the Vatican controls a radio station, the Pope's summer palace at Castel Gandolfo, and several churches in Rome. Vatican City has its own newspaper, police and railway stations, and issues its own stamps and coins.

IVORY COAST

This flag was adopted in 1960 when the country became independent from France. It combines elements from the French tricolour and the Pan-African colours. The orange represents the northern savanna, the white peace and unity and the green the forests in the south.

The Republic of the Ivory Coast, in West Africa, is officially known as Côte d'Ivoire. The south-east coast is bordered by sand bars that enclose lagoons, on one of which the former capital and chief port of Abidjan is situated. But the south-western coast is lined by rocky cliffs. Behind the coast is a coastal plain, but the land rises inland to high plains. The highest land is an extension of the Guinea Highlands in the north-west, along the borders with Liberia and Guinea. Most of the country's rivers run north–south.

Area 322,463 sq km [124,503 sq mi]
Population 17,655,000
Capital (population) Yamoussoukro (107,000)
Government Multiparty republic
Ethnic groups
Akan 42%, Voltaiques 18%, Northern Mandes 16%, Krous 11%, Southern Mandes 10%
Languages French (official), many native dialects
Religions Islam 40%, Christianity 30%, traditional beliefs 30%
Currency CFA franc = 100 centimes
Website
www.afrika.no/index/Countries/C_te_d_Ivoire/index.html

CLIMATE

Ivory Coast has a hot and humid tropical climate, with high temperatures throughout the year. There are two distinct rainy seasons in the south of the country: between May and July, and from October to November. Inland, the rainfall decreases. Northern Ivory Coast has a dry season and only one rainy season. As a result, the forests in central Ivory Coast thin out to the north, giving way to savanna.

HISTORY
The region that is now Ivory Coast came under successive African rulers until the late 15th century, when Europeans, attracted by the chance to trade in slaves and such local products as ivory, began to establish contacts along the coast. French missionaries reached the area in 1637 and, by the end of the 17th century, the French had set up trading posts on the coast. In 1842, France brought the Grand-Bassam area under its protection and Ivory Coast became a French colony in 1893. From 1895, it was ruled as part of French West Africa, a massive union which also included Benin, Burkina Faso, Guinea, Mali, Mauritania, Niger and Senegal. In 1946, Ivory Coast

ABIDJAN
Former capital of Ivory Coast, situated on Ebrié Lagoon, inland from the Gulf of Guinea. A chief port and commercial centre, Abidjan was founded by French colonists at the end of the 19th century. Although it lost capital status to Yamoussoukro in 1983, Abidjan remains a cultural and economic centre.

became a territory in the French Union. The port of Abidjan was built in the early 1950s. The country achieved autonomy from France in 1958.

POLITICS

Ivory Coast became fully independent in 1960. Its first president, Félix Houphouët-Boigny, became the longest serving head of state in Africa with an uninterrupted period in office that ended only with his death in 1993. Houphouët-Boigny was a paternalistic, pro-Western leader who made his country a one-party state. In 1983 the capital moved from Abidjan to Yamoussoukro, Houphouët-Boigny's birthplace.

Following the death of Houphouët-Boigny in 1993, the Speaker of the National Assembly, Henri Konan Bédié, proclaimed himself president. He was re-elected in 1995. In 1999 Bédié was overthrown during an army mutiny and a new administration was set up by General Robert Guei. Presidential elections, held after a new constitution was adopted in 2000, resulted in defeat for Guei. Veteran politician Laurent Gbago

became president. In 2002, economic problems and ethnic tensions led to civil war. In 2004 fighting died down, leaving the country divided into a government-held south and rebel-held, mainly Muslim, north. UN peacekeeping efforts including French and West African troops struggled to prevent ethnic conflict. Elections were postponed in 2005 and 2006. In 2007 a new peace deal attempted to revive the peace process, and rebel leader Guillaume Soro was appointed prime minister so that both sides would be represented in the government.

ECONOMY

Until the recent civil war, Ivory Coast was one of Africa's more prosperous countries. Its free-market economy attracted French commercial investment, while France's government has given much aid. Agriculture employs about three-fifths of the workforce. The chief farm products are cocoa, coffee and cotton, of which cocoa is by far the largest foreign exchange earner. Food crops include cassava, maize, plantains, rice, vegetables and yams. Manufactures include processed farm products, timber and textiles. Fluctuations in cocoa and coffee prices cause economic disruption, and unemployment is a serious problem.

YAMOUSSOUKRO

Capital of Ivory Coast since 1983. Originally a small Baouké tribal village and birthplace of Ivory Coast's first president, Félix Houphouët-Boigny, it developed rapidly into the administrative and transport centre of Ivory Coast. Yamoussoukro's Our Lady of Peace Cathedral (consecrated by Pope John Paul II in 1990) is the world's largest church.

JAMAICA

Jamaica is the third largest Caribbean island. It is a parliamentary democracy, with the monarch of the UK as its head of state. The coastal plain is narrow and discontinuous. Inland are hills, plateaux and mountains. The country's central range culminates in the Blue Mountain Peak (2,256 m [7,402 ft]). The Cockpit Country in the north-west of the island is an inaccessible limestone area, known for its many deep depressions, (cockpits). Jamaica is a lush, green island.

Area 10,990 sq km [4,244 sq mi]
Population 2,758,000
Capital (population) Kingston (104,000)
Government Constitutional monarchy
Ethnic groups Black 91%, Mixed 7%, East Indian
Languages English (official), patois English
Religions Protestant 61%, Roman Catholic 4%
Currency Jamaican dollar = 100 cents
Website www.jis.gov.jm

CLIMATE

The climate is hot and humid. Temperatures range from 25°C [77°F] in January to 27°C [81°F] in July. Moist south-east trade winds bring rain to the more temperate highlands. Annual rainfall on the northern slopes may reach 5,000 mm [200 in], but the sheltered south coast is much drier, about 750 mm [30 in] per year. The island is prone to periodic hurricanes.

HISTORY

In 1509, Spaniards occupied the island. Soon, the local Arawak Amerindian population had died out. The Spaniards imported African slaves to work the sugar plantations. The British took the island in 1655 and, with sugar as its staple product, it became a prized possession. The African slaves were the forefathers of much of the present population. The plantations on which they worked disappeared when the sugar market collapsed in the 19th century.

In 1865 the Morant Bay rebellion, a peasant uprising led by Baptist deacon, Paul Bogle, was staged by freed slaves who were suffering acute hardship. It was put down by British troops and, after 200 years of having its own elected body to help the British rule the island, Jamaica came under direct British rule as a crown colony. In the 1930s Jamaican leaders called for more power, and riots took place in 1938, with people protesting against unemployment and Britain's racial policies. In that year, the People's National Party (PNP) was founded. In 1944 Britain granted Jamaica a new constitution, providing for an elected House of Representatives. In 1958 the island became a member of the British-sponsored Federation of the West Indies, but it withdrew in 1961.

POLITICS

Jamaica became an independent nation and a member of the British Commonwealth in 1962. It joined the Organization of American States in 1969. In the 1970s, economic problems developed.

Michael Manley, leader of the PNP, became prime minister in 1972. He pursued socialist policies and advocated a policy of non-alignment. The PNP won a second term in office in 1976. It nationalized businesses and sought closer ties with Cuba. In 1980, the Jamaica Labour Party (JLP), led by Edward Seaga defeated the PNP in elections. Seaga privatized much state-owned business and distanced Jamaica from Cuba. His moderate policies led to increased investment and better relations with Western countries. In 1989, the PNP defeated the JLP and Manley was returned to power as prime minister. However, Manley broadly followed Seaga's moderate policies. Manley retired on health grounds in 1992 and was succeeded by Percival J Patterson. The PNP was re-elected in 1993, 1998, 2002 and 2006. In 2006 Portia Simpson-Miller replaced Patterson to become the country's first female prime minister.

Jamaica faces many problems, including drug trafficking. It has become a major transshipment point for cocaine being transported from South America to North America and Europe. Cannabis is produced in Jamaica. Corruption and money-laundering are major concerns. There is a very high murder rate – over 1,100 in 2004 – which is attributed to street-gang violence.

The island is frequently hit by hurricanes. In 2004 Hurricane Ivan destroyed thousands of homes, and was described as the worst disaster in living memory.

ECONOMY

Jamaica is a developing country. Agriculture employs about 20% of the workforce. The chief crop is sugar cane. Other products include allspice, bananas, citrus fruits, cocoa, coconuts, coffee, poultry, vegetables and yams. The country's chief resource is bauxite, aluminium ore, of which Jamaica is one of the world's top producers. Cement, chemicals, cigars, clothing and textiles, fertilizers, machinery, molasses and petroleum products are also produced. Service industries account for 60% of the gross domestic product. Tourism brings in vital revenue.

KINGSTON

Capital and largest city of Jamaica. It was founded in 1693 and rapidly developed into Jamaica's commercial centre, based on the export of raw cane sugar, bananas and rum. In 1872 it became the island's capital. Kingston is the cultural heart of Jamaica and the home of calypso and reggae music.

JAPAN

Japan's flag was officially adopted in 1870, though Japanese emperors had used this simple design for many centuries. The flag shows a red sun on a white background. The geographical position of Japan is also expressed in its name 'Nippon' or 'Nihon', meaning 'source of the Sun'.

Japan is an island nation in northeastern Asia containing four large islands – Honshu, Hokkaido, Kyushu and Shikoku – which make up more than 98% of the country. Thousands of small islands, including the Ryukyu island chain, make up the rest of the country.

The four main islands are mainly mountainous, while many of the small islands are the tips of volcanoes rising from the sea bed. Japan has more than 150 volcanoes, about 60 of which are active. Volcanic eruptions, earthquakes and tsunamis often occur, because the islands lie on an unstable part of the Earth's crust where the continental plates are constantly moving.

Throughout Japan, complex folding and faulting has produced an intricate mosaic of landforms. Mountains and forested hills alternate with small basins and coastal lowlands, covered by alluvium deposited there by the short rivers that rise in the uplands. Most of the population lives on the coastal plains, one being the stretch from the Kanto Plain, where Tokyo is situated, along the narrow plains that border the southern coasts of Honshu, to northern Kyushu.

The pattern of landforms is further complicated by the presence of volcanic cones and calderas. The highest mountain in Japan, Fuji-san (3,776 m [12,388 ft]), is a long dormant volcano which last erupted in 1707. It is considered sacred, and is visited by thousands of pilgrims every year.

Area 377,829 sq km [145,880 sq mi]
Population 127,464,000
Capital (population) Tokyo (12,064,000)
Government Constitutional monarchy
Ethnic groups Japanese 99%, Chinese, Korean, Brazilian and others
Languages Japanese (official)
Religions Shintoism and Buddhism 84% (most Japanese consider themselves to be both Shinto and Buddhist), others
Currency Yen = 100 sen
Website http://web-japan.org

winters. At Sapporo, temperatures below –20°C [4°F] have been recorded between December and March. Summers are warm, with temperatures often exceeding 30°C [86°F]. Rain falls throughout the year. Tokyo has the higher rainfall and temperatures while the southern islands of Shikoku and Kyushu in the south have warm temperate climates with hot summers and cold winters.

CLIMATE

The climate of Japan varies greatly. Hokkaido in the north has cold, snowy

HISTORY

Most modern Japanese are descendants of early immigrants who arrived in successive waves from the Korean Peninsula and other parts of the Asian mainland. The earliest zone of settlement included the northern part of Kyushu Island and the coastlands of Setonaikai (Inland Sea). By the 5th century AD, Japan was divided among numerous clans, of which the largest and most powerful was the Yamato. The Yamato ruled from the area which now contains the city of Nara. Shinto, a polytheistic religion based on nature worship, was practised, and the Japanese imperial dynasty established. The chiefs of the Yamato clan are regarded as ancestors of the Japanese imperial family.

The 5th century AD was a time when new ideas and technology reached Japan from China. The Japanese adopted the Chinese system of writing and their methods of calculating the calendar. Confucianism was also introduced from China and, in about 552, Buddhism reached Japan.

From the early 12th century, political power passed increasingly to military aristocrats. Government was conducted in the name of the emperor by warrior leaders called shoguns. Civil warfare between rival groups of feudal lords was endemic over long periods, but, under the rule of the Tokugawa shoguns, between 1603 and 1867, Japan enjoyed a great period of peace and prosperity. The feudal lords and their retainers, or samurai, formed a powerful military elite. During the shogun era the samurai aspired to a code of conduct called bushido, which demanded obedience to strict rules of honour and stressed loyalty to their feudal lords. As Japanese society developed, samurai became courtiers, bureaucrats and administrators as well as warriors.

European contact began with the arrival of Portuguese sailors in 1543, then in 1549 a Spanish missionary came to convert the Japanese to Christianity. The Japanese put an end to missionary work in the 1630s when they ordered all Christian missionaries to leave the country and forced Japanese converts to give up their faith. The only Europeans allowed to stay were Dutch traders, as they were not involved in missionary work. Japan opened its ports to Western trade again only in 1854 after American intervention.

The Meiji period, from 1867 to 1912, was marked by the adoption of Western ideas and technology. An educational system and a telegraph network were set up, railways built and modern systems of banking and taxation were introduced. The samurai class was abolished and a modern army and navy established.

In 1889 Japan introduced its first constitution, under which the emperor became head of state and supreme commander of the army and navy. The emperor appointed government ministers, responsible to him. The constitution also allowed for a parliament, called the Diet, with two houses.

From the 1890s, Japan began to build up an overseas empire. In 1894–5, Japan fought China over the control of Korea. Under the Treaty of Shimonoseki (1895), Japan took Taiwan. Korea was made an independent territory, leaving it open to Japanese influence. Rivalry with Russia led to the Russo-Japanese War (1904–5). Under the Treaty of Portsmouth, Japan gained the Liaodong peninsula, which Russia had leased from China, while Russia recognized the supremacy of Japan's interests in Korea. Japan became established as a world power.

In World War I Japan supported the Allies. After the war Japan's foreign policy strongly supported the maintenance of world peace, and the country became a founding member of the League of Nations in 1920. The army seized Manchuria in 1931 and made it a puppet state, which was named Manchukuo. It then extended its influence into other parts of northern China. In 1933, after the League of Nations condemned its actions in Manchuria, Japan was forced to rescind its membership.

During the 1930s, and especially after the outbreak of war between Japan and China in 1937, militarist control of Japan's government grew steadily. By the end of 1938, when Japan controlled most of eastern China, there was talk of bringing all of eastern Asia under Japanese control. In September 1939, Japan occupied the northern part of French Indo-China and, later that month, signed an agreement with Italy and Germany, assuring their co-operation in building a 'new world order', and acknowledging Japan's leadership in Asia.

In 1941 Japan launched a surprise attack on the American naval base of Pearl Harbor, in Hawaii, an action that drew the United States into World War II. On 6 August 1945, American bombers dropped the first atomic bomb on

Hiroshima. The USSR declared war on Japan and invaded Manchuria and Korea. On 9 August, the Americans dropped an atomic bomb on Nagasaki. World War II ended on 2 September 1945 when Japan officially surrendered.

POLITICS

The Allies occupied Japan in August 1945. Under a new constitution, which formally required the country to become pacifist, the emperor became a constitutional monarch. The army and navy were reduced to small defence forces.

Japan signed a Treaty of Peace that took effect on 28 April 1952. The Allied occupation ended on that day. In 1956 the Soviet Union and Japan agreed to end the state of war between them, and Japan became a member of the UN.

The conservative Liberal-Democratic Party was formed in 1955, made up of rival Japanese parties. The LDP controlled Japan's government until the 1990s, when a series of coalition governments were formed. A true opposition party emerged in the late 1990s, when the Democratic Party of Japan united with several small parties. The country underwent a serious economic crisis in 1997. In 2001, the LDP chose Junichiro Koizumi as prime minister. Koizumi promised drastic reforms to revive the economy, and sought to loosen Japan's commitment to pacifism. He won a landslide victory in 2005 elections after his plans to privatize Japan's postal system were defeated in the upper house. He was succeeded by Shinzo Abe in 2006, but the latter's period in office was dogged by political scandal and he was replaced by Yasuo Fukuda in September 2007.

ECONOMY

Japan has the world's second highest GDP after the United States. The most important sectors of the economy are financial services and manufacturing industry. Though Japan has to import raw materials and fuels, the development of high technology has given Japanese products a global market. Manufactures dominate its exports, which include machinery, electronic equipment, vehicles and transport equipment and chemicals. Economic growth, usually strong, was slowed by recession in the mid 1990s but recovered in the 2000s.

Japan has one of the world's largest fishing fleets. Only 15% of the land can be farmed, because of its rugged nature. Rice is the chief crop, taking up about half of the farmland, and Japan is usually self-sufficient in rice though heavily dependent on imports for other foods. Other farm products include fruits, sugar beet, tea and vegetables.

TOKYO

Capital of Japan, on east-central Honshu, at the head of Tokyo Bay. The modern city divides into distinct districts: Kasumigaseki, Japan's administrative centre; Marunouchi, its commercial centre; Ginza, its shopping and cultural centre; the west shore of Tokyo Bay, its industrial centre. Modern Tokyo also serves as the country's educational centre with more than 100 universities. Founded in the 12th century as Edo, it became capital of the Tokugawa shogunate in 1603. In 1868, the Japanese Reformation re-established imperial power, and the last shogun surrendered Edo Castle. Emperor Meiji renamed the city Tokyo, and it replaced Kyoto as the capital of Japan. In 1923, an earthquake and subsequent fire claimed more than 150,000 lives and necessitated the city's reconstruction. In 1944–5, intensive US bombing destroyed more than half of Tokyo, and another modernization and restoration programme began. Industries include electronics, cameras, car manufacture, metals, chemicals, textiles.

JORDAN

The green, white and black on this flag are the colours of the three tribes who led the Arab Revolt against the Turks in 1917. Red is the colour of the Hussein Dynasty. The star was added in 1928. Its seven points represent the first seven verses of the sacred book, the Koran.

The Hashemite Kingdom of Jordan is an Arab country in south-western Asia. The Great Rift Valley in the west contains the River Jordan and the Dead Sea. East of the Rift Valley is the Transjordan Plateau, where most Jordanians live. To the east and south lie vast areas of desert. Jordan has a short coastline on an arm of the Red Sea, the Gulf of Aqaba. The country's highest peak is Jabal Ram (1,754 m [5,755 ft]).

Area 89,342 sq km [34,495 sq mi]
Population 5,907,000
Capital (population) Amman (1,292,000)
Government Constitutional monarchy
Ethnic groups Arab 98% (Palestinians 50%)
Languages Arabic (official)
Religions Islam (mostly Sunni) 94%, Christianity (mostly Greek Orthodox) 6%
Currency Jordanian dinar = 1,000 fils
Website www.tourism.jo

CLIMATE

About 90% of Jordan has a desert climate, with an average annual rainfall of less than 200 mm [8 in]. Summers are hot and winters can be cold, with snow on higher areas. The north-west is the wettest area, with an average annual rainfall of 800 mm [31 in] in higher areas.

HISTORY

Jordan was first settled by Semitic peoples about 4,000 years ago, and later conquered by Egyptian, Assyrian, Chaldean, Persian and Roman forces. The area fell to Muslim Arabs in AD 636 and Arab culture remains dominant to this day.

By the end of the 12th century Christian crusaders controlled parts of western Jordan, but they were driven out by the great Muslim warrior Saladin in 1187. The Egyptian Mamelukes overthrew Saladin's successors in 1250 and ruled until

1517, when the area was conquered by the Ottoman Turks. Jordan stagnated under their rule, but the opening of a railway in 1908 stimulated the economy. Arab and British forces defeated the Turks during World War I.

After the war, the area east of the River Jordan was awarded to Britain by the League of Nations as a territory called Transjordan. It became self-governing in 1923, but Britain retained control of its defences, finances and foreign affairs. Transjordan became fully independent as Jordan in 1946.

Since the creation of the State of Israel in 1948, Jordan has suffered from instability arising from Arab-Israeli conflict. After the first Arab-Israeli War (1948-9) Jordan acquired the West Bank, which was officially incorporated into the state in 1950. This crucial area, including East Jerusalem, was captured by Israel in the Six-Day war of 1967. Many Palestinians were forced to seek refuge in Jordan. In 1970, Palestinian guerrillas using Jordan as a base became a challenge to the authority of King Hussein's government and the country fell into civil war. In 1971 Jordan ejected all guerillas operating from its soil and restored peace.

King Hussein, who had commanded great respect for his role in Middle Eastern affairs, died in 1999. He was succeeded by his eldest son who became King Abdullah II. Following the path of his father, Abdullah sought to further the Israeli-Palestinian peace process. He also worked to consolidate his country's relations with other nations in the region. Despite local opposition to the invasion of Iraq in 2003, he supported the US-led war on terrorism and worked to improve relations with Israel. However, in November 2005 suicide bombers killed 57 in Amman and terrorist group al-Qaeda claimed responsibility.

ECONOMY

Jordan's economy depends substantially on aid. The World Bank classifies Jordan as a 'lower-middle-income' developing country. Less than 6% of the land is farmed. Jordan has an oil refinery and manufactures include cement, ceramics, pharmaceuticals, processed food, fertilizers, shoes and textiles. Service industries, including tourism, employ more than 70% of the workforce.

POLITICS

In 1988 King Hussein renounced all responsibility for the West Bank, recognizing the Palestine Liberation Organization as the legitimate representative of the Palestinian people. Palestinians were still a majority of the population in the remaining part of Jordan. Refugees from the Palestinian Territories, numbering around 900,000, placed a huge burden on an economy already weakened by the loss of trade links with Israel. Jordan was further undermined by the 1991 Gulf War when, despite its neutrality, the anti-Western stance of the Palestinians in Jordan damaged prospects of trade and aid deals with Europe and the US. A ban on political parties was removed in 1991, and martial law was finally lifted 21 years after the civil war. Multiparty elections were held in 1993. In 1994 Jordan and Israel signed a peace treaty, ending a 40-year state of war and restoring some land in the south to Jordan.

AMMAN

Capital and largest city of Jordan. Known as Rabbath-Ammon, it was the chief city of the Ammonites in biblical times. Ptolemy II Philadelphus renamed it Philadelphia. A new city was built on seven hills from 1875, and it became the capital of Trans-Jordan in 1921. From 1948 it grew rapidly, partly as a result of the influx of Palestinian refugees. Industries include cement, textiles, tobacco and leather.

KAZAKHSTAN

Kazakhstan's flag was adopted on 4 June 1992, about six months after it had become independent. The blue represents cloudless skies, while the golden sun and the soaring eagle represent love of freedom. A vertical strip of gold ornamentation is on the left.

The Republic of Kazakhstan is a large country in west-central Asia. In the west, the Caspian Sea lowlands include the Karagiye Depression, which reaches 132 m [433 ft] below sea level. The lowlands extend eastwards through the Aral Sea area. The north contains high plains, but the highest land is along the eastern and southern borders. These areas include parts of the Altai and Tian Shan mountain ranges.

Eastern Kazakhstan contains several freshwater lakes, the largest of which is Lake Balkhash (Balqash Köl). The water in the rivers has been used for irrigation, causing ecological problems. The Aral Sea, deprived of water, shrank from 66,900 sq km [25,830 sq mi] in 1960, to 33,642 sq km [12,989 sq mi] in 1993. Areas which once provided fish have dried up and are now barren desert.

Kazakhstan has very little woodland. Grassy steppe covers much of the north, while the south is desert or semi-desert. Large, dry areas between the Aral Sea and Lake Balkhash have become irrigated farmland.

Area 2,724,900 sq km [1,052,084 sq mi]
Population 15,233,000
Capital (population) Astana (322,000)
Government Multiparty republic
Ethnic groups Kazakh 53%, Russian 30%, Ukranian 4%, German 2%, Uzbek 2%
Languages Kazakh (official), Russian, the former official language, is widely spoken
Religions Islam 47%, Russian Orthodox 44%
Currency Tenge = 100 tiyn
Website www.kazakhstanun.org

HISTORY

From the late 15th century, the Kazakhs built up a large nomadic empire ruled by khans, but Kazakh power declined in the 17th century. In the early 18th century, Russia became influential in the area. In 1731, the Kazakhs in the west accepted Russian rule to gain protection from attack from neighbouring peoples. By the mid-1740s, Russia ruled most of the region and, in the early 19th century, Russia abolished the khanates. They also

CLIMATE

The extreme climate reflects its position in the heart of Asia, far from the oceans. Winters are cold and snow covers the land for about 100 days, on average, at Almaty (Alma Ata). Rainfall is generally highest in spring.

CASPIAN SEA

Shallow salt lake, the world's largest inland body of water. The Caspian Sea is enclosed on three sides by Russia, Kazakhstan, Turkmenistan and Azerbaijan. The southern shore forms the northern border of Iran. It has been a valuable trade route for centuries. It is fed mainly by the River Volga; there is no outlet. The chief ports are Baku and Astrakhan. It has important fisheries and an area of 371,000 sq km [143,000 sq mi].

Soviet republic whose ethnic population is almost outnumbered by Russians, and its Muslim revival is relatively muted. Its first elected president, former Communist leader Nursultan Nazarbayev, introduced many reforms including a multiparty system. However, he has been criticized for his authoritarian rule. International observers considered the elections of 2004 and 2005 to be seriously flawed. In 2007, constitutional reforms strengthened parliament and limited the number of terms future presidents could serve, but permitted Nazarbayev to stand indefinitely.

encouraged Russians and Ukrainians to settle in Kazakhstan.

After the Russian Revolution of 1917 Kazakhs wanted independence, but the Communists prevailed. In 1936 Kazakhstan became a republic of the Soviet Union called the Kazakh Soviet Socialist Republic. During and after World War II, the Soviet government moved many people from the west into Kazakhstan. From the 1950s people were encouraged to work on a 'Virgin Lands' project, which involved bringing large areas of grassland under cultivation. The Soviets placed many of their nuclear missile sites in Kazakhstan, sited the Baikonur cosmodrome there and also built their first fast-breeder nuclear reactor at Mangyshlak.

POLITICS

Reforms in the Soviet Union in the 1980s led to its break-up 1991. Kazakhstan kept contacts with Russia and most of the former Soviet republics by joining the Commonwealth of Independent States (CIS), and in 1995 Kazakhstan announced that its army would unite with that of Russia. In 1997 the government moved the capital from Alma Ata to Aqmola, a town in the Russian-dominated north later renamed Astana. The move was intended to bring some Kazakh identity to the area.

Kazakhstan has emerged as a powerful entity, wealthier and more diversified than other Asian republics. It is the only former

ECONOMY

The World Bank classifies Kazakhstan as a 'lower-middle-income' developing country. Livestock farming, especially sheep and cattle, is an important activity, and major crops include barley, cotton, rice and wheat.

The country is rich in mineral resources, including coal and oil reserves, together with bauxite, copper, lead, tungsten and zinc. Manufactures include chemicals, food products, machinery and textiles. The oil industry has grown rapidly, with exports both to Europe, via a Russian-controlled Caspian Sea pipeline, and to China by a direct link. Growing oil exports made Kazakhstan one of the world's fastest-growing economies in the mid 2000s.

ASTANA
(formerly AQMOLA)

Capital of Kazakhstan, on the River Ishim in the steppes of north-central Kazakhstan. Under Soviet rule, Aqmola functioned as capital of the Virgin Lands. From 1961 to 1993 it was known as Tselinograd, and from 1993 to 1998 as Aqmola.

KENYA

Kenya's flag dates from 1963, when the country became independent. It is based on the flag of KANU (Kenya African National Union), the political party which led the nationalist struggle. The Masai warrior's shield and crossed spears represent the defence of freedom.

The Republic of Kenya is located in East Africa, across the Equator. Behind the narrow coastal plain on the Indian Ocean the land rises to high plains and highlands, broken by volcanic mountains including the highest peak, Mount Kenya, at 5,199 m [17,057 ft].

Crossing the country is an arm of the Great Rift Valley with several lakes including Baringo, Magadi, Naivasha, Nakuru and, on the northern frontier, Lake Turkana (formerly Lake Rudolf).

Area 580,367 sq km [224,080 sq mi]
Population 34,708,000
Capital (population) Nairobi (2,818,000)
Government Multiparty republic
Ethnic groups Kikuyu 22%, Luhya 14%, Luo 13%, Kalenjin 12%, Kamba 11%, others
Languages Kiswahili and English (both official)
Religions Protestant 45%, Roman Catholic 33%, traditional beliefs 10%, Islam 10%
Currency Kenyan shilling = 100 cents
Website www.kenya.go.ke

CLIMATE

The coast is hot and humid, but inland the climate is moderated by the height of the land. The thickly populated south-western highlands have summer temperatures 10°C [18°F] lower than the coast. Nights can be cool, but temperatures stay above zero. The main rainy season is from April to May. Only 15% of the country has a reliable rainfall of 800 mm [31 in].

HISTORY

The Kenyan coast has been an important trading centre for more than 2,000 years. Early Arab traders carried goods from eastern Asia and exchanged them for items from the local people. Portuguese explorer Vasco da Gama reached the coast in 1498. Later, the Portuguese competed with the Arabs for control of the coast.

The British took control of the coast in 1895, soon extending their influence

MOMBASA

City and seaport on the Indian Ocean, south-western Kenya, partly on Mombasa Island, partly on the mainland. From the 11th to 16th centuries, Mombasa was a centre of the Arab slave and ivory trades. From 1529 to 1648, the Portuguese held the port. Taken by Zanzibar in the mid-19th century, the city passed to Britain in 1887, when it became capital of the British East Africa Protectorate. Kenya's chief port, Mombasa exports coffee, fruit and grain. Industries include tourism, food processing, glass, oil refining.

between the political and economic policies of the countries. Hopes were revived in 1999, when a new East African Community was created. Its aim was to establish a customs union, a common market, a monetary union and, ultimately, a political union.

Jomo Kenyatta died in 1978 and was succeeded by the vice-president Daniel arap Moi, who stood down in 2002 after having been criticized for his autocratic rule, as well as corruption. The veteran Mwai Kibaki was elected president in 2002, promising to stamp out corruption, but little progress was made. In 2006 Kibaki's government became caught up in a large-scale corruption scandal.

ECONOMY
According to the United Nations, Kenya is a 'low-income' developing country. Agriculture employs about 80% of the people, but many Kenyans are subsistence farmers. The chief food crop is maize. Bananas, beans, cassava and sweet potatoes are also grown. The main cash crops are coffee and tea. Manufactures include chemicals, leather, footwear, processed food, petroleum products and textiles.

inland. Many Britons set up large farms. Opposition to British rule mounted in the 1940s and, in 1953, a secret movement called Mau Mau launched an armed struggle. Mau Mau was eventually defeated, but Kenya finally gained independence in 1963. Kenya's first president was nationalist veteran Jomo Kenyatta.

POLITICS
Many Kenyan leaders felt that the division of the population into 40 ethnic groups might lead to instability. They argued that Kenya should have a strong central government and, as a result, Kenya has been a one-party state for much of the time since independence. Multiparty democracy was restored in the early 1990s with elections in 1992, 1997 and 2002.

In the 1960s, attempts by Kenya, Tanzania and Uganda to collaborate collapsed because of the deep differences

NAIROBI

Capital and largest city of Kenya, in the south central part of the country. Founded in 1899, Nairobi replaced Mombasa as the capital of the British East Africa Protectorate in 1905. Nairobi has a national park (1946), a university (1970) and several institutions of higher education. It is an administrative and commercial centre. Industries: cigarettes, textiles, chemicals, food processing, furniture, glass.

KOREA, NORTH

The flag of the Democratic People's Republic of Korea (North Korea) has been flown since Korea was split into two states in 1948. The colours are traditional ones in Korea. The design, with the red star, indicates that North Korea is a Communist country.

The Democratic People's Republic of Korea occupies the northern part of the Korean Peninsula extending south from north-eastern China. Mountains form the heart of the country. The highest peak, Paektu-san (2,744 m [9,003 ft]) is on the northern border. East of the mountains lie the eastern coastal plains, which are densely populated, as are the coastal plains to the west which contain the capital, Pyongyang. Another small highland region in the south-east borders South Korea.

The coastal plains are mostly farmed, but some patches of chestnut, elm and oak woodland survive on the hilltops. The mountains contain forests of such trees cedar, fir, pine and spruce.

Area 120,538 sq km [46,540 sq mi]
Population 23,113,000
Capital (population) Pyongyang (3,124,000)
Government Single-party people's republic
Ethnic groups Korean 99%
Languages Korean (official)
Religions Buddhism and Confucianism (religious freedom now an illusion created by government-sponsored religious groups)
Currency North Korean won = 100 chon
Website www.korea-dpr.com

CLIMATE

North Korea has a fairly severe climate, with bitterly cold winters. Winds from across central Asia bring snow. Rivers freeze over and sea-ice may block harbours on the coast. In summer, moist winds from the sea bring rain.

HISTORY

Korea's history before North and South Korea were separated is described in pages 222–3 [see Korea, South]. A Japanese colony since 1910, North Korea was created in 1945 when Soviet forces occupied the north and US forces the south, dividing the peninsula in two. Soviet occupation led to a Communist government being established in 1948 under the leadership of Kim Il Sung.

The Korean War began in June 1950 when North Korean troops invaded the south. North Korea, aided by China and the Soviet Union, fought with South Korea, which was supported by troops from the United States and other UN members. The war ended in July 1953. An armistice was signed but no permanent peace treaty was agreed. The war caused great destruction and loss of life, with 1.6 million Communist troops killed, wounded or reported missing.

POLITICS

Between 1948 and his death in 1994 Kim Il Sung was a virtual dictator, ruling along similar lines to Stalin in the Soviet Union. After the war, North Korea adopted a hostile policy towards South Korea in pursuit of its aim of reunification. The end of the Cold War in the late 1980s eased relations between North and South and they both joined the UN in 1991. The two countries made several agreements, including one in which they agreed not to use force against each

Proliferation Treaty. Despite reports of malnutrition, North Korea formally requested an end to food aid in September 2005, probably becaue that government feared that accepting it might be seen as a sign of weakness. In 2006 North Korea tested a nuclear weapon, to widespread international condemnation; the UN imposed economic sanctions. In 2007 the country agreed to give up its nuclear programme in exchange for fuel oil and food aid.

ECONOMY

North Korea's considerable resources include coal, copper, iron ore, lead, tin, tungsten and zinc. Under Communism, North Korea has concentrated on developing heavy, state-owned industries. Manufactures include chemicals, iron and steel, machinery, processed food and textiles. Agriculture employs about a third of the population and rice is the leading crop. Economic decline and mismanagement, aggravated by three successive crop failures caused by floods in 1995 and 1996, and a drought in 1997, led to famine on a large scale.

other. However, the collapse of Communism in the Soviet Union meant that North Korea remained isolated.

In 1993, North Korea triggered a new international crisis by announcing that it was withdrawing from the Nuclear Non-Proliferation Treaty, leading to suspicions that it was developing its own nuclear weapons. Upon his death in 1994 Kim Il Sung was succeeded by his son, Kim Jong Il.

In the early 2000s, uncertainty surrounding North Korea's nuclear capabilities cast unease across the entire region. Talks between North and South Korea continued in an attempt to normalize relations between them. In 2003 North Korea's relations with the United States further deteriorated when the US accused the country of having a secret nuclear weapons programme. North Korea withdrew from international talks in early 2005 stating that it had already produced nuclear weapons. However, it later agreed to give up all its nuclear activities and rejoin the nuclear Non-

PYONGYANG

Capital of North Korea, in the west of the country, on the River Taedong. An ancient city, it was the capital of the Choson, Koguryo and Koryo kingdoms. In the 16th and 17th centuries, it came under both Japanese and Chinese rule. Pyongyang's industry developed during the Japanese occupation from 1910–45. It became the capital of North Korea in 1948. During the Korean War (1950–3), it suffered considerable damage.

KOREA, SOUTH

South Korea's flag, adopted in 1950, is white, the traditional symbol for peace. The central 'yin-yang' symbol signifies the opposing forces of nature. The four black symbols stand for the four seasons, the points of the compass, and the Sun, Moon, Earth and Heaven.

The Republic of Korea, as South Korea is officially known, occupies the southern part of the Korean Peninsula. Mountains cover much of the country. The southern and western coasts are major farming regions. There are many islands along the west and south coasts, the largest of which is Cheju-do, with South Korea's highest peak, Halla-san (1,950 m [6,398 ft]).

Area 99,268 sq km [38,327 sq mi]
Population 48,847,000
Capital (population) Seoul (9,888,000)
Government Multiparty republic
Ethnic groups Korean 99%
Languages Korean (official)
Religions No affiliation 46%, Christianity 26%, Buddhism 26%, Confucianism 1%
Currency South Korean won = 100 chon
Website www.kois.go.kr

CLIMATE

South Korea is chilled in winter by cold, dry winds blowing from central Asia. Snow often covers the mountains in the east. The summers are hot and wet, especially in July and August.

HISTORY

The Chinese conquered the north in 108 BC and ruled until AD 313. Mongol armies attacked Korea in the 13th century. In 1388 general Yi Songgye founded a dynasty of rulers which lasted until 1910.

From the 17th century Korea prevented foreigners from entering the country, earning it the name the 'Hermit Kingdom' until 1876 when Japan forced it to open some of its ports. Soon the United States, Russia and some European countries were trading with Korea. In 1910 the Japanese forcibly annexed Korea, which became a Japanese colony.

After Japan's defeat in World War II, North Korea was occupied by Soviet troops, while South Korea was occupied by United States forces. Attempts at reunification failed and, in 1948, a

SEOUL (KYONGSONG)

Capital of South Korea, on the River Han. The political, commercial, industrial and cultural centre of South Korea, it was founded in 1392 as the capital of the Yi dynasty. It developed rapidly under the Japanese (1910–45). Following the 1948 partition, it became capital of South Korea. Seoul's capture by North Korean troops precipitated the start of the Korean War (1950–3), and the following months witnessed the city's virtual destruction. In 1951, it became the headquarters of the UN command in Korea and a rebuilding programme commenced. By the 1970s, it was the hub of one of the most successful economies of South east Asia. In 1996, there were violent student demonstrations for reunification with North Korea. Seoul hosted the Summer Olympics in 1988 and the semi-final of the 2002 Fifa World Cup.

the early 1960s. Initiated by a military government and based on limited natural resources, the country used its cheap, plentiful, well-educated labour force to transform the economy. The manufacturing base of textiles remained important, South Korea also became a world leader in footwear, shipbuilding, consumer electronics, toys and vehicles.

In 1988 a new constitution came into force, enabling presidential elections to be held every five years. Evidence of the new spirit of democracy came in 1997 presidential elections when Kim Dae-jung, leader of past pro-democracy campaigns, narrowly defeated the governing party's candidate. In foreign affairs, a major breakthrough had occurred in 1991 when both North and South Korea were admitted as full members of the United Nations. The two countries signed several agreements, including one in which they agreed not to use force against each other, but tensions between them continued. In 2000, South Korea's President Dae-jung met with North Korea's Kim Jong Il in talks aimed at establishing better relations between the countries, but the prospect of reunification seemed as distant as ever. In 2002 elections Roh Moo-hyun became president.

National Assembly was elected in South Korea. This Assembly created the Republic of Korea, with North Korea becoming a Communist state. North Korean troops invaded the South in June 1950, sparking off the Korean War. The war lasted until 1953.

POLITICS

The story of South Korea after the civil war differs greatly from that of the North. Land reform based on smallholdings worked to produce some of the world's highest rice yields and self-sufficiency in food grains. The real economic miracle came with industrial expansion started in

ECONOMY

The World Bank classifies South Korea as an 'upper-middle-income' developing country. It is one of the world's fastest growing industrial economies. Resources include coal and tungsten. The main manufactures are computers and consumer electronics, cars, processed foods and textiles. Heavy industries include chemicals, fertilizers, shipbuilding and steel. Farming and fishing remain important activities. Rice is the chief food crop.

KUWAIT

The colours of Kuwait's flag are pan-Arab. The green symbolizes Kuwaiti hospitality. The white represents the commitment to peace. The red symbolizes Kuwait's determination to resist aggression. The black signifies decisiveness.

The State of Kuwait is a small, oil-rich Arab country at the head of the Persian Gulf. It consists of a mainland area and several offshore islands. The capital, Kuwait City, stands on a natural harbour called Kuwait Bay. Most of the land is a flat or gently undulating plain. The highest point is about 250 m [820 ft]. There are no rivers or lakes and water supply is a problem. Water is imported, but drinking water is also produced by desalination plants. Desert scrub covers some areas, but much of Kuwait has no vegetation.

Area 17,818 sq km [6,880 sq mi]
Population 2,418,000
Capital (population) Kuwait City (879,000)
Government Constitutional monarchy
Ethnic groups Kuwaiti 45%, other Arab 35%, South Asian 9%, Iranian 4%, other 7%
Languages Arabic (official), English
Religions Islam 85%, Christianity, Hinduism
Currency Kuwaiti dinar = 1000 fils
Website www.kuwait-info.org

CLIMATE

Kuwait has a hot desert climate. Annual rainfall is around 125 mm [5 in] and most rain occurs between November and March. Winters are mild and pleasant, but summers are hot, with average temperatures reaching 33°C to 35°C [91–95°F] between June and September. August to September are the most uncomfortable months, because the humidity is then at its highest. Periodically, hot sandstorms or duststorms blow from central Arabia.

HISTORY

In the 17th century, the north-western part of the Arabian peninsula became part of the Turkish Ottoman empire. The area was thinly populated until about 1710, when people from Arabia settled there and built the port that later became Kuwait City. They elected the head of the Al Sabah family as their ruler, and this family still rules Kuwait today.

British interest in the area began near the end of the 18th century when Kuwait's leader, Sheikh Mubarak, feared Turkish domination. In 1899 Britain became responsible for Kuwait's defence, and in 1914 the territory became a British protectorate. Britain provided naval protection, while taking control of Kuwait's external affairs. Drilling for oil began in 1936 and large reserves were discovered by the US-British Kuwait Oil Company. Production was delayed by World War II (1939–45), but oil was produced commercially in 1946. Kuwait soon became a prosperous oil exporter. The government financed great improvements to the infrastructure, and Kuwaitis soon enjoyed a high standard of living.

POLITICS

Kuwait became an independent state on 19 June 1961, and the Sheikh, the head of state, became an Amir (Emir). Kuwait joined the Arab League, and Iraq renewed its claim that Kuwait was legally part of its territory. British military intervention forced Iraq to back down. In 1963, elections were held to the National Assembly under a new constitution. However, the Amir suspended the National Assembly in 1976. The National Assembly was restored in 1981 but dissolved again in 1986.

In the Iran-Iraq War, which began in 1980, Kuwait supported Iraq with large loans. After the war, Iraq accused Kuwait of drilling across the border to take Iraqi oil. In August 1990, Iraq invaded Kuwait. The Amir and his cabinet fled to Saudi Arabia. When Iraq refused to withdraw, a United States-led and UN-supported international force began an aerial bombing campaign, called 'Operation Desert Storm', in January 1991. They took Kuwait City in late February and expelled the Iraqis, but not before the latter had set fire to more than 500 oil wells, causing massive pollution and destroying almost all the country's commercial and industrial installations. The fires took 9 months to extinguish, and repairs cost over 5 billion dollars. After the war Kuwait expelled many of its huge contingent of Palestinian immigrant workers in retaliation for PLO leader Yasser Arafat's support for Iraq. In 1994 Iraq, under UN pressure, officially recognized Kuwait's independence and boundaries. The countries still have no recognized maritime boundaries in the Persian Gulf.

In 1992, elections were held for a new National Assembly. In 1999 the Amir, Jabir al-Ahmad al-Jabir Al Sabah, suspended the Assembly. Liberals and Islamists predominated in its replacement, but the liberals did badly in elections in 2003, while Islamists again did well. In 1999 the Assembly had narrowly rejected a proposal to give women full political rights, but parliament approved these rights in May 2005. Kuwait's first woman cabinet minister was appointed in June. After Amir al-Sabah's death in 2006 he was succeeded by his half-brother Sabah al-Sabah.

Recent problems include violence by Islamist militants, some allegedly linked to al-Qaeda, who have been accused of conspiring to attack Western targets.

ECONOMY

The economy is based on oil, which accounts for more than 90% of the exports. Kuwait has about 10% of the world's known reserves. Agriculture is practically non-existent, though the country has a small fishing fleet. Kuwait has to import most of its food. The shortage of water has inhibited the development of industries. However, industrial products include petrochemicals, cement, food products and construction materials. Another industry is shipbuilding and repair.

KUWAIT CITY

Capital of Kuwait, it sits on the natural harbour Kuwait Bay in the Persian Gulf. It was first settled in the early 18th century and by the 19th century it was an important trading port. The city was invaded by Iraqi forces in the 1991 Gulf War and under Iraqi occupation renamed Saddam City, after Iraqi leader Saddam Hussein. It returned to its original name once Iraqi troops were expelled. Known as 'The City' to the people of Kuwait it includes the Majlis Al-Umma (Kuwait's parliament), most governmental offices and the headquarters of most Kuwaiti businesses.

KYRGYZSTAN

Kyrgyzstan's flag was adopted in March 1992. The flag depicts a bird's-eye view of a 'yurt' (circular tent) within a radiant sun. The 'yurt' recalls the traditional nomadic way of life. The 40 rays of the sun stand for the 40 traditional tribes.

The Kyrgyz Republic is a landlocked country between China, Tajikistan, Uzbekistan and Kazakhstan. The country is mountainous, with spectacular scenery. The highest mountain, Peak Pobedy (Peak of Victory) in the Tian Shan Range, reaches 7,439 m [24,406 ft] above sea level in the east. Less than a sixth of the country is below 900 m [2,950 ft]. The largest of the country's many lakes is Lake Issyk Kul (Ysyk-Köl) in the north-east.

Area 199,900 sq km [77,181 sq mi]
Population 5,214,000
Capital (population) Bishkek (828,000)
Government Multiparty republic
Ethnic groups Kyrgyz 65%, Russian 13%, Uzbek 13%, Ukranian 1%, others
Languages Kyrgyz and Russian (both official)
Religions Islam 75%, Russian Orthodox 20%
Currency Kyrgyzstani som = 100 tyiyn
Website www.gov.kg

CLIMATE

The lowlands of Kyrgyzstan have warm summers and cold winters. The altitude influences the climate in the mountains, where the January temperatures fall to –28°C [18°F]. Far from any sea, Kyrgyzstan has a very low annual rainfall.

HISTORY

The area that is now Kyrgyzstan was populated in ancient times by nomadic herders. Mongol armies conquered the region in the early 13th century. They set up kingdoms called khanates, ruled by chieftains, or khans. Islam was introduced in the 17th century.

China gained control of the area in the mid-18th century, but in 1876 Kyrgyzstan became a province of Russia, and Russian settlement in the area began. In 1916 Russia crushed a rebellion among the Kyrgyz, many of whom subsequently fled to China.

In 1922 the area became an autonomous *oblast* (self-governing region) of the newly formed Soviet Union. In 1936 it became one of the Soviet Socialist Republics. Under Communist rule, nomads were forced to work on government-run farms, while local customs and religious worship were suppressed. However, education and health services were greatly improved.

TIAN SHAN (TIEN SHAN)

Mountain range in central Asia, 2,400 km [1,500 mi] long, forming the border between Kyrgyzstan and Xinjiang, north-west China. At their western edge, the Tian Shan ('Celestial Mountains') divide the Tarim and Junggar Basins. The range rises to 7,439 m [24,406 ft] at Pik Pobedy, on the Chinese border with Kazakhstan and Kyrgyzstan. The Issyk Kul in Kyrgyzstan is one of the world's largest mountain lakes.

POLITICS

In 1991, following the break-up of the Soviet Union, Kyrgyzstan became an independent country. The Communist Party was dissolved, but the country retained ties with Russia through the Commonwealth of Independent States. Kyrgyzstan adopted a new constitution in 1994 and elections were held in 1995.

In the late 1990s Askar Akayev, president since 1990, introduced constitutional changes and other measures which gave him greater powers and limited press freedom. In 2000, Akayev was elected to a third five-year term as president. Alleged government interference in the parliamentary elections of March 2005 sparked massive popular protest, with the people demanding a rerun of the vote and the resignation of Askar Akayev. Official buildings in the capital were seized and, with virtually no resistance from the security forces, Akayev fled to Russia. Kurmanbek Bakiev was appointed acting president and prime minister and subsequently won a landslide victory in 2005 presidential elections. The elections were deemed to have shown clear progress in democratic standards, according to foreign observers. In 2006, after failure to tackle corruption led to mass protests, Bakiev signed a new constitution limiting his powers as president.

Kyrgyzstan has the potential to be an ethnic tinderbox, with a large Russian minority who held positions of power in Soviet days, disenchanted Uzbeks and an influx of Chinese Muslim immigrants. In the early 2000s, Islamist guerrillas staged border raids on Kyrgyzstan. They sought to set up an Islamic state in the Fergana valley, on the borders with Uzbekistan and Tajikistan.

ECONOMY

The chief activity is agriculture, especially livestock rearing. The main products include cotton, eggs, fruits, grain, tobacco, vegetables and wool. Food is imported. Manufactures include machinery, processed food, metals and textiles.

BISHKEK

Capital of Kyrgyzstan, central Asia, on the River Chu. Founded in 1862 as Pishpek, it was the birthplace of a Soviet general, Mikhail Frunze, after whom it was renamed in 1926 when it became administrative centre of the Kyrghyz Soviet Republic. Its name changed to Bishkek in 1991, when Kyrgyzstan declared independence. The city has a university (1951). Industries include textiles, food processing and agricultural machinery.

ISSYK KUL

At 182 km [113 mi] long, with a width of up to 61 km [38 mi] and a maximum depth of 701 m [2,303 ft], Issyk Kul is one of the largest mountain lakes in the world. Its name derives from a word for 'hot lake', as it does not freeze, despite being at an altitude of 1,609 m [5,278 ft]. This saltwater lake is very clear with visibility of up to 20 m [65 ft].

LAOS

Since 1975, Laos has flown the flag of the Pathet Lao, the Communist movement which won control of the country after a long struggle. The blue stands for the River Mekong, the white disc for the Moon and the red for the unity and purpose of the people.

The Lao People's Democratic Republic is a landlocked country in South-east Asia. Mountains and plateaux cover much of the country. The highest point is Mount Bia in central Laos, which reaches 2,817 m [9,242 ft].

Most people live on the plains bordering the River Mekong and its tributaries. This river, one of Asia's longest, forms much of the country's north-western and south-western borders. A range of mountains called the Annam Cordillera (Chaîne Annamatique) runs along the eastern border with Vietnam.

Area 236,800 sq km [91,428 sq mi]
Population 6,368,000
Capital (population) Vientiane (700,000)
Government Single-party republic
Ethnic groups Lao Loum 68%, Lao Theung 22%, Lao Soung 9%
Languages Lao (official), French, English
Religions Buddhism 60%, traditional beliefs and others 40%
Currency Kip = 100 at
Website www.un.int/lao

CLIMATE

Laos has a tropical monsoon climate. Winters are dry and sunny, with winds blowing in from the north-east. The temperatures rise until April, when the wind directions are reversed and moist south-westerly winds reach Laos, heralding the start of the wet monsoon season.

HISTORY

From the 9th century AD, Lao and Tai peoples set up a number of small states ruled by princes. In 1353 the area that is now Laos was united in a kingdom called Lan Xang ('land of a million elephants'). Apart from a period of Burmese rule between 1574 and 1637, the Lan Xang ruled Laos until the early 18th century. The region was divided into three separate kingdoms, Champasak, Vientiane and Louangphrabang, which became vassals of Siam (now Thailand).

In the 19th century, Chao Anou, the king of Vientiane, united his kingdom with Vietnam in an attempt to break Siamese domination, but he was defeated and Vientiane became a Siamese province. In the late 19th century, France gradually gained control of all Siamese territory east of the River Mekong and made it a protectorate, ruling it as part of French Indo-China. The region also included Cambodia and Vietnam. After France's surrender to Germany in 1940, Japanese forces moved into Indo-China. They allowed the French to continue as puppet rulers until 1945, when they interned all French authorities and military units. A Free Laos movement set up a government, but this collapsed when the French returned in 1946.

POLITICS

Under a new constitution, Laos became a monarchy in 1947. In 1949 the country became a self-governing state within the French Union. After full independence in 1954, Laos suffered from instability tourists and the opening of trade links with the country's neighbours, notably China and Japan. Laos became a member of the Association of South-east Asian Nations (ASEAN) in 1997. Choummaly Sayasone, the current president, was appointed by the Communist party in 2006.

In the 1990s and 2000s opposition to the government has led to sporadic bombings occurring in Vientiane. These have been attributed to rebels in the minority Hmong tribe. Dissent is dealt with harshly by the authorities.

ECONOMY

Laos is one of the world's poorest countries. Agriculture employs about 76% of the people, compared with 7% in industry and 17% in services. Rice is the main crop, and timber and coffee are both exported. The most valuable export is electricity, which is produced at hydroelectric power stations on the River Mekong and exported to Thailand. Most enterprises are now outside state control. Laos also produces opium, and in the early 1990s was thought to be the world's third biggest source of this illegal drug. The government is working to develop alternative crops to opium.

caused by a power struggle between royalist government forces and a pro-Communist group called the Pathet Lao. The Pathet Lao took power in 1975 after two decades of chaotic civil war in which the royalist forces were supported by American bombing and Thai mercenaries, while the Pathet Lao was assisted by North Vietnam. The king, Savang Vatthana, abdicated in 1975 and the People's Democratic Republic of Laos was proclaimed. Over 300,000 Laotians, including technicians and other experts as well as farmers and members of ethnic minorities, fled the country. Many opponents of the government who remained were sent to re-education camps.

Communist policies brought isolation and stagnation under the domination of the Vietnamese government in Hanoi, which had used Laos as a supply line in their war against the US. In 1986 the Laotian Politburo began to allow foreign

VIENTIANE (VIANGCHAN)

Capital and chief port of Laos, on the River Mekong, close to the Thai border, north central Laos. It was the capital of the Lao kingdom (1707–1828). It became part of French Indo-China in 1893, and in 1899 became the capital of the French Protectorate. It is a major source of opium for world markets. Industries include textiles, brewing, cigarettes, hides, wood products.

LATVIA

The burgundy and white Latvian flag, which dates back to at least 1280, was revived after Latvia achieved its independence in 1991. According to one legend, the flag was first made from a white sheet which had been stained with the blood of a Latvian hero.

The Republic of Latvia is one of three states on the south-eastern corner of the Baltic Sea, known as the Baltic States. Latvia consists mainly of flat plains separated by low hills, composed of moraine (ice-worn rocks) that was dumped there by ice sheets during the Ice Age. The country's highest point is only 311 m [1,020 ft] above sea level. Small lakes and peat bogs are common. The country's main river, the Daugava, is also known as the Western Dvina.

Area 64,600 sq km [24,942 sq mi]
Population 2,275,000
Capital (population) Riga (719,000)
Government Multiparty republic
Ethnic groups Latvian 58%, RUssian 30%, Belarusian, Ukranian, Polish, Lithuanian
Languages Latvian (official), Lithuanian, Russian
Religions Lutheran, Roman Catholic, Russian Orthodox
Currency Latvian lat = 100 santimi
Website www.lv

CLIMATE

Air masses from the Atlantic influence the climate of Latvia, bringing warm and rainy conditions in summer. Winters are cold. The average temperature range is 16°C to 18°C [61 to 64°F] in July, and –7°C to –3°C [19 to 27°F] in January.

HISTORY

Between the 9th and 11th centuries, the region was attacked by Vikings from the west and Russians from the east. In the 13th century, German invaders took over, naming the country Livland.

In 1561, Latvia was partitioned and most of the land came under Polish or Lithuanian rule. A Germany duchy was also established there. In 1621, the Swedish king Gustavus II Adolphus took over Riga. In 1629, the greater part of the country north of the Daugava River was

ceded to Sweden, with the south-east remaining under Lithuanian rule. But, in 1710, Peter the Great took control of Riga and, by the end of the 18th century, all of Latvia was under Russian control, although German landowners and merchants continued to exercise considerable power. The 19th century saw the rise of Latvian nationalism, and calls for independence became frequent.

After the Russian Revolution of March 1917 the Latvian National Political Conference demanded independence, but Germany occupied Riga in September. However, after the October Revolution, the Latvian National Political Conference proclaimed the country's independence in November 1918. Russia and Germany finally recognized Latvia's independence in 1920. In 1922 Latvia adopted a democratic constitution, and the elected government introduced land reforms. However, a coup in May 1934 ended this period of democratic rule. In 1939, Germany and the Soviet Union agreed to divide up much of eastern Europe. Soviet troops invaded Latvia in June 1940 and Latvia was made a part of the Soviet Union. German forces invaded the area in 1941 and held it until 1944, when Soviet troops reoccupied the country. Many Latvians opposed to Russian rule were killed or deported.

POLITICS

Under Soviet rule many Russians settled in Latvia, leading Latvians to fear that the Russians would become the dominant ethnic group. From the mid-1980s, when Mikhail Gorbachev was introducing reforms in the Soviet Union, Latvian nationalists campaigned against Soviet rule. In the late 1980s, the Latvian government ended absolute Communist rule and voted to restore the banned national flag and anthem. It also proclaimed Latvian the official language.

In 1990, Latvia established a multiparty political system. In elections in March, candidates in favour of separation from the Soviet Union won two-thirds of parliamentary seats. The parliament declared Latvia independent on 4 May 1990, though the Soviet Union claimed this act was illegal. The Soviet government finally recognized Latvia's independence in September 1991, shortly before the Soviet Union itself was dissolved. Latvia held its first free elections to its parliament, the Saeima, in 1993. Voting was limited only to those who were citizens on 17 June 1940 and their descendants. This meant that about 34% of Latvian residents were unable to vote. In 1994, Latvia restricted the naturalization of non-Latvians, denying them the vote and land ownership. In 1998 the government agreed that all children born since independence should have automatic citizenship, regardless of their parents' status, but discrimination against Russians remains an issue.

Latvia became a member of NATO and the EU in 2004.

ECONOMY

The World Bank classifies Latvia as a 'lower-middle-income' country. The country's only natural resources are land and forests, so many raw materials have to be imported.

Its industries include electronic goods, farm machinery, fertilizers, processed food, plastics, radios, washing machines and vehicles. Latvia produces only about a tenth of its electricity needs. The rest has to be imported from Belarus, Russia and Ukraine. Farm products include barley, dairy, beef, oats, potatoes and rye.

RIGA

Capital of Latvia, on the River Daugava, Gulf of Riga. Founded at the beginning of the 13th century, it joined the Hanseatic League in 1282, growing into a major Baltic port. Tsar Peter the Great took the city in 1710.
In 1918, it became capital of independent Latvia. In 1940, when Latvia was incorporated into the Soviet Union, thousands of its citizens were deported or executed. Under German occupation from 1941, the city reverted to Soviet rule in 1944 and subsequently suffered further deportations and an influx of Russian immigrants. In 1991, it again became capital of an independent Latvia.

LEBANON

Lebanon's flag was adopted in 1943. It uses the colours of Lebanese nationalists in World War I (1914–18). The cedar tree on the white stripe has been a Lebanese symbol since Biblical times. Because of deforestation, only a few of Lebanon's giant cedars survive.

The Republic of Lebanon is a country on the eastern shores of the Mediterranean Sea. Behind the coastal plain are the rugged Lebanon Mountains, or Jabal Lubnán, which rise to 3,088 m [10,131 ft]. Another range, the Anti-Lebanon Mountains or Al Jabal ash Sharqi, forms the eastern border with Syria. Between the two ranges lies the Bekaa (Beqaa) Valley, which is a fertile farming region.

Area 10,400 sq km [4,015 sq mi]
Population 3,874,000
Capital (population) Beirut (2,070,000)
Government Multiparty republic
Ethnic groups Arab 95%, Armenian 4%, others
Languages Arabic (official),French, English
Religions Islam 70%, Christianity 30%
Currency Lebanese pound = 100 piastres
Website www.lebanon-tourism.gov.lb

CLIMATE

The Lebanese coast has hot, dry summers and mild, wet winters. Inland, onshore winds bring heavy rain to the western slopes of the mountains in the winter months, with snow on the western slopes of the mountains.

HISTORY

In its early history, the area was invaded by Egyptians, Hittites, Assyrians, Babylonians and Persians. The armies of Alexander the Great seized the area in 332 BC and the Romans took control in 64 BC. Christianity was introduced in AD 325, and in 395 the area became part of the Byzantine Empire. Muslim Arabs occupied the area in the early 7th century, converting many people to Islam.

European Crusaders arrived in Lebanon in about 1100 and the area became a battlefield between Christian and Muslim armies. The Muslim

BEIRUT (BAYRUT)

Capital and chief port of Lebanon, on the Mediterranean. From AD 635 Beirut was under Arab rule. Christian crusaders made it part of the Latin Kingdom of Jerusalem from 1110–1291. In 1516, under Druze control, it became part of the Ottoman Empire and remained so until World War I. In 1920 it became capital of Lebanon under French mandate. With the creation of Israel, thousands of Arabs sought refuge there. The outbreak of civil war in 1976 saw Beirut rapidly fracture along religious lines. In 1982, Israel devastated West Beirut in the war against the PLO. Israel began a phased withdrawal in 1985. Syrian troops entered in 1987 as part of an Arab peace-keeping force and in 1990, they dismantled the 'Green Line' separating Muslim West from Christian East Beirut. All militias withdrew by 1991 and restoration began. The infrastructure, economy, and culture of Beirut suffered terribly during the civil war.

factions fought for control. The situation was complicated by interventions by Palestinian refugees, the Syrian army, Western and then UN forces as the country became a patchwork of occupied zones and 'no-go areas'.

The core religious confrontation has deep roots. In 1860 thousands of Maronites, who are aligned to the Roman Catholic Church, were murdered by Druzes, who are so different from other Islamic sects that many do not regard them as Muslims.

Although not directly involved, Lebanon was destabilized by the Arab-Israeli War of 1967 and by the exile of the PLO leadership to Beirut in 1970. By 1990 the Syrian army had crushed Christian rebels against the Lebanese government, but peace proved elusive. In 1996, Israeli forces launched a sustained attack on the pro-Iranian Hizbollah positions in southern Lebanon, with heavy civilian casualties. Fighting continued in southern Lebanon in 1997 and again flared up in early 2000. In 2005 former prime minister Rafik Hariri, a critic of Syria's presence in Lebanon, was assassinated. Following demonstrations, Syria withdrew its forces in April and ended its occupation.

In 2006 Hizbollah launched rocket attacks on Israel from positions in Lebanon. Israel responded with ground and air attacks aimed at Hizbollah forces, which caused extensive civilian casualties and damage to Lebanon's infrastructure.

Mamelukes of Egypt drove the last of the Crusaders out of the area in around 1300. In 1516, Lebanon was taken over by the Turkish Ottoman Empire. Turkish rule continued until World War I, when British and French forces defeated the Ottoman Turks. France took over Lebanon's political affairs from 1923 until 1944, and Lebanon became independent from France in 1946.

POLITICS

Lebanon made rapid economic progress until the late 1950s, when periodic conflict between Sunni and Shi'ite Muslims, Druze and Christians slowed development. In March 1975 fierce civil war broke out between Christians, Muslims and Druzes. Lebanon sank into a state of chaos. Assassinations, bombings and kidnappings became routine as numerous

ECONOMY

Civil war almost destroyed valuable trade and financial services which, together with tourism, had been Lebanon's chief source of income. Manufacturing was also hit. Manufactures include chemicals, electrical goods, processed food and textiles. Fruits, vegetables and sugar beet are farmed.

LESOTHO

Based on the national motto: white for peace, blue for rain and green for prosperity. In the white stripe is a black Basotho hat representing the indigenous people. The design was adopted in 2006 to celebrate 40 years of independence.

The Kingdom of Lesotho is a land-locked country, surrounded by South Africa on all sides. The scenic Drakensberg Range covers most of the country and forms Lesotho's north eastern border with KwaZulu Natal. It includes Lesotho's highest peak Thabana Ntlenyana, at 3,482 m [11,424 ft].

Most people live in the western lowlands, site of the capital Maseru, or in the southern valley of the Orange River which rises in north-east Lesotho and flows through South Africa to the Atlantic Ocean. Grassland covers much of Lesotho. The King holds all land in Lesotho in trust for the Sotho nation.

Area 30,355 sq km [11,720 sq mi]
Population 2,022,000
Capital (population) Maseru (180,000)
Government Constitutional monarchy
Ethnic groups Sotho 99%
Languages Sotho and English (both official)
Religions Christianity 80%, traditional beliefs 20%
Currency Loti = 100 lisente
Website www.lesotho.gov.ls

CLIMATE

The climate is greatly affected by altitude, with 66% of the country lying above 1,500 m [4,921 ft]. Maseru has warm summers, but the temperatures fall below freezing in the winter and the mountains are colder. Rainfall varies, averaging around 700 mm [28 in].

HISTORY

The early 19th century tribal wars dispersed the Sotho. The Basotho nation was founded in the 1820s by King Moshoeshoe I, who united various groups fleeing from tribal wars in southern Africa. Moshoeshoe I was forced to yield to the British, and Britain made the area a protectorate in 1868. In 1871, it became part of the British Cape Colony in South Africa. In 1884 Basutoland, as the area was called, was reconstituted as a British protectorate where whites were not allowed to own land.

POLITICS

In 1966 Sotho opposition incorporation into the Union of South Africa led to the creation of the independent Kingdom of Lesotho. Moshoeshoe II, great-grandson

SOTHO

Major cultural and linguistic group of southern Africa. It includes the Northern Sotho of Transvaal, South Africa, the Western Sotho (better known as the Tswana) of Botswana, and the Southern Sotho (Basotho or Basuto) of Lesotho. Although dominating the rural territories they inhabit, the 4 million Sotho share those areas with people of other Bantu-speaking tribes. Many work and live in the urban areas and surrounding townships.

BCP won the 1992 multiparty elections, and the military council dissolved. In 1994, Letsie III attempted to overthrow the government. Moshoeshoe II returned to the throne in 1995 but died in a car crash in 1996. Letsie III again became king. In 1997, a majority of BCP politicians formed a new governing party, the Lesotho Congress for Democracy (LCD).

In 1998 an army revolt, following an election in which the ruling party won 79 out of the 80 seats, caused much damage to the economy despite the intervention of a South African force intended to maintain order. In 2004, the government declared a state of emergency following three years of drought.

of Moshoeshoe I, became its king. In 1970, prime minister Leabua Jonathan suspended the constitution and banned opposition parties. Civil conflict between the government and Basuto Congress Party (BCP) forces characterized the next 16 years. In 1986, a military coup led to the reinstatement of Moshoeshoe II. In 1990 he was deposed, and replaced as monarch by his son Letsie III. The

ECONOMY

Lesotho is a 'low-income' developing country. It lacks natural resources except diamonds. Agriculture employs two-thirds of the workforce, but most farmers live at subsistence level. Livestock farming is important. Major crops include maize and sorghum. Tourism is developing. Other sources of income include the products of light manufacturing and remittances sent home by Basotho working abroad, mainly in the mines of South Africa.

ORANGE RIVER

Longest river of South Africa. It rises in the Drakensberg Mountains in northern Lesotho and flows generally west, forming the boundary between Free State and Cape Province. It continues west through the Kalahari and Namib deserts, forming South Africa's border with Namibia then emptying into the Atlantic Ocean at Oranjemund. It is 2,100 km [1,300 mi] in length.

MASERU

Capital of Lesotho, on the River Caledon, near the western border with South Africa. Originally a small trading town, it was capital of British Basutoland protectorate (1869–71, 1884–1966). It remained the capital when the Kingdom of Lesotho achieved independence in 1966. It is a commercial, transport and administrative centre.

LIBERIA

Liberia was founded in the early 19th century as an American colony for freed slaves who wanted to return to Africa. Its flag was adopted in 1847, when Liberia became independent. The 11 red and white stripes represent the 11 men who signed Liberia's Declaration of Independence.

The Republic of Liberia is located on the Atlantic coast of west Africa. Behind the 500 km [311 mi] long coastline lies a narrow coastal plain. Beyond, the land rises to a plateau region, with the highest land along the border with Guinea. The most important rivers are the Cavally, which forms the border with Ivory Coast, and the St Paul.

Mangrove swamps and lagoons line the coast while inland, forests cover nearly 40% of the land. Liberia also has areas of tropical savanna. Only 5% of the land is cultivated.

Area 111,369 sq km [43,000 sq mi]
Population 3,042,000
Capital (population) Monrovia (421,000)
Government Multiparty republic
Ethnic groups Indigenous African tribes 95% (including Kpelle, Bassa, Grebo, Gio, Kru, Mano)
Languages English (official), ethnic languages
Religions Christianity 40%, Islam 20%, traditional beliefs and others 40%
Currency Liberian dollar = 100 cents
Website www.un.org/Depts/dpko/missions/unmil/index.html

CLIMATE

Liberia has a tropical climate. There are high temperatures and humidity throughout the year. Rainfall is abundant all year round, but there is a particularly wet period from June to November. The rainfall generally increases from east to west.

HISTORY

In the late 18th century, some white Americans in the United States wanted to help freed black slaves to return to Africa. They set up the American Colonization Society in 1816, which bought land in what is now Liberia.

In 1822, the Society landed former slaves at a settlement on the coast which they named Monrovia. In 1847, Liberia became a fully independent republic with a constitution much like that of the United States. For many years, the Americo-Liberians controlled the government. US influence remained strong and the American Firestone Company, which ran Liberia's rubber plantations covering more than 400,000 ha [1 million acres], was especially influential. Foreign countries were also involved in exploiting Liberia's mineral resources, including its huge iron ore deposits.

POLITICS

Under the leadership (1944–71) of William Tubman, Liberia's economy grew and it adopted social reforms. In 1980, a military force composed of people from the local population killed the Americo-Liberian president William R. Tolbert, Tubman's successor. An army sergeant, Samuel K. Doe, became president. In 1985, Doe's brutal and corrupt regime won a fraudulent election.

Civil war broke out in 1989, and the Economic Community of West African States (ECOWAS) sent a five-nation peace-keeping force. Doe was assassinated and an interim government, led by

In 2001 the UN imposed an arms embargo on Liberia for trading weapons for diamonds with rebels in Sierra Leone. In 2002, Taylor imposed a state of emergency as civil war broke out again. In 2003 the fighting largely ended and Taylor was exiled. The UN helped restore order. In 2005 Ellen Johnson-Sirleaf was elected president. Taylor was arrested in Nigeria in 2006 and returned to face trial for war crimes.

ECONOMY

Civil war devastated the economy. Agriculture employs 75% of the workforce, and many families live at subsistence level. Food crops include cassava, fruits, rice and sugar cane. Rubber is grown on plantations and cash crops include cocoa and coffee. Liberia's natural resources include its forests and iron ore, while gold and diamonds are also mined. Liberia has an oil refinery, but manufacturing is small-scale. Exports include rubber, timber, diamonds, gold and coffee. Revenue is also obtained from its 'flag of convenience', used by about one-sixth of the world's commercial shipping to exploit low taxes.

Amos Sawyer, took office. Civil war raged on, claiming 150,000 lives and leaving hundreds of thousands of people homeless by 1994. In 1995 a ceasefire occurred, and the former warring factions formed a council of state. Former warlord Charles Taylor of the National Patriotic Council secured a resounding victory in 1997 elections.

AMERICAN COLONIZATION SOCIETY

Group founded in 1817 by Robert Finley to return free African-Americans to Africa for settlement. More than 11,000 African-Americans were transported to Sierra Leone and, after 1821, Monrovia. Leading members of the society included James Monroe, James Madison and John Marshall.

MONROVIA

Capital and chief port of Liberia, West Africa, on the estuary of the River St Paul. In 1822 freed US slaves settled Monrovia, on a site chosen by the American Colonization Society. The city is named after James Monroe, US president from 1817–25. Monrovia is Liberia's largest city and the administrative, commercial and financial centre of the country, though it suffered much damage in the civil war. It exports latex and iron ore. Industries – bricks and cement.

LIBYA

Libya's flag was adopted in 1977. It replaced the flag of the Federation of Arab Republics which Libya left in that year. Libya's flag is the simplest of all world flags. It represents the country's quest for a green revolution in agriculture.

The Great Socialist People's Libyan Arab Jamahiriya, as the country is officially known, is located in North Africa. The majority live on the Mediterranean coastal plains in the north-east and north-west. The Sahara, the world's largest desert, occupies 95% of Libya, reaching the Mediterranean coast along the Gulf of Sidra (Khalij Surt). The Sahara is virtually uninhabited except around scattered oases.

The land rises towards the south, reaching 2,286 m [7,500 ft] at Bette Peak (Bikku Bitti) on the border with Chad. Shrubs and grasses grow on northern coasts, with some trees in wetter areas. Few plants grow in the desert, except at oases where date palms provide protection from the hot sun.

Area 1,759,540 sq km [679,358 sq mi]
Population 5,901,000
Capital (population) Tripoli (1,733,000)
Government Single-party socialist state
Ethnic groups Libyan Arab and Berber 97%
Languages Arabic (official), Berber
Religions Islam (Sunni Muslim) 97%
Currency Libyan dinar = 1000 dirhams
Website www.libyana.org

CLIMATE

The coastal plains experience hot summers. Winters are mild with some rain. Inland, the average yearly rainfall drops to around 100 mm [4 in] or less. Daytime temperatures are high but nights are cool.

HISTORY

Libya's first known inhabitants were the Berbers. From the 7th century BC to the 5th century AD, Libya came under the Carthaginians, Greeks and Romans. The Romans left superb ruins, but the Arabs, who invaded the area in AD 642, imposed their culture, including their religion, Islam. From 1551, Libya was part of the Ottoman empire. Italy took control in 1911, but lost the territory in World War II. Britain and France then jointly ruled Libya until 1951, when it became an independent kingdom.

POLITICS

In 1969, a military group headed by Colonel Muammar Gaddafi deposed the king and set up a military government. Under Gaddafi, the government took control of the economy and used money from oil exports to finance welfare services and development projects. Although Libya claims to be democratic, political parties are not permitted, and the political system is Gadaffi's design.

BENGHAZI (BANGHAZI)

City on the north-eastern shore of the Gulf of Sidra, Libya. Founded by the Greeks in the 6th century BC, Benghazi was captured by the Italians in 1911. Libya's second largest city, Benghazi is a commercial and industrial centre for Cyrenaica province.

ECONOMY

Libya is Africa's richest country, per capita, but remains a developing country because of its dependence on oil. Oil accounts for nearly all of its export revenues.

Agriculture is important, although Libya still imports food. Crops include barley, citrus fruits, dates, olives, potatoes and wheat. Cattle, sheep and poultry are raised. Libya has oil refineries and petrochemical plants. It also manufactures cement, processed food and steel. The economy is largely controlled by the state.

The 'Great Man-Made River' is an ambitious project involving the tapping of subterranean water from rocks beneath the Sahara and piping it to the dry, populated areas in the north. The water in the aquifers is non-renewable, and will eventually run dry.

Gaddafi has attracted international criticism for his support for radical movements, such as the PLO (Palestine Liberation Organization) and various terrorist groups. In 1986, his policies led the United States to bomb installations in the capital and in Benghazi. In 1994, the International Court of Justice ruled against Libya's claim to the Aozou Strip, an area in northern Chad.

In 1999, Gaddafi sought to restore good relations with the outside world. Two Libyans suspected of planting a bomb on a PanAm plane which exploded over the Scottish town of Lockerbie in 1988 were deported for trial and Libya agreed to pay compensation to victims of the bombing. Gaddafi also accepted Libya's responsibility for the shooting of a British policewoman in London in 1984 and diplomatic relations with Britain were restored. In 2004 Libya declared it was abandoning programmes to produce weapons of mass destruction, an initiative that was rewarded by visits to Libya by many Western leaders. In 2006 diplomatic relations with the US were restored.

TRIPOLI (TARABULUS)

Capital and chief port of Libya, on the Mediterranean Sea. Founded as Oea in the 7th century BC by the Phoenicians and developed by the Romans. From the 7th century AD, the Arabs developed Tripoli as a market centre for the trans-Saharan caravans. In 1551, it was captured by the Ottoman Turks. It was made capital of the Italian colony of Libya in 1911, and was an important base for Axis forces during World War II. After intensive Allied bombing in 1941–2, Britain captured the city. In 1986, the US Air Force bombed Tripoli in retaliation for Libya's alleged support of worldwide terrorism. The city is the commercial, industrial, transport and communications centre of Libya. Its oases are the most fertile agricultural area in northern Africa.

LITHUANIA

This flag was created in 1918 when Lithuania became an independent republic. After the Soviet Union annexed Lithuania in 1940, the flag was suppressed. It was revived in 1988 and again became the national flag when Lithuania became fully independent in 1991.

The Republic of Lithuania is the southernmost of the three Baltic states. The land is essentially flat with the highest point a hill, south-east of Vilnius (292 m [958 ft]). From the south-east, the land slopes down to the fertile central lowland. In the west is an area of forested sandy ridges, dotted with lakes. South of Klaipeda, sand dunes separate a large lagoon from the Baltic Sea.

Most of the land is covered by moraine deposited by ice sheets during the Ice Age. Hollows in the moraine contain about 3,000 lakes. The longest river is the Neman, which rises in Belarus and flows through Lithuania to the Baltic Sea.

Area 65,200 sq km [25,174 sq mi]
Population 3,586,000
Capital (population) Vilnius (578,000)
Government Multiparty republic
Ethnic groups Lithuanian 80%, Russian 9%, Polish 7%, Belarusian 2%
Languages Lithuanian (official), Russian, Polish
Religions Mainly Roman Catholic
Currency 1 litas = 100 centai
Website www.lietuva.lt

CLIMATE

Winters are cold, with temperatures averaging −3°C [27°F] in January, but summers are pleasant. Average temperatures in July reach 17°C [63°F]. The average rainfall in the west is 630 mm [25 in]. Inland areas are drier.

HISTORY

The Lithuanian people were united into a single nation in the 12th century. The first great ruler was Mindaugas, who became king in 1251. By the 14th century, Lithuania's territory extended nearly to Moscow in the east and the Black Sea in the south. Lithuania and Poland became a single state in 1569. This state collapsed in the 18th century and, by 1795, Lithuania was under Russian control. Despite rebellions, Lithuania failed to regain its independence.

In 1905, a conference of elected representatives called for self-government. Russia refused. German troops occupied Lithuania during World War I, and in 1918 Lithuania declared its independence from Germany and Russia. Lithuania established a democracy, and in 1920 signed a peace treaty with Russia. Poland occupied Vilnius from 1920 until 1939, incorporating it into Poland in 1923. In 1926, a coup overthrew Lithuania's democratic regime.

In 1939, Germany and the USSR agreed to divide up much of eastern Europe. Lithuania and Vilnius were ceded to the USSR in 1940 and a government was set up. German forces invaded in 1941 and held it until 1944, when Soviet troops reoccupied the country. Many Lithuanian guerrillas fought against Soviet rule between 1944 and 1952. Thousands of Lithuanians were killed and many sent to labour camps.

POLITICS

From 1988, Lithuania led the way among the Baltic states in the drive to candidate Valdas Adamkus, a Lithuanian-American who had fled in 1944, was elected president. Lithuania now has better relations with Russia than the other two Baltic states, partly because ethnic Russians make up a lower proportion of the population than in Estonia and Latvia. Lithuania became a member of NATO and of the EU in 2004.

ECONOMY

The World Bank classifies Lithuania as a 'lower-middle-income' developing country. In the 2000s economic growth has been very rapid, leading to problems with inflation which have delayed the adoption of the Euro. Manufacturing is the most valuable activity. Products include chemicals, electronics, processed food and machine tools. Dairy and meat farming are important, as is fishing.

shed Communism and regain nationhood. In 1989, the parliament in Lithuania declared Soviet laws invalid unless approved by the Lithuanian parliament and that Lithuanian should be the official language. Religious freedom and the freedom of the press were restored, abolishing the monopoly of power held by the Communist Party and establishing a multiparty system.

Following parliamentary elections in February 1990, in which pro-independence candidates won more than 90% of the seats, Lithuania declared itself independent in March 1990. This declaration was rejected by the Soviet leaders. Most of the capital was occupied by Soviet troops and a crippling economic blockade put in place. After negotiations to end the sanctions failed, Soviet troops moved into Lithuania and 14 people were killed when the troops fired on demonstrators. Finally, on 6 September 1991, the Soviet government recognized Lithuania's independence.

Parliamentary elections in 1992 were won by the Lithuanian Democratic Labour Party, former Communists. Russian troops withdrew from the country in 1993. In 1996 elections a coalition government was set up by the conservative Homeland Union and the Christian Democratic Party. In 1998, independent

VILNIUS

Capital of Lithuania, on the River Neris. Founded in 1323 as the capital of the Grand Duchy of Lithuania, the city declined after the union of Lithuania-Poland. Vilnius was captured by Russia in 1795. After World War I, it was made capital of an independent Lithuania. In 1939, Soviet troops occupied the city and, in 1940, Lithuania became a Soviet republic. During World War II, the city was occupied by German troops, and its Jewish population was all but exterminated. In 1944, it reverted to its Soviet status. In 1990, Lithuania's declaration of independence led to clashes with Soviet troops in the city.

The old city has many historic synagogues, churches and civic buildings, and the ruins of a 14th-century castle.

LUXEMBOURG

Luxembourg's tri-colour flag derives from its coat of arms which shows a red lion on front of blue and white horizontal stripes. The first recorded use of the coat of arms is on the banner of Earl Heinrich VI in 1228.

The Grand Duchy of Luxembourg is one of the smallest and oldest countries in Europe. The north belongs to an upland region which includes the Ardennes in Belgium and Luxembourg, and the Eiffel Highlands in Germany. This scenic region contains the country's highest point, a hill in the north which reaches 565 m [1,854 ft] above sea level.

The southern two-thirds of Luxembourg, which is geographically part of French Lorraine, is a hilly or rolling plateau called the Bon Pays or Gut Land ('Good Land'). This region contains rich farmland, especially in the fertile Alzette, Moselle and Sûre (or Sauer) river valleys in the south and east.

Forests cover about a fifth of Luxembourg, mainly in the north, where deer and wild boar are found. Farms cover about 25% of the land and pasture another 20%.

Area 2,586 sq km [998 sq mi]
Population 474,000
Capital (population) Luxembourg (80,000)
Government
Constitutional monarchy (Grand Duchy)
Ethnic groups Luxembourger 71%, Portuguese, Italian, French, Belgian, Slav
Languages
Luxembourgish (official), French, German
Religions Roman Catholic 87%, others 13%
Currency Euro = 100 cents
Website www.luxembourg.lu

state in AD 963 and a duchy in 1354. In the 1440s, Luxembourg came under the House of Burgundy and, in the early 16th century, under the rule of the Habsburgs. From 1684, it came successively

CLIMATE

Luxembourg has a temperate climate. In the south of the country summers and autumns are warm. This is when the grapes ripen in sheltered southeastern valleys. Winters are sometimes severe, particularly in the Ardennes region, where snow can cover the land for some weeks.

HISTORY

Luxembourg became an independent

LUXEMBOURG

Capital of the Grand Duchy of Luxembourg, at the confluence of the Alzette and Pétrusse rivers. Luxembourg was a Roman stronghold. The walled town developed around a 10th-century fortress. The Treaty of London (1867) dismantled the fortress and demilitarized the city. It is the seat of the European Court of Justice, the Secretariat of the Parliament of the European Union, the European Monetary Fund, the European Investment Bank and the European Coal and Steel Union. Industries include iron and steel, chemicals, textiles and tourism.

Germany occupied Luxembourg in both World Wars. In 1944–5, northern Luxembourg was the scene of the Battle of the Bulge. After World War II, the economy recovered rapidly.

POLITICS

In 1948, Luxembourg joined Belgium and the Netherlands in a union by the name of Benelux and, in the 1950s, was one of the six founders of what is now the European Union. The country's capital, a major financial centre, contains the headquarters of several international agencies, including the European Coal and Steel Community and the European Court of Justice.

ECONOMY

Luxembourg has iron-ore reserves and is a major steel producer. It also has many high-technology industries, producing electronic goods and computers. Steel and other manufactures, including chemicals, glass and rubber products, are exported. Other activities include tourism and financial services. Half of the land area is farmed, but agriculture employs only 3% of the workforce. Crops include barley, fruits, oats, potatoes and wheat. Cattle, sheep, pigs and poultry are reared.

under France (1684–97), Spain (1697–1714) and Austria until 1795, when it reverted to French rule.

In 1815, following the defeat of France, Luxembourg became a Grand Duchy under the Netherlands. This was because the Grand Duke was also the king of the Netherlands. In 1890, when Wilhelmina became queen of the Netherlands, Luxembourg broke away as its laws did not permit a woman monarch. The Grand Duchy then passed to Adolphus, Duke of Nassau-Weilburg, but, in 1912, Luxembourg's laws were changed to allow Marie Adélaïde of Nassau to become the ruling grand duchess. Her sister Charlotte succeeded in 1919, but she abdicated in 1964 in favour of her son, Jean. In 2000, Grand Duke Jean handed over the role as head of state to his son, Prince Henri.

ARDENNES

Sparsely populated wooded plateau in south-eastern Belgium, northern Luxembourg and the Ardennes department of northern France. The capital is Charleville-Mézières. It was the scene of heavy fighting in both World Wars, notably in the Battle of the Bulge (1944). In the well-preserved forest regions wild game is abundant and cleared areas support arable and dairy farming.

MACEDONIA

Macedonia's flag was introduced in August 1992. The emblem in the centre of the flag was the device from the war-chest of Philip of Macedon; however, the Greeks claimed this symbol as their own. In 1995, the Macedonians agreed to redesign their flag, as shown here.

The Republic of Macedonia is in south-eastern Europe. This land-locked country is largely mountainous or hilly, the highest point being Mount Korab (2,764 m [9,068 ft]) on the border with Albania. Most of the country is drained by the River Vardar and its many tributaries. In the south-west, Macedonia shares two large lakes – Ohrid and Prespa – with Albania and Greece. Forests of beech, oak and pine cover large areas, especially in the west.

Area 25,713 sq km [9,928 sq mi]
Population 2,051,000
Capital (population) Skopje (430,000)
Government Multiparty republic
Ethnic groups Macedonian 64%, Albanian 25%, Turkish 4%, Romanian 3%, Serb 2%
Languages Macedonian and Albanian (official)
Religions Macedonian Orthodox 70%, Islam 29%
Currency Macedonian denar = 100 paras
Website www.vlada.mk/english/index_en.htm

CLIMATE

Summers are hot, though highland areas are cooler. Winters are cold and snowfall is often heavy. The climate is fairly continental with rainfall throughout the year. Average temperatures in Skopje range from 1°C [34°F] in January to 24°C [75°F] in July. The average annual rainfall in the city is 550 mm [21 in].

HISTORY

Until the 20th century, Macedonia's history was closely tied to that of a larger area, also called Macedonia, which covered of northern Greece and south-western Bulgaria. This region reached its peak in power at the time of Philip II (382–336 BC) and his son Alexander the Great (336–323 BC), who conquered an empire that stretched from Greece to India. The area became a Roman province in the 140s BC and part of the Byzantine Empire from AD 395. In the 6th century, Slavs from eastern Europe attacked and settled in the area, followed by Bulgars from central Asia in the late 9th century. The Byzantine Empire regained control in 1018. Serbia took Macedonia in the early 14th century.

The area was conquered by the Ottoman Turks in 1371 and was under their rule for more than 500 years. The Ottoman Empire began to collapse in the late 19th century and in 1913, at the end of the Balkan Wars, the area was divided between Bulgaria, Greece and Serbia.

POLITICS

As a result of the division of the area known as Macedonia, Serbia took the north and centre of the region, Bulgaria took a small area in the south-east, and Greece gained the south. At the end of World War I, Serbian Macedonia became part of the Kingdom of the Serbs, Croats and Slovenes, which was renamed Yugoslavia in 1929. Yugoslavia was conquered by Germany during World War II, but when the war ended in 1945 the Communist partisan leader Josip Broz Tito set up a Communist government.

Kosovo. In 2001, Albanian-speaking Macedonians in northern Macedonia launched an armed struggle. The uprising ended when the government introduced changes that gave Albanian-speakers increased rights, including the recognition of Albanian as an official language.

In 2004, the USA recognized the name Republic of Macedonia instead of FYROM. Despite objections from Greece, other countries began to follow. In 2005 relations with Greece improved and the EU agreed to consider Macedonia for membership.

Tito maintained unity among the diverse peoples of Yugoslavia but, after his death in 1980, ethnic and religious differences began to reassert themselves. Yugoslavia broke apart into five sovereign republics. Macedonia, declaring its independence on 18 September 1991, managed to avoid the civil war that shattered other parts of the former Yugoslavia.

However, Macedonia ran into problems concerning recognition. Greece, considering Macedonia to be a Greek name and objecting to a reference in the country's constitution to the desire to reunite the three parts of the old Macedonia, vetoed any acknowledgement of an independent Macedonia on its borders. It also objected to a symbol on Macedonia's flag, which was associated with Philip of Macedon. Macedonia adopted a new clause in its constitution rejecting all claims on Greek territory and, in 1993, joined the United Nations under the name of The Former Yugoslav Republic of Macedonia (FYROM). In late 1993 all EU countries, except Greece, established diplomatic relations with the FYROM. Greece barred Macedonian trade in 1994, but this ban was subsequently lifted in 1995.

Macedonia's stability was threatened in 1999 when Albanian-speaking refugees flooded into Macedonia from

ECONOMY

According to the World Bank, Macedonia ranks as a 'lower-middle-income' developing country. Macedonia mines coal, chromium, copper, iron ore, lead, manganese, uranium and zinc. Manufactures include cement, chemicals, cigarettes, cotton fabric, footwear, iron and steel, refrigerators, sulphuric acid, tobacco products and wool yarn.

Agriculture employs 9% of the workforce, as compared with 23% in manufacturing and mining. About a quarter of the land is farmed and major crops include cotton, fruits, maize, potatoes, tobacco, vegetables and wheat. Cattle, pigs, poultry and sheep are also raised. Forestry is another important activity in some areas.

SKOPJE

Capital of Macedonia, on the River Vardar. Founded in Roman times, it became capital of the Serbian Empire in the 14th century, fell to the Ottoman Turks in 1392 and incorporated into Yugoslavia in 1918. In 1963 an earthquake destroyed most of the city. Industries include metals, textiles, chemicals, glassware.

MADAGASCAR

The colours on this flag are those used on historic flags in South-east Asia. It was from this region that the ancestors of many Madagascans came around 2,000 years ago. This flag was adopted in 1958, when Madagascar became a self-governing republic under French rule.

The Republic of Madagascar lies 390 km [240 mi] off the south-east coast of Africa and is the world's fourth largest island. In the west, a wide coastal plain gives way to a central highland region, mostly between 600 m and 1,220 m [2,000ft to 4,000ft]. This is Madagascar's most densely populated region and home of the capital, Antananarivo. The land rises in the north to the volcanic peak of Tsaratanana, at 2,876 m [9,436 ft]. The land slopes off in the east to a narrow coastal strip.

Grass and scrub grow in the south. Forest and tropical savanna once covered much of Madagascar, but farming has cleared large areas, destroying natural habitats and seriously threatening the island's unique and diverse wildlife.

Area 587,041 sq km [226,657 sq mi]
Population 18,595,000
Capital (population) Antananarivo (1,808,000)
Government Republic
Ethnic groups Merina, Betsimisaraka, Betsileo, Tsmihety, Sakalava and others
Languages Malagasy and French (both official)
Religions Traditional beliefs 52%, Christianity 41%, Islam 7%
Currency Malagasy franc = 100 centimes
Website www.madagascar.gov.mg

CLIMATE

Altitude moderates temperatures in the highlands. Winters (April to September) are dry; heavy rains occur in summer. Coastal lands to the east are warm and humid. The west is drier, and the south and south-west are hot and dry.

HISTORY

People from South-east Asia began to settle on Madagascar around 2,000 years ago. Subsequent influxes from Africa and Arabia added to the island's diverse heritage, culture and language.

The Malagasy language is of South-east Asian origin, though it includes words from Arabic, Bantu languages and European languages.

The first Europeans to reach Madagascar were Portuguese missionaries who in the early 17th century vainly sought to convert the native population. The 17th century saw the creation of small kingdoms and later the French

ANTANANARIVO (TANANARIVE)

Capital and largest city of Madagascar. Founded around 1625, the city became the residence for Imerina rulers in 1794 and the capital of Madagascar. Antananarivo was taken by the French in 1895, and became part of a French protectorate. It is the seat of the University of Madagascar (1961). A trade centre for a rice-producing region, it has textile, tobacco, and leather industries.

French colony. In 1942, the British overthrew Vichy colonial rule and the Free French reasserted control. In 1946–8 France brutally crushed a rebellion against colonial rule, killing perhaps as many as 80,000 islanders.

POLITICS

In 1960 the island achieved full independence as the Malagasy Republic. In 1972, the military took control of government. In 1975 Malagasy was renamed Madagascar and Lt Commander Didier Ratsiraka became president. He proclaimed martial law, banned opposition parties, and nationalized many industries.

In 1992 Ratsiraka bowed to political pressure and approved a new, democratic constitution. In 1993 multiparty elections Albert Zafy became president. Zafy was impeached in 1996 and Ratsiraka regained the presidency in 1997. In 2000, floods and tropical storms devastated Madagascar.

Madagascar came to the brink of civil war in 2002 when Ratsiraka and his opponent, Marc Ravalomanana, both claimed victory in presidential elections. Ravalomanana was eventually recognized as president and Ratsiraka was exiled. In 2006 elections Ravalomanana won a second term.

ECONOMY

Madagascar is one of the world's poorest countries. The land has been eroded because of the cutting down of the forests and overgrazing of the grasslands. Farming, fishing and forestry employ about 80% of the people.

The country's food crops include bananas, cassava, rice and sweet potatoes. Coffee is the leading export. Other exports include cloves, sisal, sugar and vanilla. There is little manufacturing. Tourism is an emerging industry.

established trading posts along the east coast. The island became a haven for pirates from the late 18th to early 19th century. From the late 18th century a major part of the island was was under Merina rule. In 1817, the Merina ruler and the British governor of Mauritius agreed to the abolition of the slave trade, as a result of which the island received British military and financial assistance. British influence remained strong for several decades. France made contacts with the island in the 1860s. Finally, French troops defeated a Malagasy army in 1895 and Madagascar became a

MALAWI

The colours in Malawi's flag come from the flag of the Malawi Congress Party, which was adopted in 1953. The symbol of the rising sun was added when Malawi became independent from Britain in 1964. It represents the beginning of a new era for Malawi and Africa.

The Republic of Malawi in southern Africa is a small, landlocked country which is no more than 160 km [100 mi] wide. Its dominant physical feature is Lake Malawi, which is drained in the south by the River Shire, a tributary of the Zambezi. The land is mostly mountainous, the highest point being Mulanje, in the south-east, which reaches 3,000 m [9,843 ft].

Area 118,484 sq km [45,747 sq mi]
Population 13,014,000
Capital (population) Lilongwe (440,000)
Government Multiparty republic
Ethnic groups Chewa, Nyanja, Tonga, Tumbuka, Lomwe, Yao, Ngoni and others
Languages Chichewa and English (both official)
Religions Protestant 55%, Roman Catholic 20%, Islam 20%
Currency Malawian kwacha = 100 tambala
Website www.malawi.gov.mw

CLIMATE

The low-lying areas of Malawi are hot and humid all year round; the uplands have a pleasant climate. Lilongwe, at about 1,100 m [3,609 ft] above sea level, has a warm and sunny climate. Frosts sometimes occur in July and August, the middle of the long dry season. The wet season extends from November to May.

Wooded savanna and tropical grasslands cover much of the country, with swampy vegetation in many river valleys.

HISTORY

The Bantu-speaking ancestors of the people of Malawi first reached the area around 2,000 years ago, introducing an iron age culture and developing kingdoms in the region. In the first half of the 19th century two other Bantu-speaking groups, the Ngoni (or Angoni) and the Yao, invaded the area. The Yao took slaves and sold them to Arabs who traded along the coast. In 1859, the British missionary-explorer David Livingstone reached the area and was horrified by the cruelty of the slave trade. The Free Church of Scotland established a mission in 1875, while Scottish businessmen worked to found businesses to replace the slave trade. The British made treaties with local chiefs on the western banks of what was then called Lake Nyasa and, in 1891, the area was made the British Protectorate of Nyasaland.

The Federation of Rhodesia and Nyasaland was established by Britain in 1953. This included Northern Rhodesia (Zambia) and Southern Rhodesia (Zimbabwe). The people of Nyasaland opposed the creation of the federation, fearing domination by the white minority community in Southern Rhodesia. In 1958, Dr Hastings Banda took over leadership of the opposition to the federation and also to the continuance of British rule. Faced with mounting protests, Britain dissolved the federation in 1963. During 1964, Nyasaland became fully independent as Malawi. Banda became the country's first prime minister and, in 1966, after from most of sub-Saharan Africa in being conservative and pragmatic, hostile to its socialist neighbours, but friendly with South Africa. His austerity programme and agricultural policies seemed to have wrought an economic miracle, but a swift decline in the 1980s, combined with the arrival of a million refugees from war-torn Mozambique, led to a return to poverty despite massive aid packages. Another immediate and ongoing problem was the high incidence of AIDS putting pressure on the country's limited welfare services. Political dissent led to the restoration of a multiparty system in 1993. Banda and his party were defeated in the elections of 1994, and Bakili Muluzi became president. Banda was arrested and charged with murder, but he died in 1997.

ECONOMY

The overthrow of Banda led to a restoration of political freedoms. The abolition of school fees and school uniforms nearly doubled school enrolment. Malawi remains one of the world's poorest countries. Reforms in the 1990s included encouraging small farmers to diversify production, but free enterprise and privatization angered some farmers who have suffered from the ending of subsidies.

Agriculture dominates the economy, employing more than 80% of the workforce, although fertile farmland is limited. Tobacco is the leading export, followed by tea, sugar and cotton. The main food crops include cassava, groundnuts, maize, rice and sorghum. Many farmers raise cattle, goats and other livestock.

the adoption of a new constitution, making the country a single-party republic, Banda became the first president.

POLITICS

Banda declared himself president for life in 1971. His autocratic regime differed

LILONGWE

Capital of Malawi, south-east Africa, in the centre of the country, 80 km [50 mi] west of Lake Malawi. It replaced Zomba as the capital in 1975, and rapidly became Malawi's second-largest city.

MALAYSIA

This flag was adopted when the Federation of Malaysia was set up in 1963. The red and white bands date back to a revolt in the 13th century. The star and crescent are symbols of Islam. The blue represents Malaysia's role in the Commonwealth.

Malaysia consists of two main parts, Peninsular Malaysia (the Malay peninsula) and northern Borneo. Peninsular Malaysia is made up of 11 states and two of the three components of the federal territory (Kuala Lumpur and Putrajaya). Northern Borneo comprises two states and one component of the federal territory (Labuan)

Peninsular Malaysia is dominated by fold mountains with a north–south axis. The most important is the Main Range, which runs from the Thai border to the south-east of Kuala Lumpur, reaching 2,190 m [7,185 ft] at its highest point, Gunong Tahan. South of the Main Range lie the flat, poorly drained lowlands of Johor. Deposition of silts by the short rivers has built up a margin of lowlands around the coast.

Northern Borneo has a mangrove-fringed coastal plain, backed by hill country, with east–west fold mountains in the interior. The most striking mountain, and Malaysia's highest point, is the granite peak of Mount Kinabalu, in Sabah, at 4,101 m [13,455 ft].

Area 329,758 sq km [127,320 sq mi]
Population 24,386,000
Capital (population) Kuala Lumpur (1,392,000), Putrajaya (administrative centre)
Government Constitutional monarchy
Ethnic groups Malay and other indigenous groups 58%, Chinese 24%, Indian 8%, others
Languages Malay (official), Chinese, English
Religions Islam, Buddhism, Daoism, Hinduism, Christianity, Sikhism
Currency Ringgit = 100 cents
Website www.tourism.gov.my

HISTORY

The Malay peninsula has long been a crossroads for sea traders from China and India. Hinduism and Buddhism were introduced from India in the 9th century AD. An early golden age of Malay political power came in the 15th century with the rise of the Kingdom of Malacca (now Melaka), on the south-western coast of the Malay peninsula. Malacca controlled the important sea routes and attracted traders from all parts of Asia. Arab traders introduced Islam and, in 1414, Malacca's ruler became a Muslim. Many of the people on the peninsula soon embraced Islam, which remains the official religion of Malaysia today.

The first Europeans to reach the area were the Portuguese, and Malacca became a Portuguese possession in 1511. The Dutch, who had been trading in the area during the early 17th century, took Malacca in 1641. Many people from the Dutch-controlled Sulawesi and Sumatra settled in the peninsula, adding to the region's complex ethnic mix. The British, who had been seeking a suitable trading post in South-east Asia, took over Malac-

CLIMATE

Malaysia has a hot equatorial climate. Temperatures are high all year, though the mountains are much cooler than lowland areas. Rainfall affects the whole country and is heavy throughout the year.

KUALA LUMPUR

ca in 1794. Malacca was returned to the Dutch in 1814, but reverted to British rule in 1824. Through the activities of Stamford Raffles, an agent for the British-owned East India Company, Singapore was occupied by the British in 1819 and made a British territory in 1824. The Straits Settlement, consisting of Penang (now Pinang), Malacca and Singapore, was founded by the British in 1826. Favourable trade rules led to rapid growth and, in 1867, the Straits Settlement became a British colony. British rule was gradually extended, with Sabah and Sarawak becoming a protectorate in 1888. In 1896, Negeri Sembilan, Penang, Perak and Selangor became the Federated Malay States. Under British rule the economy developed, and thousands of Chinese and Indian workers came to work on the rubber plantations.

Japan occupied the area that is now Malaysia and Singapore during World War II, but British rule was restored in 1945 following Japan's defeat. In the late 1940s and 1950s, inspired by the Chinese revolution, Communists fought the British. Guerrilla warfare ended with the independence of the Federation of Malaya in 1957. In 1963 Malaya joined with Singapore and what are now Sabah and Sarawak, to form the nation of Malaysia. Tunku Abdul Rahman of the Alliance Party became prime minister. Brunei was invited to join, but no agreement was achieved on entry terms. Arguments between Singapore and the Malaysian government occurred from the outset, causing Singapore to withdraw in 1965 and become an independent sovereign state.

One of the problems faced by the nation has been its great ethnic and religious diversity, with Malays of both Chinese and Indian origin, many brought in by the British to work the tin mines and rubber plantations. There are also a number of Eurasians, Europeans and aboriginal peoples, notably in Sabah and Sarawak. This patchwork has caused tensions, especially between the Muslim Malays and the politically dominant, mainly Buddhist Chinese. However, while riots did break out in 1969, there

SOUTH CHINA SEA

Part of the Pacific Ocean, surrounded by south-east China, Indo-China, the Malay Peninsula, Borneo, the Philippines, and Taiwan; connected to the East China Sea by the Formosa Strait. The world's largest sea, its chief arms are the Gulf of Tonkin and Gulf of Thailand. The Si, Red, Mekong and Chao Phraya rivers flow into it. It has an area of 2.3 million sq km [848,000 sq mi] and an average depth of 1,140 m [3,740 ft].

was never any escalation into serious armed conflict, nor was economic development affected.

Malaysia faced attacks by Indonesia, which objected to Sabah and Sarawak joining Malaysia. Indonesia's policy of 'confrontation' forced Malaysia to increase its defence expenditure. Malaysia was also reluctant to have dealings with Communist countries, but at the same time was keen to remain independent of the Western bloc and aware of the need for South-east Asian nations to work together. From 1967, it was playing a major part in regional affairs, especially through its membership of ASEAN (Association of South-east Asian Nations), together with Indonesia, the Philippines, Singapore and Thailand. (Later members of ASEAN include Brunei in 1984, Vietnam in 1995, Laos and Burma (Myanmar) in 1997, and Cambodia in 1999.)

POLITICS

From the 1970s Malaysia achieved rapid economic progress, especially under the leadership of Dr Mahathir Mohamad, who became prime minister in 1981. Mahathir encouraged the development of industry in order to diversify the economy and reduce the country's reliance on agriculture and mining. The first Malaysian car, the Proton Saga, went into production in 1985. By the early 1990s, manufacturing accounted for about 20% of the gross domestic product and by 1996 its share of the GDP had risen to nearly 35%. However, as with many of the economic 'tigers' in Asia's eastern rim, Malaysia was hit by a recession in 1997–8. In response to the crisis, the government ordered the repatriation of many temporary foreign workers and initiated a series of austerity measures aimed at restoring confidence and avoiding the chronic debt problems affecting some other Asian countries. In 1998, the economy shrank by about 5%.

During the economic crisis, differences developed between Mahathir Mohamad and his deputy prime minister and finance minister, Anwar Ibrahim. Anwar wanted Malaysia to work closely with the International Monetary Fund (IMF) to promote domestic reforms and strict monetary and fiscal policies. By the summer of 1998 he had gone further, attacking corruption and nepotism in government. Mahathir, who was suspicious of international 'plots' to undermine Malaysia's economy, put much of the blame for the crisis on foreign speculators. He sacked Anwar from the government and also from the ruling United Malays National Organization (UMNO). Anwar was jailed for corruption and alleged sexual misconduct, but these charges were later overturned.

In late 1999, Mahathir called a snap election to consolidate his power and strengthen his mandate to deal with the economy. With the economy appearing to be rebounding from recession, Mahathir's coalition retained its two-thirds majority in parliament. However, many Malays voted for the conservative Muslim Parti Islam. This meant that Mahathir had to rely more on the Chinese and Indian parties in his coalition. The opposition also gained strength by forming a united front at the 1999 elections. In 2003, Mahathir was succeeded by Abdullah Ahmad Badawi, who won a landslide victory in 2004.

KUALA LUMPUR (MALAY, 'ESTUARY MUD')

Capital of Malaysia, southern Malay Peninsula. Founded in 1857, Kuala Lumpur became the capital of the Federated Malay States in 1895, capital of the Federation of Malaya in 1957, and capital of Malaysia in 1963. A commercial city, its striking modern architecture includes one of the world's tallest buildings, the twin Petronas Towers, at 452 m [1,483 ft]. Industries include tin and rubber.

ECONOMY

The World Bank classifies Malaysia as an 'upper-middle-income' developing country. Manufacturing is the most important sector of the economy and accounts for a high proportion of the exports. By the mid-1990s the country's leading exports were machinery and transport equipment, which accounted for about 55% of the value of exports. The remaining exports included other manufactures, mineral fuels, inedible raw materials and food. Electronic equipment is now a major industry, and Malaysia is one of the largest producers of consumer electronics. Other electronic products include semiconductors for computers and communications equipment. Other major industries include chemicals, petroleum products, plastics, processed food, textiles and clothing, rubber and wood products.

Malaysia is becoming increasingly urbanized, mostly as a result of industri-alization. By 2000, about 57% of the population lived in cities and towns.

Malaysia leads the world in the production of palm oil, and, in the mid-1990s, it ranked third in producing natural rubber. Malaysia also ranked fifth in the production of cocoa beans. Other important crops include apples, bananas, coconuts, pepper, pineapples and many other tropical fruits, sugar cane, tea and tobacco. The country's chief food crop is rice. Some farmers raise livestock, including cattle, pigs and poultry. The country's rainforests are exploited for timber, and wood and wood products including plywood and furniture play an important part in the economy.

The mining of tin is important with Malaysia the eighth largest producer of tin ore in the world. There is also bauxite, copper, gold, iron ore and ilmenite (an ore from which titanium is obtained). Since the 1970s, the production of oil and natural gas has steadily increased.

BRUNEI

Negara Brunei Darussalam, as Brunei is offically known, is a sultanate located in north Borneo, south-east Asia.

Bounded in the north-west by the South China Sea, Brunei consists of humid plains with forested mountains running along its southern border

CLIMATE

Brunei has an equatorial climate. Temperatures range from 23-32°C [73-90°F]. There is high humidity. Rainfall varies from 2,500 mm [98 in] on the coast to 7,500 mm [295 in] inland, but there is no defined rainy season.

HISTORY AND POLITICS

During the 16th century, Brunei ruled over the whole of Borneo and parts of the Philippines. Problems with the royal succession, combined with European colonialism, caused its influence to decline. It became a British protectorate in 1888.

Area 5,765 sq km [2,226 sq mi]
Population 379,000
Capital (population) Bandar Seri Begawan (55,000)
Government Constitutional sultanate
Ethnic groups Malay 67%, Chinese 15%, others
Languages Malay (official), Chinese, English
Religions Islam (official) 67%, Buddhist 13%, Christian 10%, indigenous beliefs and others
Currency Bruneian dollar = 100 cents
Website www.brunei.gov.bn/index.htm

Brunei achieved independence in 1983. Brunei has been ruled by the same family for over six centuries. The Sultan has executive authority.

ECONOMY

Oil and gas are the main source of income, accounting for 70% of GD, and have made the country wealthy. Recently, attempts have been made to increase agricultural production.

MALI

The colours on Mali's flag are those used on the flag of Ethiopia, Africa's oldest independent nation. They symbolize African unity. This flag was used by Mali's African Democratic Rally prior to the country becoming independent from France in 1960.

The Republic of Mali is the largest country in west Africa. It is mainly flat, with the highest land in the Adrar des Iforhas on the border with Algeria. Saharan Mali contains many wadis (dry river valleys). The old trading city of Timbuktu lies on the edge of the desert. The only permanent rivers are in the south, the main rivers being the Séné-gal, which flows westwards to the Atlantic Ocean to the north of Kayes, and the Niger, which makes a large turn, called the Niger Bend, in south-central Mali.

More than 70% of Mali is desert or semi-desert with sparse vegetation. Central and south-eastern Mali is a dry grassland region known as the Sahel. In prolonged droughts, the northern Sahel dries up and becomes part of the Sahara. Fertile farmland and tropical savanna covers southern Mali, the most densely populated region.

Area 1,240,192 sq km [478,838 sq mi]
Population 11,717,000
Capital (population) Bamako (1,379,000)
Government Multiparty republic
Ethnic groups Mande 50% (Bambara, Malinke, Soninke), Peul 17%, Voltaic 12%, Songhai 6%, Tuareg and Moor 10%, others
Languages
French (official) and many African languages
Religions Islam 90%, Traditional beliefs 9%, Christianity 1%
Currency CFA franc = 100 centimes
Website www.officetourisme-mali.com

CLIMATE

Northern Mali is part of the Sahara, with a hot, practically rainless climate. Only the south has enough rain for farming. In the south-west of the country, unpleasant weather is experienced when dry and dusty harmattan winds blow from the Sahara Desert.

HISTORY

From the 4th to the 16th centuries, Mali was part of three major black African cultures – ancient Ghana, Mali and Songhai. Reports on these empires were made by Arab scholars who crossed the Sahara to visit them. One major centre was Timbuktu (Tombouctou) in central Mali, which in the 14th century was a great centre of learning in history, law and the Muslim religion. It was also a major trading centre. At its height, the Mali Empire was west Africa's richest and most powerful state. However, following the defeat of the Songhai empire by Morocco in 1591, the area was divided into small kingdoms.

Mali was taken over by the French in the 1880s, and was incorporated into the Federation of West Africa in 1898. Nationalist movements grew more vocal in their opposition to colonialism. In 1958 Mali, then known as French Sudan, gained some autonomy. In 1959 it joined with Senegal as the Federation of Mali and split from France.

Shortly after gaining independence, Senegal seceded and, in 1960, Mali became a one-party republic. Its first president, Modibo Keita, committed

254

death sentence for corruption to life imprisonment. General Amadou Toumani Toure succeeded Konaré as president in 2002 elections and was re-elected in 2007. The opposition criticized the vote, but local and foreign observers judged it reasonably fair.

ECONOMY

Mali is one of the world's poorest countries and 70% of the land is desert or semi-desert. Only about 2% of the land is used for growing crops, while 25% is used for grazing animals. Despite this, agriculture employs nearly 85% of the workforce, many of whom still subsist by nomadic livestock rearing. Farming is hampered by water shortages, and the severe droughts in the 1970s and 1980s led to a great loss of animals and much human suffering. The farmers in the south grow millet, rice, sorghum and other food crops to feed their families.

The chief cash crops are cotton (the main export), groundnuts and sugar cane. Many of these crops are grown on land which is irrigated with river water. Only a few small areas in the south are worked without irrigation, while the barren deserts in the north are populated only by a few poor nomads.

Fishing is an important economic activity. Mali has vital mineral deposits of gold and salt.

Mali to nationalization and pan-Africanism. Mali adopted its own currency in 1962 and in 1963, it joined the Organization of African States (OAS). Economic crisis forced Keita to revert to the franc zone, and permit France greater economic influence. Opposition led to Keita's overthrow in a coup in 1968.

POLITICS

The military formed a National Liberation Committee and appointed Moussa Traoré as prime minister. During the 1970s, the Sahel suffered a series of droughts that contributed to a devastating famine. Thousands of people died.

In 1979 Mali adopted a new constitution, and Traoré was elected president. In 1991 a military coup overthrew Traoré. A new constitution in 1992 saw the establishment of a multiparty democracy. Alpha Oumar Konaré, leader of the Alliance for Democracy in Mali (ADEMA), won the ensuing presidential election. A political settlement provided a special administration for Tuaregs in northern Mali. Konaré was re-elected in 1997. In 1999, he commuted Traoré's

BAMAKO

Capital of Mali, on the River Niger, 145 km [90 mi] north-east of the border with Guinea. A centre of Muslim learning in the 11th–15th centuries, it was occupied by the French in 1883 and became capital of the French Sudan (1908). Industries include shipping, groundnuts, meat and metal products.

MALTA

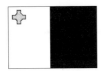

A red flag with a white cross was used by the Knights of Malta. In 1943 a George Cross was added after the award was bestowed by King George VI of Britain. Upon independence, in 1964 a red edge was added to the cross.

The Republic of Malta is an archipelago republic in the Mediterranean Sea, 100 km [60 mi] south of Sicily. Malta consists of two main islands, Malta (246 sq km [95 sq mi]) and Gozo (67 sq km [26 sq mi]). The small island of Comino lies between the two large islands and there are also two tiny islets.

The islands are low-lying. Malta island is composed mostly of limestone. Gozo is largely covered by clay, and as a result its landscapes are less arid. Malta has no forests, and 38% of the land is arable.

Area 316 sq km [122 sq mi]
Population 400,000
Capital (population) Valletta (9,000)
Government Multiparty republic
Ethnic groups Maltese 96%, British 2%
Languages Maltese and English (both official)
Religions Roman Catholic 98%
Currency Maltese lira = 100 cents
Website www.gov.mt

CLIMATE

Malta has a typical Mediterranean climate. Summers are hot and dry. Winters are mild and wet. The sirocco, a hot wind from North Africa, raises temperatures in the spring.

HISTORY

Malta has evidence of Stone Age settlement dating back 4,000 years. In around 850 BC, the Phoenicians colonized Malta. The Carthaginians, Greeks and Romans followed. In AD 395, Malta became part of the Eastern Roman (Byzantine) Empire. In 870 an Arab invasion brought Islam, but Roger I, Norman King of Sicily, restored Christian rule in 1091. In 1530, the Holy Roman Emperor gave Malta to the Knights Hospitallers. In 1565 the Knights held Malta against a Turkish siege. In 1798 the French captured Malta but, with help from Britain,

they were driven out in 1800. In 1814, Malta became a British colony and a strategic military base.

During World War I, Malta was an important naval base. In World War II, Italian and German aircraft bombed the islands. In recognition of the bravery of the Maltese resistance, the British King

KNIGHTS HOSPITALLERS

(Order of the Hospital of St John of Jerusalem) Military Christian order recognized in 1113 by Pope Paschal II. In the early 11th century, a hospital was established in Jerusalem for Christian pilgrims. They adopted a military role in the 12th century to defend Jerusalem. After the fall of Jerusalem (1187), they moved to Acre, then Cyprus, then Rhodes (1310), from where they were expelled by the Ottoman Turks (1522). The Pope then gave them Malta, where they remained until driven out by Napoleon in 1798. The order still exists as an international humanitarian charity.

George VI awarded the George Cross to Malta in 1942. Malta became a base for NATO in 1953.

POLITICS

Malta became independent in 1964, and a republic in 1974. Britain's military agreement with Malta expired in 1979, with Malta then ceasing to be a military base. In the 1980s, the people declared Malta neutral. Malta applied to join the European Union in the 1990s, but the application was scrapped when the Labour Party won the elections in 1996. Following Labour's election defeat in 1998, the bid for EU membership was renewed and Malta finally became a member in 2004.

ECONOMY

The World Bank classifies Malta as an 'upper-middle income' developing country. Although it lacks natural resources, its position and natural harbours boost trade. Tourism is the largest sector, though finance and goods transshipment are also important. Manufacturing is a significant employer, and industries include shipbuilding and ship repair, chemicals, electronic equipment and textiles. The rocky soil makes farming difficult, and Malta produces only 20% of its food. It has a small fishing industry.

MALTESE (MALTI)

Maltese is a Semitic language, that is, one of a group of languages spoken by peoples native to North Africa and the Middle East and forming one of the five branches of the Afro-Asiatic language family. It is spoken by about 340,000 people in Malta and Gozo, and is the only Semitic tongue officially written in the Latin alphabet. The modern language is closely related to western Arabic dialects, but it also shows the strong influence of the Latin that was spoken in Malta. The language developed from the Arabic spoken by the Arabs who invaded Malta in 870. French-speaking Roger I, Norman King of Sicily, ruled from 1091. In 1530 the Knights Hospitallers, who spoke Italian and Latin, were given Malta by the Holy Roman Emperor and it remained under their rule until 1798. In 1814, Malta became a British colony and the British endeavoured to make English the local language. After independence in 1964 Maltese became the national language.

VALLETTA

Port and capital of Malta, on the north-east coast of the island. Founded in the 16th century, it was named after Jean Parisot de la Valette, Grand Master of the Order of the Knights of St John, who organized the reconstruction of the city after repelling the Turks' Great Siege of 1565. Notable sights include the Royal University of Malta (1592) and the Cathedral of San Giovanni (1576).

MAURITANIA

The Islamic Republic of Mauritania adopted its flag in 1959, the year before it became fully independent from France. It features a yellow star and crescent. These are traditional symbols of the national religion, Islam, as also is the colour green.

The Islamic Republic of Mauritania in north-western Africa is nearly twice the size of France, though France's population is more than 28 times that of Mauritania. Over two-thirds of the land is barren, most of it being part of the Sahara desert. Apart from a small nomadic population, most Mauritanians live in the south, either on the plains bordering the Senegal River in the south-west or on the tropical savanna in the south-east. The highest point is Kediet Ijill (915 m [3,002 ft]). It is an area rich in haematite, a high-quality iron ore.

Area 1,025,520 sq km [395,953 sq mi]
Population 3,177,000
Capital (population) Nouakchott (735,000)
Government Multiparty Islamic republic
Ethnic groups Mixed Moor/Black 40%, Moor 30%, Black 30%
Languages Arabic and Wolof (both official), French
Religions Islam
Currency Ouguiya = 100 5 khoums
Website www.mauritania.mr

CLIMATE

The amount of rain and the length of the rainy season increases north to south. The desert has dry north-east and easterly winds throughout the year. South-westerly winds bring summer rain to the south.

HISTORY

From the 4th to the 16th centuries, parts of Mauritania belonged to the two great African empires of ancient Ghana and Mali. Portuguese explorers first explored the coast in the 1440s.

European contact did not affect the area until the 17th century, when trade in gum arabic, a substance obtained from an acacia tree, became important. Britain, France and the Netherlands competed for the trade. France made

Mauritania a protectorate in 1903 to exploit the trade in gum arabic. In 1920 the country became a French colony and a territory of French West Africa, an area that included present-day Benin, Burkina Faso, Guinea, Ivory Coast, Mali, Niger

BANC D'ARGUIN

Lying on the coast of Mauritania, the Banc d'Arguin is the most important area of intertidal flats on the coast of Africa. In winter it is home to over 2 million shorebirds, while some 40,000 waterbirds, including great white pelicans, greater flamingos, spoonbills and several species of tern also breed here. The Banc d'Arguin is also an important fishing area and the Imraguen fishing community and their predecessors have lived from the local fishery for the past 500 years or more. The sight of their lanteen sailed boats working their way up the channels between the mudflats, backed by the dunes of the Sahara, is a unique spectacle.

2003 but overthrown in a military coup led by Colonel Ely Ould Mohammed Vall in 2005. Vall's administration had popular support and promised a swift return to democracy. The country's first fair presidential elections since independence took place in 2007. Sidi Ould Sheikh Abdellahi became president.

ECONOMY

The World Bank classifies Mauritania as a 'low-income' developing country. Agriculture employs over half of the workforce, with the majority living at subsistence level. Many are still cattle herders who drive their herds from the Senegal River through the Sahelian steppelands, coinciding with the seasonal rains. However, droughts in the 1980s greatly reduced the domestic animal populations, forcing many nomadic farmers to seek help in urban areas. Plagues of locusts in 2004 also caused severe damage. Farmers in the south-east grow such crops as beans, dates, millet, rice and sorghum. Rich fishing grounds lie off the coast. The country's chief natural resource is iron ore, and the vast reserves of high quality ore around Fdérik provide a major source of revenue.

and Senegal as well as Mauritania. Mauritania became a self-governing territory in the French Union in 1958, achieving full independence in 1960.

POLITICS

In 1961 Mauritania's president, Mokhtar Ould Daddah, made the country a one-party state. In 1976 Spain withdrew from Spanish Sahara (now Western Sahara), a territory bordering Mauritania to the north. Morocco occupied the northern two-thirds of the territory, while Mauritania took the rest. POLISARIO (Popular Front for the Liberation of Saharan Territories) guerrillas began to fight for independence. In 1979 Mauritania withdrew from Western Sahara.

From 1978 Mauritania was ruled by a series of military regimes. In 1991 the people voted to create a multiparty democracy under a new constitution. In 1992 Maaouiya Ould Sidi Ahmed Taya, a colonel who had led a military administration since 1984, became president. Due to accusations of bias, subsequent elections were boycotted by opposition parties. Taya was re-elected in 1997 and

NOUAKCHOTT

Capital of Mauritania, north-west Africa, in the south-western part of the country, 8 km [5 mi] from the Atlantic Ocean. Originally a small fishing village, it was chosen as capital when Mauritania became independent in 1960. Nouakchott now has an international airport and is the site of modern storage facilities for petroleum. Light industries have been developed, but handicrafts remain important.

MAURITIUS

The flag is unique in having four equal horizontal bands. The colours derive from Mauritius' coat of arms. Red represents the blood shed in the liberation struggle, blue for the Indian Ocean, yellow for the bright future afforded by independence and green for the islands' lush vegetation.

The Republic of Mauritius is centred on the large island of Mauritius, which is situated 800 km [500 mi] east of Madagascar. This island makes up just over 90% of the country, which also includes the island of Rodrigues, about 560 km [348 mi] east of Mauritius, and several small islands. The main island is fringed by coral reefs, lagoons and sandy beaches. The land in the interior rises to a high lava plateau (828 m [2,717 ft]) enclosed by rocky peaks.

Area 2,040 sq km [788 sq mi]
Population 1,241,000
Capital (population) Port Louis (148,000)
Government Multiparty republic
Ethnic groups Indo-Mauritian 68%, Creole 27%, Sino-Mauritian 3%, Franco-Mauritian 2%
Languages English (official), Creole, French, Hindi, Urdu, Hakka, Bojpoori
Religions Hindu 50%, Roman Catholic 27%, Muslim (largely Sunni) 16%, Protestant 5%
Currency Mauritian rupee = 100 cents
Website www.gov.mu

CLIMATE

Mauritius has a tropical climate, with heavy rains in the winter. South-east winds bring rain to the interior plateau of the main island, which is also occasionally hit by destructive tropical cyclones in summer. Average annual rainfall on the interior plateau may reach 5,100 mm [200 in]. The south-west is much drier, with about 890 mm [35 in]. Temperatures range from 22°C [72°F] in the winter (June to October) to 26°C [79°F] in the summer (November to April).

HISTORY

In 1498, the fleet of Vasco da Gama saw the island. In 1510 a Portuguese navigator, Pedro Mascarenhas, landed and named it Cimé. Later Portuguese navigators used the island as a port of call, but did not establish a permanent settlement.

In 1598 the Dutch became the first nation to claim the island, and they renamed it after Maurice, Prince of Orange and Count of Nassau. However, an attempt at settlement failed in the 1650s. A second attempt was abandoned in 1710. By that time the famous dodo, which was unique to Mauritius, had become extinct through habitat loss and predation by imported species. Following the Dutch withdrawal, the island became a haven for pirates.

The French East India Company claimed Mauritius for France in 1715 and named it the Isle de France. The French developed the economy and imported African slaves. In 1767, control of the island passed to the French government, although the settlers revolted in 1796 when the French government tried to abolish slavery.

British forces landed on Mauritius in 1810, starting a period of British rule. In 1834, Britain abolished slavery on the island which they renamed Mauritius. Most former slaves refused to work on the sugar plantations and so Britain introduced indentured labourers from

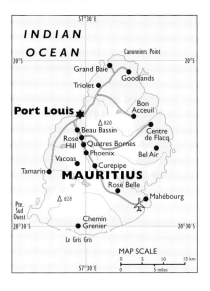

India, recruiting around 450,000 workers between 1837 and the end of indentured labour in 1910.

In 1926, the first Indo-Mauritians were elected to the government council. In 1936 a Creole politician, Dr Maurice Cure, founded the Mauritian Labour Party (MLP). In 1942, representatives from all Mauritian communities were invited to serve on consultative committees and, in 1948, many Indian and Creole were given the vote in elections to a new, enlarged legislature. Internal self-government was introduced in 1957. Elections were held under universal adult suffrage following the introduction of a new constitution in 1958. The MLP, led by Dr Seewoosagur Ramgoolam, won a majority. However, ethnic riots between Indians and Creoles occurred in 1964.

POLITICS

Mauritius became independent in 1968. In 1969, Paul Berenger founded the socialist Mauritian Militant Movement (MMM). In 1971, the MMM supported strikers and organized opposition to the government. In response, the government declared a state of emergency which lasted until 1976. The MMM won the 1992 elections and Aneerood Jugnauth became prime minister.

Mauritius became a republic in 1992 and Caseem Uteem of the MMM was elected president. In 1995 an alliance led by Navin Ramgoolam and Paul Berenger won the elections, and Ramgoolam became prime minister. Jugnauth was returned to power in 2000. He served as prime minister until 2003, when he handed over to Paul Berenger, who had been his deputy. Berenger was the first non-Hindu to become prime minister. Navin Ramgoolam again became prime minister after elections in July 2005.

Despite tensions between the Indian and Creole communities, Mauritius is a stable democracy with free elections and a good human rights record. As a result, it has attracted foreign investment.

ECONOMY

Mauritius has become one of Africa's success stories. It is now a middle-income country with a diversified economy. Arable land covers more than half of the country and sugar cane plantations cover about 90% of the cultivated land. Sugar remains a major export, though price declines have caused problems. Tea and tobacco are also grown. Agriculture and fishing employ 14% of the workforce, compared with 36% in construction and industry. Textiles and clothing are the leading exports. Mauritius has growing industrial and financial sectors and is now a major tourist centre.

PORT LOUIS

Capital of Mauritius, a seaport in the north-west of the island. It was founded by the French in 1735. Taken by the British during the Napoleonic Wars, it grew in importance as a trading port after the opening of the Suez Canal. Industries include sugar, electrical equipment and textiles.

MEXICO

Mexico's flag dates from 1821. The stripes were inspired by the French tricolour. The emblem in the centre contains an eagle, a snake and a cactus. It is based on an ancient Aztec legend about the founding of their capital, Tenochtitlán (now Mexico City).

The United Mexican States is the world's largest Spanish-speaking country. It is largely mountainous. The Sierra Madre Occidental begins in the north-west state of Chihuahua, and runs parallel to Mexico's west coast and the Sierra Madre Oriental. Monterrey lies in the foothills of the latter. Between the two ranges lies the Mexican Plateau. The southern part of the plateau contains a series of extinct volcanoes, rising to Orizaba, at 5,700 m [18,701 ft]. The southern highlands of the Sierra Madre del Sur include the archaeological sites in Oaxaca. Mexico contains two large peninsulas, Baja California (Lower California) in the north-west and the Yucatán peninsula in the south-east.

Area 1,958,201 sq km [756,061 sq mi]
Population 107,450,000
Capital (population) Mexico City (19,013,000)
Government Federal republic
Ethnic groups
Mestizo 60%, Amerindian 30%, White 9%
Languages Spanish (official)
Religions Roman Catholic 90%, Protestant 6%
Currency Mexican peso = 100 centavos
Website www.presidencia.gob.mx

CLIMATE

Mexico's climate is hugely varied according to altitude. Most rain occurs between June and September. More than 70% of Mexico has desert or semi-desert conditions.

HISTORY

Native American civilizations flourished in Mexico, including the Olmec (800–400 BC), the Maya (AD 300–900) and the Toltec Empire (900–1200). By the time Europeans arrived, the Aztec dominated the central plateau from their capital at Tenochtitlán.

In 1519 Spanish conquistadors captured the capital and the Aztec emperor Montezuma, and began to loot the Aztec empire. In 1535 the territory became the Viceroyalty of New Spain. Christianity was forcibly introduced. Spanish colonial rule was harsh and divisive.

Mexico became independent in 1821 and a republic in 1824. War with Texas escalated into the Mexican War (1846–8) with the United States. Under the terms of the Treaty of Guadalupe-Hidalgo (1848), Mexico lost 50% of its territory. Liberal forces, led by Benito Juárez, triumphed in the War of Reform (1858–61), but conservatives with support from France installed Maximilian of Austria as Emperor in 1864. In 1867, republican rule was restored and Juárez became president. In 1876 an armed revolt gave Porfirio Díaz the presidency; his dictatorship lasted until 1910. General Huerta took power in 1913, and his dictatorship prolonged the Mexican Revolution (1910–40) and led to US intervention. During the 1920s and 1930s, Mexico introduced land and social reforms. After World War II Mexico's economy was liberalized and began to grow. Relations with the US improved, but problems remain over Mexican economic migration and drug trafficking.

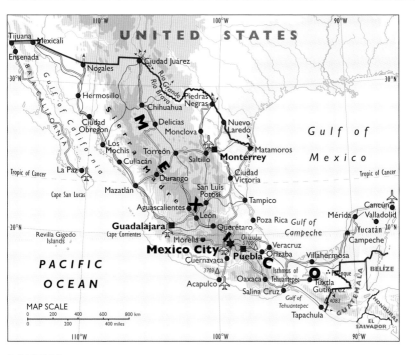

POLITICS

The Institutional Revolutionary Party (PRI) ruled Mexico from 1929 to 2000. In 1994 the Zapatista National Liberation Army (ZNLA) staged an armed revolt in the south, calling for land reforms and Native American rights. Vicente Fox became the first non-PRI leader of Mexico in 2000. In 2001 parliament passed a new rights bill for indigenous peoples. 2006 elections, marred by fraud allegations, made the conservative Felipe Calderón president by an 0.5% margin. Opposition objections led to months of disorder.

ECONOMY

The World Bank classifies Mexico as an 'upper-middle-income' developing country. Oil and oil products are major exports, while manufacturing is the most valuable activity. Factories near the northern border, known as *maquiladoras*, assemble goods for US companies.

MEXICO CITY

Capital of Mexico, in a volcanic basin at 2,380 m [7,800 ft], in the centre of the country. It is the nation's political, economic, and cultural centre and suffers from overcrowding and high levels of pollution. Hernán Cortés destroyed the former Aztec capital (Tenochtitlán), in 1521. A new city was constructed, which acted as the capital of Spain's New World colonies for 300 years. US troops occupied the city in 1847, during the Mexican War. In 1863, French troops conquered the city and established Maximilian as Emperor. Benito Juárez's forces recaptured it in 1867. Between 1914 and 1915, the revolutionary forces of Emiliano Zapata and Francisco Villa captured and lost the city three times.

MOLDOVA

Adopted in 1990, using the same colours as the Romanian flag to emphasize their strong ties. Blue stands for Transylvania, yellow for Wallachia, red for Moldavia. The eagle symbolizes the Byzantine Empire; and the bison's head, star, rose and crescent, the medieval principality of Moldavia.

The Republic of Moldova is a small country sandwiched between Ukraine and Romania. It was formerly one of the 15 republics that made up the Soviet Union. Much of the land is hilly, and the highest areas are near the centre of the country. The main river is the Dniester, which flows through the eastern side of the country.

Forests of hornbeam and oak grow in northern and central Moldova. In the drier south, most of the region is now used for farming, with rich pasture land along the rivers.

Area 33,851 sq km [13,070 sq mi]
Population 4,467,000
Capital (population) Chisinau (658,000)
Government Multiparty republic
Ethnic groups Moldovan/Romanian 65%, Ukrainian 14%, Russian 13%, others
Languages Moldovan/Romanian, Russian (official)
Religions Eastern Orthodox 98%
Currency Moldovan leu = 100 bani
Website www.moldova.org/index/eng/

CLIMATE

Moldova has a moderately continental climate, with warm summers and fairly cold winters when temperatures dip below freezing point. Most of the rain falls in the warmer months.

HISTORY

Moldavia was a historic Balkan region, between the Carpathian Mountains in Romania and the Dniester River.

Under Roman rule, it formed the major part of the province of Dacia, and today's population is Romanian-speaking. In the 14th century, it became an independent principality ruled by the Vlachs; its lands included Bessarabia and Bukovina. In 1504, the Turks conquered Moldavia and it remained part of the Ottoman Empire until the 19th century.

In 1775 the Austrians gained Bukovina, and in 1815 Russia conquered Bessarabia. After the Russo-Turkish War in 1828–9, Russia became the dominant power. In 1856, the twin principalities of Moldavia and Wallachia gained considerable autonomy. Three years later, they united under one crown to form Romania, but Russia reoccupied southern Bessarabia in 1878.

In 1920, Bessarabia and Bukovina were incorporated into the Romanian state. In 1924, the Soviet republic of Moldavia was formed, and in 1947 it was enlarged to include Bessarabia and northern Bukovina. In 1989, Moldavia asserted independence from Russia by making Romanian the official language. In 1991, following the dissolution of the Soviet Union, Moldavia became the independent republic of Moldova.

POLITICS

Following independence in 1991, the majority Moldovan population wished to rejoin Romania. This alienated the Ukrainian and Russian populations east of the Dniester, who declared their independence from Moldova as the Transdniester Republic. War broke out of the Moldovan Communists (PCRM) won the highest share of the votes. The constitution was changed in 2000, turning Moldova from a semi-presidential republic to a parliamentary republic. In 2001, the Communist leader Vladimir Voronin was elected president. The Communist party was re-elected in 2005, though it now advocates close ties with the West, a matter of some concern to Russia. Disputes over Transdniester continue.

ECONOMY

According to the World Bank, Moldova is a lower-middle income developing country, and in terms of GNP per capita, Europe's poorest country. It is fertile and agriculture remains central to the economy. Major products include fruits, maize, tobacco and grapes for wine-making. Farmers also raise livestock, including dairy cattle and pigs.

There are few natural resources within Moldova, and the government must import materials and fuels for its industries. Light industries, such as food processing and the manufacturing of household appliances, are expanding.

between the two, with Transdniester supported by the Russian 14th Army. In August 1992 a ceasefire was declared. The former Communists of the Agrarian Democratic Party won multiparty elections in 1994. A referendum rejected reunification with Romania, and Parliament instead voted to join the Commonwealth of Independent States (CIS).

In 1994 a new constitution established a presidential parliamentary republic. In 1995 Transdniester voted in favour of independence in a referendum. In 1996 Russian troops began their withdrawal. On 1 January 1997 a former Communist, Petru Lucinschi, became president. In 1998 and 2001, the Party

CHISINAU (KISHINEV)

Capital of Moldova, in the centre of the country, on the River Byk. Founded in the early 15th century, it came under Turkish then Russian rule. Romania held the city from 1918 to 1940, at which time it was annexed by the Soviet Union. In 1991 it became capital of independent Moldova. It has a 19th-century cathedral and a university (1945). Industries include plastics, rubber, textiles and tobacco.

MONGOLIA

Mongolia's flag contains blue, the national colour, together with red for Communism. The traditional Mongolian golden 'soyonbo' symbol represents freedom. Within this, the flame is seen as a promise of prosperity and progress.

Mongolia, which is sandwiched between China and Russia, is the world's largest landlocked country. It consists mainly of high plateaux, the highest of which are in the west, between the Altai Mountains (or Aerhtai Shan) and the Hangayn Mountains (or Hangayn Nuruu). The Altai Mountains contain the country's highest peaks, reaching as much as 4,362 m [14,311 ft]. The land descends towards the east and south, where Mongolia's part of the Gobi Desert is situated.

Area 1,566,500 sq km [604,826 sq mi]
Population 2,832,000
Capital (population) Ulan Bator (842,000)
Government Multiparty republic
Ethnic groups Khalkha Mongol 85%, Kazakh 6%
Languages
Khalkha Mongolian (official), Turkic, Russian
Religions Tibetan Buddhist Lamaism 96%
Currency Tugrik = 100 möngös
Website www.mongoliatourism.gov.mn

CLIMATE

Because of its remote position, Mongolia has an extreme continental climate, with long, cold winters and short, warm summers. Annual rainfall ranges from more than 500 mm [20 in] in the highlands to 125 mm [5 in] in the lowlands.

HISTORY

In the 13th century, the great Mongol conqueror Genghis Khan united the Mongol people, created a ruthless army and founded the largest land empire in history. Under his grandson, Kublai Khan, the Mongol empire stretched from Korea and China, across Asia into what is now Iraq. In the north-west, Mongol rule extended beyond the Black Sea into eastern Europe. Learning flourished under Kublai Khan, but, after his death in 1294, the empire broke up into several parts. It was not until the late 16th century that Mongol princes reunited Mongolia. During their rule they introduced Lamaism, a form of Buddhism, which became the national religion.

In the early 17th century, the Manchu leaders of Manchuria took over Inner Mongolia. They conquered China in 1644 and Outer Mongolia some 40 years later. Present-day Mongolia then became a remote Chinese province scarcely in contact with the outside world.

GOBI (SHA-MOH)

Desert area in central Asia, extending over much of southern Mongolia and northern China. One of the world's largest deserts, it is on a plateau, 900–1,500 m [3,000–5,000 ft] high. The fringes are grassy and inhabited by nomadic Mongolian tribes who rear sheep and goats. The Gobi has cold winters, hot summers, and fierce winds and sandstorms. It covers 1.3 million sq km [500,000 sq mi].

Outer Mongolia broke away from China following the collapse of the Qing Dynasty in 1911. The Mongols appointed a priest, the Living Buddha, as their king. Legally, Outer Mongolia remained Chinese territory, but China and Russia agreed to grant it control over its own affairs in 1913. Russian influence increased and, in 1921, Mongolian and Russian Communists took control of Outer Mongolia, proclaiming the Mongolian People's Republic in 1924.

POLITICS

Mongolia became an ally of the Soviet Union, its support being particularly significant from the 1950s, when the Soviet Union was in dispute with Mongolia's neighbour China. The Soviet Union helped develop Mongolia's mineral reserves, and by the late 1980s minerals had overtaken agriculture as the country's main source of revenue.

In 1990 the people, influenced by reforms taking place in the Soviet Union, held demonstrations demanding more freedom. Free elections in June 1990 resulted in victory for the Communist Mongolian People's Revolutionary Party (MPRP). The new government began to move away from Communist policies, launching into privatization and developing a free-market economy. The 'People's Democracy' was abolished in 1992 and democratic institutions were introduced.

The MPRP was defeated in elections in 1996 by the opposition Mongolian Democratic Union coalition. The Democratic Union ran into economic problems, and in the presidential elections of 1997 the MPRP candidate, Natasagiyn Babagandi, was victorious. The parliamentary elections in July 2000, which resulted in a landslide victory for the MPRP, who gained 72 out of the 76 available seats in the Great Hural (parliament). The MPRP chairman, Nambaryn Enhbayar, became prime minister. Following disputed elections in 2004 a coalition government was set up. In 2006 the coalition broke down and the MPRP once again took power.

ECONOMY

The World Bank classifies Mongolia as a 'lower-middle-income' developing country. Many Mongolians were once nomads, moving around with their livestock. Under Communist rule, most were moved into permanent homes on government-owned farms. Livestock and animal products remain important.

The Communists developed mining and manufacturing, and by 1996, mineral products accounted for nearly 60% of the country's exports. Minerals produced in Mongolia include coal, copper, fluorspar, gold, molybdenum, tin and tungsten. The leading manufactures are textiles and metal products.

ULAN BATOR

Capital of Mongolia, on the River Tola. Ulan Bator dates back to the founding of the Lamaistic Temple of the Living Buddha in 1639. It grew as a stop for caravans between Russia and China and was later a focus for the Mongolian autonomy movement, becoming the capital in 1921. It is the political, cultural and economic centre of Mongolia. Industries include textiles, building materials, leather, paper, alcohol and carpets.

MONTENEGRO

The flag of Montenegro was adopted in 2004, replacing one based on the flag of Serbia. It is based on the traditional flag of the region and specifically on the personal standard of Nikola I, Montenegro's only king, who reigned from 1910 to 1918.

Montenegro separated from the Union of Serbia and Montenegro after a 2006 referendum. The country is largely mountainous, with a narrow coastal plain. Large areas are covered with forests. The capital, Podgorica, lies at the confluence of the Ribnica and Morača rivers.

Area 13,812 sq km [5,331 sq mi]
Population 631,000
Capital (population) Podgorica (152,000)
Government Multiparty republic
Ethnic groups
Montenegrin, Serbian, Bosniak, Albanian%
Languages Serbian, Albanian
Religions Orthodox Christian, Muslim (18%)
Currency Euro = 100 cents
Website www.vlada.cg.yu/eng/

CLIMATE

The climate on the coastal plain is Mediterranean, with hot summers and mild, wet winters. Inland areas have warm summers, cold winters and high rainfall. The higher mountains are snow-covered during the winter months.

HISTORY

The region was part of the Serbian Empire until the Turkish invasion of 1355. Ottoman Turks decisively defeated Serbia in 1389, while Montenegro resisted the Sultan's rule. By 1500, most of the territory surrendered to the Ottomans.

In 1799, Turkey recognized Montenegro's independence. In 1851, a monarchy was established and in 1878 the sovereignty of the state was formally recognized. In 1910, Nicholas I assumed the title of King and sought to expel the Turks. In 1914, he declared war on Austria, and Austro-German armies quickly overran Montenegro. Nicholas was deposed in 1918, and Montenegro united with Serbia as the Kingdom of the Serbs, Croats and Slovenes. The kingdom was renamed Yugoslavia in 1929.

In 1941 Yugoslavia was invaded by the Axis forces. Montenegro was occupied and annexed by Italy. After Italy's defeat in 1943 Montenegro was occupied by Germany and, like the rest of Yugoslavia, saw bitter fighting between the occupiers and local partisans.

After the war, the Communist faction took control and established the Socialist Federal Republic of Yugoslavia. Montenegro became one of the constituent republics of Yugoslavia in 1946.

In the early 1990s Yugoslavia broke up as four of the Yugoslav republics voted to secede. In 1992 Montenegrins voted to remain part of a Yugoslav federation with Serbia, though the fairness of the referendum was questioned. Montenegro aided Serbia against Bosnia in the conflict that followed Yugoslavia's disintegration. Though it began to distance itself from Serbia in the later 1990s, Montenegro was still bombed by NATO as part of the campaign against the government of Slobodan Milošević. In 1999, many ethnic Albanians fled to Montenegro to escape Serb oppression in Kosovo.

Parliamentary elections were held in September 2006, and parliament chose a new government in December. Djukanović's finance minister, Željko Šturanović, became president.

ECONOMY

The conflicts that followed the dismantling of former Yugoslavia did severe damage to the economy. Montenegro remains industrially underdeveloped, and unemployment and corruption remain serious problems. Bauxite mining and aluminium production form the largest industrial sector. The aluminium and financial sectors were privatized not long before independence. The fastest growth area is tourism, which is attracting substantial foreign investment.

The wars severely damaged Montenegro's economy, and industry collapsed. Smuggling became the region's main livelihood. Montenegro adopted its own economic policy and adopted the German Mark as its currency in the late 1990s.

In 2003 the Federal Republic of Yugoslavia was reconstituted under a new name, the Union of Serbia and Montenegro, reflecting looser ties between its constituent parts.

POLITICS

In May 2006 a referendum was held on independence from Serbia. It was designed, moderated and closely monitored by the EU to ensure a fair process. Just over the required 55% of Montenegrins voted for independence, following a campaign led by Prime Minister Milo Djukanović. The result was accepted by Serbia, and Montenegro formally became independent in June. The new country was immediately recognized by the rest of the world, and joined the United Nations. The government has declared an intention to join the European Union and NATO.

Much of the land is barren. Agriculture is concentrated in the Zeta Valley, with much of the rest of the country suitabe only for sheep farming. Agricultural products include tobacco, grain and livestock.

PODGORICA

Capital of Montenegro, at the confluence of the Ribnica and Moraca rivers. Historically important as a junction of several trade routes, the area has been settled since Roman times. The present town was founded in the Middle Ages. During World War II, it was heavily damaged, and most of its historic buildings destroyed. From 1946 the city was named Titograd. The name Podgorica, used again since 1992, means 'under the mountain'. The city is home to much of Montenegro's industry, but in the 2000s the economy has shifted from industry to services and finance.

269

MOROCCO

Morocco has flown a red flag since the 16th century. The green pentagram (five-pointed star), called the Seal of Solomon, was added in 1915. This design was retained when Morocco gained its independence from French and Spanish rule in 1956.

The Kingdom of Morocco lies in north-western Africa. Its name comes from the Arabic Maghreb-el-Aksa, meaning 'the farthest west'. Behind the western coastal plain the land rises to a broad plateau and the Atlas Mountains. The High Atlas contains the highest peak, Djebel Toubkal, at 4,165 m [13,665 ft]. Other ranges include the Anti Atlas, the Middle Atlas, and the Rif Atlas (or Er Rif). In the east of the country lies the arid Sahara Desert.

Area 446,550 sq km [172,413 sq mi]
Population 33,241,000
Capital (population) Rabat (1,859,000)
Government Constitutional monarchy
Ethnic groups Arab-Berber 99%
Languages
Arabic (official), Berber dialects, French
Religions Islam 99%
Currency Moroccan dirham = 100 centimes
Website www.mincom.gov.ma

CLIMATE

The Atlantic coast is cooled by the Canaries Current. Inland, summers are very hot and dry while winters are mild. From October to April the south-westerly Atlantic winds bring rain; there is frequent snowfall in the High Atlas.

HISTORY

The original people of Morocco were the Berbers. In the 680s, Arab invaders introduced Islam and the Arabic language. By the early 20th century, France and Spain controlled Morocco. It finally became an independent kingdom in 1956.

POLITICS

King Hassan II ruled the country in an authoritarian way until his death in 1999. His successor, King Mohamed VI, faced a number of problems, including finding a solution to the future of Western Sahara. Relations with Spain became strained in 2002 over the disputed island of Leila (Perejil in Spanish) in the Strait of Gibraltar. Diplomatic relations were restored in 2003. Another problem faced by Morocco is activity by Islamic extremists. Its opposition to extremism led the United States to designate Morocco as a major non-NATO ally in 2004.

ECONOMY

Morocco is classified as a 'lower-middle-income' developing country. It is the world's third largest producer of phosphate rock and phosphates are the major export. Farming employs 38% of Moroccans. Fishing and tourism are important sectors.

RABAT

Capital of Morocco, on the Atlantic coast, northern Morocco. Rabat dates from Phoenician times, but the fortified city was founded in the 12th century by the Almohad ruler, Abd al-Mumin. Under French rule, it was made the capital of the protectorate of Morocco.

WESTERN SAHARA

Desert territory on the Atlantic coast of north-west Africa; the capital is El Aaiun. It comprises two districts: Saguia el Hamra in the north, and Río de Oro in the south. The population consists of Arabs, Berbers and pastoral nomads, most of whom are Sunni Muslims. Livestock-rearing dominates agriculture. The first European discovery was in 1434, but it remained unexploited until Spain took control of the coastal area in the 19th century. In 1957, a nationalist movement temporarily overthrew the Spanish but they regained control of the region in 1958 and merged the two districts to form the province of Spanish Sahara. Large phosphate deposits were discovered in 1963. The Polisario Front began a guerrilla war in 1973, eventually forcing a Spanish withdrawal in 1976. Within a month, Morocco and Mauritania partitioned the country. Polisario (backed by Algeria) continued to fight for independence, renaming the country the Saharawi Arab Democratic Republic. In 1979, Mauritania withdrew and Morocco assumed full control. In 1982, the Saharawi Republic became a member of the Organization of African Unity. By 1988 it controlled most of the desert up to the Moroccan defensive line. Fragile ceasefires were agreed in 1988 and 1991. About 200,000 Saharawis continue to live in refugee camps, mostly in Algeria. Talks between Morocco and Western Sahara began in 1997 and have been inconclusive. It covers 266,769 sq km [102,680 sq mi].

MOZAMBIQUE

Mozambique's flag was adopted when the country became independent from Portugal in 1975. The green stripe represents fertile land, the black stands for Africa and the yellow for mineral wealth. The badge on the red triangle contains a rifle, a hoe, a cogwheel and a book.

The Republic of Mozambique borders the Indian Ocean in southeastern Africa. The coastal plains are narrow in the north but broaden to the south making up nearly half of the country. Inland lie plateaus and hills, which make up another two-fifths of the country, with highlands along the borders with Zimbabwe, Zambia, Malawi and Tanzania.

Area 801,590 sq km [309,494 sq mi]
Population 19,687,000
Capital (population) Maputo (1,316,000)
Government Multiparty republic
Ethnic groups Indigenous tribal groups (Shangaan, Chokwe, Manyika, Sena, Makua, others) 99%
Languages Portuguese (official), many others
Religions Traditional beliefs 50%, Christianity 30%, Islam 20%
Currency Metical = 100 centavos
Website www.mozambique.mz

CLIMATE

Most of Mozambique has a tropical maritime climate, with two main seasons. The hot, wet season runs from November to March, while the dry, milder season lasts between April and October. Rainfall varies, being greatest on the north-western highlands and lowest on the south-eastern lowlands.

Temperatures in the lowlands vary from between 20°C and 30°C [79–86°F] in January, and between 11°C and 15°C [52–59°F] in January. The interior highlands are much cooler and are generally less humid.

HISTORY

Arab traders began to operate in the area in the 9th century AD, with Portuguese explorers arriving in 1497. The Portuguese set up trading stations in the early 16th century and the area became a source of slaves. When the European powers divided Africa in 1885, Mozambique was recognized as a Portuguese colony. Black African opposition to European rule gradually increased and, in 1961, the Front for the Liberation of Mozambique (FRELIMO) was founded to oppose Portuguese rule. FRELIMO launched a guerrilla war in 1964, which continued for ten years. Mozambique achieved independence in 1975, when the Marxist-Leninist FRELIMO took over the government.

MAPUTO (LOURENÇO MARQUES)

Capital and chief port of Mozambique, on Maputo Bay, southern Mozambique. It was visited by the Portuguese in 1502, and was made the capital of Portuguese East Africa in 1907, being known as Lourenço Marques until 1976. It is linked by rail to South Africa, Swaziland and Zimbabwe, and is a popular resort area. Industries include footwear, textiles, rubber.

ended in 1992 and multiparty elections in 1994 were won by FRELIMO, whose leader, Joaquim A Chissano, became president. RENAMO's leader, Afonso Dhlakama, accepted the result and stated that the civil war would not resume. This led to a period of relative stability. In 1995 Mozambique joined the Commonwealth. In 2004 elections, which RENAMO claimed had irregularities, Armando Guebuza of FRELIMO became president.

ECONOMY

In the early 1990s, Mozambique was one of the world's poorest countries. Battered by a civil war, which had killed around a million people and had driven 5 million from their homes, combined with devastating droughts and floods, the economy collapsed.

By the end of the twentieth century, economists were praising Mozambique for its economic recovery. Support from the World Bank and other international institutions, combined with a privatization programme and rescheduling of the country's foreign debts, led to an expansion of the economy and brought inflation under control by 1999. The improved economy attracted foreign investment. However, about 70% of the people remain impoverished. Massive floods at the start of 2000 made thousands homeless and severely damaged the economy, but in 2001 the currency was stabilized and recovery began.

Manufacturing exists only on a small scale. Agriculture is important. Crops include cassava, cotton, cashew nuts, fruits, maize, rice, sugar cane and tea. Shrimps, cashew nuts, sugar and copra are among the country's exports. Electricity is exported to South Africa from a large hydroelectric plant at the Cahora Bassa Dam on the River Zambezi.

POLITICS

After independence, Mozambique became a one-party state. Its government aided African nationalists in Rhodesia (now Zimbabwe) and South Africa. However, the white governments of these countries helped an opposition group, the Mozambique National Resistance Movement (RENAMO), to lead an armed struggle against Mozambique's government. This civil war, combined with severe droughts, caused much human suffering in the 1980s.

In 1989, FRELIMO declared that it had dropped its Communist policies and ended one-party rule. The war officially

NAMIBIA

Namibia adopted this flag in 1990 when it gained independence from South Africa. The red diagonal stripe and white borders are symbols of Namibia's human resources. The green and blue triangles and the gold sun represent the country's resources.

The Republic of Namibia lies on the Atlantic coast to the south of Angola and to the north of South Africa. The coastal region contains the arid Namib Desert, mostly between 900 m and 2,000 m [2,950–6,560 ft] above sea level, which is virtually uninhabited. Inland is a central plateau, bordered by a rugged spine of mountains stretching north–south.

Eastern Namibia contains part of the Kalahari, a semi-desert area which extends into Botswana. The Orange River forms Namibia's southern border, while the Cunene and Cubango rivers form parts of the northern borders.

Area 824,292 sq km [318,259 sq mi]
Population 2,044,000
Capital (population) Windhoek (147,000)
Government Multiparty republic
Ethnic groups Ovambo 50%, Kavango 9%, Herero 7%, Damara 7%, White 6%, Nama 5%
Languages English (official), Afrikaans, German, indigenous dialects
Religions Christianity 90% (Lutheran 51%)
Currency Namibian dollar = 100 cents
Website www.grnnet.gov.na

CLIMATE

Namibia has a warm and largely arid climate. Daily temperatures can range from about 24°C [75°F] in January to 20°C [68°F] in July. Annual rainfall ranges from about 500 mm [20 in] in northern areas to between 25 mm and 150 mm [1–6 in] in the south. Most of the rain falls in summer.

HISTORY

The earliest people in Namibia were the San, also called Bushmen, and the Damara or Hottentots. Later arrivals were people who spoke Bantu languages. They migrated into Namibia from the north and included the Ovambo, Kavango and Herero. From 1868,

Germans began to operate along the coast and, in 1884, Germany annexed the entire territory which they called German South West Africa. In the 1890s, the Germans forcibly removed the Damara and Herero from the Windhoek area. About 65,000 Herero were killed when they revolted against being forced from their land.

South African troops took over the territory in 1915 and five years later the League of Nations gave South Africa a mandate to govern the country, however, South Africa chose to rule it as though it were a South African province.

After World War II, many people challenged South Africa's right to govern the territory. A civil war began during the 1960s between African guerrillas and South African troops, with a ceasefire as finally being agreed in 1989. The country became independent in 1990.

POLITICS

After achieving independence, the government pursued a policy of 'national reconciliation'. An enclave on Namibia's coast, called Walvis Bay (Walvisbaai), remained part of South Africa unti

Farming employs around two out of every five Namibians, although many farmers live at subsistence level, contributing little to the economy. Because most of the land in Namibia has too little rainfall for arable farming, the principal agricultural activities are cattle and sheep raising. However, livestock raising has been hit in the last 20 years by extended droughts that have depleted the number of farm animals. The chief crops are maize, millet and vegetables.

Fishing in the Atlantic Ocean is also important, though overfishing has reduced the yields of Namibia's fishing fleet. The country has few manufacturing industries apart from jewellery-making, some metal smelting, the processing of farm products, such as karakul pelts (sheepskins that are used to make fur coats), and textiles. Tourism is developing, especially in the Etosha National Park in northern Namibia, which is rich in wildlife.

1994, when South Africa transferred it to Namibia. In 2004 Sam Nujoma of the South West African People's Organization (SWAPO), who had been president since independence, retired. His successor was Hifikepunye Pohama.

Namibia's Caprivi Strip is a geographical oddity. The Strip was given to Germany by European powers in the late 19th century in order that Germany would have access to the River Zambezi. It became the scene of a rebellion in 1999 when a small band of rebels tried, unsuccessfully, to seize the regional capital Kutima Mulilo as part of an attempt to make the Caprivi Strip independent. The Strip is populated mainly by Lozi people, who resent SWAPO rule. In 2002 the government declared the area safe.

ECONOMY

Namibia has important mineral reserves, including diamonds, zinc, uranium, copper, lead and tin. Mining is the most valuable economic activity and, by the mid-1990s, minerals accounted for as much as 90% of the exports, with diamonds making up over half the total revenue from minerals.

WINDHOEK

Capital and largest city of Namibia, situated some 300 km [190 mi] inland from the Atlantic at a height of 1,650 m [5,410 ft]. Originally serving as the headquarters of a Nama chief, in 1892 it was made the capital of the new German colony of South West Africa. It was taken by South African troops in World War I. In 1990, it became capital of independent Namibia. An important world trade market for karakul sheepskins, its industries include diamonds, copper and meat-packing. The German heritage is still very much in evidence with German restaurants selling traditional food and the German language still prevalent everywhere.

NEPAL

This Himalayan kingdom's uniquely shaped flag was adopted in 1962. It came about in the 19th century when two triangular pennants – the royal family's crescent moon symbol and the powerful Rana family's sun symbol – were joined together.

The Kingdom of Nepal, in central Asia, lies between India to the south and China to the north. More than three-quarters of the country is in the Himalayan mountain heartland, culminating in the world's highest peak, Mount Everest (or Chomolongma in Nepali) at 8,850 m [29,035 ft].

Nepal comprises three distinct regions. A southern lowland area (*terai*) of grassland and forests is the main location of Nepal's agriculture and timber industry. The central Siwalik mountains and valleys are divided between the basins of the Ghaghara, Gandak and Kosi rivers. Between the Gandak and Kosi lies Katmandu valley, Nepal's most populous area. The last region is the main section of the Himalayas. Vegetation varies widely according to altitude.

Area 147,181 sq km [56,827 sq miles]
Population 28,287,000
Capital (population) Katmandu (1,176,000)
Government Constitutional monarchy
Ethnic groups Brahman, Chetri, Newar, Gurung, Magar, Tamang, Sherpa and others
Languages Nepali (official), local languages
Religions Hinduism 86%, Buddhism 8%, Islam 4%
Currency Nepalese rupee = 100 paisa
Website www.welcomenepal.com

CLIMATE

The huge differences in altitude give Nepal a wide variety of climatic regions.

HISTORY

In 1482 the kingdom of Nepal was divided into three, Bhadgaon, Kathmandu and Patan. It was nearly four hundred years later, in 1768, when the three kingdoms finally resolved their differences and unified to form what is now known as Nepal. Between 1815 and 1816 the Anglo-Nepalese War took place as a result of rivalry between Nepal and the British East India Company over the annexation of minor states bordering Nepal. In exchange for autonomy the Nepalese signed The Treaty of Sugauli ceding parts of the Terrai and Sikkim to the British East India Company.

From 1846 to 1951, hereditary prime ministers from the Rana family ruled Nepal. In 1923, Britain recognized Nepal as a sovereign state. Gurkha soldiers fought in the British Army during both World Wars. In 1951, the Rana government was overthrown and the monarchy re-established. The first national constitution was adopted in 1959, and elections were held. In 1960, King Mahendra

---

HIMALAYAS

System of mountains in southern Asia, extending 2,400 km [1,500 mi] north–south in an arc between Tibet and India-Pakistan. The mountains are divided into three ranges: the Greater Himalayas (north), which include Mount Everest and K2; the Lesser Himalayas; and the Outer Himalayas (south)

dissolved parliament and introduced a political system based on village councils (*panchayat*). In 1972, Birendra succeeded his father as king.

POLITICS

In 1990, after mass protests, a new constitution limited the power of the monarchy. In 1991 the Nepali Congress Party (NCP), led by G P Koirala, won multiparty elections but stability proved elusive. A Maoist revolt arose.

In 2001 King Birendra, his queen and six other members of his family were shot dead by his heir, Crown Prince Dipendra, who then took his own life. Gyanendra, Birendra's brother, became king. Increasing Maoist activity led the new king to take direct control of the government and appoint a new cabinet early in 2005. In 2006 he was forced to reinstate parliament, which immediately removed his power of veto. Parliament then entered talks with the Maoists and reached a peace accord. The revolt had claimed more than 12,000 lives. Maoists joined an interim parliament in 2007.

ECONOMY

Ruined by the civil war, Nepal is one of the world's poorest countries. Agriculture employs over 80% of the workforce, accounting for two-fifths of the gross domestic product. Export crops include herbs, jute, rice, spices and wheat. Tourism, which is centred around the high Himalayas, has grown in importance since 1951, when the country first opened to foreigners. The country is highly dependent on aid; the government plans to use part of it to improve infrastructure and invest in hydroelectricity.

KATMANDU (KATHMANDU)

Capital of Nepal, situated 1,370 m [4,500 ft] above sea level in a Himalayan valley. Founded in AD 723, it was independent from the 15th century to 1768, when Gurkhas captured it. Katmandu is Nepal's administrative, commercial and religious centre. Sights of interest include many beautiful temples including Kasthamandap from which the city derives its name, the Royal Palace (Narayanhity Durbar) and the neo-classical Singha Durbar, former private residence of Rana prime ministers.

NETHERLANDS, THE

The flag of the Netherlands, one of Europe's oldest, dates from 1630, during the long struggle for independence from Spain which began in 1568. The tricolour became a symbol of liberty which inspired many other revolutionary flags around the world.

The Kingdom of the Netherlands lies at the western end of the North European Plain, which extends to the Ural Mountains in Russia. The country is largely flat, about 40% being below sea level at high tide. To prevent flooding, dykes have been built to hold back the waves. There are large areas called polders made up of land reclaimed from the sea.

Area 41,526 sq km [16,033 sq mi]
Population 16,491,000
Capital (population) Amsterdam (1,157,000); The Hague (seat of government, 440,000)
Government Constitutional monarchy
Ethnic groups Dutch 83%, Indonesian, Turkish, Moroccan and others
Languages Dutch (official), Frisian
Religions Roman Catholic 31%, Protestant 21%, Islam 4%, others
Currency Euro = 100 cents
Website www.holland.com

CLIMATE

Because of its position on the North Sea, the Netherlands has a temperate climate. Winters are mild, with rain coming from the Atlantic depressions which pass over the country. North Sea storms often batter the coasts. Storm waves have periodically breached the dykes, causing flooding and sometimes loss of life.

lands, then containing both Belgium and Luxembourg, became an independent kingdom. Belgium broke away in 1830, and Luxembourg followed in 1890.

The Netherlands was neutral in World War I, but occupied by German troops in World War II. Much of the Dutch fleet escaped and served with the Allies, but around three-quarters of the country's Jews were murdered, while many other people were forced to work in German factories. By the end of the war, about 270,000 Netherlanders had been killed or had died of starvation.

HISTORY

Before the 16th century, the area that is now the Netherlands was ruled by the Romans, the Germanic Franks, the French and then the Spanish. The Dutch declared their independence from Spain in 1581 and a long struggle began. Spain was finally forced to acknowledge Dutch independence in 1648. In the 17th century the Dutch built a great overseas empire, especially in South-east Asia.

France controlled the Netherlands from 1795 to 1813. In 1815 the Nether-

POLITICS

In 1948 the Netherlands formed an economic union called Benelux with Belgium and Luxembourg, and in 1949 it became a member of NATO. Economic recovery was rapid. In 1957 the country became a founder member of the EEC.

After much fighting the Dutch recognized the independence of Indonesia, their largest overseas possession, in 1949. In 1954, Suriname and the Netherlands Antilles were granted self-government. In 1962 the Dutch handed over Netherlands New Guinea to the United Nations. In 1963 the UN granted the territory to Indonesia as Irian Jaya. Suriname became fully independent in 1975.

In 1953, waves penetrated the coastal defences in the southwestern delta region. Floodwaters covered about 4.3% of the country, destroying or damaging more than 30,000 houses and killing 1,800 people. Within three weeks, a commission of enquiry had recommended the Delta Plan, a huge project to protect the delta region. Completed in 1986, it involved the construction of massive dams and floodgates which are closed during severe storms.

The Maastricht Treaty, which transformed the EEC into the European Union, was signed in the Dutch city of Maastricht in 1991. Since 1 January 2002, the euro has been its sole currency.

AMSTERDAM

Capital and largest city in the Netherlands, on the River Amstel, linked to the North Sea by the North Sea Canal. Amsterdam was chartered in 1300 and joined the Hanseatic League in 1369. The Dutch East India Company (1602) brought great prosperity to the city. It became a notable centre of learning and book printing during the 17th century. It was captured by the French in 1795 and blockaded by the British during the Napoleonic Wars. Amsterdam was badly damaged during the German occupation during World War II. A major port and one of Europe's leading financial and cultural centres, it has an important stock exchange and diamond-cutting industry.

ECONOMY

The Netherlands has the world's 14th largest economy, and is a highly industrialized country. Manufacturing and commerce are the most valuable activities. Mineral resources include china clay, natural gas, oil and salt, but most materials needed by industry are imported. Products include aircraft, chemical products, electronic equipment, machinery, textiles and vehicles. In the area south of Rotterdam, the Dutch have constructed a vast port and industrial area, Europoort. Together with Rotterdam's own facilities, the complex is the largest and busiest in the world.

Agriculture employs only 5% of the workforce, but, through the use of industrial techniques, yields are high. The Dutch cut and sell more than 3 billion flowers a year. Dairy farming is the leading farming activity. In the areas above sea level, farming includes both cattle and crops. Major food crops include barley, potatoes, sugar beet and wheat.

NEW ZEALAND

New Zealand's flag was designed in 1869 and adopted as the national flag in 1907 when New Zealand became an independent dominion. The flag includes the British Blue Ensign and four of the five stars in the Southern Cross constellation.

New Zealand lies about 1,600 km [994 mi] south-east of Australia. It consists of two main islands and several other small ones. New Zealand is mountainous and partly volcanic. The Southern Alps contain the country's highest peak, Aoraki Mount Cook, at 3,753 m [12,313 ft]. Minor earthquakes are common and there are several areas of volcanic and geothermal activity, especially on North Island.

About 75% of New Zealand lies above the 200 m [650 ft] contour. In the south-east, broad, fertile valleys have been cut by rivers between the low ranges. The only extensive lowland area of New Zealand is the Canterbury Plains. As a result of its isolation, almost 90% of the indigenous plants are unique to the country.

Much of the original vegetation has been destroyed and only small areas of the kauri forests have survived. Mixed evergreen forest grows on the western side of South Island. Forests of beech grow in the highlands, with large plantations grown for timber.

Area 104,453 sq miles [270,534 sq km]
Population 4,076,000
Capital (population) Wellington (167,000)
Government Constitutional monarchy
Ethnic groups New Zealand European 74%, New Zealand Maori 10%, Polynesian 4%
Languages English and Maori (both official)
Religions Anglican 24%, Presbyterian 18%, Roman Catholic 15%, others
Currency New Zealand dollar = 100 cents
Website www.govt.nz

CLIMATE

Auckland in the north has a warm, humid climate throughout the year. Wellington has cooler summers, while in Dunedin, to the south-east, temperatures sometimes dip below freezing in winter. The rainfall is heaviest on the western highlands.

HISTORY

Early Maori settlers arrived in New Zealand more than 1,000 years ago. The Dutch navigator Abel Janszoon Tasman reached the area in 1642, but after several of his men were killed by Maoris, he

WELLINGTON

Capital and region of New Zealand, in the extreme south of North Island, on Port Nicholson, an inlet of Cook Strait. First visited by Europeans in 1826, it was founded in 1840. In 1845 it replaced Auckland as capital. Wellington's excellent harbour furthered its development as a transport and trading centre.

mutual defence pact with Australia and the United States. Troops from New Zealand served in the Korean War from 1950 to 1953, and a few units later served in the war in Vietnam.

POLITICS

After Britain joined the EEC (now the EU) in 1973, New Zealand's exports to Britain shrank sevenfold. Along with its re-evaluation of its defence position through ANZUS, the country had to reassess its economic strategy. In the 1990s New Zealand sought new markets in Asia, cut subsidies to farmers, privatized state assets and cut back welfare programmes. The rights of Maoris and the preservation of their culture are other major political issues in New Zealand. In 1998, New Zealand completed a NZ$170 million settlement with the Ngai Tahu group on South Island in compensation for forced land purchases in the 19th century. The government expressed its profound regret for past suffering and for injustices that had impaired the development of the Ngai Tahu. Ties with Britain have been gradually reduced; in 2005 the prime minister, Helen Clark, stated that the country would eventually abolish the monarchy and become a republic.

ECONOMY

Manufacturing now employs twice as many people as agriculture. Meat and dairy products are the most valuable agricultural products. The country has more than 45 million sheep, 4.3 million dairy cattle and 4.6 million beef cattle. Major crops include barley, fruits, potatoes and other vegetables and wheat. Fishing is also important. The chief manufactures are processed food products, including butter, cheese, frozen meat and woollen products.

made no further attempt to land. His discovery was not followed up until 1769, when the British Captain James Cook rediscovered the islands.

British settlers arrived in the early 19th century. In 1840, under the Treaty of Waitangi, Britain took possession of the islands. Clashes occurred with the Maoris in the 1860s, but from the 1870s the Maoris and colonial society gradually integrated. In 1893, New Zealand became the first country in the world to give women the vote. In 1907 it became a self-governing dominion within the British Empire.

New Zealanders fought alongside the Allies in both World Wars. In 1952 New Zealand signed the ANZUS treaty, a

NICARAGUA

The colours of the flag are in homage to Argentina. Central America is represented by the white stripe; the Atlantic and Pacific Oceans are the blue stripes. The coat of arms features five volcanoes, a rainbow for hope and red Liberty cap for freedom.

The Republic of Nicaragua is the largest country in Central America. The Central Highlands rise in the north west Cordillera Isabella to more than 1,960 m [6,500 ft] and are the source for many of the rivers that drain the eastern plain. The Caribbean coast forms part of the Mosquito Coast. Lakes Managua and Nicaragua lie on the edge of a narrow volcanic region. It contains Nicaragua's major urban areas including the capital, Managua, and the second-largest city, León. This region is highly unstable, with many active volcanoes, and is prone to earthquakes.

Rainforests cover large areas in the east, with trees such as cedar, mahogany and walnut. Tropical savanna is common in the drier west.

Area 130,000 sq km [50,193 sq mi]
Population 5,570,000
Capital (population) Managua (1,109,000)
Government Multiparty republic
Ethnic groups Mestizo 69%, White 17%, Black 9%, Amerindian 5%
Languages Spanish (official)
Religions Roman Catholic 85%, Protestant
Currency Córdoba oro (gold córdoba) = 100 centavos
Website www.intur.gob.ni/index_eng.html

CLIMATE

Nicaragua has a tropical climate, with a rainy season from June to October. Cooler weather is found in the Central Highlands. The wettest part is the Mosquito Coast, with 4,200 mm [165 in] of rain.

HISTORY

Spanish explorer Christopher Columbus reached Nicaragua in 1502 and claimed the land for Spain. Colonization killed c. 100,000 Native Americans. Nicaragua became part of the Spanish Captaincy-General of Guatemala.

In 1821 Nicaragua gained independ-ence. It formed part of the Central American Federation between 1825 and 1838. In the mid-19th century, civil war and US and British interference ravaged the country. The USA sought to construct a canal through Nicaragua to link the Atlantic and Pacific. In 1855 William Walker invaded, and briefly established

THE SANDINISTA

(Sandinista National Liberation Front) Revolutionary group in Nicaragua. They took their name from Augusto César Sandino, who opposed the dominant Somoza family and was killed in 1934. The Sandinistas over-threw the Somoza regime in 1979, and formed a government led by Daniel Ortega. They were opposed by right-wing guerrillas, the Contra, supported by the USA. The conflict ended when the Sandinista agreed to free elections. They lost, but the Contra were disbanded and the Sandinista retain political influence.

wide-ranging socialist reforms. The USA, concerned about the Sandinista's ties with Communist regimes, sought to destabilize the government by supporting rebels known as Contras. Ten years of civil war devastated the country.

In 1990 elections, the National Opposition Union coalition, led by Violeta Chamorro, defeated the Sandinistas. Chamorro's coalition partners and the Sandinista-controlled trade unions blocked many of her reforms. In 1996 elections, Liberal leader Arnoldo Aleman defeated Chamorro. In 1998, Hurricane Mitch killed c. 4,000 people and caused extensive damage. Enrique Bolanos became president at elections in 2001. In 2003, former president Arnoldo Aleman was sentenced to 20 years in prison for corruption. 2006 elections returned Daniel Ortega to the presidency.

himself as president. José Santos Zemalya's dictatorship from 1893 to 1909 gained control of the Mosquito Coast and formed links with the British. From 1909 civil war raged once more. In 1912, US marines landed to protect the pro-US regime. The USA obtained exclusive rights to the planned canal to prevent competition with Panama, but later abandoned them. Opposition to US occupation resulted in guerrilla war, led by Augusto César Sandino. In 1933 the US withdrew, but set up a National Guard to fight the guerillas.

In 1934 Anastasio Somoza, director of the National Guard, assassinated Sandino. Somoza became president in 1937. His dictatorial regime led to political isolation. Somoza was succeeded by his sons Luis in 1956 and Anastasio in 1967. Anastasio's diversion of international relief aid following the devastating 1972 Managua earthquake cemented opposition.

POLITICS

In 1979, the Sandinista National Liberation Front (FSLN) overthrew the Somoza regime. The Sandinista government, led by Daniel Ortega, instigated

ECONOMY

Nicaragua faces problems in rebuilding its economy and introducing free-market reforms. Agriculture is the main activity, employing 30% of the workforce and accounting for 60% of exports. Major cash crops include coffee, cotton, sugar and bananas. Rice is the main food crop.

There is some copper, gold and silver, but mining is underdeveloped. Most of the country's small manufacturing capacity is based around Managua.

MANAGUA

Capital of Nicaragua, on the southern shore of Lake Managua, west-central Nicaragua. It became the capital in 1855. Managua suffered damage from earthquakes in 1931 and 1962. It is the economic, industrial and commercial hub of Nicaragua. Industries include textiles, tobacco and cement.

NIGER

This flag was adopted shortly before Niger became independent from France in 1960. The orange stripe represents the Sahara in the north and the green represents the grasslands in the south. Between them, the white stripe represents the River Niger, with a circle for the sun.

The Republic of Niger is a land-locked nation in north-central Africa. The northern plateaux lie in the Sahara, while north-central Niger contains the rugged Aïr Mountains, which reach a height of 2,022 m [6,632 ft] above sea level near Agadez. The rainfall in the mountains – averaging around 175 mm [7 in] per year – is sufficient in places to permit the growth of thorny scrub. Severe droughts since the 1970s have crippled the traditional lifestyle of the nomads in northern and central Niger as the Sahara has slowly advanced south. The southern region has also been hit by droughts.

The south consists of broad plains. The Lake Chad Basin lies in south-eastern Niger on the borders with Chad and Nigeria. The only permanent rivers are the Niger and its tributaries in the south-west. The narrow Niger Valley is the country's most fertile and densely populated region and includes the capital Niamey. Yet Niger, a title which comes from a Tuareg word meaning 'flowing water', seems scarcely appropriate for a country which consists mainly of hot, arid, sandy and stony basins.

Buffaloes, elephants, giraffes and lions are found in the 'W' National Park, which Niger shares with Benin and Burkina Faso. Most of southern Niger lies in the Sahel region of dry grassland. The Aïr Mountains support grass and scrub. The northern deserts are generally barren.

CLIMATE

Niger is one of the world's hottest countries. The warmest months are March to May, when the harmattan wind blows from the Sahara. Niamey has a tropical

Area 1,267,000 sq km [489,189 sq mi]
Population 12,525,000
Capital (population) Niamey (995,000)
Government Multiparty republic
Ethnic groups Hausa 56%, Djerma 22%, Tuareg 8%, Fula 8%, others
Languages French (official), Hausa, Djerma
Religions Islam 80%, indigenous beliefs, Christianity
Currency CFA franc = 100 centimes
Website www.un.int/niger

climate, with a rainy season from June to September. Rainfall decreases from south to north. Northern Niger is practically rainless. The far south consists of tropical savanna.

HISTORY

Neolithic remains have been found in the northern desert. Nomadic Tuareg settled in the Aïr Mountains in the 11th century AD, and by the 13th century had established a state centred around Agadez and the trans-Saharan trade. In the 14th century, the Hausa settled in southern Niger. In the early 16th century, the Songhai Empire controlled much of Niger, but the Moroccans supplanted the Songhai at the turn of the century.

Later on, the Hausa and then the Fulani set up kingdoms in the region. In the early 19th century, the Fulani gained control of much of southern Niger. The first French expedition arrived in 1891,

Movement for a Development Society (MNSD), but a military coup led by Colonel Ibrahim Bare Mainassara seized power. In 1995, the government and the Tuaregs signed a peace accord. In 1999, bodyguards assassinated Mainassara and he was replaced briefly by Major Daouda Malam Wanke. Parliamentary rule was restored and, later that year, Tandjou Mamadou was elected president. Niger finally banned slavery in 2003 but it remains a problem. Mamadou was re-elected in 2004.

ECONOMY

Droughts have caused great hardship and food shortages in Niger, and have destroyed much of the traditional nomadic lifestyle. Niger's chief resource is uranium, and it is the world's second-largest producer. Uranium, most of which is sent to France, accounts for more than 80% of exports and the country is highly vulnerable to uranium price fluctuations. Some tin and tungsten are also mined, but other mineral resources remain largely unexploited. Niger is one of the world's poorest countries, despite its resources, and is a major recipient of foreign aid.

Farming employs 85% of the workforce, although only a tiny proportion of the land is suitable. Food crops include beans, cassava, millet, rice and sorghum. Cotton and groundnuts are cash crops.

but Tuareg resistance prevented full occupation until 1914.

POLITICS

In 1922 Niger became a colony within French West Africa. In 1958, Niger voted to remain an autonomous republic within the French Community. It gained full independence in 1960, and Hamani Diori became Niger's first president. He maintained close ties with France.

From 1968 on, drought in the Sahel killed many livestock and destroyed crops. In 1974 a group of army officers led by Lt Colonel Seyni Kountché overthrew Hamani Diori and suspended the constitution. Kountché died in 1987 and was succeeded by his cousin General Ali Saibou. In 1991, the Tuareg in northern Niger began an armed campaign for greater autonomy. A national conference removed Saibou and established a transitional government. In 1993 multiparty elections, Mahamane Ousmane of the Alliance of Forces for Change (AFC) coalition became president. The collapse of the coalition led to fresh elections in 1995, which were won by the National

NIAMEY

Capital of Niger, West Africa, in the south-western part of the country, on the River Niger. It became capital of the French colony of Niger in 1926. It grew rapidly after World War II and is now the country's largest city and its commercial and administrative centre. Manufactures include textiles, ceramics, plastics and chemicals.

NIGERIA

Nigeria's flag was adopted in 1960 when Nigeria became independent from Britain. It was selected after a competition to find a suitable design. The green represents Nigeria's forests. The white in the centre stands for peace.

The Federal Republic of Nigeria is the most populous nation in Africa. The country's main rivers are the Niger and Benue, which meet in central Nigeria. North of the two river valleys are high plains and plateaux. The Lake Chad Basin is in the north-east, with the Sokoto plains in the north-west. Southern Nigeria contains hilly uplands and broad coastal plains, including the swampy Niger Delta. Highlands form the border with Cameroon. Mangrove swamps line the coast, behind which are rainforests. The north contains large areas of savanna with forests along the rivers. Open grassland and semi-desert occur in drier areas.

Area 923,768 sq km [356,667 sq mi]
Population 131,000,000
Capital (population) Abuja (339,000)
Government Federal multiparty republic
Ethnic groups Hausa and Fulani 29%, Yoruba 21%, Ibo (or Igbo) 18%, Ijaw 10%, Kanuri 4%
Languages English (official), Hausa, Yoruba, Ibo
Religions Islam 50%, Christianity 40%, traditional beliefs
Currency Naira = 100 kobo
Website www.nigeria.gov.ng

CLIMATE

The south of the country has high temperatures and rain all year. Parts of the coast have an average annual rainfall of 3,800 mm [150 in]. The north has a marked dry season and higher temperatures than the south.

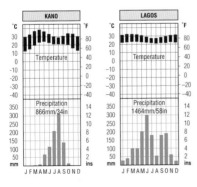

HISTORY

Nigeria's major ancient cultures include the Nok (500 BC to AD 200), the Ife, which developed c. 1,000 years ago, and the Benin, which flourished between the 15th and 17th centuries. All are known for their high quality, distinctive art.

Britain outlawed slavery in 1807 and soon afterwards the British began to trade in agricultural products. In 1851 Britain made Lagos a base from which they could continue their efforts to stop the slave trade. During the second half of the 19th century, Britain gradually extended its influence over Nigeria. By 1914 it ruled the entire country.

POLITICS

Nigeria became independent in 1960 and a federal republic in 1963. A federal constitution dividing the country into regions was necessary because Nigeria contains more than 250 ethnic and linguistic groups, as well as several religious ones. Ethnic and religious differences remain a threat to national unity. In 1967, in an attempt to meet the demands of more ethnic groups, the country's four regions were replaced by 12 states. The division of the Eastern Region provoked an uprising. In 1967 the governor of the Eastern Region, Colonel Odumegwu

Ojukwu, proclaimed it an independent republic called Biafra. Civil war continued until Biafra's surrender in 1970.

In 1998-9, civilian rule was finally restored. A former military leader, Olusegun Obasanjo, was elected president and re-elected in 2003. In the late 1990s and early 2000s, riots broke out between Yorubas and Hausas in the south-west, while the introduction of Islamic *sharia* law in northern states caused friction with Christians. In 2004 the government declared that it had put down an uprising in the north-east aimed at creating a Muslim state. In 2006 Nigeria withdrew troops from the Bakassi peninsula, ending a conflict with Cameroon. 2007 elections were marred by fraud and violence. Umaru Yar'Adua, a Muslim from the north and the ruling party's candidate, became president.

ECONOMY

Despite its many natural resources, including oil, metals, forests and fertile land, Nigeria is a 'low-income' developing economy. Oil wealth has enriched only a tiny élite. Agriculture employs 43% of the workforce and Nigeria is one of the world's leading producers of cocoa beans, groundnuts, palm oil and kernels and natural rubber. Leading food crops include beans, cassava, maize, millet, plantains, rice, sorghum and yams.

ABUJA

Nigeria's administrative capital since 1991. The new city was designed by the Japanese architect Kenzo Tange and work began in 1976.

NORWAY

This flag became the national flag of Norway in 1898, although merchant ships had used it since 1821. The design is based on the Dannebrog, the flag of Denmark, the country which ruled Norway from the 14th century until the early 19th century.

The Kingdom of Norway forms the western part of the mountainous Scandinavian Peninsula. The landscape is dominated by rolling plateaux, the vidda, which are generally between 300 m and 900 m [1,000–3,000 ft] high, but some peaks rise from 1,500 m to 2,500 m [5,000–8,000 ft] in the area between Oslo, Bergen and Trondheim. The highest areas retain permanent ice-fields, as in the Jotunheimen Mountains above Sognefjord.

Norway's jagged coastline is the longest in Europe. The vidda are cut by long, narrow, steep-sided fjords on the west coast. The largest of the fjords, is Sognefjord, which is 203 km [127 mi] long and less than 5 km [3 mi] wide.

Area 323,877 sq km [125,049 sq mi]
Population 4,611,000
Capital (population) Oslo (513,000)
Government Constitutional monarchy
Ethnic groups Norwegian 97%
Languages Norwegian (official)
Religions Evangelical Lutheran 86%
Currency Norwegian krone = 100 øre
Website www.norge.no

CLIMATE

The warm North Atlantic Drift flows off the coast and moderates the country's climate, with milder winters and cooler summers. Most of Norway's ports remain ice-free all year. Inland, away from the moderating effects of the sea, the climate becomes more severe. Winters are bitterly cold, with snow cover for at least three months of the year.

HISTORY

From about AD 800 Vikings from Norway roamed the northern seas, raiding and founding colonies around the coasts of Britain, Iceland and even North America. In about 900, Norway was united under Harold I, the country's first king. Viking power ended in the late 11th century. In 1380 Norway was united with Denmark, and in 1397 Sweden joined the union. Sweden broke away in 1523. In 1526 Denmark, which had become increasingly powerful, made Norway a Danish province.

In 1814, Denmark ceded Norway to Sweden, but retained Norway's colonies of Greenland, Iceland and the Faeroe Islands. Norway finally ended its union with Sweden in 1905. The Norwegians chose as their king a Danish prince, who took the title Haakon VII.

Despite Norway being neutral in World War I, and seeking to remain so in World War II, German troops invaded in 1940.

OSLO

Capital of Norway, southern Norway. Founded in the mid-11th century and largely destroyed by fire in 1624, Christian IV rebuilt the city, naming it Christiania. In 1905, it became the capital of independent Norway. It acquired the name Oslo in 1925.

Union. In 1960, Norway formed the European Free Trade Association with six other countries while continuing to work with its Scandinavian neighbours through the Nordic Council. In 1994, Norwegians voted against membership of the EU. In the 1990s and 2000s, Norwegian diplomats sought to broker peace deals in Sri Lanka and Palestine.

ECONOMY

Norway's chief resources and exports are oil and natural gas. Dairy farming and meat production are the chief farming activities, though Norway has to import food. Industries include petroleum products, chemicals, aluminium, wood products, machinery and clothing.

SVALBARD

Archipelago in the Arctic Ocean, 640 km [400 mi] north of Norway. Spitsbergen is the largest of nine islands. The administrative centre and largest settlement is Long-yearbyen on Spitsbergen. Ice fields and glaciers cover more than half the land, although the western edge of the islands is ice-free most of the year. The area abounds in Arctic flora and fauna. The islands are an important wildlife refuge with polar bears, walrus and whales. Protective measures have saved certain mammals from extinction. In the 17th century, Svalbard was an important whaling centre, and in the 18th century, fur traders hunted the lands. Large coal deposits were found on Spitsbergen at the end of the 19th century, and Norway, Russia and Sweden mined the area. The islands became a sovereign territory of Norway in 1925, in return for allowing mining concessions to other nations. Svalbard covers an area of 62,000sq km (24,000sq mi), with a population of 2,400.

POLITICS

After World War II, Norwegians worked to rebuild their economy and their merchant fleet. The economy was boosted in the 1970s, when Norway began producing petroleum and natural gas from wells in the North Sea. Rapid economic growth has ensured that Norwegians are among the most prosperous in Europe.

In 1949 Norway became a member of NATO, though neither NATO bases nor nuclear weapons were permitted on its soil for fear of provoking the Soviet

OMAN

White symbolizes peace. Green is a traditional Islamic colour, but also stands for the fertility of the land. Red represents the blood shed in the struggle for liberation. The Sultanate's white coat of arms consists of two crossed swords, a type of dagger called a *khnajar*, and a belt.

The Sultanate of Oman is the oldest independent nation in the Arab world. It occupies the south-eastern corner of the Arabian peninsula and includes the tip of the Musandam Peninsula which is separated from the rest of Oman by UAE territory. This peninsula overlooks the strategic Strait of Hormuz.

The Al Halar al Gharbi range, rising to 3,019 m [9,904 ft] above sea level, borders the narrow coastal plain in the north. This fertile plain along the Gulf of Oman is called Al Battinah. Inland are deserts, including part of the Rub' al Khali (Empty Quarter). Much of the land along the Arabian Sea is barren, but the province of Zufar (or Dhofar) in the south-east is a hilly, fertile region.

Area 309,500 sq km [119,498 sq mi]
Population 3,102,000
Capital (population) Muscat (41,000)
Government Monarchy with consultative council
Ethnic groups Arab, Baluchi, Indian, Pakistani
Languages Arabic (official), Baluchi, English
Religions Islam (mainly Ibadi), Hinduism
Currency Omani rial = 100 baizas
Website www.omanet.om/english/home.asp

CLIMATE

Temperatures in Oman can reach 54°C [129°F] in summer, but winters are mild to warm. Rainfall in the northern mountains can exceed 400 mm [16 in] per year, while in the south-east it can be up to 630 mm [25 in], but for most of Oman the desert climate means less than 150 mm [6 in] per year. Sandstorms, duststorms and droughts feature and occasionally, tropical cyclones bring stormy weather.

HISTORY

Oman first became a major trading region 5,000 years ago. Islam was introduced into the area in the 7th century, and today 75% of the population follow the strict Ibadi Islam sect.

The Portuguese conquered its ports in the early 16th century, but local Arabs forced them out in 1650. The Al Bu Said family came to power in the 1740s and has ruled the country ever since. British influence dates back to the end of the 18th century, when the two countries entered into the first of several treaties.

In 1920, Britain brokered an agreement whereby the interior was ruled by imams, with coastal areas under the control of the Sultan. Clashes between the two groups continued into the 1950s, but Sultan Said bin Taimur regained control of the whole country in 1959.

POLITICS

Under Sultan Said bin Taimur, Oman had been an isolated, feudal country. Its economy was backward compared to its oil-rich Gulf neighbours. However, after he was deposed by his son, Sultan Qaboos ibn Said in 1970, Oman made substantial strides. With the help of soldiers from Iran and Jordan, Qaboos saw an end to war against Yemen-backed separatist guerrillas in the province of Zufar (1965–1975). He also led the way in ship between the two countries. In 2003, elections were held to the Consultative Council. For the first time, all citizens over 21 could vote, although no parties are allowed. In 2004, the Sultan appointed the first female minister with portfolio. In 2005, nearly 100 suspected Islamists were arrested and 31 were convicted of trying to overthrow the government, but were later pardoned.

ECONOMY

The World Bank classifies Oman as an 'upper-middle-income' developing country. It has sizeable oil and natural gas deposits, a large trade surplus and low inflation. Oil accounts for more than 90% of Oman's export revenues. Huge natural gas deposits, equal to all the finds of the previous 20 years, were discovered in 1991.

Although only about 0.3% of the land is cultivated, agriculture and fishing are the traditional economic activities. Major crops include alfalfa, bananas, coconuts, dates, tobacco and wheat. Water supply is a major problem. Oman depends on water from underground aquifers, which will eventually run dry, and also from desalination plants. Industries include copper smelting, cement and chemicals, as well as food processing and import substitution. Tourism is a growing activity.

developing an expanding economy based on oil, which had been found in 1964. Production began in 1967 and reserves proved far larger than expected. Qaboos opened up Oman to the outside world, ending its isolation. At home, he avoided prestigious projects favoured by other leaders to concentrate on social programmes, including education of girls. His leadership proved popular despite the lack of a democratic government.

In 1991, Oman took part in the military campaign to liberate Kuwait. In 1997, Oman held its first direct elections to a Consultative Council. The Council advises the Sultan, but has no direct authority. Unusually for the Gulf region, two women were amongst those elected. In 1999, Oman and the United Arab Emirates signed an agreement confirming most of the borders between them. In 2001, while a military campaign was being launched in Afghanistan, Britain held military exercises in the Omani desert. This was an example of the long-standing political and military relation-

PACIFIC OCEAN

AMERICAN SAMOA

Area 199 sq km [77 sq mi]
Population 58,000
Capital (population) Pago Pago (4,000)
Government Territory of the USA
Ethnic groups
Native Pacific Islander 93%, Asian, White
Languages Samoan 91%, English 3%, Tongan
2%, other Pacific islander 2%
Religions Christian Congregationalist 50%,
Protestant 30%, Roman Catholic 20%
Currency US dollar = 100 cents
Website www.asg-gov.net

The Territory of American Samoa is an unincorporated territory of the United States and lies in the south-central Pacific Ocean. Two of its islands are coral atolls, the other five extinct volcanoes. The largest island is Tutuila.

The Samoan islands were first reached by European explorers in the 18th century. In the later 19th century, rivalries developed between Germany, Britain and the US over access to the islands. In 1899 Britain gave up its claims in return for German parts of the Solomon Islands, and Samoa was divided between Germany and the US along a line 171 degrees west of Greenwich. The US took control of the islands between 1900 and 1904 and established a naval base at Pago Pago, which was used until 1951.

Much of the population works in small-scale agriculture. The main industry is the canning of tuna, and fish products dominate the islands' economy and exports. About twice as many American Samoans live in the US as on the islands themselves. American Samoa is the recipient of substantial economic aid from the US. It has a far higher standard of living than Samoa, the independent western part of the Samoan islands.

COOK ISLANDS

Area 293 sq km [113 sq mi]
Population 21,000
Capital (population) Avarua (10,000)
Government
Self-governing parliamentary democracy
Ethnic groups
Cook Island Maori (Polynesian) 88%
Languages English (official), Maori
Religions Cook Islands Christian Church 57%,
Roman Catholic 17%, Seventh Day Saint 8%,
Church of Latter Day Saints 4%, other Protestant
6%, others
Currency New Zealand dollar = 100 cents
Website www.ck

A group of 15 islands in the south Pacific Ocean to the north-east of New Zealand, consisting of the Northern (Manihiki) Cook Islands and the Southern (Lower) Cook Islands.

Discovered in 1773 by Captain James Cook, the islands became a British protectorate in 1888 and were annexed to New Zealand in 1901. In 1965 they became a self-governing territory in free association with New Zealand.

The islands' economy is based on tourism. There is also a small offshore finance sector, and pearls are harvested for export. Manufacturing is limited to small-scale fruit processing, clothing and handicrafts. Many of the population work in small-scale agriculture. Farm products include copra, papaya and citrus fruits.

Many Cook Islanders have moved to New Zealand or Australia to work, causing the islands' population to fall.

FRENCH POLYNESIA

French Polynesia consists of 130 islands, scattered in five main groups over 2.5 million sq km [1 million sq mi] of the Pacific Ocean. The Society Islands comprise the Leewards, of which the best

[map: 170°W · AMERICAN SAMOA · Pago Pago · Manua Islands · 14°S · Tutuila · 0 50 100 km · 0 50 miles]

GUAM

Area 549 sq km [212 sq mi]
Population 171,000
Capital (population) Agana (Hagatna) (1,000)
Government Territory of the USA
Ethnic groups
Chamorro 37%, Filipino 26%, other Pacific islander
11%, white 7%, other Asian 6%
Languages English 38%, Chamorro 22%,
Philippine languages 22%, other Pacific island
languages 7%, Asian languages 7%, others
Religions Roman Catholic 85%, others 15%
Currency US dollar = 100 cents
Website www.visitguam.org

known is Bora-Bora, and the Windwards, which include Moorea and Tahiti. Tahiti is the largest island, and is home to Papeete, the capital. These islands, along with the Marquesas, most of the Tubuais and the smaller Gambier islands, are volcanic with steep-sided mountains. The Tuamotus are low-lying coralline atolls.

Europeans gradually came into contact with the islands in the 18th century, with explorers from several European nations claiming discovery of different parts of the group. European traders and missionaries brought diseases which killed many of the indigenous population.

Tribal chiefs agreed to a French protectorate in 1843. They gained increased autonomy in 1984. Some favour independence, and elections in the 2000s alternated between favouring pro-independence and pro-French governments.

The islands' relatively high standard of living is supported by income from tourism and by financial aid from France. Farming exists on a small scale. From 1966 to 1996 French nuclear testing on Mururoa led to a large military presence, but this has now been reduced.

Area 4,000 sq km [1,544 sq mi]
Population 275,000
Capital (population) Papeete (25,000)
Government Overseas territory of France
Ethnic groups Polynesian 78%, Chinese 12%,
local French 6%, metropolitan French 4%
Languages French 61%, Polynesian 31% (both
official), Asian languages
Religions Protestant 54%, Roman Catholic 30%
Currency Comptoirs Francais du Pacifique franc =
100 centimes
Website www.presidence.pf

The Territory of Guam is a strategically important 'unincorporated territory' of the USA and the largest of the Mariana Islands in the Pacific Ocean. It is composed of a coralline limestone plateau, with mountains in the south, hills in the centre and narrow coastal lowlands in the north of the island.

Guam was inhabited by indigenous Chamorro people when discovered by Magellan in 1521. Spain claimed the islands from 1565 and set up colonies from 1668. During the Spanish-American war of 1898 the island was captured by the US Navy without a fight, and after the war it was ceded to the United States.

During World War II, the island was captured by Japan in 1941 and subjected to a brutal occupation. US troops recaptured the island in 1944 after heavy fighting. A major American military base was established. During the Cold War the base was expanded and now occupies a substantial fraction of Guam's usable land area. The 2000s saw further growth.

Guam's inhabitants are US citizens. They are not represented in mainland US government, but do elect their own governor. A 1982 referendum rejected proposals to make the island a US state.

The islands' economy depends on the large US military presence and on US aid. Tourism provides further income.

KIRIBATI

Area 726 sq km [280 sq mi]
Population 105,000
Capital (population) Bairiki (on Tarawa) (32,000)
Government Multiparty republic
Ethnic groups Micronesian 99%
Languages
I-Kiribati and English (both official)
Religions Christian
Currency Australian dollar = 100 cents
Website www.janeresture.com/kirihome/index.htm

The Republic of Kiribati is an independent nation in the west Pacific Ocean. It comprises about 33 islands, including the Gilbert, Phoenix and Line Islands, spread over an area of 5 million sq km (2 million sq mi). The islands are threatened by global warming and consequent rising sea levels.

British navigators first visited the Gilbert and Ellice Islands during the late 18th century. They became a British protectorate in 1892 and a colony in 1915. In the 1970s the Ellice Islands split from the Gilbert Islands after a referendum

Japanese mandate after World War I. US forces took the main islands in 1944 and they became a US Trust Territory in 1947. Independence was achieved in 1991, but the islands remain heavily dependent on US aid. The economy is based on agriculture and tourism.

Area 181 sq km [70 sq mi]
Population 60,000
Capital (population) Majuro (20,000)
Government Constitutional in association with US
Ethnic groups Micronesian
Languages Marshallese and English (both official)
Religions Many Christian denominations
Currency US dollar = 100 cents
Website www.yokwe.net

MICRONESIA

The Federated States of Micronesia is a republic in the western Pacific Ocean, consisting of all the Caroline Islands except Belau. The 607 islands of the republic divide into four states: Chuuk, Pohnpei, Yap and Kosrae. After 1874 the islands were under a succession of rulers from Spain to Germany in 1899, to Japan in 1920. They came under US administration in 1947. In 1979, the Federated States of Micronesia came into being, with Belau remaining a US trust territory. In 1986, a compact of free association with the USA was signed. In 1991 Micronesia became a full member of the UN. The economy depends heavily on US aid. Land use is limited to subsistence agriculture.

Area 702 sq km [271 sq mi]
Population 108,000
Capital (population) Palikir (on Pohnpei) (5,000)
Government Constitutional in association with US
Ethnic groups Micronesian and Polynesian
Languages English (official), others
Religions Roman Catholic 50%, Protestant 47%
Currency US dollar = 100 at
Website www.visit-fsm.org

and became Tuvalu. The Gilbert Islands achieved independence in 1979 as the Republic of Kiribati. Kiribati exports copra and depends on foreign aid.

MARSHALL ISLANDS

The Republic of the Marshall Islands consists of 31 coral atolls, five single islands and more than 1,000 islets. It lies north of Kiribati. The islands came under German rule in 1885 and became a

PACIFIC OCEAN

NAURU

A former UN Trust Territory ruled by Australia, Nauru is a small island located in the western Pacific close to the Equator. The island is a low-lying coral atoll with a hot and humid climate.

Nauru's distinctive indigenous people were possibly of Polynesian or Melanesian descent. The first European to reach the island was British whaling captain John Fearn in 1798. In the 1870s, the import of European alcohol and firearms caused native society to break down. Violence continued until Germany annexed the islands in 1888 and imposed order.

In the early 1900s, large deposits of high quality phosphate were discovered. Mining began in 1906. In 1914, soon after World War I broke out, Nauru was taken over by Australia. During World War II the island was conquered by the Japanese, who deported most of the inhabitants for forced labour. After the war, control reverted to Australia until 1968, when Nauru achieved independence as the world's smallest republic.

Phosphate mining brought the island wealth and a very high standard of living. By the 1990s phosphate reserves were almost exhausted, and the government's financial reserves proved far smaller than intended due to poor investments and mismanagement. The country slid into bankruptcy and now depends on aid from Australia. In return Australia has used the island to detain asylum seekers, a policy which has attracted criticism.

Area 21 sq km [8 sq mi]
Population 13,000
Capital (population) Yaren (4,500)
Government Multiparty republic
Ethnic groups Nauruan 58%, other Pacific Islander 26%, Chinese 8%, European 8%
Languages Nauruan (official), English
Religions Protestant 66%, Roman Catholic 33%
Currency Australian dollar = 100 cents
Website www.un.int/nauru/

NEW CALEDONIA

New Caledonia is the most southerly of the Melanesian countries in the Pacific Ocean. It comprises a main island, Terre Grande, and several dependencies. These include the Loyalty Islands or Iles Loyauté, Ile des Pins and the Bélep archipelago as well as numerous uninhabited coral atolls.

Europeans first sighted the islands in the late 18th century. British explorer James Cook was first to sight Terre Grande, and coined the name New Caledonia. In 1853 the islands became a French possession.

During World War II, New Caledonia was a major Allied base. In 1958 it became an Overseas Territory of France. The 1980s saw demands for independence, which occasionally led to violence. In 1998, France reached an agreement with local Melanesians which allowed the islands to transition to an autonomous government, but put off any referendum on independence until at least 2014.

New Caledonia's economy is almost entirely dependent upon the mining of nickel, of which it is one of the world's largest producers. Experts claim that the islands have about a quarter of the world's nickel reserves. Nickel brings in a relatively high income, but is susceptible to price fluctuations. Tourism and financial aid from France provide additional sources of income.

Area 18,575 sq km [7,172 sq mi]
Population 219,000
Capital (population) Nouméa (76,000)
Government Overseas territory of France
Ethnic groups Melanesian 43%, European 37%, Wallisian 8%, Polynesian 4%, Indonesian 4%
Languages French (official), 33 Melanesian-Polynesian dialects
Religions Roman Catholic 60%, Protestant 30%
Currency Comptoirs Français du Pacifique franc = 100 centimes
Website www.newcaledoniatourism-south.com

NIUE

Niue is an island territory in the southern Pacific Ocean, 2,160 km [1,340 mi] north-east of New Zealand. The largest coral island in the world, Niue was first visited by Europeans in 1774. In 1901 it was annexed to New Zealand. In 1974 it achieved self-government in free association with New Zealand. Its economy is mainly agricultural; the major export is coconut.

Area 260 sq km [100 sq mi]
Population 2,000
Capital (population) Alofi (404)
Government Self-governing parliamentary democracy
Ethnic groups Niuen 78%, Pacific islander 10%, European 4%, others
Languages Niuean, English
Religions Ekalesia Niue 61%, Latter-Day Saints 9%, Roman Catholic 7%, others
Currency New Zealand dollar = 100 cents
Website www.niueisland.nu

NORFOLK ISLAND

The Territory of Norfolk Island lies in the south-west Pacific Ocean 1,450 km [900 mi] east of Australia.

Norfolk Island was first settled by Polynesians, but their colony failed. It became known to Europeans when discovered in 1774 by Captain Cook. Two attempts to found British penal colonies failed. Pitcairn Islanders, descendants of the *Bounty* mutineers, settled the empty island in 1856. The chief economic activities are agriculture and tourism.

Area 34 sq km [13 sq mi]
Population 2,100
Capital (population) Kingston
Government Territory of Australia
Ethnic groups Descendants of the Bounty mutineers, Australian, New Zealander, Polynesianss
Languages English, Norfolk
Religions Anglican 35%, Roman Catholic 12%, Uniting Church in Australia 11%, others
Currency Australian dollar = 100 cents
Website www.nf

NORTHERN MARIANA ISLANDS

The Commonwealth of the Northern Mariana Islands contains 16 mountainous islands north of Guam in the western Pacific Ocean. The islands were inhabited by Chamorro people when discovered by Magellan in 1521. Spain took control in the 17th century. Many of the native population died out and settlers were brought from the Philippines. Spain sold the islands to Germany in 1899 and Japan took control after World War I. In World War II, the US captured the Marianas after fierce fighting.

In a 1975 plebescite, islanders voted for Commonwealth status in union with the USA and in 1986 they were granted US citizenship. The economy is based on tourism and clothing manufacture.

Area 464 sq km [179 sq mi]
Population 82,000
Capital (population) Saipan (39,000)
Government Commonwealth in union with the US
Ethnic groups Asian 56%, Pacific islander 36%
Languages Philippine languages 24%, Chinese 23%, Chamorro 22%, English 10%, others
Religions Christianity
Currency US dollar = 100 cents
Website www.cnmi.net

PALAU

Area 459 sq km [177 sq mi]
Population 21,000
Capital (population) Koror (11,000)
Government Multiparty republic
Ethnic groups Palauan 70%, Filipino 15%, Chinese 5%, others
Languages Palauan (official except in Sonsoral (Sonsoralese and English official), Tobi (Tobi and English official), and Angaur (Angaur, Japanese, and English official), Filipino, English Chinese
Religions Roman Catholic 42%, Protestant 23%, Modekngei 9% (indigenous to Palau),
Currency US dollar = 100 cents
Website www.visit-palau.com

The Republic of Palau comprises an archipelago, with 26 main islands in six groups and hundreds of tiny islets. Eight of the islands are permanently inhabited, including Peleliu and Angaur.

Palau's indigenous culture is one of the oldest in the Pacific. The islands first came into contact with Europeans when the British discovered them in the 1780s. Palau was annexed by the Spanish empire in the 1880s, but sold to Germany in 1899. After the First World War, the League of Nations assigned Palau to Japan. Under Japanese rule the islands were modernized, disrupting indigenous society. During World War II, Palau was captured by the Americans in 1944 after bitter fighting. After the war it became a UN Trust Territory held by the US.

In the 1980s the island sought independence under terms that continued US aid and defence, but the US refused as Palau declared itself a nuclear-free zone. In 1994 Palau renounced the nuclear-free clause and became fully independent. Heavy US subsidies are now being reduced, and the islands have sought links with Taiwan. Other income derives from tourism, fishing and subsistence agriculture. The main crops include cassava, coconuts and copra.

PITCAIRN ISLAND

Area 55 sq km [21 sq mi]
Population 45
Capital (population) Adamstown
Government Overseas territory of the UK
Ethnic groups Descendants of the Bounty mutineers and their Tahitian wives
Languages English (official), Pitcairnese
Religions Seventh-Day Adventist
Currency New Zealand dollar = 100 cents
Website www.government.pn/homepage.htm

Pitcairn Island is a British overseas territory in the Pacific Ocean. Its inhabitants are descendents of the original settlers – nine mutineers from HMS *Bounty* and 18 Tahitians who arrived on this formerly uninhabited island in 1790. In 2004 it attracted international attention after six men, half the island's adult male population, were imprisoned for sex offences.

SAMOA

Area 2,831 sq km [1,093 sq mi]
Population 177,000
Capital (population) Apia (32,000)
Government Parliamentary democracy and constitutional monarchy
Ethnic groups Samoan 93%, Euronesians
Languages Samoan, English
Religions
Congregationalist 35%, Roman Catholic 20%, Methodist 15%, Latter-Day Saints 13%
Currency Tala = 100 sene
Website www.visitsamoa.ws

The Independent State of Samoa comprises two large and seven small islands in the South Pacific Ocean. The main islands, Upolu and Savai'i, both have central mountainous regions which are heavily forested and divided by fast-flowing rivers. The narrow coastal lowlands are surrounded by coral reefs. Upolu, the most fertile island, has two-thirds of the population.

The Samoan islands were first reached by European explorers in the 18th century. In the later 19th century, Germany, Britain and the US disputed the islands. In 1899, the Treaty of Berlin awarded Western Samoa to Germany.

In 1914, World War I broke out, and an Allied force from New Zealand immediately occupied German Samoa. After the war New Zealand governed the islands under a League of Nations mandate. The territory became an independent nation in 1962 as Western Samoa, and was the first Polynesian nation to regain independence. In 1997 the country renamed itself simply as Samoa.

Many Samoans are small-scale farmers. Coconut products are exported. Fishing is important, and there is a vert small manufacturing industry. Tourism and development aid are important.

over the islands in 1893, and they were the scene of some of the fiercest fighting in the Pacific during World War II.

The islands won full independence in 1978. In the 1990s they degenerated into political instability and ethnic violence. In 2003, Australia led a peace-keeping force sent to restore order. 2006 elections led to rioting and more peace-keeping troops were sent. The impoverished economy depends on Australian aid. Exports of fish and timber have been disrupted by the disturbances.

SOLOMON ISLANDS

Area 28,896 sq km [11,157 sq mi]
Population 552,000
Capital (population) Honiara (49,000)
Government Parliamentary democracy
Ethnic groups Melanesian 95%, others
Languages Melanesian pidgin
Religions Church of Melanesia 33%, Roman Catholic 19%, South Seas Evangelical 17%, Seventh-Day Adventist 11%, United Church 10%
Currency Solomon Islands dollar = 100 cents
Website www.solomons.com

The Solomon Islands are a chain of mainly volcanic islands in the Pacific Ocean, extending over 2,250 km [1,400 mi]. Britain established a protectorate

TOKELAU

Area 10 sq km [3.86 sq mi]
Population 1,400
Government Self-administering territory of New Zealand
Ethnic groups Polynesian
Languages Tokelauan, English
Religions Congregational Christian Church 70%, Roman Catholic 28%
Currency New Zealand dollar = 100 cents
Website www.tokelau.org.nz

Tokelau was originally settled by Polynesian emigrants from surrounding islands. It was made a British protectorate in 1889 and transferred to New Zealand administration in 1925. It is made up of three villages. There is little economic development and agriculture is at subsistence level. The people produce copra, postage stamps, souvenir coins and handicrafts, but rely heavily on aid from New Zealand.

PACIFIC OCEAN

TONGA

Area 650 sq km [251 sq mi]
Population 115,000
Capital (population) Nuku'alofa 22,000)
Government Constitutional monarchy
Ethnic groups Polynesian
Languages Tongan, English
Religions Christian (Free Wesleyan Church)
Currency Pa'anga = 100 seniti
Website http://pmo.gov.to

Originally called the Friendly Islands, the Kingdom of Tonga is an island kingdom in the South Pacific, 2,200 km [1,370 mi] north-east of New Zealand. The archipelago consists of about 170 islands in five administrative groups. Only 36 of the islands are inhabited. They are mainly coral atolls, but the western group are volcanic, with some active craters. The largest island is Tongatapu, seat of the capital Nukualofa and of the royal palace. Tongatapu is home to about two-thirds of the population.

The northern islands were discovered by Europeans in 1616, and the rest by Abel Tasman in 1643. During the 19th century, British missionaries converted the indigenous population to Christianity. In 1900, Tonga became a British Protectorate.

In 1970, the country achieved independence and became a member of the Commonwealth. It is the last Polynesian monarchy, and the only Pacific island state to have retained its original form of government through the colonial era. The king rules with the help of a parliament, of which most members are appointed from a hereditary nobility.

In 2006 King Tupou IV died after a long illness. He was succeeded by his son Tupou V, who promised political reform. The end of the year saw riots over delays in making the country more democratic, and the new king promised to make most of parliament elected by popular vote from 2008.

The economy is dominated by agriculture and many Tongans are subsistence farmers. The chief crops are coconuts, yams, tapioca and groundnuts. Fishing is also important. Tonga is not self-sufficient in food, and depends on food aid from New Zealand and Australia. The large population and limited land area have constrained the growth of agriculture and lead to unemployment.

Money sent home by Tongans working overseas is the country's largest source of external income, followed by tourism and financial aid.

TUVALU

Area 26 sq km [10 sq mi]
Population 12,000
Capital (population) Fongafale (3,000)
Government Constitutional monarchy with a parliamentary democracy
Ethnic groups Polynesian 96%, Micronesian 4%
Languages Tuvaluan, English, Samoan, Kiribati
Religions Church of Tuvalu (Congregationalist) 97%, others
Currency Tuvaluan dollar and Australian dollar = 100 cents
Website www.tuvaluislands.com

Tuvalu, formerly the Ellice Islands (see Kiribati), is an independent republic in western Pacific Ocean. None of the cluster of nine low-lying coral islands rises more than 4.6 m [15 ft] out of the Pacific, making them vulnerable to sea level rises caused by climate change.

The first European to discover the islands was the Spanish navigator Alvaro de Mendaña in 1568. Between 1850 and 1880, the population was reduced from around 20,000 to just 3,000 by Europeans abducting workers for other Pacific plantations. In 1892 the British assumed control and administered Tuvalu from the nearby Gilbert Islands (now Kiribati). In 1978, Tuvalu became a separate self-governing colony within the Commonwealth.

Poor soil restricts vegetation to coconut palms, breadfruit, and bush. The population survives by subsistence farming, raising pigs and poultry, and by fishing. Copra is the only significant export, but more foreign exchange is derived from the sale of elaborate postage stamps and from the rental of internet addresses in the islands' '.tv' internet domain.

The Republic of Vanuatu, formerly the Anglo-French Condominium of the New Herbrides, became independent in 1980. The word Vanuatu means 'Our Land Forever'. The republic consists of a chain of 80 islands in the South Pacific Ocean. Its economy is based on agriculture and it exports copra, beef and veal, timber and cocoa. Fishing, offshore financial services and tourism are also important, as is aid from Australia.

VANUATU

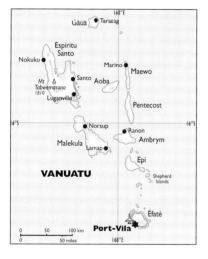

Area 12,189 sq km [4,706 sq mi]
Population 209,000
Capital (population) Port Vila (19,000)
Government Multiparty republic
Ethnic groups Ni-Vanuatu 99%
Languages Local languages (more than 100) 73%, pidgin (known as Bislama or Bichelama) 23%, others
Religions Presbyterian 31%, Anglican 13%, Roman Catholic 13%, Seventh-Day Adventist 11%, indigenous beliefs 6% (including Jon Frum cargo cult), others
Currency Vatu
Website www.vanuatugovernment.gov.vu

WALLIS & FUTUNA

Area 200 sq km [77 sq mi]
Population 16,000
Capital (population) Mata-Utu (1,000)
Government Overseas territory of France
Ethnic groups Polynesian
Languages Wallisian 59%, Futunian 30%, French 11%
Religions Roman Catholic
Currency Comptoirs Français du Pacifique franc = 100 centimes
Website www.wallis.co.nc

The Territory of the Wallis and Futuna Islands in the South Pacific Ocean forms the smallest and the poorest of France's overseas territories. They were reached by Dutch and British explorers in the 17th and 18th centuries.

A French dependency since 1842, the territory comprises two groups of islands. The Isles de Hoorn, which includes Futuna, is situated to the north-east of the Fiji Islands. The other is the Wallis Archipelago. In 1959 the inhabitants of the islands voted to become a French overseas territory.

The economy is based on subsistence agriculture, and 80% of the workforce makes their living from either coconuts and vegetables, livestock or fishing. Other revenue comes from the licensing of fishing rights to Japan and South Korea. French government subsidies are still needed to maintain the islands' economy.

301

PAKISTAN

Pakistan's flag was adopted in 1947, when the country gained independence. The colour green, the crescent Moon and the five-pointed star are all traditional symbols of Islam. The white stripe represents the other religions in Pakistan.

The Islamic Republic of Pakistan contains a wide range of terrain. The river Indus runs the length of the country in a broad, fertile valley, reaching the sea at the eastern end of the coast. West of the Indus delta lie arid coastal plains, rising into the Makran mountain range and the Baluchistan plateau. Higher mountains rise all along the north-west border with Afghanistan. In the far north, the North-West Frontier province contains parts of the massive Hindu Kush and Himalayan mountain ranges. K2, on the border with China, is the world's second highest peak at 8,611 m [28,251 ft] and lies in the northern part of Jammu and Kashmir. The Thar, or Great Indian, Desert straddles the border with India in the south-east.

Area 796,095 sq km [307,372 sq mi]
Population 165,804,000
Capital (population) Islamabad (791,000)
Government Federal republic
Ethnic groups Punjabi, Sindhi, Pashtun (Pathan), Baluchi, Muhajir
Languages Urdu (official), many others
Religions Islam 97%, Christianity, Hinduism
Currency Pakistani rupee = 100 paisa
Website www.infopak.gov.pk

CLIMATE
The climate varies widely across Pakistan, but most areas have hot summers and cool winters. The coast has more moderate weather, while inland summers can be very hot. Winters in the mountains are bitterly cold and snowy. Rainfall is sparse over much of the country.

HISTORY
Pakistan was home to the Indus Valley civilization, one of the world's earliest urban cultures after Egypt and Mesopotamia. It was highly developed by about 2500 BC. It broke into smaller cultures in about 1700 BC, possibly as a consequence of changes in the course of the river Indus. The great cities of Harappa and Mohenjo-Daro were lost until their rediscovery by archaeologists in the 1920s.

Later, the region became part of a number of empires in succession. It was ruled by Persia until conquered by Alexander the Great. After his death, it became part of the Mauryan empire. A culture based on a mixture of Indian and Greek elements survived several further conquests, and by the 8th century the region had once again fallen under the control of Persia.

In the early 8th century the country was invaded by Arabs, who conquered Sind in 712 and introduced Islam. Over the following centuries, Muslim influence grew as the population gradually converted. In 1211, Pakistan became part of the Delhi Sultanate.

In 1526 the Mogul Empire supplanted the Sultanate. The Urdu language developed under their rule. In the late 18th century, Ranjit Singh conquered the Punjab and introduced Sikhism there.

The early 19th century saw the emergence of the British East India Company as the dominant force. The British conquered Sind in 1843, the Punjab in 1849 and much of Baluchistan in the 1850s. Pathans in the north-west resisted subjection, and the British created a separate province in 1901. The dominance of Hindus in British India led to the formation of the Muslim League in 1906. In the 1940s the League's leader, Muham-

mad Ali Jinnah, gained popular support for the idea of a separate state in Muslim-majority areas. The Muslim League proposed the name Pakistan, from the Urdu for 'land of the pure'.

POLITICS

After World War II, British India's demands for independence grew too strong for Britain to ignore. The Muslim League played a major role in convincing the British to divide the region into two states along religious lines, and in 1947 British India was divided into Pakistan and India. Pakistan, which in the British partition also included the entirety of

KARACHI

Karachi is a city and seaport on the Arabian Sea in south-east Pakistan. The area contained only villages until the end of the 17th century, when it fell under the control of the rulers of Sind who began to develop a city. It was conquered by the British in 1843 and annexed to the British Empire in India. The British built a military settlement, or cantonment. Recognizing the city's potential for trade because of its strategic location in the Indus basin, the British later invested in the city's infrastructure and developed Karachi into a major city and seaport.

When Pakistan achieved independence in 1947, Karachi was chosen as the capital. In 1958 the national capital was moved to Rawalpindi, and Karachi is now only the capital of Sind province. The city received less government attention and investment but continued to grow, remaining the largest and most important city in Pakistan. The city's population is now about 12 million.

Karachi is a major centre of commerce and industry. It is Pakistan's financial hub, and its two large ports handle almost all of the country's overseas trade. There is a large base of heavy industry including steelmaking and motor vehicle manufacture as well as lighter industries such as textiles. Publishing, media and IT are growing sectors.

Muslims fled India. As many as 15 million people moved between the two states, and law and order broke down as ethnic tensions led to violence. Estimates of the number of people who died or were killed range between 500,000 and a million. The partition also left ownership of the Kashmir region in dispute.

In 1948 Pakistan declared Urdu its sole official language, leading to riots in East Pakistan where most spoke only Bengali. In the 1950s Bengali was made a joint official language, but relationships between the two geographically separate parts of the country deteriorated as the West Pakistan-based government continued to favour its own region and neglect the east. After a bitter civil war, in which India declared war on Pakistan to support the eastern territories, East Pakistan broke away in 1971 as Bangladesh.

In 1948–9, 1965 and 1999, Pakistan and India's dispute over the territory of Kashmir flared into war. The first divided the territory along approximately the boundary that persists today, with two-thirds of the territory under Indian control. The 1965 war was costly but inconclusive, while the 1999 conflict was on a smaller scale.

Military dictatorships and elected civilian governments have alternately ruled Pakistan for most of the time since independence. In 1997 Narwaz Sharif was elected prime minister, but a military coup brought General Pervez Musharraf to power in 1999.

In 1998, while tensions over Kashmir were high, India conducted nuclear weapon tests. Pakistan responded by revealing that it too had developed nuclear weapons, performing several successful nuclear tests. Pakistan was also involved in proliferating nuclear technology to other states including North Korea.

In 2001 Pakistan, a US ally since the Cold War, supported the Western assault on Taliban forces in Afghanistan. Musharraf then changed the constitution to increase his powers and, in 2004, announced that he would remain army

what is now Bangladesh, was to be the Muslim-dominated state while India's population were mostly Hindu. However, millions found themselves on the wrong side. Neither state was prepared for the mass migrations that occurred as Hindus and Sikhs fled Pakistan and chief as well as head of state. Pakistan's declaration of support for the coalition against terrorism provoked a backlash by Islamic fundamentalists. From 2003, India and Pakistan began to move towards a peace settlement over the Kashmir dispute. In October 2005 nearly 75,000 people were killed and 3 million left homeless in an earthquake centred on Pakistan-administered Kashmir.

In 2006–7, Taliban and al-Qaeda forces operating from Pakistan against NATO forces in Afghanistan became a major problem as the Pakistani government struggled to control the border.

ECONOMY

Pakistan is a poor country, classed by the World Bank as a 'low-income' developing country, though since 2000 the economy has begun to grow. Unemployment is a problem because of the rapid growth of the population. Industries include motor vehicles and vehicle components, ship-building, cement, industrial chemicals and textiles. IT and communications are rapidly growing sectors.

Agriculture employs over 40% of the workforce. Major crops are cotton, fruits, rice, sugar cane, vegetables and wheat. Livestock include goats and sheep.

THE KHYBER PASS

Mountain pass in the Safid Kuh range, on the frontier between Pakistan and Afghanistan. It links Afghanistan's Kabul valley, which lies to the west, to Peshawar in Pakistan to the east. It is about 50 km [30 mi] long, and its height reaches 1,073 m [3520 ft]. The surrounding mountains are much higher and the pass is walled by steep cliffs.

The pass has long been a strategic location. Alexander the Great marched his armies through it in 326 BC to begin his attempt to conquer India, and many other forces used it throughout history. It was a key location in all three Anglo-Afghan wars in the 19th and early 20th century and the British constructed the first road through the pass in 1879 during the second of these.

The pass is also a key route for trade. The local population, mostly Pashtun, have traditionally lived by levying tolls from travellers and traders. They are heavily armed and fiercely independent and are known for crafting their own firearms, copies of modern and antique Western models.

ISLAMABAD

Capital of Pakistan, in the north of the country. It is a planned city on a grid layout, designed from its beginning to be the national capital as a replacement for Karachi. Islamabad's location was chosen both to try to improve the development of Pakistan's northern regions and because the surrounding mountains make it relatively defensible. Pakistan's government feared that Karachi would be vulnerable in the event of war with India.

Construction began in 1960. In 1967 Islamabad became the official capital, replacing the interim capital at nearby Rawalpindi. The city's architecture follows modern styles.

Islamabad lies at the heart of an agricultural region. Administration and government dominate the city, which is home to many large government ministries. Islamabad is also the site of many of Pakistan's institutions of higher education. Private commerce is relatively small-scale, though it has begun to grow through foreign investment. The industrial sector remains small.

PANAMA

The blue quarter stands for the Conservative Party. The red quarter represents the Liberal Party. The white quarters symbolize peace between the parties The blue star stands for purity and honesty. The red star denotes government and law.

The Republic of Panama forms an isthmus linking Central America to South America. The narrowest part of Panama is less than 60 km [37 mi] wide. The Panama Canal, which is 80 km [50 mi] long and cuts straight across the isthmus, has made the country a major transport centre. Most Panamanians live within 20 km [12 mi] of it. Much of the land between the Pacific and Caribbean coastal plains is mountainous, rising to 3,475 m [11,400 ft] at the volcano Barú.

Tropical forests cover approximately 50% of Panama. Mangrove swamps line the coast, though in recent years more than 400 sq km [150 sq mi] have been lost to agriculture, ranching and shrimp mariculture. Subtropical woodland grows on the mountains, while tropical savanna occurs along the Pacific coast.

Area 75,517 sq km [29,157 sq mi]
Population 3,191,000
Capital (population) Panamá (1,173,000)
Government Multiparty republic
Ethnic groups Mestizo 70%, Black and Mulatto 14%, White 10%, Amerindian 6%
Languages Spanish (official), English
Religions Roman Catholic 85%, Protestant 15%
Currency US dollar; Balboa = 100 centésimos
Website www.visitpanama.com

Spain established control, and the indigenous population was soon wiped out by Spanish troops and exposure to European diseases. In 1821, Panama became a province of Colombia. The USA exerted great influence from the

CLIMATE

Panama has a tropical climate, though the mountains are much cooler than the coastal plains. The rainy season is between May and December. The Caribbean side of has about twice as much rain as the Pacific side.

HISTORY

Christopher Columbus landed in Panama in 1502. In 1510, Vasco Núñez de Balboa became the first European to cross Panama and see the Pacific Ocean.

PANAMA CANAL

Waterway connecting the Atlantic and Pacific oceans across the Isthmus of Panama. A canal, begun in 1882 by Ferdinand de Lesseps, was subsequently abandoned because of bankruptcy. The US government decided to finance the project to provide a convenient route for its warships. The main construction took about ten years to complete, and the first ship passed through in 1914. The 80 km [50 mi] waterway reduces the sea voyage between San Francisco and New York by about 12,500 km [7,800 mi]. Control of the Canal passed from the USA to Panama at the end of 1999.

Pérez Balladares became president in 1994 elections. In 1999 Mireya Moscoso, Panama's first woman president, succeeded Balladares. She was succeeded in 2004 by Martin Torrijos, son of a former military dictator.

Revenues from the canal rose in the early 21st century, but the economy slowed overall, causing social discontent. In 2006 the government announced major expansion of the canal.

mid-19th century. After a revolt in 1903, Panama declared independence from Colombia. In 1904, the USA began construction of the Panama Canal and established the Panama Canal Zone. Since it opened in 1914, the status of the canal has dominated Panamanian politics. US forces intervened in 1908, 1912 and 1918 to protect US interests.

POLITICS

Panama was politically unstable throughout the 20th century, with a series of dictatorial regimes and military coups.

Civil strife during the 1950s and 1960s led to negotiations with the USA for the transfer of the Canal Zone. In 1977 a treaty confirmed Panama's sovereignty over the canal, while providing for US bases in the Canal Zone. The USA agreed to hand over control of the canal on 31 December 1999. In 1979 the Canal Zone was disestablished, and the canal was controlled jointly by Panama and the US.

In 1983 General Noriega took control of the National Guard and ruled Panama through a succession of puppet governments. In 1987 the USA withdrew its support for Noriega after he was accused of murder, electoral fraud and aiding drug smuggling. It imposed sanctions the following year. In 1989 Noriega annulled elections, made himself president and declared war on the USA. On 20 December 1989, 25,000 US troops invaded Panama. Noriega was quickly captured, and taken to the USA for trial.

ECONOMY

The World Bank classifies Panama as a 'lower-middle-income' developing country. The Panama Canal is a major source of revenue, generating jobs in commerce, trade, manufacturing and transport.

After the canal, the main activity is agriculture, which employs 27% of the workforce. Rice is the main food crop. Bananas, shrimps, sugar and coffee are exported. Tourism is also important. Many foreign-owned ships are registered under Panama's flag due to its low taxes.

PANAMA CITY

Capital of Panama, on the shore of the Gulf of Panama, near the Pacific end of the Panama Canal. It was founded by Pedro Arias de Avila in 1519, and was destroyed and rebuilt in the 17th century. It includes an area known as Casco Antiguo (Colonial Panama), which was constructed inland after the destruction of the first city. Casco Antiguo has been declared 'Patrimony of Humanity' by UNESCO. The city became the capital of Panama in 1903 and it developed rapidly after the construction of the Panama Canal in 1914. Industries include brewing, shoes, textiles, oil-refining, and plastics.

PAPUA NEW GUINEA

Papua New Guinea's flag was first adopted in 1971, four years before the country became independent from Australia. It includes a local bird of paradise, the 'kumul', in flight, together with the stars of the Southern Cross. The colours are those often used by local artists.

The Independent State of Papua New Guinea is part of a south-west Pacific island region called Melanesia, and lies 160 km [100 mi] north-east of Australia. Papua New Guinea includes the eastern part of New Guinea, the Bismarck Archipelago, Solomon Islands, New Hebrides, the Trobriand and D'Entrecasteaux Islands, the Louisiade Archipelago and the Tanga group.

New Guinea island is largely mountainous, rising to Mount Wilhelm, at 4,508 m [14,790 ft], in the east. In 1995, two volcanoes erupted in Eastern New Britain. East New Guinea also has extensive coastal lowlands.

Forests cover more than 70% of the land. The dominant vegetation is rainforest. Mangrove swamps line the coast. 'Cloud' forest and tussock grass are found on the higher peaks.

Area 462,840 sq km [178,703 sq mi]
Population 5,671,000
Capital (population) Port Moresby (193,000)
Government Constitutional monarchy
Ethnic groups Papuan, Melanesian, Micronesian
Languages English (official), Melanesian Pidgin, more than 700 other indigenous languages
Religions Traditional beliefs 34%, Roman Catholic 22%, Lutheran 16%, others
Currency Kina = 100 toea
Website www.pngonline.gov.pg

Dutch took western New Guinea (now part of Indonesia) in 1828, but it was not until 1884 that Germany took north-eastern New Guinea as German New Guinea and Britain formed the protectorate of British New Guinea in south-

CLIMATE

The climate is tropical. It is hot all year with most rain occurring during the monsoon from December to April, when winds blow from the northeast. Winds blow from the southwest during the dry season.

HISTORY

The Portuguese made the first European sighting of the island in 1526, although no European settlements were established until the late 19th century. The

<table>
<tr><td colspan="2">PORT MORESBY</td></tr>
</table>

Temperature
Precipitation
1011mm/40in
J F M A M J J A S O N D

BOUGAINVILLE

Volcanic island in the south-west Pacific Ocean, east of New Guinea; a territory of Papua New Guinea. It was discovered in 1768 by Louis de Bougainville. The island was under German control from 1884, and then under Australian administration after 1914 and again in 1945 (after the Japanese wartime occupation). It has been the scene of guerrilla warfare since the late 1980s. Kieta is the chief port. Industries include copper mining, copra, cocoa and timber. It covers an area of 10,049 sq km [3,880 sq mi], with a population of 204,800.

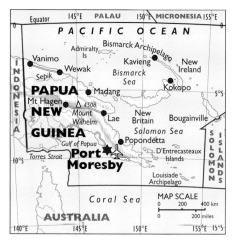

created unrest in the army. In 1997, troops and civilians surrounded Parliament, forcing the resignation of Prime Minister Sir Julius Chan. He was succeeded by Bill Skate. In April 1998 a ceasefire was declared on Bougainville, ending the civil war. An estimated 20,000 people had been killed. Local autonomy was granted to Bougainville in 2000.

Michael Somare became president in 2002 elections. In 2004 Australia sent police to help fight rapidly rising crime. In 2005 the government began the evacuation of the Carteret Islands, which are slowly sinking. In 2007 presidential elections Somare won a second term. Crime, corruption and rising HIV infection rates remain problems.

east New Guinea. In 1906 Britain transferred the south-east to Australia. It then became known as the Territory of Papua. When World War I broke out in 1914, Australia took German New Guinea. In 1921 the League of Nations gave Australia a mandate to rule the area, which was named the Territory of New Guinea.

Japan invaded New Guinea in 1942, but the Allies reconquered it in 1944. In 1949, Papua and New Guinea were combined into the Territory of Papua and New Guinea. In 1973, the Territory achieved self-government as a prelude to full independence as Papua New Guinea in 1975.

POLITICS

Since independence, the government has worked to develop mineral reserves. One of the most valuable reserves was a copper mine at Panguna on Bougainville. Conflict developed when the people of Bougainville demanded a larger share in mining profits.

Following an insurrection, the Bougainville Revolutionary Army proclaimed independence in 1990. Bougainville's secession was not recognized internationally. In 1992 and 1996, Papua New Guinea launched offensives against the rebels. The use of highly paid mercenaries

ECONOMY

Papua New Guinea is a 'lower-middle-income' developing country. Agriculture employs 75% of the workforce, many at subsistence level. Minerals, notably copper and gold, are the most valuable exports. Unemployment is high and aid from Australia makes up a significant proportion of the economy.

PORT MORESBY

Capital of Papua New Guinea, on the south-east coast of New Guinea, built around Fairfax Harbour, the island's largest harbour. Settled by the British in the 1880s and named after British explorer John Moresby, its sheltered harbour was the site of an important Allied base in World War II. It developed rapidly in the post-war period. In recent years it has experienced problems with a growing disparity in income, which has led to an increase in crime. Exports include gold, copper and rubber.

PARAGUAY

The front (obverse) side of Paraguay's tricolour flag, which evolved in the early 19th century, contains the state emblem, which displays the May Star, commemorating liberation from Spain in 1811. The reverse side shows the treasury seal – a lion and staff.

The Republic of Paraguay is a landlocked country in South America. Rivers form most of its borders. They include the Paraná in the south and the east, the Pilcomayo (Brazo Sur) in the south-west, and the Paraguay in the north-east. West of the River Paraguay is a region known as the Gran Chaco, which extends into Bolivia and Argentina. The Gran Chaco is mostly flat, but the land rises to the north-west. East of the Paraguay is a region of plains, hills and, in the east, the Paraná Plateau region.

Area 406,752 sq km [157,047 sq mi]
Population 6,506,000
Capital (population) Asunción (1,750,000)
Government Multiparty republic
Ethnic groups Mestizo 95%
Languages Spanish and Guarani (both official)
Religions Roman Catholic 90%, Protestant
Currency Guarani = 100 céntimos
Website www.paraguay.com

CLIMATE

The northern half of Paraguay lies in the tropics, while the southern half is subtropical. Most of the country has a warm, humid climate while the Gran Chaco is the dry and hot. Rainfall is higher on the Paraná Plateau in the south-east.

HISTORY

The Guarani, an Amerindian people, were the indigenous people of what is now Paraguay. Spanish and Portuguese explorers reached the area in the early 16th century. In 1537 a Spanish expedition built a fort at Asunción, which later became the capital of Spain's colonies in south-eastern South America. The Spaniards were attracted by the potential labour supply of the Guarani and the chance to find a short cut to the silver mines of Peru. From the late 16th century, Jesuit missionaries arrived to convert the Guarani to Christianity and to protect them against those who wanted to exploit them as cheap labour. Complaints against the Jesuits' power led to their expulsion in 1767.

From 1776 Paraguay formed part of the Rio de la Plata Viceroyalty, with its capital at Buenos Aires. This proved unpopular, however, and Paraguay broke free in 1811, achieving independence from Buenos Aires in 1813.

Between 1865 and 1870, the disastrous War of the Triple Alliance against Brazil, Argentina and Uruguay cost the country more than half of its 600,000 population and much of its territory. Some territory was regained after the Chaco Wars against Bolivia between 1920 and 1935. A 1947 civil war was followed by a spell of political and economic stability, but while most other South American countries attracted European settlers and foreign capital, Paraguay remained isolated.

POLITICS

In 1954, General Alfredo Stroessner seized power and took the presidency.

his former running mate, General Lino Oviedo, who had been imprisoned for attempting a coup against the previous president, Juan Carlos Wasmosy. In March 1999 Paraguay's vice-president, an opponent of Cubas, was assassinated. Congress impeached Cubas, who resigned and fled to Argentina. In 2003, Nicanor Duarte Frutos was elected president.

ECONOMY

The World Bank classifies Paraguay as a 'lower-middle-income' developing country. Agriculture and forestry are the leading activities, employing 48% of the work force. The country has very large cattle ranches, while crops are grown in the fertile soils of eastern Paraguay. Major exports include cotton, soya beans, timber, vegetable oils, coffee, tannin and meat products. The country has abundant hydroelectricity and exports power to Argentina and Brazil. Its factories produce cement, processed food, leather goods and textiles.

His dictatorship placed great emphasis on infrastructure development. Large hydro-electric power developments made the country self-sufficient in electricity in the 1970s, but displaced tens of thousands of indigenous people. In the 1980s the Itaipu dam, a $20 billion joint project with Brazil, was developed to produce power for export. However, demand slackened and income declined, making it difficult for Paraguay to repay foreign debts incurred on the projects. High inflation and balance of payments problems followed. Stroessner's regime, which had US backing thanks to its anti-Communist stance, was corrupt and nepotistic. He ruled with an increasing disregard for human rights during nearly 35 years of fear and fraud until his former supporters deposed him in 1989. Archives documenting the extent of the Stroessner regime's use of torture and kidnapping were discovered in 1992.

Three elections were held in the 1990s, but democracy remained fragile. In 1998 the newly elected president, Raul Cubas Grau, was threatened with impeachment after issuing a decree freeing

ASUNCIÓN

Capital, chief port and largest city of Paraguay, located on the east bank of the Paraguay River near its junction with the River Pilcomayo. Founded by the Spanish 1536 as a trading post, Asunción was the scene of the Communeros rebellion against Spanish rule in 1721 and was later occupied by Brazil (1868–76). City sites include the Pantéon Nacional, Encarnación Church, National University (1889) and the Catholic University (1960). It is an administrative, industrial and cultural centre. Industries include vegetable oil and textiles.

PERU

Peru's flag was adopted in 1825. The colours are said to have been inspired by a flock of red and white flamingos which the Argentine patriot General José de San Martín saw flying over his marching army when he arrived in 1820 to liberate Peru from Spain.

The Republic of Peru lies in the tropics in western South America. A narrow coastal plain borders the Pacific Ocean in the west. Inland are ranges of the Andes Mountains, which rise to 6,768 m [22,205 ft] at Mount Huascarán, an extinct volcano. The Andes also contain active volcanoes, windswept plateaux, broad valleys and, in the far south, part of Lake Titicaca, the world's highest navigable lake. To the east the Andes descend to a hilly region and a huge plain. Eastern Peru is part of the Amazon basin.

Area 1,285,216 sq km [496,222 sq mi]
Population 28,303,000
Capital (population) Lima (8,180,000)
Government Constitutional republic
Ethnic groups Mestizo (Spanish-Indian) 44%, Creole (mainly African American) 30%, Mayan Indian 11%, Garifuna (Black-Carib Indian) 7%, others 8%
Languages English (official), Creole, Spanish
Religions Roman Catholic 62%, Protestant 30%
Currency Belize dollar = 100 cents
Website www.peru.info/perueng.asp

CLIMATE

The coastal plain is arid. It is cooled by the cold Humboldt Current. El Niño periodically disrupts the current and brings heavy rain. The Andes are cooled by altitude, and many are snow-capped. The eastern lowlands are hot and humid.

HISTORY

Amerindian people reached the area about 12,000 years ago. Several civilizations developed in the Andes region. By about AD 1200, the Inca were established in southern Peru. In 1500, their empire extended from Ecuador to Chile. The Spanish adventurer Francisco Pizarro visited Peru in the 1520s. Hearing of Inca riches, he returned in 1532. By 1533, he had conquered most of Peru.

In 1820, the Argentinian José de San Martín led an army into Peru and declared the country independent. However, Spain still held large areas. In 1823, the Venezuelan Simón Bolívar led another army into Peru and, in 1824, one of

LIMA

Capital and largest city of Peru, on the River Rímac at the foot of the Cerro San Cristóbal. Founded in 1535, it functioned as the capital of Spain's New World colonies until the 19th century. Chilean forces occupied Lima during the War of the Pacific (1881–3). It is the commercial and cultural centre of Peru. With the oil-refining port of Callao, the Lima metropolitan area forms the third-largest city of South America, and handles more than 75% of all Peru's manufacturing. Lima has the oldest university (1551) in the Western Hemisphere.

1993, giving Fujimori increased power. In 1996, Tupac Amaru (MRTA) rebels seized the Japanese ambassador's residence, taking hostages and demanding the release of guerrilla prisoners. The stalemate ended in April 1997, when Peruvian troops freed the remaining 72 hostages.

Fujimori began his third term as president in 2000, but, in November, the Congress declared him 'morally unfit' to govern. He resigned and sought sanctuary in Japan. In his absence he was banned from holding office until 2011. In 2005 the government began extradite proceedings for financial corruption and sanctioning death squads and he was extradited from Chile in 2007. In 2001, Alejandro Toledo became the first Amerindian president of Peru.

2003–4 saw a resurgence of Shining Path guerilla activity. By the time they were finally suppressed in 2006 about 70,000 people had been killed in their rebellion. Guzmán was sentenced to life imprisonment in 2006.

Toledo struggled to fight poverty, and was replaced by Alan Garcia in 2006 elections. In 2007 he claimed limited emergency powers in order to tackle organized crime.

his generals defeated the Spaniards at Ayacucho. The Spaniards surrendered in 1826. Peru suffered much instability throughout the 19th century.

POLITICS
Instability continued into the 20th century. When civilian rule was restored in 1980, a left-wing group called the Sendero Luminoso (Shining Path), began guerrilla warfare against the government. In 1990 Alberto Fujimori, son of Japanese immigrants, became president. In 1992, he suspended the constitution and dismissed the legislature. The guerilla leader, Abimael Guzmán, was arrested but instability continued. A new constitution was introduced in

ECONOMY
The World Bank classifies Peru as a 'lower-middle-income' developing country. Agriculture employs 35% of the workforce and major food crops include beans, maize, potatoes and rice. Coffee, cotton and sugar are the chief cash crops. Many farmers live at subsistence level. Fishing is important, but subject to interruption by El Niño.

Peru is one of the world's main producers of copper, silver and zinc. Iron ore, lead and oil are also produced, while gold is mined in the highlands. Most manufacturing is small-scale.

PHILIPPINES

This flag was adopted in 1946, when the country won its independence from the United States. The eight rays of the large sun represent the eight provinces which led the revolt against Spanish rule in 1898. The three smaller stars stand for the three main island groups.

The Republic of the Philippines is an island country in south-eastern Asia. It includes about 7,100 islands, of which 2,770 are named and about 1,000 are inhabited. Luzon and Mindanao, the two largest islands, make up more than two-thirds of the country.

The land is mainly mountainous. It is also unstable and prone to earthquakes. The islands have several active volcanoes, one of which is the highest peak, Mount Apo, and reaches 2,954 m [9,692 ft].

Area 300,000 sq km [115,830 sq mi]
Population 89,469,000
Capital (population) Manila (10,677,000)
Government Multiparty republic
Ethnic groups Christian Malay 92%, Muslim Malay 4%, Chinese and others
Languages Filipino (Tagalog) and English (both official), Spanish and many others
Religions Roman Catholic 83%, Protestant 9%, Islam 5%
Currency Philippine peso = 100 centavos
Website www.gov.ph

CLIMATE

The climate is tropical, with high temperatures all year. The dry season runs between December and April. The rest of the year is wet. Typhoons periodically strike the east coast, bringing high rainfall.

MANILA

°C / °F

Temperature

Precipitation
2083mm/82in

J F M A M J J A S O N D

HISTORY

The first European to reach the Philippines was Ferdinand Magellan in 1521. Spanish explorers claimed the region in 1565 when they established their first permanent settlement on Cebu. Manila was founded in 1571. The Spaniards regarded their new territory as a stepping-stone to the Spice Islands to the south. Spain also converted most of the people, except the Muslims on Mindanao and Sulu, to Roman Catholicism.

The economy grew from the late 18th century when the islands were opened up to foreign trade. In 1896 a secret rev-olutionary society called Katipunan launched a revolt against Spanish rule. The revolt was put down and the rebel leader Emilio Aguinaldo left the country. In 1898 the United States declared war

MANILA

Capital of the Philippines, on Manila Bay, south-west Luzon island. It is the industrial, commercial and administrative heart of the Philippines. The River Pasig bisects the city. On the south bank stands the old walled city (Intramuros), built by the Spanish in the 16th century on the site of a Muslim settlement. It became a trading centre for the Pacific area. Farther south lies Ermita, the administrative and tourist centre. Japan occupied the city in 1942 and in 1945 a battle between Japanese and Allied forces destroyed the old city.

the islands. The Philippines finally achieved independence in 1946.

POLITICS

Until 1971, the country was governed under a constitution based on that of the United States. In 1971 constitutional changes were proposed, but President Ferdinand Marcos declared martial law before they could be ratified. In 1977 the opposition leader, Benigno Aquino Jr, was sentenced to death. He was granted a stay of execution and fled to the US. Martial law was lifted in 1981, but Aquino was killed on his return to the Philippines in 1983.

Marcos claimed the presidency again after fraudulent 1986 elections. His opponent Corazon Aquino, Benigno Aquino's widow, launched a campaign of civil disobedience. Marcos lost the support of the US, and Aquino became president.

Gloria Macapagal-Arroyo was elected president in 2001. Her government sought to suppress Muslim separatists in the southern Philippines. Allegations of corruption led to an unsuccessful coup attempt in 2003. Gloria Arroyo was re-elected in 2004. A ceasefire was agreed in the south with the Moro Islamic Liberation Front, but it broke down in 2005. 2007 saw government successes against the Islamists.

ECONOMY

The Philippines is a developing country with a 'lower-middle-income' economy. Agriculture employs 40% of the workforce. Rice and maize are the main food crops, along with cassava, coconuts, coffee, cocoa, fruits, sugar cane, sweet potatoes and tobacco. Farm animals include water buffalo, goats and pigs.

Forests cover nearly half of the land and forestry is a valuable industry. Sea fishing is also important and shellfish are obtained from inshore waters.

on Spain, and the first major engagement was the destruction of all the Spanish ships in Manila Bay. Aguinaldo returned to the Philippines and formed an army which fought alongside the Americans. He proclaimed the Philippines an independent nation and a peace treaty between Spain and the United States was signed with the US taking over the government of the Philippines. However, Aguinaldo still wanted independence and fighting continued between 1899 and 1901.

The Philippines became a self-governing US Commonwealth in 1935 and were guaranteed full independence after a ten-year transitional period. During World War II Japanese troops occupied

POLAND

Poland's flag was adopted when the country became a republic in 1919. Its colours were taken from the 13th-century coat of arms of a white eagle on a red field. This coat of arms still appears on Poland's merchant flag.

The Republic of Poland faces the Baltic Sea in north-central Europe. Behind the lagoon-fringed coast is a broad plain. The land rises to a plateau region in the south-east of the country. The Sudeten Highlands straddle the border with the Czech Republic. Part of the Carpathian Range lies on the south-eastern border with the Slovak Republic.

Area 323,250 sq km [124,807 sq mi]
Population 38,537,000
Capital (population) Warsaw (1,626,000)
Government Multiparty republic
Ethnic groups
Polish 97%, Belarusian, Ukranian, German
Languages Polish (official)
Religions Roman Catholic 95%, Eastern Orthodox
Currency Zloty = 100 groszy
Website www.poland.pl

CLIMATE

Poland's climate is influenced by its geographical position. Warm, moist air masses come from the west, while cold air masses come from the north and east. Summers are warm, winters cold and snowy.

HISTORY

Poland first became a unified kingdom in the 11th century. It reached its greatest heights in the 16th century and was united with Lithuania in 1569. In the 17th century it fell into decline and in the 18th century Russia took control. In the 1790s it was divided between Russia and Prussia, and Poland ceased to exist as an independent state. In 1815 the country was partitioned between Austria, Prussia and Russia. 19th century uprisings against Russian rule were suppressed.

In World War I the region was conquered by Germany. Poland regained its independence in 1918 and captured Warsaw from Russia in 1920. In 1939 Germany and the Soviet Union secretly agreed to divide Poland, then overran the country in a sudden invasion. Germany conquered the remainder of the country in 1941 and killed c. 6 million during their occupation, including almost all of the country's 3 million Jews. After Germany's defeat in 1945, the Soviet Union reconstituted Poland under new boundaries. It lost land and population to the Soviet Union, but was granted parts of Germany as far west as the River Oder. Soviet pressure imposed a Communist government in 1947.

WARSAW

Capital and largest city of Poland, on the River Vistula. It dates from the 11th century and became Poland's capital in 1596. Controlled by Russia from 1813 to 1915, German troops occupied it during World War I. The city was devastated in World War II. After the war the old town was painstakingly reconstructed and Warsaw became a major transport and industrial centre.

POLITICS

In the 1970s, economic difficulties heightened opposition to Communist rule. In 1980 Lech Walesa founded Solidarity, an independent union which sought political reform. Despite repression, Solidarity weakened Communist power, and in 1989 a coalition government was formed between Solidarity and the Communists. In 1990, the Communist Party was dissolved and Walesa became president. He faced many problems in Poland's rapid but disruptive shift to a free-market economy. Solidarity divided in 1990 over the speed of reform.

In 1995, former Communist Aleksander Krasniewski defeated Walesa in presidential elections, but continued to follow westward-looking policies. Poland became a member of NATO in 1999 and of the EU in 2004. Having lost elections in 1997, Krasniewski was re-elected president in 2000. In 2005, right-wing candidate Lech Kaczynski was elected president. In 2006 his twin brother Jaroslav became prime minister.

ECONOMY

The economy has grown rapidly, but unemployment remains a problem. Manufacturing is important, and products include chemicals, machinery, ships, steel and textiles. Coal is mined on a large scale.

There is a large but inefficient agricultural sector. Crops include barley, potatoes, rye, sugar beet and wheat.

PORTUGAL

Portugal's colours, which were adopted in 1910 when the country became a republic, represent the soldiers who died in the war (red) and hope (green). The armillary sphere – an early navigational instrument – reflects Portugal's leading role in world exploration.

The Portuguese Republic shares the Iberian Peninsula with Spain. It is the most westerly of Europe's mainland countries. The land rises from the coastal plains on the Atlantic Ocean to the western edge of the huge plateau, or Meseta, which occupies most of the Iberian Peninsula. In central Portugal, the Sera da Estrela contains Portugal's highest point, at 1,993 m [6,537 ft]. Portugal also contains two autonomous regions, the Azores and Madeira island groups.

Area 88,797 sq km [34,285 sq mi]
Population 10,606,000
Capital (population) Lisbon (1,977,000)
Government Multiparty republic
Ethnic groups Portuguese 99%
Languages Portuguese (official)
Religions Roman Catholic 94%, Protestant
Currency Euro = 100 cents
Website www.portugal.org

CLIMATE

Winds blowing in from the Atlantic Ocean moderate the climate. Portugal experiences cooler summers and milder winters than other lands on the same latitude.

HISTORY

The Romans completed their conquest of the Iberian Peninsula around 2,000 years ago and Christianity was introduced in the 4th century AD. The Romans called Portugal Lusitania. Following the collapse of the Roman Empire in the 5th century, Portugal was conquered by the Christian Visigoths, but in the early 8th century, the Iberian Peninsula was conquered by Muslim Moors. The Christians strove to drive out the Muslims and, by the mid-13th century, they had retaken Portugal and most of Spain.

In 1143, Portugal became a separate country, independent from Spain. In the 15th century, the Portuguese, who were skilled navigators, led the 'Age of Exploration', pioneering routes around Africa onwards to Asia.

Portugal set up colonies in Africa and Asia, though the most valuable was Brazil. Portugal became wealthy through trade and the exploitation of its colonies, but its power began to decline in the 16th century, when it could no longer defend its far-flung empire. Spain ruled Portugal from 1580 until 1640, when Portugal's independence was restored by John, Duke of Braganza, who took the title of John IV. England supported Portuguese independence and several times defended it from invasion by Spain and its allies. Brazil declared independence in 1822, dramatically reducing the size of the Portuguese empire.

POLITICS

Portugal became a republic in 1910, but its first attempts at democracy led to great instability. Portugal fought alongside the Allies in World War I. A coup in 1926 brought an army group to power. They abolished the parliament and set up a dictatorial regime. In 1928, they selected António de Oliviera Salazar, an economist, as minister of finance. He country's colonies. Free elections were held in 1978 and full democracy was restored in 1982, when a new constitution abolished the military government and reduced the powers of the president.

Portugal joined the European Community (now the EU) in 1986, and in 1999 became one of the 12 EU countries to adopt the euro, the single currency of the EU. In 2005 the Socialists, led by the moderate José Socrates, won a decisive victory in parliamentary elections.

ECONOMY

Although its economy was growing strongly in the late 1990s, Portugal remains one of the EU's poorer members. Agriculture and fishing were the mainstays of the economy until the mid-20th century, but manufacturing is now the most valuable sector. Textiles, processed food, paper products and machinery are important manufactures. Major crops include grapes for wine-making, olives, potatoes, rice, maize and wheat. Cattle and other livestock are raised and fishing catches include cod, sardines and tuna.

Forest products including timber and cork are important, though forest fires often cause much damage.

LISBON (LISBOA)

Capital, largest city and chief port of Portugal, at the mouth of the River Tagus, on the Atlantic Ocean. An ancient Phoenician settlement, the Romans conquered the city in 205 BC. After Teutonic invasions in the 5th century AD, it fell to the Moors in 716. In 1147, the Portuguese reclaimed Lisbon and in 1260 it became the capital. It declined under Spanish occupation (1580–1640). In 1755, an earthquake devastated the city and Marques de Pombal oversaw its reconstruction. It is an international port and tourist centre.

became prime minister in 1932 and ruled as a dictator from 1933. After World War II, when other European powers' colonies began to gain independence, Salazar was determined to maintain his country's empire. Colonial wars weakened Portugal's economy. Salazar suffered a stroke in 1968 and died two years later. His successor, Marcello Caetano, was overthrown by another military coup in 1974 and the new military leaders set about granting independence to the

QATAR

The vertical serrated white stripe, added at the request of the British, denotes friendly Arab states. The nine-point serrated line indicates that Qatar is the ninth member of the reconciled Emirates of the Arabian Gulf. The maroon area represents blood shed in the 19th century wars.

The State of Qatar occupies a long, narrow peninsula jutting into the Persian Gulf. The peninsula is about 200 km [124 mi] long, with a greatest width of 90 km [56 mi]. The land is mostly flat desert covered by gravel and loose, wind-blown sand. Sand dunes occur in the south-east. There are also some barren salt flats. The highest point, on a central limestone plateau, is only 98 m [321 ft] above sea level. Qatar also includes several offshore islands and coral reefs. Fresh water is scarce and much of the water supply comes from desalination plants.

Area 11,437 sq km [4,415 sq mi]
Population 885,000
Capital (population) Doha (264,000)
Government Absolute monarchy
Ethnic groups Arab 40%, Pakistani 18%, Indian 18%, Iranian 10%
Languages Arabic (official), English
Religions Islam 95% (all native Qataris are Wahhabi Sunni)
Currency Rial = 100 dirham
Website http://english.mofa.gov.qa

CLIMATE

The weather from May to September is extremely hot and dry, with the temperatures soaring to 49°C [120°F]. Sand and dust storms are common. Winters are mild to warm, with the weather generally sunny and pleasant. The total annual rainfall seldom exceeds 100 mm [4 in]. Most of the rain occurs in the winter months.

HISTORY

In the 18th century, Bedouin established trading settlements along the coast of the peninsula. Since the mid-19th century, members of the Al-Thani family have been the leaders of Qatar. Between 1871 and 1913 the Ottoman Turks, with Qatar's consent, occupied a garrison on the peninsula. In 1916, Qatar agreed that Britain would take responsibility for the country's foreign affairs. Oil was struck in 1939 but exploitation was delayed by World War II. Commercial exploitation began in 1949, leading to rapid development. Oil revenues contributed to the modernization of the country's infrastructure.

In 1968, Britain announced that it would withdraw its forces from the Gulf. Qatar negotiated with Bahrain and the United Arab Emirates concerning the formation of a federation, but this proposal was finally rejected.

POLITICS

Qatar became fully independent on 3 September, 1971. In 1972, because of rivalries in the ruling family, the deputy ruler Khalifa bin Hamad Al Thani seized power from his cousin, Emir Ahmad in Al-Thani, in a coup. In 1982 Qatar, together with Bahrain, Kuwait, Oman, Saudi Arabia and the United Arab Emirates, united to form the Gulf Co-operation Council, which is concerned with such matters as defence and economic development.

MAP SCALE 51°E
Persian Gulf
0 10 20 30 km
0 10 miles

Qatar is an emirate, ruled by the Emir and his appointed Council of Ministers. Municipal elections in 1999 heralded moves towards democracy. A new constitution introduced in 2004 provided for a Consultative Council. This Council consisted of 45 members, two-thirds of whom would be elected by the public and one-third appointed by the Emir. The new constitution came into force in 2005, and elections were planned for 2007.

Qatar resolved long-standing boundary disputes with Bahrain and Saudi Arabia in 2001. In 2003, the US Central Command forward base in Qatar became the main centre for the US-led invasion of Iraq.

ECONOMY

The people of Qatar enjoy a high standard of living, deriving from oil revenues. The country has a comprehensive welfare system, and many of its services are free or highly subsidized. Oil production has given Qatar one of the world's highest per capita incomes and accounts for more than 80% of the country's export revenues. Qatar has about 5% of the world's proven oil reserves and more than 15% of the world's proven natural gas reserves.

Besides oil refining, Qatar produces ammonia, cement, fertilizers, petrochemicals and steel. It is trying to attract investment to diversify away from oil. Wells have been dug to develop agriculture, and products include beef, dairy products, fruits, poultry and vegetables.

In 1990, following Iraq's invasion of Kuwait, Qatar agreed to allow foreign troops on its soil. In 1991, Qatari troops were involved in the military campaign to free Kuwait. In 1995, Qatar signed a security pact with the United States. A bloodless coup occurred in 1995, when the heir apparent, Sheikh Hamad bin Khalifa Al-Thani, deposed his father while he was abroad. An attempted counter-coup failed in 1996.

In 1996, the Al-Jazeera satellite television station was launched in Qatar. It won a reputation for tackling controversial issues connected with the Arab world. In 2001, it became famous when it aired recorded statements by al-Qaeda leader Osama bin Laden. From 2003 it provided graphic coverage of the conflict in Iraq.

DOHA

Capital of Qatar, on the east coast of the Qatar peninsula, in the Persian (Arabian) Gulf. Doha was a small fishing village until oil production began in 1949. It is now a modern city and trade centre. Industries include oil refining, shipping, engineering.

ROMANIA

Romania's flag, adopted in 1948, uses colours from the arms of the provinces, which united in 1861 to form Romania. A central coat of arms, added in 1965, was deleted in 1990 after the fall of the Communist regime of the dictator Nicolae Ceaucescu.

Romania is on the Black Sea in eastern Europe. Eastern and southern Romania form part of the Danube River Basin. The delta region where the river flows into the Black Sea is one of Europe's finest wetlands. The southern part of the coast contains several resorts.

The country is dominated by the Carpathian mountains which curve around the plateaux of Transylvania in central Romania. The southern arm of the mountains, including Mount Moldoveanu (2,543 m [8,341 ft]), is known as the Transylvanian Alps. On the border with Serbia, the River Danube (Dunav/Dunărea) has cut a gorge, the Iron Gate (Portile de Fier) whose rapids have been tamed by a huge dam. Forests cover large areas in Transylvania and the Carpathians, while farmland dominates in the Danubian lowlands and the country's central plateaux.

Area 238,391 sq km [92,043 sq mi]
Population 22,304,000
Capital (population) Bucharest (1,764,000)
Government Multiparty republic
Ethnic groups Romanian 89%, Hungarian 7%, Roma 2%, Ukranian
Languages Romanian (official), Hungarian, German
Religions Eastern Orthodox 87%, Protestant 7%, Roman Catholic 5%
Currency Leu = 100 bani
Website www.gov.ro/engleza/

CLIMATE

Romania has hot summers and cold winters. Rainfall is heaviest in spring and early summer, when thundery showers are common.

HISTORY

Around 2,300 years ago, Romania was called Dacia. After the Romans conquered the area in AD 106, the Dacians embraced Roman culture and language so completely that the region became known as Romania. The first step towards the creation of the modern state occurred in the 14th century when two principalities were formed, Walachia or Valachi in the south and Moldavia in the east. Both were conquered by the Ottoman Turks around 1500.

Walachia and Moldavia united in 1861 to form modern Romania. After World War I Romania, which had fought with the Allies, gained much land, including Transylvania. This almost doubled the country's size and population. In 1939 Romania lost territory to Bulgaria, Hungary and the Soviet Union. Romania fought alongside Germany in World War II, and was occupied by the USSR in 1944. Hungary returned northern Transylvania to Romania in 1945, but Bulgaria and the Soviet Union kept former Romanian territory when King Michael was forcibly deposed.

In the 1960s, Romania's Communist Party, led by Gheorghe Gheorghiu-Dej, began to oppose Soviet control. Nicolae Ceaucescu, who became Communist Party chief in 1965, continued the policy.

Under Ceaucescu, Romania developed industries based on its oil and natural gas reserves. His rule was corrupt and ment in 1991. There were strikes and protests against the new authorities and also against the effects of the switch to a market economy, which caused food shortages, rampant inflation and increased unemployment. Foreign investment was sluggish, deterred by the political instability. Presidential elections in 1996 led to defeat for Iliescu and victory for the centre-right Emil Constantinescu. In 2000, Iliescu was re-elected president. His government continued privatization policies. In 2004, Traian Baiescu was elected to succeed him. Romania became a member of NATO in 2004 and joined the EU in January 2007. In June the EU criticised Romania for insufficient progress at reducing corruption.

ECONOMY

According to the World Bank, Romania is a 'lower-middle-income' economy. Oil and natural gas are the chief mineral resources and the aluminium, copper, lead and zinc industries use domestic supplies. Manufactures include cement, processed food, petroleum products, textiles and wood. Agriculture employs nearly a third of the workforce. Crops include fruits, maize, potatoes, sugar beet and wheat. Sheep are the chief livestock.

self-seeking, but he won plaudits from the West for his independent stance against Soviet control, including a knighthood from Queen Elizabeth II. However, he pursued a strict Stalinist approach and the remorseless industrialization and urbanization programmes of the 1970s caused severe debt. In the 1980s, he cut imports and diverted output to exports. Self-sufficiency turned to subsistence and shortages, with savage rationing of food and energy.

In December 1989 mass anti-government demonstrations were held in Timisoara, along with protests across Romania. Security forces fired on crowds, causing many deaths. After army units joined the protests, Nicolae Ceaucescu and his wife Elena fled from Bucharest. Both were executed on Christmas Day on charges of genocide and corruption. A provisional government of the National Salvation Front (NSF), took control, much of the old administrative apparatus was dismantled, and the Communist Party was dissolved.

POLITICS

In May 1990, the NSF under Ion Iliescu won Romania's first free elections since World War II, a result judged to be flawed but not fraudulent. A new constitution enshrining pluralist democracy and a market economy was passed by parlia-

BUCHAREST (BUCURESTI)

Capital and largest city of Romania, on the River Dimbovita, southern Romania. Founded in the 14th century on an important trade route, it became capital in 1862 and was occupied by Germany in both World Wars. It is an industrial, commercial and cultural centre. The seat of the patriarch of the Romanian Orthodox Church, it has notable churches, museums and galleries.

RUSSIA

In August 1991, Russia's traditional flag, which had first been used in 1699, was restored as Russia's national flag. It uses colours from the flag of the Netherlands. This flag was suppressed when Russia was part of the Soviet Union.

The Russian Federation is the world's largest country. About 25% lies west of the Ural Mountains (Uralskie Gory) in European Russia, where 80% of the population lives. It is mostly flat or undulating, but the land rises to the Caucasus Mountains in the south, with Russia's highest peak, Elbrus (5,633 m [18,481 ft]). Siberia contains vast plains and plateaux, with mountains in the east and south. The Kamchatka peninsula in the far east has many active volcanoes. Russia contains many of the world's longest rivers, including Yenisey-Angara and the Ob-Irtysh. It also includes part of the world's largest inland body of water, the Caspian Sea, and Lake Baikal, the world's deepest lake.

Area 17,075,400 sq km [6,592,812 sq mi]
Population 142,894,000
Capital (population) Moscow (10,672,000)
Government Federal multiparty republic
Ethnic groups Russian 82%, Tatar 4%, Ukrainian 3%, Chuvash 1%, more than 100 others
Languages Russian (official), many others
Religions Russian Orthodox, Islam Judaism
Currency Russian rouble = 100 kopeks
Website www.kremlin.ru/eng

CLIMATE

The climate of European Russia, including Moscow, is continental with cold and snowy winters and warm summers. South and central Siberia have a harsher, drier climate. The far north has a severe, frozen arctic climate.

HISTORY

In the 9th century AD, a state called Kievan Rus was formed at the junction of the forest and the steppe in what is now Ukraine. Other states then formed farther to the north and all were eventually united under the principality of Muscovy. In the 13th century, Mongol armies from the east penetrated the forests and held sway over the Slavic peoples there. It was only in the 16th century that the Mongol yoke was thrown off as the Russians under Ivan the Terrible (1530–84) began to advance across the steppes.

There began a period of expansion from the core area of Slavic settlement to the south, east and west. Expansion across Siberia was rapid and the first Russian settlement on the Pacific, Okhotsk, was established in 1649. By 1696 Azov, the key to the Black Sea, was secured. A series of struggles in the 17th and 18th centuries against the Swedes and the Poles resulted in the addition of the Gulf of Finland, the Baltic coast and part of Poland to the growing Russian Empire, while, in the 19th century, the Caucasus, Central Asia and new territories in the Far East were added.

The Russian Revolution took place in 1917. Tsar Nicholas II was forced to abdicate and a Communist Bolshevik government was established under Vladimir Ilyich Lenin (1870–1924). The Union of Soviet Socialist Republics (the USSR or the Soviet Union) was established in 1922.

From 1924 Joseph Stalin introduced a socialist economic programme, suppressing all opposition both within the party and among the population. His authority was consolidated with the Great Purge, a period of widespread arrests and executions which reached its peak in 1937. His introduction of five-year plans and collective farming transformed the USSR from a largely peasant society to a major world industrial power by the end of the 1930s. Collectivization was violently resisted by many peasants, resulting in millions of casualties from famine and mass repression of peasants (*kulaks*) by the authorities. After Stalin's death the Soviet leaders modified some policies, but remained true to the principles of Communism until Mikhail Gorbachev changed the face of Russia in the 1980s.

The USSR joined World War II (the Great Patriotic War) in June 1941. The armed forces of the USSR inflicted about 80% of losses suffered by German land forces in World War II (about 3 million soldiers). The USSR suffered enormous losses, with 25 million dead.

Under Soviet rule, changes took place in the distribution of the population so that the former pattern of a small highly populated core and 'empty' periphery began to break down as the government encouraged development in the east. A far higher proportion of the population lives east of the Ural Mountains than before the Revolution. Migration to the towns and cities has also been marked, and by 1997, 73% of the population lived in cities and towns.

In the 1980s, Mikhail Gorbachev sought to introduce economic and political reforms necessitated by the failures of Communist economic policies. This was a time of *glasnost* (openness) and *perestroika* (restructuring). The Soviet Union broke up in December 1991. Russia maintained contact with 11 of the 15 former Soviet republics through a loose confederation called the Commonwealth of Independent States (CIS).

POLITICS

Despite Gorbachev's efforts at reform, his successor Boris Yeltsin inherited an economy in crisis. The abolition of price controls sent the cost of basic commodities rocketing, there were food shortages,

MOSCOW (MOSKVA)

Capital of Russia and largest city in Europe, on the River Moskva. Inhabited since Neolithic times, but not recorded until 1147. It was a principality by the end of the 13th century, and in 1367 the first stone walls of the Kremlin were constructed. By the end of the 14th century, Moscow emerged as the focus of Russian opposition to the Mongols. Moscow was the capital of the Grand Duchy of Russia from 1547 to 1712, when the capital moved to St Petersburg. Occupied by Napoleon in 1812 who was forced to flee when the city burned to the ground, in 1918, following the Russian Revolution, it became the capital of the Soviet Union. The failure of the German army to seize the city in 1941 was the Nazis' first major setback in World War II. The Kremlin is the centre of the city, and the administrative heart of the country. Adjoining it are Red Square, the Lenin Mausoleum, and the 16th-century cathedral of St Basil the Blessed.

and unemployment rose rapidly. Despite these difficulties, including rising corruption and crime, the government's programme of reforms was supported in a 1993 referendum and Yeltsin was returned as president in July 1996. Yeltsin resigned in 1999 due to poor health, and appointed the prime minister Vladimir Putin as the acting president. Putin was elected president by a landslide in 2000.

Secessionists in Chechnya began fighting during the 1990s which flared up into full-scale war in 1999. The conflict slowed in 2000, but Chechen terrorists began attacks on Russian cities. After the attacks on the USA on 11 September 2001 Putin supported US campaigns against terrorism and Afghanistan's Taliban, but relations soured when Russia opposed the attack on Iraq in 2003. The secessionist conflict in Chechnya had been largely suppressed by 2006, leaving the region devastated. In 2005 and 2006 high oil and gas prices boosted the economy and government funds and gave Russia massive global influence once again. Putin's government has concentrated political power and media control in the president's hands, and democratic institutions remain weak.

ECONOMY

In the early 1990s the World Bank described Russia as a 'lower-middle-income' economy. In 1997 Russia was admitted to the Council of Europe, the same year Russia attended the G7 summit, suggesting that it was now counted among the world's leading economies. Industry is the chief activity and light industries producing consumer goods are becoming important. Russia's resources include oil and natural gas, coal, timber, metal ores and hydroelectric power. Russia is a major producer of farm products. Major crops include barley, flax, fruit, oats, rye, potatoes, sugar beet, sunflower seeds, vegetables and wheat.

RWANDA

Rwanda's new flag was adopted in 2002. The colour blue is used to symbolize peace and tranquillity. Yellow represents wealth as the country works to achieve sustainable economic growth, while green denotes prosperity, work and productivity. The 24-ray golden sun symbolizes new hope.

The Republic of Rwanda is Africa's most densely populated country. It is a small state in the heart of Africa. The western border is formed by Lake Kivu and the River Ruzizi. Rwanda has a rugged landscape, dominated by high, volcanic mountains, rising to Mount Karisimbi, at 4,507 m [14,787 ft]. The capital, Kigali, stands on the central plateau. East Burundi consists of stepped plateaux, which descend to the lakes and marshland of the Kagera National Park on the Tanzania border.

The lush rainforests in the west are one of the last refuges for the mountain gorilla. Many of Rwanda's forests have been cleared and 35% of the land is now arable. The steep mountain slopes are intensively cultivated. Despite contour ploughing, heavy rains cause severe soil erosion.

Area 26,338 sq km [10,169 sq mi]
Population 8,648,000
Capital (population) Kigali (234,000)
Government Republic
Ethnic groups Hutu 84%, Tutsi 15%, Twa 1%
Languages French, English and Kinyarwanda (all official)
Religions Roman Catholic 57%, Protestant 26%, Adventist 11%, Islam 5%
Currency Rwandan franc = 100 centimes
Website www.gov.rw

CLIMATE

Temperatures in Kigali are moderated by the altitude. The rainfall is abundant, but much heavier rain falls on the western mountains. The dry season is June–August. The floor of the Great Rift Valley has a warmer and drier climate than the rest of the country.

HISTORY

The Twa, a pygmy people, were the first known people to live in Rwanda. About 1,000 years ago, a farming people, the Hutu, settled in the area, gradually displacing the Twa.

From the 15th century, a cattle-owning people from the north, the Tutsi, began to dominate the Hutu, who had to serve the Tutsi overlords.

By the late 18th century, Rwanda and Burundi formed a single Tutsi-dominated state, ruled by a King (Mwami). In 1890, Germany conquered the area and subsumed it into German East Africa. During World War 1, Belgian forces occupied both Rwanda and Burundi in 1916. In 1919, it became part of the Belgian League of Nations mandate territory of Ruanda-Urundi (which in 1946 became a UN Trust Territory). The Hutu majority intensified their demands for political representation. In 1959, the Tutsi Mwami died. The ensuing civil war between Hutus and Tutsis claimed more than 150,000 lives. Hutu victory led to a mass exodus of Tutsis. The Hutu Emancipation Movement, led by Grégoire Kayibanda, won the 1960 elections. In 1961, Rwanda declared itself a republic. Belgium granted independence in 1962, and Kayibanda became president.

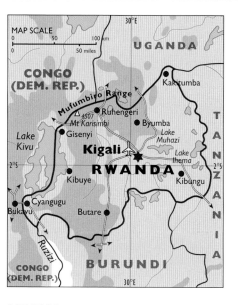

the entire region. In 1997, Rwandan troops supported Laurent Kabila's successful overthrow of President Mobutu in Zaïre. Kabila failed to expel the Hutu militia from Congo, and Rwanda switched to supporting rebel forces. In 1998, the UN International Criminal Tribunal sentenced Rwanda's former prime minister Jean Kambanda to life imprisonment for genocide. Paul Kagame became president in 2000. His government brought stability but suppressed opposition. He was re-elected in biased 2003 elections.

In the 2000s, prosecutions of the genocide's perpetrators began in both Belgium and Tanzania. Rwanda finally withdrew from DR Congo in late 2002 after signing a peace deal with Kinshasa.

POLITICS

Rwanda was subject to continual Tutsi incursions from Burundi and Uganda. In 1973, Major General Habyarimana overthrew Kayibanda in a military coup. In 1978, Habyarimana became president. Drought devastated Rwanda in the 1980s. More than 50,000 refugees fled to Burundi. In 1990, the Tutsi-dominated Rwandan Patriotic Front (RPF) invaded Rwanda, forcing Habyarimana to adopt a multiparty constitution. In April 1994, Habyarimana and the president of Burundi died in a rocket attack. The Hutu army and militia launched an act of genocide against the Tutsi minority, massacring more than 800,000 of them.

In July 1994, an RPF offensive toppled the government, creating 2 million Hutu refugees. A government of national unity, comprising Tutsis and Hutus, emerged. More than 50,000 people died in refugee camps in eastern Zaïre (now DR Congo). Hutu militia controlled the camps, and their leaders later faced prosecution for genocide. The sheer number of refugees (in 1995, 1 million in Zaïre and 500,000 in Tanzania) destabilized

ECONOMY

According to the World Bank, Rwanda is a 'low-income' developing country. Agriculture employs 90% of the workforce, many at subsistence level. Chief food crops include bananas, beans, cassava, plantains, potatoes, sorghum and sweet potatoes. Some farmers raise cattle and other livestock. The chief cash crop and export is coffee, followed by tea, hides and skins. Rwanda also produces pyrethrum, which is used to make insecticide. The country produces some cassiterite (tin ore) and wolframite (tungsten ore). Manufacturing is small-scale and include beverages, cement and sugar.

KIGALI

Capital city lying in the centre of Rwanda. It was a trade centre during the period of German and Belgian colonial administration, becoming the capital when Rwanda achieved independence in 1962. Industries include tin mining, cotton and coffee.

SAUDI ARABIA

Saudi Arabia's flag was adopted in 1938. It is the only national flag with an inscription as its main feature. The Arabic inscription above the sword means 'There is no God but Allah, and Muhammad is the Prophet of Allah.'

The Kingdom of Saudi Arabia occupies about three-quarters of the Arabian Peninsula in south-west Asia. The land is mostly desert and includes the largest expanse of sand in the world, the Rub' al Khali (Empty Quarter), covering an area of 647,500 sq km [250,000 sq mi]. Mountains to the west border the Red Sea plains.

Area 2,149,690 sq km [829,995 sq mi]
Population 27,020,000
Capital (population) Riyadh (5,514,000)
Government Absolute monarchy
Ethnic groups Arab 90%, Afro-Asian 10%
Languages Arabic (official)
Religions Islam 100%
Currency Saudi riyal = 100 halalas
Website www.saudinf.com

CLIMATE

Saudi Arabia has a hot, dry climate. In the summer, the temperatures are extremely high and often exceed 40°C [104°F], although the nights are cool.

HISTORY

Saudi Arabia contains the two holiest places in Islam. Mecca was the birthplace of the Prophet Muhammad in 570, while Medina was where Muhammad and his followers settled in 622 .

In the mid-15th century, the Saud Dynasty established control over a small area near present-day Riyadh. In the mid-18th century an alliance was established with a religious leader, Muhammad Ibn Abd al-Wahhab, who wanted to restore strict observance of Islam. The Wahhabi movement swept across Arabia and the Saud family took over areas converted to the Wahhabi beliefs. By the early 19th century, they had taken Mecca and Medina. The Ottoman governor of Egypt attacked to halt their expansion, and by the late 19th century, most of the Arabian Peninsula was under the rule of Ottoman Turks.

In 1902 Abd al-Aziz Ibn Saud led a force from Kuwait, where he had been living in exile, and captured Riyadh. From 1906, the Saud family gradually won control over the territory held by their ancestors and extended their land following the defeat of the Ottoman Empire in World War I. After further conquests in the 1920s, Ibn Saud proclaimed the country the Kingdom of Saudi Arabia in 1932.

POLITICS

The first major oil discovery was made in 1938, and full-scale production began after World War II. Saudi Arabia eventually became the world's leading oil exporter and highly influential in the Arab world, where it played a major role in supplying development aid.

Saudi Arabia supported Egypt, Jordan and Syria in the Six-Day War against Israel in 1967. It did not send troops, but gave aid to the Arab combatants.

King Fahd suffered a stroke in 1995 and appointed his half-brother, Crown Prince Abdullah Ibn Abdulaziz, to act on his behalf. Fahd died in 2005 and Abdullah succeeded him as king.

Although assisted by a Consultative Council, the monarch holds executive and legislative powers and is also the imam (supreme religious ruler). Saudi Arabia is an absolute monarchy with no formal constitution.

Saudi Arabia supported Iraq in its 1980s war with Iran. After Iraq's invasion of Kuwait in 1990, Saudi Arabia asked for the protection of Western forces against possible Iraqi aggression. In 1991, the country assisted in the quick victory over Iraq in the Gulf War.

Relations between Saudi Arabia and the United States became strained following the terrorist attacks on the US on 11 September 2001, in part because Osama bin Laden and many of his followers were Saudi-born. Saudi authorities denounced the attacks and severed relations with the Taliban in Afghanistan. In 2003 and 2004 Saudi Arabia was attacked by terrorists linked to Al-Qaeda.

The government held nationwide municipal elections in 2005, its first exercise in democracy. However, political parties are banned and activists who publicly broach the subject of reform risk jail.

ECONOMY

Saudi Arabia is a wealthy country. It has about 25% of the world's known oil reserves, and oil and oil products make up 85% of its exports.

RIYADH

Capital of Saudi Arabia, in the east-central part of the country, 380 km [235 mi] inland from the Persian Gulf. In the early 19th century it was the domain of the Saudi dynasty, and it became capital of Saudi Arabia in 1932. The chief industry is oil refining.

331

SENEGAL

This flag was adopted in 1960 when Senegal became independent from France. It uses the three colours that symbolize African unity. It is identical to the flag of Mali, except for the five-pointed green star. This star symbolizes the Muslim faith of most of the people.

The Republic of Senegal is situated on the north-west coast of Africa. The volcanic Cape Verde (Cap Vert), on which Dakar stands, is the most westerly point in Africa. The country entirely surrounds Gambia. The Atlantic coastline from St Louis to Dakar is sandy. Plains cover most of Senegal, though the land rises gently in the southeast. The north forms part of the Sahel. The main rivers are the Sénégal, which forms the north border, and the Casamance in the south. The River Gambia flows into the Gambia.

Desert and semi-desert cover northeast Senegal. In central Senegal, dry grasslands and scrub predominate. Mangrove swamps border parts of the south coast. The far south is a region of tropical savanna, though large areas have been cleared for farming. Senegal has several protected parks, of which the largest is the Niokolo-Kobo Wildlife Park.

Area 196,722 sq km [75,954 sq mi]
Population 11,987,000
Capital (population) Dakar (2,313,000)
Government Multiparty republic
Ethnic groups Wolof 44%, Pular 24%, Serer 15%
Languages French (official), tribal languages
Religions Islam 94%, Christianity (mainly Roman Catholic) 5%, traditional beliefs 1%
Currency CFA franc = 100 centimes
Website www.senegalembassy.co.uk

CLIMATE

Dakar has a tropical climate, with a short rainy season between June and September when moist winds blow from the southwest. Temperatures are higher inland. Rainfall is greatest in the south.

HISTORY

From the 6th century to the 10th, Senegal formed part of the Empire of ancient Ghana. Between the 10th and 14th centuries, the Tukolor state of Tekrur dominated the Sénégal valley. The Almoravid dynasty of Zenega Berbers introduced Islam, and it is from the Zenega that Senegal got its name. In the 14th century, the Wolof established the Jolof Empire. The Songhai Empire began to dominate the region.

In 1444, Portuguese sailors became the first Europeans to reach Cape Verde. Trading stations were rapidly established in the area. In the 17th century, France and the Netherlands replaced Portuguese influence. France gradually gained control of the valuable slave trade and founded St Louis in 1658. By 1763 Britain had expelled the French from Senegal and in 1765, set up

THE SAHEL

A band of semi-arid scrub and savanna grassland in Africa to the south of the Sahara. Over the past 30 years the Sahara has encroached on the northern Sahel in the world's most notorious example of desertification.

a coup in the Gambia. In 1982 the two countries joined to form the Confederation of Senegambia, but the union collapsed in 1989. From 1989 to 1992, Senegal was at war with Mauritania.

In 2000, Diouf was surprisingly beaten in presidential elections by veteran opposition leader Abdoulaye Wade of the Senegalese Democratic Party, ending 40 years of Socialist Party rule. In 2004, the government announced a peace treaty with separatist rebels in the southern Casamance province. 2007 elections gave Wade a second term, though the opposition accused them of unfairness and boycotted parliamentary elections later in the year.

Senegambia, the first British colony in Africa. In 1783 France regained control and in the mid-19th century, battled for control of the interior. The French founded Dakar in 1857. In 1895, Senegal became a French colony within the Federation of French West Africa. In 1902, the capital of this huge empire transferred from St Louis to Dakar. Dakar became a major trading centre. In 1946, Senegal joined the French Union.

POLITICS

In 1959, Senegal joined French Sudan to form the Federation of Mali. Senegal separated in 1960 to become the Republic of Senegal, while the remainder of the federation became Mali. Senegal's first post-colonial president, Léopold Sédar Senghor, was a noted African poet.

After a failed coup against him in 1962, Senghor gradually assumed wider powers and made the country a one-party state. During the 1960s Senegal's economy deteriorated and a succession of droughts caused starvation and widespread civil unrest. In 1974, Senegal was a founding member of the West African Economic Community.

Senghor continued in office until 1981, when he was succeeded by the prime minister, Abdou Diouf. In that same year, Senegalese troops suppressed

ECONOMY

According to the World Bank, Senegal is a 'lower-middle-income' developing country. Agriculture still employs 65% of the population, though many farmers produce little more than they need to feed their families. Food crops include cassava, millet and rice. Senegal is the world's sixth largest producer of groundnuts. Phosphates are the chief resource mined, and Senegal also refines oil imported from Gabon and Nigeria. Fishing is important.

DAKAR

Capital and largest city of Senegal. Founded in 1857 as a French fort, the city grew rapidly with the arrival of a railway (1885). A major Atlantic port, it later became capital of French West Africa. There is a Roman Catholic cathedral and a presidential palace. Dakar has excellent educational and medical facilities, including the Pasteur Institute. Industries include textiles, oil refining, brewing.

SERBIA

The tricolour flag uses the Pan-Slavic colours of blue, white and red. These colours derive from the 19th-century flag of Russia.

Serbia is a landlocked country in eastern Europe, formerly part of Yugoslavia. When Yugoslavia broke up in the early 1990s Serbia included Montenegro, and in 2003 it adopted the name of the Union of Serbia and Montenegro. In 2006 they divided into separate countries.

Serbia's mountainous regions include the Dinaric Alps and part of the Balkan Mountains. The Pannonian Plains, drained by the River Danube, are in the north.

Area 102,173 sq km [39,449 sq mi]
Population 9,396,000
Capital (population) Belgrade (1,116,000)
Government Federal republic
Ethnic groups Serb 66%, Albanian 17%, Hungarian 3%, others
Languages Serbian (official), Albanian
Religions Orthodox 65%, Islam 19%, others
Currency New dinar = 100 paras
Website www.srbija.sr.gov.yu/?change_lang=en

CLIMATE

The country is mostly composed of upland areas with a continental climate. The highlands have cold, snowy winters while the Pannonian Plains have hot, arid summers, and heavy rains in the spring and autumn.

HISTORY

Slavs moved into the area c. 1,500 years ago. They adopted Orthodox Christianity under Byzantine rule. Serbia was the leading Balkan power until its defeat by the Turks in 1389. In 1459, it became a province of the Ottoman Empire.

In 1829, Serbia gained autonomy under Russian protection. In 1867, Milan Obrenović began a war in support of a rebellion against Turkish rule in Bosnia and Herzegovina. Russia intervened to aid Serbia and, in 1878, Turkey finally granted Serbia independence.

In 1908 Serbia joined with Bosnia and Herzegovina in the Balkan League, which defeated Turkey in 1912 but split into feuding factions. In 1913 Serbia defeated Bulgaria in the second Balkan War, but its expansion antagonized Austria and was a major contributing factor to the outbreak of World War 1.

In 1918 the region united in the Kingdom of the Serbs, Croats and Slovenes, ruled by Peter I of Serbia. Alexander I succeeded Peter I in 1921. In 1929 he renamed the country Yugoslavia and abolished the constitution, ruling as a dictator. After the Germans invaded in 1941, the royalist *chetniks* and Communist partisans under Josip Broz Tito fought both the Germans and each other.

POLITICS

Yugoslavia split in 1991–2 as Bosnia-Herzegovina, Croatia, Macedonia and Slovenia each proclaimed their independence. Serbia and Montenegro were all that remained of Yugoslavia.

Fighting broke out in Croatia and Bosnia-Herzegovina as rival groups struggled for power. In 1992 the United Nations withdrew recognition of Yugoslavia because of its failure to halt from Kosovo and the KLA was disbanded. In 2000, the Yugoslav leader Slobodan Milošević was defeated in presidential elections. From 2002 he faced charges at the UN War Crimes Tribunal in The Hague, but he died in 2006 before his trial could be completed.

Serbia and Montenegro made their first steps towards separation in 2003, renaming the country the Union of Serbia and Montenegro and making both semi-independent. Montenegro voted for full independence in a 2006 referendum, which Serbia accepted.

In 2007 the UN unveiled a draft plan for an independant Kosovo, which currently remains under NATO occupation and UN governance. Serbia rejected the plan, which then stalled.

ECONOMY

Resources include bauxite, coal, copper and other metals, together with oil and natural gas. Manufactures include aluminium, machinery, plastics, steel, textiles and vehicles. Agriculture remains important.

atrocities committed by Serbs living in Croatia and Bosnia-Herzegovina. In 1995 Yugoslavia took part in talks that led to the Dayton Peace Accord, but it had problems of its own as international sanctions struck the war-ravaged economy.

In 1998 the fragility of the region was again highlighted in Kosovo, a region in southern Serbia where most people are Albanian-speaking Muslims. Serbians forced Muslim Albanians to leave their homes, but were opposed by the Kosovo Liberation Army (KLA). The Serbs hit back and thousands of civilians fled.

In March 1999, after failed attempts to find an agreement, NATO forces launched aerial attacks on administrative and industrial targets in Kosovo and Serbia. Serbian forces stepped up attacks on Albanian-speaking villages, forcibly expelling the people, who fled into Albania and Macedonia. The NATO offensive ended when Serbian forces withdrew

BELGRADE (BEOGRAD)

Capital of Serbia, at the confluence of the Sava and Danube rivers. Belgrade became capital of Serbia in the 12th century, but fell to the Ottoman Turks in 1521. Freed from Ottoman rule in 1867, it became capital of the newly created Yugoslavia in 1929. The city suffered much damage under German occupation in World War II. In 1999 Belgrade was further damaged by Allied air strikes after Milosevic sent federal troops into Kosovo. In October 2000, more than 300,000 people marched through the streets of Belgrade, forcing Milosevic to step down as president.

SIERRA LEONE

The green of the flag represents the nation's agriculture and its lush mountain slopes. Blue stands for the waters of the Atlantic that lap Sierra Leone's coast. White symbolizes the desire for peace, justice and unity.

The Republic of Sierra Leone, on the west coast of Africa, is about the same size as the Republic of Ireland. The coast contains several deep estuaries in the north, with lagoons in the south. The most prominent feature is the mountainous Freetown (or Sierra Leone) peninsula. North of the peninsula is the River Rokel estuary, west Africa's best natural harbour. Behind the coastal plain, the land rises to mountains, with the highest peak, Loma Mansa, reaching 1,948 m [6,391 ft].

Swamps cover large areas near the coast. Inland, much of the rainforest has been destroyed. The north is largely covered by tropical savanna.

Area 71,740 sq km [27,699 sq mi]
Population 6,005,000
Capital (population) Freetown (470,000)
Government Single-party republic
Ethnic groups Native African tribes 90%
Languages English (official), Mende, Temne, Krio
Religions Islam 60%, traditional beliefs 30%, Christianity 10%
Currency Leone = 100 cents
Website www.visitsierraleone.org

CLIMATE

The climate is tropical, with heavy rainfall. In the north, it is dry between December and March. In the south, it is dry in January and February.

HISTORY

Sailors from Portugal reached the coast in 1460. In the 16th century, the area became a source of slaves. Freetown was founded in 1787 as a home for freed slaves, and in 1808 the settlement became a British Crown Colony. The interior was made a British Protectorate in 1896, and in 1951 the Protectorate and Colony united.

Sierra Leone gained independence in 1961. In 1978 it became a one-party state.

POLITICS

A 1991 referendum voted for the restoration of multiparty democracy, but the military seized power in 1992. A civil war raged between government forces and the Revolutionary United Front (RUF). The RUF fought to end foreign interference and to nationalize the country's diamond mines. After 1996 elec-

FREETOWN

Capital and chief port of Sierra Leone, west Africa. First explored by the Portuguese in the 15th century and visited by Sir John Hawkins in 1562. Freetown was founded by the British in 1787 as a settlement for freed slaves from England, Nova Scotia and Jamaica. It was the capital of British West Africa (1808–74). West Africa's oldest university, Fourah Bay, was founded here in 1827. Freetown was made capital of independent Sierra Leone in 1961. Industries include platinum, gold, diamonds, oil refining and palm oil.

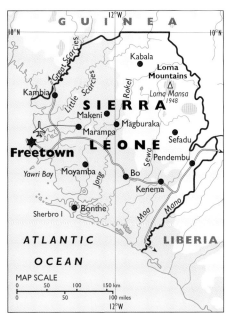

arrived to bolster the UN peace-keeping effort. Disarmament continued throughout 2001 through a UN-brokered peace plan. Sankoh was captured and, in 2002, the war appeared to be over. About 50,000 people had been killed. Rebel raids from Liberia in 2003 failed to disturb the country's fragile peace. Stability was gradually restored and, in late 2005, the last contingent of UN soldiers left the country. Ernest Bai Koroma was elected president in 2007.

ECONOMY

The World Bank classifies Sierra Leone among the 'low-income' economies. Agriculture provides a living for 70% of the workforce, though farming is mostly at subsistence level. Food crops include cassava, maize and rice, the staple food, and export crops include cocoa and coffee. The most valuable exports include diamonds, bauxite and rutile (titanium ore).

tions, Ahmad Tejan Kabbah led a civilian government. In 1997, Major Johnny Paul Koroma seized power in a military coup. The Economic Community of West African States (ECOWAS) imposed sanctions and Nigeria led an intervention force that restored Kabbah as president in 1998.

A 1999 peace treaty and the arrival of UN peace-keeping forces seemed to signal an end to the civil war, but in 2000 RUF rebels, led by Foday Sankoh and backed by Liberia, abducted UN troops and renewed the war. British soldiers

ROKEL RIVER

The Rokel River rises in the Guinea Highlands in northern Sierra Leone. It drains a 10,620 sq km [4,100 sq mi] basin and flows for 400 km [250 mi] in the direction of the Atlantic, emptying into the River Rokel estuary, the best natural harbour in West Africa.

DIAMOND

Crystalline form of carbon (C). The hardest natural substance known, it is found in kimberlite pipes and alluvial deposits. Appearance varies according to impurities. Bort, inferior in crystal and colour, carborondo, an opaque grey to black variety, and other non-gem varieties are used in industry. Industrial diamonds are used as abrasives, bearings in precision instruments such as watches, and in the cutting heads of tools. Most synthetic diamonds, made by subjecting graphite and a catalyst to high pressure and temperatures of 3,000°C [5,400°F], are fit only for industry. Diamonds are weighed in carats (0.2 g).

SINGAPORE

Singapore's flag was adopted in 1959 and it was retained when Singapore became part of the Federation of Malaysia in 1963. The crescent stands for the nation's ascent. The stars stand for Singapore's aims of democracy, peace, progress, justice and equality.

The Republic of Singapore is an island country at the southern tip of the Malay Peninsula. It consists of the large Singapore Island and 59 small islands, 20 of which are inhabited.

Singapore Island is 42 km [26 mi] wide and 28 km [14 mi] across. It is linked to the peninsula by a 1,056 m [3,465 ft] long causeway. The land is mostly low-lying; the highest point, Bukit Timah, is only 176 m [577 ft] above sea level. Its strategic position, at the convergence of some of the world's most vital shipping lanes, ensured its growth.

Rainforest once covered Singapore, but forests now grow on only 5% of the land. Today, about 50% of Singapore is built up. The distinction between island and city has all but disappeared. Most of the rest consists of open spaces, including parks, granite quarries and inland waters. Farmland covers 4% of the land and plantations of permanent crops make up 7%.

Area 683 sq km [264 sq mi]
Population 4,492,000
Capital (population) Singapore City (4,372,000)
Government Multiparty republic
Ethnic groups
Chinese 77%, Malay 14%, Indian 8%
Languages Chinese, Malay, Tamil and English (all official)
Religions Buddhism, Islam, Hinduism, Christianity
Currency Singaporean dollar = 100 cents
Website www.gov.sg

CLIMATE

Singapore has a hot, humid equatorial climate, with temperatures averaging 30°C [86°F]. Total average annual rainfall is, 2,413 mm [95 in], with rain occuring (on average) 180 days each year.

HISTORY

According to legend, Singapore was founded in 1299. It was first called Temasak ('sea town'), but was renamed Singapura ('city of the lion'). Singapore soon became a busy trading centre within the Sumatran Srivijaya kingdom. Javanese raiders destroyed it in 1377. Singapore became a trading centre for the powerful Malacca sultanate. Later, from the 16th century, it came under the control of the sultanate of Johor.

In 1819, Sir Thomas Stamford Raffles, agent of the British East India Company, made a treaty with the Sultan of Johor which allowed the British to build a settlement on Singapore Island. In 1826,

SIR THOMAS STAMFORD RAFFLES (1781–1826)

British colonial administrator, founder of Singapore City. When Java returned to Dutch rule (1816), Raffles bought the island of Singapore for the British East India Company (1819). Under his guidance, it developed rapidly into a prosperous free port.

Singapore, Pinang and Malacca formed the Straits Settlement. Singapore soon became the most important British trading centre in South-east Asia, and the Straits Settlement became a Crown Colony in 1867. Despite British defensive reinforcements in the early 20th century, Japanese forces seized the island in 1942.

POLITICS

British rule returned in 1945. In 1946, the Straits Settlement dissolved and Singapore became a separate colony. In 1959, Singapore achieved self-government. Following a referendum in 1963, Singapore merged with Malaya, Sarawak, and Sabah to form the Federation of Malaysia. In 1965 Singapore broke away from the Federation to become an independent republic within the Commonwealth of Nations.

The People's Action Party (PAP) has ruled Singapore since 1959. Its leader, Lee Kuan Yew, served as prime minister from 1959 until 1990, when he resigned and was succeeded by Goh Chok Tong. Under the PAP the economy has expanded rapidly, although some people consider that the PAP's rule has been dictatorial and oversensitive to criticism. In 2004 Lee Hsien Loong, eldest son of Lee Kuan Yew, succeeded Goh Chok Tong as prime minister and called for a more open society. Support for political opposition groups has slowly increased, but the electoral system remains heavily in favour of the PAP.

ECONOMY

The World Bank classifies Singapore as a 'high-income' economy. It is one of the world's fastest growing 'tiger' economies. Historically, Singapore's economy has been based on transshipment, and this remains a vital component. It is one of the world's busiest ports, annually handling more than 290 million tonnes of cargo. Post-1945 the economy diversified. Singapore has a highly skilled and productive workforce. The service sector employs 65% of the workforce; banking and insurance provide many jobs.

Manufacturing is the largest export sector. Industries include computers and electronics, telecommunications, chemicals, machinery, scientific instruments, ships and textiles. It has a large oil refinery. Agriculture is relatively unimportant. Most farming is highly intensive, and farmers use the latest technology and industrial methods.

SINGAPORE CITY

The capital of Singapore, on Singapore Island, the largest island in the Republic of Singapore at the mouth of the Singapore River. The city is home to an ethnic mix of Chinese, Malaysians and Indians, and English is the main language. It has a high standard of living due to its healthy export-based economy. Tourism is an important industry, with attractions including the Singapore Zoological Gardens and the Jurong Bird Park, well-known shopping areas such as Orchard Road and the city's famous cuisine.

SLOVAK REPUBLIC

The flag uses the typical red, white and blue Slavic colours. The coat of arms is taken from part of the Hungarian arms and shows a double cross set on three hills to commemorate the arrival of Christianity in the Carpathian region in the 9th century.

The Slovak Republic (Slovakia), is a predominantly mountainous country and part of the Carpathians which divide the Slovak Republic from Poland is found in the north. The highest peak, Gerlachovka, reaches 2,655 m [8,711 ft]) and lies in the scenic Tatra (Tatry) Mountains on the Polish border.

Forests cover much of the mountain slopes and there is also extensive pasture. The south-western Danubian lowlands form a fertile lowland region. The Danube forms part of the southern border with Hungary.

Area 49,012 sq km [18,924 sq mi]
Population 5,439,000
Capital (population) Bratislava (449,000)
Government Multiparty republic
Ethnic groups Slovak 86%, Hungarian 11%
Languages Slovak (official), Hungarian
Religions Roman Catholic 60%, Protestant 8%, Orthodox 4%, others
Currency Slovak koruna = 100 halierov
Website www.government.gov.sk/english

CLIMATE

Slovakia has a transitional climate, in between the mild conditions of western Europe and the continental conditions of Russia to the east. The conditions in Kosice, eastern Slovakia, are fairly typical. Temperatures can range from −3°C [27°F] in January to 20°C [68°F] in July. Kosice has an average annual rainfall of 600 mm [24 in]. The mountains have a more extreme climate, and snow or rain falls throughout the year.

HISTORY

Slav peoples settled in the region in the 5th century AD. In the 9th century, the region, together with Bohemia and Moravia in what is now the Czech Republic, became part of the Greater Moravian Empire. Hungarians conquered this empire in 907 and ruled for nearly a thousand years. Religious wars in the 15th century led many Czech nobles to settle in what is now the Slovak Republic. Hungary was defeated by the Turkish Ottomans in 1526 and, soon afterwards, the Ottomans occupied much of eastern and central Hungary. As a result, the centre of Hungarian power shifted into Slovakia.

Slovak nationalism developed from the late 18th century, but it was kept in check by the Hungarians, who enforced 'Magyarization'. In 1867, Hungary and Austria were united to form the dual monarchy of Austria-Hungary. At the end of World War I, Austria-Hungary collapsed and the Czechs and Slovaks united to form a new nation called Czechoslovakia. In 1938, Hungary forced Czechoslovakia to give up several areas with large Hungarian populations. These areas included Kosice in the east.

In 1939, fearing that it might be divided up between Germany, Poland and Hungary, Slovakia declared itself independent. The country was then conquered by Germany. At the end of World War II, Slovakia again became part of

Czechoslovakia. Communists seized control in 1948. In the late 1960s many Czechs and Slovaks, led by Alexander Dubček, tried to reform the Communist system. This movement, known as 'the Prague Spring', was put down in 1968 by Soviet troops. Demands for democracy re-emerged in the 1980s, when Soviet leader Mikhail Gorbachev launched a series of reforms in the USSR.

POLITICS

At the end of November 1989, Czechoslovakia's parliament abolished the Communist Party's sole right to govern. In December, the head of the Communist govermnent resigned. Non-Communists led by dissident playwright Václav Havel formed a new government, which won a majority in 1990 elections.

In the elections of 1992, the Movement for Democratic Slovakia, led by Vladimir Mečiar, campaigned for Slovak independence and won a majority in Slovakia's parliament. The Slovak National Council then approved a new constitution for the Slovak Republic, which came into existence on 1 January 1993.

The Slovak Republic became a member of the OECD in 1997 and maintained close contacts with its former partner. Slovak independence raised national aspirations among the Magyar-speaking community. Relations with Hungary deteriorated in 1996 when the Slovak government re-arranged administrative regions, which the Hungarian

minority claimed under-represented them politically. The government also made Slovak the only official language. The government's autocratic rule and apparent tolerance of organized crime led to mounting international criticism. In 1998, Mečiar's party was defeated in a general election by a four-party coalition and Mikuláš Dzurinda, leader of the centre-right Slovak Democratic Coalition, became prime minister. Dzurinda narrowly won the parliamentary elections of 2002 and his government continued its policy of strengthening ties with the West. Slovakia became a member of both NATO and the EU in 2004. In 2006 elections Dzurinda was replaced by Robert Fico.

ECONOMY

Communist governments developed manufacturing industries, producing chemicals, machinery, steel and weapons. Since the late 1980s, many state-run businesses have been handed over to private owners. Manufacturing employs around 33% of workers. Bratislava and Kosice are the chief industrial cities. Products include ceramics, machinery and steel. The armaments industry is based at Martin, in the north-west.

Farming employs about 12% of the workforce. Major crops include barley, grapes for wine-making, maize, sugar beet and wheat.

BRATISLAVA

Capital of Slovakia, on the River Danube, western Slovakia. It became part of Hungary after the 13th century, and was the Hungarian capital from 1526–1784. Incorporated into Czechoslovakia in 1918, it became the capital of Slovakia in 1992. Industries include oil refining, textiles, chemicals, electrical goods.

SLOVENIA

Slovenia's flag, which was based on the flag of Russia, was originally adopted in 1848. Under Communist rule, a red star appeared at the centre. This flag, which was adopted in 1991 when Slovenia proclaimed its independence, has a new emblem, the national coat of arms.

The Republic of Slovenia was one of the six republics which made up Yugoslavia. Much of the land is mountainous and forested. The highest peak is Mount Triglav (2,863 m [9,393 ft]) in the Julian Alps (Julijske Alpe), an extension of the main Alpine ranges in the north-west. Much of central and eastern Slovenia is hilly. The River Sava which flows through central Slovenia is a tributary of the Danube, as is the Drava in the north-east.

Central Slovenia contains the limestone Karst region, with numerous underground streams and cave networks. The Postojna Caves, south-west of Ljubljana, are among the largest in Europe. The country has a short coastline on the Adriatic Sea.

Forests cover about half of Slovenia. Mountain pines grow on higher slopes, with beech, oak and hornbeam at lower levels. The Karst region has relatively sparse vegetation because of the lack of surface water. Farmland covers about a third of Slovenia.

Area 20,256 sq km [7,821 sq mi]
Population 2,010,000
Capital (population) Ljubljana (264,000)
Government Multiparty republic
Ethnic groups Slovene 92%, Croat 1%, Serb, Hungarian, Bosniak
Languages Slovenian (official), Serbo-Croatian
Religions Mainly Roman Catholic
Currency Tolar = 100 stotin
Website www.slovenia-tourism.si

HISTORY

The ancestors of the Slovenes, the western branch of a group of people known as the South Slavs, settled in the area around 1,400 years ago. An independent Slovene state was formed in AD 623, but the area came under Bavarian-Frankish rule in 748. The ruling family of Austria, the Habsburgs, took control of the region in 1278. Apart from a short period of French rule between 1809 and 1815, it remained under Austrian control until 1918, when the dual monarchy of Austria-Hungary collapsed.

At the end of World War I, Slovenia became part of a new country called the Kingdom of the Serbs, Croats and Slovenes, renamed Yugoslavia in 1929. Slovenia was invaded by Germany and Italy in 1941 and was partitioned between them and Hungary. At the end of the war, Slovenia again became one of the six republics of Yugoslavia.

In the late 1960s and early 1970s, some Slovenes called for the secession of their federal republic from Yugoslavia, but the dissidents were removed from the Communist Party by President Josip Broz Tito, whose strong rule maintained the unity of his country.

CLIMATE

The Slovenian coast has a very mild Mediterranean climate. The climate inland is more continental, with snow capping the mountains in winter. Eastern Slovenia has cold winters and hot summers. Rain occurs in every month in Ljubljana, late summer being the rainiest.

became the new president. Janez Drnovšek, of the centre-left Liberal Democratic Party, became prime minister, heading a coalition government. The Liberal Democrat coalition government was returned again in 1996 and 2000, and Drnovšek became president in 2002. Slovenia became a member of NATO and the EU in 2004. Later that year, the centre-right Slovenian Democratic Party topped the polls in parliamentary elections and a centre-right coalition was formed. In 2007 Slovenia adopted the euro as sole currency.

POLITICS

After Tito's death in 1980, the federal government in Belgrade found it increasingly difficult to maintain the unity of the disparate elements of the population. It was also weakened by the fact that Communism was increasingly seen to have failed in Eastern Europe and the Soviet Union. In 1990, Slovenia held multiparty elections and a non-Communist coalition was formed to rule the country.

Slovenia and neighbouring Croatia proclaimed their independence in June 1991, but these acts were not accepted by the central government. After a few days of fighting between the Slovene militia and Yugoslav forces, Slovenia, the most ethnically homogenous of Yugoslavia's six component parts, found ready support from Italy and Austria (which had Slovene minorities of about 100,000 and 80,000, respectively), as well as Germany (an early supporter of Slovene independence). After a three-month moratorium, during which there was a negotiated, peaceful withdrawal, Slovenia became independent on 8 October 1991, thereby avoiding the conflict that was to plague several other former Yugoslav states.

Slovenia's independence was recognized by the European Community in 1992. Multiparty elections were held and Milan Kučan, a former Communist,

ECONOMY

The reform of the formerly state-run economy, and the fighting in areas to the south caused problems for Slovenia. It remains one of the fastest-growing economies in Europe.

Manufacturing is the principal activity and manufactures include chemicals, machinery and transport equipment, metal goods and textiles. Slovenia mines some iron ore, lead, lignite and mercury. The farming sector's leading crops are maize, potatoes and wheat.

LJUBLJANA

Capital and largest city of Slovenia, at the confluence of the rivers Sava and Ljubljanica. In 34 BC Roman Emperor Augustus founded Ljubljana as Emona. From 1244 it was the capital of Carniola, an Austrian province of the Habsburg Empire. During the 19th century, it was the centre of the Slovene nationalist movement. The city remained under Austrian rule until 1918, when it became part of the Kingdom of Serbs, Croats, and Slovenes (later Yugoslavia). When Slovenia achieved independence in 1991, Ljubljana became the national capital.

SOMALIA

This flag was adopted in 1960, when Italian Somaliland in the south united with British Somaliland in the north to form Somalia. The colours are based on the United Nations flag and the points of the star represent the five regions of East Africa where Somalis live.

Somalia lies in a region known as the 'Horn of Africa'. A narrow, mostly barren, coastal plain borders the Indian Ocean and the Gulf of Aden. In the interior, the land rises to a plateau at 1,000 m [3,300 ft]. In the north is a highland region. The south contains the only rivers, the Juba and the Scebeli.

Much of Somalia is dry grassland or semi-desert. There are areas of wooded grassland, with trees such as acacia and baobab. Plants are most abundant in the the lower Juba valley.

Area 637,657 sq km [246,199 sq mi]
Population 8,863,000
Capital (population) Mogadishu (1,257,000)
Government
Transitional, parliamentary federal government
Ethnic groups Somali 85%, Bantu, Arab, others
Languages
Somali (official), Arabic, English, Italian
Religions Islam (Sunni Muslim)
Currency CFA franc = 100 centimes
Website www.unsomalia.net

CLIMATE

Rainfall is light throughout, the wettest regions being in the south and the northern mountains. The country is prone to droughts, with temperatures on the plateaux and the plains often reaching 32°C [90°F].

HISTORY

In the 7th century, Arab traders established coastal settlements and introduced Islam. Around 900, Mogadishu was founded as a trading centre. The interest of European imperial powers increased after the opening of the Suez Canal in 1869. In 1887, Britain established a Protectorate in northern Somalia. Italy formed a Protectorate in the central region in 1889, and extended its power to the south by 1905. In 1896 France established a colony in Djibouti.

Colonial boundaries split Somalis into five areas: the two Somalilands, Djibouti, Ethiopia and Kenya. In 1936 Italian

MOGADISHU

Capital and chief port of Somalia, on the Indian Ocean. It was founded by Arabs in the 10th century. In the 16th century, the Portuguese captured the city and it became a cornerstone of their trade with Africa. In 1871 the Sultan of Zanzibar took control. He first leased (1892) and then sold (1905) the port to the Italians. The city then became the capital of Italian Somaliland. It was occupied by the British during World War II. In 1960, Mogadishu became the capital of independent Somalia. The civil war of the 1980s/1990s devastated the city, its population swelled by refugees escaping famine and drought in the outlying regions. In 1992, UN troops flew in to control aid distribution but withdrew in 1995 after little success.

was overthrown and the United Somali Congress, led by Ali Mahdi Muhammad, gained power. Somalia disintegrated into civil war between rival clans. The Ethiopian-backed Somali National Movement gained control of the north-west and seceded as the Somaliland Republic. An attack by the Somali National Alliance, led by General Muhammad Aideed, shattered Mogadishu. War and drought resulted in a devastating famine. The UN was slow to provide relief; US marines led a taskforce to aid food distribution, but became embroiled in conflict with Somali warlords.

In 1994 30 US marines died in the fighting and US forces withdrew. Civil strife continued, and in 1996 Aideed was killed. In 2004 an interim government was set up, but it controlled so little of Somalia that it withdrew to Kenya for safety. In mid 2006 the Union of Islamic Courts defeated the warlords and took power in Mogadishu, with considerable public support. In December 2006 the transitional government, backed by Ethiopian forces, attacked and captured Mogadishu and claimed the country, though fighting continued in the south-west. The transitional government struggled to control the capital and prevent a return to warlord rule.

Somaliland united with the Somali regions of Ethiopia to form Italian East Africa. During World War II, Italy invaded British Somaliland, but British forces conquered the region in 1941 and ruled both Somalilands until 1950, when Italian Somaliland returned to Italy as a UN Trust Territory. In 1960, both Somalilands gained independence and joined together to form the United Republic of Somalia.

POLITICS

In 1969 the army, led by Siad Barre, seized power and formed a socialist Islamic republic. During the 1970s Somalia and Ethiopia fought for control of the Ogaden Desert, inhabited mainly by Somali nomads. In 1978 Ethiopia forced Somalia to withdraw but resistance continued, forcing 1 million refugees to flee to Somalia. In 1991 Barre

ECONOMY

Somalia is a developing country whose economy has been shattered by drought and war. Catastrophic flooding in late 1997 displaced tens of thousands of people, further damaging the country's infrastrucure, destroying hopes of economic recovery.

Many Somalis are nomads who raise livestock. Live animals, meat and hides are major exports, plus bananas grown in the wetter south. Other crops include citrus fruits, cotton, maize and sugar cane.

345

South Africa's flag was first flown in 1994 when the country adopted a new, non-racial constitution. It incorporates the red, white and blue of former colonial powers, Britain and the Netherlands, together with the green, black and gold of black organizations.

The Republic of South Africa is geologically very ancient, with few deposits less than 600 million years old. The country can be divided into two main regions: the coastal fringes and the the interior plateau. The plateau is, the southern part of the huge plateau that makes up most of southern Africa.

The interior consists of two main parts. Most of Northern Cape Province and Free State are drained by the Orange River and its right-bank tributaries that flow over level plateaux, varying in height from 1,200 m to 2,000 m [4,000–6,000 ft]. The Northern Province is occupied by the Bushveld, an area of granites and igneous intrusions.

The Fringing Escarpment divides the interior from the coastal fringe. This escarpment makes communication within the country very difficult. In the east the massive basalt-capped rock wall of the Drakensberg, at its most majestic near Mont-aux-Sources, rises to more than 3,000 m [10,000 ft]. The Drakensberg range overlooks KwaZulu-Natal and Eastern Cape coastlands.

In the west there is a similar, though less well developed, divide between the interior plateau and the coastlands. The Fringing Escarpment also parallels the south coast, where it is fronted by a series of ranges, including the folded Cape Ranges.

CLIMATE

Most of South Africa has a mild, sunny climate. Much of the coastal strip, including the city of Cape Town, has warm, dry summers and mild, rainy winters, just like the Mediterranean lands in northern Africa. Inland, large areas are arid.

Area 1,221,037 sq km [471,442 sq mi]
Population 44,188,000
Capital (population) Cape Town (legislative, 2,930,000); Tshwane/Pretoria (administrative, 1,590,000); Bloemfontein (judiciary, 350,000)
Government Multiparty republic
Ethnic groups Black 76%, White 13%, Coloured 9%, Asian 2%
Languages Afrikaans, English, Ndebele, Pedi, Sotho, Swazi, Tsonga, Tswana, Venda, Xhosa and Zulu (all official)
Religions Christianity 68%, Islam 2%, HInduism 1%
Currency Rand = 100 cents
Website www.gov.za

HISTORY

Early inhabitants were the Khoisan (also called Hottentots and Bushmen). However, the majority of the people today are Bantu-speakers from the north, who entered the country and introduced a cattle-keeping, grain-growing culture. Arriving via the plateaux of the northeast, they continued southwards into the well-watered zones below the Fringing Escarpment of KwaZulu-Natal and Eastern Cape. By the 18th century, these people had reached the south-east. They formed large groups, including the Zulu, Xhosa, Sotho and Tswana.

During this time, a group of Europeans was establishing a supply base for the Dutch East India Company on the site of present-day Cape Town. The first group was led by Jan van Riebeeck, who founded the base in 1652. In 1657, some company employees set up their own farms and became known as Boers (farmers). After Britain took over the Cape Town settlement in the early 19th century many Boers, who resented British rule, began to move inland to develop their own Afrikaaner culture. Beginning in 1836, this migration was known as the Great Trek. Their advance

was channelled in the south by parallel coastal ranges, and eventually black and white met near the Kei River. To the north, once the Fringing Escarpment had been overcome, the level plateau surfaces allowed a rapid spread northwards. The Boers founded the Transvaal in 1852 and Orange Free State in 1854.

In 1870, diamonds were found near the site where Kimberley now stands. Both the British and the Boers claimed the area, but Britain annexed it in 1871. In 1880, the Boers rebelled and defeated the British in the First Boer War. In 1886, gold was discovered in the Witwatersrand in what is now Gauteng. Many immigrants, called *uitlanders* (foreigners), flooded to the area. Most of them were British and, to maintain their control, the Boers restricted the British immigrants' freedom. Tension developed, culminating in the Second Boer War (1899–1902). The defeated Boer republics of Orange Free State and Transvaal then surrendered and became British colonies. Meanwhile, British forces had defeated the Zulus and overcome Zulu resistance to European settlement. By 1898, all opposition had been suppressed and the black people had lost their independence.

POLITICS

In 1906, Transvaal was granted self-rule, followed by Orange Free State in 1907. The other two parts of the country, Cape Colony and Natal, already had self-rule. In 1910, the entire country was united as the Union of South Africa, a self-governing country within the British Empire. During World War I, two Boer generals led South African forces against Germany. In German South West Africa (now Namibia), General Louis Botha conquered the Germans, while General Jan Christiaan Smuts led Allied forces in German East Africa (now Tanzania). In 1920, the League of Nations gave South Africa control over South West Africa under a trusteeship agreement. In 1931, Britain granted South Africa full independence as a member of the Commonwealth of Nations.

The development of minerals and urban complexes in South Africa caused an even greater divergence between black and white. The African farmers gained little from the mineral boom. With taxes to pay, they had little alternative but to seek employment in the mines or on European-owned farms. Migrant labour became the normal way of life for many men, while agriculture in black areas stagnated. Groups of Africans took up urban life, living in communities set apart from the white settlements. These townships, with their rudimentary housing often supplemented by shanty dwellings and without any real services, mush-

roomed during World War II and left South Africa with a major housing problem in the late 1940s. Nowhere was this problem greater than in Johannesburg, where a vast complex of brick boxes called SOWETO (South-Western Townships) was built. The contrast between the living standards of blacks and whites increased rapidly.

At the start of World War II, opinion was divided as to whether South Africa should remain neutral or support Britain. The pro-British General Smuts triumphed. He became prime minister, and South African forces served in Ethiopia, northern Africa and Europe. During the war Daniel Malan, a supporter of Afrikaner nationalism, reorganized the National Party. The Nationalists came to power in 1948, with Malan as prime minister, and introduced the policy of apartheid. The African National Congress, which had been founded in 1912, became the leading black opposition group. Opposition to South Africa's segregationist policies mounted around the world. Stung by criticism from Britain and other Commonwealth members, South Africa became a republic and withdrew from the Commonwealth in 1961. In 1966, the United Nations voted to end South Africa's control over South West Africa, although it was not until 1990 that the territory finally became an independent state and was named Namibia.

PRETORIA (TSHWANE)

Administrative capital of South Africa, Gauteng province. Founded in 1855 and named after Andries Pretorius. It became the capital of the Transvaal in 1860, and of the South African Republic in 1881. The Peace of Vereeniging, which ended the South African Wars, was signed here in 1902. In 1910, it became the capital of the Union of South Africa. Pretoria is an important communications centre.

In response to continuing opposition, South Africa repealed some apartheid laws. In 1984, under a new constitution, a new three-house parliament was set up. The three houses were for whites, Asians, and the so-called 'Coloured' non-white minority, but the black majority were still unrepresented. In 1986, the European Community (now the European Union), the Commonwealth and the United States applied sanctions on South Africa, banning trade in certain areas. In 1989, F W de Klerk was elected president and in 1990 he released the banned ANC leader Nelson Mandela from prison.

In the early 1990s, more apartheid laws were repealed. The country began to prepare a new constitution giving all non-whites the right to vote, though progress towards majority rule was marred by fighting between the Zulu-dominated Inkatha Freedom Party and the ANC.

Elections held in 1994 resulted in victory for the ANC, and Nelson Mandela became president. Mandela advocated reconciliation between whites and non-whites, and his government sought to alleviate the poverty of Africans in the townships. The slow rate of progress disappointed many, as did other problems, including an increase in crime and the continuing massive gap in living standards between races. In 1999, following the retirement of Nelson Mandela, his successor Thabo Mbeki led the African National Congress to an overwhelming electoral victory.

Besides poverty, one of the biggest problems facing the country is the high HIV and AIDS rate. It is estimated that one in five South Africans is infected with HIV. The ANC government has been criticized for its poor response to the crisis.

ECONOMY

South Africa is Africa's most developed country. However, most of the black people – rural and urban – are poor, with low standards of living. Natural resources include diamonds and gold, which formed the basis of its economy from the late 19th century. Today, South Africa ranks first in the world in gold production and fifth in diamond production. South Africa also produces coal, chromite, copper, iron ore, manganese, platinum, phosphate rock, silver, uranium and vanadium. Mining and manufacturing are the most valuable economic activities and gold, metals and metal products, and gem diamonds are the chief exports.

Manufactures include chemicals, processed food, iron and steel, machinery, motor vehicles and textiles. The main industrial areas lie in and around the cities of Cape Town, Durban, Johannesburg, Port Elizabeth and Pretoria. Investment in South African mining and manufacturing declined in the 1980s, but foreign companies began to invest again following the abolition of apartheid.

Farmland is limited by the aridity of many areas, but the country produces most of the food it needs and food products make up around 7% of South Africa's exports. Major crops include apples, grapes (for wine-making), maize, oranges, pineapples, sugar cane, tobacco and wheat. Sheep-rearing is important on land which is unfit for arable farming. Other livestock products include beef, dairy products, eggs and milk.

CAPE TOWN

City and seaport at the foot of Table Mountain, South Africa. It is South Africa's legislative capital and the capital of Western Cape province. Founded in 1652 by the Dutch East India Company, it came under British rule in 1795. Places of interest include the Union Parliament, a 17th-century castle, the National Historic Museum and the University of Cape Town (founded 1829). It is an important industrial and commercial centre. Industries: clothing, engineering equipment, motor vehicles, wine.

SPAIN

The colours on the Spanish flag date back to those used by the old kingdom of Aragon in the 12th century. The present design, in which the central yellow stripe is twice as wide as each of the red stripes, was adopted in 1938, during the Civil War.

The Kingdom of Spain is the second largest country in Western Europe after France. It shares the Iberian Peninsula with Portugal. A plateau, called the Meseta, covers most of Spain. Much of it is flat, but crossed by several mountain ranges (*sierras*).

The northern highlands include the Cantabrian Mountains (Cordillera Cantabrica) and the high Pyrenees, which form Spain's border with France. Mulhacén, the highest peak on the Spanish mainland, is in the Sierra Nevada in the south-east. Spain also contains fertile coastal plains. Other lowlands are the Ebro River Basin in the north-east and the Guadalquivir River Basin in the south-west.

Spain also includes the Balearic Islands (Islas Baleares) in the Mediterranean Sea and the Canary Islands off the north-west coast of Africa. Tenerife in the Canary Islands contains Pico de Teide, Spain's highest peak, which reaches 3,718 m [12,918 ft].

Forests lie to the rainier north and north-west, with beech and deciduous oak being common. Towards the drier south and east, Mediterranean pines and evergreen oaks take over, and the forests resemble open parkland. Large areas are matorral, a Mediterranean scrub. Where soils are thin and drought is prevalent, matorral gives way to steppe.

CLIMATE

Spain has the widest range of climate in Western Europe. One of the most striking contrasts is between the humid north and north-west, where winds from the Atlantic bring mild, wet weather throughout the year, and the mainly arid

Area 497,548 sq km [192,103 sq mi]
Population 40,398,000
Capital (population) Madrid (3,017,000)
Government Constitutional monarchy
Ethnic groups Mediterranean and Nordic types
Languages Castillian Spanish (official) 74%, Catalan 17%, Galician 7%, Basque 2%
Religions Roman Catholic 94%, others
Currency Euro = 100 cents
Website www.spain.info

remainder of the country. Droughts are common in much of Spain, though these are occasionally interrupted by thunderstorms.

The Meseta, removed from the influence of the sea, has a continental climate with hot summers and cold winters. In winter, frosts often occur and snow blankets the mountain ranges that rise above the plateau surface. By contrast, the Mediterranean coastlands and the Balearic Islands have mild, moist winters. Summers along the Mediterranean coast are hot and dry. The Canary Islands have mild to warm weather throughout the year.

HISTORY

5,000 years ago, Spain was inhabited by farming people called Iberians. Some historians believe the Basques of northern Spain may be descendants of these people. Around 3,000 years ago, Phoenicians from the eastern Mediterranean reached the Iberian Peninsula and began to establish trading colonies, some on the sites of modern cities such as Cádiz and Málaga. Celtic peoples arrived later from the north, while Greeks reached the east coast of Spain around 600 BC.

In the 5th century BC, Carthaginians conquered much of Spain, but after the Second Punic War (218–201 BC) the Iberian Peninsula gradually came under Roman rule. The Romans made Iberia a Roman province called Hispania.

By 573, the Visigoths had conquered the entire peninsula, including what is now Portugal, and they ruled until the early 8th century when the Muslim Moors invaded from North Africa. They introduced their culture and scholarship, building superb mosques and palaces. In the 11th century, the country began to divide into many small Moorish kingdoms, leaving them open to attack by the Christian kingdoms in the north. Portugal broke away from Spain in the 11th–12th centuries. By the late 13th century, Muslim power was confined to the southern Kingdom of Granada.

The rest of Spain was ruled by the Christian kingdoms of Aragon, Navarre and, the most powerful of all, Castile. In 1469, Prince Ferdinand of Aragon married Princess Isabella of Castile. Ferdinand and Isabella started the Spanish Inquisition which persecuted Jews, Muslims and other non-Roman Catholics. Ferdinand's forces captured the last

351

Muslim stronghold of Granada in 1492 and the Kingdom of Navarre in 1512. This completed the union of Spain.

Ferdinand and Isabella also sponsored the expeditions that began to make Spain a colonial power. By the mid-16th century, Spain ruled a vast overseas empire controlling much of Central and South America, parts of Africa and the Philippines in Asia. A major disaster occurred in 1588, when King Philip II sent a fleet, the Armada, to conquer England, but the English navy and bad weather destroyed half of the Spanish ships. The empire remained strong but went into decline in the late 17th century. By the 20th century only small African territories remained.

A military government was established in 1923 and King Alfonso III allowed General Miguel Primo de Rivera, the prime minister, to rule as a dictator. After Primo de Rivera was forced to resign in 1930, Alfonso called for city elections. Republican candidates scored such a major victory in these elections that he left the country, which subsequently became a republic.

MADRID

Capital and largest city of Spain, lying on a high plain in the centre of Spain on the River Manzanares. It is Europe's highest capital city, at 655 m [2,149 ft]. Founded as a Moorish fortress in the 10th century, Madrid was captured by Alfonso VI of Castile in 1083. In 1561, Philip II moved the capital to Madrid. The French occupied the city during the Peninsular War (1808–14). Madrid expanded considerably in the 19th century. During the Spanish Civil War, it remained loyal to the Republican cause and was under siege for almost three years. Its capitulation in March 1939 brought the war to an end. Modern Madrid is a thriving centre of commerce and industry.

In 1936, the socialist Popular Front won elections. Nationalists under General Francisco Franco (1892–1975) rebelled and started a brutal civil war. Supported by fascist Italy and Nazi Germany, the Nationalists defeated the Reupblican government. In 1939 the war ended and Franco became dictator. During World War II, Spain was pro-Axis but officially neutral.

POLITICS

The revival of Spain's shattered economy began in the 1950s through the growth of manufacturing industries and tourism. As standards of living rose, people began to demand more freedom. After Franco died in 1975 the monarchy was restored and Juan Carlos, grandson of Alfonso III, became king. The ban on political parties was lifted and, in 1977, elections were held. A new constitution making Spain a parliamentary democracy, with the king as head of state, came into effect in December 1978.

From the late 1970s, Spain began to tackle the problem of its regions. In 1980, a regional parliament was set up in the Basque Country (Euskadi in Basque and Pais Vasco in Spanish). Similar parliaments were initiated in Catalonia (Cataluña) in the north-east and Galicia in the north-west. While regional devolution was welcomed in Catalonia and Galicia, it did not end the terrorist campaign of the Basque separatist movement, Euskadi Ta Askatasuna (ETA). ETA announced an indefinite ceasefire in September 1998, but the truce was ended in December 1999 and the conflict continued. The Supreme Court voted in 2003 to ban Batasuna, the Basque separatist party deemed to be the political wing of ETA.

In March 2004 terrorist bombs exploded in Madrid killing 191 people. Though the government sought to blame ETA, the bombings proved to be the work of Islamists linked to Al-Qaeda. In elections three days later, the right-wing government was voted out, as the people blamed the bombings on government support for the US-led invasion of Iraq. The new Socialist prime minister, Jose Zapatero, immediately withdrew all Spanish troops from Iraq. In 2006-7 ETA resumed its own terror campaign.

ECONOMY

Spain has the fifth-largest economy in the EU. By the early 2000s, agriculture employed 6% of the workforce, compared with industry at 17% and services including tourism who employ 77%. Farmland makes up two-thirds of the land, and forest most of the rest. Major crops include barley, citrus fruits, grapes for wine, olives, potatoes and wheat.

There is some high-grade iron ore in the north. Spain's many manufacturing industries include cars, chemicals, clothing, electronics, processed food, metal goods, steel and textiles.

ANDORRA

Andorra is a tiny state sandwiched between France and Spain in the Pyrenees Mountains. Winters are cold and dry and summers a little wetter.

Andorra is a co-principality, sharing the position of head of state between the Bishop of Urgel in Spain and the current President of France. An elected PM, Albert Pintat, governs the country.

Tourism is the main source of income, particularly for winter sports. The valleys are farmed, and cattle and sheep are grazed on the mountain slopes.

Area 468 sq km [181 sq mi]
Population 71,000
Capital (population) Andorra La Vella (22,000)
Government Co-principality
Ethnic groups Spanish 43%, Andorran 33%, Portuguese 11%, French 7%
Languages Catalan (official)
Religions Mainly Roman Catholic
Currency Euro = 100 cents
Website www.turisme.ad

GIBRALTAR

Gibraltar is a tiny British dependency on the south coast of Spain, occupying a strategic position overlooking the narrow Strait of Gibraltar, which links the Mediterranean Sea with the Atlantic Ocean. The majority of the populous works for the government or in the tourist trade.

Most of the land is a huge mass of limestone, known as the Rock of Gibraltar. Between AD 711 and 1309, and again between 1333 and 1462, Gibraltar was held by Moors from North Africa. Spaniards retook the area in 1462, but it became a British territory in 1713. Gibraltar became a vital British military base, but was still claimed by Spain.

In 1967 the Gibraltarians voted to remain British. Between 1969 and 1985

Area 6.5 sq km [2.5 sq mi]
Population 28,000
Capital (population) Gibraltar Town (28,000)
Government British dependency
Ethnic groups English, Spanish, Maltese, Italian, Portuguese
Languages English (official), Spanish, Italian, Portuguese
Religions Mainly Roman Catholic
Currency Gibraltar pound = 100 pence
Website www.gibraltar.gov.uk

Spain closed its border with Gibraltar. Britain withdrew its military forces in 1991. In 2002, proposals that Gibraltar should come under joint Anglo-Spanish sovereignty were rejected by nearly all Gibraltarians in a referendum.

SRI LANKA

Sri Lanka's unusual flag was adopted in 1951, three years after the country, then called Ceylon, became independent from Britain. The lion banner represents the ancient Buddhist kingdom. The stripes symbolize the minorities – Muslims (green) and Hindus (orange).

The Democratic Socialist Republic of Sri Lanka is an island nation, sometimes called the 'pearl of the Indian Ocean'. It lies on the same continental shelf as India, separated by the shallow Palk Strait. Most of the land is low-lying but, in the south-central part of Sri Lanka, it rises to a mountain massif. The nation's highest peak is Pidurutalagala (2,524 m [8,281 ft]). The nearby Adam's Peak, at 2,243 m [7,359 ft], is a place of pilgrimage. The south-west is also mountainous, with long ridges.

Around the south-central highlands are broad plains, while the Jaffna Peninsula in the far north is made of limestone. Cliffs overlook the sea in the south-west, while elsewhere lagoons line the coast. Forests cover nearly two-fifths of the land, with open grasslands in the eastern highlands. Farmland, including pasture, covers another two-fifths of the country's area.

Area 65,610 sq km [25,332 sq mi]
Population 2,222,000
Capital (population) Colombo (642,000)
Government Multiparty republic
Ethnic groups
Sinhalese 74%, Tamil 18%, Moor 7%
Languages Sinhala and Tamil (both official)
Religions Buddhism 70%, Hinduism 15%, Christianity 8%, Islam 7%
Currency Sri Lankan rupee = 100 cents
Website www.gov.lk

CLIMATE

The western part of Sri Lanka has a wet equatorial climate. Rainfall is heavy and Temperatures are high. October and May, when the summer monsoon retreats and advances are the wettest months. Eastern Sri Lanka is drier.

HISTORY

The ancestors of the Sinhalese people settled on the island around 2,400 years ago. They pushed the Veddahs, descendants of the earliest inhabitants, into the interior. The Sinhalese founded the city of Anuradhapura, which was their centre from the 3rd century BC to the 10th century AD. Tamils arrived around 2,100 years ago and the early history of Ceylon, as the island was known, was concerned with a struggle between the Sinhalese and the Tamils. Victory for the Tamils led the Sinhalese to move south.

From the early 16th century, Ceylon was ruled successively by the Portuguese, Dutch and British. Independence was achieved in 1948 and the country was renamed Sri Lanka in 1972.

POLITICS

After independence, rivalries between the two main ethnic groups, the Sinhalese and Tamils, marred progress. In the 1950s, the government made Sinhala the official language. Following protests, the prime minister made provisions for Tamil to be used in some areas. In 1959, the prime minister was assassinated by a Sinhalese extremist and was succeeded by Sirimavo Bandanaraike, the world's first woman prime minister.

Sinhalese Buddhists, who believe that the temple's treasured tooth belonged to Buddha. This led to rioting, provoked President Chandrika Kumaratunga to ban the LTTE, and caused some of the fiercest fighting in the civil war including several suicide bombings. The government lost most of the gains it had made in the mid-1990s. A long-term ceasefire agreement was signed in 2002. In December 2004, Sri Lanka was hit by a tsunami, which killed more than 30,000 people. In 2005 Mahinda Rajapakse was elected president and promised to end the conflict. In 2006–7 violence intensified once again, with both sides openly violating the ceasefire.

ECONOMY

The World Bank classifies Sri Lanka as a 'low-income' developing country. Agriculture employs around a third of the workforce, coconuts, rubber and tea are the cash crops. Rice is the chief food crop. Cattle, water buffalo and goats are the chief farm animals, while fish provide another source of protein. Manufacturing is mainly the processing of agricultural products and textile production. The leading exports are clothing and accessories, gemstones, tea and rubber.

Conflict between Tamils and Sinhalese continued in the 1970s and 1980s. In 1987, India helped to engineer a ceasefire. Indian troops arrived to enforce the agreement. They withdrew in 1990 after failing to subdue the main guerrilla group, the Tamil Tigers, who wanted an independent Tamil homeland in northern Sri Lanka. In 1993 the country's president, Ranasinghe Premadasa, was assassinated by a suspected Tamil separatist. A ceasefire was signed in May 1993, but fighting soon broke out. In 1995, government forces captured Jaffna, the stronghold of the 'Liberation Tigers of the Tamil Eelam' (LTTE). The 1998 bombing of the Temple of the Tooth in Kandy created great outrage among the

COLOMBO

Capital and chief seaport of Sri Lanka, on the south-west coast. Settled in the 6th century BC, it was taken by Portugal in the 16th century and later by the Dutch. It was captured by the British in 1796, and gained its independence in 1948. Sights include the town hall and the Aqua de Lupo Church.

SUDAN

Adopted in 1969, Sudan's flag uses colours associated with the Pan-Arab movement. The Islamic green triangle symbolizes prosperity and spiritual wealth. The flag is based on the one used in the Arab revolt against Turkish rule in World War I (1914–18).

The Republic of the Sudan is the largest country in Africa. It extends from the arid Sahara in the north to an equatorial swamp region (the Sudd) in the south.

Much of the land is flat, but there are mountains in the north-east and south-east; the highest point is Kinyeti, at 3,187 m [10,456 ft]. The River Nile (Bahr el Jebel) runs south to north, entering Sudan as the White Nile, converging with the Blue Nile at Khartoum, and flowing north to Egypt.

Khartoum is prone to summer dust storms (*haboobs*). From the bare deserts of the north, the land merges into dry grasslands and savanna. Dense rain-forests grow in the south.

Area 2,505, 813 sq km [967,494 sq mi]
Population 41,326,000
Capital (population) Khartoum (947,000)
Government Military regime
Ethnic groups Black 52%, Arab 39%, Beja 6%, others
Languages Arabic (officia)l, Nubian, Ta Bedawie
Religions Islam 70%, traditional beliefs
Currency Sudanese dinar = 10 Sudanese pounds
Website www.sudan.net

CLIMATE

Northern Sudan is hot and arid. The centre has an average annual rainfall of 100 mm to 510 mm [4–32 in], while the tropical south has between 810 mm and 1,400 mm [32–55 in] of rain per year.

HISTORY

One of the earliest civilizations in the Nile region of northern Sudan was Nubia, which came under Ancient Egyptian rule around 4,000 years ago. Another Nubian civilization, called Kush, developed from about 1000 BC, finally collapsing in AD 350. Christianity was introduced to northern Sudan in the 6th century. From the 13th to 15th centuries, northern Sudan came under Muslim control and Islam became the dominant religion.

In 1821 Muhammad Ali's forces occupied Sudan. Anglo-Egyptian forces, led by General Gordon, attempted to extend Egypt's influence into the south. Muhammad Ahmad led an Islamist Mahdi uprising in the 1880s which briefly freed Sudan from Anglo-Egyptian control. In 1898, General Kitchener's forces defeated the Mahdists. Sudan became Anglo-Egyptian Sudan, governed jointly by Britain and Egypt.

POLITICS

After Sudan's independence in 1952 the southern Sudanese, who are predominantly Christians or followers of traditional beliefs, revolted against the dominance of the Muslim north, and civil war broke out. In 1958, the military seized power. Civilian rule was re-established in 1964 but overthrown again in 1969, when Gaafar Muhammad Nimeri seized control. In 1972 southern Sudan received considerable autonomy, but unrest persisted.

In 1983, the imposition of strict Islamic law sparked off further conflict region in the west, primarily involving rebels and Arab militias. A severe humanitarian crisis developed, and the militias were accused of ethnic cleansing. In the south, government and rebels signed a peace deal in 2005 but the Darfur conflict worsened. By mid-2006 over 200,000 had died, most killed by the government-backed militias, and 2 million had become refugees. In 2006-7 the fighting spilled over into neighbouring countries and UN and African Union peace-keepers proved ineffective.

ECONOMY
The World Bank classifies Sudan as a 'low-income' economy. Food shortages and a refugee crisis worsened its economic plight 80% of the population are farmers or herders, most on a subsistence level. Ongoing conflict has hindered food aid.

Industries include processed foods, cement, fertilizers and textiles. Exports include oil, cotton, gum arabic and sesame seeds.

between the government and the Sudan People's Liberation Army (SPLA) in the south. In 1985, Nimeri was deposed and a civilian government installed. In 1989, the military, led by Omar Hassan Ahmed al-Bashir, established a Revolutionary Command Council. Civil war continued in the south. In 1996 Bashir became president. The National Islamic Front (NIF) dominated the government and was believed to have strong links with Iranian terrorist groups.

In 1996, the UN imposed sanctions on Sudan. A South African peace initiative in 1997 led to the formation of a Southern States' Co-ordination Council. The US imposed sanctions on Bashir's regime and American Secretary of State Madeleine Albright met rebel leaders. In 1998, the USA bombed a pharmaceuticals factory in Khartoum in the mistaken belief that it produced chemical weapons. In 2003 conflict broke out in the Darfur

KHARTOUM
Capital of Sudan, at the junction of the Blue Nile and White Nile. Khartoum was founded in the 1820s by Muhammad Ali and was besieged by the Mahdists in 1885, when General Gordon was killed. In 1898, it became the seat of government of the Anglo-Egyptian Sudan, and from 1956 the capital of independent Sudan. It was at the centre of controversy in 1998 when the US bombed a pharmaceuticals plant, believing it was producing chemical weapons. Industries include cement, gum arabic, chemicals, glass, cotton and textiles.

SURINAME

The star symbolizes national unity – each point being one of Suriname's five main ethnic groups. Yellow is for Suriname's golden future. Red stands for progress and the struggle for a better life. Green signifies hope and fertility. White symbolizes freedom and justice.

The Republic of Suriname is on the Atlantic Ocean in north-eastern South America bordered by Brazil to the south, French Guiana to the east and Guyana to the west.

Suriname is made up of the Guiana Highlands plateau, a flat coastal plain and a forested inland region. Its many rivers serve as a source of hydroelectric power. The narrow coastal plain was once swampy, but it has been drained and now consists mainly of farmland. Inland lie hills and low mountains which rise to 1,280 m [4,199 ft].

Area 163,265 sq km [63,037 sq mi]
Population 439,000
Capital (population) Paramaribo (216,000)
Government Multiparty republic
Ethnic groups
Hindustani/East Indian 37%, Creole (mixed White and Black) 31%, Javanese 15%, Black 10%, Amerindian 2%, Chinese 2%, others
Languages Dutch (official), Sranang Tonga
Religions Hinduism 27%, Protestant 25%, Roman Catholic 23%, Islam 20%
Currency Surinamese dollar = 100 cents
Website www.parbo.com/tourism/

CLIMATE

Suriname has a hot, wet and humid climate. Temperatures are high throughout the year.

HISTORY

Spanish explorer Alfonso de Ojeda discovered Suriname in 1499, but it was the British who founded the first colony in 1651. In 1667, Britain handed Suriname to the Dutch in return for New Amsterdam, an area that is now the state of New York. Slave revolts and Dutch neglect hampered development.

In the early 19th century Britain and the Netherlands disputed the ownership of the area. The British gave up their claims in 1813 and in 1815 the Congress of Vienna gave the Guyana region to Britain and reaffirmed Dutch control of 'Dutch Guiana'. Slavery was abolished in 1863 and soon afterwards Indian and Indonesian labourers were introduced to work on plantations. Dutch Guiana gained autonomy in 1954.

POLITICS

Suriname became fully independent from the Netherlands in 1975 and gained membership of the United Nations, but the economy was weakened when thousands of skilled people emigrated to the Netherlands.

Following a coup in 1980 Suriname was ruled by a military dictator, Dési Bouterse, who banned all political parties. Guerrilla warfare disrupted the

---

BAUXITE

Ore from which aluminium is extracted. Bauxite is a mixture of several minerals, such as diaspore, gibbsite, boehmite and iron. It is formed by prolonged weathering and leaching of rocks containing aluminium silicates.

ident in 1988 elections, but he was overthrown by a military coup in 1990.

Democracy returned in 1991 Ronald Venetiaan, leader of the New Front for Democracy and Development, became president. In 1992 the government negotiated a peace agreement with the *boschneger*, descendants of African slaves, who had launched a struggle against the government. That same year, the constitution was amended in order to limit the power of the military and a peace agreement was reached with the rebels. Elections were then held regularly, most recently in 2006. Venetiaan became president again.

In 1999, Bouterse was convicted in absentia in the Netherlands of having led a cocaine-trafficking ring during and after his tenure in office. In 2004, the government announced that he and others would face trial over the killings of 15 people in 1982.

economy. In 1987, a new constitution provided for a 51-member National Assembly, with powers to elect the president. Rameswak Shankar became pres-

PARAMARIBO

Capital of Suriname, a port on the River Suriname. It was founded in the early 17th century by the French and became a British colony in 1651. It was held intermittently by the British and the Dutch until 1816, when the latter finally took control until independence. Paramaribo is the administrative and economic centre. The name is derived from Paramurubo, meaning 'city of parwa blossoms' after an old Arrawak village. Places of interest include Fort Zeelandia/Suriname Museum, the Palm Gardens and the Presidential Palace. Industries include bauxite, timber, sugar cane, rice, rum, coffee and cacao.

ECONOMY

The World Bank classifies Suriname as an 'upper-middle-income' developing country. Its economy is based on mining and metal processing. Suriname is a leading producer of bauxite, from which the metal aluminium is made.

The chief agricultural products are rice, bananas, sugar cane, coffee, coconuts, timber and citrus fruits.

COPPENAME RIVER

The Coppename River is located on the Atlantic Coast of Suriname and its estuary is an important wetland region. The wide, tidal mud flats, lagoons and swamps are typical of the coastal wetlands of the Guyanas and northern Brazil and have been protected since 1953.

SWAZILAND

The oxhide shield with two spears and a staff represent the defence of the country abd the tassels are symbols of the Swazi monarchy. Black and white represent racial harmony, blue denotes peace and yellow stands for the nation's mineral wealth. Red signifies blood shed in past struggles.

The Kingdom of Swaziland is a small, landlocked country in southern Africa bounded by South Africa to the north, west and south and by Mozambique to the east.

The country has four regions which run north–south. In the west, the Highveld, with an average height of 1,200 m [3,937 ft], makes up 30% of Swaziland. The Middleveld, between 350 m and 1,000 m [1,148–3,281 ft], covers 28% of the country. The Lowveld, with an average height of 270 m [886 ft], covers another 33%. The Lebombo Mountains, stretching along the eastern border, reach 800 m [2,600 ft].

Meadows and pasture cover 65% of Swaziland. Arable land covers 8% of the land, and forests only 6%.

Area 17,364 sq km [6,704 sq mi]
Population 1,136,000
Capital (population) Mbabane (38,000)
Government Monarchy
Ethnic groups African 97%, European 3%
Languages Siswati and English (both official)
Religions
Zionist (a mixture of Christianity and traditional beliefs) 40%, Roman Catholic 20%, Islam 10%
Currency Lilangeni = 100 cents
Website www.gov.sz

CLIMATE

The Lowveld is almost tropical, with an average temperature of 22°C [72°F] and a low rainfall of 500 mm [20 in] a year. The altitude moderates the climate in the west of the country. Mbabane has a climate typical of the Highveld with warm summers and cool winters.

HISTORY

In the 18th century, according to tradition, a group of Bantu-speaking people under the Swazi Chief Ngwane II crossed the Lebombo range and united with local African groups to form the Swazi nation. In the 1840s, under attack from the Zulu, the Swazi sought British protection. Gold was discovered in the 1880s, and many Europeans sought land concessions from the king, who did not realize that in acceding to their demands he lost control of the land. In 1894, Britain and the Boers of South Africa agreed to put Swaziland under the control of the South African Republic (the Transvaal).

BANTU

Group of African languages generally considered as forming part of the Benue-Congo branch of the Niger-Congo family. Swahili, Xhosa and Zulu are among the most widely spoken of the several hundred Bantu languages spoken from the Congo Basin to South Africa, and almost all are tone languages. There are more than 200 million speakers of Bantu. The language of Swaziland, Siswati (also known as Swati or Swazi) is a member of the Bantu family of languages.

huza died in 1982 after a reign of 82 years.

In 1983 Sobhuza's son, Prince Makhosetive, was chosen as his heir. In 1986, he became King Mswati III. Elections in 1993 and 1998, in which political parties were banned, failed to satisfy pro-testers who opposed the absolute monarchy.

Mswati continued to rule by decree and in 2004 he announced plans to build palaces for each of his 11 wives. At the same time the government appealed for aid in the face of a national disaster caused by the spread of HIV and a severe drought. In 2006 Mswati announced a new constitution reinforcing his powers.

ECONOMY

The World Bank classifies Swaziland as a 'lower-middle-income' developing country. Agriculture employs 50% of the workforce, with many farmers living at subsistence level. Farm products and processed foods, including sugar, wood pulp, citrus fruits and canned fruit, are the leading exports. Swaziland exhausted its high-grade iron ore reserves in 1978, while demand for its asbestos fell. Swaziland is heavily dependent on South Africa and the two countries are linked through a customs union.

Britain took control at the end of the second South African War (1899–1902).

POLITICS

In 1968, when Swaziland became fully independent as a constitutional monarchy, the head of state was King Sobhuza II. In 1973, Sobhuza suspended the constitution and assumed supreme power. In 1978, he banned all political parties. Sob-

LOBAMBA

The traditional royal capital of Swaziland, lying in the Ezulwini Valley 16 km [10 mi] from Mbabane. It is the home of the Queen Mother. The National Assembly, National Museum and parliament are all based here.

MBABANE

Capital of Swaziland, in the north-west of the country, at the northern end of the Ezulwini Valley in the Dlangeni Hills, which are part of the Highveld region of southern Africa. It is both an administrative and commercial centre, serving the surrounding agricultural region. Tin and iron ore are mined nearby.

SWEDEN

Sweden's flag was adopted in 1906, though it had been in use since the time of King Gustavus Vasa (reigned 1523–60). This king won many victories for Sweden and laid the foundations of the modern nation. The colours on the flag come from a coat of arms dating from 1364.

The Kingdom of Sweden is the largest of the countries of Scandinavia in both area and population. It shares the Scandinavian Peninsula with Norway. The western part of the country, along the border with Norway, is mountainous. The highest point is Kebnekaise, which reaches 2,117 m [6,946 ft] in the north-west.

Area 449,964 sq km [173,731 sq mi]
Population 9,017,000
Capital (population) Stockholm (1,729,000)
Government Constitutional monarchy
Ethnic groups Swedish 91%, Finnish, Sami
Languages Swedish (official), Finnish, Sami
Religions
Lutheran 87%, Roman Catholic, Orthodox
Currency Swedish krona = 100 öre
Website www.sweden.gov.se

CLIMATE

The northerly latitude and high mountains and plateaux of Norway cut Sweden off from the mild influences of the Atlantic in the west. The Gulf Stream warms the southern coastlands. The February temperature in the central lowlands is just below freezing, but in the north it is –15°C [5°F].

Precipitation is low, but lies as snow for more than six months in the north. In summer there is little difference between the north and south. Most areas have an average temperature range between 15°C and 20°C [59–68°F].

HISTORY

Sweden was first settled at the close of the last ice age, c. 8,000 years ago. From c. 1800–600 BC it was an influential centre of Bronze Age culture, but after 600 worsening climate caused it to decline.

By the seventh century AD, Teutonic peoples had occupied much of central Sweden. Between the 9th and 11th centuries the Swedish Vikings sailed to the east, across Russia and down to the Black and Caspian seas.

In the 11th century, Sweden, Norway and Denmark were separate kingdoms. In 1388 Sweden, fearing the growing influence of Germany, turned to Queen Margaret of Denmark and Norway for help. The Germans were defeated in 1389 and, in 1397, Sweden, Denmark and Norway were united by a treaty called the Union of Kalmar. Sweden defeated the Danes in 1523 and under Gustavus Vasa, a Swedish noble, Sweden broke away from the union. Gustavus encouraged Lutheranism, which became the official religion by 1540.

From the late 16th century Sweden became involved in a series of wars, during which it gained territory around the Baltic Ocean. In 1658, Sweden forced Denmark to give up its provinces on the Swedish mainland. Following defeat at the hands of Tsar Peter the Great in 1709, a coalition of Russia, Poland and Denmark forced Sweden to give up most of its European possessions.

Sweden lost Finland to Russia in 1809, though it gained Norway from Denmark in 1814. By the late 19th cenfare programmes in the world. In turn, the tax burden is the world's highest.

The elections of September 1991 saw the end of the Social Democratic government, which had been in power since 1932, with voters swinging towards parties advocating lower taxes. The Social Democrats returned to power in 1994, advocating economic stringency.

A founder member of EFTA (the European Free Trade Association), Sweden joined the European Union in 1985 following a referendum. However, it did not adopt the euro in 2001. In 2003, the government launched a referendum on replacing the krona with the euro, a plan Swedish voters rejected. In 2006 elections the ruling Social Democrat party lost to a centre-right coalition. Fredrik Reinfeldt became prime minister.

ECONOMY

Sweden is a highly developed industrial country. Major products include iron and steel goods. Steel is used in the engineering industry to manufacture aircraft, motor vehicles, machinery and ships. Sweden has some of the world's richest iron-ore deposits.

STOCKHOLM

Port and capital of Sweden, on Lake Mälaren's outlet to the Baltic Sea. Founded in the mid-13th century, it became a trade centre dominated by the Hanseatic League. Gustavus I made it the centre of his kingdom, and ended the privileges of Hanseatic merchants. Stockholm became the capital of Sweden in 1436, and developed as an intellectual centre in the 17th century. Industrial development dates from the mid-19th century. Industries include textiles, clothing, paper and printing, rubber, chemicals, shipbuilding, beer and electronics.

tury, Sweden was a major industrial nation. The Social Democratic Party was set up in 1889 to improve the conditions of workers. In 1905, Norway's parliament voted for independence from Sweden.

POLITICS

Sweden has a high standard of living, and more than 70% of the national budget is spent on one of the widest ranging wel-

Switzerland has used this square flag since 1848, though the white cross on the red shield has been Switzerland's emblem since the 14th century. The flag of the International Red Cross, which is based in Geneva, was derived from this flag.

The Swiss Confederation is a landlocked country in Western Europe. Much of the land is mountainous. The Jura Mountains lie along Switzerland's western border with France, while the Swiss Alps make up about 60% of the country in the south and east. Four-fifths of the people of Switzerland live on the fertile Swiss Plateau, which contains most of Switzerland's large cities.

Area 41,284 sq km [15,940 sq mi]
Population 7,524,000
Capital (population) Bern (124,000)
Government Federal republic
Ethnic groups German 65%, French 18%, Italian 10%, Romansch 1%, others
Languages French, German, Italian and Romansch (all official)
Religions Roman Catholic 46%, Protestant 40%
Currency Swiss franc = 100 centimes
Website www.vlada.hr/default.asp?ru=2

CLIMATE

The climate varies greatly according to the height of the land. The plateau region has a central European climate with warm summers and cold snowy winters. Rainfall occurs throughout the year.

HISTORY

In 1291, three small cantons (states) united to defend their freedom against the Habsburg rulers of the Holy Roman Empire. They were Schwyz, Uri and Unterwalden, and they called the confederation 'Switzerland'. In the 14th century, Switzerland defeated Austria in three wars of independence. After a defeat by the French in 1515 the Swiss adopted a policy of neutrality, which they still follow.

In 1815, the Congress of Vienna expanded Switzerland to 22 cantons and guaranteed its neutrality. Switzerland's 23rd canton, Jura, was created in 1979 from part of the capital Bern (Berne).

POLITICS

In 1993 the Swiss voted against joining the European Union. However, in 2002, the Swiss voted by a narrow majority to end its centuries-old political isolationism and join the United Nations.

ECONOMY

Although lacking in natural resources, Switzerland is a wealthy, industrialized country with many highly skilled workers. Major products include chemicals, electrical equipment, machinery and machine tools, precision instruments, processed food, watches and textiles.

BERN (BERNE)

Capital of Switzerland, on the River Aare in Bern region. Founded in 1191 as a military post, it became part of the Swiss Confederation in 1353. Bern was occupied by France during the French Revolutionary Wars (1798). It has a Gothic cathedral and a 15th-century town hall and is the headquarters of the Swiss National Library.

Farmers produce about three-fifths of the country's food – the rest is imported. Livestock raising, especially dairy farming, is the chief agricultural activity.

Crops include fruits, potatoes and wheat. Tourism and banking are also important. Swiss banks attract investors from all over the world.

LIECHTENSTEIN

The Principality of Liechtenstein is sandwiched between Switzerland and Austria. The River Rhine flows along its western border, while Alpine peaks rise in the east and the south. The capital, Vaduz, is situated on the Oberland Plateau above the fields and meadows of the Rhine Valley. The climate is relatively mild and the average annual precipitation is about 890 mm [35 in].

Area 160 sq km [62 sq mi]
Population 34,000
Capital (population) Vaduz (5,000)
Government Hereditary constitutional monarchy
Ethnic groups Alemannic 86%, Italian, Turkish
Languages German (official), Alemannic dialect
Religions Roman Catholic 76%, Protestant 7%
Currency Swiss franc = 100 centimes
Website www.liechtenstein.li

Liechtenstein, whose people speak a German dialect, has been an independent principality since 1719. Switzerland has represented Liechtenstein abroad since 1918 and the Swiss currency was adopted in 1921. It has been in customs union with Switzerland since 1924.

Liechtenstein is best known abroad for its postage stamps, but is a haven for international companies, attracted by the low taxation and the strictest banking codes in the world.

In 2003, the people voted to give the head of state, Prince Hans Adam III, sovereign powers. In 2004, he handed the running of the country to his son, Prince Alois, but remained titular head of state.

SYRIA

Syria has used this flag since 1980. The colours are those used by the Pan-Arab movement. This flag is the one that was used by the United Arab Republic between 1958 and 1961, when Syria was linked with Egypt and North Yemen.

The Syrian Arab Republic is in south-western Asia. The narrow coastal plain is overlooked by a low mountain range which runs north–south. Another range, the Jabal ash Sharqi, runs along the border with Lebanon. South of this range is a region called the Golan Heights, which Israel has occupied since 1967. East of the mountains, the bulk of Syria consists of fertile valleys, grassy plains and large sandy deserts. This region contains the valley of the River Euphrates (Nahr al Furat).

Area 185,180 sq km [71,498 sq mi]
Population 18,881,000
Capital (population) Damascus 2,317,000)
Government Multiparty republic
Ethnic groups
Arab 90%, Kurdish, Armenian, others
Languages Arabic (official), Kurdish, Armenian
Religions Sunni Muslim 74%, other Islam 16%
Currency Syrian pound = 100 piastres
Website www.syriatourism.org

CLIMATE

The coast has a Mediterranean climate, with dry, warm summers and wet, mild winters. The low mountains cut off Damascus from the sea. It has less rainfall than the coastal areas and becomes drier to the east.

HISTORY

Syria is rich in historic sites from a wide range of periods. The earliest known settlers were Semites who arrived around 3,500 years ago. They set up city-states, such as Ebla, which existed between about 2700 and 2200 BC. The people of Ebla used clay tablets inscribed in cuneiform, an ancient system of writing developed by the Sumer people of Mesopotamia, to write one of the earliest recorded Semitic languages. Later conquerors of the area included the Akkadi-

ans, Canaanites, Phoenicians, Amorites, Aramaeans and the Hebrews, who introduced monotheism. The Assyrians occupied the area from 732 BC until 612 BC, when the Babylonians took over. The ancient Persians conquered the Babylonians in 539 BC, but the armies of Alexander the Great swept into the region in 331 BC, introducing Greek culture in their wake. The Romans took over in 64 BC, and Syria remained under Roman law for nearly 700 years.

Christianity became the state religion of Syria in the 4th century AD, but, in 636, Muslims from Arabia invaded the region. Islam became the main religion, and Arabic the chief language. From 661, Damascus became the capital of a vast Muslim empire which was ruled by the Ummayad Dynasty. When the Abbasid Dynasty took over in 750, the centre of power passed to Baghdad.

From the late 11th century, Crusaders from western Europe sought to reconquer the region from the Muslims. They were unsuccessful in their aim as Saladin, a Muslim ruler of Egypt, defeated the Crusaders and ruled most of the area by the end of the 12th century. The Mameluke Dynasty of Egypt ruled Syria flict, greatly improved its standing in the West. In the mid-1990s, Syria had talks with Israel over the future of the Golan Heights. Negotiations were suspended after the Israelis elected Binyamin Netanyahu's right-wing government in 1996. Assad died in 2000 and was succeeded by his son, Bashar al Assad.

Syria has been criticized for supporting Palestinian terrorist groups and for its long occupation of Lebanon. In 2005, following demonstrations against its continuing military presence in Lebanon, Syria withdrew its troops. However, it has been accused of continuing to interfere in Lebanese politics.

from 1260–1516, when the region became part of the Turkish Ottoman Empire. During World War I, Syrians and other Arabs fought alongside British forces and overthrew the Turks.

POLITICS

After the collapse of the Turkish Ottoman empire in World War I, Syria was ruled by France. Syria became fully independent from France in 1946. The partition of Palestine and the creation of Israel in 1947 led to the first Arab-Israeli war, when Syria and other Arab nations failed to defeat Israeli forces. In 1949, a military coup established a military regime, starting a long period of revolts and changes of government. In 1967, in the third Arab-Israeli war (known as the Six-Day War), Syria lost the strategically important Golan Heights to Israel.

In 1970 Lieutenant-General Hafez al Assad led a military revolt. He became Syria's president in 1971. His repressive but stable regime attracted much Western criticism and was heavily reliant on Arab aid. Syria's anti-Iraq stance in the 1991 Gulf War, and the involvement of about 20,000 Syrian troops in the con-

ECONOMY

The World Bank classifies Syria as a 'lower-middle-income' developing country. Its main resources are oil, hydro-electricity and fertile land. Agriculture employs about 26% of the population. Oil is the chief mineral product, and phosphates are mined to make fertilizers.

DAMASCUS

Capital of Syria, on the River Barada, south-west Syria. Thought to be the oldest continuously occupied city in the world, in ancient times it belonged to the Egyptians, Persians and Greeks, and under Roman rule was a prosperous commercial centre. It was held by the Ottoman Turks for 400 years, and after World War I came under French administration. It became capital of an independent Syria in 1941. Sites include the Great Mosque and the Citadel. It is Syria's administrative and financial centre. Industries include damask fabric, metalware, leather goods, sugar.

TAIWAN

In 1928, the Chinese Nationalists adopted this design as China's national flag and used it in the long struggle against Mao Zedong's Communist army. When the nationalists were forced to retreat to Taiwan in 1949, their flag went with them.

Taiwan (formerly Formosa), is an island about 140 km [87 mi] off the south coast of mainland China. The country administers a number of islands close to the mainland. They include Quemoy (Jinmen) and Matsu (Mazu).

High mountain ranges, extending the length of the island, occupy the central and eastern regions. Only a quarter of the island's surface is used for agriculture. The highest peak is Yü Shan (Morrison Mountain), 3,952 m [12,966 ft] above sea level. Several peaks in the central ranges rise to more than 3,000 m [10,000 ft], and carry dense forests of broadleaved evergreen trees, such as camphor and Chinese cork oak. Above 1,500 m [5,000 ft], conifers, such as pine, larch and cedar, dominate. In the east, where the mountains often drop steeply down to the sea, the short rivers have cut deep gorges. The western slopes are more gentle.

Area 13,900 sq km [36,000 sq mi]
Population 23,036,000
Capital (population) Taipei (2,619,022)
Government Unitary multiparty republic
Ethnic groups
Taiwanese 84%, mainland Chinese 14%
Languages
Mandarin Chinese (official), Min, Hakka
Religions Buddhism, Taoism, Confucianism
Currency New Taiwan dollar = 100 cents
Website www.roc-taiwan.org.uk

CLIMATE

Taiwan has a tropical monsoon climate. The annual rainfall exceeds 2,000 mm [79 in] in almost all areas. From July to September, the island is often hit by typhoons. When humidity is high, the heat can be oppressive.

HISTORY

Chinese settlers arrived in Taiwan from the 7th century AD, displacing the native population, but large settlements were not established until the 17th century. When the Portuguese first reached the island in 1590, they named the island Formosa (meaning 'beautiful island'), but chose not to settle there. The Dutch occupied a trading port in 1624, but they were driven out in 1661 by refugees from the deposed Ming Dynasty on the mainland. A Ming official tried to use the island as a base for attacking the Manchu Dynasty, but without success. The Manchus took the island in 1683 and incorporated it into what is now Fujian province.

The Manchus settled the island in the late 18th century and, by the mid 19th century, the population had increased to about 2.5 million. The island was a major producer of sugar and rice, which were exported to the mainland. In 1886, the island became a Chinese province and Taipei became its capital in 1894. However, in 1895, Taiwan was ceded to Japan following the Sino-Japanese War. Japan used the island as a source of food crops and, from the 1930s, developed manufacturing industries based on hydroelectricity.

1971. It was abandoned diplomatically by the United States in 1979, when the US switched its recognition to mainland China. However, in 1987, with continuing progress in the economy, martial law was lifted by the authoritarian regime in Taiwan. In 1988, a native Taiwanese became president and in 1991 the country's first general election was held.

China continued to regard Taiwan as a Chinese province and, in 1999, tension developed when the Taiwanese President Lee Teng-hui stated that relations between China and Taiwan should be on a 'special state-by-state' basis. This angered the Chinese President Jiang Zemin, whose 'one-nation' policy was based on the concept that China and Taiwan should be regarded as one country with two equal governments. Tension mounted in 2000, when Taiwan's opposition leader, Chen Shui-bian, was elected president, because Chen had adopted a pro-independence stance. However, after the elections, Chen adopted a more conciliatory approach to mainland China.

POLITICS

In 1945, the Japanese army surrendered Taiwan to General Chiang Kai-shek's Nationalist Chinese forces. From 1947, when Communists began to take control of the mainland, Nationalists fled to Taiwan. The influx was met with hostility by the 8 million Taiwanese, which was suppressed when Chiang Kai-Shek's Kuomintang government took control of the island and established military rule. By the time mainland China became a Communist state in 1949, about 2 million Nationalists had occupied Taiwan.

Aided by the United States, Chiang's government set about ambitious programmes for land reform and industrial expansion. By 1980, Taiwan had become one of the top 20 industrial nations. Economic development was accompanied by a marked rise in living standards.

Nevertheless, Taiwan remained politically isolated and it lost its seat in the United Nations to Communist China in

ECONOMY

The economy depends on manufacturing and trade. Manufactures include electronic goods, footwear and clothing, ships and television sets. The western coastal plains produce large rice crops. Other products include bananas, pineapples, sugar cane, sweet potatoes and tea.

TAIPEI

Capital and largest city of Taiwan, at the northern end of the island. A major trade centre for tea in the 19th century, the city grew under Japanese rule (1895–1945), and became the seat of the Chinese Nationalist government in 1949. Industries include textiles, chemicals, fertilizers, metals and machinery. The city expanded from 335,000 people in 1945 to 2,619,022 in 2005.

TAJIKISTAN

Tajikistan's flag was adopted in 1993. It replaced the flag used during the Communist period which showed a hammer and sickle. The new flag shows an unusual gold crown under an arc of seven stars on the central white band.

The Republic of Tajikistan is one of the five central Asian republics that formed part of the former Soviet Union. Only 7% of the land is below 1,000 m [3,280 ft], while almost all of eastern Tajikistan is above 3,000 m [9,840 ft]. The highest point is Ismail Samani Peak, formerly known as Communism Peak, which reaches 7,495 m [24,590 ft]. The main ranges are the westwards extension of the Tian Shan Range in the north and the snow-capped Pamirs in the south-east. Earthquakes are common throughout the country.

Vegetation varies greatly according to altitude. Much of Tajikistan consists of desert or rocky mountain landscapes capped by snow and ice.

Area 143,100 sq km [55,521 sq mi]
Population 7,321,000
Capital (population) Dushanbe (529,000)
Government Republic
Ethnic groups Tajik 65%,Uzbek 25%, Russian
Languages Tajik (official), Russian
Religions Islam (Sunni Muslim 85%)
Currency Somoni = 100 dirams
Website www.tajiktour.taknet.com

CLIMATE

Tajikistan has an extreme continental climate. Summers are hot and dry in the lower valleys, and winters are long and bitterly cold in the mountains. Much of the country is arid, but the south-east has heavy snowfalls.

HISTORY

The ancestors of the people of Tajikistan were Persians, who settled in the area about 2,500 years ago. Macedonian Greeks led by Alexander the Great conquered the region in 331 BC. From 323 BC, the area was split into several independent states. Arab armies conquered the area in the mid 7th century and introduced Islam, which remains the chief religion today. In the 9th century the area became part of the Iranian empire. In the 13th century, Tajikistan was overrun by the Mongol hordes of Genghis Khan. Uzbeks, a Turkic people, ruled the area as the Khanate of Bukhara from the 16th to the 19th centuries.

PAMIRS

A mountainous region in central Asia, lying mostly in Tajikistan and partly in Pakistan, Afghanistan and China. The region forms a geological structural knot from which the Tian Shan, Karakoram, Kunlun and Hindu Kush mountain ranges radiate. The climate is cold during winter and cool in the summer. The terrain includes grasslands and sparse trees. The main activity is sheep herding and some coal is mined. The highest peak is Ismail Samani Peak at 7,495 m [24,590 ft].

democrats and Islamic forces. The government maintained control, but it relied heavily on aid from the Commonwealth of Independent States. Presidential elections in 1994 resulted in victory for Imomali Rakhmonov of the People's Democratic Party, though the Islamic opposition refused to recognize the result.

A ceasefire was signed in December 1996. Further agreements in 1997 provided for the opposition to have 30% of ministerial posts in the government, but many small groups excluded from the agreement continued to undermine the peace process through killings and military action. In 1999, Rakhmonov was re-elected president. Changes to the constitution in 2003 enabled him to serve two more seven-year terms. In 2006 he was again reappointed president after elections in which opposition parties were heavily restricted. International observers criticized the polls as neither free nor fair.

The fragmentation of the region aided Russian conquest from 1868. After the Russian Revolution in 1917, Tajikistan rebelled against Russian rule. Although Soviet troops annexed northern Tajikistan into Turkistan in 1918, the Bukhara Emirate held out against the Red Army until 1921. In 1924 Tajikistan became an autonomous part of the Republic of Uzbekistan. In 1929 Tajikistan achieved full republic status, but Bukhara and Samarkand remained in the Republic of Uzbekistan. During the 1930s vast irrigation schemes increased agricultural land. Many Russians and Uzbeks were settled in Tajikistan.

POLITICS

While the Soviet Union began to introduce reforms in the 1980s, many Tajiks demanded freedom. In 1989, the Tajik government made Tajik the official language instead of Russian and, in 1990, it stated that its local laws overruled Soviet laws. Tajikistan became fully independent in 1991, following the break-up of the Soviet Union. As the poorest of the former Soviet republics, Tajikistan faced many problems in trying to introduce a free-market economic system.

In 1992 a civil war broke out between the government, which was run by former Communists, and an alliance of

ECONOMY

The World Bank classifies Tajikistan as a 'low-income' developing country. Agriculture, mainly on irrigated land, is the main activity and cotton is the chief product. Other crops include fruits, grains and vegetables. The country has large hydroelectric power resources and it produces aluminium.

DUSHANBE

Capital of Tajikistan, at the foot of the Gissar Mountains, central Asia. Founded in the 1920s, it was known as Stalinabad from 1929–61. An industrial, trade and transport centre, it is the site of Tajik University and Academy of Sciences. Industries include cotton milling, engineering, leather goods and food processing.

TANZANIA

Tanzania's flag was adopted in 1964 when mainland Tanganyika joined with the island nation of Zanzibar to form the United Republic of Tanzania. The green represents agriculture and the yellow minerals. The black represents the people, while the blue symbolizes Zanzibar.

The United Republic of Tanzania consists of the former mainland country of Tanganyika and the island nation of Zanzibar, which also includes the island of Pemba.

Behind a narrow coastal plain, the majority of Tanzania is a plateau lying between 900 m and 1,500 m [2,950–4,920 ft] above sea level. The plateau is broken by arms of the Great African Rift Valley. The western arm contains lakes Nyasa (Malawi) and Tanganyika, while the eastern arm contains lakes Natron, Eyasi and Manyara. Lake Victoria occupies a shallow depression in the plateau, outside the Rift Valley.

Kilimanjaro, the highest peak, is an extinct volcano. At 5,895 m [19,340 ft], it is Africa's highest mountain. Zanzibar and Pemba are coral islands.

Area 945,090 sq km [364,899 sq mi]
Population 37,445,000
Capital (population) Dodoma (204,000)
Government Multiparty republic
Ethnic groups Native African 99% (Bantu 95%)
Languages Swahili (Kiswahili) and English (both official)
Religions Islam 35% (99% in Zanzibar), traditional beliefs 35%, Christianity 30%
Currency Tanzanian shilling = 100 cents
Website www.tanzania.go.tz/index2E.html

CLIMATE

The coast has a hot, humid climate. The greatest rainfall is in April and May. Inland mountains and plateaux are cooler and less humid. The Rift Valley is hot. Mount Kilimanjaro was formerly ice-covered, but is now almost bare through climate change.

HISTORY

Around 2,000 years ago, Arabs, Persians and Chinese traded along the Tanzanian coast. Arab traders often intermarried with local people and the Arab-African people produced the distinctive Arab-Swahili culture. The Portuguese took control of coastal trade in the early 16th century, but the Arabs regained control in the 17th century.

In 1698, Arabs from Oman took control of Zanzibar. They developed inland trade, bringing gold, ivory and slaves from the interior. In the 19th century, European explorers mapped the country while missionaries tried to stop the slave trade. In the 1880s the country was carved up between European powers as part of the 'Scramble for Africa'.

LAKE TANGANYIKA

Second largest lake in Africa and the second deepest freshwater lake in the world. It lies in east-central Africa and borders Tanzania, DR Congo, Zambia and Burundi in the Rift Valley. The lake's fish are a vital source of protein for the local peoples. It has an area of 32,893 sq km [12,700 sq mi] and a depth of 1,437 m [4,715 ft].

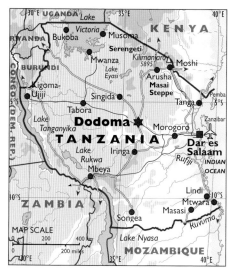

elected in 2000, pursued more liberal economic policies. In 2005, Mkapa was succeeded by Jakaya Kikwete, another CCM (Chama Cha Mapinduzi) candidate.

ECONOMY

Tanzania is one of the world's poorest countries. Although crops are grown on only 5% of the land, agriculture employs 85% of the people. Most farmers grow only enough to feed their families. Food crops include bananas, cassava, maize, millet, rice and vegetables. Export crops include coffee, cotton, cashew nuts, tea and tobacco. Other crops grown for export include cloves, coconuts and sisal. Some farmers raise animals, but sleeping sickness and drought restrict the areas available for livestock farming.

Diamonds and other gems are mined, together with some coal and gold. Industry is mostly small-scale. Manufactures include processed food, fertilizers, petroleum products and textiles.

Tourism is increasing. Tanzania has beautiful beaches, but its main attractions are its magnificent national parks and reserves, including the celebrated Serengeti and the Ngorongoro Crater. These are renowned for their wildlife and are among the world's finest.

Tanzania also contains a major archaeological site, Olduvai Gorge, west of the Serengeti. Here, in 1964, British archaeologist Louis Leakey discovered 1.75-million-year-old fossils of *Homo habilis*, an early ancestor of modern humans.

POLITICS

Mainland Tanganyika became a German territory in the 1880s, while Zanzibar (including Pemba) became a British protectorate in 1890. The Germans introduced a system of forced labour to develop plantations. This led to a major rebellion in 1905, which was put down with great brutality.

Following Germany's defeat in World War I, Britain gained control of Tanganyika and was granted a mandate to rule it by the League of Nations. Tanganyika remained a British territory until winning its independence in 1961, followed by Zanzibar in 1963. Tanganyika and Zanzibar united to form the United Republic of Tanzania in 1964.

The country's first president, Julius Nyerere, pursued socialist policies of self-help (called *ujamaa* in Swahili) and egalitarianism. While many of its social reforms were successful, the country failed to make economic progress. Nyerere resigned as president in 1985, though he remained influential until his death in 1999. His successors, Ali Hassan Mwinyi, who served from 1985 until 1995, and Benjamin Mkapa, who was re-

DODOMA

Capital of Tanzania, located in the centre of the country. Dodoma replaced Dar es Salaam as capital in 1974. It is in an agricultural region, crops include grain, seeds and nuts.

THAILAND

Thailand's flag was adopted in 1917. In the late 19th century, it featured a white elephant on a plain red flag. In 1916, white stripes were introduced above and below the elephant, but in 1917 the elephant was dropped and a central blue band added.

The Kingdom of Thailand is one of ten nations in South-east Asia. Central Thailand is a fertile plain drained mainly by the Chao Phraya. A densely populated region, it includes the capital, Bangkok. The highest land occurs in the north and includes the second largest city,, Chiang Mai, and the highest peak, Doi Inthanon, which reaches 2,595 m [8,514 ft].

The Khorat Plateau, in the north-east, makes up about 30% of the country and extends to the River Mekong border with Laos. In the south, Thailand shares the finger-like Malay Peninsula with Burma and Malaysia.

The vegetation of Thailand includes many hardwood trees to the north. The south has rubber plantations. Grass, shrub and swamp make up 20% of land. 33% of the land is arable, mainly comprising rice fields.

Area 513,115 sq km [198,114 sq mi]
Population 64,632,000
Capital (population) Bangkok (6,604,000)
Government Constitutional monarchy
Ethnic groups Thai 75%, Chinese 14%, others
Languages Thai (official), English, ethnic and regional dialects
Religions Buddhism 95%, Islam, Christianity
Currency Baht = 100 satang
Website www.thaigov.go.th

CLIMATE

Thailand has a tropical climate. Monsoon winds from the south-west bring heavy rains between May and October. Bangkok is drier than many parts of South-east Asia because mountains shelter the country's central plain from the rain-bearing winds.

HISTORY

The Mongol capture in 1253 of a Thai kingdom in south-west China forced the Thai people to move south. A new kingdom was established around Sukothai. In the 14th century it expanded and the capital moved to Ayutthaya.

European contact began in the early 16th century, but in the late 17th century the Thais, fearing interference in their affairs, forced all Europeans to leave. This policy continued for 150 years. Thailand remained the only South-east Asian nation to resist colonization.

In 1782 a Thai General, Chao Phraya Chakkri, became king, founding a dynasty which continues today. The country became known as Siam, and Bangkok became its capital. From the mid-19th century, contacts with the West were restored. In World War I, Siam supported the Allies against Germany and Austria-Hungary. In 1932 the country became a constitutional monarchy.

POLITICS

In 1938, Pibul Songkhram became premier and changed the country's name to Thailand. In 1941 Pibul, despite opposition, invited Japanese forces into Thailand. Pibul was overthrown in a military coup in 1957. The military governed Thailand until 1973. Thailand became a imate and the king approved a re-run, but a military coup took place before it could be carried out. Retired general Surayat Chulanont became prime minister. In 2007 the military government, though it promised a return to democracy, banned the former ruling party.

ECONOMY

Despite its rapid progress, the World Bank classifies the country as a 'lower-middle-income' developing country. Manufactures, including commercial vehicles, food products, machinery, timber products and textiles, are exported.

Agriculture still employs two-thirds of the workforce. Rice is the chief crop, while other major crops include cassava, cotton, maize, pineapples, rubber, sugar cane and tobacco. Thailand also mines tin and other minerals.

Tourism is a major source of income, though the December 2004 tsunami, which killed more than 5,000 people, cast a shadow over its future growth.

BANGKOK

Capital and chief port of Thailand, located on the east bank of the River Chao Phraya. Bangkok became the capital in 1782, when King Rama I built a royal palace here. It quickly became Thailand's largest city. The Grand Palace (including the sacred Emerald Buddha) and more than 400 Buddhist temples (*wats*) are notable examples of Thai culture. It has a large Chinese minority. During World War II it was occupied by the Japanese. Today, Bangkok is a busy market centre, part of the city's commerce taking place on the numerous canals (*klongs*). The port handles most of Thailand's imports and exports. Industries include tourism, building materials, rice processing, textiles, jewellery.

member of ASEAN (Association of South-east Asian Nations) in 1967 and its economy grew rapidly, especially its manufacturing and service industries. In 1997, however, it suffered recession along with other eastern Asian countries.

A military group seized power in 1991, but elections were held in 1992, 1995 and 2001. In 2004 Thailand was rocked by sectarian violence in the south, where a Muslim minority claimed to suffer discrimination by the central government. In 2006 the government of Thaksin Shinawatra, accused of corruption, called elections. These were annulled as illegit-

TOGO

The five stripes represent action and the five regions of Togo, while the alternation of colours is for unity in diversity. Red represents the blood shed in the struggle for independence, the star life, liberty and labour. Green is for hope and agriculture and yellow for Togo's mineral wealth.

The Republic of Togo is a long, narrow country in West Africa. From north to south, it extends about 500 km [311 mi]. Its coastline on the Gulf of Guinea is only 64 km [40 mi] long and it is only 145 km [90 mi] at its widest point. The coastal plain is sandy. North of the coast is an area of fertile, clay soil. North again is the Mono Tableland, which reaches an altitude of 450 m [1,500 ft] and is drained by the River Mono. The Atakora Mountains are the fourth region. The vegetation is mainly open grassland.

Area 56,785 sq km [21,925 sq mi]
Population 5,549,000
Capital (population) Lomé (658,000)
Government Multiparty republic
Ethnic groups Native African 99%
(largest tribes are Ewe, Mina and Kabre)
Languages French (official), African languages
Religions Traditional beliefs 51%, Christianity 29%, Islam 20%
Currency CFA franc = 100 centimes
Website www.republicoftogo.com

CLIMATE

Togo has year-round high temperatures. The main wet season runs from March to July, with a minor wet season in October and November.

HISTORY

The historic region known as Togoland comprised what is now the Republic of Togo and West Ghana. From the 17th century to the 19th, the Ashanti of Ghana raided Togoland and sold the indigenous inhabitants, the Ewe, to Europeans as slaves.

Togo became a German protectorate in 1884; it developed economically and Lomé was built. At the start of World War I, Britain and France captured Togoland from Germany. In 1922 it was divided into two mandates, became UN Trust Territories in 1946. In 1956 the people of

British Togoland voted to join Ghana, while French Togoland gained independence from France as the Republic of Togo in 1960.

In 1961, Sylvanus Olympio became Togo's first president. He was assassinated in 1963. Nicolas Grunitzky became president, but he was overthrown in a military coup of 1967. The coup's leader, armed forces head General Gnassingbé Eyadéma, then became president. In 1969, a new constitution confirmed Togo as a single-party state, the sole legal party being the Rassemblement du Peuple Togolais (RPT).

POLITICS

Re-elected in 1972 and 1986, Eyadéma was forced to resign in 1991 after pro-democracy riots. Kokou Koffigoh led an interim government. Unrest continued with troops loyal to Eyadéma attempting to overthrow Koffigoh.

A new constitution was adopted in 1992. In 1993 Eyadéma won rigged elections, and the EU cut off aid in response to the country's poor human rights record. Multiparty elections were held in 1994 and were won by an opposition general elections in 1999. In late 2002 the constitution was changed to allow Eyadéma to stand for re-election. He won the subsequent elections in 2003.

Eyadéma died in 2005 and his son, Faure, became president. After international pressure he stepped down and called elections. Faure won these two months later amid claims by the opposition that the vote was rigged. In addition, political violence surrounding the presidential poll was such that around 40,000 Togolese fled to neighbouring countries.

These events called into question Togo's 2004 declaration of commitment to democracy which had been declared in 2004, which aimed to normalize ties with the EU and restore access to aid.

ECONOMY

Togo is a poor developing country. Farming employs 65% of the people, but most farmers grow little more than they need to feed their families. Major food crops include cassava, maize, millet and yams. The chief cash crops are cocoa, coffee and cotton. The leading exports are phosphate rock, which is used to make fertilizers, and palm oil.

Togo's small-scale manufacturing and mining industries employ only about 6% of the people.

LOMÉ

Capital and largest city of the Republic of Togo, on the Gulf of Guinea. Made capital of German Togoland in 1897, it later became an important commercial centre. It was the site of two conferences (1975, 1979) that produced a trade agreement (known as the Lomé Convention) between Europe and 46 African, Caribbean and Pacific states. Its main exports are coffee, cocoa, palm nuts, copra and phosphates.

alliance, but Eyadéma formed a coalition government. In 1998 paramilitary police prevented the completion of the count in presidential elections when it became clear that Eyadéma had been defeated. Eyadéma continued in office and the main opposition parties boycotted the

TRINIDAD & TOBAGO

The colours represent earth, water and fire. The black stripe stands for the country's abundant resources of oil and gas, plus the unity and determination of the people. The white stripes symbolize the Caribbean Sea, as well as purity and equality. The red field represents the warm Caribbean sun.

The Republic of Trinidad and Tobago consists of two main islands and is the most southerly in the Lesser Antilles. The largest island, Trinidad, is just 16 km [10 mi] off Venezuela's Orinoco delta. Tobago, a detached extension of Trinidad's hilly Northern Range, lies 34 km [21 mi] to the north. The country's highest point is Mount Aripo (940 m [3,085 ft]) in Trinidad's rugged and forested Northern Range. Fertile plains cover much of the country.

Area 5,130 sq km [1,981 sq mi]
Population 1,066,000
Capital (population) Port of Spain (51,000)
Government Multiparty republic
Ethnic groups Indian (South Asian) 40%, African 38%, mixed 21%, others
Languages English (official), Hindi, French, Spanish, Chinese
Religions Roman Catholic 26%, Hindu 23%, Anglican 8%, Baptist 7%, Pentecostal 7%, others
Currency Trinidad and Tobago dollar = 100 cents
Website www.visittnt.com

CLIMATE

Temperatures are high throughout the year, ranging from 18°C to 33°C [64°F to 92°F]. Rainfall is heavy, with the wettest months from June to November. Annual rainfall ranges from 1,270 mm [50 in] on south-western Trinidad to more than 2,540 mm [100 in] on the highlands of Tobago.

HISTORY

The islands were inhabited by Arawak and Carib Amerindians when first visited by Columbus in 1498. He named Trinidad after three peaks at its southern tip, and Tobago after a local tobacco pipe. Spain colonized Trinidad in 1532, while Dutch settlers planted sugar on plantations in Tobago in the 1630s. In 1781, France colonized Tobago and further developed its plantation economy. The British captured Trinidad from Spain in 1797 and, in 1802, Spain formally ceded the island to Britain. In 1814 France ceded Tobago to Britain and in 1869 the two islands were combined into one colony. Black slaves worked on the plantations until slavery was abolished in 1834. To meet the problem of labour shortages, the British then recruited Indian and Chinese indentured labourers. The presence of people of African, Asian and European origin has resulted in a complex cultural mix in present-day Trinidad and Tobago.

POLITICS

Independence was achieved in 1962. Eric Williams, moderate leader of the People's National Movement (PNP), which he had founded in 1956, became prime minister. In 1970 the Black Power movement, who called for an end to foreign influence and high unemployment, called strikes. The government declared a state of emergency. From the mid-1970s, rising oil prices revived the economy. Trinidad and Tobago became a republic in 1976, with Williams continuing as prime minister. In 1986, after 30

378

years in office, the PNP was defeated in elections. The National Alliance for Reconstruction (NAR) coalition took office under Arthur Robinson. In 1990, Islamists seized parliament and held Robinson and other officials hostage for several days. In 1991, Patrick Manning became prime minister following an election victory for the PNP, but, in 1994, Baseo Panday, leader of the Indian-based United National Congress (UNC), became prime minister, leading a coalition with the NAR. In the 2002 elections the PNP was victorious and Patrick Manning returned as prime minister.

Trinidad and Tobago is a major trans-shipment point for cocaine being moved from South America to North America and Europe. Cannabis is also produced in the country. The drug trade has fuelled gang violence and corruption. The death penalty was reintroduced in 1999, despite strong international pressure. In 2005, a Caribbean Court of Justice was set up in Trinidad as a final court of appeal to replace the British Privy Council.

ECONOMY

Oil is vital to the economy. Chief exports include refined and crude petroleum, anhydrous ammonia, and iron and steel.

PORT OF SPAIN

Capital of Trinidad and Tobago, on the north-west coast of Trinidad. Founded by the Spanish in the late 16th century, it was seized by Britain in 1797. From 1958 to 1962 it was the capital of the Federation of the West Indies. It is a major tourist and shipping centre.

TUNISIA

Tunisia's flag originated in about 1835 when the country was officially under Turkish rule. It became the national flag in 1956, when Tunisia became independent from France. The flag contains two traditional symbols of Islam, the crescent and the star.

The Republic of Tunisia is the smallest country in North Africa. The mountains in the north are an eastwards and comparatively low extension of the Atlas Mountains.

To the north and east of the mountains lie fertile plains, especially between Sfax, Tunis and Bizerte. South of the mountains lie broad plateaux which descend towards the south. This low-lying region contains a large salt pan, called the Chott Djerid, and part of the Sahara.

Area 163,610 sq km [63,170 sq mi]
Population 10,175,000
Capital (population) Tunis (2,063,000)
Government Multiparty republic
Ethnic groups Arab 98%, European 1%
Languages Arabic (official), French
Religions Islam 98%, Christianity 1%, others
Currency Tunisian dinar = 1,000 millimes
Website www.tourismtunisia.com

CLIMATE

Northern Tunisia has a Mediterranean climate, with dry summers, and mild winters with a moderate rainfall. The average yearly rainfall decreases greatly towards the south, which forms part of the Sahara desert.

HISTORY

Tunisia has come under the influence of a succession of cultures, each of which has left its mark on the country, giving Tunisia a distinct identity and a long tradition of urban life. The Phoenicians began the Carthaginian Empire in Tunisia around 1100 BC and, according to legend, the colony of Carthage was established in 814 BC on a site near present-day Tunis. At its peak Carthage controlled large areas in the eastern Mediterranean but, following the three Punic Wars with Rome, was destroyed in

146 BC. The Romans ruled the area for 600 years until the Vandals defeated them in AD 439. The Vandals were in turn conquered by the Byzantine Empire. Arabs reached the area in the mid-7th century, introducing Islam and the Arabic language. In 1547, Tunisia came under the rule of the Turkish Ottoman Empire.

In 1881, Tunisia became a French protectorate. French rule aroused nationalist sentiment, but it was not until 1934 that Habib Bourguiba founded the first effective opposition group, the Neo-Destour (New Constitution) Party, which was renamed the Socialist Destour Party in 1964 and is now known as the Constitutional Assembly.

Tunisia supported the Allies during World War II, and the country was the scene of much fierce fighting. Tunisia became independent from France in 1956. In 1957, the new parliament abolished the monarchy and declared Tunisia a republic. The nationalist leader, Habib Bourguiba, became president.

POLITICS

In 1975, Bourguiba was elected president for life. His government introduced many reforms, including votes for

1999 and 2004 with his party dominating the Chamber of Deputies. Some seats were reserved for opposition parties whatever their proportion of the popular vote, but much of the opposition boycotted the flawed elections.

Occasional violence and suppression of human rights marred Ali's presidency. He faced opposition from Islamic fundamentalists, and responded by banning al-Nahda, the main Islamic party. Islamic fundamentalism was successfully suppressed in Tunisia, in contrast to its successes in neighbouring Algeria.

ECONOMY

The World Bank classifies Tunisia as a 'middle-income' developing country. Its main natural resources are oil and phosphates. Agriculture employs 22% of the people. Chief crops are barley, citrus fruits, dates, grapes, olives, sugar beet, tomatoes and wheat. Sheep are the most important livestock.

Since independence, new industries and have transformed a number of coastal towns. Major manufactures include cement, flour, phosphoric acid, processed food and steel. An important stimulus was the signing of a free-trade agreement with the EU in 1995. Tunisia was the first Arab country on the Mediterranean to sign such an agreement. Tourism has become a substantial sector of the economy.

women. The pace of reform brought its own problems. A national school system was established, although its success was not matched by the economy, leading to a rapid increase in the number of educated people who were unable to find jobs that measured up to their qualifications. The growth of tourism, which provided a valuable source of foreign currency, led conservatives to fear that Western influences might undermine Muslim values.

The prime minister, Zine el Abidine Ben Ali, removed Bourguiba from office in 1987 and succeeded him as president. He was elected president in 1989, 1994,

TUNIS

Capital and largest city of Tunisia. Tunis became the capital in the 13th century under the Hafsid dynasty. Seized by Barbarossa in 1534 and controlled by Turkey, it attained infamy as a haven for pirates. The French assumed control in 1881. Tunis gained independence in 1956. Products include olive oil, carpets, textiles and handicrafts. The ruins of Carthage are nearby.

TURKEY

Turkey's flag was adopted when the Republic of Turkey was established in 1923. The crescent moon and the five-pointed star are traditional symbols of Islam. They were used on earlier Turkish flags used by the Turkish Ottoman Empire.

The Republic of Turkey lies in two continents. The European section, sometimes known as Thrace, lies west of a waterway between the Black and Mediterranean seas. This waterway consists of the Bosphorus, on which the city of Istanbul stands, the Sea of Marmara (Marmara Denizi) and a narrow strait called the Dardanelles.

Most of the Asian part of Turkey consists of plateaux and mountains, which rise to 5,165 m [16,945 ft] at Mount Ararat (Agri Dagi) near the border with Armenia. Earthquakes are common.

Deciduous forest grow inland with conifers on the mountains. The plateau is mainly dry steppe.

Area 774,815 sq km [299,156 sq mi]
Population 70,414,000
Capital (population) Ankara (3,203,000)
Government Multiparty republic
Ethnic groups Turkish 80%, Kurdish 20%
Languages Turkish (official), Kurdish, Arabic
Religions Islam (mainly Sunni Muslim) 99%
Currency New Turkish lira = 100 kurus
Website www.kultur.gov.tr/EN

CLIMATE

Central Turkey has a dry climate, with hot, sunny summers and cold winters. The driest part of the central plateau lies south of Ankara, around Lake Tuz. The west of Turkey has a Mediterranean climate, while the Black Sea coast has cooler summers.

HISTORY

In AD 330, the Roman Empire moved its capital to Byzantium, renaming it Constantinople. Constantinople became the capital of the East Roman (or Byzantine) Empire in 395. Muslim Seljuk Turks from central Asia invaded Anatolia in the 11th century. In the 14th century another group of Turks, the Ottomans, conquered the area. In 1453, the Ottoman Turks took Constantinople, which they called Istanbul. The Ottoman Turks built up a large empire, which finally collapsed during World War I (1914–18). In 1923, Turkey became a republic. Its leader Mustafa Kemal, or Atatürk ('father of the Turks'), launched policies to modernize and secularize the country.

The country joined NATO in 1951 and was a US ally during the Cold War. In 1974, Turkey invaded Northern Cyprus, leading to an ongoing dispute with Greece and damaging relations with Europe.

POLITICS

After a military coup in 1980, civilian government was restored with a new constitution in 1982. In 1987 Turkey applied to join the European Economic Community and was rejected.

In 1998, the government banned the Islamist Welfare Party for violating secular principles. In 1999, the largest numbers of parliamentary seats were won by the ruling Democratic Left Party and the far-right Nationalist Action Party. In 2001 the Turkish parliament adopted reforms to ease the country's entry into the European Union. In 2002 Turkey finally agreed to recognize Cyprus as an EU member, though other issues were not resolved. Negotiations towards Turkey's accession to the EU were launched in 2005 and expected to take about 10 years, but were delayed in 2007 over the continuing Cyprus dispute.

In the elections of 2002 the Islamic Justice and Development Party (AKP) won 362 of the 500 seats in parliament. None of the parties in the former ruling coalition achieved parliamentary seats. The AKP won further elections in 2007 and appointed Abdullah Gül as president. The rise of the pro-Islamic AKP has angered the country's secular establishment, particularly the army.

In the 1980s and 1990s civil war was a problem in the east and south-east of Turkey. Fighting took place between Turkish forces and those of the secessionist Kurdistan Workers' Party (PKK). Over 30,000 people have died, and the Turkish government has frequently been accused of violating the human rights of Kurds. A ceasefire was reached in 1999, but broke down in 2004 as violence resumed. In 2007 Turkey threatened to extend its military actions against the PKK into northern Iraq.

ECONOMY

Turkey is a 'lower-middle-income' developing country. Agriculture employs 40% of the people, and barley, cotton, fruits, maize, tobacco and wheat are major crops. Livestock farming is important and wool is a leading product. Manufacturing is the chief activity, including processed farm products and textiles, cars, fertilizers, iron and steel, machinery, metal products and paper products. Turkey receives more than 9 million tourists a year.

ANKARA

Capital of Turkey, at the confluence of the Cubuk and Ankara rivers. In ancient times it was known as Ancyra, and was an important commercial centre as early as the 8th century BC. It flourished under Augustus as a Roman provincial capital. Tamerlane took the city in 1402. Kemal Atatürk set up a provisional government here in 1920. It replaced Istanbul as the capital in 1923, changing its name to Ankara in 1930. It is noted for its angora wool and mohair.

383

TURKMENISTAN

Turkmenistan's flag was adopted in 1992. It incorporates a typical Turkmen carpet design. The crescent is a symbol of Islam, while the five stars and the five elements in the carpet represent the traditional tribal groups of Turkmenistan.

The Republic of Turkmenistan is one of five central Asian republics which once formed part of the Soviet Union. Most of the land is low-lying, with mountains on the southern and south-western borders.

In the west lies the salty Caspian Sea. A depression called the Kara Bogaz Gol Bay contains the country's lowest point. Most of the country is arid and Asia's largest sand desert, the Garagum, covers 80% of the country, though parts of it are irrigated by the Garagum Canal.

Area 488,100 sq km [188,455 sq mi]
Population 5,043,000
Capital (population) Ashkhabad (521,000)
Government Single-party republic
Ethnic groups Turkmen 85%, Uzbek 5%, Russian 4%, others
Languages Turkmen (official), Russian, Uzbek
Religions Islam 89%, Eastern Orthodox 9%
Currency Turkmen manat = 100 tenesi
Website
www.turkmenistan.gov.tm/index_eng.html

CLIMATE

Turkmenistan has a continental climate, with average annual rainfall varying from 80 mm [3 in] in the desert to 300 mm [12 in] in the mountains. Summers are very hot, but winter temperatures drop below freezing.

HISTORY

Turkmenistan was originally part of the Parthian Empire. At the end of the 1st millennium AD Turkic people settled in the lands east of the Caspian Sea and the name 'Turkmen' comes from this time. Genghis Khan and his Mongol armies conquered the area in the 13th century and it subsequently became part of Tamerlane's vast empire. With the break up of the Timurid dynasty, Turkmenistan came under Uzbek control. Islam was introduced in the 14th century.

Russia took over the region during the 1870s and 1880s. In 1899, despite resistance, Turkmenistan became part of Russian Turkistan. After the Russian Revolution of 1917, the area came under Communist rule and, in 1924, as part of the Turkistan Autonomous Soviet Socialist Republic, it joined the Soviet Union. The Communists strictly controlled all aspects of life and, in particular, discouraged religious worship.

CASPIAN SEA

Shallow salt lake, the world's largest inland body of water. The Caspian Sea is enclosed on three sides by Russia, Kazakhstan, Turkmenistan and Azerbaijan. The southern shore forms the northern border of Iran. It has been a valuable trade route for centuries. It is fed mainly by the River Volga; there is no outlet. The chief ports are Baku and Astrakhan. It important fisheries and covers an area of 371,000 sq km [143,000 sq mi].

However, the Soviet government did help develop education, health services, housing and transport.

POLITICS

During the 1980s, the Soviet Union introduced reforms, and the Turkmen began to demand more freedom. In 1990, the Turkmen government stated that its laws overruled Soviet laws. In 1991, Turkmenistan became fully independent as the Soviet Union broke up. Like other former Soviet republics, it kept ties with Russia through the Commonwealth of Independent States (CIS).

In 1992 Turkmenistan adopted a new constitution, allowing for political parties providing that they were not ethnic or religious in character. Despite this, Turkmenistan remained effectively a one-party state. Saparmurad Niyazov, the former Communist and now Democratic leader, was the only candidate in 1992 elections. In 1999 parliament declared him president for life. 2004 parliamentary elections were described as a 'sham' because all the candidates supported the president. In 2005 he surprised observers by calling for contested presidential elections to take place in 2009.

Niyazov sought to influence every aspect of his people's lives, requiring all Turkmen to take 'spiritual guidance' from a book he published and imposing bans on things such as opera and young men wearing beards. He spent the country's newfound oil wealth on grandiose projects while heavily damaging the country's education, health and welfare systems. Inequality rose steeply.

Niyazov died at the end of 2006. In early 2007 his aide, Gurbanguly Berdimuhammedov, became president after elections widely condemned as rigged.

ECONOMY

The World Bank classifies Turkmenistan as a 'lower-middle-income' country. Turkmenistan has joined an Economic Co-operation Organization with Iran, Pakistan and Turkey. In 1996 a rail link from Turkmenistan to the Iranian coast improved communications. Agriculture is important, and cotton is the chief cash crop, grown on irrigated land. Manufactures include cement, glass, petrochemicals and textiles. Turkmenistan's extensive hydrocarbon and natural gas reserves have brought wealth, but limited export routes restrict growth. In 2006 a dispute with Russia's Gazprom, the main customer, ended with Turkmenistan obtaining a larger share of oil and gas profits.

ASHGABAT (ASHKHABAD)

Capital of the central Asian republic of Turkmenistan, located 40 km [25 mi] from the Iranian border. Founded in 1881 as a Russian fortress between the Garagum Desert and the Kopet Dagh Mountains, it was largely rebuilt after a severe earthquake in 1948. The city was known as Poltaratsk from 1919 to 1927. Its present name was adopted after the republic attained independence from the former Soviet Union in 1991.

UGANDA

The flag used by the party that won the first national election was adopted as the national flag when Uganda became independent from Britain in 1962. The black represents the people, the yellow the sun and the red brotherhood. The crested crane is the country's emblem.

The Republic of Uganda is a landlocked country on the East African Plateau. It contains part of Lake Victoria, Africa's largest lake and a source of the River Nile, which occupies a shallow depression in the plateau.

The plateau varies in height from about 1,500 m [4,921 ft] in the south to 900 m [2,953 ft] in the north. The highest mountain is Margherita Peak, which reaches 5,109 m [16,762 ft] in the Ruwenzori Range in the south-west. Other mountains, including Mount Elgon at 4,321 m [14,177 ft], rise along Uganda's eastern border.

Part of the Great African Rift Valley, which contains lakes Edward and Albert, lies in western Uganda. The landscapes range from rainforests in the south, through savanna in the centre, to semi-desert in the north.

Area 241,038 sq km [93,065 sq mi]
Population 28,196,000
Capital (population) Kampala (1,345,000)
Government Republic
Ethnic groups Baganda 17%, Ankole 8%, Basogo 8%, Iteso 8%, Bakiga 7%, Langi 6%, Rwanda 6%, Bagisu 5%, Acholi 4%, Lugbara 4% and others
Languages English and Swahili (both official), Ganda
Religions Roman Catholic 33%, Protestant 33%, traditional beliefs 18%, Islam 16%
Currency Ugandan shilling = 100 cents
Website www.statehouse.go.ug

CLIMATE

The Equator runs through Uganda and the country is warm throughout the year, though the high altitude moderates the temperature. The lands to the north of Lake Victoria, and the western mountains, especially the high Ruwenzori Range are the wettest regions. Much of Uganda has two rainy seasons from Apri to May and from October to December. In the centre and the north, these merge into one, with a distinct dry season.

HISTORY

In around AD 1500, the Nilotic-speaking Lwo people formed various kingdoms in south-western Uganda, including Buganda (kingdom of the Ganda) and Bunyoro. During the 18th century, the Buganda kingdom expanded and trade flourished. In 1862 a British explorer, John Speke, became the first European to reach Buganda. He was closely followed in 1875 by Sir Henry Stanley. The conversion activities of Christian missionaries led to conflict with Muslims. The Kabaka (king) came to depend on Christian support. In 1894, Uganda became a British Protectorate.

In 1962, Uganda gained independence with Buganda's Kabaka, Sir Edward Mutesa II, as president and Milton Obote as prime minister. In 1966, Mutesa II was forced into exile. Obote also abolished the traditional kingdoms, including Buganda. Obote was overthrown in 1971 in a military coup led by General Idi Amin Dada. Amin quickly established a personal dictatorship and launched a war against foreign interfer-

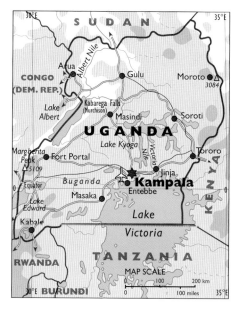

began to rebuild the economy and improve foreign relations.

In 1987 the Lord's Resistance Army began a rebellion in the north. The governement failed to suppress them or protect civilians from massacres and mutilations. The LRA abducted children, forcing them to serve as soldiers.

In 1996 Museveni claimed victory in Uganda's first direct presidential elections, although opposition groups were suppressed. In 2005 the people voted in favour of restoring multiparty politics, but attacks on the opposition continued. LRA attacks spread to the east of the country. 2006 saw ceasefires, but a final peace deal proved elusive.

ECONOMY

Stability was restored to the economy under President Museveni, and it finally expanded. Agriculture dominates, employing 80% of the people. Food crops include bananas, cassava, maize, millet, sorghum and sweet potatoes, while the chief cash crops are coffee, cotton, sugar cane and tea. The only important metal is copper. The Owen Falls Dam at Jinja, on the outlet of Lake Victoria, produces cheap electricity.

ence that resulted in the mass expulsion of Asian settlers. Amin's regime was responsible for the murder of more than 250,000 Ugandans. Obote loyalists resisted the regime from neighbouring Tanzania. In 1976, Amin declared himself president for life and Israel launched a successful raid on Entebbe Airport to end the hijack of one of its passenger planes. In 1978 Uganda annexed the Kagera region of north-west Tanzania.

POLITICS

In 1979 Tanzanian troops helped the Uganda National Liberation Front (UNLF) to overthrow Amin and capture Kampala. In 1980, Apollo Milton Obote led his party to victory in the national elections. After charges of fraud, Obote's opponents the National Resistance Movement (NRA) began guerrilla warfare. More than 200,000 Ugandans sought refuge in Rwanda and Zaïre. A military group overthrew Obote in 1985.

Strife continued until 1986, when the NRA captured Kampala and Yoweri Museveni became president. Musveni

KAMPALA

Capital and largest city in Uganda, on the northern shore of Lake Victoria. Founded in the late 19th century on the remains of a royal palace of the Kings of Buganda, it replaced Entebbe as capital when Uganda attained independence in 1962. It is the trading centre for the agricultural goods and livestock produced in Uganda. Industries include textiles, food processing, tea blending, coffee and brewing.

UKRAINE

Ukraine's flag was first used between 1918 and 1922. It was readopted in September 1991. The colours were first used in 1848. They are heraldic in origin and were first used on the coat of arms of one of the Ukrainian kingdoms in the Middle Ages.

Ukraine is the second largest country in Europe, after Russia. The mostly flat country faces the Black Sea in the south. The Crimean Peninsula includes a highland region overlooking Yalta. The highest point of the country is in the eastern Carpathian Mountains. The most extensive land region is the central plateau which descends in the north to the Dnipro-Pripet Lowlands. A low plateau occupies the north-east.

Area 603,700 sq km [233,089 sq mi]
Population 46,711,000
Capital (population) Kiev (2,621,000)
Government Multiparty republic
Ethnic groups Ukranian 78%, Russian 17%, Belarusian, Moldovan, Bulgarian, Hungarian, Polish
Languages Ukranian (official), Russian
Religions Mainly Ukranian Orthodox
Currency Hryvnia = 100 kopiykas
Website www.president.gov.ua/en

CLIMATE

Ukraine has warm summers, but the winters are cold, becoming more severe from west to east. In the summer, the east of the country is often warmer than the west. The heaviest rainfall occurs in the summer.

HISTORY

In the 9th century, Varangians united the northern regions as Kievan Rus with a capital at Kiev. In the 13th century the country was invaded by Mongol hordes, and broke apart. In succeeding centuries, large areas fell under foreign rule.

Poland took control in the 16th century. In 1648 the Cossacks, refugees from oppressive Polish rule, liberated Ukraine. A succession of wars with Russia ended in the country's division into three Russian provinces in 1775.

After the Bolshevik Revolution of 1917, Ukraine set up an independent, non-Communist republic. The Red Army invaded to secure Communist rule. In 1921 Poland took control of western Ukraine, and in 1922 the remainder became a republic of the Soviet Union.

In the 1930s, forced agricultural collectivization caused famines which killed between 3 and 6 million people. The 1939 Nazi-Soviet partition of Poland reunified the Ukraine, but in World War II the country was conquered by the Nazis. Millions were killed during the occupation. Ukraine was recaptured by the Soviet Union in 1945. In 1954 the Crimea was annexed to Ukraine, which became one of the most powerful republics in the Soviet Union.

POLITICS

The country finally became independent when the Soviet Union broke up in 1991. Ukraine continued to work with Russia through the Commonwealth of Independent States but differed with Russia on some issues, including control over the Crimea. In 1999, Russia rejected a treaty confirming Ukraine's present boundaries. Leonid Kuchma, who became president in 1994, came under fire in the early 2000s for maladministration and alleged involvement in the murder of a journalist. In 2004 prime minister Viktor Yukanovich, a supporter of Kuchma, was declared winner in presidential elections. After massive demonstrations, the election was declared invalid and was re-run. The pro-Western opposition leader Victor Yuschenko was elected president, leading to tensions with Russia. A dispute with Russia over the price of gas supplies to Ukraine in 2005–6 was said to be politically motivated. After inconclusive 2006 elections Yanukovich again became prime minister, and the country returned to instability.

ECONOMY

The World Bank classifies Ukraine as a 'lower-middle-income' economy. Agriculture is important, and major export crops are wheat and sugar beet. Livestock rearing and fishing are also important. Manufacturing is the chief economic activity and includes iron and steel, machinery and vehicles. The country has large coalfields and hydroelectric and nuclear power stations, but it imports oil and natural gas. In 1986, an accident at the Chernobyl nuclear power plant caused widespread nuclear radiation. The plant was finally closed in 2000.

KIEV (KYYIV)

Capital of Ukraine and a seaport on the Dnieper River. Founded in the 6th century AD, Kiev was the capital of Kievan Russia. It later came under Lithuanian, then Polish rule before being absorbed into Russia. It became the capital of the Ukrainian Soviet Socialist Republic in 1934, and of an independent Ukraine in 1991.

UNITED ARAB EMIRATES

The flag of the United Arab Emirates was adopted on 2 December 1971 when the country was formed by a union of seven sheikdoms. Red, white, black and green are the Pan-Arab colours, historically linked to the Arab people and Islamic faith. They stand for Arab unity and independence.

The United Arab Emirates (UAE) is a union of seven small Arab emirates or sheikhdoms. Swamps and salt marshes border much of the coast in the north. The land is a flat, stony desert, with occasional oases. Sand dunes occur in the east. Highlands rise in the east, near the border with Oman. In the south, the land merges into the bleak Rub' al Khali (Empty Quarter) of Saudi Arabia.

Area 83,600 sq km [32,278 sq mi]
Population 2,603,000
Capital (population) Abu Dhabi (928,000)
Government Federation of Sheikdoms
Ethnic groups South Asian 50%, other Arab and Iranian 23%, Emirati 19%
Languages Arabic (official), Persian, English, Hindi, Urdu
Religions Muslim 96% (Shi'a 16%), others
Currency Emirati dirham = 100 fils
Website www.government.ae/gov/en/index.jsp

CLIMATE

In most of the country, the average annual rainfall is less than 130 mm [5 in], most of it occurring between November and March. In summer (May to September), temperatures can soar to 49°C [120°F], with high humidity along the coast. Winters are warm to mild. The eastern highlands are generally cooler and rainier than the rest of the country. Sandstorms and duststorms are common.

HISTORY

The area has its roots as a trading centre between the Mesopotamian and Indus Valley civilizations, later coming under Persian control and, in the 7th century AD, embracing Islam. In the 16th century various European nations set up coastal trading posts. The emirates of today began to develop in the 18th century. Their economies were based on pearl fishing and trading. In 1820, conflict between local rulers and piracy along the coast led Britain to force the states to sign a series of truces. Britain took control of the foreign affairs of the states, while promising protection from attack by outsiders. The states retained control over internal affairs. Because of these truces, the region became known as the Trucial States. In 1952, the emirates set up a Trucial Council to increase co-operation between them. Oil was

ABU DHABI (ABU ZABY)

Largest and wealthiest of the United Arab Emirates, lying on the south coast of the Persian Gulf. Also the name of its capital city, the federal capital of the UAE. Ruled since the 18th century by the Al-bu-Falah clan of the Bani Yas tribe. There are long-standing frontier disputes with Saudi Arabia and Oman. Abu Dhabi's economy is based almost entirely on crude oil production.

discovered in 1958 and first exported in 1962. In 1968, Britain announced the withdrawal of its forces.

POLITICS

The country became independent in 1971, when six of its seven states, Abu Zaby (Abu Dhabi), Ajman, Dubayy (Dubai), Al Fujayrah, Ash Shariqah (Sharjah) and Umm-al-Qaywayn, agreed to form a single country, the United Arab Emirates. A seventh state, Ras al Khaymah, joined the country in 1972. Each of the seven Emirates has its own Emir, who controls internal affairs. The federal government controls foreign affairs and defence and plays a leading role in the social and economic development of the country. The seven Emirs form a Federal Supreme Council, which elects the federation's president and vice-president who serve five-year terms. The president appoints the prime minister. The only elections, introduced in 2006, are for half of the members of an advisory council which has no direct powers. The country is one of the most liberal and tolerant of the Persian Gulf countries. The UAE joined the allied force against Iraq in 1991 following the invasion of Kuwait, and the United States stationed forces there during the 2003 invasion of Iraq.

ECONOMY

The wealthy economy is based on oil production, and the country is a major oil exporter. In the 1990s and 2000s, oil revenues were invested in diversifying the economy. Dubai has become a tourist and financial centre, with many extravagant architectural landmarks.

The flag of the United Kingdom was officially adopted in 1801. The first Union flag, combining the cross of St George (England) and St Andrew (Scotland), dates back to 1603. In 1801, the cross of St Patrick, Ireland's emblem, was added to form the present flag.

The United Kingdom of Great Britain and Northern Ireland consists of England, Scotland, Wales and Northern Ireland, the first three of which make up Great Britain. The Isle of Man and the Channel Islands are not part of the UK, but are British dependencies with their own governments.

Much of Scotland and Wales is mountainous, the highest peak is Scotland's Ben Nevis at 1,342 m [4,404 ft]. England has some highland areas, including the Cumbrian Mountains (Lake District) and the Pennine range in the north. England also has large areas of fertile lowland. Northern Ireland is a mixture of lowlands and uplands and contains the UK's largest lake, Lough Neagh.

Area 241,857 sq km [93,381 sq mi]
Population 60,609,000
Capital (population) London (8,089,000)
Government Constitutional monarchy
Ethnic groups English 82%, Scottish 10%, Irish 2%, Welsh 2%, Ulster 2%, West Indian, Indian, Pakistani, others
Languages English (official), Welsh, Gaelic
Religions Christianity, Islam, Sikhism, Hinduism, Judaism
Currency Pound sterling = 100 pence
Website www.pm.gov.uk

CLIMATE

The UK has a mild climate, influenced by the Gulf Stream flowing across the Atlantic from the Gulf of Mexico. Moist winds from the south-west bring rain, which diminishes west to east. Winds from the east and north bring cold conditions in winter. The weather is markedly changeable, as low-pressure systems over the Atlantic form weather fronts which pass rapidly across the country.

HISTORY

The isolation of the United Kingdom from mainland Europe has made a major impact on its history. Despite insularity, Britons are of mixed stock.

In ancient times, Britain was invaded by many peoples, including Iberians, Celts, Romans, Angles, Saxons, Jutes, Norsemen, Danes and Normans, who arrived in 1066 and were the last people successfully to invade Britain. They overcame Welsh resistance in 1282, when Edward I annexed Wales and united it with England. Union with Scotland was achieved by the Act of Union of 1707. This created a country known as the United Kingdom of Great Britain.

Ireland came under Norman rule in the 11th century, and much of its later history was concerned with a struggle against English domination. In 1801, Ireland became part of the United Kingdom of Great Britain and Ireland, but in

393

UNITED KINGDOM

1921 southern Ireland broke away to become Irish Free State. Most of the people in Irish Free State were Roman Catholics. In Northern Ireland, where the majority were Protestants, most wanted to remain citizens of the United Kingdom. Ireland was partitioned, and as a result the country's official name was changed to the United Kingdom of Great Britain and Northern Ireland.

The British empire began to develop in the 18th century, despite the loss in 1783 of its North American colonies. In the late 18th century the UK was the first country to industrialize its economy.

The British Empire broke up after World War II (1939–45), though the UK still administers many small territories around the world. The empire was transformed into the Commonwealth of Nations, a free association of independent countries, numbering 53 in 2005.

POLITICS

A welfare state was set up in 1945, with a social security system that provided welfare for people 'from the cradle to the grave'. In 1960, the UK helped to set up the European Free Trade Association-with six other nations. In 1963, Britain's request to join the EEC was rejected. The UK finally joined the EEC in 1973, though a strong body of opinion still feared that the development of a federal Europe would jeopardize British sovereignty. Membership was endorsed by a referendum in 1975 but, at the turn of the century, Britons were still debating whether it was advisable for Britain to adopt the euro – the single European currency adopted by 12 of the 15 European Union members in 1999.

From the 1960s, Northern Ireland was the scene of conflict between the Protestant majority, who mostly favour continuing union with the UK, and the Roman Catholic minority, many of whom are republicans who would like to see Ireland reunified. British troops were sent to the province in 1969 to control violence between the communities and, at various times, Britain has imposed direct rule. In 1998, the 'Good Friday' agreement held out hope for the future, when unionists and nationalists agreed that Northern Ireland would remain part of the United Kingdom until a majority of its people voted in favour of a change. The agreement also allowed the Republic of Ireland a consulting role in Northern Ireland, and the Republic amended its constitution to remove all claims to Northern Ireland. A Northern Ireland Assembly was set up to handle local

LONDON

Capital of the United Kingdom, second-largest city in Europe. Located on the River Thames, 65km [40mi] from its mouth in the North Sea. Greater London, comprises the City of London 'square mile' plus 13 inner and 19 outer boroughs, covering a total of 1,580 sq km [610 sq mi]. The Romans called it Londinium. In the 9th century, Alfred the Great made it the seat of government. Edward the Confessor built Westminster Abbey and made Westminster his capital in 1042. The plague of 1665 killed 75,000 here, and in 1666 the Fire of London destroyed many buildings. Sir Christopher Wren designed many churches, including St Paul's. The 19th century saw the population reach 4 million and London become the world's biggest city. Further growth between the World Wars was accompanied by extensions to the transport system. Much of London was rebuilt after World War II, and the docklands were regenerated in the late 1980s. London is one of the world's most important administrative, financial and commercial cities.

affairs. In July 2005 the IRA issued a statement of full disarmament. Negotiations led in 2007 to full power-sharing in the Northern Ireland Assembly.

Before 1999, Scotland and Wales were directly ruled by the British parliament in London. In 1997, following the landslide victory of the Labour Party under Tony Blair, 74% of voters in Scotland and 50.3% of voters in Wales opted for the setting up local assemblies.

The Scottish parliament is responsible for local affairs, with limited powers to raise or reduce taxes. The Welsh Assembly has no powers over taxation. Both met for the first time in 1999. Devolution has caused concern among those who fear that it might lead to the break-up of the UK. Regional elections in 2007 led to an increased share of seats for nationalists in the Welsh Assembly and the Scottish Nationalists becoming the largest party in the Scottish Parliament.

The high cost of welfare services is a matter of political controversy. There is also concern about the changing economy, with a decline in traditional manufacturing and the growth of service industries, both of which affect employment. Another issue is immigration and the fear that economic migrants entering the UK will lessen the job opportunities of the indigenous workforce.

After the terrorist attacks on the United States on 11 September 2001 Britain was prominent in its support for the United States, joining the attack on the Taliban government of Afghanistan. Britain also joined the 2003 invasion of Iraq and subsequent occupation, despite public opposition. In July 2005 four suicide bombers struck in central London, killing 52 and injuring hundreds. In 2007 Tony Blair stepped down and was replaced as PM by Gordon Brown.

ECONOMY

The UK is a major industrial and trading nation. Its natural resources are coal, iron ore, oil and natural gas, but it has to import most of the materials for industry. It also has to import food. Service industries are vital. Financial and insurance services bring in foreign exchange, while tourism is a major earner.

Agriculture employs only 1% of the workforce. Production is high. Major crops include barley, potatoes, sugar beet and wheat. Sheep are the leading livestock, beef and dairy cattle, pigs and poultry are also important, as is fishing.

CHANNEL ISLANDS

Group of islands at the south west end of the English Channel, 16 km [10 mi] off the west coast of France. The main islands are Jersey, Guernsey, Alderney and Sark; the chief towns are St Helier (Jersey) and St Peter Port (Guernsey). A dependency of the British crown since the Norman Conquest, they were under German occupation during World War II. They are divided into the administrative bailiwicks of Guernsey and Jersey, each with its own legislative assembly. The islands have a warm, sunny climate and fertile soil. The major industries are tourism and agriculture. They cover an area of 194 sq km [75 sq mi].

ISLE OF MAN

Island off the north-west coast of England, in the Irish Sea; the capital is Douglas. In the Middle Ages, it was a Norwegian dependency, subsequently coming under Scottish then English rule. It has been a British crown possession since 1828, but has its own government (the Tynwald). The basis of the economy is tourism although agriculture is important, the chief products being oats, fruit and vegetables. It covers an area of 572 sq km [221 sq mi].

UNITED STATES OF AMERICA

This flag, known as the 'Stars and Stripes', has had the same basic design since 1777, during the War of Independence. The 13 stripes represent the 13 original colonies in the eastern United States. The 50 stars represent the 50 states of the Union.

Area 9,629,091 sq km [3,717,792 sq mi]
Population 298,444,000
Capital (population) Washington, DC (3,934,000)
Government Federal republic
Ethnic groups White 77%, African American 13%, Asian 4%, Amerindian 2%, others
Languages English (official), Spanish, more than 30 others
Religions Protestant 56%, Roman Catholic 28%, Islam 2%, Judaism 2%
Currency US dollar = 100 cents
Website www.firstgov.gov

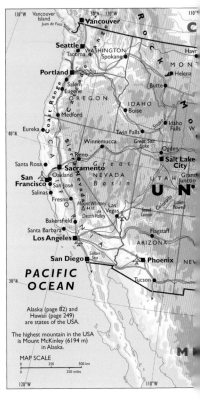

Alaska (page 82) and Hawaii (page 249) are states of the USA.

The highest mountain in the USA is Mount McKinley (6194 m) in Alaska.

MAP SCALE

The United States of America is the world's fourth largest country in area and the third largest in population. It contains 50 states, 48 of which lie between Canada and Mexico. The other two are Alaska in north-western North America, and Hawaii, a group of islands in the North Pacific Ocean.

Densely populated coastal plains lie to the east and south of the Appalachian Mountains. The central lowlands, drained by the Mississippi-Missouri rivers, stretch from the Appalachians to the Rocky Mountains in the west. The Pacific region contains fertile valleys separated by mountain ranges.

CLIMATE

The climates of the United States vary greatly, ranging from the Arctic conditions in northern Alaska, where average temperatures plummet to –13°C [9°F], to the intense heat of Death Valley, which holds the record for the highest shade

temperature ever recorded in the United States at 57°C [134°F].

The Midwest, New England and the Middle Atlantic States experience cold winters and warm summers. By contrast, the southern states have long, hot summers and mild, wet winters. In the central United States, a lack of topographical features allows the northwards movement of hot, moist air from the Gulf of Mexico, and in winter the southwards movement of dry, cold air from the Arctic. These air masses produce contrasts of climate, exacerbated by storms, blizzards and tornadoes. Parts of California have a pleasant Mediterranean-type climate, but the mountains of the west are much cooler and wetter. The central plains are arid, while deserts occur in parts of the west and south-west.

HISTORY

The first people in North America, the ancestors of the Native Americans, arrived around 40,000 years ago from Asia. Although Vikings probably reached North America 1,000 years ago, European exploration did not begin until the late 15th century.

The first Europeans to settle in large numbers were the British, who founded settlements on the eastern coast in the early 17th century. British rule ended with the War of Independence (1775–83). The country expanded in 1803 when a vast territory in the south and west was acquired through the Louisiana Purchase, while the border with Mexico was fixed in the mid-19th century. The Civil War (1861–5) ended slavery and the serious threat that the nation might split into two parts. In the late 19th century the West was opened up, while immigrants flooded in from Europe and elsewhere.

POLITICS

The United States has long played a leading role in industrial, economic, social and technological innovation, and the majority of Americans continue to enjoy one of the world's highest material

UNITED STATES OF AMERICA

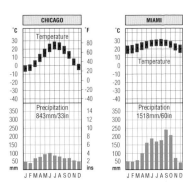

standards of living. At the same time, the country faces many problems. One concerns the maintenance of social cohesion as the composition of American society changes. Another is the issue of poverty and the low standards of living of a sizeable underclass of poor and inadequately educated people, many of whom are members of ethnic minorities. Other associated problems include crime, drug addiction and racial conflict.

The United States has one of the most diverse populations of any country in the world. Until about 1860 the population, with the exception of the Native Americans and the southern African Americans, was made up largely of immigrants of British and Irish origin with small numbers of Spaniards and French. However, after the Civil War, increasing numbers of immigrants arrived from the countries of central and south-eastern Europe, including Italy, the Balkans, Poland, Scandinavia and Russia. This vast influx of Europeans, numbering about 30 million between 1860 and 1920, was vastly different in culture and language from the established population. More recently, the country has received lesser influxes of Japanese, Chinese, Filipinos, Cubans, Puerto Ricans and large numbers of Mexicans, many of them illegal immigrants. Although strong influences and pressures towards Americanization still exist, members of these groups have tended to maintain their own culture, establishing social and cultural enclaves

within American society. Although the nation has never adopted an official language, English was readily adopted by most immigrants in the late 19th and early 20th century, because they sought acceptance in the 'melting pot' that makes up the United States. However, many of the recent Hispanic immigrants persist in speaking Spanish, which has become the country's second language. Many Americans are concerned about this trend towards 'cultural pluralism' rather than integration through the 'melting pot'. They argue that Hispanics who do not speak English are at a disadvantage in American society and believe that everyone should speak English, either as a first or second language. According to some population forecasts, today's white majority will be outnumbered by other ethnic groups in 2050. With a total projected population of 380 million, Hispanics are expected to number around 80 million by 2050, while African Americans will account for another 62 million.

From the 1890s, the United States developed into a world power, and played a leading role in international affairs throughout the 20th century. It played a key role in both World Wars. After World War II, the US and Soviet Union had become the world's sole superpowers and the US led the west into the Cold War with the Soviet Union. After the fall of Communism in 1991, the United States has faced new threats from terrorists and rogue states. Disputed 2000 elections made the conservative Republican candidate, George W Bush, president despite receiving fewer votes than his Democrat opponent Al Gore.

September 2001 saw terrorist attacks on New York City and on Washington, DC Al-Qaeda terrorists claimed responsibility. The United States responded vigorously, creating an international alliance to combat terrorism and the nations which shelter or aid terrorists. In 2001 it led a coalition force against the Taliban regime in Afghanistan, which was accused of protecting al Qaeda terrorists. In 2003 the US led another coalition force to overthrow the repressive regime of Saddam Hussein in Iraq, but the subsequent occupation proved troubled and costly.

Bush was re-elected in 2004. Discontent with the occupation of Iraq led to the opposition Democrats gaining control of Congress and the House of Representatives in 2006 elections.

ECONOMY

Agriculture employs only 2.4% of the labour force. The western plains are the main centres of production. Much of the land farmed by the Pilgrim Fathers and other settlers is now built over, or has reverted to forest. The US has become a leading producer of meat, dairy products, soya beans, maize, oats, wheat, barley, cotton, sugar and many other crops.

The spread of prosperity generated new consumer industries to satisfy demands of a large middle class for ever-increasing standards of comfort. The United States was a pioneer of large-scale industrial production. With almost every raw material available within its own boundaries, or readily gained through trade, its mining and extractive industries have been heavily exploited. Anthracite from eastern Pennsylvania, good bituminous and coking coals from the Appalachians, Indiana, Illinois, Colorado and Utah are still in demand, and vast reserves remain.

Oil, first drilled in Pennsylvania in 1859, was subsequently found in several major fields underlying the Midwest, the eastern and central mountain states, the Gulf of Mexico, California and Alaska. Home consumption of petroleum products has grown steadily. Although the United States is a major producer, it is also by far the world's greatest consumer and has long been a net importer of oil. In the Gulf Coast states, the exploitation of oil in Oklahoma, Texas and Louisiana has shifted the former dependence on agriculture to the refining and petrochemical industries. Oil has transformed Dallas-Fort Worth into a major conurbation, while Denver has changed from a small railhead town into a wealthy state capital. Natural gas is also found in abundance, usually associated with oil.

WASHINGTON, DC

Capital of the USA, on the east bank of the Potomac River, covering the District of Columbia and extending into the neighbouring states of Maryland and Virginia. The site was chosen as the seat of government in 1790, and French engineer Pierre Charles L'Enfant planned the city. Construction of the White House began in 1793, and the building of the Capitol in the following year. In 1800, Congress moved from Philadelphia to Washington. During the War of 1812, the British occupied the city and many public buildings were burned, including the White House and the Capitol. Washington is the legislative, judicial and administrative centre of the USA. Despite its role, Washington has severe social problems; many of the large African-American population live in slum housing.

URUGUAY

Uruguay has used this flag since 1830. The nine stripes represent the nine provinces which formed the country when it became an independent republic in 1828. The colours and the May Sun had originally been used by Argentina during its struggle against Spanish rule.

The Oriental Republic of Uruguay, as Uruguay is officially known, is South America's second smallest independent nation after Suriname. The River Uruguay, which forms the country's western border, flows into the Río de la Plata (River Plate). The River Plate is a large estuary, fringed with lagoons and sand dunes, which leads into the South Atlantic Ocean.

The land consists mainly of low-lying plains and hills. The highest point lies south of Minas and is only 501 m [1,644 ft] above sea level. The main river in the interior is the Rio Negro.

Area 175,016 sq km [67,574 sq mi]
Population 3,432,000
Capital (population) Montevideo (1,353,000)
Government Multiparty republic
Ethnic groups White 88%, Mestizo 8%, Mulatto or Black 4%
Languages Spanish (official)
Religions Roman Catholic 66%, Protestant 2%, Judaism 1%
Currency Uruguayan peso = 100 centésimos
Website www.turismo.gub.uy

CLIMATE

Uruguay has a mild climate, with rain throughout the year, though droughts sometimes occur. The summer is pleasantly warm, especially near the coast. The weather remains relatively mild in the winter months.

HISTORY

The first people of Uruguay were Amerindians, but the Amerindian population has largely disappeared. Most were killed by Spanish settlers or died from European diseases to which they had no resistance. The majority of Uruguayans today are of European origin, though there are some *mestizos* of mixed European and Amerindian descent. The first European to arrive in Uruguay was a Spanish navigator, Juan Diaz de Solis, in 1516, but he and part of his crew were killed by the local Charrúa Amerindians when they went ashore.

Few Europeans settled until the late 17th century. Spanish settlers founded Montevideo in order to prevent the Portuguese from gaining influence in the area. Uruguay was then little more than a buffer zone between the Portuguese territory to the north and Spanish territories to the west. By the late 18th century, Spaniards had settled in most of the country. Uruguay became part of a colony called the Viceroyalty of La Plata, which included Argentina, Paraguay, and parts of Bolivia, Brazil and Chile.

Uruguay was annexed by Brazil in 1820, bringing about an end to Spanish rule. In 1825 Uruguayans, supported by Argentina, began a struggle for independence from Brazil.

POLITICS

Uruguay was recognized as an independent republic by Brazil and Argentina in 1828. Social and economic developments were slow in the 19th century, but, from 1903 governments made

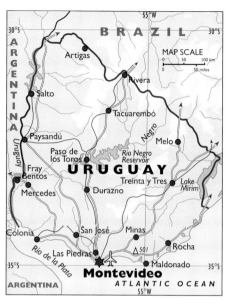

lems in trying to rebuild its weakened economy and reinforce its democratic traditions. In 1991, Uruguay joined with Argentina, Brazil and Paraguay to form Mercosur, which aimed to create a common market. Mercosur's secretariat is in Montevideo. The early 21st century brought economic problems, many of which were the result of the economic crisis in Argentina and its imposition of banking controls. Uruguay elected its first left-wing president, Tabare Vasquez, in 2004.

ECONOMY

Uruguay is classed by the World Bank as an 'upper-middle-income' developing country. Although 90% of the population live in urban areas and agriculture employs 3% of the population, the economy depends on the exports of hides and leather goods, beef and wool. Main crops include maize, potatoes, rice, sugar beet and wheat.

Manufacturing concentrates on food processing and packing. The economy has diversified into cement, chemicals, leather goods, textiles and steel. Uruguay depends largely on hydroelectric power for energy, and produces sufficient surplus to export electricity to Argentina.

Uruguay a democratic and stable country. Since 1828, two political parties – the Colorados (Liberals) and the Blancos (Conservatives) – have dominated.

During World War II, Uruguay prospered because of its export trade, especially in meat and wool. However, from the 1950s, economic problems caused unrest. Terrorist groups, notably the Tupumaros (Marxist urban guerrillas), carried out murders and kidnappings in the 1960s and early 1970s. In 1972, President Juan Maria Bordaberry declared war on the Tupumaros and the army crushed them. In 1973, the military seized power, suspended the constitution and ruled with great severity, committing major human rights abuses.

Military rule continued until 1984, when elections were held. General Gregorio Alvarez, who had been president since 1981, resigned and Julio Maria Sanguinetti, leader of the Colorado Party, became president in February 1985, leading a government of National Unity. He ordered the release of all political prisoners. In the 1990s, Uruguay faced prob-

MONTEVIDEO

Capital of Uruguay, in the south of the country, on the River Plate. Originally a Portuguese fort (1717), the Spanish captured Montevideo in 1726, and it became the capital of Uruguay in 1828. One of South America's major ports, it is the base of a large fishing fleet and handles most of the country's exports. Products include textiles, dairy goods, wine and packaged meat.

UZBEKISTAN

The white crescent moon in the upper hoist is a traditional symbol of Islam and represents the rebirth of the nation. The white stars recall the 12 signs of the zodiac. Blue stands for water and the eternal sky. Red represents life. White symbolizes peace and green denotes nature.

The Republic of Uzbekistan is one of five republics in Central Asia which were once part of the Soviet Union. Plains cover most of western Uzbekistan, with highlands in the east. The main rivers, the Amu (or Amu Darya) and Syr (or Syr Darya), drain into the Aral Sea. So much water has been taken from these rivers for irrigation that the Aral Sea is now only a quarter of its size in 1960. Much of the former sea is now desert.

Area 447,400 sq km [172,741sq mi]
Population 27,307,000
Capital (population) Tashkent (2,160,000)
Government Socialist republic
Ethnic groups Uzbek 80%, Russian 5%, Tajik 5%, Kazakh 3%, Tatar 2%, Kara-Kalpak 2%
Languages Uzbek (official), Russian
Religions Islam 88%, Eastern Orthodox 9%
Currency Uzbekistani sum = 100 tyiyn
Website www.gov.uz

CLIMATE

Uzbekistan has a continental climate. Winters are cold, but temperatures soar in the west conditions are extremely arid with an average annual rainfall of about 200 mm [8 in].

HISTORY

Uzbekistan lies on the ancient Silk Road between Europe and Asia. Great cities such as Samarkand and Bukhara, famed for their architectural opulence, were important trade and cultural centres. Russia annexed the area in the 19th century. After the Russian Revolution of 1917, Communists took over, setting up the Uzbek Soviet Socialist Republic in 1924. Under Communism, all aspects of Uzbek life were controlled and religious worship was discouraged. The country did benefit though and health, housing, education and transport were all improved. In the late 1980s, people demanded more freedom and, in 1990, the government stated that its laws overruled those of the Soviet Union.

POLITICS

Uzbekistan became independent in 1991 with the break-up of the Soviet

---

SAMARKAND

City in the fertile Zeravshan Valley, south-east Uzbekistan. One of the oldest cities in Asia, it was conquered by Alexander the Great in 329 BC. A vital trading centre on the Silk Road, it flourished in the 8th century AD as part of the Umayyad Empire. Samarkand was destroyed in 1220 by Genghis Khan but became capital of the Mongol empire of Tamerlane in 1370. Ruled by the Uzbeks from the 16th century, it was captured by Russia in 1868, though it remained a centre of Muslim culture. It is now a major scientific research centre and has a population of over 350,000.

Karimov accused fundamentalists out to destabilize the country, but his opponents blamed the determination of those in power to crush all dissent and maintain a repressive state. There were calls for an international enquiry which the government rejected, as a result of which the US threatened to withold aid. Uzbekistan reacted by ordering US forces to leave the country.

Union, but retained links with Russia through the Commonwealth of Independent States (CIS). It subsequently pulled out because of the leader's opposition to closer integration on post-Soviet territory. Islam Karimov, leader of the People's Democratic Party (formerly the Communist Party), was elected president in December 1991. In 1992–3, many opposition leaders were arrested because the government said that they threatened national stability. In 1994–5, the PDP claimed victory in flawed national elections, and in 1995 a referendum extended Karimov's term in office until 2000. In 2000 he was again re-elected.

In 2001, Karimov declared Uzbekistan's support for the United States in its campaign against the terrorist al Qaida bases in Afghanistan. He sought US favour by allowing American forces a base on Uzbek territory. Because of the government's suppression of opposition and poor record on human rights, the European Bank for Reconstruction and Development announced in 2004 that it would cut aid to Uzbekistan.

Recent years have seen bombings and shootings for which the authorities have blamed Islamic extremists. In 2005 protests against the jailing of several people charged with Islamic extremism in the city of Andijan turned to violence, with troops opening fire. Several hundred civilians were killed, though the government claimed a toll of 180.

ECONOMY

The World Bank classifies Uzbekistan as a 'lower-middle-income' developing country. The government still controls most economic activity and economic reform has been very slow. Uzbekistan produces coal, copper, gold, oil and natual gas, while manufacturing industries include agricultural machinery, chemicals and textiles.

Agriculture is important, with cotton the main cash crop. Soviet-era drives to increase production caused widespread environmental damage. Other crops include fruits, rice and vegetables; cattle, sheep and goats are raised.

TASHKENT

Largest city and capital of Uzbekistan, in the Tashkent oasis in the foothills of the Tian Shan (Celestial Range) mountains (a 2,400 km [1,500 mi] long mountain range). Tashkent is watered by the River Chirchik. It was ruled by the Arabs from the 8th until the 11th century. The city was captured by Tamerlane in 1361, and by the Russians in 1865. The modern city is the transport and economic centre of the region. Industries include textiles, chemicals, food processing, mining machinery, paper, porcelain, clothing, leather and furniture.

VENEZUELA

Venezuela's flag, adopted in 1954, has the same basic tricolour as the flags of Colombia and Ecuador. The colours were used by the Venezuelan patriot Francisco de Miranda. The seven stars represent the provinces in the Venezuelan Federation in 1811.

The Bolivarian Republic of Venezuela, in northern South America, contains the Maracaibo Lowlands in the west. The lowlands surround the oil-rich Lake Maracaibo (Lago de Maracaibo). Arms of the Andes Mountains enclose the lowlands and extend across most of northern Venezuela. Between the northern mountains and the scenic Guiana Highlands in the south-east, where the Angel Falls are found, lie the *llanos* (tropical grasslands), a low-lying region drained by the River Orinoco and its tributaries. The Orinoco is Venezuela's longest river.

Area 912,050 sq km [352,143 sq mi]
Population 25,730,000
Capital (population) Caracas (3,276,000)
Government Federal republic
Ethnic groups Spanish, Italian, Portuguese, Arab, German, African, indigenous people
Languages Spanish (official), indigenous dialects
Religions Roman Catholic 96%
Currency Bolivar = 100 céntimos
Website www.venezlon.co.uk

CLIMATE

Venezuela has a tropical climate. Temperatures are high throughout the year on the lowlands, though far cooler in the mountains. There is a marked dry season in much of the country that falls between December and April. Most rainfall is in the mountains.

HISTORY

Arawak and Carib Amerindians were the main inhabitants of Venezuela before the arrival of Europeans. The first European to arrive was Christopher Columbus, who sighted the area in 1498. Spaniards began to settle in the early 16th century, but economic development was slow.

In the early 19th century, Spain's colonies in South America began their struggle for independence. The Venezuelan patriots Simón Bolívar and Francisco Miranda were prominent in the struggle. Venezuela was the first South American country to demand freedom and, in July 1811, it declared independence, though Spaniards still held most of the country. In 1819, Venezuela became part of Gran Colombia, a republic led by Simón Bolívar that also included Colombia, Ecuador and Panama.

The country became fully independent in 1821, after the Venezuelans had defeated the Spanish in a battle at Carabobo, near Valencia. Venezuela broke away from Gran Colombia in 1829 and in 1830 a new constitution was drafted. The country's first president

ANGEL FALLS

The world's highest uninterrupted waterfall, in La Gran Sabrana, eastern Venezuela. Part of the River Caroni, it was discovered in 1935 and named after its discoverer Jimmy Angel, a US aviator. The total drop is 980 m [3,212 ft].

official name to the Bolivarian Republic of Venezuela and held a referenum on a new constitution. This gave the president increased power over military and civilian institutions, which he claimed to need to counter corruption. In 2002, Chavez himself survived a coup, and in 2004 he won a majority in a referendum which the opposition had intended to remove him from office. He was re-elected in 2006. In 2007 he granted himself extensive 'emergency powers' and withdrew from the World Bank and IMF.

ECONOMY

The World Bank classifies Venezuela as an 'upper-middle-income' developing country. Oil accounts for 80% of the exports. Other exports include bauxite and aluminium, iron ore and farm products. Agriculture employs 9% of the people. Major crops include bananas, cassava, citrus fruits, coffee, maize, plantains, rice and sorghum. Commercial crops are grown on large farms, but many people in remote areas farm at subsistence level.

Manufacturing industries now employ 21% of the population. The leading industry is petroleum refining, centred on Maracaibo. Other manufactures include aluminium, cement, processed food, steel and textiles.

was General José Antonio Páez, who had been one of the leaders of Venezuela's independence movement.

POLITICS

The development of Venezuela in the 19th century and the first half of the 20th century was marred by instability, violence and periods of harsh dictatorial rule. However, the country has had elected governments since 1958.

Venezuela has greatly benefited from its oil resources, which were first exploited in 1917. In 1960, Venezuela helped to form OPEC (the Organization of Petroleum Exporting Countries) and, in 1976, the government of Venezuela took control of the entire oil industry. Money from oil exports has helped Venezuela to raise living standards, but has had little success at diversifying the economy.

Financial problems in the late 1990s led to the election of Hugo Chávez as president in February 1999. Chávez, leader of the Patriotic Pole left-wing coalition, had led a failed coup in 1992. As President he adopted populist left-wing policies, embarked on a nationalization programme, changed the country's

CARACAS

Capital of Venezuela, on the River Guaire. Caracas was under Spanish rule until 1821. It was the birthplace of Venezuelan patriot Simón Bolívar. The city grew after 1930, encouraged by the exploitation of oil. It has the Central University of Venezuela (1725) and a cathedral (1614). Industries include motor vehicles, oil, brewing, chemicals and rubber.

VIETNAM

Vietnam's flag was first used by forces led by the Communist Ho Chi Minh during the liberation struggle against Japan in World War II (1939–45). It became the flag of North Vietnam in 1945 and it was retained when North and South Vietnam were reunited in 1975.

The Socialic Republic of Vietnam occupies an S-shaped strip of land facing the South China Sea in South-east Asia. The coastal plains include two densely populated, fertile river delta areas. The Red (Hong) Delta faces the Gulf of Tonkin in the north, while the Mekong Delta is in the south.

Inland are thinly populated highland regions, including the Annam Cordillera (Chaîne Annamitique), which forms much of the boundary with Cambodia. The highlands in the north-west extend into Laos and China.

Area 331,689 sq km [128,065 sq mi]
Population 84,403,000
Capital (population) Hanoi (4,147,000)
Government Socialist republic
Ethnic groups Vietnamese 87%, Chinese, Hmong, Thai, Khmer, Cham, mountain groups
Languages Vietnamese (official), English, French, Chinese, Khmer, mountain languages
Religions Buddhism, Christianity, indigenous beliefs
Currency Dong = 10 hao - 100 xu
Website www.vietnamtourism.com

CLIMATE

Vietnam has a tropical climate, though the drier months of January to March are cooler than the wet, hot summer months, when monsoon winds blow from the south-west. Typhoons sometimes hit the coast, causing much damage.

HISTORY

In 111 BC, China seized Vietnam, naming it Annam. In AD 939, it became independent. In 1558, it split into two parts. Tonkin, in the north, was ruled from Hanoi, while Annam, in the south, was ruled from Hué. In 1802, with French support, Vietnam was united as the Empire of Vietnam under Nguyen Anh. In 1859, the French seized Saigon, and by 1887 had formed Indo-China from the union of Vietnam and Cochin China.

Japan conquered Vietnam during World War II, and established a Vietnamese state under Emperor Bao Dai. After the war, Bao Dai's government collapsed, and the nationalist Viet Minh, led by Ho Chi Minh, set up a

---

MEKONG RIVER

River in south-east Asia that rises in Tibet as the Lancang Jiang and flows south through Yünnan province, China. It forms the Burma-Laos border and part of the Laos-Thailand border and then flows south through Cambodia and Vietnam creating a vast river delta that is one of the most important rice-producing regions in Asia. It is 4,180 km [2,600 mi] long.

South Vietnam through the Viet Cong irregular army. The USA became increasingly involved in what they saw as a fight against Communism. The conflict escalated into the Vietnam War, which devastated the country. In 1975, after the withdrawal of US troops, Ho Chi Minh's forces overran South Vietnam.

In 1976, the reunited Vietnam became a Socialist republic. In 1979 Vietnam helped overthrow the Khmer Rouge government in Cambodia, only withdrawing in 1989. The United States opened an embassy in Hanoi in 1995 and in 2002 a trade agreement opened access to US markets. The early 2000s saw economic liberalization and rapid development, and the country joined the WTO in 2007.

ECONOMY

The World Bank classifies Vietnam as a 'low-income' developing country, but in the 21st century the economy has grown rapidly. Manufacturing is the major activity. Products include electronics, garments and textiles, cement, fertilizers, processed food, machinery and steel.

Agriculture is still a major employer. Products include rice, maize and sweet potatoes; commercial crops include bananas, coffee, groundnuts, rubber, soya beans and tea. Fishing is also important. Natural resources include coal, chromium, oil, phosphates and tin.

Vietnamese republic. In 1946, the French tried to reassert control and war broke out. Despite aid from the USA, the French were defeated by the Viet Minh at Dien Bien Phu.

POLITICS

In 1954, Vietnam was divided along the 17th Parallel. North Vietnam fell under the communist government of Ho Chi Minh and South Vietnam under the French-supported Bao Dai. In 1955, Bao Dai was deposed and Ngo Dinh Diem was elected president. Many western countries recognized Diem as the legal ruler of the whole of Vietnam. North Vietnam, supported by China and the Soviet Union, extended its influence into

HANOI

Capital of Vietnam and its second largest city, on the Red River. In the 7th century the Chinese ruled Vietnam from Hanoi; it later became capital of the Vietnamese empire. Taken by the French in 1883, the city became the capital of French Indo-China (1887–1945). In 1946–54, it was the scene of fierce fighting between the French and the Viet Minh. Hanoi was heavily bombed by the US during the Vietnam War.

YEMEN

Yemen's flag was adopted in 1990 when the Yemen Arab Republic (or North Yemen) united with the People's Democratic Republic of Yemen (or South Yemen). This simple flag is a tricolour of red, white and black – colours associated with the Pan-Arab movement.

The Republic of Yemen faces the Red Sea and the Gulf of Aden in the south-western corner of the Arabian Peninsula. Behind the narrow coastal plain along the Red Sea, the land rises to a mountain region called High Yemen. Beyond the mountains, the land slopes down towards the Rub' al Khali Desert. Other mountains rise behind the coastal plain along the Gulf of Aden. To the east lies a fertile valley called the Hadramaut and also the deserts of the Arabian Empty Quarter.

Palm trees grow along the coast. Plants such as acacia and eucalyptus flourish in the interior. Thorn shrubs and mountain pasture are found in the highlands.

Area 527,968 sq km [203,848 sq mi]
Population 21,456,000
Capital (population) Sana'a (1,621,000)
Government Multiparty republic
Ethnic groups Predominantly Arab
Languages Arabic (official)
Religions Islam
Currency Yemeni rial = 100 fils
Website
www.yemeninfo.gov.ye/ENGLISH/home.htm

CLIMATE

The climate in San'a is moderated by its altitude. Temperatures are much lower than in Aden (Al' Adan), which is at sea level. In summer, south-west monsoon winds bring thunderstorms. But most of Yemen is arid. The south coasts are particularly hot and humid, especially from June to September. There are two seasonal rainfalls, during March to May and from July to September. The average rainfall is about 50 mm [2 in] on most parts of the plateaux, but may rise to 1,000 mm [40 in] in the highlands, while the coastal lowlands may have no more than 12 mm [0.5 in].

HISTORY

From around 1400 BC, Yemen lay on an important trading route, with frankin-

ADEN (AL'ADAN)

Commercial capital, and historic capital of the Aden Protectorate (1937–67) and the former People's Democratic Republic of Yemen (1967–90). A sea port city on the Gulf of Aden, 160 km [100 mi] east of the Red Sea, Aden was an important Roman trading port. With the opening of the Suez Canal in 1869 its importance increased. It was made a crown colony in 1937 and the surrounding territory became the Aden Protectorate. Industries include cigarettes, oil and salt refining.

ernment forces. In 1995 Yemen resolved border disputes with Oman and Saudi Arabia, but clashed with Eritrea over uninhabited islands in the Red Sea.

In 1998 and 1999, militants in the Aden-Abyan Islamic Army sought to destabilize the country. In 2000, a suicide bomb attack on the USS *Cole* in Aden killed 17 US personnel. In 2001, President Saleh offered support to the USA in its 'war on terrorism'. President Saleh was reappointed in 2006 elections, the first in which opposition candidates were permitted. 2007 saw clashes between government forces and Islamist rebels.

cense, pearls and spices being the major commodities. But its prosperity declined in the 4th century AD, when it became divided between warring groups.

Islam was introduced during the 7th century by the son-in-law of the Prophet Muhammad. From 897, the country was ruled by a Muslim leader. In 1517, the area was taken over by the Turkish Ottoman Empire and remained under Turkish rule for the next 400 years.

POLITICS

After World War I, northern Yemen, which had been ruled by Turkey, began to evolve into a separate state from the south, where Britain was in control. Britain withdrew in 1967 and a left-wing regime took power in the south. North Yemen became a republic in 1962 when the monarchy was abolished.

Clashes occurred between the traditionalist Yemen Arab Republic in the north and the formerly British Marxist People's Democratic Republic of Yemen. In 1990 they were resolved when the two Yemens merged to form one country. Marrying the needs of the two parts of Yemen has proved difficult. In 1994 civil war erupted when President Ali Abdallah Saleh, a northerner, attempted to remove the vice-president, a southerner. The war ended when Aden was captured by gov-

ECONOMY

The World Bank classifies Yemen as a 'low-income' developing country. Agriculture employs up to 63% of the people. Herders raise sheep and other animals, while farmers grow such crops as barley, fruits, wheat and vegetables in highland valleys and around oases. Cash crops include coffee and cotton.

Imported oil is refined at Aden and petroleum extraction began in the northwest in the 1980s. Handicrafts, leather goods and textiles are manufactured.

SAN'A

Capital and largest city of Yemen, 65 km [40 mi] north-east of the Red Sea port of Hodeida. Situated on a high plateau at 2,286 m [7,500 ft], it claims to be the world's oldest city, founded by Shem, eldest son of Noah. During the 17th century and from 1872 to 1918, it was part of the Ottoman Empire. In 1918, it became capital of an independent Yemen Arab Republic, and in 1990 capital of the new, unified Yemen. It is noted for its handicrafts. Agriculture (grapes) and industry (iron) are also important.

ZAMBIA

Zambia's flag was adopted when the country became independent from Britain in 1964. The colours are those of the United Nationalist Independence Party, which led the struggle against Britain and ruled until 1991. The flying eagle represents freedom.

The Republic of Zambia is a land-locked country in southern Africa. The country lies on the plateau that makes up most of southern Africa. Much of the land is between 900 m and 1,500 m [2,950–4,920 ft] above sea level. The Muchinga Mountains in the north-east rise above this flat land.

Lakes include Bangweulu, which is entirely within Zambia, together with parts of lakes Mweru and Tanganyika in the north. Most of the land is drained by the river Zambezi, from which the country takes its name, and its two main tributaries, the Kafue and Luangwa. Occupying part of the Zambezi Valley and stretching along the southern border Lake Kariba, which was dammed in 1961 is the largest artificial lake in Africa and one of the largest in the world (280 km [175 mi] long and 40 km [25 mi] across at its widest point). Zambia shares Lake Kariba and the Victoria Falls with Zimbabwe.

Grassland and wooded savanna cover much of Zambia. There are also swamps. Evergreen forests exist in the drier south-west of the country.

Area 752,618 sq km [290,586 sq mi]
Population 11,502,000
Capital (population) Lusaka (1,450,000)
Government Multiparty republic
Ethnic groups Native African (Bemba, Tonga, Maravi/Nyanja)
Languages English (official), Bemba, Kaonda
Religions Christianity 70%, Islam, IHinduism
Currency Zambian kwacha = 100 ngwee
Website www.zambiatourism.com

the country. The average annual rainfall ranges from about 1,300 mm [51 in] in the north down to between 510 mm and 760 mm [20–30 in] in the south.

HISTORY

European contact with Zambia began in the 19th century, when the explorer David Livingstone crossed the River Zambezi. In the 1890s, the British South Africa Company, set up by Cecil Rhodes (1853–1902), the British financier and statesman, made treaties with local chiefs and gradually took over the area. In 1911, the Company named the area Northern Rhodesia. In 1924, Britain took over the government of the country and the discovery of copper led to a large influx of Europeans in the late 1920s.

After World War II, the majority of Europeans living in Zambia wanted greater control of their government and some favoured a merger with their southern neighbour, Southern Rhodesia (now Zimbabwe). In 1953, Britain set up a federation of Northern Rhodesia, Southern Rhodesia and Nyasaland (now Malawi). Local Africans opposed the setting up of the federation arguing that it concentrated power in the hands of the

CLIMATE

Zambia lies in the tropics, although temperatures are moderated by the altitude. The rainy season runs from November to March, when the rivers sometimes flood. Northern Zambia is the wettest region of president. In 2005 the Supreme Court rejected a challenge to his election, but stated that the 2001 ballot had been flawed. In 2006 Mwanawasa was re-elected, although opposition allegations of fraud led to violent unrest.

ECONOMY
Zambia holds 6% of the world's copper reserves and copper is the leading export, accounting for 49% of Zambia's total exports. Zambia also produces cobalt, lead, zinc and various gemstones, but the country's dependence on minerals has created problems, especially when prices fluctuate. Agriculture employs 69% of the workforce, compared with 4% in mining and manufacturing. Major food crops include cassava, fruits and vegetables, maize, millet and sorghum, while cash crops include coffee, sugar cane and tobacco.

The Copperbelt, centred on Kitwe, is the main urban region, while Lusaka, provides the other major growth pole. Rural to urban migration has increased since 1964, but work is scarce. The production of copper products is the leading industrial activity. Other manufactures include beverages, processed food, iron and steel, textiles and tobacco.

white minority in Southern Rhodesia. Their opposition proved effective and the federation was dissolved in 1963. In 1964, Northern Rhodesia became an independent nation called Zambia.

POLITICS
The leading opponent of British rule, Kenneth Kaunda, became president in 1964. His government enjoyed reasonable income until copper prices crashed in the mid-1970s, but his collectivist policies failed to diversify the economy and neglected agriculture. In 1972, he declared the United Nationalist Independence Party (UNIP) the only legal party, ending democratic rule.

Under a new constitution, adopted in 1990, elections were held in 1991 in which Kaunda was trounced by Frederick Chiluba of the Movement for Multiparty Democracy (MMD). Chiluba was re-elected in 1996, but he stood down in 2001 after an MMD proposal to amend the constitution to allow Chiluba to stand for a third term met with substantial popular and parliamentary opposition. In the 2001 elections the MMD candidate, Levy Mwanawasa, was elected

LUSAKA
Capital and largest city of Zambia, in the south-central part of the country, at an altitude of 1,280 m [4,200 ft]. Founded by Europeans in 1905 to service the local lead-mining, it replaced Livingstone as the capital of Northern Rhodesia (later Zambia) in 1935. A vital road and rail junction, Lusaka is the centre of a fertile agricultural region, and is a major financial and commercial city.

ZIMBABWE

Zimbabwe's flag, adopted in 1980, is based on the colours used by the ruling Zimbabwe African National Union Patriotic Front. Within the white triangle is the Great Zimbabwe soapstone bird, the national emblem. The red star symbolizes the party's socialist policies.

The Republic of Zimbabwe is a land-locked country in southern Africa. Most of the country lies on a high plateau between the Zambezi and Limpopo Rivers between 900 m and 1,500 m [2,950–4,920 ft] above sea level.

The principal land feature is the High Veld, a ridge that crosses Zimbabwe from north-east to south-west. Harare lies on the north-east edge and Bulawayo on the south-west edge. Bordering the High Veld is the Middle Veld, the country's largest region and the site of many large ranches. Below 900 m [2,950 ft] is the Low Veld.

The country's highest point is Mount Inyangani, which reaches 2,593 m [8,507 ft] near the Mozambique border. Zimbabwe's best-known physical feature, Victoria Falls, is in the north-east. The Falls are shared with Zambia, as is the artificial Lake Kariba which is also on the River Zambezi.

Wooded savanna covers much of Zimbabwe. The Eastern Highlands and river valleys are forested. There are many tobacco plantations.

Area 390,757 sq km [150,871 sq mi]
Population 12,237,000
Capital (population) Harare (1,527,000)
Government Multiparty republic
Ethnic groups Shona 82%, Ndebele 14%, other African groups 2%, mixed and Asian 1%
Languages English (official), Shona, Ndebele
Religions Christianity, traditional belief
Currency Zimbabwean dollar= 100 cents
Website www.zim.gov.zw

HISTORY

The Shona people were dominant in the region about 1,000 years ago. They built the Great Zimbabwe, a city of stone buildings. Under the statesman Cecil Rhodes (1853–1902), the British South Africa Company occupied the area in the 1890s, after obtaining mineral rights from local chiefs. The area was named Rhodesia and later Southern Rhodesia. It became a self-governing British colony in 1923. In 1953, Southern and Northern Rhodesia (now Zambia) were joined to Nyasaland (Malawi) in the Central African Federation.

POLITICS

In 1965, the European government of Southern Rhodesia (then known as Rhodesia) declared their country independent. However, Britain refused to accept this declaration. Finally, after a civil war, the country became legally independent in 1980.

After independence, rivalries between the Shona and Ndebele people threatened its stability. Order was restored when the Shona prime minister, Robert Mugabe, brought his Ndebele rivals into his government. In 1987 Mugabe

CLIMATE

The subtropical climate varies greatly according to altitude. The Low Veld is much warmer and drier than the High Veld. November to March is mainly hot and wet. Winter in Harare is dry but cold. Frosts have been recorded between June and August.

inflation, perhaps the worst ever recorded. Rising political opposition was brutally suppressed.

ECONOMY

The World Bank classifies Zimbabwe as a 'low-income' economy. Its economy improved rapidly after independence, with successful agrarian policies and the exploitation of the country's mineral resources. However, a fast-growing population continued to exert pressure both on land and resources of all kinds. Under Mugabe's regime the economy has collapsed, self-sufficiency in food has ended and exports have fallen sharply. The imposition of price controls has led to mass shortages and a substantial black market. Unemployment is crippling, with the vast majority of people out of work.

Most of the limited employment is in farming. Maize is the chief food crop. Cash crops include cotton, sugar and tobacco but production has fallen sharply. The country is a major recipient of aid, including much of its food supply.

Gold, asbestos, chromium and nickel are mined and the country also has some coal and iron ore. Manufactures include beverages, chemicals, iron and steel, metal products, processed food, textiles and tobacco.

became the country's executive president, and in 1991 the government renounced its Marxist ideology. In 1990, the state of emergency that had lasted since 1965 was allowed to lapse – three months after Mugabe had secured a landslide election victory. Mugabe was re-elected in 1996. In the late 1990s, Mugabe threatened to seize white-owned farms without paying compensation to owners. His announcement caused much disquiet among white farmers. The situation worsened in the early 2000s, when landless 'war veterans' began to occupy white-owned farms, resulting in violence and deaths.

Food shortages have become a major problem with aid agencies blaming the land reform programme while the government blames drought.

In 2002, amid accusations of electoral irregularities, Mugabe was re-elected president. Mounting criticism of Mugabe led the Commonwealth to suspend Zimbabwe's membership. Later Zimbabwe confirmed that it had pulled out of the Commonwealth permanently. In 2004 the European Union renewed sanctions against the country. In 2006–7 the country's problems worsened, as economic mismanagement led to crippling hyper-

HARARE

Capital of Zimbabwe, in the north east of the country. Settled by Europeans in 1890 as Fort Salisbury, it became capital of Southern Rhodesia in 1902. The city served as capital of the Federation of Rhodesia and Nyasaland (1953–63) and of Rhodesia (1965–79). It has a university (1957) and two cathedrals. Industries include gold mining, textiles, steel, tobacco, chemicals and furniture.

INDEX

Places are usually indexed to the largest scale map on which they appear.

439